THE MAPS
OF GETTYSBURG

An Atlas of the Gettysburg Campaign,
June 3 – July 13, 1863

Bradley M. Gottfried

SB

Savas Beatie

New York and California

The Maps of Gettysburg: An Atlas of the Gettysburg Campaign, June 3 – July 13, 1863

Cataloging-in-Publication Data is available from the Library of Congress.

ISBN-10: 1-932714-30-8
ISBN-13: 978-1932714302

10 9 8 7 6 5 4 3 2 1
First Edition, First Printing

SB

Published by
Savas Beatie LLC
521 Fifth Avenue, Suite 3400
New York, NY 10175
Phone: 610-853-9131

Editorial Offices:

Savas Beatie LLC
P.O. Box 4527
El Dorado Hills, CA 95762
Phone: 916-941-6896
(E-mail) editorial@savasbeatie.com

Savas Beatie titles are available at special discounts for bulk purchases in the United States by corporations, institutions, and other organizations. For more details, please contact Special Sales, P.O. Box 4527, El Dorado Hills, CA 95762. You may also e-mail us at sales@savasbeatie.com, or click over for a visit to our website at www.savasbeatie.com for additional information.

For Linda Nieman and Theodore P. Savas,
whose support and interest made this book possible

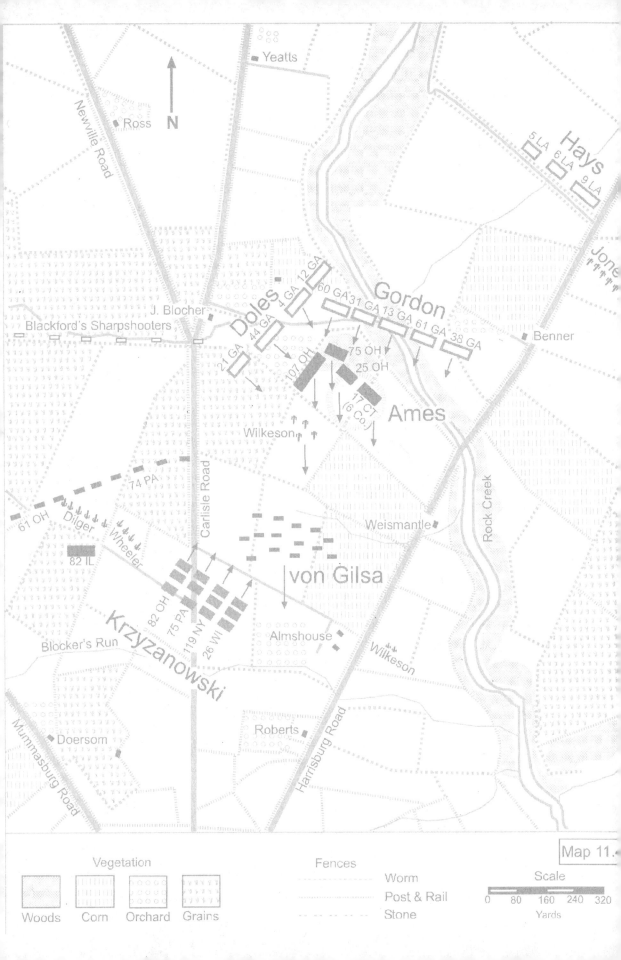

Map 11.

Vegetation
Woods · Corn · Orchard · Grains

Fences
Worm
Post & Rail
Stone

Scale
0   80   160   240   320
Yards

Contents

Contents (continued)

Contents (continued)

List of Maps

List of Maps (continued)

List of Maps (continued)

List of Maps (continued)

List of Maps (continued)

List of Maps (continued)

List of Maps (continued)

List of Maps (continued)

List of Maps (continued)

Introduction

Another book on Gettysburg?

A few years ago, a distinguished Civil War historian decried the continual flow of books, articles, and research on the battle of Gettysburg. As far as he was concerned, the energy poured into the battle directed attention away from other important events that needed scholarly attention. One of the books he focused attention on in his article was my own recently released *Brigades of Gettysburg: The Union and Confederate Brigades at the Battle of Gettysburg* (Da Capo, 2002). That title, and others like it, intoned the historian, was what was wrong with modern Civil War historiography. Although I respect his broad body of work, and own many of his books, I disagree entirely with his assessment.

First, no other campaign has uncovered so many first-person accounts of those pivotal weeks in 1863. These recollections make it easier for anyone writing on the subject to understand—at a much broader and deeper level—what really occurred during that campaign. This is true not only at the strategic level, but from the eyes of men who served in the ranks and from the perspective of ordinary civilians. Newly discovered accounts on this subject appear with regularity. As ongoing research turns up new sources, it is the historian's job to synthesize that material and produce something useful from it. The recently published and well received *Plenty of Blame to Go Around: Jeb Stuart's Controversial Ride to Gettysburg*, by Eric J. Wittenberg and J. David Petruzzi (Savas Beatie, 2006) is a classic example of what good historians can do with new material.

Second, the national interest in Gettysburg continues unabated. Attendance at the national park dedicated to memorializing the battle has fallen recently, but nearly 2,000,000 people still visit each year. Books on the subject continue to sell well because the interest in reading about the campaign remains vibrant.

All of this is a roundabout way of coming back to how this Introduction opened. In your hands is another book with Gettysburg in the title (twice). My own work on the subject is concentrated on topics I think others want to read more about, including reference material that will hopefully assist experts and laymen alike. I am a firm believer that plowing ground that will help others in the future is a worthwhile endeavor.

Researching and preparing *Brigades of Gettysburg* in the late 1990s was much more difficult than I expected it might be. A dearth of easy-to-read complete maps on the campaign made tracking the daily movement of the opposing armies and individual units much more difficult than it would otherwise have been. To understand fully any campaign or battle, a student must appreciate how and when the individual armies and their component parts marched to the battlefield and their proximity to one another along the way at any given time. Being able to visualize this information makes it come alive and weaves the threads of understanding together into a tighter picture that usually explains why commanders marched when and where they did, or why they made one decision and not another. Knowing the precise movements of the opposing forces also sheds light on why and when a particular battle took place. Understanding how the opposing armies reached the field of battle goes a long way toward explaining why the subsequent fighting unfolded as it did. This is true of every military campaign of every age.

When it comes to Gettysburg, readers have several cartographic works from which to choose. Each has its own strengths and weaknesses. Any serious study of Gettysburg must include time with John Bachelder's maps. These maps are invaluable for studying the battle. However, Bachelder's maps only cover the events on the field at Gettysburg, and although crafted with care, contain many inaccuracies. John Imhof's *Gettysburg—Day Two: A Study in Maps* (Butternut and Blue, 1997) is an outstanding work designed to cover only a slice of the battle (the second day); it does so admirably. Another similar study includes Jeffrey Hall's *The Stand of the U.S. Army at Gettysburg* (Indiana University Press, 2003). The topographical maps are impressive and helpful, but Hall's pro-Northern point of view, coupled with his sequential approach, makes it less valuable than it might otherwise have been.

The Maps of Gettysburg: An Atlas of the Gettysburg Campaign, June 3 – July 13, 1863 takes a different approach on two levels. First, its neutral coverage includes the entire campaign from both points of view. The text and maps carry the armies from the opening step of the campaign during the early days of June all the way to the battlefield in Pennsylvania, through the three days of fighting, and then south again until the Army of Northern Virginia crossed the Potomac River in mid-July. My purpose is to offer a broad and full understanding of the complete campaign, rather than a micro-history of one day or one sector of the battle itself.

Second, *The Maps of Gettysburg* dissects the actions within each sector of the battlefield for a deeper and hopefully more meaningful experience. Each section of this book includes a number of text and map combinations. Every left-hand page includes descriptive text corresponding with a facing right-hand page original map. An added advantage of this arrangement is that it eliminates the need to flip through the book to try to find a map to match the text. Some sections, like the defeat of the 157th New York north of Gettysburg on July 1, are short and required only two maps. Others, like the prolonged bloody combat in the Wheatfield on July 2, required a large number of maps and text pages. Wherever possible, I utilized relevant firsthand accounts to personalize the otherwise straightforward text.

To my knowledge, no single source until now has pulled together the myriad of movements and events of this mammoth campaign and offered it in a cartographic form side-by-side with reasonably detailed text complete with end notes. I hope readers find this method of presentation useful. Newcomers to Gettysburg should find the plentiful maps and sectioned coverage easy to follow and understand. Hopefully, it makes digesting what is an otherwise complex campaign easier to grasp in its broad strokes. The various sections may also trigger a special interest or two and so pry open avenues for further study. I am optimistic that readers who approach the subject with a higher level of expertise will find the maps and text not only interesting to study and read, but truly helpful. If someone, somewhere, places this book within reach to refer to it now and again as a reference guide, the long hours invested in this project will have been worthwhile.

The Maps of Gettysburg is not the last word or definitive treatment of the campaign, battle, or any part thereof—nor did I intend it to be. Given space and time considerations, I decided to cover the major events of the campaign and battle, with smaller transition sections to flesh out the full campaign story. For example, a light overview of Jeb Stuart's orders and subsequent ride to Gettysburg is included, but I did not dedicate space to the major combats and skirmishes he waged along the way. The important cavalry actions on the field of Gettysburg, however, are discussed in great detail in two separate sections.

Original research was kept to a minimum. My primary reliance was upon firsthand accounts, battle reports, and quality secondary scholarship. I am also intimately familiar with the entire battlefield, having walked nearly every yard of it many times over the years. Thus, there are no new theories or evaluations of why the campaign or battle unfolded as it did.

Whenever a book uses short chapters or sections, as this one does, there will inevitably be some narrative redundancy. As far as possible, I have endeavored to minimize those occurrences. I am also keenly aware that Gettysburg is a very hot topic of debate in many circles, and even relatively bland observations can spark rancorous discourse and a challenge to a duel with pistols at dawn. And of course, the sources can and often do conflict on many points, including numbers engaged and casualties. I have tried to follow a generally accepted interpretation of the campaign and battle, and (I hope with some success) portray the information accurately and with an even hand.

Inevitably, a study like this makes it likely that mistakes of one variety or another have slipped into the text (or on a map) despite my endless hours of proofreading. I apologize in advance for any errors and assume full responsibility for them.

* * *

Many obstacles stood in the way of the completion of this project. Discussions with publishers and editors early on were problematic as they struggled to understand the project as I envisioned it should be. At best, they wanted to modify its scope dramatically. Theodore P. "Ted" Savas, who had signed on to publish my *Brigades of Gettysburg* book in 1999 before selling Savas Publishing Company to an east coast conglomerate, took an immediate interest in the project because he understood my vision, saw a need for the book, and believed in its potential. Ted has been all that an author could ask for in a publisher and developmental editor. With a mixture of tough-love and encouragement, he saw the project through to fruition. This book would not have been possible without his ongoing support and interest.

Ted arranged to have David Wieck thoroughly review the text and edit where necessary. David is a government analyst and independent editor with a strong background in historical, technical, and governmental materials. He is also co-author, with David Shultz, of *The Battle between the Farm Lanes: Hancock Saves the Union Center: Gettysburg July 2, 1863* (Ironclad, 2006). David's suggestions were always helpful, and his keen eye and knowledge of the battle helped make this a better book.

Many others also graciously assisted me. Cavalry experts Eric J. Wittenberg and J. David (J.D.) Petruzzi (*Plenty of Blame to Go Around: Jeb Stuart's Controversial Ride to Gettysburg*, 2006) read the sections dealing with mounted operations, identified some key mistakes, and made this work that much stronger. J.D. then took it upon himself to review the entire manuscript, bringing to the table his familiarity of the entire campaign and battle. Jay Jorgenson (*Gettysburg's Bloody Wheatfield*, 2001), Dr. David G. Martin (*Gettysburg: Day 1*, 1995), and Dr. Earl J. Hess (*Pickett's Charge: The Last Attack at Gettysburg*, 2000) perused sections dealing with their areas of expertise and offered a wide variety of observations and ideas for improving this study. I cannot begin to thank each of these gentlemen enough.

And then there were the maps. I initially intended to co-write the book with a cartographer. My goal was to focus on the text and rough out scores of maps before turning both over to an experienced mapmaker to breathe life into my crude renditions. Two cartographers signed on over the course of several years. Unfortunately (or fortunately, depending upon one's perspective now that the heavy labor is over), creative differences ended each collaboration. My options narrowed quickly. I could either scuttle the project entirely or learn how to produce the maps myself. Linda Nieman, one of my coworkers, encouraged me to take the plunge and learn how to draft them on my own. She also helped me learn a computer graphics program. There would probably not be a book without Linda's patient instruction and encouragement.

In addition to the learning curve for the software, it took literally hundreds and hundreds of hours to complete the scores of maps. In spite of the more than occasional tedium of working long hours after midnight with a drawing program, I actually enjoyed preparing them.

Bradley M. Gottfried
La Plata, Maryland

THE MAPS

OF GETTYSBURG

An Atlas of the Gettysburg Campaign,
June 3 – July 13, 1863

Map Set 1: The March to Gettysburg

Map 1.1 (June 3-4)

By early 1863, the Federals held large chunks of Southern territory, supply shortages plagued the South, and foreign recognition remained elusive.[1] In the West, Ulysses S. Grant's army threatened Vicksburg, Mississippi. In the East, Robert E. Lee's Army of Northern Virginia was in winter quarters, cold and hungry but encouraged by the winter defensive victory at Fredericksburg the previous December.

General Lee contemplated a move north of the Potomac River as early as February 23.[2] Major General Joseph Hooker interrupted Lee's planning in late April when he put his Army of the Potomac into motion toward Richmond. Despite the absence of Lt. Gen. James Longstreet and two First Corps divisions (on duty in southwestern Virginia) and being heavily outnumbered, Lee moved to meet Hooker at Chancellorsville in early May and scored one of the most stunning victories of the war. However, Lt. Gen. Thomas "Stonewall" Jackson was mortally wounded and casualties were heavy.

The loss of Jackson prompted Lee to reorganize his army (something he had contemplated for some time) to improve its efficiency and make it easier to handle. He divided his infantry into three corps (three divisions each) and reorganized his artillery. Richard S. Ewell was promoted to lieutenant general to replace Jackson at the head of the Second Corps. The new Third Corps was created for Ambrose P. Hill, who was also promoted to lieutenant general.

Lee's thoughts turned once again to an invasion of the North. His reinforced army numbered as many as 75,000 soldiers—far more than he had for his earlier invasion that had ended in a bloody tactical draw and strategic defeat at Sharpsburg (Antietam) the previous September. Virginia needed a respite from war, the shock of an invasion might dispirit Northerners, and a decisive military success on foreign soil might ease the pressure against

Vicksburg and compel other nations to recognize the Confederacy. The rich farms and towns of Pennsylvania also offered food, forage, and supplies for Lee's army. First, Lee had to convince President Jefferson Davis and his cabinet. Davis wanted to send troops west to relieve Vicksburg. Lee, however, prevailed.

His plan was bold. He would leave A. P. Hill's Third Corps in front of Fredericksburg to watch the Federal army while his other two corps slipped around the enemy right flank and pushed north down the Shenandoah Valley, using the Blue Ridge Mountains to screen his movements.[3]

Two of Longstreet's divisions led the way north. Lafayette McLaws' men broke camp near Fredericksburg and marched for Culpeper Court House on the morning of June 3. According to Samuel Pickens, 5th Alabama (O'Neal's Brigade), "it was a very warm day & we were in a cloud of dust most of the time . . . my eyes, mouth, face & hair were covered with dust."[4] John Hood's Division on the Rapidan River moved later that day. George Pickett's Division remained far to the south at Hanover Court House. Two divisions of Richard Ewell's Second Corps (Jubal Early and Edward Johnson) stayed in camp near Hamilton Crossing, while the third division under Robert Rodes began moving north on June 4.[5] Hood arrived at Culpeper about 1:00 p.m. that day; McLaws stopped at Raccoon Ford on the Rapidan; Rodes camped about one mile from Spotsylvania Court House. Hill's Corps remained around Fredericksburg.[6]

Hooker's seven corps remained in their camps north of the Rappahannock River. John F. Reynolds' I Corps and John Sedgwick's VI Corps camped near White Oak Church, Winfield S. Hancock's II Corps near Falmouth, Daniel E. Sickles' III Corps at Boscobel, George G. Meade's V Corps near Banks' and United States fords, Oliver O. Howard's XI Corps near Brooke's Station on the Aquia Creek Railroad, and Henry Slocum's XII Corps near Stafford Court House and Aquia Landing. Two cavalry divisions, commanded by Brig. Gens. John Buford and David McMurtrie Gregg, remained near Warrenton Junction, while the third, under Colonel Alfred Duffié, occupied the area around Brooke's Station.[7]

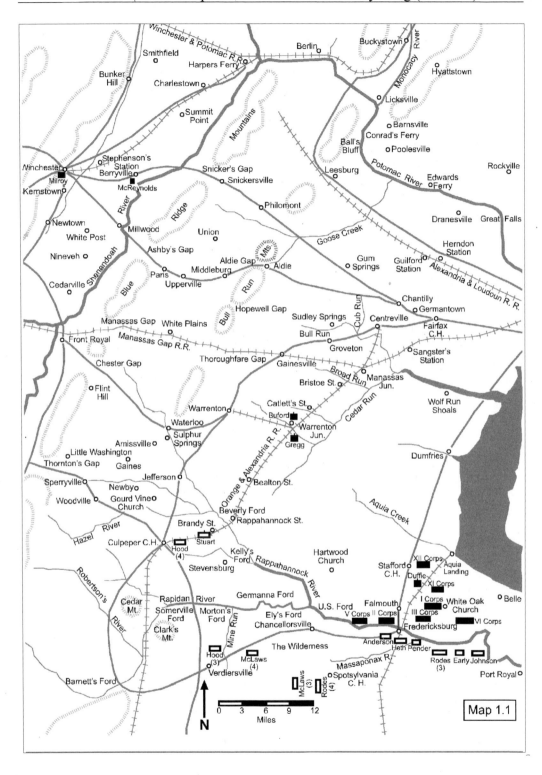

Map 1.1

Map 1.2 (June 5-8)

June 5 found Hood's Division at Brandy Station, witnessing Maj. Gen. J. E. B. Stuart's grand cavalry review for President Jefferson Davis and other Richmond dignitaries. After the festivities, Hood's veterans marched back to Culpeper Court House. Rodes' Division advanced to Verdiersville, while Early's and Johnson's men broke camp after midnight and marched through the darkness, finally joining Rodes at Verdiersville on June 6.[8]

Joe Hooker was not blind to the clouds of dust to the southwest and the absence of men to his front. Suspecting an enemy movement might be underway, he ordered Sedgwick to reconnoiter, throwing his entire VI Corps across the river to support his scouts, if necessary. Sedgwick dispatched two regiments, the 5th and 26th New Jersey, across in pontoon boats, capturing some 150 rebels from A. P. Hill's Corps in the process.[9]

Sedgwick did not know it, but he had sent men to an area recently vacated by Rodes, Early, and Johnson. A. P. Hill promptly rushed Pender's Division east to counter the Federal probe. What appeared to be a promising excursion bogged down when Brig. Gen. Albion Howe's division met stiff resistance on the south side of the river. Sedgwick wrote at 10:30 a.m., "I cannot move 200 yards without bringing on a general fight. Before bringing over the rest of my corps, I await orders." Hooker quickly responded that the one division would suffice. Meanwhile, Brig. Gen. James Wadsworth's First Corps division headed to Franklin's Crossing to support Sedgwick's probe.[10]

The movement of Howe's division across the Rappahannock River froze most of the Confederate movements early on June 6. Lee quickly resumed the march when he realized that Hooker was merely testing his strength and intentions. As Hood's Division returned to Brandy Station from Culpeper Court House, McLaws' Division veered to the right of the Court House, halting at Stevensburg. These two powerful units were now in a position to cross the Rappahannock River and strike Hooker's right flank near Hartwood Church. Ewell's Second Corps continued its slow march toward Culpeper Court House, covering less than five miles that day.[11]

The Federal V Corps also caused Hooker grief. Ordered to probe across Banks' and United States fords, Brig. Gen. George Sykes protested to his corps commander, George Meade. "I am opposed to any movement across the river with the forces I have . . . it is hardly to be expected that anything reliable would be gained, even supposing it could be obtained from such sources," he wrote. An angry Hooker fired back, "You are not to disregard the order to feel the enemy a little."[12]

Still unsure of Lee's movements, Hooker sent units of Buford's cavalry to Jefferson to gather information on June 6, but the usually reliable Buford produced little by way of results. Frustrated by his inability to get definitive information on Lee's positions and intentions, Hooker wired General Henry Halleck at 3:00 p.m. that all of his cavalry and 3,000 of his infantry were on the road toward Culpeper Court House. He ordered Maj. Gen. Alfred Pleasonton to take his cavalry across the Rappahannock at Beverly and Kelly fords and head for Brandy Station.[13]

The three divisions of Ewell's II Corps marched to Culpeper Court House on June 7. Rodes reached the town that night, while Pender and Johnson camped their two divisions within three miles of the place. Five Southern infantry divisions were now concentrated near Culpeper Court House by the evening of June 8. To the south on the same day, three of the five brigades of Pickett's Division left Hanover Court House.

The Federal army spent June 8 quietly, save for Pleasonton's cavalry, which advanced toward Brandy Station, and Brig. Gen. Horatio Wright's division, which relieved Howe's south of the Rappahannock River on June 7.[14]

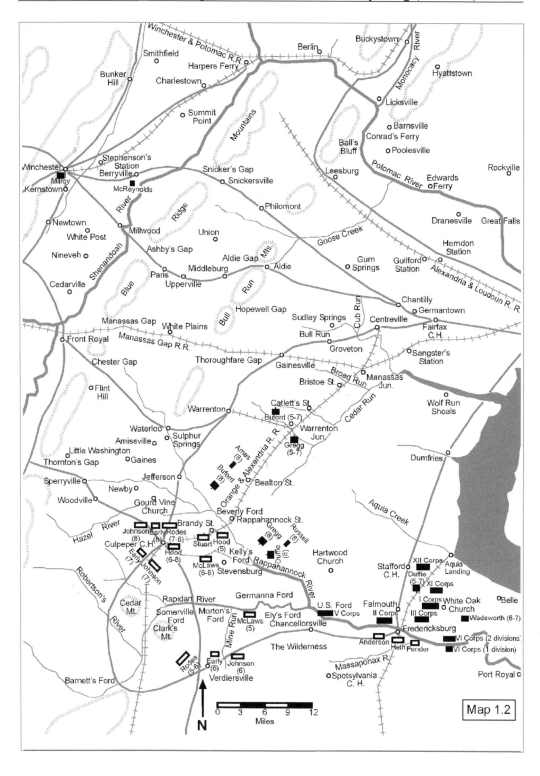

Map 1.2

Map 1.3 (June 9-11)

During the early morning hours of June 9, Buford's division, with Brig. Gen. Adelbert Ames' infantry brigade in support, splashed across the Rappahannock River at Beverly Ford, while Gregg's and Duffié's divisions and Brig. Gen. David A. Russell's infantry brigade crossed at Kelly's Ford. The movement triggered the greatest cavalry battle ever fought on American soil.

Pleasonton's 11,000 troopers only slightly outnumbered Stuart's 9,500, but they held one critical advantage: surprise. On Hooker's orders, Pleasonton had split his command to attack Stuart's cavalry near Brandy Station.

Buford's wing opened the battle with immediate success, driving the Confederates from the ford and toward Fleetwood Heights. The battle raged back and forth as Stuart fed reinforcements into the fast-moving combat as quickly as they arrived on the scene. Gregg's and Duffié's divisions entered the battle from the south, but persistent Confederate counterattacks stymied their advance. Both sides mounted charges and countercharges, battle lines became mingled, and troopers fought saber to saber. Although his men fought well, Pleasonton realized the futility of continuing the offensive and pulled his troopers back across the river, ending the battle. His men had acquitted themselves better than ever before against Stuart's veterans. However pleased they may have been with their performance, they still had not secured the vital information Hooker so desperately needed.[15]

The five Confederate divisions near Culpeper Court House had not remained idle during the fight. They quickly marched toward Brandy Station to help Stuart's beleaguered cavalry, but arrived too late to render assistance and returned to their camps. The timing was probably good for Lee because Pleasonton's troopers withdrew without ever registering their presence. Meanwhile, Pickett's Division continued its northward march.[16]

Lee waited 18 hours after the battle for Hooker's next move. When none came, he struck north again on June 10. Taking the Old Richmond Turnpike, Early and Johnson's divisions marched to Woodville. Rodes marched his division along a parallel road and camped for the night at Gourd Vine Church. After a rapid march, Pickett's men halted for the night about eight miles south of Culpeper Court House.

Hooker was still unsure of Lee's intentions, so the Federal army did not move save for Pleasonton's cavalry, which returned to Warrenton Junction, and Maj. Gen. John Newton's division, which relieved Brig. Gen. Horatio Wright's division of the Federal VI Corps on the south side of the Rappahannock River. In the midst of all his activity, Pleasonton reorganized his three divisions into two, consolidating the Second and Third divisions under the command of General Gregg.[17]

Four Confederate divisions were on the march on June 11. Three in Ewell's Second Corps continued toward the Shenandoah Valley. Johnson's and Early's divisions reached Little Washington that afternoon and went into camp while Rodes' Division bivouacked about two miles north of Flint Hill. Of Longstreet's I Corps, Pickett's Division made a short march, ending within three miles of Culpeper Court House, while McLaws and Hood remained in camp near Culpeper Court House.[18]

The Federal army's positions remained unchanged on June 11, save for the III Corps, which marched from Boscobel to Hartwell Church in response to General Pleasonton's urgent request for an infantry corps to move between his cavalry and Stuart's. The corps also patrolled the area between Kelly's and Beverly fords. The XI Corps took up the III Corps' positions at Boscobel. The Union corps commanders received orders to prepare to march the next day. O. O. Howard was to "march . . . without delay by the most direct route to Catlett's Station." Pleasonton threw out patrols to ascertain enemy movements. Unbeknownst to Hooker, none ventured farther north than Waterloo Bridge, only ten miles beyond Beverly Ford. As a result, they were unaware that Ewell's Second Corps was marching toward the Shenandoah Valley.[19]

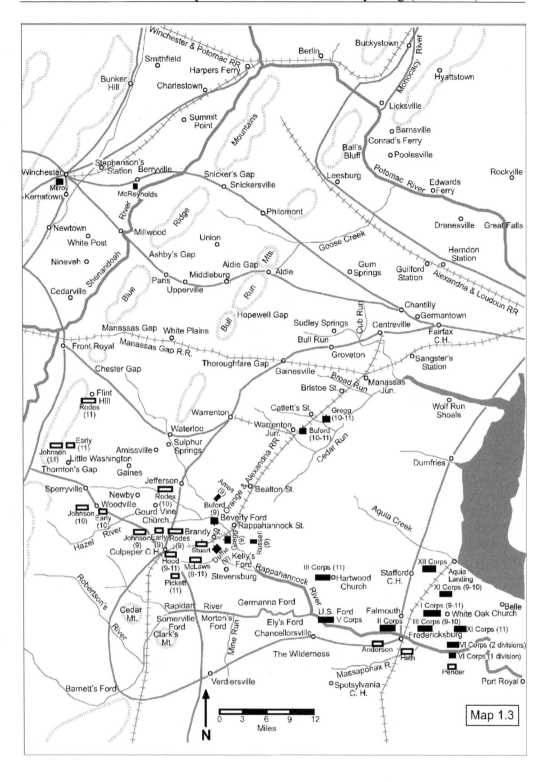

Map 1.3

Map 1.4 (June 12)

On June 12, Ewell's Second Corps entered the Shenandoah Valley through Chester Gap, accompanied by Brig. Gen. Albert Jenkins' Brigade of cavalry and the 35th Virginia Cavalry Battalion. The lush countryside impressed the men. Samuel Pickens of Alabama commented about the "most luxuriant clover [and] the splendid fields of wheat." The corps next marched through Front Royal, forded the Shenandoah River, and went into camp just north of Cedarville.

Upon learning that Maj. Gen. Robert Milroy held Winchester with about 8,000 men and that Colonel Andrew McReynolds commanded another 1,800 in Berryville, Ewell quickly formulated a plan. His goal was to clear the Shenandoah Valley for the advance of Lee's army, and the first step was the destruction of Milroy's men at Winchester. Rodes' Division (with Jenkins' cavalry brigade) was ordered to attack McReynolds at Berryville and then quickly march on Martinsburg to liquidate its garrison. Anxious to get a head start, Rodes ordered his men back on the road and they marched until they reached Stone Bridge that night.[20]

A stream of information now reached Hooker, confirming that most of Lee's units had moved west and north. This was not a surprise; Hooker had spent much of the last week requesting permission from President Lincoln to drive south and capture Richmond. Leaving Washington uncovered was unacceptable, and Lincoln denied each request. Hooker could no longer wait in place for an order that would never come, and so sent units to interpose themselves between Lee's army and the capital. The I and III Corps marched toward Bealton—the latter corps reaching its destination that night, the former reaching Deep Run. The XI Corps marched to Hartwood Church, halting for the night in preparation for its march to Catlett's Station. The XII Corps moved in behind them. Sedgwick also pulled his troops back from across the Rappahannock River while the II and V Corps remained in camp. Hooker placed I Corps commander Major General John Reynolds in charge of the army's left wing, composed of the I, III, V, and XI Corps, and Pleasonton's cavalry. A cavalry division under Maj. Gen. Julius Stahel arrived from Baltimore to patrol beyond the Bull Run Mountains toward New Baltimore, Salem, Middleburg; Dranesville and Leesburg, and from there through the Blue Ridge Mountains to Front Royal and Winchester.[21]

These were hard marches for the Federals. A soldier in the III Corps recalled the misery: "the dust combined with the heat caused great suffering. The nostrils of the men, filled with dust, became dry and feverish, and even the throat did not escape. The grit was felt between the teeth, and the eyes were rendered almost useless. There was dust in eyes, mouth, ears, and hair. The shoes were full of sand, and the dust penetrating the clothes and getting in at the neck, wrists, and ankles, mixed with perspiration produced an irritant almost as active as cantharides."[22]

In response to the sluggishness of the army, Hooker issued General Order No. 62. Stern in tone, it reminded the officers of prior General Orders, set rules on the treatment of stragglers and non-military personnel in the camps, denied the use of horses and mules for non-military reasons, and restricted the use of enlisted men as waiters or servants. Hooker also reminded the officers of the importance of drill at all levels of the army. The orders were read to the men of each company and battery.[23]

Northwest of Hooker, General Milroy threw out cavalry patrols to ascertain the enemy's position in the Shenandoah Valley. His troopers encountered and engaged enemy horsemen, and one patrol claimed to have seen long lines of Confederate infantry approaching Cedarville. "Impossible," thought Milroy.[24]

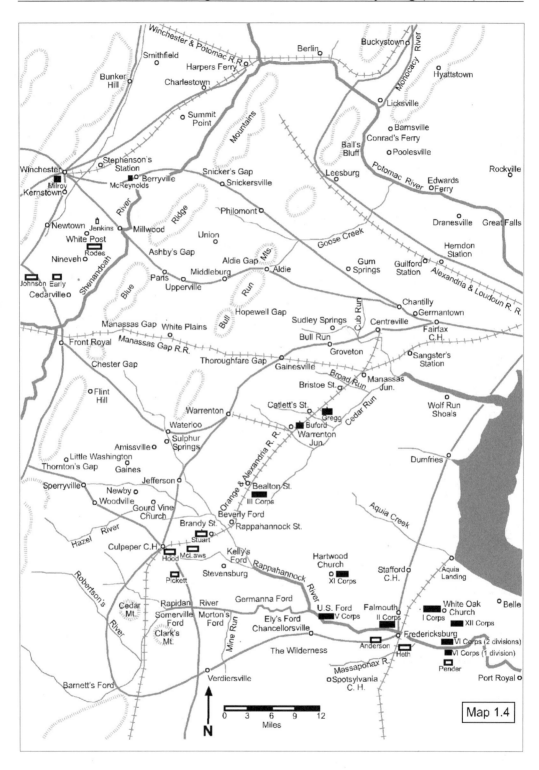

Map 1.4

Map 1.5 (June 13)

June 13 found both armies on the move. Hooker divided the Army of the Potomac into two wings and sent the advance (or left) wing toward the Orange and Alexandria Railroad to get between Lee and Washington. John Reynolds, in charge of the left wing, marched north toward Manassas Junction while the rest of the army remained behind to cover the withdrawal of government property.[25]

The I Corps marched from Deep Run to Bealton Station, joining the III Corps which had reached it the day before. The men of the III Corps were happy to remain there after a 25-mile march. The V Corps broke camp near Banks' Ford in a driving rain and marched until midnight to Hartwood Church, where they replaced Howard's XI Corps, which began its 24-mile march to Weaverville, near Catlett's Station. They halted there at 4:00 a.m. Buford's cavalry division was ordered toward Thoroughfare Gap that evening, while Gregg's cavalry division remained in camp near Catlett's Station.[26]

Federal units from the right wing were also on the move. Portions of the VI Corps re-crossed the Rappahannock River, assisted in removing the pontoon boats, and marched north toward Brooke's Station, reuniting with the remainder of the corps the following day at Stafford Court House. The XII Corps began its march to Dumfries, halting for the night at Brooke's Station. After laying out their camps, they were ordered back into line. Their march consumed the night of June 13-14. The men first backtracked toward Stafford Court House before striking north toward Dumfries. The II Corps remained at Falmouth, acting as the army's rear guard to keep an eye on A. P. Hill's Corps lingering on the far side of the river.[27]

The Confederates were less active on June 13. Tracking the Federal withdrawal, Hill's Third Corps prepared to break camp and march on Culpeper Court House to join Longstreet's First Corps. Only the Second Corps was on the march this day. According to the day's plan, Jenkins' cavalry brigade was to ride into Millwood without alerting Col. Andrew McReynolds to the

invasion, but this did not occur. Rodes sent Jenkins north to bottle-up McReynolds at Berryville, but the latter fled toward Winchester. Jenkins continued north in pursuit of a wagon train. The Confederate horsemen encountered enemy infantry at Bunker Hill and, although outnumbered twenty to one, the Federal troops tenaciously held their ground. They ultimately took refuge in blockhouses, which Jenkins' men stormed several times. Realizing the futility of these efforts and that he had no time to spare, Jenkins finally broke off the action and headed north after the wagons but it was too late; they had already reached safety. Rodes, meanwhile, put his infantry back on the road to pursue McReynolds and finally reached Summit Point, where the men bivouacked in a pouring rain.[28]

Farther west, Ewell sent Early's Division down the Valley Turnpike to turn Milroy's right flank at Winchester, while Johnson's Division marched along the Front Royal and Winchester Road to attack the Federal division from the south. Marching through Newtown, Early's Division reached the environs of Kernstown and was shelled by Federal artillery on Pritchard's Hill. General Early deployed his men against the battery, which quickly withdrew but not before inflicting losses on the advancing infantry. When Early's men heard horses galloping toward them, John B. Gordon's and Harry T. Hays' brigades shifted to meet an ill-advised attack by the 12th Pennsylvania Cavalry. The Confederate infantry fired before the cavalry came within effective range, giving the Pennsylvanians time to rein in their horses and beat a hasty retreat.

Early's men spent the night resting just south of Abram's Creek, near Winchester. Johnson's Division was not as heavily engaged, but encountered a tenacious enemy picket line about four miles south of Winchester. Units of the Stonewall Brigade moved forward and chased off the Federal infantry.[29]

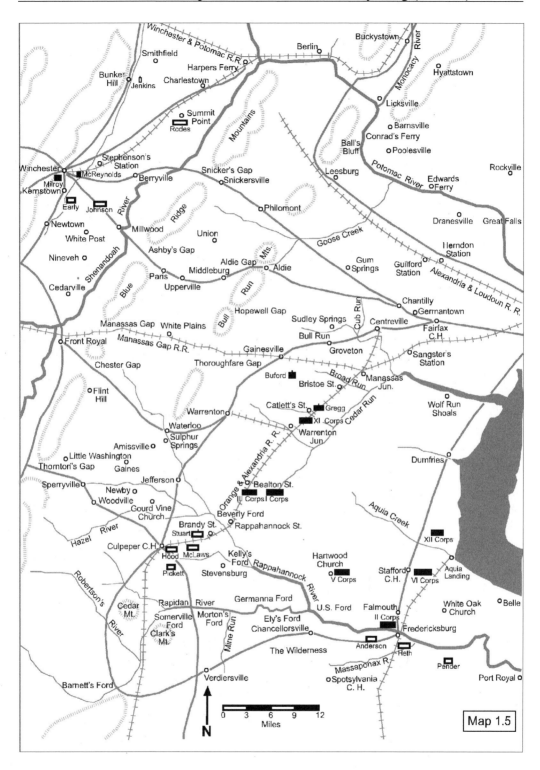

Map 1.5

Map 1.6 (June 14)

President Abraham Lincoln anxiously followed the frenzied activity in Northern Virginia as he tried to piece together Lee's movements. "The enemy have Milroy surrounded at Winchester and Tyler at Martinsburg," he wrote Hooker. "If they could hold out a few days, could you help them?" Then Lincoln added one of his most memorable lines: "if the head of Lee's army is at Martinsburg and the tail of it on the Plank Road between Fredericksburg and Chancellorsville, the animal must be very slim somewhere. Could you not break him?"[30]

The Federal army continued its long marches on June 14. The I and III Corps of Reynolds' wing left Bealton Station by a road paralleling the Orange and Alexandria Railroad. Passing Warrington Junction, they drove on toward Manassas Junction. As midnight struck, the III Corps reached Catlett's Station and halted for the night. The I Corps was not so lucky, continuing its march through the night. The V Corps reached Catlett's Station about 7:00 p.m. after a 20-mile march. A soldier in Weed's brigade remembered, "some of them [the men] fell out of the ranks, just as though they had been shot." The XI Corps started the day at Catlett's Station, marched north to Bristoe Station, and finally halted a few miles from Centreville. The widely dispersed VI Corps assembled at Stafford Court House and marched through the night of June 14 and into the early morning hours of June 15. Congested road conditions slowed the march. The XII Corps completed an all-night march on June 13-14, reaching Dumfries at 9:00 a.m. on June 14, where the men rested and recuperated for the rest of the day. The II Corps broke camp but did not make much progress on June 14.[31]

These were miserable marches for the Federal troops. According to John Halsey of the 17th Maine, Colonel Philippe de Trobriand's brigade, "it is difficult to get sufficient water for drinking, and as for ablutions, a mud puddle would be deemed an inestimable treasure." Darkness brought moderating temperatures, but there were other hazards, such as "falling off bridges, stumbling into ditches, tearing the face and injuring the eyes against the bushes and projecting limbs of trees often sprung back from a soldier ahead."[32]

With the Federals abandoning their camps at Falmouth Heights, Lee put Richard H. Anderson's Division of the Third Corps on the road to Culpeper Court House on June 14; the other two divisions of Hill's Third Corps remained near Fredericksburg. The First Corps remained in camp at Culpeper Court House, while the Second Corps closed its trap on Milroy's division sitting at Winchester. With McReynolds beyond his grasp, Rodes decided to follow his original orders and marched his division through Smithfield and Bunker Hill, finally reaching Martinsburg at 9:00 p.m. The town had been occupied by Colonel Benjamin Smith and 1,200 Federals troops. Prior to Rodes' arrival, however, Jenkins' cavalry drove back the Federal picket line, which made it plain that an attack was imminent. While waiting for Rodes' infantry to arrive, Jenkins demanded the garrison's surrender; Smith declined. The Confederates did not know that Smith had decided to withdraw after dark. When Rodes reached the town, he directed Jenkins to dismount his command and advance from the west to cut off the retreat while his infantry attacked in the darkness from the east and south.

It was too late; Smith was already gone. Rodes had to be content with five abandoned cannon and a variety of important supplies. As he lamented in his report, "could the division have reached the town an hour or two earlier . . . I would have captured the whole force." To the south, Early's and Johnson's divisions continued their advance on Winchester and Milroy's main body on June 14.[33]

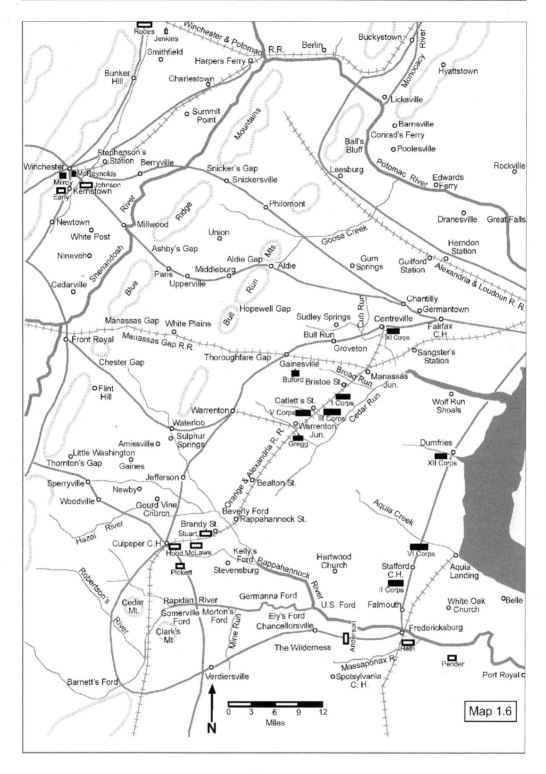

Map 1.6

Map 1.7 (June 15)

June 15 found Hooker's entire army on the march toward its rendezvous points along the Orange . and Alexandria Railroad. Reynolds aimed his wing for Centreville, and the XI Corps reached it first about 9:00 a.m. The exhausted I Corps was the next to arrive. It had been marching all night—25 miles in nearly 20 hours. The men finally reached Manassas Junction at 3:30 a.m. Their wake was littered with blankets, rations, and other belongings they had shed to lighten their loads. At 8:30 a.m. they were ordered back into column and marched to Centreville, which they reached about noon. Several hours behind trudged the III Corps, which had not marched through the night. Its 15-hour march brought it to Bull Run at 10:00 p.m. Tramping along the Orange and Alexandria Railroad, the V Corps reached Manassas Junction by noon. After an hour's rest the men were back on the march, halting a few miles from Centreville for the night. Gregg's cavalry division rode to the Bull Run battlefield, where it joined Buford's division. During the next 48 hours, patrols fanned outward looking for signs of enemy movements.[34]

Farther east, the Federal right wing was also on the move. The VI Corps had marched all through the night of June 14-15. After a brief respite at Aquia Creek, the footsore men continued their trek to Dumfries, arriving there at 11:00 a.m., where they rested and ate. The XII Corps, which had left Dumfries at 2:30 a.m., was well ahead by this time. Its 25-mile march ended at Fairfax Court House about 9:00 p.m. Far to the south the II Corps brought up the rear, finally camping about a mile north of Aquia Creek.[35]

All of the Confederate infantry was on the march on June 15. The First Corps broke camp around Culpeper Court House and followed the Second Corps toward the Shenandoah Valley. Hood's Division made the longest march, halting just across the Hazel River. McLaws' and Pickett's divisions followed. The Third Corps, with Anderson's Division in the lead, continued toward Culpeper Court House. Anderson's men camped for the night about four miles south of Stevensburg. Henry Heth's Division left

Fredericksburg and marched about nine miles, reaching the vicinity of the Chancellorsville battlefield. Only William Pender's Division remained behind at Fredericksburg. Stuart's cavalry, by this time well rested near Brandy Station, broke camp and prepared to ride north to screen the Confederate advance. The road was so clogged with wagons, however, that Stuart decided to postpone his movement until June 16.[36]

On the evening of June 14, General Jenkins received orders to ride to Chambersburg, Pennsylvania, to gather supplies. His men were in the saddle early the next morning and Jenkins headed north, but the hit-and-run tactics of Captain William Boyd and his 1st New York (Lincoln) Cavalry impeded his progress. Warned of Jenkins' plans, bankers and storekeepers either hid their valuables or sent them north. Two young Confederate officers entered Chambersburg about 11:00 p.m., where former soldiers and other townspeople seized them. The Confederate main body rode in soon after, and a furious Jenkins demanded their release. The rest of Jenkins' horsemen camped about a mile north of the town.[37]

The Confederate Second Corps won a stirring victory north of Winchester at Stephenson's Depot on June 15 (see Map Set 3). While Johnson's Division took on Milroy's men, Early's soldiers remained within supporting distance at Winchester. Rodes' Division continued its march down the Valley, reaching the Potomac River across from Williamsport about 11:00 p.m. Rodes threw the brigades of Stephen D. Ramseur, Alfred Iverson, and George P. Doles across the river with three batteries, retaining Edward O'Neal's and Junius Daniel's brigades on the Virginia side with the remainder of his artillery.[38]

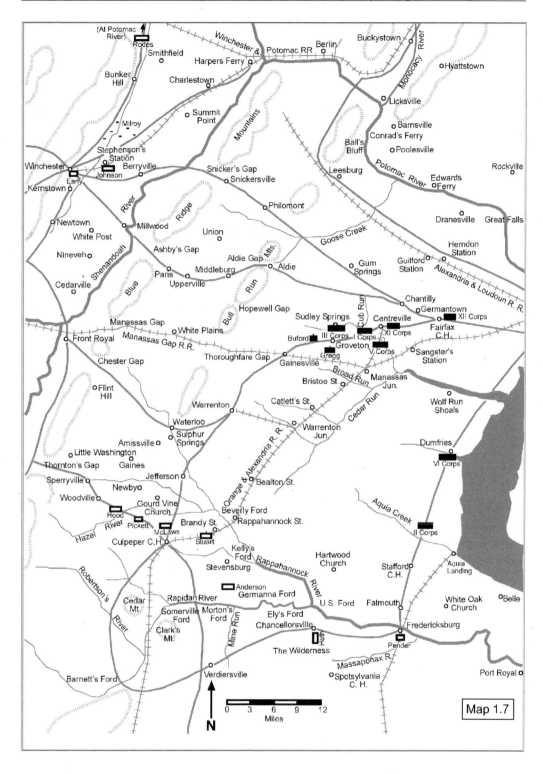

Map 1.7

Map 1.8 (June 16)

June 16 found all but two Federal corps resting in their camps. The I and XI Corps occupied Centreville, the III Corps camped near the old Bull Run battlefield, the V Corps remained near Manassas Junction, and the XII Corps was near Fairfax Court House. Only the II and VI Corps were on the march. The former reached Dumfries at 8:00 a.m., quickly pushing on to Wolf Run Shoals. "One would scarce have recognized his best friend through the sweat and dust," Captain George Bowen of the 12th New Jersey wrote in his diary, "our faces would be wet with perspiration, the dust would settle on it, then a drop would start running down and wash a path through, this would soon fill, and again it would be washed off."[39]

Following the routine established the day before, the VI Corps was back on the road shortly before midnight and marched all through the early morning hours of June 16. The column passed through Wolf Run Shoals ahead of the II Corps before resting. The cool waters provided a large measure of relief. The men bathed their blistered feet, poured it on their heads, slaked their thirst, and refilled their canteens. Then it was on to Fairfax Court House, which the men reached that evening. Determined to find Lee's infantry, Hooker sent Pleasonton's cavalry west toward Aldie Gap in the Bull Run Mountains, which opened into the Shenandoah Valley. Gregg's division led the column, followed by Buford's division.[40]

Unlike Hooker's army, most of Lee's was on the march on June 16. Well ahead, Ewell's Second Corps continued concentrating along the Potomac River. Rodes' Division already straddled the river at Williamsport, and now Johnson's Division marched toward Shepherdstown, halting for the night just south of Smithfield. Brig. Gen. John M. Jones' Brigade left the division to destroy boats and parts of the Chesapeake and Ohio Canal. Early's Division remained in camp at Winchester.

Hood's Division led Longstreet's First Corps advance. Instead of following Ewell's Second Corps into the Shenandoah Valley, Longstreet guided his troops east of the Blue Ridge Mountains. The high heat and humidity wore on the men as they marched in the hilly country from Marcum Station on the Manassas Gap Railroad. Far to the rear, General Pickett's three First Corps brigades splashed across the Hazel River and eventually camped near Gaines' Crossroads. "The dust is almost suffocating," one soldier recalled. "[I]t forms a fine impalpable powder, sufficiently light to fill the air like smoke; and penetrate the eyes, ears, nostrils, hair, and skin, until its power of annoyance is unbearable. Then, when one's clothing is utterly saturated with perspiration mixing with the dust in a grimy paste; and above all weighs the heavy musket . . . and the chafing canteen straps, is it strange that one sees hundreds of men gasping for breath, and lolling out their tongues like mad men?" Bringing up the rear, McLaws' First Corps division marched to Sperryville.

With the departure of Pender's Division of the Third Corps from Fredericksburg at 4:00 a.m., Lee's entire army was now on the march. Anderson's Division reached Culpeper Court House and Heth's Division camped within twelve miles of it. Jenkins' cavalry remained in Chambersburg, scrounging the countryside for supplies, impressing both runaway slaves and free blacks and creating panic in the state—particularly in Harrisburg, which was being evacuated. As one observer keenly noted, the movement "[is] no longer a flight—it is a flood."[41]

Stuart established his headquarters that evening at Salem. With him were Beverly Robertson's and W. H. F. "Rooney" Lee's brigades. Wade Hampton's and John M. Jones' brigades were resting to the rear between Hill's and Longstreet's corps, and three regiments of Fitzhugh Lee's Brigade were at Piedmont while two others occupied Upperville.[42]

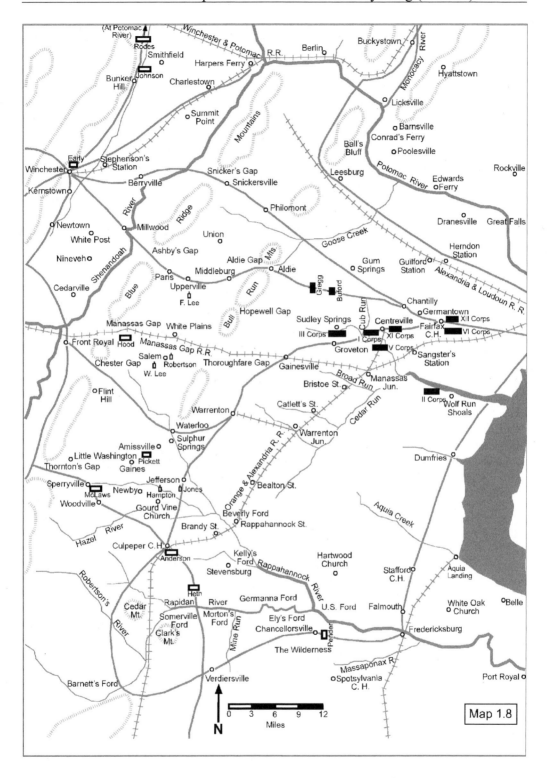

Map 1.8

Map 1.9 (June 17)

Several of Hooker's corps traveled northward from their camps along the Orange and Alexandria Railroad. The XI Corps made the longest march—23 miles from Centreville to Goose Creek. The V Corps made a 10-mile march to Gum Springs. General Samuel Crawford's Pennsylvania Reserve division joined the corps here after spending the last few months around Washington. The I Corps broke camp near Centreville and marched 14 miles to Herndon Station on the Alexandria and Loudoun Railroad. The III Corps marched a mere three miles to Centreville, as the XII Corps moved to within two or three miles of Dranesville near the Potomac. The II Corps, the army's rearguard, reached Sangster's Station on the Orange and Alexandria Railroad. Only the VI Corps, which had marched through the night, remained in camp near Fairfax Court House.[43]

Far to the north, Ewell's Second Corps occupied the lower Shenandoah Valley. Only Johnson's Division was on the march, moving 12 miles to within three miles south of Shepherdstown. Early's Division remained in camp at Winchester. Rodes' Division straddled the Potomac River (Daniel's Brigade crossed to join the three brigades already in Maryland). Longstreet's First Corps continued its march on the eastern side of the Blue Ridge range. Hood's Division in the van struck a fast pace in the hilly countryside and ended its march about two miles beyond Upperville. Pickett's Division marched to Brice's Crossroads, and McLaws' Division halted for the night beyond Gaines' Crossroads. Hill's Third Corps brought up the army's rear. Anderson's Division left Culpeper Court House and camped on the opposite side of the Hazel River. Heth's Division reached Culpeper Court House and camped about two miles beyond it, while Pender's Division halted about 12 miles south of the Court House.[44]

Pleasonton's cavalry units continued their trek toward Aldie Gap. In search of rebel activity, Colonel Duffié's 1st Rhode Island rode to Loudoun Valley. When the rest of Pleasonton's command was about nine miles from Aldie, the general ordered Gregg to spin off a brigade to

reconnoiter through Aldie Gap before pushing toward Front Royal in the Shenandoah Valley. Gregg selected the brigade riding at the head of his column, an outfit commanded by Brig. Gen. Judson Kilpatrick.[45]

These movements put the two cavalry forces on a collision course. Stuart was deploying his Confederate troopers at the critical mountain passes. W. H. F. Lee's Brigade, under Colonel John Chambliss, rode toward Thoroughfare Gap, and Jones' Brigade headed for Warrenton and then Salem. Hampton's Brigade remained behind on the Rappahannock River. Robertson's Brigade took up a position at Rectortown, where it could support either unit. Fitz Lee's Brigade, under the command of Colonel Thomas Munford, rode to Aldie, where it collided with Kilpatrick's brigade. Munford was at a disadvantage as only a portion of his brigade was up during the initial encounter. Kilpatrick did not take advantage of this opportunity, choosing instead to throw his troops into the fight piecemeal, never bringing his superior force to bear. What should have been a sharp Union victory resulted in a bloody stalemate as Munford threw his units into action as they arrived. By the time the action ended, Kilpatrick had lost 20% of his command; Munford's losses totaled less than half that figure.[46]

Duffié rode through Thoroughfare Gap and headed for Middleburg, where his men encountered large numbers of Confederate horsemen. He quickly ordered his men to barricade themselves in the town and called for immediate aid, but none came. The resulting fight with Chambliss' Brigade was bloody and decisive. Only Duffié and eighty of his original 300 men made their way to safety, and only because darkness hid them as the battle waned.[47]

Farther north, upon hearing that Federal troops were approaching, General Jenkins quickly left Chambersburg and headed south. He spun off a 250-man contingent under Col. Milton J. Ferguson at Greencastle to search the McConnellsburg region for additional supplies. Jenkins continued riding south and eventually linked up with Rodes' Division at Williamsport.[48]

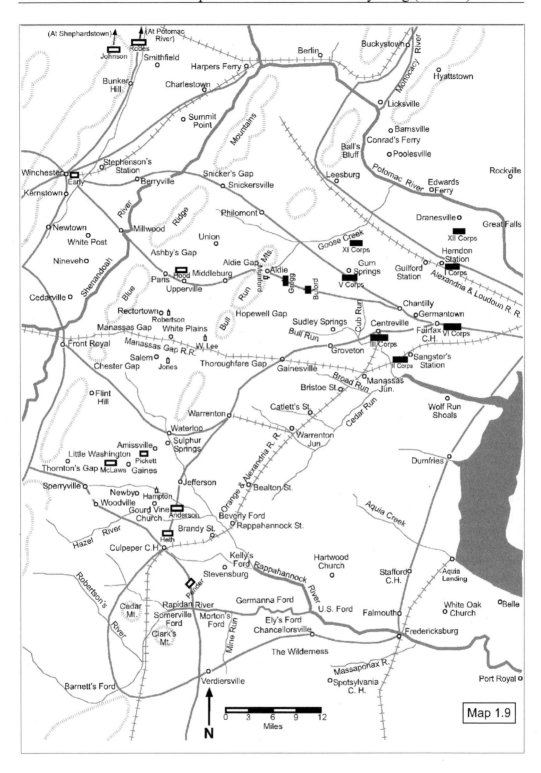

Map 1.10 (June 18)

June 18 found the Federal II, III, V, and XI Corps ensconced in their camps, with the I Corps reestablishing its camp at nearby Guilford Station. The VI Corps marched to Fairfax Court House, where the men halted to have breakfast. When the expected orders to resume the march failed to materialize, the men remained in camp. Only the XI Corps made a significant march, moving 20 miles to Leesburg, where it guarded the Potomac River fords.

Help was on the way for Maj. Gen. Darius Couch, commander of the newly formed Department of the Susquehanna. A militia brigade composed of two New York regiments numbering 800 men arrived in Harrisburg. Couch put Brig. Gen. Joseph Knipe in command of the unit.[49]

On the Confederate side, Johnson's Division splashed across the Potomac River at Boteler's Ford. Marylanders in Brig. Gen. George Steuart's Brigade kissed the ground when they stepped on their home soil. The division spent the night near Sharpsburg. Rodes' Division remained in camp in Maryland and Early's Division finally left Winchester and marched to Shepherdstown. Hood's Division of the First Corps, which had been marching east of the Blue Ridge Mountains, finally entered the Shenandoah Valley through Ashby's Gap. After wading the Shenandoah River, the men marched another mile before going into camp. Laws' and Anderson's brigades peeled off to guard Snicker's Ford. Pickett's Division remained east of the Blue Ridge Mountains, ending the day at Paris, where Hood's Division had begun it. To the south, McLaws' Division halted at Piedmont Station on the Manassas Gap Railroad.

The beauty of the countryside helped to temper the harshness of the marches. "I was never more struck with the grandeur of mountain scenery than on this march," remembered Surgeon Charles Lippitt of Pickett's Division. "No other scenery can equal it."[50]

A. P. Hill's Third Corps was also on the march. Anderson's Division reached the vicinity of Flint Hill, Heth's Division passed Sperryville and camped between it and Gaines' Crossroads,

and Pender's Division finally marched through Culpeper Court House and camped about four miles beyond it.

Stuart consolidated his cavalry command near the vital mountain passes on June 18. Chambliss' and Robertson's brigades occupied areas near Middleburg, Munford's Brigade shifted back from Aldie to Union to remain within reach of Snicker's Gap and within supporting distance of Chambliss and Robertson to the south. William E. "Grumble" Jones' Brigade, riding from Rector's Crossroads, would join Munford the next day and Wade Hampton's Brigade still guarded the Rappahannock River. Partisan ranger Colonel John Mosby captured a Federal courier carrying dispatches with the positions of all Federal units on June 17, as well as their orders for the following day. This information was sent to Stuart and on to General Lee. Hampton's Brigade rode to Warrenton, also the destination of a reconnaissance by General Julius Stahel's Union cavalry division.[51]

While Stuart plugged the mountain passes in an attempt to keep the Federals from gaining information about Lee's movements, Alfred Pleasanton mounted four ambitious expeditions to do just that. Colonel Thomas Devin's brigade of Buford's division rode toward Thoroughfare Gap in the Bull Run Mountains to scout for enemy infantry and remained there until June 20, when it returned to the division. Colonel William Gamble's brigade moved toward Snicker's Gap, where it encountered Munford's Brigade (which had ridden from Union to Philomont). Gamble decided to return to headquarters without engaging the Virginians. Major J. Irvin Gregg, who commanded a brigade in his cousin's Brig. Gen. David McMurtrie Gregg's division, approached the Blue Ridge Mountains via Middleburg to test Confederate strength there. Pushing aside elements of Chambliss' and Robertson's brigades in a series of skirmishes, Colonel Gregg moved his troopers into Middleburg and occupied Duffié's barricades. Gregg pulled back that night about halfway to Aldie without venturing beyond Ashby's Gap.[52]

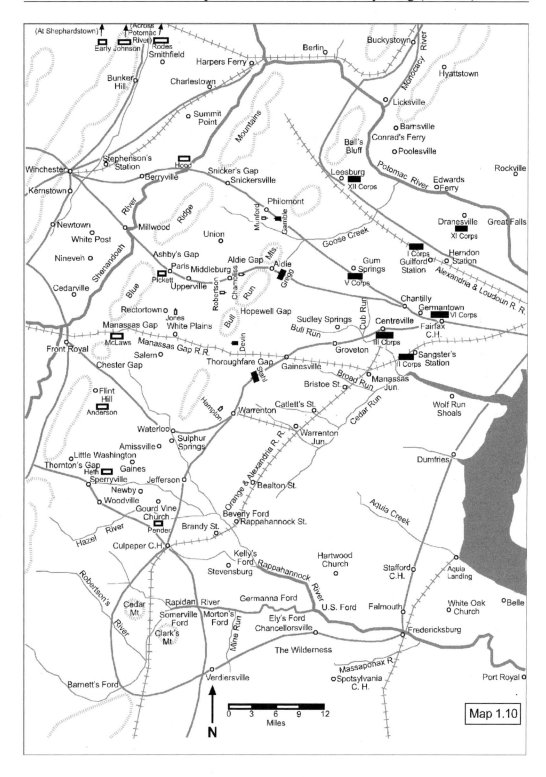

Map 1.10

Map 1.11 (June 19-20)

June 19 found three of Hooker's seven infantry corps on the move. As the II Corps marched from Sangster's Station to Centreville to join the rest of the army, the V Corps advanced from Gum Springs toward Aldie near the Bull Run Mountains where they could support Pleasonton's cavalry forays. The III Corps took up a position at Gum Springs. General Gregg's cavalry division, along with Gamble's brigade from Buford's division, rode at dawn from Aldie to Middleburg. Upperville was their destination, but the troopers never reached it because they encountered Chambliss' Brigade approaching from Middleburg. A series of hand-to-hand actions ended near Middleburg when Chambliss pulled his troopers back to a good defensive line that protected the mountain passes. While Gregg battled Chambliss, Gamble's detached brigade collided with Grumble Jones' Brigade about three miles to the northwest. The Virginians tried several times to drive Gamble from their path, but every effort failed. They finally withdrew a short distance, ending the fight. Neither Union cavalry brigade succeeded in penetrating the passes or locating any of Lee's infantry.[53]

Early's and Johnson's divisions of Ewell's Second Corps remained in camp on June 19. O'Neal's Brigade, the last in Rodes' Division to leave Virginia, crossed the Potomac and the combined unit marched to Hagerstown, Maryland, then two miles farther to Funkstown, screened all the while by Jenkins' cavalry brigade. Far to the south, Anderson's Division led the Third Corps through Chester Gap into the Shenandoah Valley. It marched through Front Royal, crossed the Shenandoah River, and went into camp in an exceptionally muddy area. Heth's Division, marching in the middle of the corps, reached Chester Gap that night, and Pender's Division, bringing up the rear, crossed Hazel River and camped at Gaines' Crossroads. Longstreet's First Corps helped Stuart's cavalry hold the Blue Ridge Mountain gaps. Laws' and Robertson's brigades of Hood's Division defended Snicker's Gap, while Anderson's and Benning's brigades marched to Snickersville.

McLaws' Division marched through heavy mud to reach Ashby's Gap, where they took up defensive positions. Pickett's Division camped midway between the two where it could provide support to either.[54]

The Federal II Corps marched on June 20. Leaving Centreville, it headed for Thoroughfare Gap. Hays' division camped at Gainesville while Gibbon's and Caldwell's divisions continued on to Haymarket. Barnes' division of the V Corps broke camp about 3:00 a.m. and marched toward Middleburg to support Pleasonton's cavalry. Heavy rains hindered cavalry movement, and a sharp skirmish erupted between Gamble's brigade and the 5th Virginia of Munford's Brigade. Howe's division of the VI Corps was also on the move, marching about 18 miles to Bristoe Station to cover the army's left flank.[55]

June 20 found the Confederate Second Corps in its camps in western Maryland and Northern Virginia. Jenkins' cavalry brigade rode into Pennsylvania again, camping just south of Greencastle. Anderson's Division of the Third Corps reached White Post in the evening. Heth's Division entered the Shenandoah Valley, closing on Anderson's Division while Pender's Division camped near Chester Gap, poised to enter the Shenandoah Valley. After reconsolidating his division at Snicker's Gap and building strong breastworks, Hood left the gap and re-crossed the Shenandoah River. Pickett's Division crossed the same river at Snicker's Ferry and promptly went into camp. McLaws' Division crossed at Berry's Ford, and went into camp. Hampton's Brigade, riding from Warrenton, finally joined the rest of Stuart's Division in Loudoun Valley. Because Snicker's Gap was guarded by Hood and McLaws, Stuart believed he could safely station only one cavalry brigade there. He selected Munford's and sent the balance of his brigades to Upperville and Ashby's Gap, which he deemed to be the most vulnerable. Chambliss' and Jones' Brigades were stationed near Union, Robertson's and Hampton's at Middleburg.[56]

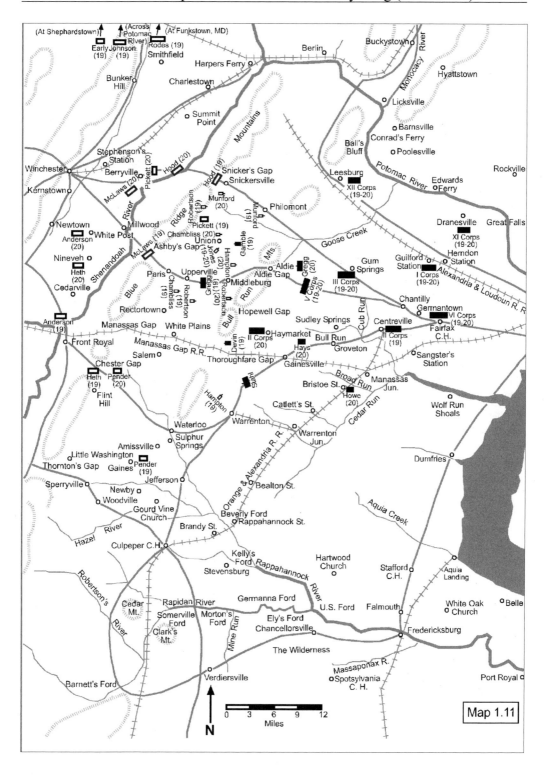

Map 1.11

Map 1.12 (June 21-22)

Except for Barnes' division of the V Corps, which marched to Middleburg to join Pleasonton's cavalry in its attack against Stuart's troopers, Hooker's units remained in camp. Pleasonton assembled all 12,000 of his cavalry to attack Stuart. According to the plan, Buford's division would ride north around Stuart's left flank just below Goose Creek, while Gregg's division, supported by Col. Strong Vincent's infantry brigade of the V Corps, distracted the enemy by attacking his center and right.

The lead elements of Gregg's division encountered Hampton's and Robertson's brigades east of Upperville at 3:00 p.m. The outnumbered Confederates resorted to a leap-frogging defense to delay the Federal advance. Stuart finally ordered the two brigades to ride through Upperville to avoid a fight in the town. As Hampton's men took position on the opposite side, the lead elements of Gregg's column barreled into Robertson's rearguard as it was leaving. Hampton ordered a counterattack, driving the enemy out of Upperville. Federal reinforcements forced Hampton back, but he ordered another attack, forcing the Yanks back again. Both sides pulled back to reorganize. When he spotted what he believed was Vincent's approaching infantry, Hampton retreated with Robertson's Brigade to Ashby's Gap.

Meanwhile, Buford moved against what he thought was Stuart's left flank at Middleburg. The movement began two hours late. By this time both men and horses were fractious, as neither had eaten in two days. Buford quickly learned that his information about Stuart's positions was incorrect and that he was not moving against Stuart's vulnerable flank. Finding Jones' Brigade in his path, Buford's men pushed it back toward Upperville. The Virginians resorted to delaying actions, forcing Buford's men to redeploy to push the tenacious troopers from their front. Outside of Upperville, Jones and Chambliss joined forces and deployed their brigades to put up another fight. Jones attacked Buford's men, who had taken position behind a stone wall, but could not dislodge them. Jones broke off the action and rode toward Ashby's

Gap. Following the retreating Confederates, Buford's men approached the gap and observed McLaws' infantry beyond it, confirming that Confederate infantry was in the region.[57]

Five of Lee's nine divisions remained in camp on June 21. The Third Corps passed Longstreet's First Corps, which was delayed at the Blue Ridge Mountain passes. Anderson's Division, leading the corps, reached Berryville about noon, and Heth's Division joined it that night. Pender's Division camped at White Post. Only McLaws' Division of the First Corps was in motion, re-crossing the Shenandoah River and taking position at Ashby's Gap to help repel an expected Federal cavalry attack. The attack never materialized, and the men spent a miserable night without blankets or fires.[58]

June 22 found only Barnes' division and Pleasonton's cavalry on the move. The former rejoined the V Corps at Aldie; the latter withdrew east toward Middleburg. Stuart collected his troopers and camped at Rector's Cross Roads. With the last remaining divisions of Confederate infantry approaching the Potomac River, he had completed his job of guarding the passes. The cavalier approached Lee with a bold plan to ride around the Federal army, collect supplies, and guard Ewell's right flank. Lee agreed—but only if Stuart left two brigades behind to guard the Blue Ridge passes. It was a fateful decision.[59]

With Anderson's Division approaching Shepherdstown on June 22, Early's Division received orders to cross the Potomac River and move to Sharpsburg, finally camping three miles beyond Boonesborough. Johnson's Division was already in Sharpsburg, having reached it a few days before. Rodes' Division, which had camped near Funkstown since June 19, crossed into Pennsylvania and went into camp two miles beyond Greencastle. Anderson's Division reached Charlestown that night, and Pender's Division approached Berryville. Heth's Division remained in camp. Pickett's Division also remained in camp; three-quarters of Hood's Division marched to Millwood. Only Anderson's Brigade remained behind at Snicker's Gap. With the Federal cavalry gone, McLaws' Division re-crossed the Shenandoah River.[60]

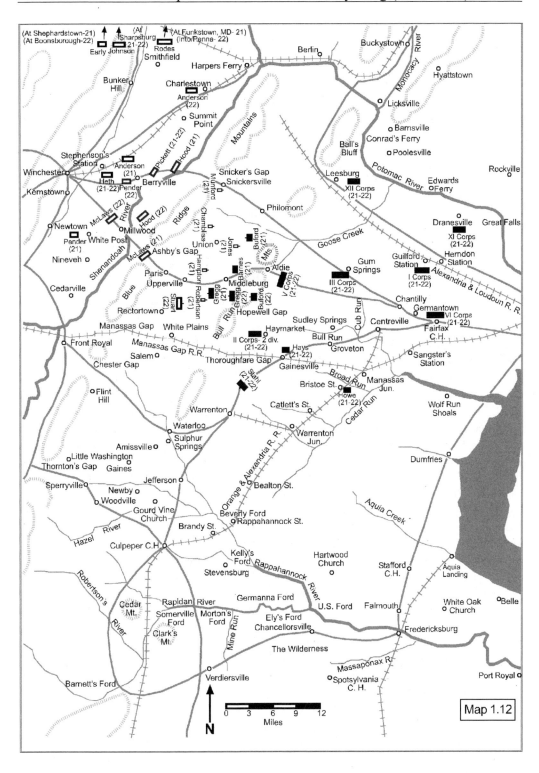

Map 1.12

Map 1.13 (June 23-24)

June 23 found all of the Federal infantry and some of the Confederates resting in their camps. After a few days of rest, Johnson's Division marched to Hagerstown, then on toward Pennsylvania, camping within a few miles of the border. Early's Division marched through Cavetown, Smithburg, and finally entered Pennsylvania at Waynesboro. Rodes' Division rested near Greencastle. Jenkins' cavalry brigade reentered Chambersburg less tentatively than on its earlier visit; this time around the general demanded rations from the citizens. The Confederate First Corps remained in camp far to the south in Virginia. The entire Third Corps was on the road. Anderson's Division marched through Charlestown to Shepherdstown, within a few miles of the Potomac River. Heth's Division passed Charlestown and continued on toward Shepherdstown. Pender's Division marched through Berryville and continued north.[61]

Lee sent Stuart additional orders on June 23, telling him to cross the Blue Ridge Mountains and ride to Frederick to ensure that Hooker was not contemplating a strike south toward Richmond. He left Stuart with discretionary powers that the cavalry chief quickly used. After conferring with partisan ranger John Mosby, Stuart decided to ride through the Federal army by crossing a gap in the Bull Run Mountains below Middleburg, turn north, ford the Potomac River at Seneca Ford, and move into Maryland.[62]

Meanwhile, Pleasonton's Federal cavalrymen rested near Aldie. Hooker was receiving information hourly on Lee as he prepared to move his army into Maryland, but only the XI Corps was on the march on June 24, approaching Edwards' Ferry in preparation for the crossing of the Potomac River.

For the first time in quite a while, virtually all of Lee's army was on the move. Rodes' Division, which was farthest north, broke camp at 5:00 a.m. and reached Chambersburg by noon. Ewell rode in a buggy at the head of the column. Rodes was again upset with Jenkins. His cavalry had not held Chambersburg until the infantry arrived, which led to the loss of valuable supplies. Rodes'

men marched another three miles to the banks of the Conococheague River while Jenkins' command reconnoitered toward Carlisle by way of Shippensburg. Fired on by a detachment of the 1st New York (Lincoln) Cavalry, Jenkins panicked and requested infantry support. Rodes quickly sent Junius Daniel's Brigade to his aid. Johnson's Division also resumed its march, entering Pennsylvania and camping within three miles of Chambersburg. Steuart's Brigade was detached and marched to McConnellsburg on the opposite side of Cove Mountain to collect supplies and guard the left flank. Along the way, the brigade stopped at Mercersburg, where the men "shopped" before continuing on toward McConnellsburg. There, the men encountered Federal militia under Colonel Jacob Szink and easily scattered them in all directions. Early's Division marched from Waynesboro, through Quincy and Mount Alto, halting for the night at Greenwood. Splashing across the Potomac River, Anderson's Division of the Third Corps marched through Sharpsburg. Pender's Division marched to Shepherdstown, where it joined an idle Heth's Division. Farther south, Pickett's Division led the First Corps advance. Marching through Berryville, it halted for the night at Darksville. Reunited with Anderson's Brigade, Hood's Division marched steadily toward Shepherdstown, halting for the night at Summit Point. McLaws' Division arrived a short time later.[63]

General Stuart, meanwhile, finalized his plans on June 24. He decided to leave one small brigade under Beverly Robertson and a larger one under Grumble Jones to guard the gaps while he rode north with his remaining three brigades. Some believe Stuart left behind his weakest and least efficient brigades to accompany Lee's army. Stuart moved his headquarters from Rector's Crossroads to Salem to be closer to the Bull Run Mountains. Having recovered from a bout of arthritis, General Fitz Lee returned to command his brigade, sending Colonel Munford back to his regiment.[64]

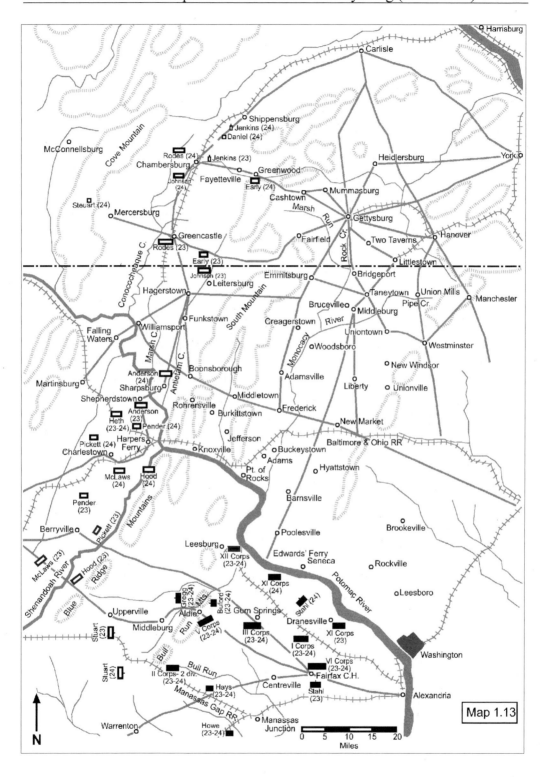

Map 1.13

Map 1.14 (June 25)

Hooker quickly finalized his plans to move the army north into Maryland on June 25. Reynolds, commanding the I, III, and XI Corps of the left wing, would cross the Potomac River and seize the vital Crampton's and Turner's gaps. Stahel's cavalry division would guard Reynolds' right flank while Buford's cavalry division guarded the rear of the wing. The XI Corps crossed the river first at Edwards Ferry, marching a total of 24 miles before camping for the night at Jefferson. The III Corps crossed next and marched along the slippery banks lining the Chesapeake and Ohio Canal. Its 25-mile march ended at 10:00 p.m. at the Monocacy Aqueduct. The I Corps crossed the river last, marching through Poolesville before ending the day at Barnsville.

The rest of the army would move in stages. The II Corps marched from Thoroughfare Gap to Gum Springs, where it replaced the III Corps. The V Corps remained near Aldie to support Pleasonton's cavalry; the VI Corps remained near Centreville, where it waited for Howe's division to rejoin it. The XII Corps remained in camp near Leesburg, watching the army's right flank. Gregg's cavalry division guarded the rear and continued to do so through June 27.[65]

Knowing that they were back in friendly territory made the long and fatiguing marches in the steady rain easier to bear. "It seemed pleasant once more to see smiling faces and to be greeted with friendly words," noted Charles Davis of the 13th Massachusetts, Paul's brigade. At Poolesville, "the women cheered us and waved their handkerchiefs as well. This is the first place for them to do so," wrote John McMahon of Smith's brigade. The rain made the marches even more difficult and the respites from the marches were not much better. Colonel Regis de Trobriand recalled that his men spent that night "without shelter, without supper, in a driving rain, we slept in the mud that sound sleep which is known only to soldiers worn with fatigue."[66]

Lee's army was also on the move. Anderson's Division at the van of the Third Corps tromped through Hagerstown and entered Pennsylvania at Middleburg (State Line).

Heth's and Pender's divisions crossed the Potomac River into Maryland and camped within ten miles of Hagerstown. Bringing up the rear of Lee's army, Longstreet's First Corps also approached the Potomac River. Pickett's Division forded the river at Falling Waters and advanced about a mile before bedding down. Hood's and McLaws' divisions bypassed Martinsburg and camped within a few miles of the Potomac. Already in Pennsylvania, the Second Corps rested. Despite the bountiful countryside, the officers discouraged foraging and food was scarce. "I ate my day's rations at one mouthful—not one meal," grumbled a soldier in the 3rd South Carolina, Kershaw's Brigade.[67]

During the earliest minutes of June 25, Stuart led Hampton's, Fitz Lee's, and Chambliss' brigades south from Salem to Glasscock's Gap in the Bull Run Mountains. The 5,300 men saw few Federal troops as they swept through the pass. Noon found the column near Haymarket, where the cavalrymen encountered Hancock's II Corps as they rode north. At this point Stuart should perhaps have aborted his plan to ride through the Union army and sought to rejoin Lee in the most direct manner possible. He had no intention of doing so. Instead, he altered his course to swing still farther south and east around the Federal troops. Stuart deployed a battery that opened fire on the Union infantry, triggering considerable consternation but not much damage. The battery limbered up and quickly departed, as the rest of Stuart's column headed for Gainesville on the Manassas Gap Railroad, where it spent the night. Stuart sent information to Lee that the Federal army was again on the march, but his message never reached the Confederate commander. Lee would not hear from his best cavalry officer for almost one week.[68]

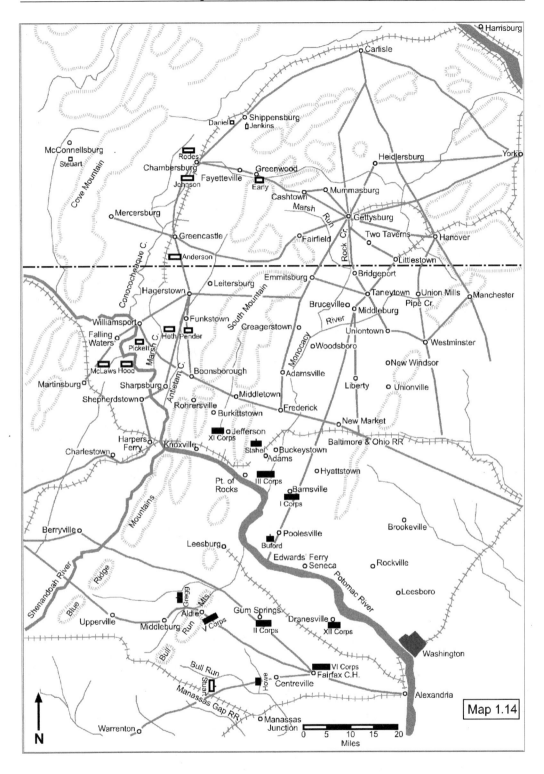

Map 1.15 (June 26)

The entire Federal army was in motion on June 26. The left wing under Reynolds began concentrating in the mountainous region west of Frederick, Maryland. A brigade in Francis C. Barlow's division of the XI Corps moved forward to secure Crampton's Gap, while a brigade in Adolph von Steinwehr's division advanced to Boonesborough Gap. Allowed to rest until noon, the remainder of the corps reached Middletown by evening. The III Corps continued its march along the Baltimore and Ohio Railroad to Point of Rocks, and the I Corps crossed Catoctin Mountain to Jefferson, where it spent the night. The XII Corps, which had rested for about seven days in the Leesburg area, crossed the Potomac River at Edwards Ferry and followed the route used by the III Corps the day before to the Monocacy Aqueduct, where the men spent the night. Federal troops again filled Leesburg when the V Corps arrived. They remained but a short time, crossing the Potomac River about 9:00 p.m. and marching to Poolesville, where they bivouacked.

The right wing was also moving. The II Corps left Gum Springs, Virginia, crossed the Potomac River that night, and camped within two miles of Frederick. Howe's division of the VI Corps was marching when June 25 became June 26, reaching Centreville at 1:00 a.m., where it rejoined the rest of the VI Corps. The division did not have much time to rest, for the corps broke camp at 3:00 a.m. and marched through the day, camping for the night at Dranesville. Buford's and Gregg's cavalry divisions occupied the Leesburg sector, and Stahel's division approached Frederick, Maryland.[69]

The Confederate Second Corps split into two parts on June 26, each assigned a different destination in Pennsylvania. Rodes' and Johnson's divisions marched from Chambersburg toward Carlisle while Early's Division headed for Gettysburg and then York. Rodes' Division got as far as Dykeman Spring, just beyond Shippensburg, where it reunited with Daniel's Brigade, which had been supporting Jenkins' cavalry. Marching behind it, Johnson's Division spent the night about half a mile west

on Timber Hill where it awaited Steuart's Brigade, which had begun its trek back from McConnellsburg about 4:00 p.m. Heavy rains delayed the departure of Early's Division, but it eventually left Greenwood, destroying along the way the Caledonia Iron Works owned by abolitionist Thaddeus Stevens. At Mummasburg, Early detached Gordon's Brigade and, with Colonel E. V. White's 35th Virginia cavalry battalion, the Georgians headed for a small crossroads town called Gettysburg. Early sent Hays' Brigade to support Gordon's men, while William Smith's and Robert Hoke's brigades went into camp. Hoke had been wounded at Chancellorsville and command of his brigade had devolved to Colonel Isaac Avery. As they approached Gettysburg, White's cavalry tangled with the 26th Pennsylvania Militia. They captured about 175 prisoners and drove the rest away before entering the town. They did not make a favorable first impression. A Gettysburg professor likened the Confederates to "so many savages from the wilds of the Rocky Mountains." Early ordered the authorities to provide supplies, but they pleaded that none existed.

Anderson's Division of the Third Corps crossed into Pennsylvania and camped two miles beyond Greencastle while Heth's and Pender's divisions ended their march just south of Hagerstown. Pickett's Division of the First Corps marched through Hagerstown and entered Pennsylvania, camping about a mile from Greencastle. Far to the south, McLaws' and Hood's divisions reached Williamsport, Maryland, where they forded the Potomac River. Hood's men continued their long march. They crossed into Pennsylvania that evening and camped near Greencastle. McLaws' soldiers camped just beyond Williamsport. All of Lee's infantry was now on Northern soil.[70]

With uncharacteristic and perhaps undue caution, Stuart directed his troopers on June 26 to circle farther to the east. Instead of riding through Centreville, he directed his men to Brentsville and then to Wolf Run Shoals on the Occoquan River. He rested his men and mounts there for several hours before moving toward Fairfax Station.[71]

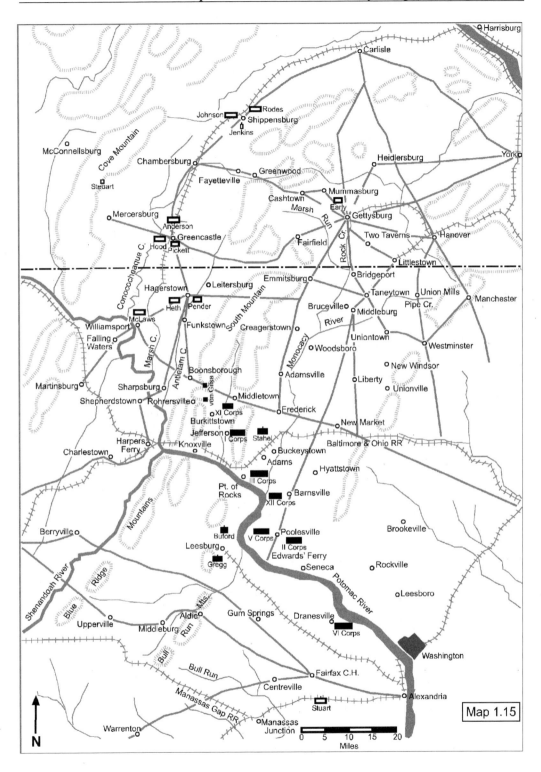

Map 1.15

Map 1.16 (June 27)

The entire Federal army continued concentrating in central Maryland on June 27. Reynolds' left wing consolidated its hold on the mountain passes. The I Corps marched about eight miles before halting just north of Middletown, where it joined the XI Corps. The III Corps marched a short distance to Burkittsville, just southwest of Middletown and within striking distance of Crampton's Gap. Colonel Leopold Von Gilsa's brigade of the XI Corps was already there as was Stahel's cavalry, scouring Catoctin Mountain. Buford's cavalry division rode from Edwards Ferry to Jefferson via Point of Rocks. Hooker's right wing was also on the move. The XII Corps left Point of Rocks and marched along the Potomac River to Knoxville, about five miles from Harpers Ferry and directly south of the left wing. The II Corps marched due north, from Poolesville to Barnsville, continuing along the base of Sugar Loaf Mountain and following the tracks of the Baltimore and Ohio Railroad. The VI Corps moved into Poolesville after it crossed the Potomac River. The V Corps marched through Buckeystown and then to Ballinger's Creek, a few miles from Frederick. Gregg's cavalry division also closed in on Frederick.[72]

The feuding between Joe Hooker and President Lincoln drew to a close when the president again rebuffed the general's efforts to secure additional reinforcements from the Harpers Ferry garrison. General Halleck wrote to Hooker, "Maryland Heights have always been regarded as an important point to be held by us . . . I cannot approve their abandonment." Receiving intelligence that Lee's army outnumbered his own, and unable to follow Lincoln's directive to stop Lee's advance, Hooker wrote, "I earnestly request that I may at once be relieved from the position I occupy."[73]

Carlisle, the northern-most community to host Confederate troops, was visited first by Jenkins' cavalry brigade and then by Rodes' and Johnson's divisions, which entered from different directions. Charged with guarding the town, Knipe's militia brigade quickly departed before the Confederates arrived. Jenkins did not

enjoy the fruits of Carlisle, for Ewell ordered him to ride west to begin scouting the approaches to Harrisburg. Steuart's Brigade reached Shippensburg and turned north to rendezvous with the rest of Johnson's Division. Meanwhile, Early's Division, minus Gordon's Brigade, trudged east from Mummasburg, spending the night outside of East Berlin. Its destination was York. Gordon's Brigade marched four miles ahead. Reaching Chambersburg, Anderson's Division of the Third Corps turned east and marched to Fayetteville, where it spent the night. The remainder of the corps reached it that evening. Greencastle, Pennsylvania hosted the arrival of the entire First Corps on June 27. Pickett's Division led the way, continuing on through Chambersburg and camping about three miles north where Hood's Division joined it. McLaws' Division camped about six miles south of Chambersburg.[74]

No one was happy with Lee's General Orders No. 73, which reiterated an earlier order about respecting private property: "It must be remembered that we make war only upon armed men, and that we cannot take vengeance for the wrongs our people have suffered without lowering ourselves in the eyes of all whose abhorrence has been excited by the atrocities of our enemies."[75]

June 27 found Stuart's men in the saddle early, riding toward Fairfax Court House. Stuart detached Fitz Lee's Brigade to Burke's Station to cut the telegraph wires and tear up railroad tracks. All three brigades finally reunited at Dranesville. Recent heavy rains caused a change in the fording site from Seneca Ford to Rowser's Ford. Hampton's Brigade led the difficult crossing of the Potomac. The deep water completely submerged the cannons. The artillerymen emptied their caissons and carried the ammunition across by hand. It was exhausting work for both man and beast, but they managed it without losing a gun. It also cost Stuart valuable time he could not spare.[76]

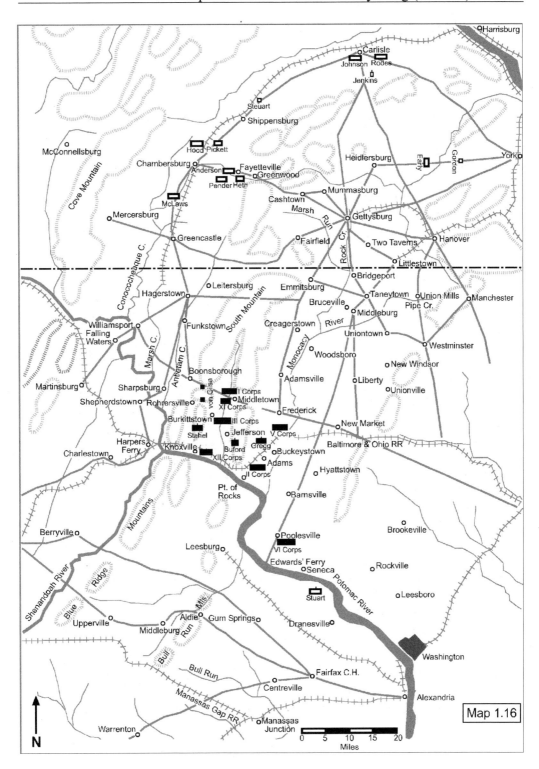

Map 1.16

Map 1.17 (June 28)

President Lincoln accepted Joe Hooker's resignation and named Maj. Gen. George Meade as his replacement. Informed of his new command at 3:00 a.m., Meade immediately sought information on the location of his far-flung army, which by the end of the day occupied a 30-mile arc from the Potomac River to Frederick. Many soldiers voiced concern, considering it unwise to change commanders in the middle of a campaign. Others felt differently. "I felt assured that the President would not place in command a person, in whom he had not the utmost confidence of his ability as a leader," wrote one soldier, "and especially at a time when we were so near the enemy and in daily expectation of coming in contact with him." Meade ordered the left wing to abandon the mountain passes and march on Frederick, which the three corps accomplished that night after crossing Catoctin Mountain. The XII Corps also crossed the mountain to reach Frederick, while the II Corps arrived at Monocacy Junction within view of Frederick. The VI Corps headed north from Poolesville, halting for the night at Hyattstown. Cherry trees lined many of the roads, providing the men with enjoyment and nourishment.[77]

Citizens came out to greet the soldiers, waving flags, cheering, and distributing food and water to the weary men. "This act of generosity and kindness brought forth repeated and hearty cheers from the ranks," recalled Thomas Marbaker of Carr's brigade. The III Corps received a hero's welcome when it reached Frederick. One old man waving a flag from a second-story window yelled, "Still they come! Still they come!" at the seemingly endless column of troops. A pretty young girl ran over to Colonel Regis de Trobriand with a bouquet of flowers. He called the march through the town "triumphal."[78]

Pleasonton convinced Meade to replace Stahel with Judson Kilpatrick to form the Third Division of his cavalry corps. This prompted a quick reorganization that jumped Captains Wesley Merritt, Elon Farnsworth, and George Custer to the rank of Brig. Gen. and command of

their own brigades in the new division. Buford's division patrolled the Pleasant Valley, looking in vain for Confederate infantry, before riding along the eastern base of South Mountain to Middletown. Meanwhile, Gregg received word from Pleasonton that Stuart's men had crossed the Potomac and that two of his brigades were to ride quickly to protect the vital Baltimore and Ohio Railroad and its associated telegraph wires. Gregg took six hours to comply, finally sending McIntosh's brigade to Ridgeville and Huey's brigade toward Mount Airy. McIntosh split his command at Ridgeville, throwing regiments out to Cooksville, Lisbon, and Poplar Springs.[79]

As Meade pulled his army together near Frederick and studied his strategic situation, Lee rested most of his troops on June 28. Only a few units were on the march. Early's Division captured and ransomed York, while Gordon's Brigade continued to the Susquehanna River, where it encountered militia who burned the Columbia Bridge at Wrightsville. Sparks from the fire scattered to neighboring buildings and set them ablaze. Forming a bucket brigade, Gordon's Georgians helped extinguish the flames. Albert Jenkins' cavalry brigade reached Mechanicsburg by 9:00 a.m., after riding most of the night. Knipe's militia brigade was in the area, and an artillery duel broke out near Sporting Hill. Farther south, McLaws' Division of the I Corps was also on the march, finally reaching Chambersburg.[80]

Stuart's troopers, who began crossing the Potomac River on the evening of June 27, finally completed their task at 3:00 a.m. on June 28. After destroying some property along the Chesapeake and Ohio Canal and capturing about 300 Federal soldiers, the men rested until the late morning. Chambliss' Brigade spotted a long wagon train near Rockville and captured approximately 125 wagons. The wagons considerably slowed Stuart's progress toward Westminster. While Chambliss' men were capturing the wagons, Fitz Lee's and Hampton's brigades were riding north to Hood's Mill to destroy large stretches of the Baltimore and Ohio Railroad.[81]

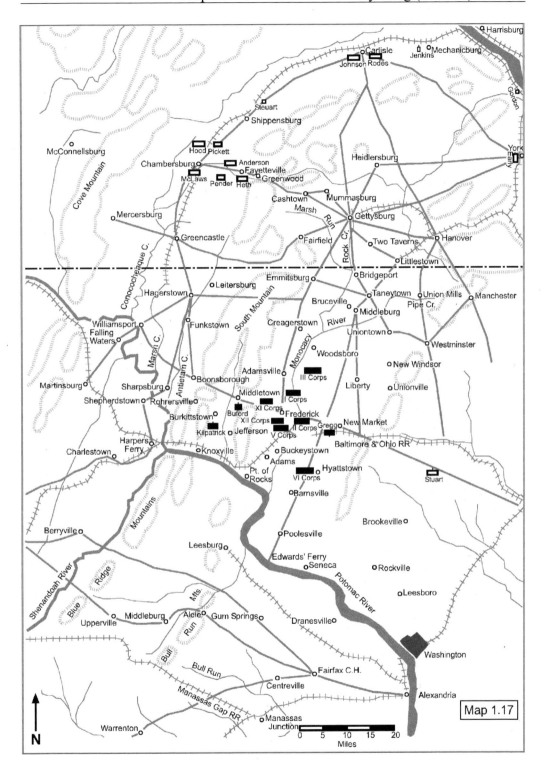

Map 1.17

Map 1.18 (June 29)

With his troops concentrated near Frederick on June 29, Meade prepared to push north to counter Lee's threat. The left wing traveled almost due north while the right wing swung northeast and then north. In the left wing, the I Corps marched to Emmitsburg by way of Mechanicstown (Thurmont), the XI Corps also headed for Emmitsburg, but through Utica and Creagerstown, and the III Corps aimed for Taneytown, east of Emmitsburg, moving through Woodsboro and Middleburg. Each was a long and difficult march of about twenty-five miles; the I and XI Corps reached Emmitsburg that evening. The XII Corps of the right wing ended its march at Bruceville, just south of Emmitsburg and Taneytown, after passing through Woodsboro. The II Corps' march began at 8:00 a.m., four hours later than planned because its orders arrived late. The corps made up the time by marching fourteen hours, tramping through Liberty and camping one mile beyond Uniontown. Straggling was widespread during these rapid marches in the high heat and humidity. The V and VI Corps' marches ended far to the south. The V Corps marched along Baltimore Pike through Ceresville before halting for the night at Liberty, while the VI ended its march just to the east at New Windsor.[82]

The Federal cavalry continued scouting Lee's movements while simultaneously providing a screen for Meade's rapid northward push. Now with three cavalry divisions, Pleasonton divided his forces. Buford's division operated on the left (west), attempting to locate Hill's and Longstreet's corps, while Gregg's division operated on the right, looking for Stuart's cavalry while protecting the Army of the Potomac's flank. Kilpatrick's division rode between them searching for Ewell's Corps. Buford led Gamble's and Devin's brigades northwest from Middletown through Turner's Gap, to Boonesborough. Turning northeast, the column rode toward Fairfield and camped about ten miles south of Gettysburg. Meanwhile, newly promoted Wesley Merritt moved his reserve brigade from Middletown to Mechanicstown, Maryland, to guard his comrades' right flank. To the east, Gregg received word that Stuart's troopers were smashing equipment near Hood's Mill. He reconsolidated his dispersed division and headed toward the enemy. However, VI Corps infantrymen clogged the road, slowing his passage. Finally reaching New Windsor, Gregg permitted his men to rest, but soon they were up and back on their mounts for an all-night ride to Westminster. Some called this the most difficult ride they had ever made; troopers fell asleep in the saddle and horses broke down on the march. Kilpatrick divided his force at Frederick, sending Farnsworth's brigade northeast toward Taneytown and Custer's Wolverines toward Emmitsburg. The division would reunite in Littlestown, Pennsylvania.[83]

Lee sent Ewell orders to march on Harrisburg on June 29. Jenkins reached the Susquehanna shoreline, collecting information on the approaches to the city. It was never put to use because Lee aborted the mission when he received word of Meade's movement toward Pennsylvania. While Rodes' Division remained at Carlisle and Early's at York, Johnson's began its march south toward Chambersburg. Lee sent Ewell orders to move to Gettysburg or Cashtown after Johnson's departure, instructing the latter to turn south at Green Village, march through Fayetteville, and cross the Blue Ridge Mountains to Cashtown. Johnson's Division march ended later that night just north of Shippensburg. While Pender's and Anderson's divisions (Hill's Third Corps) remained near Fayetteville, Heth's Division was marching toward Cashtown by 4:30 a.m., which it reached later that day. Longstreet's First Corps remained at Chambersburg.[84]

Stuart's destruction of the Baltimore and Ohio Railroad at Hood's Mill continued on June 29. His troopers also destroyed other military targets, including telegraph lines and bridges. The Confederate troopers rode on to Westminster, reaching that place about 5:00 p.m. Perhaps 100 Federal troopers opened fire on the column, forcing Stuart to halt, deploy, and drive them off. The Confederate horsemen camped around Westminster that night.[85]

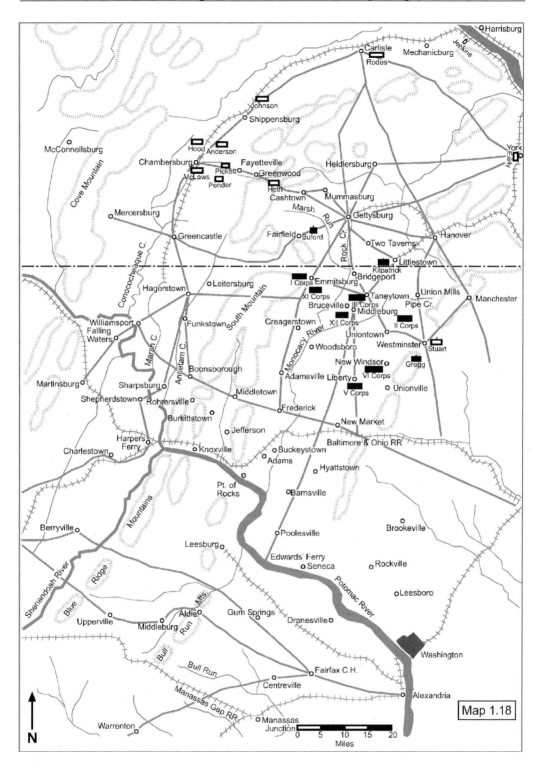

Map 1.18

Map 1.19 (June 30)

As his army moved north on June 30, Meade notified Halleck that he expected a major engagement at or near Gettysburg. The Federal army did not make much progress that day. Wadsworth's division of the I Corps camped near Marsh Creek after a six-mile march and Robinson's and Doubleday's divisions camped three miles away at Moritz Tavern. The XI Corps' march was even shorter. After marching through Emmitsburg, the corps moved another mile and bivouacked at St. Joseph's Academy. While resting in camp at Taneytown, the men of the III Corps watched as the XII Corps trudged past. Continuing north, the XII Corps reached the Pennsylvania border about noon and, after some celebration, continued to Littlestown, where Alpheus Williams' division went into camp one mile beyond it. Hearing reports of Confederate cavalry at Hanover, David Geary's division moved in that direction. The III Corps marched about nine miles from Taneytown, through Bridgeport, camping near Emmitsburg. Marching through New Windsor, the VI Corps continued northwest to Manchester, while the V Corps marched to Union Mills. The II Corps received a day's rest at Uniontown.[86]

Judson Kilpatrick's cavalry division reached Littlestown just before midnight and spent the first few hours of June 30 being fed and feted by the townspeople. Kilpatrick had his men riding toward Hanover just before sunup, his ultimate destination York, Pennsylvania. As the 18th Pennsylvania Cavalry regiment—the last unit in Kilpatrick's division—approached Hanover, Chambliss' Brigade, at the head of Stuart's column, attacked it. Earlier in the day, the Confederate horsemen had given Littlestown a wide berth when they learned Federal troopers were in the town. Unfortunately for the Southern cavalry, Chambliss blundered into a fight Stuart wanted to avoid. The initial Confederate attack drove the Pennsylvanians into Hanover. Elon Farnsworth heard the shooting and turned his command around, leading the 5th New York in a headlong counterattack that forced Chambliss' retreat. Farnsworth's troopers threw up barricades and waited for support from Custer.

Because the Confederate wagon-laded column stretched for miles, Southern reinforcements were slow to arrive. Custer dismounted his men and his brigade drove the enemy back, but the weight of Confederate reinforcements shoved the Wolverines rearward a short time later. A stalemate developed as darkness fell on the field. Stuart quickly disengaged his troopers and sent them north toward Jefferson in an all-night search for General Ewell's Second Corps.

After riding through the night, David Gregg's cavalry division reached Westminster at daybreak on June 30, where Gregg learned Stuart had passed through the town about 12 hours earlier. Unsure that the enemy had really gone, Gregg unlimbered a battery and lobbed a few shells toward the town. The command remained there through the day. John Buford's division completed its ride to Gettysburg just in time to encounter three regiments from James Pettigrew's Brigade marching from Cashtown on a reconnaissance and supply-gathering mission. Pettigrew quickly withdrew toward Cashtown.[87]

Lee's army continued concentrating near Gettysburg and Cashtown on June 30. Anderson's Division of Hill's Corps approached Cashtown where Heth's Division was already resting. Pender's Division remained in camp near Fayetteville. Ewell's Second Corps was also on the march. Johnson's Division trudged through Shippensburg, Green Village, and Scotland, where it camped for the night, while Rodes' Division marched due south through Papertown (York Springs), Petersburg, and halted for the night near Heidlersburg. Early's Division, which began its march near York, also aimed for Heidlersburg. After marching through East Berlin, the division bivouacked three miles from Rodes. Hood's and McLaws' divisions of Longstreet's First Corps left Chambersburg and marched east through Fayetteville, halting for the night at Greenwood at the base of South Mountain. Prior to the march, General Evander Law's Brigade peeled off toward New Guilford to prevent a Federal thrust from that direction. Pickett's Division remained in Chambersburg, where it protected the rear of Lee's army. The road east was so clogged with traffic it could not have moved even it had had orders to do so.[88]

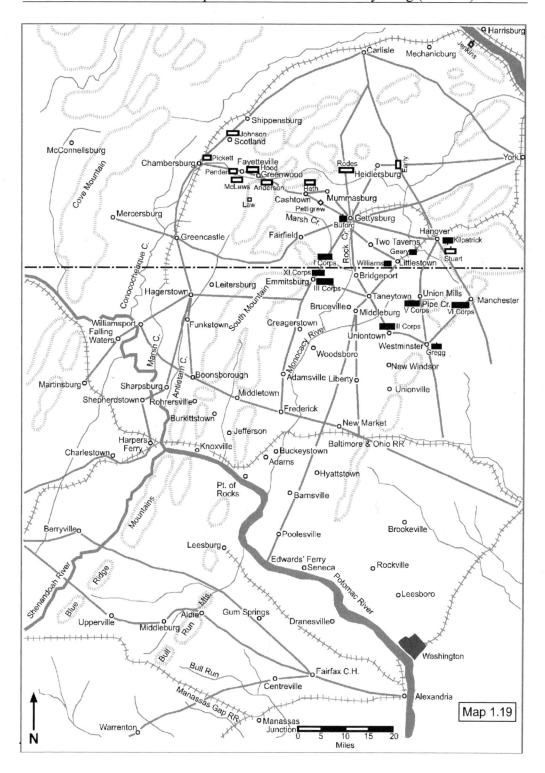

Map 1.19

Map 1.20 (July 1)

The battle of Gettysburg began on July 1 when Heth's Division, with Pender's trailing behind it, encountered Buford's cavalry division along the Chambersburg Pike west of town. Reynolds' I Corps was on the way to Gettysburg, having begun its march at Marsh Creek about 9:00 a.m. The head of the corps arrived from the south along the Emmitsburg Road around 10:00 a.m. Howard's XI Corps also approached the battlefield. Barlow's division was in the lead behind the rear of the I Corps, while the XI Corps' remaining two divisions marched north along Taneytown Road. The roads were sloppy from the rain, which made marching more difficult and tiresome. The head of the column reached Gettysburg about noon.[89]

Most of Lee's other infantry and artillery units were also converging on Gettysburg. To the north, Rodes' Division marched to Middletown before turning south to Gettysburg. It took up a position on Oak Hill northwest of town. Early's Division arrived later, marching on Harrisburg Road, where it encountered Barlow's division aligned on Blocher's Knoll. Anderson's Division left Fayetteville soon after first light and made good progress to Cashtown, where it halted. Johnson's Division was on the same road and arrived at Gettysburg in the late afternoon. Because the latter division and Ewell's wagon train clogged the road in front of them, McLaws' and Hood's divisions waited impatiently near Greenwood until 4:00 p.m. when the road finally cleared. Midnight came and went, and the column was still on the road. Pickett's Division tore up railroad tracks in the Chambersburg area.[90]

The rest of the Federal army was also marching on Gettysburg. The XII Corps began its march near Littlestown and Hanover and headed toward Two Taverns. The men rested there for several hours despite the fact that many insisted they could hear the sounds of battle ahead of them. Resuming the march to Gettysburg about 2:30 p.m., the corps arrived at Wolf Hill about 4:00 p.m. The III Corps reached the battlefield next. Breaking camp about noon at Emmitsburg, the corps marched toward Gettysburg on Emmitsburg Road. De Trobriand's and Burling's brigades were left behind to watch for Confederates coming through the Fairfield Gap in the Blue Ridge Mountains. The corps finally reached the battlefield about 5:30 p.m. The II Corps broke camp at Uniontown after 7:00 a.m., marched to Taneytown, then on toward Gettysburg, arriving about three miles from the town around 9:00 p.m. The II Corps deployed across Taneytown Road.[91]

Two Federal corps were still in motion at midnight on July 1. The V Corps broke camp at Union Mills after 8:00 a.m. on July 1 and reached the Pennsylvania border by late morning. Resting near Manchester, the VI Corps heard the hooves of couriers' horses about 6:00 p.m., and the men were ordered back into column. Marching back toward Westminster, they learned they had taken the wrong road.[92]

General Stuart, meanwhile, continued his frantic search for Lee's army. Stuart pushed his men from Hanover to York, only to learn that the Confederate infantry had departed hours before. The exhausted troopers rested and ate at Dover. After reading local newspapers filled with conflicting information, Stuart sent aides galloping in different directions to find Lee. The rest of the column rode through Dillsburg toward Carlisle, negotiating steep and dangerous roads that were especially challenging for the exhausted men and horses. Reaching Carlisle, Stuart was again frustrated to find only Federal militia under General William Smith who would not surrender. Confederate artillery opened fire on them.[93]

Thinking (incorrectly) that Lee's army was near East Berlin, about ten miles north of Hanover, Kilpatrick rode in that direction on July 1. The ride took him well west of Stuart's route. In Gettysburg, Buford's men stoutly battled advancing infantry from A.P. Hill's III Corps. Gregg's division finally entered Pennsylvania. Despite conflicting orders, Gregg sent Huey's brigade to Manchester to protect supplies and turned McIntosh's and Irvin Gregg's brigades northeast toward Hanover, where he was told to join Kilpatrick's division.[94]

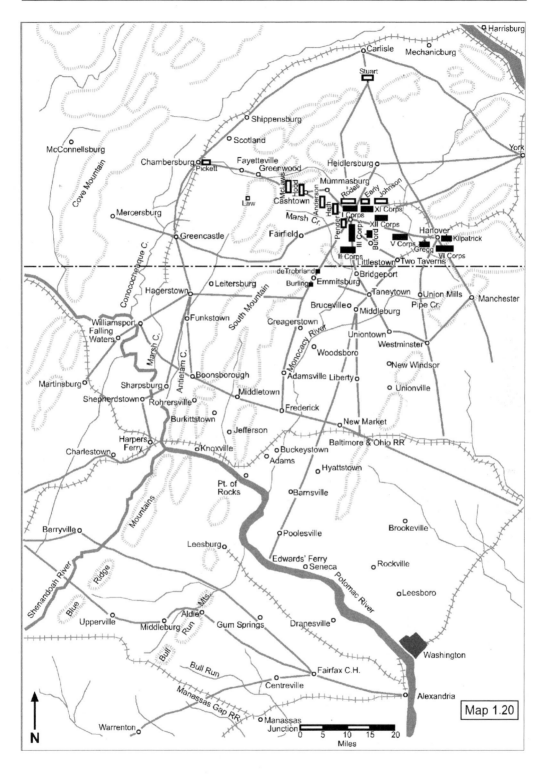

Map 1.20

Map 1.21 (July 2)

General Gregg's two cavalry brigades reached Hanover around midnight on July 1 and rested until 3:00 a.m. on July 2, when the men remounted and rode toward Gettysburg. Meanwhile, Stuart continued his efforts to find Lee's army. He decided to abandon his attempt to capture Carlisle and moved south toward Heidlersburg and Hunterstown at 1:00 a.m., having finally learned that Lee was at Gettysburg. Hampton's Brigade encountered Kilpatrick's division at Hunterstown and the resulting combat was short but severe. Charge followed countercharge, with neither side able to gain a decided advantage. After dark, Stuart pulled Hampton from the combat and proceeded to Gettysburg. Kilpatrick likewise withdrew.

Lee was finally reunited with his errant cavalry officer. Although Stuart brought with him supplies and wagons, his men and horses were beyond the point of exhaustion and he had little in the way of intelligence as to the dispositions of the Union army. Buford, on the other hand, had provided Meade with excellent information on Lee's location.[95]

July 2 brought the final infantry units to the vicinity of the battlefield. McLaws' and Hood's divisions of Longstreet's First Corps had halted near Marsh Creek after midnight, but resumed their march at 4:00 a.m. While Hood's men were resting, Law's Brigade began its march back to rejoin the division from its mission at New Guilford. Longstreet later called its 28-mile trek "the best marching done in either army to reach the field of Gettysburg." Finally relieved by Imboden's cavalry brigade, Pickett's Division began marching to the battlefield from Chambersburg at 2:00 a.m. The division reached Marsh Creek about 2:30 p.m. after a 23-mile journey.[96]

Federal units were also making early morning marches in the darkness. The V Corps, which had rested at 1:00 a.m. near Bonaughtown (Bonneville), was back on the road two hours later. A clear and moonlit night helped speed the march, and the head of the corps reached the field about 5:00 a.m. Only a few halts were permitted for the VI Corps, which finally crossed into Pennsylvania and continued toward Gettysburg. James Bowen of the 37th Massachusetts described the misery of the march: "It was a hot, breathless July day. The sun poured down with merciless, unbroken heat, and the dust that rose in great lazy clouds from the highway enveloped man and horse . . . in its all-embracing mantle of torture. How the exhausted lungs panted for one full breath of pure, cool fresh air! Panted only to be mocked by the bitter, burning, dust-laden blast that seemed to come from the mouth of a furnace . . . strong men gasped and staggered and fell, while the thick blood burst forth from mouth and nostrils and the tortured frame was placed tenderly in some shaded nook." The column reached Littlestown and continued to Rock Creek south of Gettysburg, where it arrived about 3:00 p.m. The march of the VI Corps was one of the most remarkable in American military history. Although most of the units in this corps would not be engaged in the battle, they did provide a powerful reserve for the Army of the Potomac. Burling's and de Trobriand's brigades of the III Corps left Emmitsburg at 5:00 a.m. and reached the field about 10:00 a.m.[97]

The marches to the battlefield were now at an end. The two armies had traversed 150-odd miles in fits and starts over the past month. While both armies covered approximately the same distance, the Federal troops as a whole covered the last portion of the trek in a much more arduous manner and arrived in a more exhausted state. Fighting on their own soil energized the Federals, who would fight the Confederates with an intensity that belied their exhaustion.

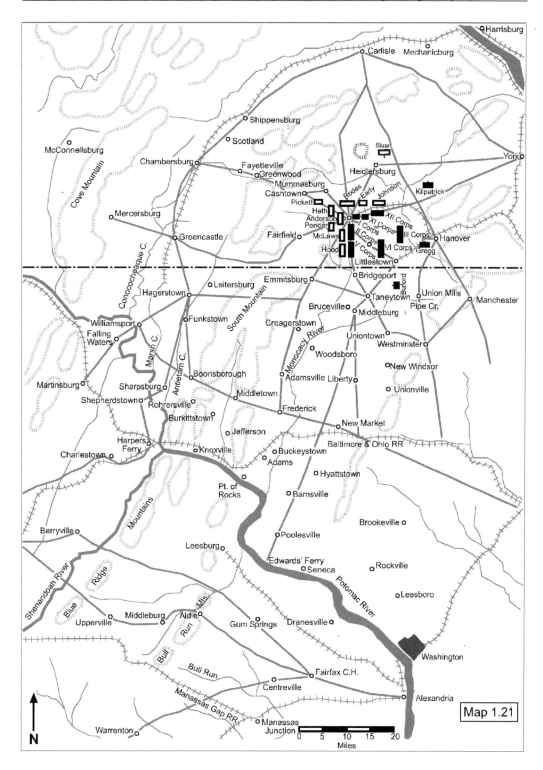

Map 1.21

N

Map Set 2: The Battle of Second Winchester

Map 2.1 (June 10-12)

Lieutenant General Richard Ewell pushed his men of the Second Corps northward from Culpeper Court House on June 10 on a march that would have made even Stonewall Jackson proud. His foot cavalry entered the Shenandoah Valley via Chester Gap on June 12; Ewell led the way in a carriage. This was his first campaign since losing a leg at Groveton during the Second Manassas Campaign and by June 12, he was simply worn out.

After conferring with his three division commanders that evening, Ewell crafted a plan to clear the Federal forces out of the lower Shenandoah Valley. Robert Rodes' Division would march to Berryville accompanied by Albert Jenkins' cavalry brigade. Once there, he would capture the 1,800 men of Col. Andrew McReynolds' brigade of Maj. Gen. Robert Milroy's division. After reducing Berryville, Rodes and Jenkins would turn their attention to Col. Benjamin Smith's command of 1,300 men guarding the Baltimore and Ohio Railroad at Martinsburg. Ewell's other two divisions under Early and Johnson would attack Milroy's main body of approximately 8,000 men at Winchester. Johnson would march on the Front Royal Road toward Winchester while Early turned west at Nineveh and marched to Newtown, where his division would pick up the Valley Turnpike. Ewell was going to strike Winchester from two directions.[1]

Despite frequent requests from Henry Halleck to vacate Winchester and head toward Harpers Ferry, Milroy had thus far refused. He believed his command occupied good defensive positions and could repel any Confederate attack. He did not know that more than twelve thousand men were bearing down on him, intent on his destruction.

The first clash between Milroy's and Ewell's troops occurred on the morning of June 12 when a Federal cavalry patrol encountered Johnson's Division south of Winchester. The patrol quickly alerted Milroy, who rushed reinforcements to the area—about 600 men from the 87th Pennsylvania, 18th Connecticut, and 13th Pennsylvania Cavalry, along with a section of Spooner's battery. Milroy intended to lay a trap for the approaching enemy of the 1st Maryland Battalion and the 14th Virginia Cavalry. The latter fell into the snare, losing about 50 men.[2]

Milroy was still in denial that night about his circumstances. "I deemed it impossible that Lee's army, with its immense artillery and baggage trains, could have escaped from the Army of the Potomac, and crossed the Blue Ridge," he wrote. Although Milroy was skeptical that the enemy was approaching in great force, he disposed his troops to defend the town. He doubled the number of pickets and ordered Col. McReynolds to return with his brigade to Winchester if he heard two cannon shots. He also deployed parts of his remaining two brigades in positions to guard the Valley and Front Royal turnpikes. To the former, commanded by Brig. Gen. Washington Elliott, went the 110th and 123rd Ohio, 12th West Virginia, 13th Pennsylvania Cavalry, and John Carlin's Battery D. Colonel William Ely took his brigade, composed of the 87th Pennsylvania, 18th Connecticut, 5th Maryland, 12th Pennsylvania Cavalry, and a section of E. D. Spooner's Battery L, south along the Fort Royal Turnpike.[3]

Ewell's plan for defeating Milroy was remarkably similar to Stonewall Jackson's design during his First Winchester Campaign one year earlier—and it was to Ewell's advantage that he had participated in it. Johnson's Division would advance up the Front Royal Turnpike in full view of Milroy's soldiers while Early's Division left the Valley Turnpike, looped around to the left, and hit Milroy's fortifications from the west. "From all of the information I could gather," explained Ewell, "the fortifications of Winchester were only assailable from the west and northwest." It was a good plan, and one made more likely to succeed by Milroy's blind determination.[4]

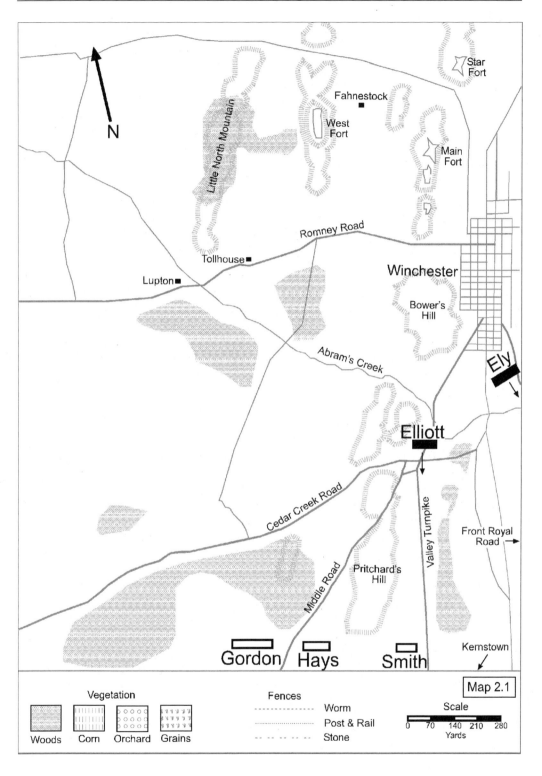

Star Fort

Fahnestock

West Fort

Main Fort

Little North Mountain

N

Romney Road

Tollhouse

Lupton

Winchester

Bower's Hill

Abram's Creek

Ely

Elliott

Cedar Creek Road

Valley Turnpike

Front Royal Road

Pritchard's Hill

Middle Road

Gordon   Hays   Smith

Kernstown

Map 2.1

Vegetation

Woods   Corn   Orchard   Grains

Fences

— — — — — — Worm
.... Post & Rail
- - - - - - Stone

Scale

0   70   140   210   280
Yards

Map 2.2 (June 13)

The Confederates were on the road early on June 13. Johnson's Division broke camp at Cedarville at first light and marched north, encountering Federal pickets a few miles from Winchester about noon. Thrown out on the skirmish line, the 2nd Virginia drove the Federal pickets back toward the town. Spooner's Federal battery arrived, unlimbered to the right of the road, and began shelling the advancing Virginians. Johnson responded by deploying Carpenter's battery, which forced the Federal artillery from the field. The issue was far from over, however. Milroy's big guns in the forts around Winchester opened fire, driving the Virginians to cover. A stalemate developed. Johnson decided not to press the matter, and instead rested his troops for the fight he hoped would take place on the morrow.[5]

As Johnson's men advanced along Front Royal Road, Early moved his division down the Valley Turnpike. When he reached Kernstown, Early learned that Federal cavalry were in the area and that a section of Carlin's battery was posted on Pritchard's Hill. Suspecting that Federal infantry was nearby, Early dispatched Harry Hays' Louisiana Brigade west to Middle Road. With the Valley Turnpike to its right and Middle Road to its left, the brigade deployed in front of Pritchard's Hill. The Tigers immediately advanced and occupied the hill without loss as the Federal artillery had already withdrawn. Hays quickly realized a Union regiment occupied the heights to the northwest. The enemy was the 12th West Virginia, anchoring the right of a Federal line occupied by General Elliott's brigade. The rest of Elliott's brigade was also in position, with the 110th Ohio on the 12th's left, and Carlin's battery deployed behind them. The 123rd Ohio was across the Valley Turnpike, and the 13th Pennsylvania Cavalry formed the brigade's left flank.[6]

About 4:00 p.m., Gordon's Brigade marched to support Hays' men and deployed to their left. (See #1 on facing map). Partially hidden in a stand of timber, the West Virginians watched Gordon's infantry approach. Although inexperienced, the West Virginians fired destructive volleys into the Georgians, forcing them to pull back. Gordon extended his line to flank the West Virginians. With the 31st Georgia on the right and the 13th Georgia on the left, Gordon's men again advanced, their line now extending far beyond the right of the stubborn Federal regiment. Gordon's solid tactics forced the West Virginians from the heights, but their withdrawal was orderly and they filed to their left, away from the Georgians, across Middle Road toward the Valley Turnpike.[7]

The West Virginians joined with the 110th and 123rd Ohio, deployed near Abram's Creek. (See #2 on facing map). The latter regiment was south of the creek, the former north of it with the 87th Pennsylvania. Carlin's four guns also unlimbered, having recently moved north to these new positions. As Early's men advanced, Carlin's guns opened fire. A Federal soldier recalled that when the artillery fire hit the massed Confederate infantry, "the cry of 'Oh Lord! Oh Lord! Oh Lord!' came loud and plaintive, full one-fourth of a mile away."[8]

With the Confederate infantry in disarray, General Elliott launched the 123rd Ohio and several companies of the 12th West Virginia in a stunning and well-timed counterattack. General Gordon's Georgians slowly fell back before the onslaught. When a portion of the 12th Pennsylvania Cavalry made an ill-advised sortie against Early's veterans, however, the troopers were beaten back.[9]

Gordon's men bivouacked to the left of Middle Road, with Hays' Brigade to their left. After Elliott pulled his troops back across Abram's Creek, Milroy ordered them to continue their retreat to the safety of the forts ringing Winchester. Heavy rains fell that night, soaking the Federal troops, but they were in good spirits as they had accounted themselves well against General Ewell's veterans.[10]

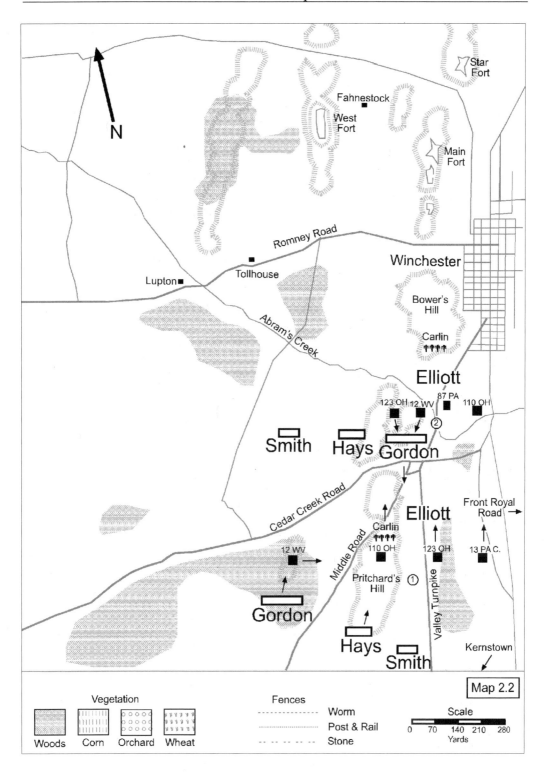

N

Star Fort

Fahnestock

West Fort

Main Fort

Romney Road

Winchester

Lupton

Tollhouse

Bower's Hill

Abram's Creek

Carlin

Elliott

123 OH 12 WV 87 PA 110 OH

Smith Hays Gordon ②

Cedar Creek Road

Front Royal Road →

Carlin

Elliott

12 WV 110 OH 123 OH 13 PA C.

Middle Road

Pritchard's Hill ①

Gordon

Hays Smith

Valley Turnpike

Kernstown

Map 2.2

Vegetation

Woods   Corn   Orchard   Wheat

Fences

-------------- Worm
·················· Post & Rail
-- -- -- -- Stone

Scale

0   70   140   210   280
Yards

Map 2.3 (June 14)

Dawn of Sunday, June 14 found Milroy's cavalry scouting the east and northeast approaches to Winchester, but they were quickly beaten back by Confederate sharpshooters. Jubal Early was also up early, surveying his line of battle. It stretched from the base of Bower's Hill to the west to just across the Valley Turnpike to the east. The three Virginia regiments making up General William Smith's Brigade formed Early's left, Gordon's Brigade held the right, and Hays' Louisiana brigade was between them. Early's fourth brigade under Col. Isaac E. Avery was in Kernstown guarding the wagons.

Early's line advanced that morning. The 123rd Ohio on Bower's Hill retreated after firing a few volleys at the powerful approaching enemy. The 12th West Virginia, which had valiantly held its position against long odds the day before, moved to the western slope of Bower's Hill. From that vantage point, the West Virginians watched the deadly effects of Milroy's artillery against the left of Early's line. The artillery fire did not deter Early's combat veterans, who continued pacing up the hill until they forced the Union defenders to vacate their position.[11]

Some of Gordon's men entered Winchester, but their stay was short-lived when Milroy rushed the 87th Pennsylvania and 18th Connecticut through the town. Street fighting and in some cases house-to-house combat erupted, and the Georgians were forced to vacate the town. Meanwhile, Generals Early and Ewell met on Bower's Hill, where they had a good view of the Federal forts. They decided to leave Gordon's battered brigade behind on Bower's Hill to distract the enemy while Hays, Avery, and Smith looped their brigades to the left (west) to storm the West Fort later that afternoon. The trek of eight miles would be an exhausting one because the day was sweltering hot. West Fort was a minor emplacement that blocked the approaches to Main and Star forts. Defended by the 110th Ohio, a company of the 116th Ohio, and Spooner's battery, the smaller position was more of a trap for its defenders than a defensive bastion.[12]

Johnson's Division created a diversion while the flank march got underway. The 5th Virginia of James A. Walker's Stonewall Brigade formed as a skirmish line between Millwood and Berryville roads while its sister regiments advanced about 500 yards behind it. General George Steuart's Brigade deployed within supporting distance. The 5th Virginia encountered the 18th Connecticut, triggering a skirmish that lasted for several hours.[13]

Although Federal troops patrolled the area, none detected Early's movement west of Winchester. Hays' and Smith's brigades marched south about two miles from Bower's Hill, where they met Avery's Brigade coming from Kernstown. Turning onto Cedar Creek Turnpike, they marched west and then left the road to march north, struggling through fields and woods. Early spun off the 54th North Carolina (Avery's Brigade) to act as a rearguard on Romney Road while the rest of his men continued moving north. Wherever possible, Early used roads to move his men, and he wisely rested them a few times along the way. When they reached Little North Mountain the men rested while the guns of Jones' Artillery battalion were pulled, dragged, and manhandled into position through woods, gullies, brush, and rocky terrain. Eight guns under Captain James Carrington deployed north of West Fort, while twelve more under Captain Willard Dance dropped trail in an orchard southwest of it. This deployment ensured that the fort would be the target of a deadly converging fire. Both sides could hear cannon fire to the northwest just after 5:00 p.m. when Early's troops began attacking Milroy's forts from the west.[14]

While Early was preparing to attack the West Fort, Milroy sent three regiments to retake Bower's Hill. The 122nd Ohio on the left (east) and the 12th West Virginia on the right (west) advanced up the hill with the 123rd Ohio in reserve. From behind stone walls and in rifle pits, Gordon's men fired destructive volleys into the Buckeyes. Though outnumbered, the Georgians held their ground, forcing the Federal troops to abort their attack.[15]

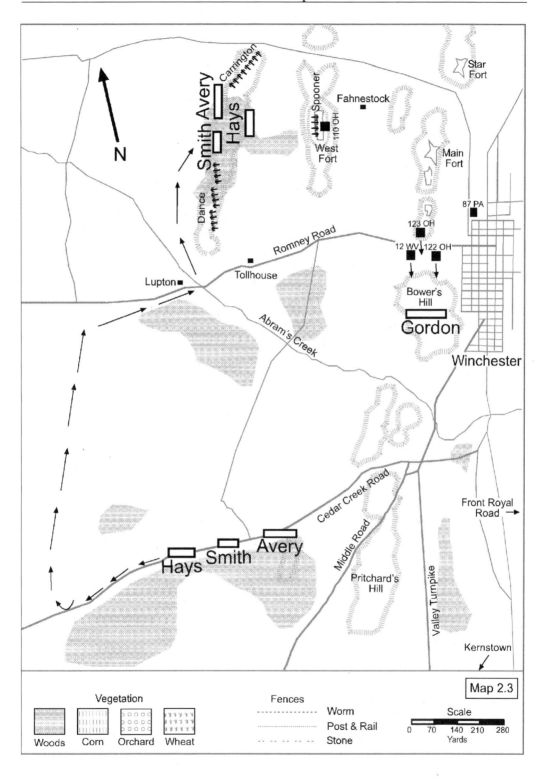

Map 2.3

Vegetation

Woods Corn Orchard Wheat

Fences

------------- Worm

·············· Post & Rail

-- -- -- -- Stone

Scale

0   70   140 210   280

Yards

Map 2.4 (June 14)

Early chose Hays' Louisiana Tigers to lead the charge on the West Fort. Hays ordered the 6th, 7th, and 9th Louisiana into the front line, with the 5th and 8th Louisiana forming the second. Avery's and Smith's brigades deployed behind the Tigers.[16]

The 110th Ohio in the West Fort was blissfully ignorant of what was about to befall them. Twenty Confederate guns opened fire as one, creating havoc in the Federal fort. The guns also fired on the other forts to prevent Federal reinforcements from reaching them. Enemy iron pounded Spooner's battery until only two guns were serviceable. Early refused to let Hays' infantry advance until the artillery fire knocked out the Federal guns. Waiting was hard for the impatient and aggressive Hays, especially when counter-battery fire began crashing through the trees that sheltered his men. Hays sent an aide back to Early to request permission to begin the charge. Early told the aide to tell Hays to wait a few more minutes, but Hays launched the attack before the aide returned with Early's reply.[17]

As they approached the fort, Hays' men realized that the Federal infantry were hugging the ground to avoid being hit by Confederate shrapnel. When the Louisianans stepped within 150 yards of the fort and launched themselves into a dead run, the Buckeyes appeared and fired several volleys into them at point-blank range. The Tigers, however, were not to be denied. They swarmed into the fort and shot down those Federal troops and horses that had not fled for their lives. The greatest resistance was mounted not by the infantry but by the gunners, who refused to abandon their pieces. The surviving Federal infantry made their way to Main and Star forts on Apple Pie Ridge. The Confederate attack slowed when the hungry men stopped to plunder the Federal haversacks left behind. Other infantrymen spun the two cannons around, loaded them with canister, and fired a few rounds at the retreating enemy. The withdrawing Federals ran into the 116th Ohio and 87th Pennsylvania, which were marching to the aid of the West Fort. The Buckeyes and Pennsylvanians were relieved when orders arrived to turn around and return to the safety of the forts.[18]

Losses on both sides were surprisingly low. Hays lost 79 men (12 killed and 67 wounded) and captured a number of prisoners and an entire Federal battery. Warren Keifer's 110th Ohio lost about 40 killed, wounded, and missing.[19]

Meanwhile, in front of Bower's Hill, the men of the three Federal regiments clung to the ground for safety. Milroy needed these troops quickly, so he ordered them back to the forts on Apple Pie Ridge. One Federal soldier was relieved, writing home, "it was the luckiest thing for us that ever happened . . . if we had made the charge we would have been all cut to pieces for they had 3 regiments and some cannon waiting for us." The three regiments quickly took position in the Main Fort, where they awaited an attack.[20]

With the West Fort now in Confederate hands, Early ordered Carrington to move all eight of his pieces and four of Dance's guns to the captured stronghold and open fire on the forts atop Apple Pie Ridge. No sooner had they deployed in the West Fort than the Federal artillery in Star Fort opened fire, devastating the Southern batteries. The shots quickly dismounted two guns and exploded a limber. The Confederate gunners, however, kept up a brisk counter-battery fire until the setting sun ended the stalemate.[21]

Although no one knew it, the Second Battle of Winchester was over. That night, Milroy decided his only option was to abandon his works and retreat to Harpers Ferry. If there was any doubt about Richard Ewell's ability to handle a corps-level action, the combat at Winchester seemed to answer it.

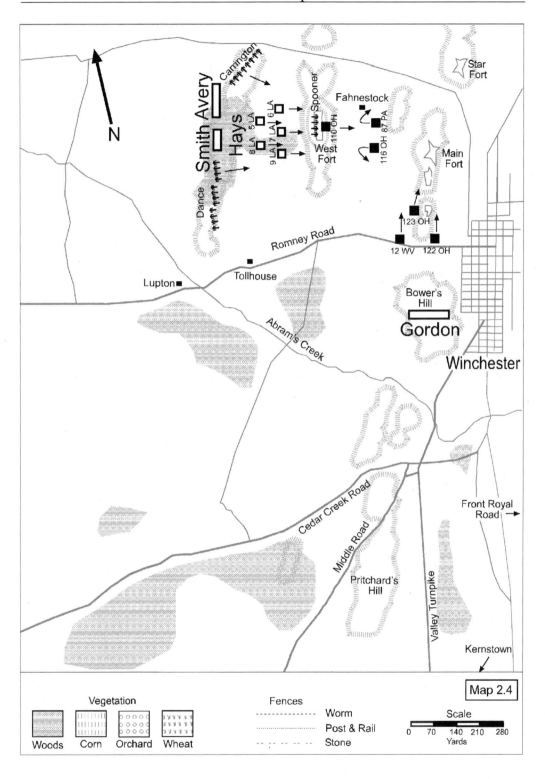

Map 2.4

Map Set 3: The Battle of Stephenson's Depot

Map 3.1 (June 15)

Major General Robert Milroy assembled his brigade commanders at 9:00 p.m. on June 14 to decide how to deal with the Confederate offensive against Winchester. West Fort was in enemy hands and Ewell's forces were pressuring the town from several directions. Milroy knew if he left now, it was tantamount to admitting the Federal high command was right when it earlier ordered his retreat. Still, remaining in place was no longer viable and he decided to pull back during the night to Harpers Ferry and its Federal garrison.[1]

Milroy planned to put his division on the Martinsburg Pike at 1:00 a.m., with the hope that by sunrise his troops would be out of harm's way. He ordered the cannons spiked and left behind, and ammunition dumped into wells. He also abandoned the wagons, but not before the men destroyed their wheels. Only the horses and mules could accompany the infantrymen. Orders to leave their sick and wounded behind infuriated the men.[2]

The moonless night helped cover the preparations for the retreat and the actual movement north. Early's infantrymen busily digging entrenchments in West Fort did not see them go. None of the Confederates knew until the following morning of Milroy's successful escape from Winchester. General Ewell, however, had planned ahead. Realizing that Milroy was outnumbered and outgunned, he anticipated that his adversary would retreat rather than fight it out. Ewell gambled by sending General Johnson's Division north of town to close the escape route in that direction.[3]

Leaving Jones' Brigade east of town to block a possible Federal retreat on the Berryville Pike, Ewell ordered Johnson to take his remaining three brigades and eight guns from Colonel Snowden Andrews' artillery battalion from their current position near Berryville Pike to a point on the Martinsburg Pike about two and a half miles northeast of Winchester. Johnson put three regiments of Steuart's Brigade on the road at 9:00 p.m., followed by Nicholls' Brigade. Walker's Stonewall Brigade was slated to bring up the rear, but it had pushed a skirmish line into Winchester to ascertain the Federal troop dispositions prior to receiving Johnson's orders. Dr. R. T. Coleman, Johnson's surgeon, rode to General Walker with the news that the rest of the division was marching away and the Virginians were expected to bring up the rear of the column. Unsure how to proceed, Walker sent an aide to find General Johnson and establish the proper course of action. While waiting, Walker pushed his skirmish line quickly into Winchester and found it abandoned. The enemy had retreated into his forts. His aide finally returned at 11:00 p.m. with orders to join Johnson's column without further delay.[4]

As Johnson led his two brigades northward, a knowledgeable guide warned him that Ewell's designated route was not the best available, and suggested an alternate route via Jordan Springs. This road converged with the Martinsburg Pike farther north of Winchester than Ewell ordered, but one of the route's advantages was a wooded embankment associated with the Winchester and Potomac Railroad near the crossroads that could conceal Johnson's men. The crossroads was just southwest of Stephenson's Depot. Johnson accepted the guide's advice and set out.[5]

Milroy's column began its march later than Johnson's, between 1:00 and 2:00 a.m., but enjoyed a more direct route. General Washington Elliott's brigade led the column, with the 12th Pennsylvania Cavalry in the lead. Next marched Colonel William Ely's brigade, followed by the horses and mules, and then the 13th Pennsylvania Cavalry. The 13th Pennsylvania was part of Elliott's brigade, but Milroy placed it closer to the rear because he thought the greatest threat was from that direction. Colonel Andrew McReynolds' third brigade, with the 1st New York (Lincoln) Cavalry serving as rear guard, brought up the rear of Milroy's column.[6]

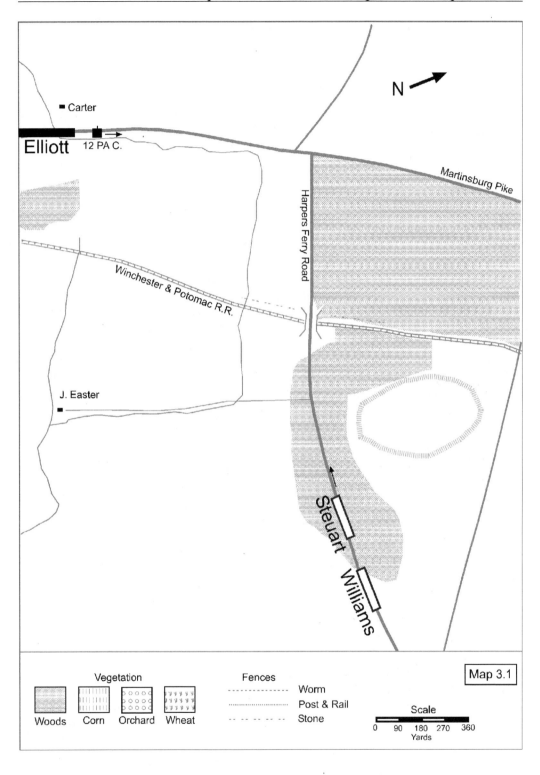

N

Carter

Elliott   12 PA C.

Martinsburg Pike

Harpers Ferry Road

Winchester & Potomac R.R.

J. Easter

Steuart

Williams

Map 3.1

Vegetation

Woods   Corn   Orchard   Wheat

Fences
- - - - - - - - - - - - -   Worm
....   Post & Rail
- - - - - - - -   Stone

Scale
0   90   180   270   360
Yards

Map 3.2 (June 15)

As the sky brightened, Maj. Gen. Edward Johnson halted his column at a tiny bridge that crossed the Winchester and Potomac Railroad. He rode forward a few hundred yards toward Martinsburg Pike with his staff and a group of sharpshooters. They could hear horses neighing somewhere ahead of their position.

Because of Lt. Gen. Richard Ewell's anticipation, the local guide's expertise, and good fortune, Johnson's troops arrived at the junction before the Federals. Quickly deploying his sharpshooters, Johnson galloped back to his infantry and ordered his men to advance at the double-quick. A stone wall stretched along the edge of a railroad cut and Johnson positioned his men behind it, the 10th Virginia and 1st and 3rd North Carolina of Brig. Gen. George Steuart's Brigade on the right and the 2nd, 10th, and 15th Louisiana regiments of Brig. Gen. Francis Nicholls' Brigade on the left. A cannon from Capt. William F. Dement's Battery dropped trail on the small bridge and another deployed to its left and rear. The remaining artillery pieces took position on the high ground behind the infantry. Nicholls' remaining two regiments supported the artillery.[7]

When Johnson's sharpshooters opened fire in the day's first light, the shock and surprise to the 12th Pennsylvania Cavalry was total. They had anticipated a threat from the rear of the column, not from the front. Drawing sabers, the Federal cavalry turned to their right (east) and charged toward the sharpshooters, who had taken up position in Carter's Woods between Martinsburg Pike and the railroad. Some of the troopers later claimed that the enemy had strung telegraph wires between the trees, unhorsing several riders. That the sharpshooters would have had either the time or equipment to do such a thing seems unlikely, but there is no question that the lead riders went down hard. The horsemen behind them quickly sheathed their sabers and took up their pistols and carbines, blazing away at Confederates they could barely see.[8]

Hearing the gunfire up ahead, General Elliott deployed his first three regiments in line

of battle. Because of the limited visibility, Elliott could not see his adversaries and assumed they were positioned across the road. As a result, he deployed his 123rd Ohio across the road with the 110th Ohio on its left and the 122nd Ohio behind the 123rd Ohio. When he realized the enemy was actually to his right, Elliott swung the 123rd Ohio around to face the woods. The 110th Ohio quickly filed by the left flank to parallel the road. The 122nd Ohio responded less quickly as it formed into column first before redeploying. Just as the 12th Pennsylvania Cavalry began breaking off its attack, the 110th Ohio arrived on the scene.[9]

Colonel Warren Keifer of the 110th Ohio saw Steuart's line of Virginia and North Carolina infantry beyond the woods. He rode to his brigade commander, General Elliott, and asked permission to attack. Elliott assented, and Keifer prepared his men to assault the Confederate line.

The first advance, which was against the center of Steuart's line, was more of a probe than a full assault. Intense Confederate volleys, combined with the effective firing of Dement's two advanced artillery pieces, forced the Buckeyes back to the road. Keifer moved his men to the left and charged again, this time more forcefully.

This time the regiment drove forward with its left flank extending beyond the 10th Virginia on the right of Johnson's line. It did not help the Confederates that the Virginians were almost out of ammunition. "My regiment," Colonel Keifer later reported, "outflanked him on his right, and driving him through the woods upon his artillery, occupying the woods upon the east of the road, opening a destructive fire into the enemy's ranks, throwing him into confusion, and killing large numbers. We also silenced two of the enemy's guns (12-pounders) immediately in our front, capturing one of his caissons."

However, with no support on his right flank, Keifer could not successfully continue his advance. A counterattack by the two North Carolina regiments forced Keifer to retreat.[10]

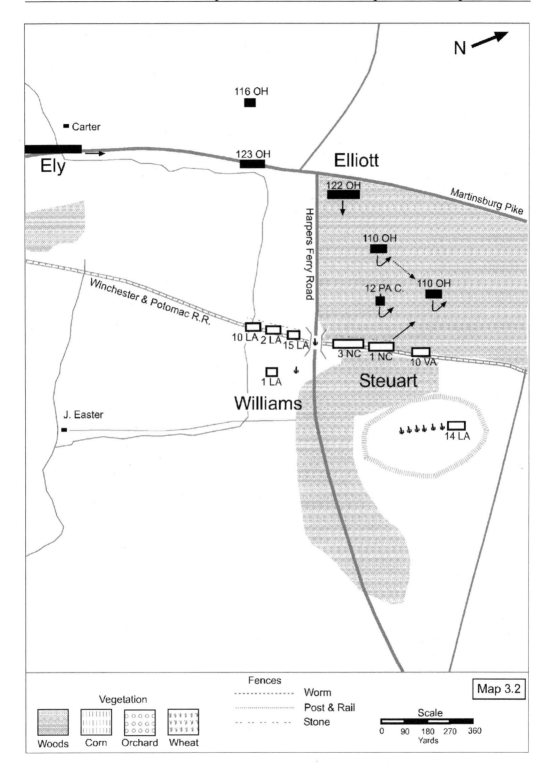

N

116 OH

Carter

Ely

123 OH

Elliott

122 OH

Martinsburg Pike

110 OH

Harpers Ferry Road

Winchester & Potomac R.R.

12 PA C.

110 OH

10 LA 2 LA 15 LA

3 NC 1 NC

10 VA

1 LA

Steuart

Williams

J. Easter

14 LA

Fences

--------------- Worm

Vegetation

.... Post & Rail

- -- -- -- - Stone

Scale

Woods   Corn   Orchard   Wheat

0   90   180   270   360
Yards

Map 3.2

Map 3.3 (June 15)

Additional Federal units appeared at this time. The 122nd Ohio of Elliott's brigade took position on the 110th Ohio's right flank and within 20 minutes, the two Buckeye regiments resumed the attacks on Johnson's line, pushing it back from the railroad. The two guns from Dement's Battery, deployed near the small bridge that helped blow apart the Buckeye lines during the last Federal charge, now came under intense enemy small arms fire that dropped men and horses alike. The surviving artillerists kept firing and, when several companies of the 14th Louisiana arrived to bolster the line, the Confederate right held a second time.[11]

Colonel Ely's brigade arrived and formed on Elliott's right flank parallel to the road facing Nicholls' Brigade. Most of Nicholls' Louisianans occupied the defensive line to the left of Harpers Ferry Road; only the 14th Louisiana was to the right of it. The 87th Pennsylvania, commanded by Colonel John Schall, was the lead regiment in Ely's brigade and it quickly deployed into line of battle. There was not yet enough light to see clearly the 122nd Ohio, aligned on Schall's left flank. The Pennsylvanians immediately charged without waiting for the regiments marching behind them to deploy and join in the attack.

Next to form in line of battle was the 18th Connecticut, which leveled its rifled muskets and fired into the shadowy figures moving to its front. The unfortunates before them proved to be Schall's Pennsylvanians. Seeing the effects of this "friendly fire," General Milroy wrote, he "dashed along in front of them and by the fiercest yelling and knocking up their guns with my sword I got their firing stopped and got them to understand that they were firing on their friends and that the enemy was beyond them." The beleaguered Pennsylvanians also received killing volleys from Nicholls' Confederates in front of them. Realizing the futility of continuing the charge, Colonel Schall pulled his battered Pennsylvanians back to safety, no doubt cursing at the Connecticut boys within earshot.

Milroy, meanwhile, deployed the 123rd Ohio of Elliott's brigade, which had been standing idly along the road, into position to the right of the 18th Connecticut. Milroy now had five regiments in line, but the darkness and confusion mingled with his haste, all of which conspired to make cooperation impossible. The right of Milroy's line managed to attack Nicholls but ran into problems again when the left of the 123rd Ohio ran into the right of the 18th Connecticut, throwing both regiments into disorder.[12]

Over on the Federal left, Colonel Keifer launched the 110th Ohio and 122nd Ohio regiments against the right of Steuart's line and again drove it backward. Supported by Dement's guns, the Confederates counterattacked, forcing the Buckeyes to withdraw. It was at this point that Milroy mistakenly believed his entire column had passed the crossroads, so he ordered Elliott's brigade to disengage and resume its march to Harpers Ferry. Elliott's men began their retreat just as Ely's brigade launched its third attack against Nicholls' line.[13]

Major Noah Ruhl claimed that his 87th Pennsylvania, on the left of Ely's line, charged the enemy line three separate times. During the second attack, the right of the Pennsylvania's line apparently threatened to overlap the left flank of Steuart's Brigade and get into its rear, so Steuart ordered the 3rd North Carolina to face west and engage it. Before his men could do so, the 1st and 15th Louisiana appeared and drove the Pennsylvanians back to the road.[14]

As Ely's brigade prepared for its third charge against Johnson's line, the horses and mules arranged between it and the third Federal brigade—fully 1,000 of them—became crazed by the gunfire and panicked, stampeding through the lines of battle, knocking men about and creating much disorder. Ely's charge finally got underway, but it suffered the same fate as those that had come before it. Milroy ordered the brigade to retreat.[15]

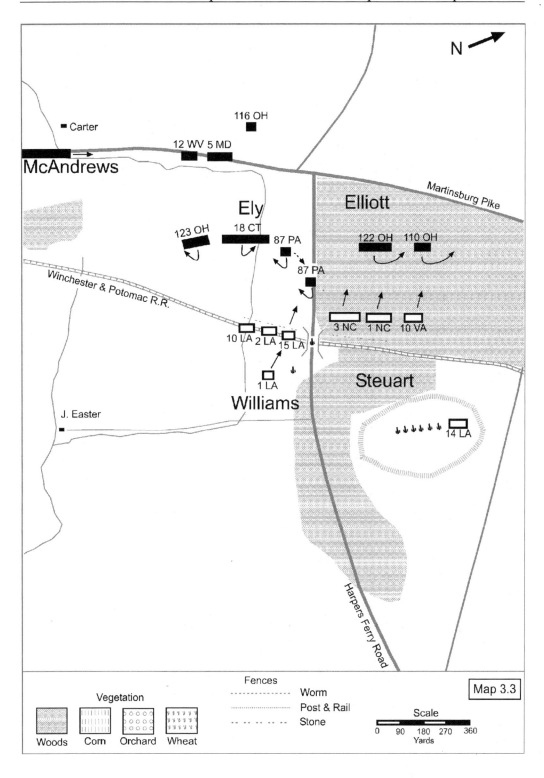

N

- Carter

116 OH

12 WV 5 MD

McAndrews

Ely

Elliott

Martinsburg Pike

123 OH   18 CT

87 PA

122 OH   110 OH

Winchester & Potomac R.R.

87 PA

3 NC 1 NC 10 VA

10 LA 2 LA 15 LA

1 LA

Williams

Steuart

J. Easter

14 LA

Harpers Ferry Road

Fences
.... Worm
.... Post & Rail
-- -- -- -- -- Stone

Map 3.3

Vegetation

Scale

Woods Corn Orchard Wheat

0   90   180 270   360
Yards

Map 3.4 (June 15)

With ammunition running low and Federal attacks becoming more persistent, Johnson looked behind him for the arrival of the Stonewall Brigade. It soon appeared with the 2nd and 5th Virginia, the two largest regiments in the brigade, in the van. Directed to the right to bolster Steuart's line, these regiments quickly crossed the railroad and reached Martinsburg Road. Their arrival posed a serious threat to Milroy's men: two veteran Confederate regiments now blocked the road to Harpers Ferry.[16]

The remaining units of the Stonewall Brigade, the 4th, 27th, and 33rd Virginia, hurried to the left to relieve Nicholls' regiments. Since Ely's final assault on this part of the line had already been repulsed, the three regiments retraced their steps to rejoin the 2nd and 5th Virginia on the road. About this time, Milroy ordered Ely to continue his march to Harpers Ferry. The 18th Connecticut and part of the 87th Pennsylvania immediately complied, but the smoke and fog were so dense they could not see the Confederate infantry in front of them. Brigadier General James Walker, however, spotted the Federals and ordered his men to open fire. "The enemy gave way, and retreated back from the pike in disorder at the first fire, returning only a straggling and inaccurate fire . . . they made no stand, but hoisted a white flag, and surrendered to the two regiments [2nd and 5th Virginia] before the others came up," wrote Walker in his battle report.[17]

Without orders to pull back, the 123rd Ohio on the right of Ely's line continued firing at Nicholls' Brigade, but the Buckeyes were surrounded quickly and most of them surrendered. Milroy's handling of the situation was less than effective. Instead of giving orders to his two brigade commanders, he communicated directly with the regiments, disrupting his chain of command and adding to the confusion. Several regiments, including the 116th Ohio, 12th West Virginia, and 5th Maryland of Ely's brigade had been left to languish, awaiting orders to no avail while marking time on Martinsburg Pike. The first two

regiments finally did form into line of battle, whether at their own volition or because of a staff officer's orders, but before they could move forward they were ordered to begin their retreat to Harpers Ferry.[18]

While Elliott's brigade was battling Steuart and Ely's brigade was about to join in, Milroy encountered Colonel McReynolds. He ordered McReynolds to rush his brigade forward. McReynolds advanced his troops on the double-quick. Noting the devastation being wrought by the Confederate artillery against Ely's brigade, McReynolds ordered his 13th Pennsylvania Cavalry to ride around the left of the Confederate line and charge. The Confederate artillerists saw the movement and quickly wheeled about and blasted the oncoming column of horsemen, leaving many of them dead and wounded in the grassy meadow. McReynolds also sent the 6th Maryland and 67th Pennsylvania around the Confederate left, where they took up a position behind a stone wall. The Confederate artillery opened on them as well, forcing a move farther to the east and closer to the rear of the enemy line. The 2nd and 10th Louisiana regiments rushed to this area and opened fire, forcing the two Federal regiments to retreat. The officers of the 67th Pennsylvania could not keep the regiment together, and the men scattered in every direction. Only 44 of the regiment's 700 men ever reached the safety of Harpers Ferry. The 6th Maryland, on the other hand, remained intact and, using back roads, made its way to Harpers Ferry with few losses.[19]

Few engagements in the war were as decisive as the often overlooked combat at Stephenson's Depot. Estimates vary, but Milroy probably lost about half of his men: 4,443. Most of them (up to 3,856) were captured. In a daring escapade, General Johnson captured 30 Federal soldiers on his own. By comparison, Confederate losses were small: 47 killed, 219 wounded, and three missing, for a total of 269. Ewell's men also captured 200,000 rounds of small arms ammunition, 300 loaded wagons, 23 cannon, over 300 horses, and a large quantity of supplies.[20]

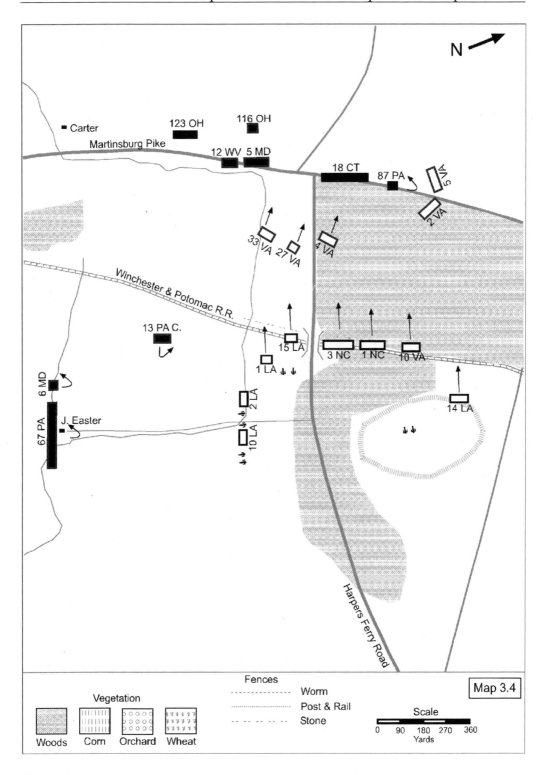

Map Set 4: The Initial Fighting West of Gettysburg, North of Chambersburg Pike

Map 4.1 (July 1)

Major General Henry Heth's Division, led by Maj. William Pegram's artillery battalion, set out for Gettysburg about 5:00 a.m. on July 1. Heth suspected a Federal force occupied the town, but did not know its character or strength. Regardless, he intended to push it away and enter the town on reconnaissance.

Watching for Heth just east of Marsh Creek were videttes of Brig. Gen. John Buford's First Cavalry Division. Buford occupied Gettysburg with two brigades under Cols. William Gamble and Thomas C. Devin, slightly more than 3,200 troopers. Buford's third brigade under Brig. Gen. Wesley Merritt was still near Mechanicstown, Maryland, guarding his trains and watching the mountain passes. When the head of Heth's column reached Marsh Creek, one of Buford's men fired—the discharge was the first shot of the battle.[1]

The opening fire prompted Gamble to send more men from his regiments to the reserve line along Herr Ridge and to the west to reinforce his skirmishers. They dismounted, and every fourth man led the horses back to McPherson Ridge. Heth sent out a skirmish line both north and south of the Chambersburg Pike, which outnumbered Buford's men 5 to 1. Pushed heavily on the front and flanks, Gamble's troopers (assisted by some of Devin's men) waged a fighting withdrawal toward Herr Ridge. Pegram's cannons unlimbered and added their metal to the mismatch developing west of town. Heth held a firm advantage in both numbers and firepower, but the sharp resistance offered by Buford's troopers slowed his advance to a crawl.[2]

The Federal skirmishers gave ground stubbornly for about one and one-half miles while Buford readied the rest of his men on McPherson Ridge. His artillery consisted of one battery of six 3-inch ordnance rifles under Lt. John Calef. This "flying artillery" was lighter and more mobile than the guns associated with the

infantry. Calef had spent the prior evening near the Lutheran Seminary south of Chambersburg Pike. To give the impression of strong artillery support, Buford ordered Calef to disperse his guns. One section under Lt. John Roder deployed on McPherson Ridge north of Chambersburg Pike. A second section under Sgt. Joseph Newman dropped trail on the opposite side of the road near the McPherson farm. The last section, under Sgt. Charles Pergel, unlimbered in the southeast corner of McPherson Woods.[3]

Colonel Gamble's brigade held Buford's left half of his line. Gamble positioned the 3rd Indiana (six companies) to the right of the unfinished railroad cut north of Chambersburg Pike. The 12th Illinois (four companies) occupied the area between the cut and the road. Colonel George Chapman of the 3rd Indiana commanded both regiments. The 8th Illinois deployed between the road and McPherson Woods, and the 8th New York anchored the left of the line just south of the woods. Colonel Devin's brigade was deployed north of the railroad cut, aligned from left to right as follows: 3rd West Virginia – 6th New York – 9th New York – 17th Pennsylvania. The right flank of the 17th Pennsylvania covered the Mummasburg Road.[4]

Heth's skirmishers, eight companies from Brig. Gen. James Archer's Brigade, approached McPherson Ridge. Buford reinforced his line and the fighting intensified. Heth responded by deploying more men from Archer's and Brig. Gen. Joe Davis' brigades, now moving in battle line. The rest of the division waited in column along the road. When it became obvious the fight was more than he was expecting, Heth deployed the balance of his first two infantry brigades. It was about 9:30 a.m. Davis' men fell into line north of Chambersburg Pike; Archer's infantry regiments formed south of the road.[5]

As Heth's infantry began their slow advance upon McPherson Ridge, the First Brigade of Maj. Gen. John Reynolds' I Corps, commanded by Brig. Gen. Lysander Cutler, arrived on the field and quickly approached Chambersburg Pike. Buford and his men had masterfully completed their task.

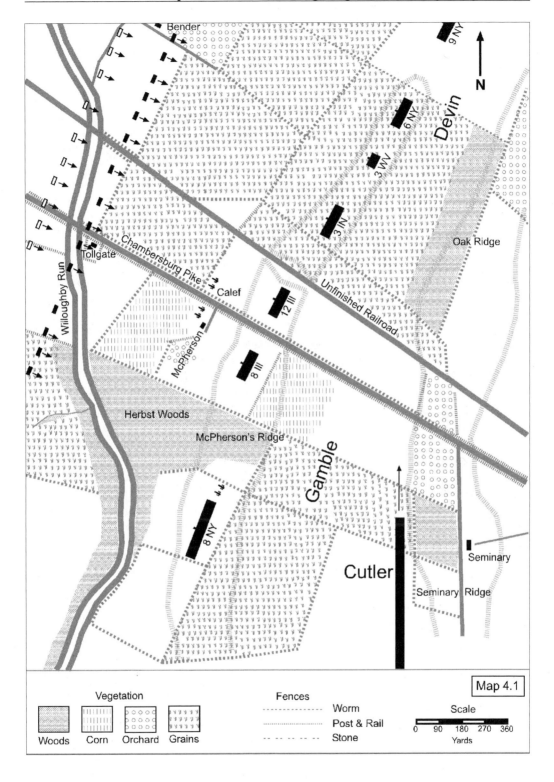

Vegetation

Woods Corn Orchard Grains

Fences

.... Worm
.... Post & Rail
- - - - - - - Stone

Map 4.1

Scale
0   90   180   270   360
Yards

Map 4.2

John Reynolds' I Corps led the Union Army's march to Gettysburg on July 1, and Brig. Gen. Lysander Cutler's brigade led the I Corps. As they approached the Codori house along the Emmitsburg Road, the men left the road and angled northwest, cutting across fields and knocking down fences as they tramped. Artillery fire from Lt. John H. Calef's Battery A, 2nd U.S. Artillery, was clearly audible and served to quicken their pace. The first two regiments in the brigade's column, the 76th New York and 56th Pennsylvania, crossed Chambersburg Pike. In its haste to relieve sections of Calef's battery north of the road, Captain James Hall's six-gun 2nd Maine battery made a sudden dash between the 56th Pennsylvania and the next regiment in line, the 147th New York. The result was that the latter regiment remained on the south side of Chambersburg Pike with the 84th and 95th New York near the McPherson farm buildings. Hall's battery finally dropped trail between Chambersburg Pike and the unfinished railroad while Calef's guns withdrew to the Lutheran Theological Seminary, where the men rested and restocked their ammunition. As Cutler's men took up their new positions, Maj. William Pegram's Confederate artillery battalion on Herr Ridge hurled shells in their direction. Casualties appeared almost immediately.[6]

As the six hundred Federal infantry of the 76th New York and 56th Pennsylvania continued moving north from the unfinished railroad cut, 1,700 men in the 2nd Mississippi, 42nd Mississippi, and 55th North Carolina of Brig. Gen. Joseph Davis' Brigade rapidly approached from the west. These were large regiments, each numbering more than 500 men, but only the 2nd Mississippi had significant combat experience. The three regiments were part of Heth's Division of A. P. Hill's Third Corps, and had marched behind Brig. Gen. James Archer's Brigade on Chambersburg Pike as they approached Gettysburg. Archer deployed on the right (south) of the road, while Davis formed his regiments into line of battle on Archer's left. Davis' entire sizable command numbered 2,300 muskets, but the 11th

Mississippi was in the rear guarding the trains. At about 10:30 a.m., with the veteran 2nd Mississippi in the middle of the line and the two inexperienced regiments deployed on either side—the 55th North Carolina on the left flank and the 42nd Mississippi on the right—the brigade advanced about one mile preceded by a skirmish line. The 55th North Carolina began curving its march to the northeast as it passed the Bender farm.[7]

Davis' men suddenly materialized in the wheat fields in front of the 76th New York and 56th Pennsylvania as the Federal troops reached their positions north of the unfinished railroad cut. General Cutler reported that the enemy was "advancing in two lines, at short range, in front and on my right flank." Although second in line, the 56th Pennsylvania completed its deployment from column into line of battle before the 76th New York to its right. Seeing troops in front of him, Col. William Hofmann of the 56th Pennsylvania asked General Cutler, "Is that the enemy?" Cutler, who had been watching the movements through his binoculars, answered in the affirmative. Hofmann yelled to his men, "Ready, Right Oblique! Aim! Fire!" The rounds struck two members of the 55th North Carolina's color guard—the first recorded shots fired by Federal soldiers during the battle.

The 2nd Mississippi and 55th North Carolina quickly responded. The men leveled their weapons and fired, killing and wounding an unrecorded number of Pennsylvanians. Still moving into position, the 76th New York received a raking fire and several men fell. Unable to see any enemy soldiers, its commanding officer, Maj. Andrew Grover, assumed the fire was coming from Federal troops and ordered his New Yorkers to hold their fire. Another volley ripped through his line. Grover, still unconvinced of the source, continued cautioning his men to hold their fire. When he finally spotted the 2nd Mississippi rising out of the fields in front of him, the major ordered his embattled men to defend themselves.[8]

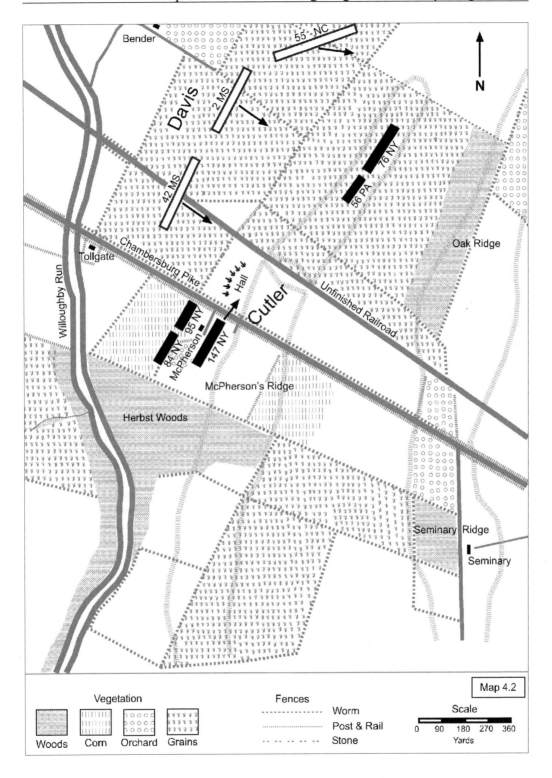

Map 4.2

Map 4.3

Seeing the right flank of the 76th New York hanging in the air, Col. John Connelly grabbed the flag of his 55th North Carolina as the regiment continued its wheeling movement. With a yell he rushed toward the enemy with his color guard in tow. The advancing colors drew the New Yorkers' attention, and Connelly quickly suffered a debilitating wound. The regiment's second in command rushed over to Connelly, who told him, "Take the colors and keep ahead of the Mississippians." Recognizing the threat to his right flank, Major Grover ordered the right wing of his 76th New York to "change front to the rear," which refused the right flank to face the 55th North Carolina. The left side of the regiment continued facing the 2nd Mississippi and that part of the 55th North Carolina in front of it. Grover fell with a mortal wound almost as soon as he gave the order. Few men saw their leader fall as they were too busy firing at the approaching enemy troops, who were sending gunfire into the 76th's front, flank, and rear.[9]

The 147th New York crossed Chambersburg Pike and, seeing the enemy closing in on Hall's battery, quickly advanced to a wheat field just north of the unfinished railroad cut, approximately 100 yards in advance (west) of the position held by the 56th Pennsylvania and 76th New York. The 42nd Mississippi, Davis' leading regiment, fired volley after volley into the newly arrived Federal troops. In an effort to stay alive, many of the New Yorkers slid down into the wheat to reload, rose quickly to fire, and repeated the cycle. As a result, those who were struck were usually hit in the upper body, where wounds tended to be more serious. A thick layer of smoke enveloped the area and visibility diminished considerably.[10]

Realizing that his men were in an untenable position with their entire right flank exposed, division commander Maj. Gen. James Wadsworth ordered them to pull back 300 yards to Sheads' Woods. The 76th New York and 56th Pennsylvania lost heavily during their twenty minutes on the ridge. The former left about 62% on the field, and the latter about 50%. A line of

dead and wounded marked their original line of defense.[11]

Because of the smoke, deafening sound, and confusion, Lt. Col. Francis Miller of the 147th New York was unaware of the retreat of the two Federal regiments. He also did not know that he had both the 42nd Mississippi approaching obliquely against his front and the 2nd Mississippi advancing nearly perpendicular to his exposed right flank. His situation grew even more critical when Davis' third regiment, the 55th North Carolina, finished wheeling about and moved against the right-rear of the isolated New Yorkers. General Wadsworth quickly sent an aide to Miller, ordering him to pull the regiment back to safety, but Miller went down with a severe wound before he could comply. Major George Harney displayed sound tactics when he refused the right companies to take on the new threat from the north, though to no avail. According to one survivor, "the boys on the right were falling like autumn leaves; the air was full of lead." Another messenger from Wadsworth arrived and ordered an immediate withdrawal. Executing such a move under fire from three sides was nearly impossible to do while maintaining any sort of discipline. The men were ordered to leave everything behind except their weapons and cartridge boxes. Their dash for the rear understandably had little, if any, semblance of order. Only 79 of the 380 men who had marched into the battle found their way to safety (79 percent casualties). The three Federal regiments north of Chambersburg Pike lost half of their men in about 30 minutes of fighting.[12]

When the 147th New York withdrew, Captain Hall had no choice but to limber his guns and get out as best he could. Heth's advance had shattered the Federal right flank, and Davis' men (most of whom were as inexperienced as their commander) seemed on the verge of exploiting their stunning early-morning victory.[13]

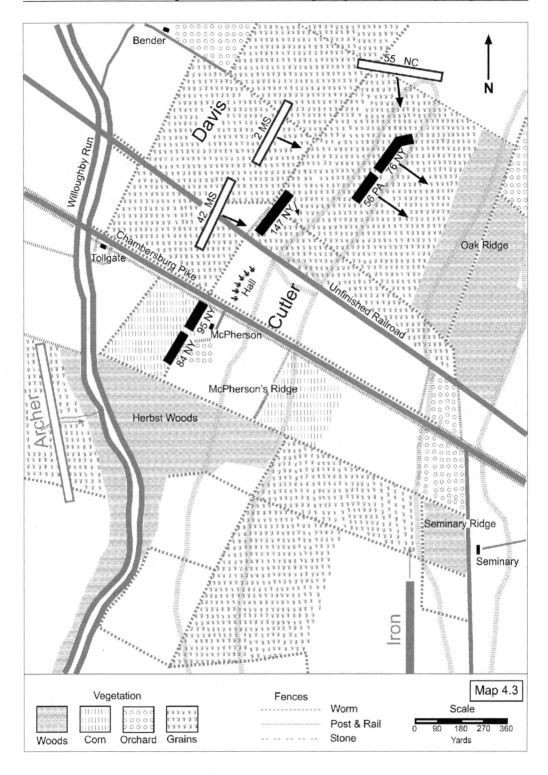

Bender

55 NC

N

Davis

2 MS

76 NY

56 PA

Willoughby Run

42 MS

147 NY

Oak Ridge

Chambersburg Pike

Tollgate

Hall

Cutler

Unfinished Railroad

95 NY

84 NY

McPherson

McPherson's Ridge

Herbst Woods

Archer

Seminary Ridge

Seminary

Iron

Vegetation

Woods Corn Orchard Grains

Fences

------------- Worm

.... Post & Rail

-- -- -- -- Stone

Map 4.3

Scale

0   90   180   270   360

Yards

Map 4.4

Reinforcements streamed toward the beleaguered Federal right flank. One of the 3-inch rifles from Lt. John Roder's section of Calef's battery unlimbered near the unfinished railroad cut and opened fire with double canister on the Confederates trying to capture Hall's guns. To the right of Hall's battery, three Federal regiments prepared to attack Davis' Brigade from the south side of Chambersburg Pike.[14]

The 84th and 95th New York of Cutler's brigade initially occupied the unit's left flank near the McPherson farm buildings. Under the command of Col. Edward Fowler of the 84th New York, they had skirmished earlier with Archer's approaching brigade. The Iron Brigade arrived on Fowler's left and took up position in Herbst Woods. North of Fowler's position (on his right), the remainder of Cutler's brigade was in full retreat. Fowler could see the seriousness of the situation, for enemy troops were advancing from both the west and the north on fronts much longer than his own. About-facing his two regiments, he marched them in line a short distance to the rear before ordering them to pivot and face Chambersburg Pike and the approaching Confederate threat to the north.

During this time, Maj. Gen. Abner Doubleday ordered the 6th Wisconsin of the Iron Brigade to leave its reserve position near the Seminary and "Go like hell!" toward Chambersburg Pike. The 100-man Iron Brigade Guard, composed of 20 men from each regiment, also moved to join the New Yorkers. Seeing the Rebels advancing on the opposite side of the railroad cut and moving perpendicular to his line, Col. Rufus Dawes halted his Wisconsin troops, filed them to the right (east) to extend into line of battle, then moved by the left flank to take up position along a rail fence on the south side of the road. This movement put his regiment just to the right (east) of Cutler's 84th and 95th New York regiments.[15]

Flushed with victory, Davis' men rushed after Cutler's three retreating regiments north of the pike. The attacking force was not as powerful as many may have thought. The headlong pursuit of the Federals disordered Davis' lines, two of

his three regimental commanders had been knocked out of action, and the remaining officers appeared to have lost control of their men. The inexperienced Davis apparently gave little thought to halting his troops to re-dress his lines before continuing the pursuit.[16]

Resting their rifles on the lowest rail, the men of the 84th and 95th New York and 6th Wisconsin fired several volleys into Davis' Mississippians and North Carolinians. The well-executed walls of fire stopped them in their tracks. And then a strange thing occurred: many of the Confederates simply disappeared from view. Only later did these Federal troops learn that their enemy had sought refuge in an unfinished railroad cut.[17]

The withering small arms fire from the newly arrived Federal regiments lying along Chambersburg Pike, as one soldier described it, caused Davis' line to "sway and bend." The officers of the 42nd Mississippi on the right (west) and the 2nd Mississippi to its left tried to wheel their regiments to face the new threat, but the shelter of the unfinished railroad cut was just too tempting. The Mississippians literally piled into the defile. "Our men thought [it] would prove a good breastwork," recalled a sergeant, "but it was too steep and in changing front the men were all tangled up and confused." Once in the cut, most of the Confederates found themselves trapped (the 42nd Mississippians less so because the cut was shallower where they entered it). It was too deep to even see the enemy, much less shoot at them. Worse, they could not move forward or backward, and trying to move laterally was just as difficult because of the shear confusion and masses of men milling in the narrow cut.

Major John Blair was now in command of the 2nd Mississippi. "All the men were jumbled together without regard to regiment or company," he explained. Some of the officers urged an attack on the Federal line to the south, but Davis overruled them and ordered a retreat. It was too late for either effort.[18]

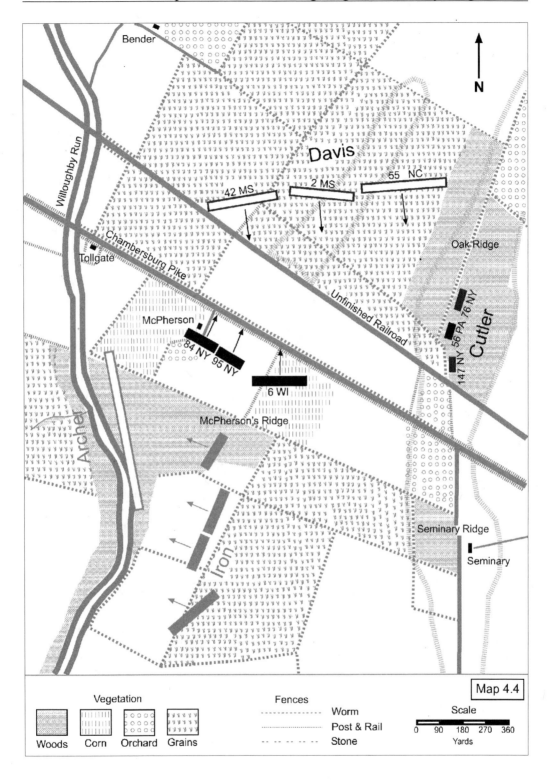

Map 4.5

With the Confederates in disarray, Lt. Col. Dawes recognized his opportunity. He passed the word through the 6th Wisconsin to prepare to attack and rushed over to the 95th New York and its commander, Maj. Edward Pye, yelling, "We must charge!" Pye agreed and the two officers relayed orders through the ranks.

The 6th Wisconsin led off, followed by the 95th New York. The 84th New York, on the left of the line, launched its attack after the other regiments had already moved out. The Federals faced immediate obstacles. Chambersburg Pike was lined with rail fences on both sides, which the men had to scale while under fire. As Dawes later put it, crossing the first fence "was a sure test of metal and discipline." A veteran of the 6th Wisconsin recalled that the Confederate small arms fire his men faced as they traversed the open area north of Chambersburg Pike was "the worst I ever experienced." Men fell at every step, but still they advanced at the double-quick. Dawes repeated his orders over and over: "Align on the colors! Close up on that color!" Because of Dawes' urging, the 6th Wisconsin's line bent to form an inverted "V" with the flag at its apex. It sustained its highest losses within fifteen feet of the railroad cut, where Davis' men fired a volley that ripped sizeable holes in the Badger line. The 6th continued running to the very lip of the Railroad Cut, where Col. Dawes was shocked to find "hundreds of rebels . . . four feet deep." The Wisconsin men lined the cut and yelled, "Throw down your muskets! Down with your muskets!" Several reckless soldiers jumped into the cut in an effort to engage the trapped Confederates in hand-to-hand combat. Others fired from above, slaughtering the Confederates where they stood. Seeing a potential escape route to his right, the adjutant of the 6th Wisconsin led a detachment of 20 men to block it. The score of soldiers quickly took up their position and emptied their weapons into the exposed flank of the trapped Mississippians. Some of the soldiers of the 42nd Mississippi escaped by rushing to their right (west) and scaling the shallower walls there, but many of the men were trapped. Realizing the futility of further resistance, Davis'

men began throwing down their arms and surrendering.[19]

The men in the 55th North Carolina were luckier than their Mississippi comrades, for those who had entered the Railroad Cut did so well to the east, where it was shallow and easier to exit. Many other Tarheels opted to line up just north of the shallow defile; either decision allowed them to escape the terrible fate of their friends. Most of the 2nd Mississippi was sandwiched between its two sister regiments. Though the walls were shallower in their sector, they were still difficult to traverse. The soldiers of the 2nd Mississippi were also victims of topography, caught between Dawes' 20-man detachment on their left and the panic-stricken men of the 42nd Mississippi on their right. Trapped in the defile, hundreds were captured or shot down trying to flee.

The fight for the 2nd Mississippi's flag was especially intense and memorable, largely because there were eyewitnesses who lived to tell the tale. Several men were killed and wounded in hand-to-hand combat for the swath of colorful wool. The 6th Wisconsin's Cpl. Francis Waller finally seized the Mississippi flag-bearer with one hand and the flag with the other. The former was subdued and the banner captured. Waller received the Medal of Honor for his actions.[20]

The situation was still unsettled when Dawes asked, "Where is the colonel of this regiment?" When Maj. John Blair of the 2nd Mississippi approached, Dawes said, "I command this regiment. Surrender or I will fire." Blair did not say a word and handed over his sword. More than 225 Confederates, most from the 2nd Mississippi, threw down their arms.[21]

The bloody victory at the Railroad Cut was a spectacular coup and a measure of redemption for Cutler's brigade. Just as Davis' Brigade had decisively bested three of Cutler's regiments earlier in the action, Dawes' Wisconsin soldiers from the Iron Brigade and two New York regiments from Cutler's brigade had evened the score. The 6th Wisconsin paid a terrible price for the victory, losing about half its men during the action.[22] After the war, the New York and Wisconsin veterans sparred over their respective roles in the morning combat.

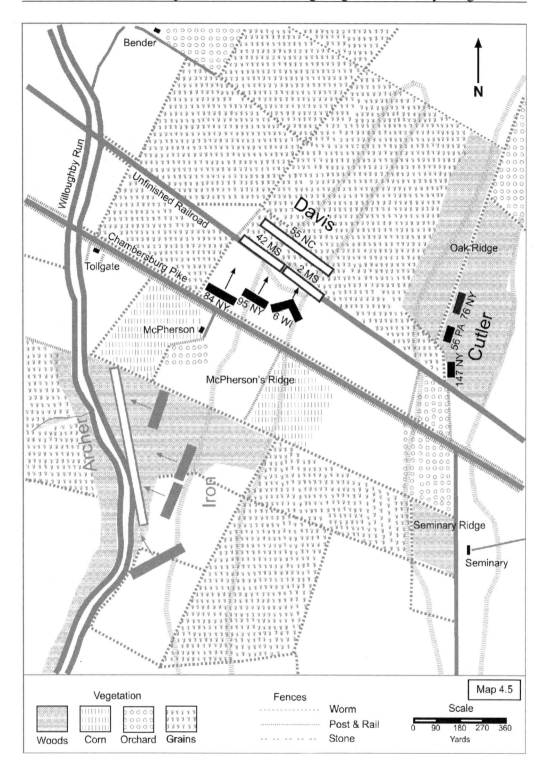

N

Bender

Willoughby Run

Unfinished Railroad

Davis

55 NC

42 MS

2 MS

Chambersburg Pike

Tollgate

84 NY   95 NY

6 WI

McPherson

Oak Ridge

76 NY

56 PA   Cutler

147 NY

McPherson's Ridge

Archer

Iron

Seminary Ridge

Seminary

Vegetation

Woods   Corn   Orchard   Grains

Fences

--------------- Worm

.... Post & Rail

– · – · – · – · – Stone

Scale

0   90   180   270   360

Yards

Map 4.5

Map Set 5: The Morning Fight Between Archer's Brigade and the Iron Brigade

Map 5.1

Brigadier General James Archer's 1,100-man brigade trudged toward Gettysburg on Chambersburg Pike in the van of Maj. Gen. Henry Heth's Division. Second in line, Brig. Gen. Joseph Davis deployed his brigade on the opposite side (north) of the pike. Heth's other two brigades under Brig. Gen. James J. Pettigrew and Col. John M. Brockenbrough marched behind Davis, with Maj. Gen. W. Dorsey Pender's Division following Heth. None of these foot soldiers expected a serious fight on what promised to be another muggy summer day.

Two brigades of Maj. Gen. John Buford's cavalry division, slightly more than 2,700 men, stood between Gettysburg and almost 13,500 Confederates approaching from the west. Buford intended to fight a delaying action, knowing the Federal I and XI Corps were closing on the battlefield. He knew he could not stop an entire enemy division, but he could force Heth to shift from marching column into line of battle.[1]

Approaching Herr Ridge, Archer deployed his men into line of battle on the right (south) of Chambersburg Pike. The 5th Alabama Battalion, with 50 men from the 13th Alabama, formed the skirmish line that first encountered the dismounted 8th Illinois Cavalry of Col. William Gamble's brigade, slowly pushing it back toward Willoughby Run. Behind the skirmish line, Archer deployed his line of battle from left to right: 7th Tennessee – 14th Tennessee – 1st Tennessee – 13th Alabama. Because of gentler terrain, the regiments on the left outdistanced those on the right, forcing Archer to order the advanced units to halt until the others caught up. One foot soldier in the 13th Alabama recalled that we "halted to reform, reload, catch our breath, and cool off a little." Willoughby Run was up ahead, clear water nearly knee-deep with "pebbles in bottom," recalled an Alabama foot soldier. The cautious Archer halted his brigade. General Heth rode up and ordered him to test

the "strength and line of battle of the enemy." Archer demurred, stating that his "brigade was [too] light to risk so far in advance of support." Unconvinced, Heth ordered Archer to continue advancing.[2]

Neither Archer nor any of his men knew of the rapid approach of the Iron Brigade on the opposite side of Willoughby Run. Major General James Wadsworth's division of the I Corps approached Gettysburg from the south along Emmitsburg Road, having spent the night at Marsh Creek. Near the Codori House, the men abandoned the road and marched overland in a northwest direction toward the Lutheran Theological Seminary on the ridge that bore its name. In the van, Lysander Cutler's brigade straddled Chambersburg Pike. The 1,800-man Iron Brigade under Brig. Gen. Solomon Meredith hurried after Cutler's men as they crossed the fields leading to Herbst Woods.[3]

The 2nd Wisconsin led the Iron Brigade, followed by the 7th Wisconsin, 19th Indiana, 24th Michigan, and 6th Wisconsin. Lieutenant Colonel John Kress of General Wadsworth's staff met the column as it approached the Seminary. When General Meredith could not be found and with Archer's men swarming across Willoughby Run, Kress ordered each regiment to shift from column of fours into line of battle with two ranks, and sent them west toward the enemy. This resulted in an en echelon attack formation as the units were fed into the combat as soon as they arrived. The 6th Wisconsin formed the reserve near the seminary.[4]

The 2nd Wisconsin barreled toward Herbst (McPherson's) Woods without waiting for the other regiments to form beside it. On its left, Sergeant Charles Pergel's two-gun section of Calef's battery continued firing at the approaching enemy.[5]

The left flank of Archer's brigade line extended as far as the northern portion of Herbst Woods. The 5th Alabama Battalion, still deployed as a skirmish line, thinly extended the line north to Chambersburg Pike. The men from the battalion exchanged musket fire with the 84th and 95th New York regiments of Cutler's brigade that occupied the McPherson farm buildings.[6]

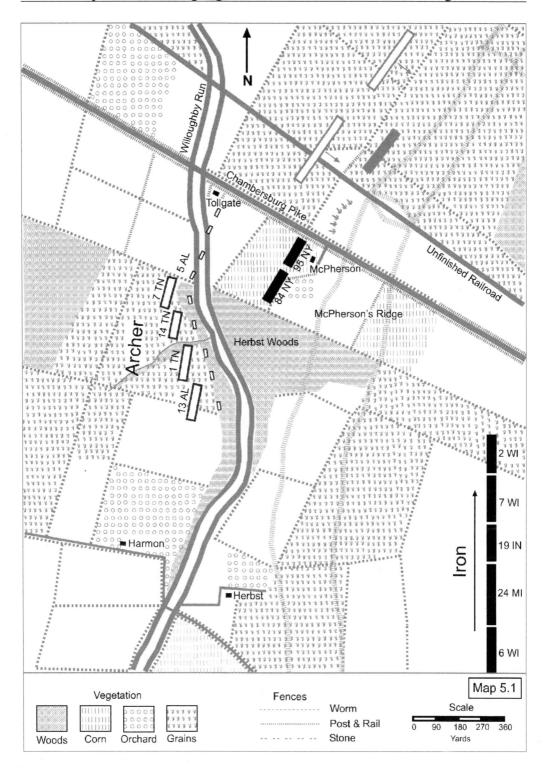

Map 5.1

Vegetation

Woods Corn Orchard Grains

Fences

---------- Worm
.... Post & Rail
-- -- -- -- Stone

Scale

0   90   180   270   360
Yards

Map 5.2

Lieutenant Colonel Samuel Shepard of the 7th Tennessee was deeply concerned about the terrain around Willoughby Run. The landscape included "a fence and undergrowth, which was some disadvantage to our line in crossing." Still, his men "rushed across with a cheer" and began climbing the steep bank on the opposite side of the stream. The rugged terrain opened gaps between several of the regiments. Archer's men were no longer advancing as a solid, cohesive brigade.[7]

The 2nd Wisconsin moved to meet the advancing Confederates. Just prior to reaching Herbst Woods, the regiment encountered a fence that disorganized its lines. The men were also ordered to load their weapons on the run, which threw them into further disarray. They took no time to halt and dress their lines but moved quickly down the sloping pasture toward Willoughby Run. As the infantry advanced, Pergel's section of Calef's battery pulled back to safety.[8]

A heavy volley from the 7th and 14th Tennessee met the men of the 2nd Wisconsin as they descended the slope. Dozens of men—possibly as many as 30% of the regiment—fell killed or wounded. The 7th's Col. S. G. Shepard reported this initial volley was delivered at a range of only 40-50 yards. Although it will never be known with certainty, the volley may have also killed Maj. Gen. John Reynolds. (Some claim a sharpshooter's bullet killed him, but this is very unlikely as there were no sharpshooters operating in that sector.) "Our men fired with great coolness and deliberation," Shepard later reported, "and with terrible effect." [9]

The 2nd Wisconsin's advance ground to a halt as the officers reformed the men and judged their losses. The rest of the brigade had not yet arrived. As the men of the 13th Alabama on the right of Archer's line finally reached the stream bed that provided some shelter from the Federal bullets, they halted momentarily to rest, re-form, and reload before moving up the slope. One Alabama soldier recalled seeing the Tennesseans on their left fan out as they moved up the ridge

from Willoughby Run. At the same time, an officer, probably from the 14th Tennessee, requested that the unopposed 13th Alabama on the right of the line oblique slightly to the left and throw enfilade fire into the 2nd Wisconsin. The Alabamians complied, moving slowly up the slope while swinging its left toward its crest until it was only 75 yards from the left flank of the 2nd Wisconsin. The subsequent converging fire killed and wounded several Federal infantrymen. The Tennessee soldiers in front of the 2nd Wisconsin loaded while lying on their backs and rolled over to fire at the enemy, repeating the process again and again.[10]

Help was on the way in the form of the 7th Wisconsin. Approaching the seminary behind the 2nd Wisconsin, Lt. Col. John Kress quickly sent it toward Willoughby Run after it formed into line of battle. Colonel William Robinson rushed his men forward at the double-quick with orders to load their rifles as they moved. Robinson explained in his report that just moments earlier "no one expected that we were to be engaged so quickly."

When the regiment reached the crest of the hill, several men were struck by fire from Archer's men. A heavy layer of smoke made it difficult for Colonel Robinson to evaluate the surrounding terrain and identify the troops firing into his unit. When he inquired of an aide as to the source of the fire, the subordinate merely pointed to the left, where the colonel spotted a Confederate flag. Rather than pitching forward like the 2nd Wisconsin, Robinson decided to wait until the 19th Indiana and the 24th Michigan regiments arrived and formed on his left.

As it happened, the 19th Indiana had been on picket duty the night before so its men's rifles were already loaded. The 24th Michigan had halted to load its weapons upon arriving on the crest of the McPherson Ridge, but a staff officer ordered the regiment to hurry forward to catch up with the other two regiments now rushing toward Willoughby Run.[11]

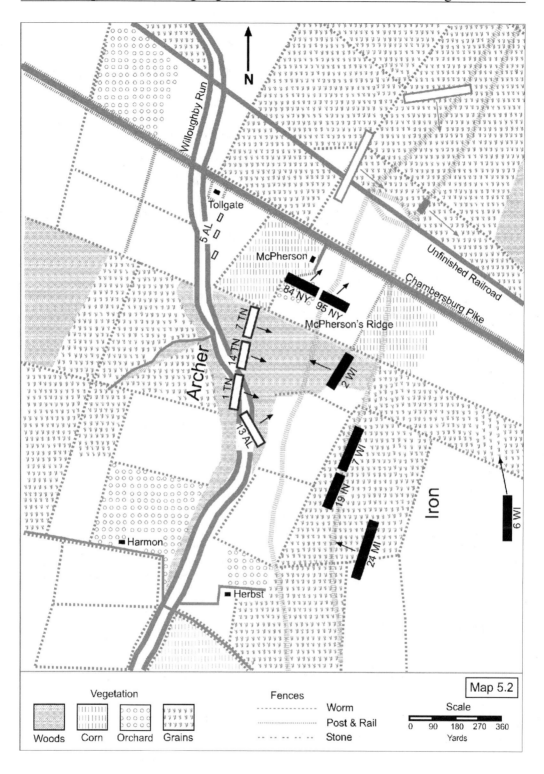

Map 5.2

Map 5.3

On the right side of Archer's line, officers of the 13th Alabama apparently spotted the 7th Wisconsin, 19th Indiana, and 24th Michigan approaching and ordered a hasty retreat. Other soldiers in Archer's remaining regiments did not see the Federal threat and were confused by the sudden withdrawal. "We could see no reason for the order, as the Tennesseans were keeping the blue boys busy, and things seemed to be going pretty well for us," explained one soldier.

After driving the 13th Alabama back to Willoughby Run, the 7th Wisconsin, 19th Indiana, and 24th Michigan delivered a final volley and then, in the words of Col. William Robinson of the 7th Wisconsin, "rushed into the ravine with a yell."[12] According to a member of the 13th Alabama, "all of a sudden a heavy line of battle rose up out of the wheat, and poured a volly into our ranks, it wavered and they charged us, and we fell back to the ravine again, and before we could rally, it seemed to me there were 20,000 Yanks down in among us hollowing surrender." The newly arrived Federal troops scooped up scores of Alabamians and sent them to the rear as prisoners. Private E. Boland, a member of the 13th Alabama, recalled that "we discovered that we had tackled a hard proposition . . . we had Yankees on the front, Yankees on the flanks, and seen Yankees behind us. . . . After a short, furious fight," Boland continued, "surrounded by infantry and cavalry, nothing was left for us to do but lay down in the field and allow the enemy to come on or surrender, which we did." [13]

Although the 1st and 14th Tennessee in the center of Archer's line could not see the advancing Federals, they knew they were there because of the heavy musketry and rifle fire zipping in from the right. Every man in the ranks knew what the increasing regularity and intensity of the fire meant. According to Captain Jacob Turney of the 1st Tennessee, when the Federal shooting suddenly ceased, "[I] dropped on my knees, and, looking beneath the hanging smoke, saw the feet and legs of the enemy moving to our left." Rushing over to General Archer, Turney told him what he saw. "I guess not, Captain, since Gen. Joe Davis is to occupy that timber to our left," Archer is said to have replied.[14]

The men of the 2nd Wisconsin could see Confederates darting from tree to tree as they sought out better defensive positions. Colonel Lucius Fairchild realized the Confederates were reforming their lines and that three other Federal regiments had come up to join him on the left. He ordered his 2nd Wisconsin to resume its charge. A bullet ripped into his arm soon after, forcing him to relinquish command to Maj. John Mansfield. The Tennesseans held their ground until the 2nd Wisconsin came to within about fifteen paces before falling back across the stream. Finding no resistance in their front, the 24th Michigan on the left of the line splashed across Willoughby Run and wrapped behind the remnants of the retiring 13th Alabama and 1st Tennessee, capturing additional men as it did so. With increasing pressure against their front, and with the 24th Michigan curling around their left flank and rear, Archer's men fell back as quickly as possible to avoid the closing enemy jaws.[15]

The threat posed to the right flank of the Federal line by Joe Davis' Brigade resulted in the 6th Wisconsin and the 84th and 95th New York regiments of Cutler's brigade being moved in that direction. The shifting of these regiments prevented them from participating in the repulse of James Archer's Brigade.

Archer's heavy losses totaled about 375 men, including 240 captured. As the soldiers of the 2nd Wisconsin crossed the stream to round up additional prisoners, they captured a knot of men in the thick undergrowth. One of them was General Archer himself—the first general officer from the Army of Northern Virginia to be captured on the field of battle. Just moments before, Archer was observed to be "very much exhausted with fatigue." Colonel Birkett Fry of the 13th Alabama assumed command of the shattered brigade after it fell back and regrouped.[16]

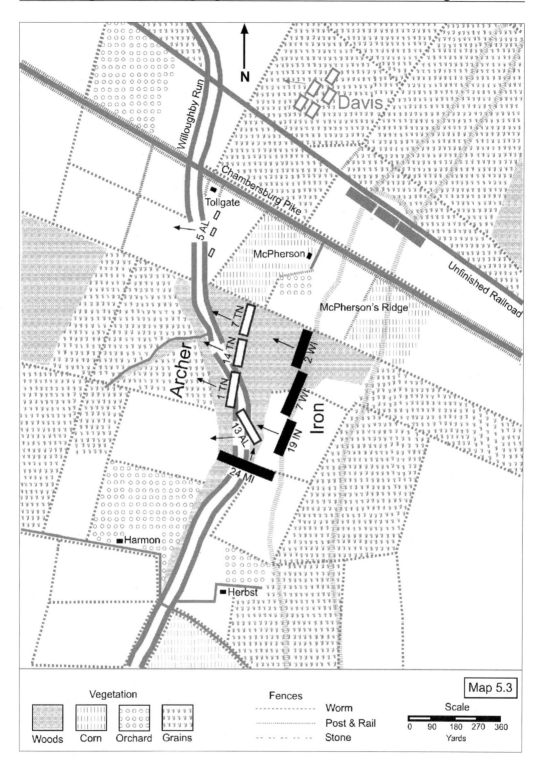

Map 5.3

Vegetation

Woods Corn Orchard Grains

Fences

.... Worm
.... Post & Rail
-- -- -- -- Stone

Scale

0   90   180   270   360

Yards

Map Set 6: Oak Ridge: Initial Attacks

Map 6.1

Major General Robert Rodes quickly deployed his Second Corps Confederate division as it arrived on Oak Hill during the early afternoon. Brigadier General George Doles' Georgia brigade moved left (east) toward Carlisle Road to keep a watch out for the arriving Federal XI Corps. Colonel Edward O'Neal's Alabama brigade occupied Oak Hill, and to its right, Brig. Gen. Alfred Iverson's North Carolina brigade deployed in the Forney Woods south of Mummasburg Road. Rodes' fourth brigade, the North Carolinians of Brig. Gen. Junius Daniel, formed on the right end of the division 200 yards behind Iverson with its left also in the Forney Woods. (Brigadier General Stephen D. Ramseur's Brigade was not yet up.) The four batteries of Lt. Col. Thomas Carter's artillery battalion arrived and unlimbered on Oak Hill.[1]

The initial deployment of O'Neal's Brigade was, from left to right: 5th Alabama – 6th Alabama – 26th Alabama – 12th Alabama – 3rd Alabama. This changed when Rodes detached the 5th Alabama to fill the gap between Doles' right and the rest of the division. He also sent the 3rd Alabama, on the opposite end of the line, to connect with the left of Daniel's Brigade. Why he did this is unclear. Rodes may have believed the 3rd Alabama did not have sufficient room to deploy and not enough protection. "For reasons explained to Colonel O'Neal," he penned in his after-battle report, "the Third having been permitted by Colonel O'Neal to move with Daniel's Brigade." O'Neal, however, protessed to know nothing about the reason for the dismantling of his brigade. "The Third Alabama on the right of the brigade . . . was ordered by General Rodes to connect with the brigade of General Daniel, on my right, and the Fifth Alabama . . . on the left," wrote O'Neal in his Gettysburg report. "General Rodes said he would command in person, so I only moved forward with the Twelfth, Twenty-sixth, and Sixth Alabama Regiments. Why my brigade was

thus deprived of two regiments, I have never been informed."[2]

By about 1:00 p.m., the Federal forces aligned against Rodes consisted of Brig. Gen. Henry Baxter's fresh brigade (Robinson's division, I Corps), Brig. Gen. Lysander Cutler's battered brigade (Wadsworth's division, I Corps), and the van of the XI Corps. On the right, Col. George von Amsberg's brigade (Schimmelfennig's division, XI Corps) took position just south of the McClean farm near the Hagy homestead. Four companies of the 45th New York arrived first and immediately confronted a battalion of sharpshooters from the 5th Alabama of O'Neal's Brigade. Pushing them back, they waited for the rest of the brigade to arrive. The remaining six companies of the 45th New York came up and deployed behind them. The 61st Ohio and 74th Pennsylvania regiments deployed to the right of the four advanced companies of the 45th New York as a skirmish line. Because this limited number of men had to cover an extended front, these units were spread very thinly, all facing generally north. The 157th New York and 82nd Illinois assumed a reserve role in support of Captain Hubert Dilger's 1st Ohio Light, Battery I, and Lieutenant William Wheeler's 13th New York Independent Battery, which had also recently arrived.[3]

On Oak Ridge, on von Amsberg's left, the position held by Baxter's brigade resembled something of an arrowhead. The 11th Pennsylvania and 97th New York faced northwest along Forney's field. The 12th Massachusetts deployed to their right, however, facing north forming the tip of the arrow. Its left flank connected with the 97th New York while its right flank was refused to form a right angle to connect with the 90th Pennsylvania, which also faced generally north. To the right, facing northeast along Mummasburg Road were the 83rd New York and the 88th Pennsylvania.[4]

The remnants of Cutler's battered brigade were reorganizing on Baxter's left. The 56th Pennsylvania and the 147th New York faced north along Forney's field at almost right angles to Baxter's left wing, while the 76th, 95th, and 84th New York regiments deployed to their left facing west.[5]

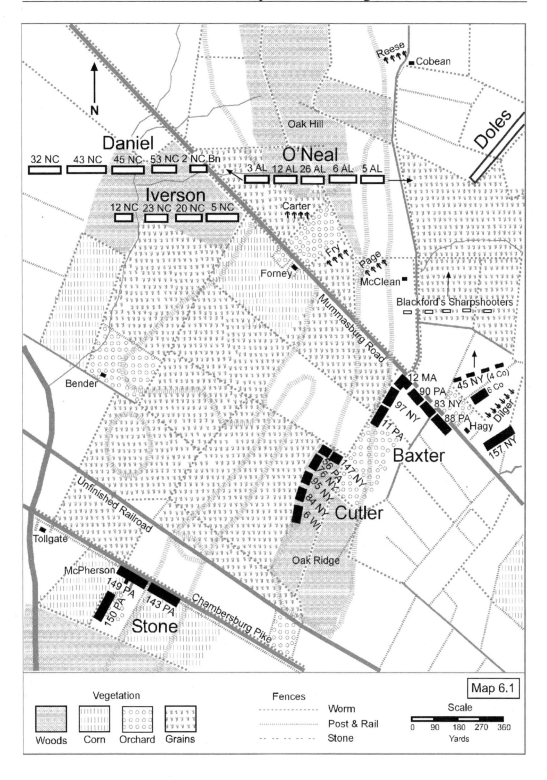

Map 6.1

Map 6.2

Although extraordinarily well positioned to strike the Federal right flank, Rodes' assault went awry from the beginning. O'Neal committed the first obvious error when he launched his brigade into the attack prematurely and in piecemeal fashion. According to Rodes, "the Alabama brigade went into action in some confusion, and with only three of its regiments . . . the three . . . regiments moved forward with alacrity (but not in accordance with my orders as to direction) and in confusion into the action."[6] Colonel O'Neal sent forward little more than half of his available manpower. Only 1,000 of his 1,700 effectives engaged about the same number of men in four regiments of Baxter's brigade along Mummasburg Road.

The Federals O'Neal attacked were deployed from left to right as follows: 12th Massachusetts – 90th Pennsylvania – 83rd New York – 88th Pennsylvania. According to Col. Samuel Pickens of O'Neal's 12th Alabama, "we attacked them in a strong position. After a desperate fight of about fifteen minutes, we were compelled to fall back, as the regiments on our left gave way, being flanked by a large force." O'Neal and his men apparently had not spotted the 45th New York of Col. George von Amsberg's brigade lurking along their left flank, accompanied by a section of Dilger's battery. Both poured enfilade fire into the 6th Alabama's left flank while the 88th and 90th Pennsylvania and 83rd New York regiments threw volleys into its front. The 45th New York was a mere 50-100 yards away when it opened a devastating fire against the Confederates. With musketry fire on their front, flank, and rear, and canister from Dilger's battery ripping into his left, O'Neal's attack collapsed.[7]

General Rodes watched the attack closely. "We were making no impression upon the enemy," he later reported. Disgusted with the way O'Neal was directing his attack, Rodes rode forward and ordered the 5th Alabama to the left of the line to assist the beleaguered 6th Alabama. The commander of the 5th Alabama, Col. Josephus Hall, could see the enemy line composed of "two heavy lines of infantry in front and a line of sharpshooters, supported by infantry and artillery, on my left flank." After the regiment passed the McClean farmhouse, Hall sent his right companies toward Mummasburg Road while refusing his left flank at right angles to handle the threat in that direction. The addition of the 5th Alabama had little impact on the success of the attack against Baxter's position. "My command was under a front and enfilading fire, with no support, and suffering a very severe loss," Hall bitterly remarked in his report. As Rodes put it, "the whole brigade . . . was repulsed quickly, and with loss."[8]

John Vautier of the 88th Pennsylvania vividly recalled the Confederate charge after the war. "Their line of battle, covered by a cloud of busy skirmishers, came driving through the woods from the right of the Mummasburg Road," wrote Hall. "Waiting until they were in easy range, the order was given, 'Commence firing.' With the sharp crack of the muskets a fleecy cloud of smoke rolled down the front of the brigade [Baxter's] and the Minie balls zipped and buzzed with a merry chorus toward the Southern line, which halted, and after a brief contest, retired to the shelter of the woods." Hall pitied the Southerners, noting that they marched "over the hill, through the brush, over fences and rocks, and being in the advance, came in collision with Baxter before Iverson was up."[9]

O'Neal's shattered remnants retreated northwest along the axis of Mummasburg Road and reformed along a fence about 300 yards in the rear, where most of the men fell to the ground to rest. Samuel Pickens of the 12th Alabama remarked in his diary, "I never saw troops so scattered & in such confusion . . . the Brig. was rallied by Col. O'Neal & Genl Rodes."[10] In the wake of the sharp repulse of O'Neal's Brigade, the four lead companies of the 45th New York advanced swiftly to the McClean barn, where they captured a number of his Alabamians.[11]

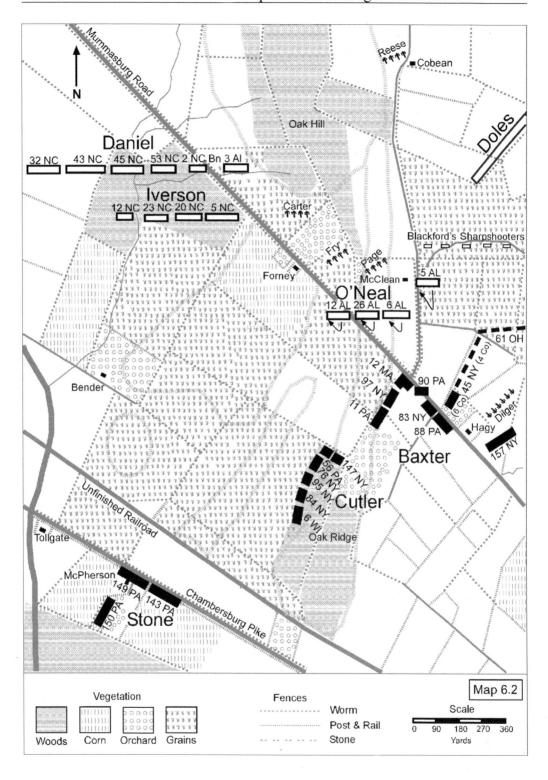

Map 6.2

Map 6.3

When he learned that Col. Edward O'Neal's Brigade had advanced without him, Brig. Gen. Alfred Iverson quickly ordered his men forward. It was between 2:00 and 2:30 p.m.

The brigade marched across Mummasburg Road aligned from left to right as follows: 5th North Carolina – 20th North Carolina – 23rd North Carolina – 12th North Carolina. Inexplicably, it did so without a skirmish line to uncover any unpleasant surprises that might await them. The line veered to the left, aiming toward the southeast corner of the open clover-planted Forney Field, where a gap yawned between Cutler's and Baxter's brigades. Because of O'Neal's premature attack, Iverson's left flank hung dangerously in the air as the brigade marched obliquely toward Baxter's position. When he received word that Iverson's regiments were advancing, General Daniel prepared his large brigade to move south as well. Rodes' Division was attacking in dribs and drabs, a sure recipe for disaster.[12]

Soldiers on both sides commented on the splendor of Iverson's advance. According to John Vautier of the 88th Pennsylvania, "Iverson's men, with arms at a right shoulder, came on in splendid array, keeping step with an almost perfect line." Nothing obstructed their march except a rail fence running roughly parallel and 700 yards south of the Mummasburg Road.[13]

Like O'Neal before him, Iverson did not accompany his brigade during its charge. Captain V. E. Turner and Sergeant H. C. Wall of the 12th North Carolina wrote, "Iverson's part in the heroic struggle of his brigade seems to have begun and ended with the order to move forward and 'Give them hell.'" The brigade had suffered heavily at the battle of Chancellorsville two months earlier, where many of the officers were killed and wounded. The North Carolinians were marching into action without the leadership they would so soon desperately require.[14]

Baxter's men, who had effectively halted O'Neal's advance just a few minutes before, did not have much time to savor their victory, for they could see Iverson's men advancing from the northwest. Concerned about the gap between Baxter's and Cutler's brigades, division commander John Robinson ordered the 11th Pennsylvania and 97th New York regiments southward to plug the hole. At the same time, the 83rd New York and 88th Pennsylvania on the right of the line received orders to "About face, right half wheel, halt; right dress; front." The order brought them into the positions vacated by the 11th Pennsylvania and 97th New York. The 12th Massachusetts and 90th Pennsylvania also filed to the left. The right side of the 90th Pennsylvania extended beyond Mummasburg Road. It was refused to face north to watch for any renewed threat from that sector. Baxter's brigade faced Iverson deployed from left to right as follows: 11th Pennsylvania – 97th New York – 83rd New York – 88th Pennsylvania – 12th Massachusetts – 90th Pennsylvania. Robinson could see that the enemy substantially outnumbered Baxter's brigade, so he summoned Brig. Gen. Gabriel Paul's brigade from its reserve position on Seminary Ridge and rushed it north to support the Oak Ridge line.[15]

Baxter's men were concealed behind a low stone wall, crouching behind it on one knee and taking careful aim at the advancing enemy. As a result, no one in Iverson's ranks knew what awaited them. Lieutenant Walter Montgomery of the 12th North Carolina recalled that the "troops bounded forward not knowing certainly where the enemy was, for his whole line, with every flag, was concealed . . . not one of them was to be seen."[16] According to the 88th Pennsylvania's John Vautier, "the field in our front was swarming with Confederates who come sweeping on in magnificent order with perfect alignment, guns at right shoulder and colors to the front." Closer and closer the North Carolinians marched, oblivious to the hundreds of fingers waiting on triggers to shoot them down. Every one of Baxter's men "with rifles cocked and fingers on the triggers, waited and bided their time." Orders were to "await command and aim low."

As Iverson's men marched ahead, General Daniel ordered the 3rd Alabama, which had been detached by O'Neal earlier to join his brigade, to move forward in support of Iverson.[17]

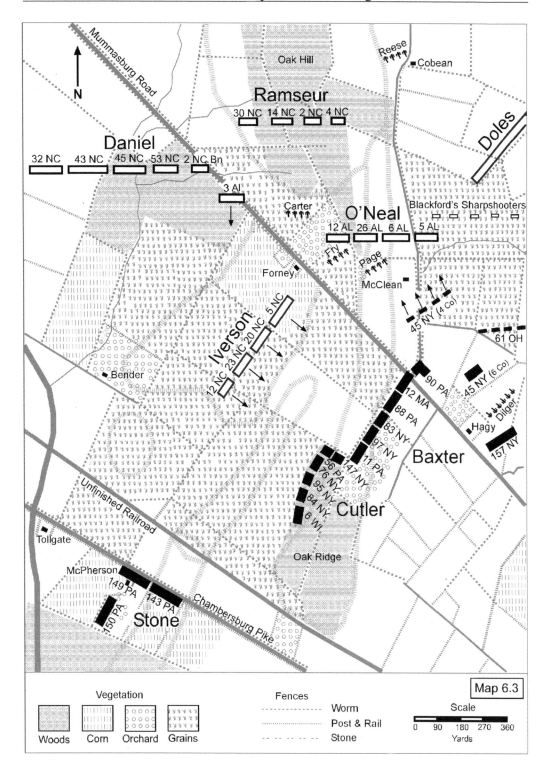

Map 6.4

The 5th North Carolina on the left of Iverson's line advanced within fifty yards of Baxter's line when Union officers screamed, "Open fire!" "A sheet of fire and smoke belched from the wall, flashing full in the faces of the Confederates," remembered John Vautier. "Hundreds of the Confederates fell at the first volley, plainly marking their line with the ghastly row of dead and wounded men, whose blood trailed the course of their line with a crimson stain clearly discernable for several days after the battle, until the rain washed the gory record away." New Yorker Charles Blacknall confirmed the surprise: "A solid wall of blue rose behind the one of stone and poured in a plunging, crushing fire. The range was point blank and largely enfilading." George Hussey of the 83rd New York wrote, "rarely has such a destructive volley been fired on any field of battle."[18]

A young Confederate artilleryman commented on the effect of this initial volley the following day: "There were . . . seventy-nine North Carolinians laying dead in a straight line. I stood on their right and looked down their line. It was perfectly dressed. Three had fallen to the front, the rest had fallen backward; yet the feet of all these dead men were in a perfectly straight line. . . . They had evidently been killed by one volley of musketry and they had fallen in their tracks without a single struggle." The three Confederate regiments on the left of the line (closest to Baxter's position) sustained the highest losses. The more fortunate regiment on the right, the 12th North Carolina, suffered relatively few casualties because it was farthest from the Federal line and afforded some shelter by a knoll.[19]

While Iverson's Brigade was being slaughtered without the benefit of the presence of its namesake, General Daniel—in a desperate effort to take some pressure off the beleaguered North Carolinians—launched his command against Cutler's brigade in Sheads' Woods and Stone's brigade along Chambersburg Pike. Daniel's regiments, also Tarheels to a man, filed to the left and advanced through the fields toward the Bender house. Daniel split his brigade

into two parts, sending the 2nd North Carolina Battalion, 32nd North Carolina, and 45th North Carolina toward Stone's brigade along Chambersburg Pike while the 12th and 53rd North Carolina turned east toward Cutler's position. The 3rd Alabama was already advancing toward Iverson's devastated brigade.[20]

Although in a state of shock and disarray because of the sudden change of events, many of Iverson's survivors attempted to return fire. The Federal troops, secure behind the stone wall, continued shooting into the stricken regiments. It was a mismatch the Southerners could not win. "The men [Iverson's] were falling like leaves in a storm . . . but no troops could long withstand that pelting fire," observed a Pennsylvanian. A young officer in the 88th Pennsylvania described how a "steady death-dealing fire was kept up, our men loading in comparative safety, and then resting rifle on boulders before them, would fire coolly with unerring aim."[21]

Iverson's men had few options, all of them bad. To retreat would mean re-crossing the open field behind them and presenting their backs to the enemy. Advancing was suicide; those who attempted it were promptly shot down. One was Col. Daniel Christie of the 23rd North Carolina, who was mortally wounded almost as soon as he rose to his feet to lead another charge against Baxter's men.[22]

Most of the Southern soldiers pressed themselves into the ground or sought cover in whatever ruts or depressions they could find. One gully in particular held a number of men. Others took shelter behind the bodies of the fallen. As Captain V. C. Turner of the 23rd North Carolina put it, "unable to advance, unwilling to retreat, the brigade lay down in the hollow or depression in the field and fought as best it could." Many men were hit several times as they lay exposed before Baxter's position. As a testament to their courage, the irregular fire the trapped soldiers managed to maintain killed and wounded several Federal infantrymen.[23]

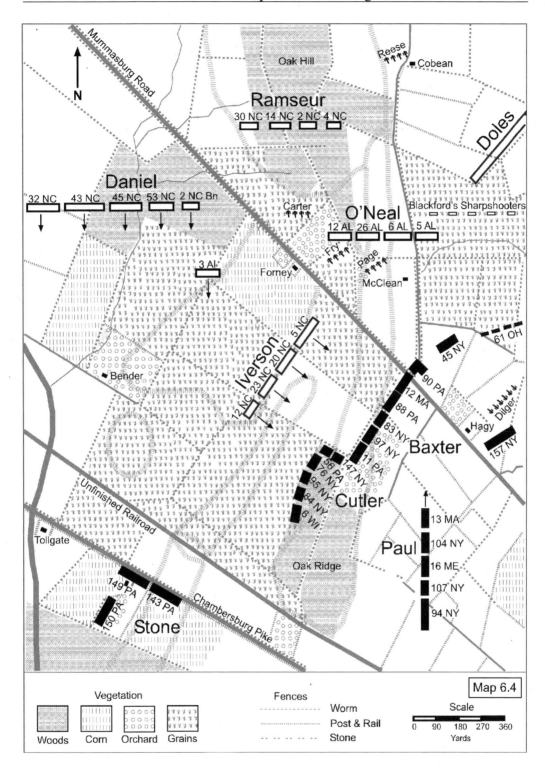

Map 6.4

Map 6.5

The situation facing Iverson's Brigade was beyond desperate. The fact that many of its officers were out of action only exacerbated the plight of the trapped rank and file.

After about ten minutes in the open field, the survivors realized help would not be forthcoming, there was no one to lead them, and that surrender was their only viable option. Those without white items hoisted boots or hats on their bayonets to show they were giving up. Seeing these tokens of surrender, soldiers from Baxter's brigade rose and ran toward Iverson's men. "It was not a charge at all," recalled Sergeant George Kimball of the 12th Massachusetts, "only a run forward to drive in Iverson's men who were willing enough to surrender." Several regiments of Cutler's brigade, which had changed front from west to northwest, joined the ragged advance. Only the 12th North Carolina, sheltered behind the knoll on the left side of the decimated brigade, escaped destruction and capture. The men bided their time until help arrived.[24]

The glee of the victorious Federals soon turned to horror and then anger when many Confederates opened fire on them almost as soon as they ventured forth to collect the prisoners. Some of the firing was from a handful of Iverson's infantrymen who were unwilling to surrender or not yet fully convinced it was necessary. (Brigadier General Stephen Ramseur's recently arrived brigade also contributed heavily to the musketry fire.) Collecting as many prisoners as they could together with several battle flags, the Federals quickly returned to their defensive positions.[25]

Iverson's losses amounted to about 900 out of the nearly 1,400 he sent (but did not lead) into battle. Most of them fell within the first few minutes of the lopsided combat. This nearly 65 percent loss tied with Richard Garnett's Brigade (July 3) as the highest in Lee's army. The regiment that suffered the heaviest loss was the 23rd North Carolina, which left about 9 of every 10 men on the field.[26]

As the 53rd North Carolina (Daniel's Brigade) and the 3rd Alabama (O'Neal's Brigade)

swept forward, a crossfire ripped into them from Cutler's brigade to their front and Stone's brigade to their right. The commander of the 53rd North Carolina halted his men when the Alabamians on his left suddenly stopped and fell back, uncovering his flank. Without this support, the North Carolinians withdrew about 50 yards to reconnect with the Alabamians. Almost immediately, the 3rd Alabama moved again, this time to the left to reconnect with the rest of O'Neal's Brigade. While the 43rd North Carolina halted at the Bender farm lane, the rest of Daniel's Brigade swept toward Chambersburg Pike and Stone's brigade.[27]

Returning to their original positions, Baxter's men found that Brig. Gen. Gabriel Paul's brigade had arrived to reinforce them. Because two brigades now occupied a position previously occupied by one, the officers had to redeploy their men. Paul split his brigade into two sections. The regiments arriving first continued marching northward to strengthen Baxter's right flank along Mummasburg Road, while the remaining regiments joined the left of Baxter's main line and faced west. Fronting Forney's field looking west, the regiments of the two brigades were aligned left to right as follows: 94th New York – 16th Maine – 107th Pennsylvania – 11th Pennsylvania – 97th New York – 83rd Pennsylvania – 88th Pennsylvania – 12th Massachusetts – 90th Pennsylvania. On their right along Mummasburg Road were the 104th New York and the 13th Massachusetts.[28]

The victory against Iverson's troops would be short-lived. Fresh Confederate soldiers had reached the field and were preparing to attack the Federal positions along Oak Ridge. Brigadier General Stephen Ramseur's Brigade, North Carolinians all, had been guarding the wagon train. They were now on Oak Hill and ready to be inserted into the developing battle.

Rodes promptly split Ramseur's Brigade in half, sending the 2nd and 4th North Carolina regiments to the left flank to support O'Neal's Brigade, while the 14th and 30th North Carolina regiments marched south to assist Iverson. Almost immediately, perhaps in anticipation of a Union attack on his position, Rodes ordered the first two regiments back to Oak Hill.[29]

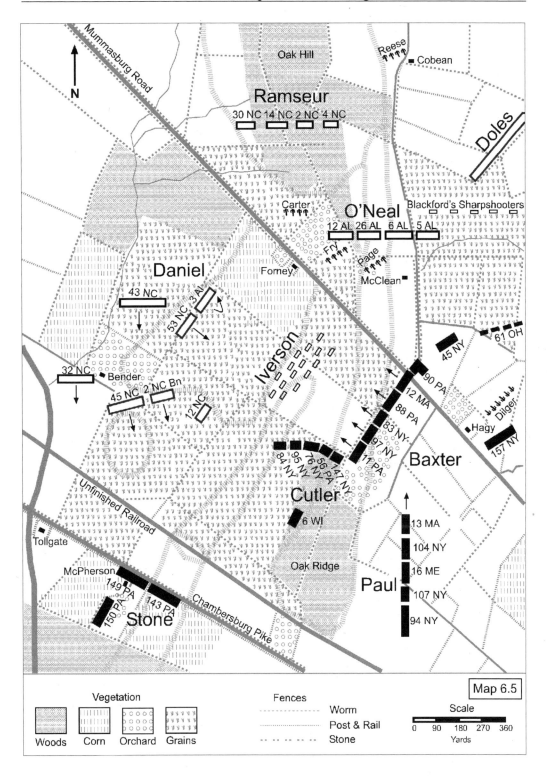

Map 6.5

Map Set 7: Along Chambersburg Pike

Map 7.1

Arriving on the battlefield shortly before noon, Col. Roy Stone's brigade (Brig. Gen. Thomas A. Rowley's division, I Corps) deployed near the McPherson farm buildings south of Chambersburg Pike. While Maj. Gen. Robert Rodes deployed his division on Oak Hill, Stone rearranged his three regiments. He shifted the 143rd and 149th Pennsylvania to parallel Chambersburg Pike facing north, and made sure the 150th Pennsylvania faced Maj. Gen. Harry Heth's Division to the west. Although there was little evidence at this point that Heth was preparing another assault, the massed Confederate artillery on Herr Ridge continually barraged Stone's men, forcing them to hunt for cover as casualties mounted. In an effort to lessen the effectiveness of the enemy fire, Stone decided to use the colors of the 149th Pennsylvania as a decoy. The color guard advanced to a position behind a pile of fence rails north of the pike. The ruse worked, tricking the Confederate artillerymen to concentrate their efforts against the Federal flags.[1]

Federal artillery also occupied the sector near Stone. Two sections of Calef's battery unlimbered north of Chambersburg Pike. When he received a severe enfilading fire from Capt. Thomas Brander's battery to the northwest and the rest of Maj. William J. Pegram's battalion to the west, Calef shifted his guns southeast. He unlimbered them just east of Herbst Woods, a good position that offered his tubes and men protection from Pegram's guns. From this new position Calef opened on Oak Hill. Captain Gilbert Reynolds' battery reached Calef's former position, found it too hot there, and crossed the road to take up a position next to Calef.[2]

The sight of Brig. Gen. Alfred Iverson's attack against Oak Ridge excited Stone's inexperienced men. Some opened fire though they were too far away to be effective. Their fire caught the attention of Brig. Gen. Junius Daniel, whose North Carolina brigade formed the right

flank of Rodes' Division. Daniel's orders were to "protect the right of the division, and to support Iverson's right." Daniel advanced the 2nd North Carolina battalion and 32nd and 45th North Carolina regiments southeast to confront Stone's brigade along Chambersburg Pike, while the 43rd and 53rd North Carolina regiments swung southeast at a sharper angle to front Oak Ridge and assist Iverson.[3]

Stone's two regiments along Chambersburg Pike—915 men in all—watched as the 2nd North Carolina battalion and the 45th North Carolina advanced obliquely toward them. When the two regiments reached a point about 500 yards from the Federal position, Confederate batteries on Oak Hill opened fire. The North Carolinians threw themselves to the ground to avoid the shells screaming over their heads. Colonel Stone ordered the 149th Pennsylvania to leave its position along Chambersburg Pike and advance to the unfinished railroad cut about 160 yards away. Because the cut at this point was steep, many men slid or tumbled to the bottom with a variety of cuts, bruises, and even broken bones. Those who could still walk climbed up the northern bank of the cut, took up a position there, and rested their muskets on the lip. Their orders were "to take deliberate aim at the knees of the front rank of the enemy as he came up."[4]

With the short artillery barrage at an end, the North Carolinians rose and continued their attack on Chambersburg Pike and the Federal flank, not realizing that a Federal regiment occupied the unfinished railroad cut in front of them. Reaching a fence about 75 yards from the cut (which was already littered with the killed and wounded from the earlier fight), Daniel's men finally spotted the waiting Pennsylvanians and opened fire. The volley was ineffective because, as one Federal put it, "our bodies were so well protected below the edge of the railroad cut." The Pennsylvanians received orders to fire "as long as a man was seen moving in that field in front of us," noted Francis Jones of the 149th Pennsylvania. One of the Confederates who escaped the carnage about to ensue recalled, "the enemy were some five or six hundred yards in front, and results showed that they had set a most deadly trap for us."[5]

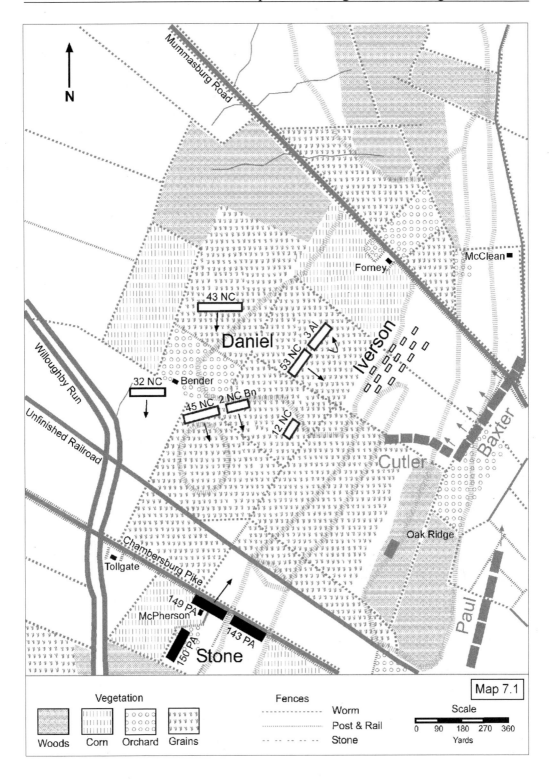

Map 7.2

The 149th Pennsylvania's initial volley could not have come at a worse time for the 2nd North Carolina Battalion and the 45th North Carolina. The Southerners were in the act of climbing a rail fence when it hit. According to Lt. Col. Walton Dwight of the 149th Pennsylvania, "the effect on the enemy was terrible, he being at the time brigade en masse, at 9-pace interval. He now broke to the rear in great confusion." General Daniel sent the 32nd North Carolina to assist in storming the pike, but it arrived too late to participate in this action. Two of Brander's Napoleons also arrived, crossing Willoughby Run and deploying southeast of the Bender homestead.[6]

The 2nd North Carolina Battalion and the 45th North Carolina made another attempt to pry the 149th Pennsylvania from the railroad cut, but were repulsed again with heavy loss. According to Lt. Col. Dwight, his men held their fire until "we could almost reach him with the muzzles of our pieces." Reynolds' and Calef's batteries, firing from almost perfect enfilade positions to the southeast, played a major role in beating back these attacks. The North Carolina units took fire from infantry to the front and artillery from the flank; losses on both sides mounted. Finally realizing the folly of their efforts, the two Confederate units retreated.

The 149th Pennsylvania's stay in the unfinished railroad cut ended when Brander's two guns unlimbered west of its position and poured a deadly fire into the Pennsylvanians, forcing them back to Chambersburg Pike. When they arrived, Dwight berated the men for their "cowardice" in vacating the railroad cut.[7]

As the 149th Pennsylvania withdrew to Chambersburg Pike, the 150th Pennsylvania changed front. The 150th Pennsylvania had been positioned to receive an attack from the west by Heth's Division, but when his troops remained inactive, Stone shifted the 150th regiment to face north against the more imminent threat emanating from Daniel north of Chambersburg Pike. Before making the movement, Col. Langhorne Wister divided his regiment into two wings, with Lt. Col. Henry Huidekoper commanding the right and Maj. Thomas Chamberlin the left. The movement drew Confederate artillery fire and Daniel launched still another attack. This time the 32nd North Carolina moved to the right a bit to drive against Stone's left flank from the northwest while the 2nd North Carolina Battalion and the 45th North Carolina attacked once again from the north.

The North Carolinians faced a deadly fire from the 143rd and 149th Pennsylvania regiments. Many took refuge in the unfinished railroad cut, which must have resembled a slaughterhouse after all the fighting it had witnessed this day. From this shelter, they opened an effective fire against the Federal position along Chambersburg Pike. When some of the Confederates advanced toward the 143rd Pennsylvania, its commander, Col. Edmund Dana, yelled to his men, "Steady now my men. Every one of you pick your man, ready now, Fire!" Much of the North Carolinians' first line fell, but a second rank quickly took its place. Some Confederates came as close as the fence lining the northern side of Chambersburg Pike before being driven back by point-blank fire from the two Pennsylvania regiments. Dana remarked that they had advanced "with a determination that was brave, and which befitted a better cause."[8]

A bullet tore into Col. Stone's hip about this time, and while he remained with the troops, he passed command of the brigade to Colonel Wister of the 150th Pennsylvania.[9]

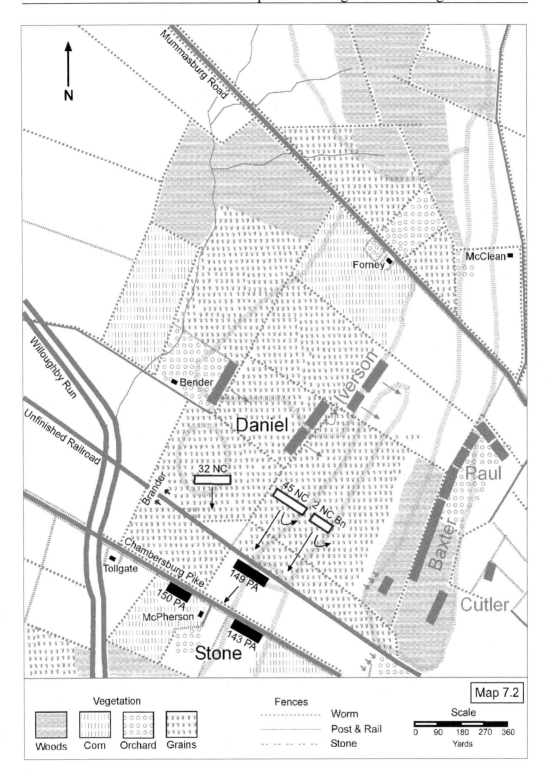

N

Mummasburg Road

Forney

McClean

Iverson

Willoughby Run

Unfinished Railroad

Bender

Daniel

Paul

Brander

32 NC

45 NC

2 NC Bn

Baxter

Tollgate

Chambersburg Pike

149 PA

Cutler

150 PA

McPherson

143 PA

Stone

Vegetation

Woods   Corn   Orchard   Grains

Fences

---------- Worm

.... Post & Rail

– – – – – Stone

Map 7.2

Scale

0   90   180   270   360

Yards

Map 7.3

With Confederates firing from the shelter of the railroad cut, Colonel Wister realized that he must act or continue to lose men. He ordered the 149th Pennsylvania, which had just returned from the cut, to turn and attack it once again. Although wounded in the thigh, Lieutenant Colonel Dwight again led his troops forward using his sword as a cane. The assault successfully drove the 2nd North Carolina Battalion and 45th North Carolina from the cut. However, the 32nd North Carolina still posed a threat along the brigade's left flank and Brander's battery was still firing from west of the cut. Thus, Dwight was again forced to pull his 149th Pennsylvania rearward to the relative shelter of Chambersburg Pike.[10]

Any Confederates returning to the unfinished railroad cut quickly scrambled for safety when Lieutenant James Stewart's Battery B (4th U.S.) opened on them with canister from its position near Sheads' Woods to the east. Elements of Cutler's brigade and the 6th Wisconsin of the Iron Brigade supported Stewart's guns. The two battered Confederate units retreated about halfway back to Oak Hill, where the men collapsed to the ground to await further orders.[11]

While the 149th Pennsylvania was charging back toward the railroad cut, Wister ordered the three right companies of his own 150th Pennsylvania, now under Lt. Col. Henry Huidekoper, to cross Chambersburg Pike and form at an oblique angle to the rest of the regiment. After successfully forcing the 149th Pennsylvania back to Chambersburg Pike, the 32nd North Carolina continued its attack south toward the McPherson barn.

The Southern soldiers entered a wheat field but did not spot the three companies of the 150th Pennsylvania crouching behind a fence. "At a distance of 50 yards, a volley was poured into the rebels, which staggered them so completely that a second one was fired before an attempt was made to advance or retreat," noted an officer. Two companies of the 149th Pennsylvania also crossed the road and formed behind the three companies of the 150th. With

the Confederates in disarray, the three companies of the 150th Pennsylvania, probably numbering no more than 130 men, counterattacked, driving the North Carolinians rearward. "[T]his regiment charged up to the barn [McPherson's], and dislodged the enemy," wrote the 32nd North Carolina commander Col. E. C. Brabble, "but, being unsupported on the right and left, and the battery on the hill opening a terrific fire upon it, it again fell back near the cut."[12] Stewart's battery supported the advance from its position straddling the unfinished railroad cut. Confederate artillery opened fire, forcing an end to the Federal attack. The detached Pennsylvania companies returned to Chambersburg Pike, where they rejoined their regiments.[13]

While the detachment of the 150th Pennsylvania took on the front of the 32nd North Carolina and the men on the right side of the regiment hit the North Carolinians on their flank, the left side opened fire on a body of about 70 Confederates to the northwest. These troops were probably part of Davis' shattered brigade, which had been torn apart in the railroad cut earlier that morning. The Federal volleys drove the Confederates back to their original positions.

General Daniel watched his men advance on two fronts, the 43rd and 53rd North Carolina attacking Oak Ridge, as his remaining three regiments drove against Stone's brigade. Linking with the 12th North Carolina of Iverson's Brigade on their left, the North Carolinians advanced on Baxter's brigade in Sheads' Woods.[14]

A bullet struck Colonel Wister in the mouth, but he refused to quit the field. Because he could not speak, he turned command of the brigade over to Col. Edmund Dana of the 143rd Pennsylvania. Losses were also heavy within the ranks of Confederate leadership. Both Lt. Col. Hezikiah Andrews of the 2nd North Carolina Battalion and Lt. Col. Samuel Boyd of the 45th North Carolina were wounded and out of the fight.[15]

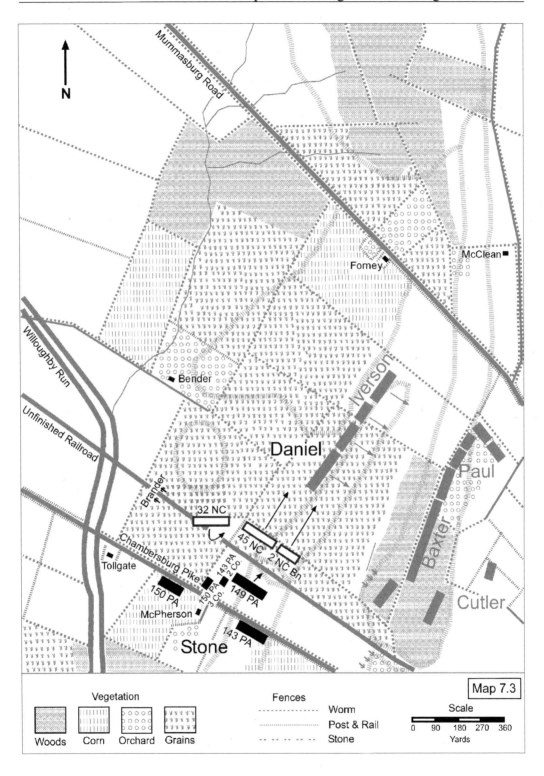

Map 7.3

Map 7.4

Despite repeated setbacks, Brig. Gen. Junius Daniel refused to give up. His brigade was new to the Army of Northern Virginia, having served in North Carolina for most of the war. If Daniel and his men believed they had something to prove to General Lee and his veterans, they were going to do it on July 1.

Daniel pulled the 2nd North Carolina Battalion and 45th North Carolina back about 40 paces from where they had begun their charge and reorganized the shattered ranks. Using "stentorian tones audible in command a quarter of a mile or more away," Daniel tried to hearten his men. Realizing that the capture of the southern portion of Oak Ridge was more important than taking Stone's position along Chambersburg Pike, he sent the 2nd North Carolina Battalion and the 45th North Carolina to join his 43rd and 53rd North Carolina, and together they successfully attacked Sheads' Woods. Meanwhile, Daniel ordered the 32nd North Carolina to continue its efforts to pry Stone's troops from their positions along Chambersburg Pike. Even if they could not dislodge Stone, their actions would cover the right flank of Daniel's Brigade as it moved against Baxter's men aligned in Sheads' Woods.[16]

While the men of the 32nd North Carolina hurled themselves against Stone's position along Chambersburg Pike, Heth's Division remained immobile. Perhaps Heth was mindful of Lee's order "not to bring on a general engagement" (even though a general engagement was already underway). This situation changed about 3:00 p.m. when Brockenbrough's Virginia brigade advanced. In response, the 150th Pennsylvania, "with no undue excitement, and in thoroughly good order . . . swung back to its original position, facing the west, leaving, however, a large gap between our left and the woods [Herbst], which was impossible to fill," recalled Maj. Thomas Chamberlin. This meant the 149th Pennsylvania's left flank was hanging in the air, a weakness quickly exploited by the 32nd North Carolina charging from the northwest. Caught between Brockenbrough's Brigade to the west and the 32nd North Carolina (Daniel) from the northwest, Stone's prospects for defending his position darkened considerably.[17]

Lieutenant Benjamin Wilber's section of three-inch ordnance rifles from Reynolds' battery galloped to the left of the 150th Pennsylvania and unlimbered, but it was too late to alter the tactical situation. They may not have had time to fire a shot. Johnston Pettigrew's Brigade, also part of Heth's Division, was knocking down the regiments of the Iron Brigade from the left like a game of dominos, and the steady advance of Brockenbrough's Brigade forced the Pennsylvanians to withdraw.

Stone's remaining two regiments were also in a precarious position. As the 32nd North Carolina attacked Stone's line along Chambersburg Pike from the northwest, Brockenbrough moved slowly forward from the west and some of Pettigrew's men approached from the south. Caught in a vise, Col. Dana reluctantly ordered the two regiments to vacate their positions along Chambersburg Pike. The exhausted Federals retreated toward a new defensive position on Seminary Ridge.[18]

Losses on both sides were exceptionally heavy. The 149th Pennsylvania, which launched two attacks against Daniel's Brigade, lost 336 men or 75 percent of its strength. The 150th Pennsylvania lost 66 percent of its men, and the 143rd Pennsylvania on the right of the line lost more than 54 percent. Losses in the 2nd North Carolina Battalion, which repeatedly attacked the two Federal regiments ensconced along Chambersburg Pike, were even more severe— 199 out of 240, or 83 percent. (Only one regiment in Brig. Gen. Richard Garnett's Brigade of Maj. Gen. George Pickett's Division and another one in Brig. Gen. Alfred Iverson's Brigade, Maj. Gen. Rodes' Division, lost a higher percentage of men at Gettysburg.) Stone's brigade also sustained another indignity. In the confusion of battle and withdrawal, no one remembered to order the detached 149th Pennsylvania color guard to fall back from its isolated position north of Chambersburg Pike. Mississippians in Davis' Brigade captured the flag later that afternoon. Despite losing most of its men before falling back, Stone's brigade had acquitted itself bravely in its first battle.[19]

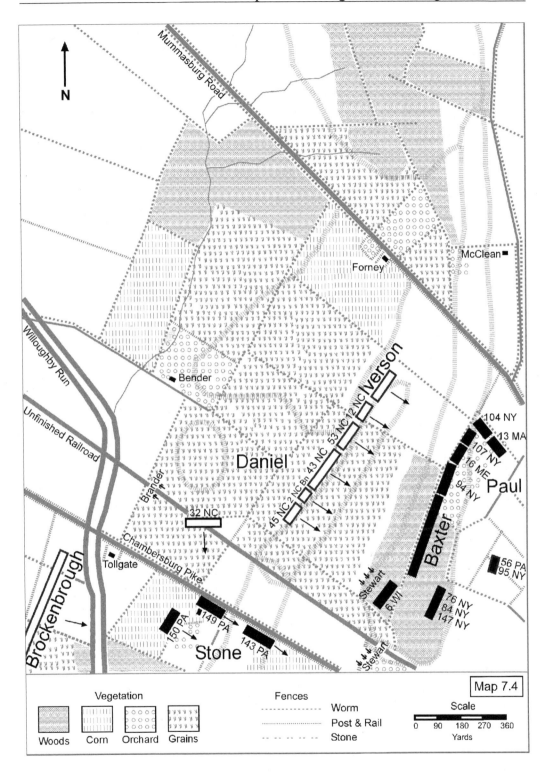

Map 7.4

Vegetation

Woods   Corn   Orchard   Grains

Fences

Worm
Post & Rail
Stone

Scale

0   90   180   270   360
Yards

Map Set 8: The Fight for McPherson Ridge

Map 8.1

The sector along Willoughby Run was relatively quiet after the bloody repulse of Archer's Brigade that morning. The lull permitted Brig. Gen. Solomon Meredith time to realign his Iron Brigade on McPherson Ridge.

Meredith placed the 7th Wisconsin on the right of the line, the 2nd Wisconsin on its left, followed by the 24th Michigan and finally the 19th Indiana. The alignment was fine, but the manner of their deployment was not. The front was too long for the Iron Brigade to cover, and the regiments were positioned in such a manner that they could not provide mutual support. The men of the 24th Michigan and 19th Indiana (on the left) were particularly unhappy. In order to connect with the 2nd Wisconsin, the right wing of the 24th Michigan bent back to form an obtuse angle in the line. The men on one end of the regiment could not see those on the other and their fields of fire were similarly restricted. The 24th's commander, Col. Henry Morrow, sent several aides to report that his position was untenable. Each returned with the same response: "the position was ordered to be held, and must be held at all hazards." The men of the 19th Indiana were also worried about their position because their left flank hung dangerously in the air. When protests were lodged with General Meredith, he replied that he was merely following orders. It is not clear whether division commander Maj. Gen. James Wadsworth heard any of these complaints.[1]

Colonel Chapman Biddle's brigade arrived to support the Iron Brigade. However, instead of closing the gap between units and extending the line to the left, the brigade formed about 200 yards to the rear midway between McPherson and Seminary ridges. The 19th Indiana's left flank remained in the air, as did both flanks of Biddle's brigade. The latter was aligned from left to right as follows: 121st Pennsylvania – 80th New York – 142nd Pennsylvania – 151st Pennsylvania. Reynolds' battery deployed between the 80th New York and the 142nd Pennsylvania; the infantry was ordered to lie down. About 2:00 p.m., the 151st Pennsylvania withdrew to the Lutheran Seminary, where it became the I Corps' last reserve unit.[2]

The Confederates were also active during this period preparing a fresh assault. Major General Harry Heth's last two fresh brigades advanced toward McPherson Ridge between 2:30 and 3:00 p.m. The front was composed of Johnston Pettigrew's large North Carolina Brigade on the right and John Brockenbrough's much smaller Virginia brigade on the left. The remnants of Archer's Brigade, now commanded by Col. Birkett D. Fry, aligned themselves on Pettigrew's right flank. Pettigrew's 2,600-man brigade deployed from left to right as follows: 26th North Carolina – 11th North Carolina – 47th North Carolina – 52nd North Carolina. The regiments aligned en echelon on the 26th North Carolina, a large regiment of nearly 900 men. Lieutenant Colonel John Lane of the 26th North Carolina recalled after the war that "all kept the step and made as pretty and perfect a line as a regiment ever made, every man endeavoring to keep dressed on the colors." Brockenbrough's Brigade, which numbered only about 800 effectives, deployed from left to right as follows: 55th Virginia – 47th Virginia – 40th Virginia – 22nd Virginia Battalion.[3]

The 26th North Carolina advanced directly toward the 24th Michigan while the 11th North Carolina closed on the 19th Indiana. The rest of Pettigrew's Brigade extended hundreds of yards south of the 19th Indiana and its exposed left flank. The 24th Michigan opened fire as the 26th North Carolina approached Willoughby Run, but most of the men shot high and found little Southern flesh. When Federal batteries opened on Pettigrew's line, an enlisted man in the 24th Michigan observed that the North Carolinians closed "up the gaps made by our guns, the slow advance not being checked in the least—banners flying proudly, voices ringing out defiantly above the roar of artillery." After the war, Pettigrew's adjutant wrote that the brigade "marched out in perfect alignment, and under as hot a fire as was ever faced, moved steadily through the wheat."[4]

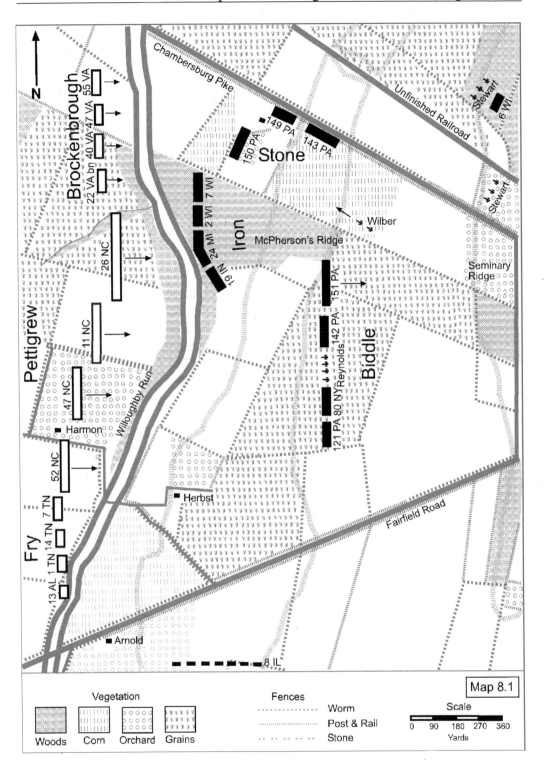

N

Chambersburg Pike

Brockenbrough

55 VA
47 VA
40 VA
22 VA bn

Unfinished Railroad

Stewart
6 Wi.

149 PA
150 PA
143 PA

Stone

Stewart

7 Wi
2 Wi
24 Mi
19 Il

Iron

Wilber

McPherson's Ridge

26 NC

Pettigrew

11 NC

47 NC

Harmon

52 NC

Herbst

151 PA

142 PA

80 NY
121 PA

Reynolds

Biddle

Seminary
Ridge

Fairfield Road

Fry

7 TN
14 TN
1 TN
13 AL
1 AL

Willoughby Run

Arnold

8 Il

Map 8.1

Vegetation

Woods   Corn   Orchard   Grains

Fences

- - - - - - - - Worm
· · · · · · · · Post & Rail
- - — - - — - Stone

Scale

0   90   180   270   360
Yards

Map 8.2

Effective Federal artillery fire forced the left end of the 26th North Carolina to crowd toward the center. As the men picked their way through the dense undergrowth bordering Willoughby Run, the lines became further disordered. Once across the stream, the regiment halted and the line re-dressed. As the range closed, small arms fire from the Iron Brigade became more deadly. George Underwood of the 26th North Carolina found the whizzing balls as "thick as hail stones in a storm." Officers were everywhere in evidence, cheering on their raw troops.[5]

As the Confederates advanced, an officer in the Iron Brigade bravely yelled to his men, "Boys, we must hold our colors on this line, or lie here under them," but the 24th Michigan's best efforts could not halt the 26th North Carolina. According to Col. Henry Morrow, "their advance was not checked, and they came on with rapid strides, yelling like demons." The lines closed to within point blank range, firing into each other with horrific effect.

To the left of the 24th Michigan, the 19th Indiana held its fire as the 11th North Carolina approached. According to a Union private, "they kept coming steadily on, and in as good [a] line as ever troops did on parade and their muskets a glittering. It was ·an awe-inspiring sight to observe them." The Hoosiers' commander, Col. Samuel J. Williams, noted that because Biddle's brigade had taken position "en echelon, to my left and rear, which . . . did not prevent a heavy fire on my flank . . . the enemy attacked this position—coming forward in three battle lines far overlapping me on the left . . . whose intention evidently . . . was to sweep round upon my left and rear, thus subjecting my command to capture." Besides the 26th North Carolina, the other two battle lines Morrow referred to were the 47th and 52nd North Carolina regiments.

The noise and chaos of battle affects each man differently. Despite seeing clearly that the regiment was about to be engulfed, many of the Federal officers refused to take action to prevent the looming disaster about to break upon their left. One enlisted man wrote bitterly that his regiment was "shamefully ordered to stand there without support of either troops or cannon." As the 11th North Carolina approached, the 19th Indiana finally opened fire. The Tarheels stopped, re-dressed their lines, and continued forward. When they struck the Hoosier left flank, its left-most companies crumbled quickly, forcing those men who did not immediately turn and flee toward the center. The Southerners pressed on and rolled up the Federal line.

Their position untenable, the men of the 19th Indiana began trickling backward to assume a new defensive position about 100 yards distant. The trickle soon became a torrent, and the torrent became a rout. "We drove the enemy like sheep . . . we just mowed them down," Lt. William Taylor of the 11th North Carolina wrote to his mother. The cost to both units was enormous. The 19th Indiana left about 40% of its men on the field. The 11th North Carolina also sustained heavy casualties. One of its companies entered the battle with 38 men, but only four remained unhurt when the sun set on July 1.[6]

The situation was not as desperate on the right end of the Iron Brigade's line, where the 2nd and 7th Wisconsin regiments faced Brockenbrough's Virginians. At first it seemed that the Virginians' drive would take them beyond the right flank of the Wisconsin troops, but several of the Confederate regiments changed direction as they approached Herbst Woods, apparently to skirt a quarry. The right side of Brockenbrough's Brigade (the 22nd Virginia Battalion, the 40th Virginia, and part of the 47th Virginia) slowly advanced against the Wisconsin regiments. While Pettigrew's Brigade was one of the largest units in the army, Brockenbrough's Virginia outfit was one of the smallest (and one of the least reliable in Lee's entire army). Brockenbrough's advance was slow and methodical, and the Virginians periodically fell to the ground to fire into the exposed Federal troops before standing to continue moving forward.[7]

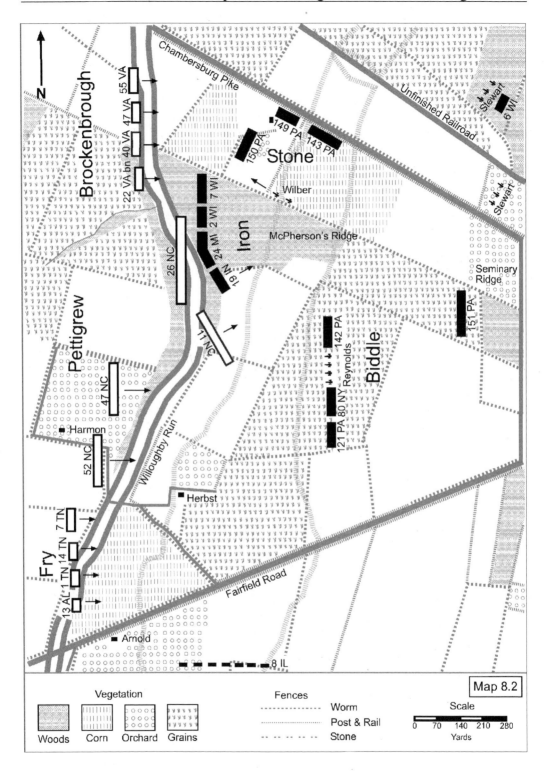

N

Chambersburg Pike

Brockenbrough

55 VA

47 VA

40 VA

22 VA bn

Unfinished Railroad

Stewart

6 WI

149 PA

143 PA

150 PA

Stone

7 WI

2 WI

24 MI

Iron

19 IN

26 NC

Wilber

Stewart

McPherson's Ridge

Seminary Ridge

151 PA

11 NC

142 PA

Biddle

Pettigrew

47 NC

80 NY

Reynolds

Harmon

121 PA

Willoughby Run

52 NC

Herbst

7 TN

14 TN

1 TN

13 AL

Fry

Fairfield Road

Arnold

8 IL

Vegetation

Woods   Corn   Orchard   Grains

Fences

.... Worm

.... Post & Rail

– - – - – - Stone

Scale

0   70   140   210   280

Yards

Map 8.2

Map 8.3

As Pettigrew's men attacked, an artillery shell felled Iron Brigade commander Solomon Meredith. Because of the noise and confusion, for a time no one took his place. Each regiment fought independently until Col. William Robinson of the 7th Wisconsin assumed command of the brigade.[8]

The withdrawal of the 19th Indiana exposed the left flank of the 24th Michigan, the next regiment in line. Within minutes, its men began "falling like grass before the scythe." Even those lying on the ground were not safe, and many were hit several times while lying prone. The two left companies were refused to face the looming threat on the flank, but they were too few against far too many. A few minutes later they too were swept away, and eventually the entire regiment began making its way to the rear. Heth's attack was methodically prying loose the defenders, one regiment at a time.[9]

The 19th Indiana and 24th Michigan took up new positions about 100 yards to the rear, where they again opened fire and exacted a terrible toll on Pettigrew's men. At one point, the two lines stood less than 20 paces apart. According to an officer of the 26th North Carolina, "we raised a cheer [and] the Yankee line gave way; we charged to the top of the hill where we found another line, which we charged."

The two Federal regiments, fighting independently, were flanked again and again, and forced to fall back as many as four more times. Casualties among the flag bearers were staggering for both sides. A total of fifteen men in the 26th North Carolina carried the flag during this attack including two of its regimental commanders (both gravely wounded). Ten men carried the 24th Michigan banner. The toll among the flag bearers was so great in the 19th Indiana that the banners were furled for a while to stop others from taking them up in the excitement of combat and being killed or maimed for the effort.[10]

On the right of the Iron Brigade's defensive line in Herbst Woods, the 2nd and 7th Wisconsin were faring much better. Brockenbrough's Virginians made only two "half-hearted"

approaches against them. These Confederates had initially faced the 150th Pennsylvania of Stone's brigade, before shifting to their right to avoid the quarry.[11]

Meanwhile, the right side of Pettigrew's Brigade, composed of the 47th and 52nd North Carolina regiments, passed beyond the right flank of the Iron Brigade and advanced toward Biddle's brigade deployed in the saddle between McPherson and Seminary ridges. According to Lt. J. Rogers of the 47th North Carolina, "in the line of the Forty-seventh there are over 650 muskets, the men marching steadily to meet the foe . . . artillery which at every step rakes through our lines, cutting great gaps, which are quickly filled up by our boys." They did not see Biddle's infantry until they had passed through a wheat field.[12]

Archer's Brigade (under Colonel Fry) advanced on the right of Pettigrew's men. Seeing the 8th Illinois of Gamble's cavalry brigade on the opposite side of Fairfield Road, Colonel Fry wheeled his line in its direction. This unexpected movement was a great relief to Colonel Biddle; if Fry had continued to advance along his original axis, his brigade would have overlapped Biddle's left flank and tramped right into his rear. And then something else unexpected occurred: Fry decided he was content to watch the cavalrymen rather than attack them. His veteran infantrymen did not participate further in the attack already under way. Our brigade, wrote a disgusted Capt. Jacob Turney of the 1st Tennessee, acted as a "body of observation." Lieutenant Colonel Samuel G. Shepard of the 7th Tennessee observed that when the brigade changed front, "the cavalry did not advance upon us, but hung around during the entire engagement of the evening of July 1."[13]

Help, however, was on the way for the beleaguered Federal troops on McPherson Ridge. The 467-man 151st Pennsylvania (School Teachers' Regiment) of Biddle's brigade, which had been in reserve near the Lutheran Seminary, was moving forward to reinforce the embattled Iron Brigade in Herbst Woods.[14]

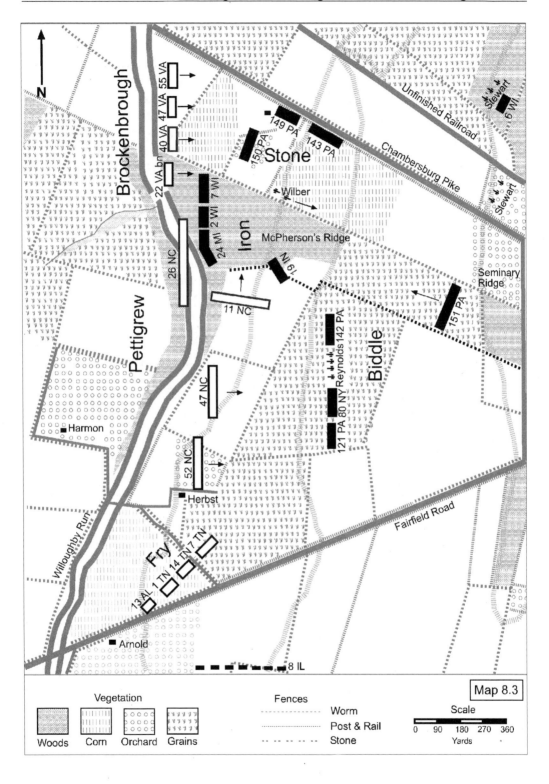

Map 8.3

Vegetation

Woods   Corn   Orchard   Grains

Fences

-------- Worm

············ Post & Rail

— - — - — Stone

Scale

0   90   180   270   360

Yards

Map 8.4

As the 19th Indiana and 24th Michigan fell back, the right of the Iron Brigade, composed of the 2nd and 7th Wisconsin, held securely against John Brockenbrough's half-hearted attacks. Given how lightly they were pushing, the Virginians must have been surprised when many of the Federal troops in front of them suddenly fell back. They did not know that the collapse of the 24th Michigan had uncovered their left flank and, with the 26th North Carolina approaching them, their position had become untenable.

The retreat was in unplanned installments. Seven companies of the 7th Wisconsin retreated while the rest of the regiment and the 2nd Wisconsin attempted to hold fast. Hit by small arms fire in their front and flank, they too fell back. The 2nd Wisconsin's Capt. Robert Beecham did not recall receiving orders to retire. As he later colorfully put it, his men vacated their positions like a flock of birds that "are seen to quit their tree at the same instant." The men reformed with the rest of the 7th Wisconsin behind a fence between the two ridges.

According to Colonel Williams of the 19th Indiana, his regiment was on the left of the 7th Wisconsin at this time. This was the second time these Hoosiers had been forced back since retreating from their original position. Their latest position proved just as untenable as their earlier one. The two regiments continued their withdrawal to Seminary Ridge with the men stopping, singly or in small knots, to fire into the advancing 26th North Carolina as it pressed rapidly after them.[15]

About 2:30 p.m., while the left regiments of Pettigrew's Brigade and Brockenbrough's Virginians were rolling up the Iron Brigade and driving the survivors to the rear, the 47th and 52nd North Carolina on the Confederate right closed on Biddle's brigade. The men of the 121st Pennsylvania could see a line of gray rising steadily over the rise of McPherson Ridge. To their dismay, the enemy battle front overlapped their left flank by more than 100 yards. "I saw the line of the enemy slowly approaching up the hill, extending far beyond our left flank, for which we had no defense," Maj. Alexander Biddle, commander of the 121st Pennsylvania and the brigade commander's cousin, wrote in his official report. Captain Frank Sterling of the same regiment noted that the 52nd North Carolina's advance was "a beautiful sight . . . to see the rebels advancing from the woods in line of battle with their flags flying as they marched steadily on until they were within the range." They could also see another regiment, the 47th North Carolina, approaching from their right. Because the advance of the 52nd North Carolina was initially screened by McPherson Ridge, the Confederates materialized so quickly in front of Biddle's line that Reynolds' battery was in danger of being captured. The gunners could not get off a shot before limbering up and galloping back to the safety of Seminary Ridge.[16]

From his position near the Lutheran Seminary, General Rowley could see that the Iron Brigade was in serious trouble. He sent forward his last reserve, Lt. Col. George McFarland's 151st Pennsylvania. McFarland moved his regiment into the gap between the right flank of the 142nd Pennsylvania of Biddle's brigade and the left flank of the 19th Indiana of the Iron Brigade.

The unfortunately timed advance of the 151st Pennsylvania (through no fault of McFarland's) coincided with the precipitous withdrawal of the rest of the Iron Brigade. On the right of the 151st Pennsylvania, shattered regiments were pulling back to Seminary Ridge. Colonel Henry Morrow of the 24th Michigan reported that his men were "forced back, step by step, contesting every foot of ground, to the barricade." Morrow was wounded during this retreat and Capt. Albert Edwards assumed command of the regiment. To the left, Biddle's brigade wavered in the face of Pettigrew's unrelenting onslaught.

McFarland and his men of the 151st Pennsylvania quickly discovered they were alone without any visible means of support.[17]

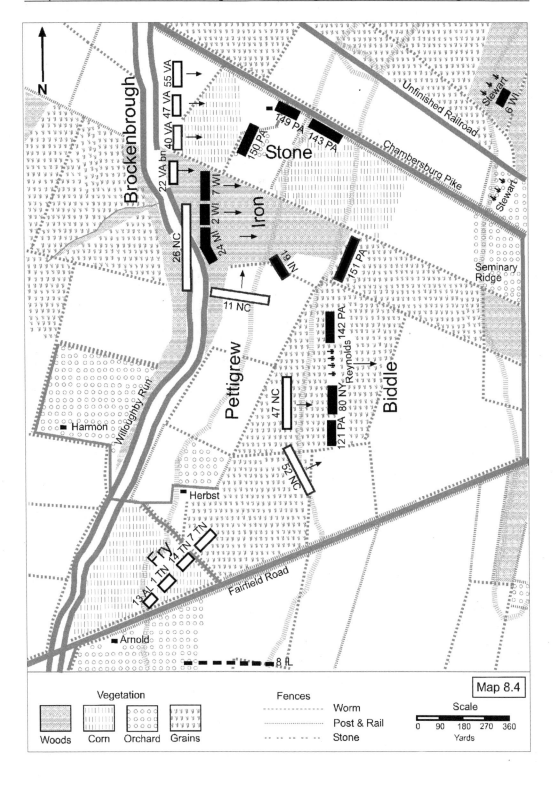

Map 8.4

Map 8.5

Edwin Gearhart of the 142nd Pennsylvania watched as North Carolinians "kept steadily advancing until we could see their officers stepping in front swinging their swords. Suddenly a cloud of smoke arose from their line and almost instantly the balls began to whistle about us and the men next to my right fell." The 121st Pennsylvania held its fire until the 52nd North Carolina "had reached within a few yards of the top of the ridge, [when] the men arose and delivered their fire directly in their faces, staggering them and bringing them to a stand," noted one Federal soldier. "As the enemy's faces appeared over the crest of the hill [McPherson Ridge], we fired effectually into them, and soon after, [we] received a crushing fire from their [Confederate] right, under which our ranks were broken and became massed together as we endeavored to change front to the left to meet them," noted Col. Chapman Biddle.[18]

Several North Carolinians recalled cresting McPherson Ridge and entering a breast-high wheat field. They could see Biddle's line of battle about 75 yards distant. The Federals, remembered one Tar Heel, "leveled their shining line of gun barrels on the wheat heads." The first volleys by both regiments were devastating. "The earth just seemed to open and take in that line which five minutes ago was so perfect," recalled a North Carolinian fortunate enough to live to write about it. Major Alexander Biddle, now commanding the 121st Pennsylvania, believed his men almost annihilated the North Carolinians as they appeared above the wheat. Though casualties were horrific on both sides, it was an unequal contest. Attacked in front and flank, the Federal losses mounted rapidly. Captain Frank Sterling believed that the majority of the soldiers of the 121st Pennsylvania were lying on the ground by this point, and the remainder would be soon enough if they remained in their position for another minute. Biddle reached the same conclusion and ordered the broken regiment back to Seminary Ridge. The speed with which the troops crossed the quarter-mile stretch to the seminary was,

according to one of the men who made the dash, "remarkable, probably the best on record."[19]

While the 121st Pennsylvania was being overwhelmed, the center and right of Biddle's brigade, composed of the 80th New York and 142nd Pennsylvania, engaged the 47th North Carolina and the right of the 11th North Carolina. Captain John Cook of the 80th New York remarked that the Tarheels "could shoot all right as they stood out there in line in the open field and poured in a rapid fire of musketry they gave us no time to criticize their appearance. Our men sprang to their feet, returned their fire, and the battle was on." After the initial Confederate volleys the two Federal regiments reciprocated and brought the Southern attack to a grinding, if temporary, halt. The Federal troops fired so quickly their weapons became too hot to handle. Many soldiers flung them down, but they did not lack for weapons—the ground was littered with small arms for the choosing. As one veteran recalled, "there was no scarcity of muskets, as the dead and wounded were largely in the majority of the regiment." The Confederates' rifled-muskets were also overheating. John Thorpe of the 47th North Carolina recalled their guns became so hot and fouled with power that they had trouble ramming home charges, so they pounded the ramrods with rocks and against the ground.[20]

When they reached the eastern edge of Herbst Woods, a volley from the 11th North Carolina greeted the 151st Pennsylvania. The lead knocked scores from the ranks. This was the 151st's first battle, and aside from those who had taken target practice, the Pennsylvanians had never fired their weapons. The regiment's commander, Col. George McFarland, cautioned his men to fire individually "as he saw an enemy on which to take a steady aim."

Despite their advanced and isolated position, and utter inexperience, the men fought tenaciously. "I know not how men could have fought more desperately, exhibited more coolness, or contested the field with more determined courage," reported McFarland.[21]

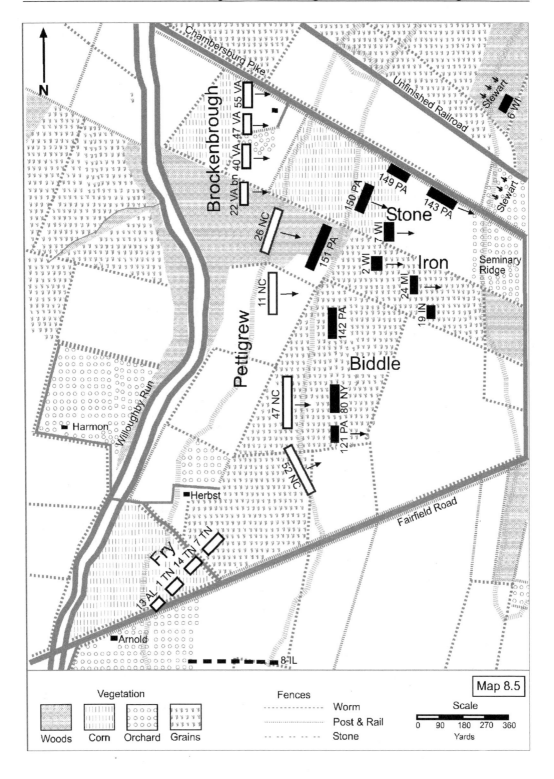

Map 8.5

Map 8.6

The departure of the 121st Pennsylvania exposed the 80th New York's left flank to the enemy, causing the same dilemma the Pennsylvanians experienced a few minutes before. Seeing the Confederates gaining his rear, Col. Theodore Gates had no choice but to take hold of his regiment's flag and order his men to retreat toward Seminary Ridge—but not before signaling them to fire a final volley at the approaching foe.[22]

With the 80th New York heading to the rear, all that remained of Biddle's line was the 142nd Pennsylvania on the far right. The regiment was in a terrible position, with the 52nd North Carolina advancing against its flank and the 47th North Carolina moving against its front. Seeing the hopelessness of their situation, the men began inching backward, but "the enemy giving us a heavy volley at pretty close range we broke," noted one of the men.[23]

Colonel Biddle rode forward and grabbed the 142nd Pennsylvania's fluttering colors, yelling, "Rally round the flag!" Gathering a number of men, he led a counterattack against the 47th North Carolina. It was a foolhardy effort that wasted more men, including Col. Robert Cummins, the 142nd's commander. As he lay mortally wounded, Cummins managed to urge, "For God's sake men, rally, we can whip them yet."

A Confederate soldier from the 47th North Carolina recalled how "the scattered Federals swarmed around him [Cummins] as bees cover their queen." Another Southern soldier wrote that the counterattack was "an act of personal gallantry . . . but unwise, rash, leading to misfortune which might not otherwise have occurred." The Pennsylvanians saw that to remain was folly, so they broke and ran, making for the relative safety of Seminary Ridge. Some tried to make a stand at a broken fence before reaching the ridge, but they too were swept away. Edwin Gearhart of the 142nd Pennsylvania admitted that the men "were running in retreat without order." The regiment lost its colors during the confusion.[24]

Seeing that his 151st Pennsylvania was about to be surrounded near Herbst Woods, Colonel McFarland ordered the regiment to fall back toward Seminary Ridge. Few of his men made it that far. Trapped in a deadly crossfire delivered by the 11th and 26th North Carolina, the regiment lost almost three-quarters of its men during its brief ill-advised sojourn on McPherson Ridge. The rest of the brigade also suffered heavy casualties, with each regiment reporting the loss of more than 60 percent of its men.

The toll was also high on the Confederate side. The cost of successfully forcing two Federal brigades from McPherson Ridge cut away more than 1,000 men from Pettigrew's large brigade in just thirty minutes. The victorious 26th North Carolina paid the heaviest price—549 men out of 840 or 65 percent of its opening strength. In the middle of the attacking line, the 11th North Carolina left more than half of its men on the field.[25]

The Federals did not run far. Even as the last of Biddle's men and the Iron Brigade fell or fled, their survivors were busy coalescing to form a strong defensive position on Seminary Ridge. They had been bested in the first round, but they had not been defeated. Fresh batteries arrived and unlimbered to support their new effort.

For the Confederates, however, no order arrived to continue the pursuit. General Heth had fallen earlier in the attack when a rifled ball struck him in the head. The blow knocked him unconscious; the paper wadding stuffed into the brim of his oversized hat probably saved his life. The inexperienced Johnston Pettigrew assumed command of the division.

Heth's men took heart, however, for behind them were thousands of fresh veteran reinforcements in the form of Maj. Gen. Dorsey Pender's approaching division.

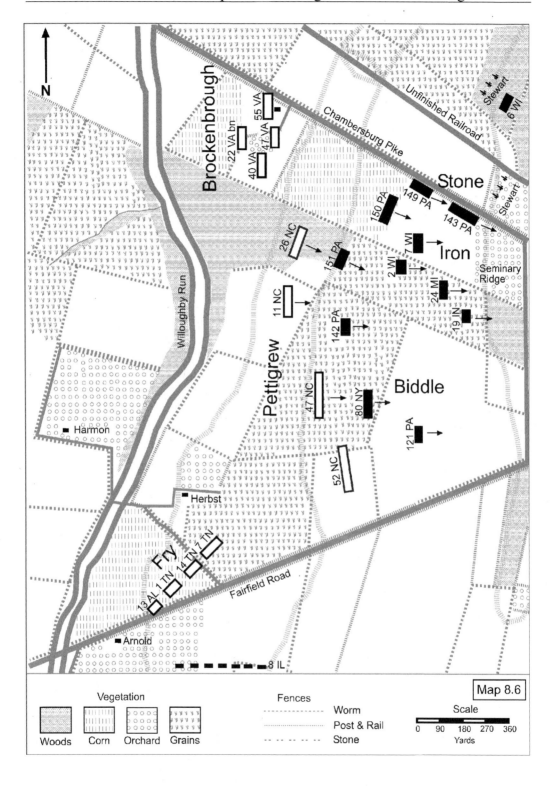

Map 8.6

Map Set 9: Seminary Ridge

Map 9.1

With the McPherson Ridge line broken, the battered remnants of three Union brigades sought refuge in a new Federal line forming on Seminary Ridge. Colonel Roy Stone's brigade probably arrived first and took position astride Chambersburg Pike. The next units to arrive were from the Iron Brigade, probably in this order: 19th Indiana, 24th Michigan, 7th Wisconsin, and finally the 2nd Wisconsin. The survivors of Col. Chapman Biddle's brigade arrived last, with the 151st Pennsylvania the final regiment to arrive. Its men had found the 142nd Pennsylvania's flag and brought it with them. Their commander reported that he planted it to the left of his regiment, and the remnants of the 142nd formed on it. As the men regrouped, they could see a line of Federal I Corps artillery already in action.[1]

The men of the Iron Brigade found a two-foot high barricade on Seminary Ridge "of loose rails, which . . . had been thrown together by some of our troops in the earlier part of the day, behind which I threw the regiment," reported Col. William Robinson of the 7th Wisconsin. Paul's brigade of Brig. Gen. John C. Robinson's division, I Corps, had probably thrown up these defenses when it occupied this position earlier in the day. Two Federal batteries were in action about 40 yards behind these infantrymen. Biddle's men were less fortunate. Not only did they lack the artillery support, they had to scrounge around for fence posts or any other materials they could use to form a rough barricade.[2]

Biddle's brigade to the left of the seminary probably aligned as it had on McPherson Ridge, with the 121st Pennsylvania on the left and the 151st Pennsylvania on the right. The devastation suffered by the Iron Brigade made its regimental alignment less coherent as they occupied barricades to the right of the seminary. On the right of the Iron Brigade, Stone's three regiments deployed with the 150th Pennsylvania on the left, the 149th Pennsylvania in the center, and the 143rd Pennsylvania extending the line across Chambersburg Pike to the north. The 6th Wisconsin of the Iron Brigade also deployed north of the road, supporting the three guns of Lt. James Stewart's battery north of the unfinished railroad cut. The 76th, 84th, and 147th New York regiments of Cutler's brigade supported the other three guns of Stewart's battery firing from south of the cut.[3]

Unlike the Federal infantry, the nineteen artillery pieces deployed on Seminary Ridge were relatively fresh and full of fight. Two sections of Capt. Gilbert Reynolds' battery, now under Lt. George Breck, dropped trail just north of Fairfield Road. Three guns of Captain James Cooper's battery deployed just north of the seminary behind the Iron Brigade, and Captain Greenleaf Stevens' four Napoleons unlimbered to their right. A third section of Reynolds' battery under Lt. Benjamin Wilber deployed along Chambersburg Road.[4]

Brigadier General John Buford's cavalry supported the Federal left flank. Three horse regiments of Col. William Gamble's brigade, the 3rd Indiana, 12th Illinois, and half of the 8th New York, extended the Federal line to the south. These units were at three-quarter strength on the firing line because one man in four held the reins of the horses. To the southwest, Maj. John Beveridge's 8th Illinois maintained its threat to the Confederate right flank. Colonel Fry of Archer's Brigade had stopped his men to face the cavalry outfit during Heth's final assault on McPherson Ridge. Although it had pulled back from Fairfield Road, the Illiniois regiment still posed a danger to the Confederates.[5]

Despite gaps arising from having too few men to defend so long a line, the Federal position was formidable, manned by desperate soldiers and well supported by artillery. Harry Heth's two brigades, Pettigrew's and Brockenbrough's, drove the Federal troops off McPherson Ridge, but had taken a beating in the process. The new line and heavy Federal artillery fire convinced them to pull back. In their stead stepped three fresh brigades from Maj. Gen. Dorsey Pender's Division, about 5,000 fresh Southern infantry anxious for a fight.[6]

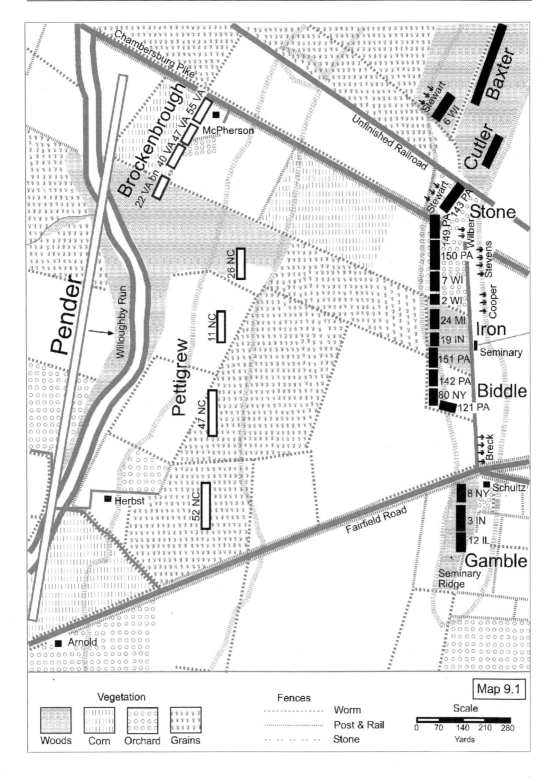

Map 9.1

Vegetation

Woods   Corn   Orchard   Grains

Fences

---------- Worm

················· Post & Rail

-- -- -- -- -- Stone

Scale

0   70   140   210   280

Yards

Map 9.2

Major General Dorsey Pender's three Confederate brigades passed through Heth's Division and prepared for the new assault on the Federal line recently established along Seminary Ridge. On the right, Brig. Gen. James Lane led his North Carolinians forward near Hagerstown (Fairfield) Road, deployed from left to right as follows: 33rd North Carolina – 18th North Carolina – 28th North Carolina – 37th North Carolina. The 7th North Carolina formed a skirmish line on the right of the brigade with the 52nd North Carolina of Pettigrew's Brigade.[7]

On Lane's left tramped Col. Abner Perrin's South Carolina brigade. Perrin was in temporary command of the brigade because its permanent commander, Brig. Gen. Samuel McGowan, had been wounded at Chancellorsville. Because of Perrin's inexperience, General Pender issued him a string of specific orders, including instructions to form a line of battle "leaving sufficient room between my left and the Gettysburg Road [Chambersburg Pike] for General Scales' brigade, and to throw out skirmishers to cover my right flank." With Lane advancing on the right, Perrin did not have to send skirmishers to that flank. He deployed his brigade left to right as follows: 14th South Carolina – 1st South Carolina – 12th South Carolina – 13th South Carolina.[8]

Brigadier General Alfred Scales' Brigade formed the left side of the division, deployed in line of battle from left to right as follows: 38th North Carolina – 13th North Carolina – 34th North Carolina – 22nd North Carolina – 16th North Carolina. Scales reported that his left flank was 50-60 "steps" from Chambersburg Pike. Prior to taking position, his men encountered Brockenbrough's Virginians on McPherson Ridge. The Virginians "were without ammunition, and would not advance farther," Scales later wrote. "I ordered my men to march over them, they did so."[9]

Before the attack column stepped off, Colonel Perrin received another order from General Pender instructing him to follow and support Heth's Division as it renewed its attack on McPherson Ridge. Pender added that Perrin should do so by "preserving my alignment with General Scales, on my left." Pender believed that by ordering Perrin to follow the movements of his more experienced brigade commander, the attack should go more smoothly.[10]

The order to advance reached Pender's brigade commanders about 4:00 p.m. Colonel Perrin recalled that the orders were to "advance, and to pass General Heth's division should I come up to it at a halt, and to engage the enemy as circumstances might warrant," meaning that Perrin should press on even if Heth's men were repulsed or exhausted. Before advancing his line of battle Perrin had a few words for his soldiers: "Men, the order is to advance; you will go to the crest of the hill. If Heth does not need you, lie down and protect yourselves as well as you can; if he needs you, go to his assistance at once. Do not fire your guns; give them the bayonet; if they run, then see if they can outrun the bullet." Colonel Joseph Brown of the 14th South Carolina recalled another part of the order—the men were not to stop for any reason until they had driven the enemy from Seminary Ridge.[11]

Perrin's Brigade advanced slowly, with Lane's men on the right and Scales' soldiers on the left. They could see Pettigrew's regiments well to the front, bloodied and worn out after defeating two Federal brigades. As the new line advanced Pettigrew's men yelled out, "Go in, South Carolina! Go in, South Carolina!" One of the Palmetto warriors advancing that afternoon was Captain Washington Shooter. "Our line passed over Hill's [Heth's] and drove the enemy rapidly before us without firing a gun," recalled the captain. "We could see the Yankees running in wild disorder and everything went merry as a marriage bell until we ascended a hill where we saw their batteries and their last line of entrenchment—a stone wall."[12]

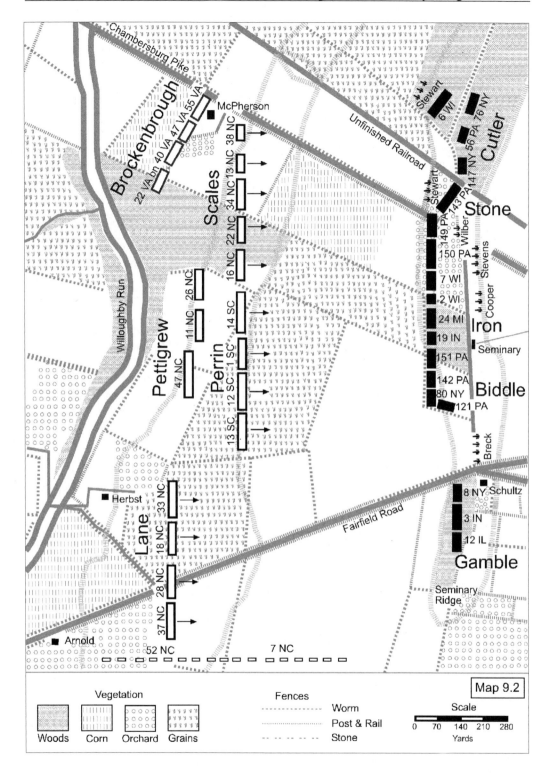

Map 9.2

Vegetation

Woods   Corn   Orchard   Grains

Fences
---------------- Worm
.... Post & Rail
— — — — — — Stone

Scale
0   70   140   210   280
Yards

Map 9.3

Major General Dorsey Pender's "final" assault on the Federal positions west of town began without his fourth brigade under Brig. Gen. Edward Thomas, which was well to the rear guarding Confederate artillery.

Confronting Pender's fresh division were fewer than 2,300 exhausted Federal troops hunkered down behind their makeshift barricades or behind nothing at all. Abner Perrin's South Carolinians advanced against the remnants of Chapman Biddle's brigade and the left side of the Iron Brigade, while Alfred Scales' men faced the right of the Iron Brigade and the left of Roy Stone's brigade; William Gamble's three cavalry regiments confronted James Lane's Brigade.[13]

Pender's attack against Seminary Ridge resembled Heth's earlier advance against McPherson Ridge. Federal artillery on the ridge opened fire as soon as the Confederate troops stepped into range. According to Thomas Littlejohn of the 12th South Carolina, "they began throwing grapeshot at us by the bushel it seems. They shot too high for us as the shot went over our heads. Had they been a little lower, I don't see how any of us could have escaped." Several of Pender's men fell during this part of the advance.[14]

The Federal troops grimly watched from behind their barricades as Scales and Perrin expertly guided their brigades forward. Major Mark Finnicum of the 7th Wisconsin watched as the Rebels "came moving on in gallant and splendid style, not withstanding the shot and shell that ploughed through their ranks from our artillery." It was too much for the defenders to hope that their artillery alone would be enough to break up the Confederate advance.[15]

J. F. J. Caldwell of the 1st South Carolina remembered the fire of the long-arm that afternoon. "The artillery of the enemy now opened upon us with fatal accuracy. They had a perfectly clear, unobstructed fire upon us," he wrote after the war. "Still we advanced, with regular steps and a well-dressed line. Shell and canister continued to rain upon us." Great gaps appeared in the brigade's line. "Never have I seen such a charge. Not a man seemed to falter," Col. Charles Wainwright, commander of the I Corps' artillery, wrote in his diary. "Lee may well be proud of his infantry; I wish ours was equal to it."[16]

The 38th North Carolina advanced on the north side of Chambersburg Pike directly into the path of the three Napoleons from Stewart's battery deployed south of the unfinished railroad cut. The artillery rounds from these pieces tore into the Tarheels and the men bowed their heads as if walking into a strong wind, but still they advanced.[17]

Looking to his right, Perrin could not see Lane's Brigade. Like Colonel Fry before him, Lane had become preoccupied with the 8th Illinois cavalry situated beyond his right flank. Lane threw out the 7th North Carolina to move as skirmishers and continued forward, but deploying the skirmish line slowed his brigade's progress to little more than a crawl. As a result, it lagged behind the rest of the division. Lane was relieved to see the 52nd North Carolina of Pettigrew's Brigade line up beside the 7th North Carolina, both facing the threatening (if heavily outnumbered) horsemen.

By not maintaining his line of march, however, Lane exposed the right flank of Perrin's advancing brigade to a murderous enfilading fire that dropped scores of Confederates. Lane's tactical mistake angered Perrin, who wrote after the battle, "Lane's Brigade never came up at all until the Yankees were clear out of reach."[18]

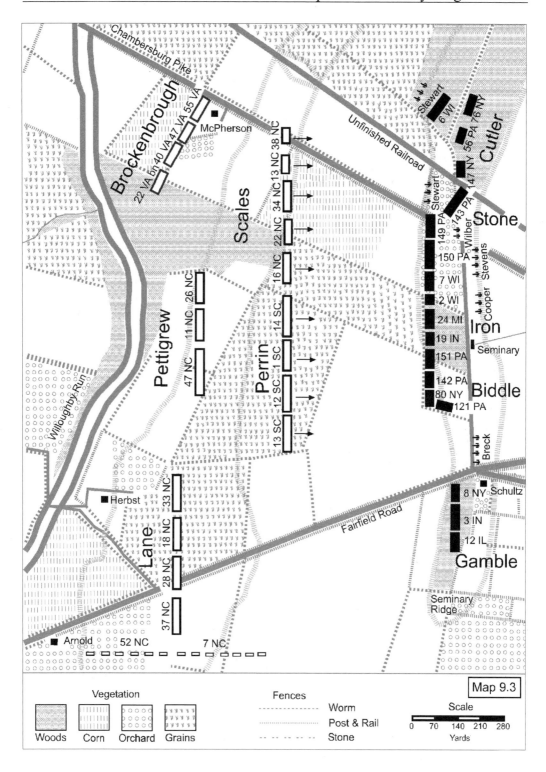

Map 9.3

Map 9.4

Colonel William Robinson of the 7th Wisconsin, now commanding the Iron Brigade, watched as the Confederates approached his position on Seminary Ridge. "It was with some difficulty I restrained the men from firing until the enemy got as near as I wanted them," he later wrote. "When they were within easy range, the order was given, and their ranks went down like grass before the scythe . . . very few, if any, of that brigade escaped death or wounds."

North of Chambersburg Pike, Col. Rufus Dawes ordered his 6th Wisconsin to open fire on the 38th North Carolina. His men screamed, "Come on, Johnny! Come on!" and "when within a hundred paces of us, a sheet of flame burst from our line hurling its leaded hail with such deadly certainty that their confident ranks were checked . . . literally annihilating the Rebel line . . . not a man was left standing, what few if any were unhurt, sought safety behind the dead bodies of their fallen comrades," Dawes recalled.[19]

South of the unfinished railroad cut, the men in Stewart's battery shifted their aim from the 38th North Carolina, wheeling their three guns 90 degrees to the left to enfilade the flank of the 13th North Carolina on the opposite side of Chambersburg Pike. They opened fire with canister with devastating effect. "From our second round on a gray squirrel could not have crossed the road alive," wrote cannoneer Augustus Buell with pride.[20]

Although Buell was not at Gettysburg (he wrote in the first person but probably received his information secondhand), the carnage was indeed almost unimaginable. Scales reported that his brigade "encountered a most terrific fire of grape and shell on our flank, and grape and musketry in our front. Every discharge made sad havoc in our line, but still we pressed on at a double-quick until we reached . . . a distance of about 75 yards from the ridge we had just crossed, and about the same distance from the college [Seminary] . . . Our line had been broken up, and now only a squad here and there marked the place where regiments had rested."[21]

According to Perrin, the Federal infantry opened fire at a range of only 200 yards. He called it "the most destructive fire of musketry I have ever been exposed to." His men continued forward, still without firing, and were hit by yet another deadly volley. Daniel Tompkins of the 14th South Carolina could hear the Federal officers "distinctly encouraging their men to hold their fire, until the command to fire was given. . . . They . . . [finally] rose to their feet and took as deliberate aim as if they were on dress parade, and to show you how accurate their aim was, 34 out of 39 men fell at the first fire." Perrin agreed with Tompkins' grim assessment, writing, "The Fourteenth Regiment was staggered for a moment by the severity and destructiveness of the enemy's musketry."[22]

As his men staggered forward, Perrin rode to the front of his line to rally his wavering troops. Men flung away their knapsacks and blankets, everything save weapons and ammunition, and pressed on. According to Colonel Brown of the 14th South Carolina, "to stop was destruction. To retreat was disaster. To go forward was orders." As the colonel noted, "not a foot of ground presented a place of safety. The Union troops fired low, and their balls swept close to the ground."[23]

Finally, the North Carolinians advancing under Scales could advance no further. Every field officer in his brigade fell killed or wounded, save one. The 13th North Carolina lost 150 of 180 men. Hit on the flank and front by artillery and small arms fire, the survivors were forced to lie down about 75 yards from the ridge. Stevens' battery in Scales' front expended 57 rounds of deadly canister in a few short minutes. As one artilleryman noted, "the whole line of battle from right to left was one continuous blaze of fire . . . completely filled with the thick blue smoke of infantry, making it difficult to distinguish friend from foe."[24]

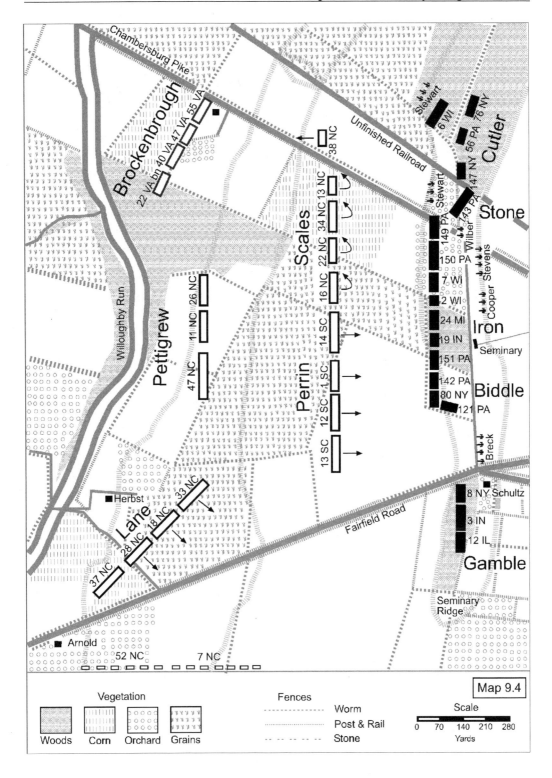

Chambersburg Pike

Unfinished Railroad

Brockenbrough

22 VA.bn 40 VA 47 VA 55 VA

38 NC

Scales

13 NC
34 NC
22 NC
16 NC

Pettigrew

26 NC
11 NC
47 NC

Willoughby Run

Perin

14 SC
1 SC
12 SC
13 SC

Stewart

6 WI
56 PA 76 NY
47 NY

Cutler

Stewart

149 PA 143 PA

Stone

Wilber

150 PA

Cooper Stevens

7 WI

2 WI

24 MI

Iron

19 IN

Seminary

151 PA

142 PA

80 NY

Biddle

121 PA

Breck

8 NY Schultz

3 IN

12 IL

Gamble

Seminary
Ridge

Herbst

Lane

33 NC
18 NC
28 NC

37 NC

Fairfield Road

Arnold

52 NC   7 NC

| Vegetation | | | | Fences | | Scale |
| Woods | Corn | Orchard | Grains | | | |

Fences
- - - - - - - - - Worm
. . . . Post & Rail
- - - - - - Stone

Scale
0   70   140   210   280
Yards

Map 9.4

Map 9.5

Colonel Abner Perrin and his men faced a desperate situation. He had lost support on both flanks. Scales' attack had been blown apart on his left, and Lane had slowed down, partially turned away (and may have formed a hollow square) to face what he believed was a threat from Federal cavalry on his right. While his flank protection fell away, Perrin's South Carolinians continued to advance alone. His orders were to take the ridge, and he was determined to do so.[25]

About this time, Perrin spotted a gap in the Federal line just north of Fairfield Road between the left of Col. Chapman Biddle's brigade and the right of Colonel Gamble's cavalry brigade. A Federal battery manned the gap, but Perrin "directed the First Regiment . . . to oblique to the right, to avoid a breastwork of rails behind which I discovered the enemy was posted, and then to change front to the left, and attack in flank."[26]

While the 1st South Carolina maneuvered to the right, and the 14th South Carolina continued its frontal attack, Perrin ordered the 12th and 13th South Carolina to oblique far more sharply to the right and take on Gamble's cavalry brigade. With their shift to the right complete, the 1st South Carolina obliqued left and drove toward the gap in the Federal line. As they approached it, the men of the 1st South Carolina turned sharply left and fired into the exposed flank of the 121st Pennsylvania, forcing Biddle's men to vacate their position and flee to the rear. J. F. J. Caldwell recalled the men "struggling and panting, but cheering and closing up, they [1st South Carolina] went, through the shell, through the Minie balls, heeding neither the dead who sank down by their sides, nor the fire from the front which killed them, until they threw themselves desperately on the line of Federals and swept them from the field."

With the first clear-cut tactical victory of the assault in evidence, the 1st and 14th South Carolina proceeded to roll up the Union flank. Their advance struck first Biddle's brigade, then the Iron Brigade, and finally Stone's brigade. The perfectly delivered attack pried the exhausted enemy regiments from the ridge and sent them fleeing eastward in retreat toward Gettysburg.

According to Colonel Williams of the 19th Indiana, "we could have held out against the line in front but their maneuvers on the left made the position untenable and I gave the order to retreat." He noted that the "men were loath to obey the order . . . [and] returned again to the barricade to pay the enemy one more compliment."[27]

Captain Nat Rollins of the 2nd Wisconsin knew it was time to withdraw when he saw Confederates flanking his position. Looking to his right, he could see Chambersburg Pike clogged with hundreds of retreating Union soldiers. "There was no time to waste; so we stood not on order of our going, but went at once."[28]

Only the capture of Federal artillery could have made the Southern victory more complete. Despite a hail of bullets that killed gunners and horses alike, all of the Federal guns were hauled safely to Cemetery Hill. (Gamble's cavalry helped cover the withdrawal of Lt. George Breck's guns.) As Perrin later lamented to the governor of South Carolina, "If we had any support at all we could have taken every piece of artillery they had and thousands of prisoners." They captured four Federal colors, however, including the old flag of Reynolds' I Corps.[29]

Meanwhile, the 12th and 13th South Carolina regiments of Perrin's Brigade took on Gamble's dismounted cavalry. "They rushed up to the crest of the hill and the stone fence, driving everything before them, the Twelfth gaining the stone fence, and pouring an enfilading fire upon the enemy's right flank," reported Perrin after the battle. "The Thirteenth now coming up, made it an easy task to drive the enemy down the opposite slope and across the open field west of Gettysburg." What he failed to mention was the heavy losses sustained by these two regiments. According to Surgeon Spencer Welch, "as the enemy were concealed, they killed a great many of our men before we could get at them."[30]

The Federal line had broken in at least two places and its position atop Seminary Ridge was no more. As the troops retreated toward town, the screaming and victorious Confederates assumed sole possession of the hills and ridges west of Gettysburg.

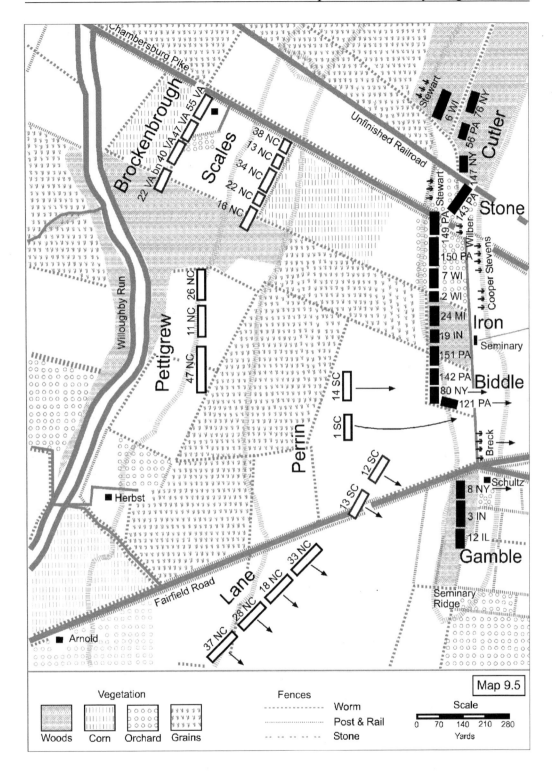

Chambersburg Pike

Unfinished Railroad

Brockenbrough

Scales

22 VA bn 40 VA 47 VA 55 VA

38 NC
13 NC
34 NC
22 NC
16 NC

Stewart

6 WI   76 NY

56 PA

147 NY

Cutler

Stewart

149 PA   143 PA

Stone

150 PA

Wilber

7 WI

Cooper Stevens

2 WI

24 MI

Iron

19 IN

Seminary

151 PA

142 PA

Biddle

80 NY

121 PA →

14 SC →

1 SC

Breck →

Willoughby Run

Pettigrew

26 NC
11 NC
47 NC

Perrin

12 SC
13 SC

Schultz

8 NY

3 IN

12 IL

Gamble

Herbst

Lane

33 NC
18 NC
28 NC
37 NC

Fairfield Road

Seminary Ridge

Arnold

Vegetation

Woods   Corn   Orchard   Grains

Fences

-------------- Worm
.... Post & Rail
— — — — Stone

Map 9.5

Scale

0   70   140   210   280

Yards

Map Set 10: The Defeat of the Federal Troops on Oak Ridge

Map 10.1

The survivors of Iverson's, O'Neal's, and Daniel's brigades regrouped in the fields south of Oak Hill. Rodes' fourth brigade under Brig. Gen. Stephen Ramseur, a small organization (about 1,000 soldiers) that had been in the rear guarding wagons, joined them under the shadow of Oak Hill. Ramseur's Brigade was a veteran unit and its commander was widely considered to be one of the finest young combat officers in Lee's army. Once reorganized, Rodes issued orders for his men to move south and help drive Federal troops off Oak Ridge.[1]

General Ramseur divided his brigade. The 2nd and 4th North Carolina marched east to support O'Neal's Brigade while Ramseur accompanied the 14th and 30th North Carolina south with Daniel's men and Iverson's shattered brigade. On the way, Ramseur encountered Col. Cullen Battle of the 3rd Alabama (O'Neal's Brigade) and asked if the Alabamians would assist him. Battle responded affirmatively and the three regiments maneuvered into line of battle. Ramseur was about to attack across the same deadly ground that Iverson's unfortunates had recently traversed when an officer suggested Ramseur shift his regiments leftward and attack the apex of the Federal line. The 2nd and 4th North Carolina, meanwhile, had traveled only a few hundred yards before Rodes recalled them. He feared the Federals were planning to attack his own position on Oak Hill. The two North Carolina regiments remained near Oak Hill for only a few minutes before orders were issued to carry out their original directive to attack the Federal positions on Oak Ridge.[2]

With the 3rd Alabama on the right, the 30th North Carolina in the center, and the 14th North Carolina on the left, Ramseur prepared to strike Paul's line. Other Confederate troops also maneuvered into position. When Rodes released the 2nd and 4th North Carolina, they moved due east before turning south. O'Neal's Alabama brigade moved up into the gap between the two wings of Ramseur's Brigade and, on the right of the 3rd Alabama, the remnant of Iverson's Brigade, including the fresh 12th North Carolina, prepared its advance. The 43rd and 53rd North Carolina of Daniel's Brigade angled into position to attack the Federal line in the woods south of Forney field, where the remnants of Cutler's and Paul's brigades had formed a line.[3]

Looking west across Forney's field, the 94th New York, 16th Maine, and 107th New York of Paul's brigade watched Iverson's regiments approach. Paul's other regiments, the 104th New York and 13th Massachusetts, faced north by northwest—at nearly a right angle to the rest of the line. They faced Mummasburg Road, where O'Neal's Brigade and the left wing of Ramseur's Brigade closed on them from the north.[4]

Holding the far right of Rodes' attenuated divisional front was Daniels, whose brigade advanced on a line extending well beyond the flank of the 94th New York and across the front of Cutler's bloodied brigade. To counter this threat, all but one regiment of Baxter's brigade marched quickly south from Oak Ridge to reinforce Cutler and support Stewart's battery, deployed on either side of Chambersburg Pike. Baxter's 97th New York remained behind briefly before joining its comrades in their shift south. Its men were almost out of ammunition. Cutler's brigade soon received orders to move farther south to support Federal batteries on Seminary Ridge, which left the protection of that part of the field and Stewart's guns to Baxter.[5]

Heavy skirmishing erupted prior to the final Confederate push against the right wing of the I Corps on Oak Ridge. On the north end of the Federal line, the 13th Massachusetts and 104th New York of Paul's brigade engaged Ramseur's skirmish line along Mummasburg Road. Both regiments attacked the Confederate skirmishers, scooping up scores of prisoners. The men of the 97th New York (Baxter) and the 94th New York, the 16th Maine, and the 107th Pennsylvania (Paul) exchanged fire with Iverson's regiments. Some of these Federals charged across Forney's Field, but were quickly driven back. Although no one fighting on Oak Ridge or in Shead's Woods could have known it, the battle was about to take a dramatic turn.[6]

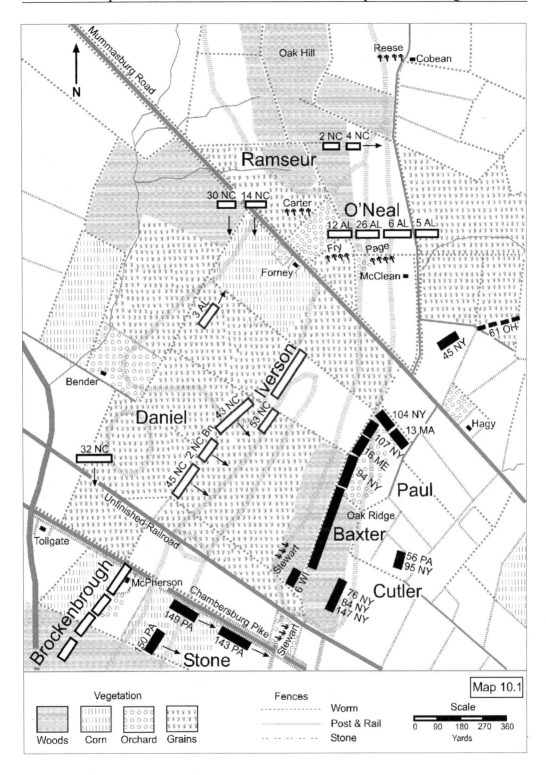

Map 10.1

Map 10.2

A fresh Confederate division under Maj. Gen. Jubal Early arrived north of Gettysburg about 3:30 p.m. With the substantial help of Robert Rodes' fifth brigade, an all-Georgia outfit under George Doles, Early's men broke Oliver O. Howard's XI Corps' defensive line north of town.

The rout of Howard's corps exposed the right flank of Brig. Gen. Gabriel Paul's brigade on the northern tip of Oak Ridge. On Paul's left, the remainder of the I Corps was already in full retreat to Seminary Ridge. General Robinson could see that his men were in danger of being cut off and captured en masse and finally allowed Paul's men to retreat. He chose the 16th Maine to delay the Confederates as long as possible while the rest of the brigade made its way to safety. Riding up to Col. Charles Tilden of the 16th Maine, Robinson pointed to the stone wall bordering Forney's Field where it intersected with Mummasburg Road and ordered, "Take that position and hold it as long as there is a single man left." Tilden protested that his 200 men could not possibly halt the Confederate advance, but when he realized that his commander's mind was made up, he replied, "All right, General we'll do the best we can." From his assigned position, Tilden placed the left of his regiment behind the stone wall facing west and refused the other wing to face Mummasburg Road to the north. The regiment's flag occupied the angle between the two wings.[7]

Rodes coordinated the final Confederate attack on Oak Ridge. From the right, the Confederate line was comprised of the 45th North Carolina, 2nd North Carolina Battalion, 43rd and 53rd North Carolina, all of Daniel's Brigade, with Iverson's Brigade aligned on Daniel's left. Together, they drove east across the southern portion of Forney Field. In the center came the 3rd Alabama, advancing southeast with the 30th and 14th North Carolina of Ramseur's Brigade. O'Neal's Brigade attacked from due north, the 12th, 26th, 6th, and 5th Alabama regiments aligned from right to left. Finally, the remaining two regiments of Ramseur's Brigade,

the 2nd and 4th North Carolina, flanked Paul's position as they advanced from the northeast.

"We heard distinctly the commands of a rebel officer directing his men to fire; and a volley crashed, and we saw some of our men fall," wrote Adjutant Abner Small of the 16th Maine. The men returned the fire, and several of Ramseur's North Carolinians fell, including a flag bearer (probably from the 14th or 30th North Carolina). Colonel R. Tyler Bennett of the 14th North Carolina wanted to swing around the 16th Maine and "lift him into the air," but Ramseur merely replied, "No, let's go directly in upon them."[8]

The Maine infantrymen fell by the score and the survivors retreated under the crushing weight of the attack. "They came on, firing from behind the wall, from fences, from the road; they forced us, fighting, back along the ridge," wrote Small. Remnants of the small regiment halted periodically to face the enemy, only to be driven back each time.[9]

Ramseur directed the 12th North Carolina of Iverson's Brigade to swing around the rear of the 16th Maine as it attempted to escape. Meanwhile, Ramseur's 2nd and 4th North Carolina on the left of the Confederate line drove forward and scooped up hundreds of prisoners from Paul's brigade. When the men of the 16th Maine finally reached the unfinished railroad cut, they encountered more of Daniel's men swinging around their flank. Faced with Daniel's men on their right and in front of them, and the 3rd Alabama and 12th North Carolina behind them, the remnants of the 16th Maine realized that there was no hope. Several members of the regiment ripped up their flag, hid pieces in their pockets, and broke the staff. Colonel Tilden thrust his sword into the ground and snapped it in two. Of the 200 men who began the fight, all but four officers and 38 men were killed, wounded, or captured, a loss of nearly 80%.[10]

The retreat of Robinson's division from its position north of town signaled the end of a major phase of the prolonged and bloody fighting on July 1. The Confederates were now firmly in control of the high ground west of Gettysburg.

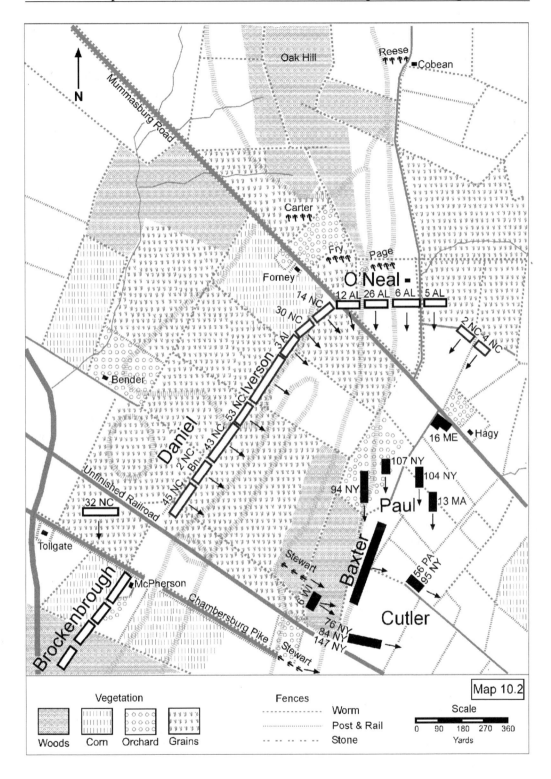

N

Oak Hill

Reese

Cobean

Mummasburg Road

Carter

Fry

Page

Forney

O'Neal

14 NC

12 AL   26 AL   6 AL   5 AL

30 NC

2 NC 4 NC

3 AL

Bender

Iverson

53 NC

16 ME

Hagy

43 NC

107 NY

Daniel

2 NC Bn.

104 NY

94 NY

13 MA

Unfinished Railroad

45 NC

Paul

32 NC

Baxter

56 PA
95 NY

Tollgate

Stewart

Cutler

Brockenbrough

McPherson

6 WI

Chambersburg Pike

76 NY
84 NY
147 NY

Stewart

Map 10.2

Vegetation

Fences

Scale

Woods   Corn   Orchard   Grains

Worm

Post & Rail

Stone

0   90   180   270   360

Yards

Map Set 11: Defeat of Barlow's Division on Blocher's Knoll

Map 11.1

Brigadier General Francis Barlow's division of the XI Corps followed the I Corps to Gettysburg on Emmitsburg Road. It arrived after its two sister XI Corps divisions, which had marched on Taneytown Road. To his left, Barlow could see the fight between the Federal I Corps and elements of Heth's Division on McPherson Ridge. When XI Corps commander Oliver Howard (who was in command of the troops on the field because of the death of John Reynolds) learned Confederates were in strength on Oak Hill on the I Corps' right flank, he sent Brig. Gen. Alexander Schimmelfennig's and Barlow's divisions into the fields north of town to reinforce that vulnerable flank.[1]

The artillerists of Carter's Battalion deploying on Oak Hill could not resist throwing shells at the massed Federal XI Corps column winding its way north out of Gettysburg. According to a private, "as soon as we got clear of the town we received another reception, but this was in the shape of solid shot, shells . . . and everything that could be shot out of a cannon." The column continued moving quickly north. "The shells were coming pretty thick before we reached the barn [Almshouse]," he continued. This long-range fire inflicted few casualties, but the cannonade chipped away psychologically on the men marching into battle.[2]

The weary soldiers halted at the Almshouse, massed in double column of companies. One soldier wrote, "I dropped on the ground like a dead person, all exhausted and very tired." Barlow inspected the terrain as his men rested. Brigadier General Adelbert Ames' brigade moved off Harrisburg Road to the east, deployed from left to right as follows: 107th Ohio – 25th Ohio – 17th Connecticut. The 75th Ohio formed a supporting line. Colonel Leopold von Gilsa's brigade occupied the left of the road. Von Gilsa did not file a report, so the arrangement of his regiments is unclear. Schimmelfennig's division of two brigades occupied the open ground to the left of Barlow's division. Colonel Wladimir Krzyzanowski's brigade deployed from left to right as follows: 82nd Ohio – 75th Pennsylvania – 119th New York – 26th Wisconsin in double column of companies to the west (left) of Carlisle Road. According to Capt. Alfred Lee of the 82nd Ohio, the regiments deployed in "solid squares," which were dense and so highly vulnerable to artillery fire. Colonel George von Amsberg's brigade took position to the northwest between Mummasburg and Carlisle roads. The 45th New York, 61st Ohio, and 74th Pennsylvania were thrown out on a skirmish line extending from Mummasburg Road toward Carlisle Road. The 157th New York and the 82nd Illinois supported Capt. Hubert Dilger's 1st Ohio Light, Battery I, and Lt. William Wheeler's New York Light, 13th Battery, deployed near the Hagy farmhouse. A third battery, Lt. Bayard Wilkeson's 4th U.S. Battery G, attached to Barlow's division, awaited orders. Southern artillery on Oak Hill found the range of Schimmelfennig's men and casualties mounted.[3]

From his excellent vantage atop Oak Hill, Maj. Gen. Robert Rodes watched the 5,600 Federal troops spilling north out of the town. Rodes led the largest division in Lee's army (five brigades, 8,000 effectives). Three of his brigades—Edward O'Neal's, Alfred Iverson's, and Junius Daniel's—were preparing to attack Oak Ridge. Rodes knew Maj. Gen. Jubal Early's Division was marching south toward Gettysburg and would arrive via Harrisburg Road. Rodes needed to protect his exposed left flank and buy time until Early arrived. He advanced a fourth brigade, 1,300 Georgians under Brig. Gen. George Doles, toward Carlisle Road to confront the growing XI Corps threat. Doles deployed his soldiers on either side of Newville Road just north of where Carlisle Road branches at the Smithy Farm. Most of the brigade deployed to the right of the road, facing town, from left to right as follows: 12th Georgia – 4th Georgia – 44th Georgia – 21st Georgia. The 12th Georgia extended the line beyond Newville Road to the east. The large gap between Doles' right and Oak Hill was partially filled by skirmishers from the 5th Alabama (O'Neal), which extended its line eastward.[4]

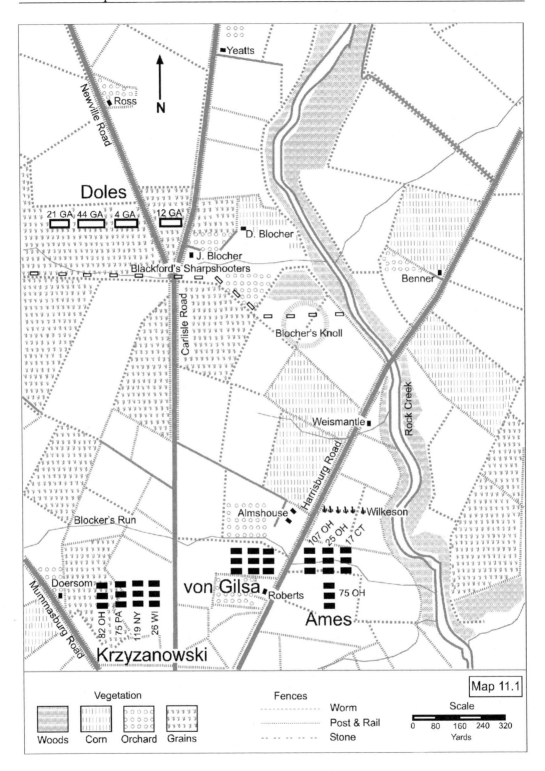

Map 11.1

Map 11.2

Brigadier General Francis Barlow did not care for his assigned position. He much preferred Blocher's Knoll in front of him, which offered a more promising artillery platform for Wilkeson's guns. On his own initiative, he ordered Colonel von Gilsa to occupy the hill with his 1,140-man brigade. "I had an admirable position," Barlow later wrote in a letter to his mother. "The country was an open one for a long distance around and could be swept by our artillery." Major General Carl Schurz, who was commanding the XI Corps because Howard was temporarily in charge of the troops on the entire field, saw it differently. As Schurz put it, Barlow had either misunderstood his orders or had been "carried away by the ardor of the conflict."[5]

From the Almshouse, von Gilsa pushed two companies of the 153rd Pennsylvania and the small 54th and 68th New York regiments forward on the skirmish line. The remaining eight companies marched behind them. They quickly cleared the sharpshooters from Major Eugene Blackford's Battalion of the 5th Alabama (O'Neal's Brigade) off the knoll. Von Gilsa ordered his men forward to occupy the elevation, deploying them in two lines facing Rock Creek to the northeast. The first line was essentially the skirmish line, with two companies of the 153rd Pennsylvania in the middle and part of the 68th New York on its right. The 54th New York extended the line eastward, with its right flank ending at Harrisburg Road at the bridge over Rock Creek. The remaining eight companies of the 153rd Pennsylvania formed the second line, which stretched from the middle of the small detachment of the 153rd Pennsylvania on the left to the center of the 54th New York on the right. The remainder of the 68th New York formed a widely-spaced skirmish line, linking the left of the small detachment of the 153rd Pennsylvania with the right of the 74th Pennsylvania of von Amberg's brigade. Upon reaching the knoll, von Gilsa ordered his men to lie down to protect themselves. Ames' brigade marched toward the knoll, halting en echelon about one-quarter mile to the rear.[6]

When he spotted Barlow's Federals approaching Blocher's Knoll, General Doles moved his brigade left (east) to face the threat more directly. According to Doles, "the enemy moved his force from our front, made a strong demonstration on our left, driving our skirmishers from the hill . . . the command was then moved by the left flank, to meet any attack the enemy might attempt on our left and rear. We found the enemy strongly posted with infantry and artillery." The brigade retained its original orientation, from left to right as follows: 12th Georgia – 4th Georgia – 44th Georgia – 21st Georgia.[7]

While Doles prepared to engage von Gilsa on Blocher's Knoll, General Early's Division made its inaugural appearance on Harrisburg Road. Early quickly deployed, placing Brig. Gen. Robert Hoke's Brigade (under Col. Isaac Avery) on his left, Brig. Gen. John B. Gordon's on the right, and Brig. Gen. Harry Hays' in the center astride Harrisburg Road. Brigadier General William Smith's Brigade formed the divisional reserve. Spotting an opportunity before him, Early immediately ordered Gordon's Georgians to prepare to attack Barlow on Blocher's Knoll. Lieutenant Colonel Hilary Jones' artillery battalion unlimbered east of Harrisburg Road and opened fire on the knoll.

The arrival of Early's Division triggered Barlow into action. He immediately called up four Napoleons from Lt. Bayard Wilkeson's battery, which dropped trail near the 153rd Pennsylvania. Wilkeson's remaining pair of pieces were left in the rear on the east side of Harrisburg Road near the Almshouse, where they defended the division's right flank. Barlow also ordered the 25th Ohio of Ames' brigade to move to the knoll to support these guns. A short time later, Barlow ordered the rest of Ames' brigade up to reinforce the knoll. The 17th Connecticut was shy four companies, which had earlier crossed Rock Creek to form a skirmish line near the Benner farm.[8]

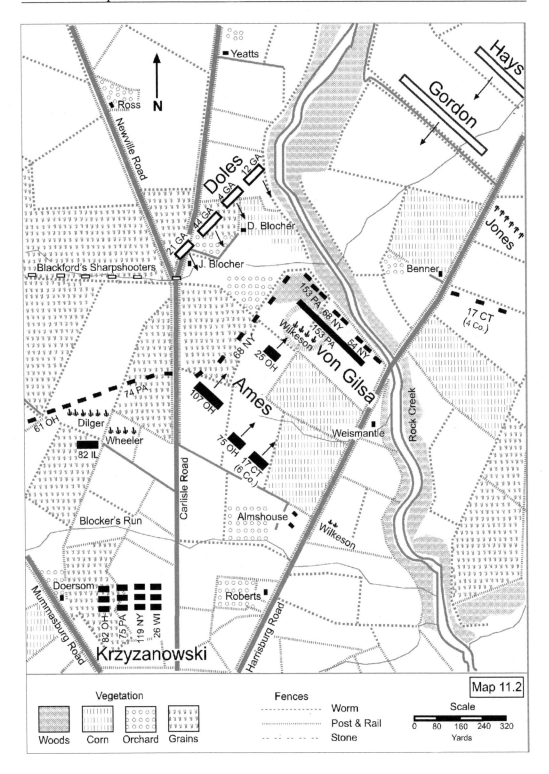

Map 11.2

Map 11.3

Pursuant to General Early's orders, General Gordon deployed his men in line of battle along a sunken farm lane west of the Benner house, from left to right as follows: 38th Georgia – 61st Georgia – 13th Georgia – 31st Georgia – 60th Georgia. Despite their fatigue from the long marches, the men quickly formed in anticipation of an attack against von Gilsa's position.[9]

On the Federal side, the 107th Ohio of Ames' brigade arrived and formed on the left of the 25th Ohio and at a right angle to it, facing northwest, creating a salient. The 75th Ohio and six companies of the 17th Connecticut formed a general reserve behind the main line.

Barlow was initially confident that he could hold Blocher's Knoll against the Confederate onslaught. He wrote to his mother after the battle, "We ought to have held the place easily for I had my entire force at the very point where the attack was made." What he did not know until events unfolded was that he had chosen poor ground to defend and deployed his men badly by separating his brigade from any support.

When his brigade was ready, Gordon ordered the attack. Rock Creek posed an almost immediate difficulty for the Georgians. The water was only about two feet deep, but according to Gordon, the stream's "banks were so abrupt as to prevent a passage excepting at certain points."

Barlow ordered von Gilsa's first line to hold its fire until the Georgians closed to within 75 yards. They did exactly that and offered a stiff, if short-lived, wall of resistance. "We met the enemy at Rock Creek. We attacked them immediately, but we had a hard time moving them," remembered a private from the 61st Georgia. "We advanced with our accustomed yell, but they stood firm until we got near them." Standing less than 50 paces apart, the two lines opened fire into each other."[10]

Doles was also on the move. His Georgia brigade struck the three regiments of Ames' brigade—about 1,200 men—from the northwest while Gordon attacked from the north. According to a soldier fighting under Doles, "our brigade charged with that soul-stirring rebel yell,

which once heard on the field of battle can never be forgotten."[11]

The 107th Ohio, left-most on the line and facing northwest, was in a terrible position, subject to a deadly enfilading fire from both sides. Lead missiles from the 21st Georgia and part of the 44th Georgia raked the Buckeyes along their left flank, and similar devastation confronted them along their right flank when the 31st and 60th Georgia regiments opened upon them. Compounding 107th Ohio's difficulties was small arms fire delivered from the front by the 4th, 12th, and part of the 44th Georgia regiments.

On the right of the 107th, the 25th Ohio was in similar straits, hit on its front and flanks. The reserves Ames had deployed behind these two regiments could not fire for fear of hitting their own men. All they could do was wait and watch while their comrades were mowed down holding an untenable position. The two Ohio regiments fought back with assistance from Wilkeson's battery, firing from the high ground behind them. One of Doles' men remembered that his unit "advanced through a field midst grape shot and cannister." The two lines fought close together—so close that the flag bearers of the 25th Ohio and 31st Georgia actually fought each other with their flag staffs.[12]

Wilkeson's four guns opened large holes in the lines of attacking Confederate infantry moving against the knoll. "We suffered severely from the enemy's batteries," Doles admitted in his report. Private Reuben Ruch of the 153rd Pennsylvania also remembered the artillery work performed that afternoon. "A battery in the rear of us, on higher ground than we were, opened fire over us and we could feel the heat of the balls as they passed over us," he recalled. "About this time the Rebels made a charge, away to the left of us, and the battery in the rear turned guns on them, taking them by flank. . . . We could see balls plowing up the ground along the rear of the line, and if ever Johnnies ran for cover those fellows did."[13]

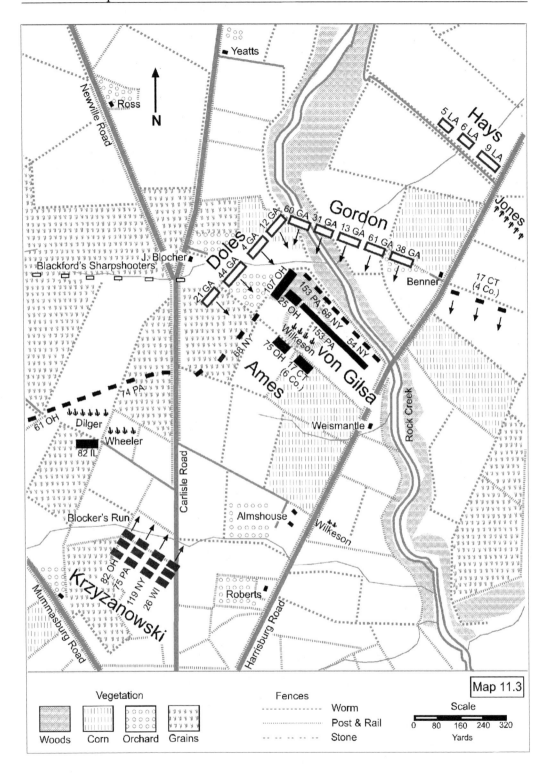

Map 11.3

Map 11.4

Lieutenant Bayard Wilkeson's position on Blocher's Knoll was only 1,200 yards from the four Confederate batteries belonging to Lt. Col. Hilary Jones' artillery battalion. As a result, the four Federal guns received an immediate and severe counter-battery fire.

Major Thomas Osborn, the commander of the XI Corps artillery, reported that he found the four guns "unfortunately near the enemy's line of infantry, with which they were engaged, as well as two of his batteries, the concentrated fire of which no battery could withstand." One of the early casualties was Lieutenant Wilkeson, whose leg was severed below the knee. The young officer cut away the remnants of his limb with his pocket knife, but died later that day from shock and loss of blood. Lieutenant Eugene Bancroft took charge of the battery and, by changing its position frequently, was able to maintain its fire.[14]

With pressure along both wings and in front, von Gilsa's first defensive line began to crumble and the men retired toward Gettysburg. A private in Gordon's Brigade noted that von Gilsa's men "stood firm until we got near them. They then began to retreat in fine order, shooting at us as they retreated." Von Gilsa's second line, composed of the large but inexperienced 153rd Pennsylvania, briefly held its ground until the officers realized that they were about to be overwhelmed and ordered a withdrawal. One soldier recalled that the brigade had been in position for only about ten minutes before the attack began. While running for his life, Private Ruch of the 153rd Pennsylvania looked back upon the carnage. The ground was littered with "a regular swath of blue coats as far as I could see along the line. They were piled up in every shape."[15]

The withdrawal of von Gilsa's brigade left Ames' brigade in a precarious situation. The general ordered the 75th Ohio to "fix bayonets, pass to the front between the 107th and 25th Ohio, and if possible check the advance of the enemy," recalled its commander, Col. Andrew Harris. "It was a fearful advance and made at a dreadful cost of life. We could go no farther, we

halted and opened fire. We checked them in our immediate front, but they continued to press on around both flanks." Colonel Harris expected orders to fall back, but none arrived, and he became increasingly distressed.[16]

In their haste to reach safety, von Gilsa's men overran the other reserve, six companies of the 17th Connecticut. A soldier in the latter regiment recorded in his diary that a "german regt came running back, hooting & hollowing, right through our lines which broke our regt all up & scattered us." The 17th Connecticut reformed and advanced with the 75th Ohio. Its commander, Lt. Col. Douglas Fowler, swung his sword and yelled, "Now, Seventeenth, do your duty! Forward, double quick! Charge bayonets!" Reaching the top of the knoll, the men engaged in hand-to-hand combat with Gordon's Georgians. Scores of Connecticut soldiers, including Fowler, were cut down. "An effort was here made by the enemy to change his front and check our advance, but the effort failed," was how Gordon reported the effort after the battle.[17]

Time had run out for Adelbert Ames and his men. Major W. Willis of the 4th Georgia Infantry reported that the "enemy was a little stubborn, but soon gave way, with considerable loss." Gordon later wrote that, "under the concentrated fire from front and flank, the marvel is that any escaped." The Federal position on Blocher's Knoll had completely collapsed.

The XI Corps troops retreated with Doles' and Gordon's men screaming after them in hot pursuit. The Confederates were not content to hold Blocher's Knoll, but followed the retreating Federal troops south straight toward Gettysburg.[18]

Early's victorious infantry, however, did not have a clear run to Gettysburg. Additional Federal troops had arrived in the form of Col. Wladimir Krzyzanowski's brigade of the XI Corps, which was at that moment crossing Carlisle Road and advancing from the southwest.

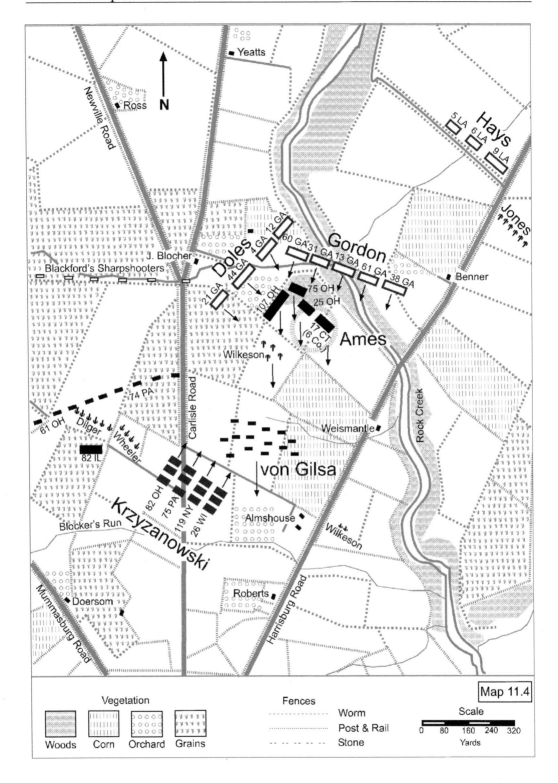

Map 11.4

Vegetation

Woods   Corn   Orchard   Grains

Fences

------ Worm
.... Post & Rail
– – – – – Stone

Scale

0   80   160   240   320
Yards

Map Set 12: The Defeat of Krzyzanowski's Brigade

Map 12.1

As Brig. Gen. Francis Barlow's men took their advanced positions on Blocher's Knoll, Maj. Gen.1 Carl Schurz, the temporary commander of XI Corps, ordered Col. Wladimir Krzyzanowski's brigade forward to support Barlow's left flank.

The men were relieved to leave their exposed position between Mummasburg and Carlisle roads, where Confederate artillery on Oak Hill was pounding them. One soldier noted that the artillery fire was "lively, and their shot and shell ricocheted splendidly over the open fields." Colonel Krzyzanowski was less than enthusiastic, however, since he fully realized that Barlow's men were about to be overwhelmed. An officer from the 82nd Ohio noted that his commander's face became "pale and distressed" when he received the order to advance. The Confederate batteries again found the brigade as it moved north across the open fields. According to Capt. Alfred Lee of the 82nd Ohio, Confederate batteries opened on the brigade from two or three different directions. "Their shells plunged through our solid squares making terrible havoc," he wrote. To speed its movement to Barlow's aid, the brigade remained in "column of divisions," but this increased its vulnerability to the Confederate batteries. When Krzyzanowski realized this, he ordered his brigade to halt and formed his regiments into line of battle, from left to right as follows: 119th New York – 82nd Ohio – 75th Pennsylvania – 26th Wisconsin.[1]

Rail fences made the march across the open fields more difficult and the ranks were forced to halt as the men tore down the rails, "which had to be taken down under a heavy fire of musketry from the enemy." Although they could hear the sound of heavy fighting coming from the direction of Blocher's Knoll, because of the rolling terrain many of the men could not see a single enemy soldier. Within a few minutes, however, an "irregular line of butternut and gray hove gradually in sight—their officers all mounted, waving their swords and cheering on their men," recalled an officer in the 119th New York. The Confederates were from the 21st Georgia, the rightmost regiment in George Doles' line of battle. The 21st Georgia had been attacking Adelbert Ames' brigade on Blocher's Knoll.[2]

Seeing the threat from Krzyzanowski's brigade advancing from the south, the 21st Georgia wheeled to the right and entered a wheatfield. The Federals apparently fired first when one of their officers yelled, "Let them have it!" One of Krzyzanowski's officers later wrote, "This [the opening volley] in no way checked the enemy's advance, but it drew their fire; and they continued slowly to push on, keeping it up in a desultory manner as they drew near."[3]

Colonel John Mercer, the commander of the 21st Georgia, did not immediately realize that his 287 soldiers were up against an entire Federal brigade of 1,425 men. After battling the Federal troops for a few minutes, however, Mercer recognized he was hopelessly outnumbered and pulled his men back to Blocher's farm lane. "Having attracted their fire, and finding their force too strong for the exposed position we then occupied," reported Mercer, "we fell back some 40 yards to a lane, where we awaited their approach." Mercer ordered his Georgians to lie down to reduce the risk of exposure. An officer in the 75th Pennsylvania gleefully put the withdrawal of the 21st Georgia another way: "we charged upon them and drove them back."[4]

Krzyzanowski's brigade continued its advance, moving north in a line of battle paralleling Carlisle Road. Two batteries west of the road—Capt. Hubert Dilger's Battery I, 1st Ohio Light Artillery, and Lt. William Wheeler's 13th New York Independent Battery—threw in their support. Dilger's guns had arrived first. When Wheeler's pieces rolled up in support, Dilger advanced his own guns into the wheatfield and unlimbered them there, where they could take Doles' Brigade in the flank.[5]

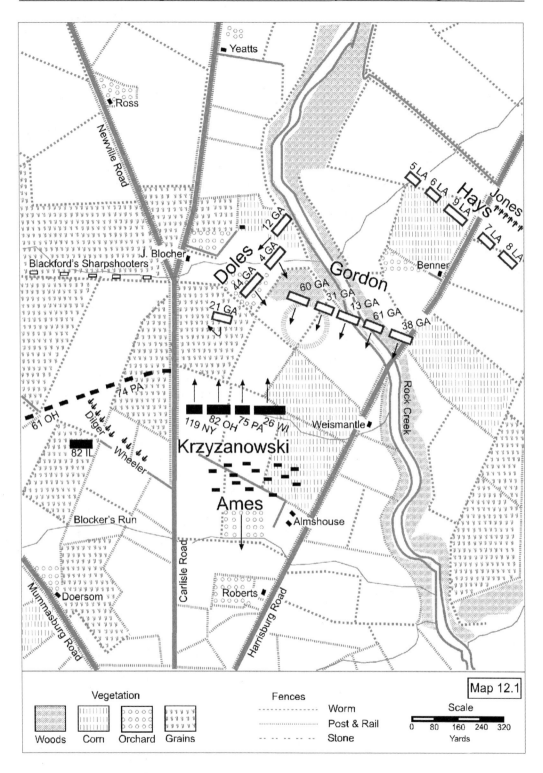

Map 12.1

Vegetation

Woods Corn Orchard Grains

Fences

Worm

Post & Rail

Stone

Scale

0   80   160   240   320

Yards

Map 12.2

Although the initial movement looked promising, time was against Col. Wladimir Krzyzanowski. With Brig. Gen. Francis Barlow's division knocked off Blocher's Knoll, the balance of Brig. Gen. George Dole's Georgia brigade was free to focus on the approaching Federals. The Georgians wheeled to face Krzyzanowski's men. There is no record of who ordered this change in position "by the right flank," but the veterans smoothly completed the complex large-scale movement.

Captain Alfred Lee of the 82nd Ohio watched Doles' men approach. "Their movements were firm and steady, as usual, and their banners, bearing the blue Southern cross, flaunted impudently and seemed to challenge combat. On they came, one line after the other, in splendid array."[6]

The 31st and 60th Georgia regiments of Gordon's Brigade joined in the advance. These two regiments had participated in the fight with Barlow's division on Blocher's Knoll, but now formed on Gordon's left flank. The additional regiments extended the Confederate line to the east, overlapping the 26th Wisconsin, which formed the right end of Krzyzanowski's brigade. Disaster loomed for the newly arrived Federal brigade.[7]

While Doles took on Krzyzanowski's left and center, Gordon's two regiments attacked the brigade's right flank and rear. The two opposing lines stood less than 75 feet apart at some places—so close "names of battles printed on the Confederate flags might have been read, had there been time to read them," remembered one Federal soldier. Casualties rapidly mounted on both sides. An officer from the 119th New York recalled that "every five or six seconds some poor fellow would throw up his arms with an 'ugh!' and drop." General Early's artillery battalion north of Blocher's Knoll fired into the Federals, while Dilger's and Wheeler's batteries unlimbered to the southwest blasted round after round into Doles' Georgians.

The 26th Wisconsin on the right side of Krzyzanowski's line was shattered in the assault, losing 26 men killed and 129 wounded within a matter of minutes. The 75th Pennsylvania broke next, leaving 111 of its 208 men on the field after fewer than fifteen minutes of fighting. Included among the dead was the regiment's commander, Col. Francis Mahler. His brother was also a casualty.[8]

As Gordon's two regiments rolled up Krzyzanowski's right flank, Doles continued pressuring the brigade's left and center. Caught within this powerful Confederate two-brigade infantry vise, Krzyzanowski's remaining regiments had no choice but to stand and fall or turn and flee. They chose the latter option. An officer of the 119th New York admitted after the war that there was "no disguising the fact that we were fairly driven off the field." Confederate brigade commander John Gordon agreed, adding that the Federal troops were driven back in the "greatest confusion."[9]

When his horse fell wounded, Colonel Krzyzanowski hit the ground hard. He later recalled that his troops battled as best they could, "sweaty, blackened by gun-powder, and they looked more like animals than human beings." The open fields north of town on July 1, wrote Krzyzanowski with complete accuracy, were a "portrait of hell." Despite difficulty in breathing because of his fall, Krzyzanowski refused to leave his men. By the time he ushered his command back to the town, his losses were high—669 out of 1,420 or 47% in less than half an hour of fighting. The 82nd Ohio suffered the greatest loss, leaving 58 percent of its manpower on the field. The losses may have been considerably higher had not the 157th New York of von Amsberg's brigade approached to distract the advancing and victorious enemy.[10]

The two Federal batteries also withdrew, though not before putting up a desperate fight to hold their ground. "The enemy then massed his infantry and threw them upon the troops on our right, who fell back after some severe fighting. I changed the direction of my right section, and fired into the advancing column of the enemy with canister, but did not succeed in checking them," reported Lieutenant Wheeler.[11]

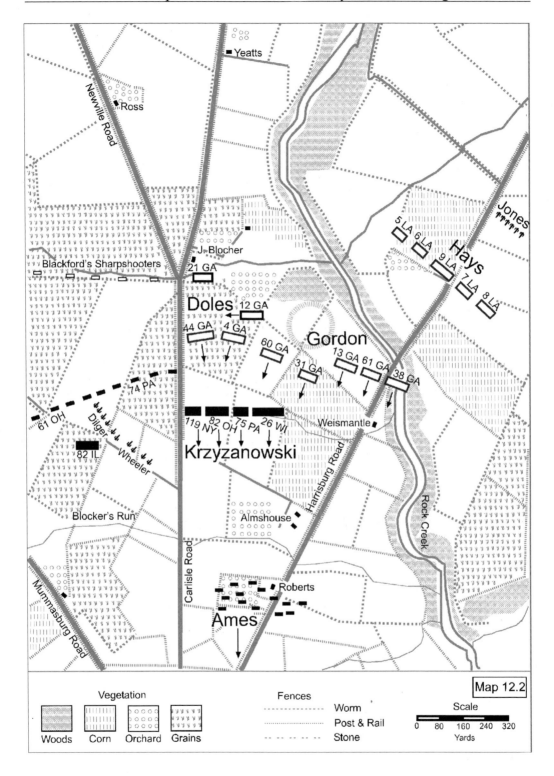

Map 12.2

Vegetation

Woods Corn Orchard Grains

Fences

-------------- Worm
.... Post & Rail
-- -- -- -- Stone

Scale

0   80   160   240   320

Yards

Map Set 13: The Defeat of the 157th New York

Map 13.1

After defeating first Brig. Gen. Francis Barlow's division on Blocher's Knoll, and then Col. Wladimir Krzyzanowski's brigade to the southwest, Brig. Gen. George Doles pushed his brigade toward Gettysburg. Although somewhat disordered, the Georgians were still full of fight and relatively fresh.

Doles marched his brigade due southward, aligned with the 12th Georgia on the left, the 44th Georgia in the center, and the 4th Georgia on the right. Doles' fourth regiment, the 21st Georgia, remained at the Blocher house, where it had retreated during its initial fight with Krzyzanowski's brigade. The two regiments of Gordon's Brigade that had helped defeat Krzyzanowski, the 31st and 60th Georgia, remained in place on Doles' left and advanced simultaneously with Doles.[1]

When the acting 3rd Division commander, Brig. Gen. Alexander Schimmelfennig, spotted Doles' Brigade moving forward to attack the advanced XI Corps units, Schimmelfennig looked around for a unit that could strike the enemy's vulnerable right flank. The two most advanced units on that portion of the field were the 157th New York and the 82nd Illinois, both of von Amsberg's brigade, 3rd Division. The brigade occupied the sector near the Hagy farm along Mummasburg Road, with the 45th New York, 61st Ohio, and 74th Pennsylvania manning the skirmish line while the 82nd Illinois and 157th New York supported Dilger's and Wheeler's batteries. When Dilger advanced his guns, the two supporting regiments advanced with him.

Schimmelfennig chose the 400-man 157th New York and quickly ordered it north, leaving the 82nd Illinois alone to support the two batteries. The New Yorkers marched up the west side of Carlisle Road until its commander, Col. Philip Brown, ordered the men to change front to the right to form a line of battle parallel to the road. To their south and east were the remnants of Krzyzanowski's brigade fleeing to the rear. Hundreds of Georgians from Doles' and Gordon's brigades, most in reasonably good alignment, were in hot pursuit.[2]

As he was pursuing the withdrawing Federals to the south, an organized force of Federal troops suddenly appeared on Doles' right flank and rear. Colonel Brown's 157th New York had assumed a perfect tactical position. The New Yorkers opened fire on the 44th Georgia from a distance of perhaps 40 yards.[3] The rolling ground west of Doles' right flank had obscured Brown's advance from Confederate eyes. Colonel Brown must have been excited when he realized his quick march had placed him undetected on the flank of the 44th Georgia. That same ground, however, also concealed the men of the 21st Georgia near the Blocher farm lane on Brown's left flank. These Georgians, lying prone, received orders to load their weapons and prepare to fire a volley into the unsuspecting New Yorkers. Brown's sudden good fortune was about to reverse itself.[4]

Few first-person accounts exist from the men who served that day in the 157th New York. This is partly so because many members of the regiment were eventually killed or wounded that afternoon. One of the few soldiers who left his recollections was Jonathon Boynton. "We moved forward, obliqued to the right, passed through and over a rail fence, and halted, then received orders to fire," he wrote in his unfortunately sketchy account of the combat. "Then came the order to load and fire at will. The noise of shells and bullets hurtling through the air was terrible. We continued to advance and all at once the regiment charged bayonets."[5]

It was at this point that, far from any reinforcements, Colonel Brown discovered his single regiment was facing an entire brigade of veteran Confederate infantry.

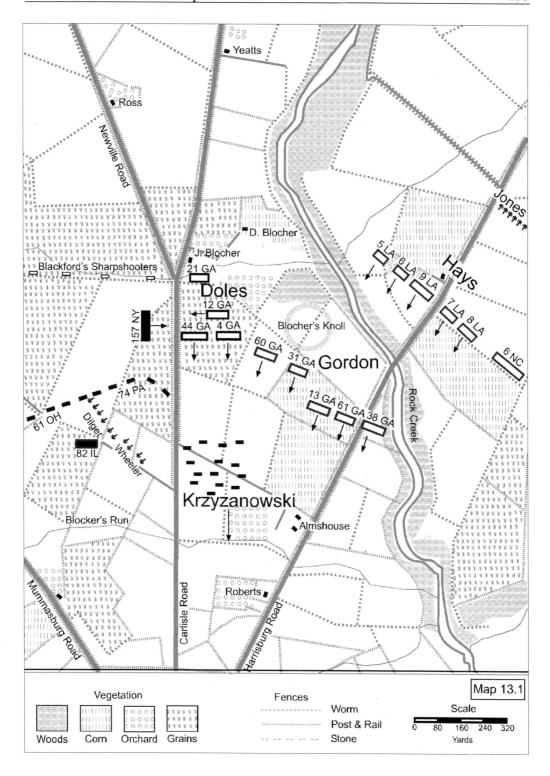

Yeatts

Ross

Newville Road

Jones

D. Blocher

J. Blocher

Blackford's Sharpshooters

21 GA

Doles

12 GA

157 NY

44 GA   4 GA

Blocher's Knoll

60 GA

31 GA   Gordon

13 GA   61 GA   38 GA

74 PA

61 OH

Dilger

Wheeler

82 IL

Krzyzanowski

Blocker's Run

Almshouse

Rock Creek

5 LA   6 LA   9 LA   Hays

7 LA   8 LA

6 NC

Mummasburg Road

Carlisle Road

Harrisburg Road

Roberts

Map 13.1

Vegetation

Woods   Corn   Orchard   Grains

Fences

--------- Worm

·············· Post & Rail

– ·· – ·· – Stone

Scale

0   80   160   240   320

Yards

Map 13.2

The fire delivered by the 157th New York created a shock wave that rippled through the 44th Georgia. The surprise at the sudden attack, however, lasted for only a few moments as the veterans took stock of the new situation and responded to the threat accordingly.

Major William H. Peebles wrote the battle report for the 44th Georgia after its colonel, Samuel P. Lumpkin, fell with what proved to be a mortal wound. According to Peebles, "as soon as it was discovered that we were flanked, we made a wheel to the right, faced the new foe, and began to fire upon him. Thus checked in his movement, he faced us, and opened a severe fire upon us."

Next in line was the 4th Georgia, which also wheeled to face the New Yorkers. Doles sent the 12th Georgia, which had been on the far left of his line of battle, by the right flank around the rear of the 4th and 44th Georgia regiments to aid the 21st Georgia. The 12th Georgia formed on the right of the 21st regiment.

The New Yorkers watched these ominous movements to their front and flanks with what must have been growing dismay, but they did not see what was developing along their left flank, where the 21st Georgia occupied the Blocher's farm lane. These Georgians now rose from their prone position and fired a withering volley into the 157th New York's vulnerable left front and flank. The 44th Georgia, reported Peebles, "charged over two fences, across the turnpike, under a raking fire from some batteries near the edge of the town, firing grape at us as we crossed the road." The 12th Georgia extended the line around the left flank of the New Yorkers and also opened fire.[6]

Hit in front, on both flanks, and in parts of their rear, the men of the 157th New York fell in droves. Colonel Brown recalled that "the men were falling rapidly and the enemy's line was taking the form of a giant semi-circle . . . concentrating the fire of their whole brigade upon my rapidly diminishing numbers." Without orders to withdraw, Brown refused to allow his men to retreat. He learned later that one of Brig. Gen. Alexander Schimmelfennig's aides had "hallooed" him from a distance to retreat, but no one in the regiment saw or heard the man. While the lead was flying into the 157th New York from several points of the compass, a Southern battery on Oak Hill opened fire on the regiment's exposed rear with "fearful execution."[7]

According to Major Peebles, "we captured, killed, or wounded nearly every man that came upon our right flank." Peebles was not exaggerating: the 157th New York lost seventy-five percent of its men: 27 killed, 166 wounded, 114 captured or missing. The New Yorkers suffered the highest regimental losses in the XI Corps, and the sixth highest of any Federal regiment at Gettysburg. Among the captured was Jonathon Boynton, who was firing near a fence when members of the 44th Georgia overran him. "I dropped my gun at once and stood facing the gray boys at attention," he later wrote. The remnants of the regiment finally withdrew when Brown realized his outfit faced the very real possibility of elimination to a man.

Some Confederates felt sorry for the regiment's plight. "One time I felt sad, one Yankee regiment charge [sic] us," Cpl. Sidney Richardson of the 21st Georgia wrote home soon after the battle. "[W]e fired a volley into them and then charged them as quick as we could, they turned to run and we continued the charge untill [sic] they got away."[8]

With the defeat of the 157th New York, George Doles wheeled his brigade back toward Gettysburg in a magnificent display of tactical control and unit cohesion. The brigades from the XI Corps that had advanced north of town were now in full retreat. With no infantry left to support, or to support them, Dilger's and Wheeler's batteries limbered and rolled south toward town. Everywhere one looked, all that could be seen of the XI Corps was its soldiers fleeing toward the town and the safety of Cemetery Hill beckoning beyond it.

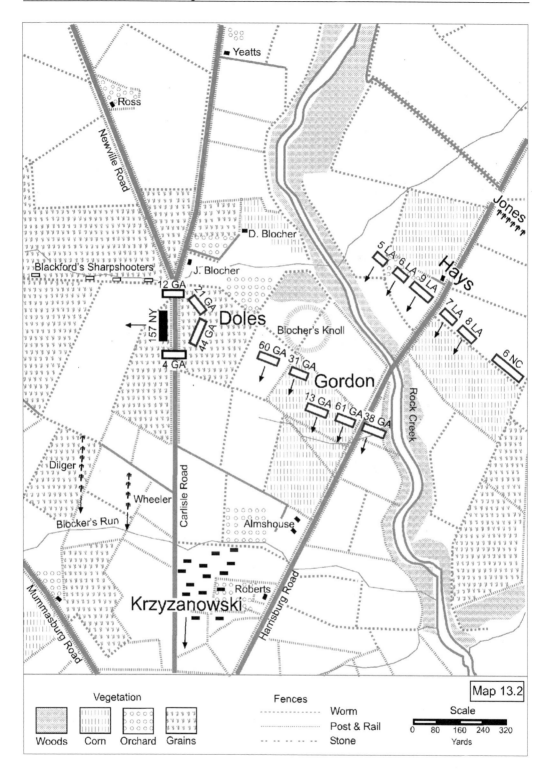

Map 13.2

Map Set 14: The Brickyard Fight

Map 14.1

The XI Corps deployed quickly during the early afternoon of July 1. While Brig. Gen. Francis Barlow's First Division and Brig. Gen. Alexander Schimmelfennig's Third Division marched into the fields north of town to confront the Confederate threat looming there, Brig. Gen. Adolph von Steinwehr's Second Division assumed a reserve position on Cemetery Hill. And there the division remained.

Despite frequent requests for additional support, temporary XI Corps commander Maj. Gen. Carl Schurz (Maj. Gen. Oliver O. Howard assumed command of the army on the field after Maj. Gen. John Reynolds fell early in the day) stubbornly refused to release any men from von Steinwehr's reserve division. Finally, with Barlow's division heavily engaged on Blocher's Knoll and Krzyzanowski's brigade of the Third Division moving to its aid, Schurz called for reinforcements. Von Steinwehr ordered Col. Charles Coster's First Brigade down the slope and through the town. Coster's men had been supporting Capt. Michael Weidrich's Battery I, 1st New York on northeast Cemetery Hill.[1]

Coster's men marched through the town past hundreds of XI Corps soldiers, many wounded, fleeing toward the safety of Cemetery Hill. Coster detached the 73rd Pennsylvania at the town square near the railroad station and continued north with his three remaining regiments, about 900 men. The brigade halted and deployed in John Kuhn's brickyard on the edge of town, taking up a position east of Stratton Street just south of its junction with Harrisburg Road. Captain Lewis Heckman's 1st Ohio Light, Battery K, composed of four Napoleons, unlimbered on the west side of the road on the brigade's left flank. Heckman's guns commanded the length of Harrisburg Road, but it was a frustrating time for the gunners because the flood of blue uniforms masked the guns and prevented them from firing at the approaching Confederates.[2]

After destroying the better part of three Federal XI Corps brigades and a regiment from a fourth, Jubal Early's Division approached Gettysburg. John Gordon's Georgia brigade, which had played a major role in the victory north of town, earned a well-deserved rest and did not continue the pursuit. Early sent Harry Hays' Louisiana brigade and Isaac Avery's North Carolina brigade toward the town, scooping up scores of prisoners in the process. Coster's Federal brigade was standing in their way, hoping to slow or stop their advance.

While Hays advanced in line of battle with his right flank astride Harrisburg Road, Avery moved his brigade south on the east side of Rock Creek. The brigade was shy two regiments, which had remained in Virginia to help transport the prisoners captured at Winchester and Stephenson's Depot. His men could see Coster's brigade ahead, taking position behind "a strong fence, portions of which were made of stone." "Our advance was made with great deliberation until we approached a sluggish stream, or slough, about 200 yards in front of the enemy's lines, when the batteries opened upon us with grape and canister, seconded by a very destructive fire from the infantry," wrote Col. Archibald Godwin of the 57th North Carolina, who would later command the brigade. Avery immediately yelled for his men to double-quick across the stream to close with the enemy.[3]

To the right of Avery's Brigade, a young lieutenant of the 8th Louisiana fighting under Hays recalled, "we crossed about 20 fences & 1 creek and at last came right slap up on the '11th corps' & a battery." Because of the topography, Avery made better progress toward Coster's brigade. As a result, when Avery's right reached Coster's position in the brickyard, Hays' left flank lagged some distance behind.[4]

Hays' Brigade was deployed from right to left as follows: 5th Louisiana – 6th Louisiana (both west of Harrisburg Road) – 9th Louisiana (astride the road) – 7th Louisiana – 8th Louisiana (both east of the road). After crossing Rock Creek, Avery's regiments deployed on Hays' left flank with the 6th North Carolina closest to the Louisianans, followed by the 21st North Carolina and the 57th North Carolina. The latter two regiments advanced east of Stevens Run.[5]

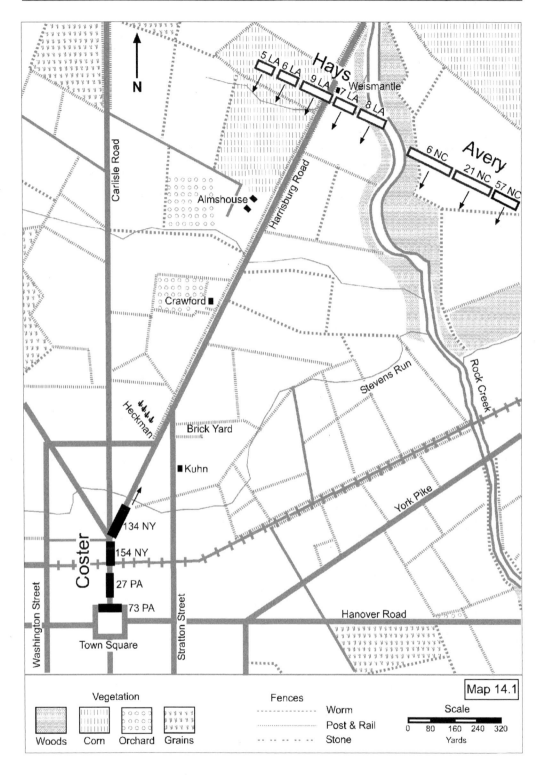

N

5 LA 6 LA 9 LA 7 LA 8 LA

Hays

Weismantle

6 NC 21 NC 57 NC

Avery

Carlisle Road

Harrisburg Road

Almshouse

Crawford

Rock Creek

Stevens Run

Heckman

Brick Yard

Kuhn

York Pike

134 NY

154 NY

Coster

27 PA

73 PA

Washington Street

Stratton Street

Hanover Road

Town Square

Vegetation

Woods   Corn   Orchard   Grains

Fences

- - - - - - - - Worm

· · · · · · · · · · · · Post & Rail

- · · - · · - · · Stone

Map 14.1

Scale

0   80   160   240   320

Yards

Map 14.2

Two fresh Southern brigades, in excess of 2,500 men, advanced against fewer than 1,000 Federals. Deployed behind a fence abutting Stratton Street, Col. Charles Coster's regiments were aligned as follows: the 27th Pennsylvania on the left and the 154th New York in the center (both facing north), and the 134th New York on the right (facing northeast).

Theirs was not a good position. "The ground in our front was higher than at our position, gently rising until, 40 rods away, it was perhaps 20 feet above us and covered with wheat just ready for the sickle," recalled Pvt. Charles McKay of the 154th New York. The 27th Pennsylvania, populated mainly with German immigrants, found itself in a depression near Stratton Street on the left end of the line. The result of this unfortunate deployment was that its members could only fire at a right oblique angle. In an unnerving turn of events, Coster's soldiers could hear their veteran enemy approaching in their front but could not see them. The rising terrain to their front extended toward the center of the line, and the colonel of the 154th New York later admitted that his regiment should have advanced and deployed along this high ground, but there was not sufficient time to do so. The Confederates, he wrote, "came down upon us almost before we had got in line."[6]

Hit with canister from Heckman's battery and small arms fire, probably from the 134th New York, Avery's North Carolinians began taking casualties as soon as they crossed Rock Creek about 200 yards from the Federal position. This fire, however, did nothing to deter their confident advance.

Those who could see the approaching Confederate line of battle never forgot it. One soldier wrote after the war, "it seemed as though they had a battle flag every few rods, which would indicate the formation was in solid column." The men were ordered to "reserve our fire until the enemy were close enough to make our volley effective." They did not have long to wait before "the whole line is a blaze of fire." The 134th New York (on the right of the line) opened fire when the 57th North Carolina tramped within sixty yards of its position.[7]

When some Federal officers realized that a gap existed between the two New York regiments, a battalion of the 27th Pennsylvania on the left moved quickly to the right to plug the hole. However, in the din of battle only 50 men heard the order and moved to obey it.

Outnumbered almost three to one, Coster's men somehow managed to hold their ground and fire effective volleys into the advancing Confederates. One Federal soldier estimated that each member of the 154th New York fired six to nine rounds into the enemy's closely-packed ranks. On the east side of Harrisburg Road, the effect of the fire stopped the advance of the 6th and 21st North Carolina regiments. The 57th North Carolina, on the left flank of Avery's line, swung farther left to hit the front, flank, and rear of the 134th New York on the right of Coster's line.

Realizing that they were about to be engulfed by an enemy approaching from beyond their flank, the men of the 134th began drifting away from the firing line. The regiment's commander, Lt. Col. D. B. Allen, later wrote that the enemy line "so far overlapped the 134th on our right that they swung around almost in their rear, and had such an enfilading fire upon them and our whole line, that that regiment was compelled to give way."

Many North Carolinians waited until the New Yorkers on the right of the line got up from their prone positions behind the fence. Once fully visible, the Southern infantry shot them as they bolted for the rear. The remainder of the Federal regiment, however, gamely held its ground.[8]

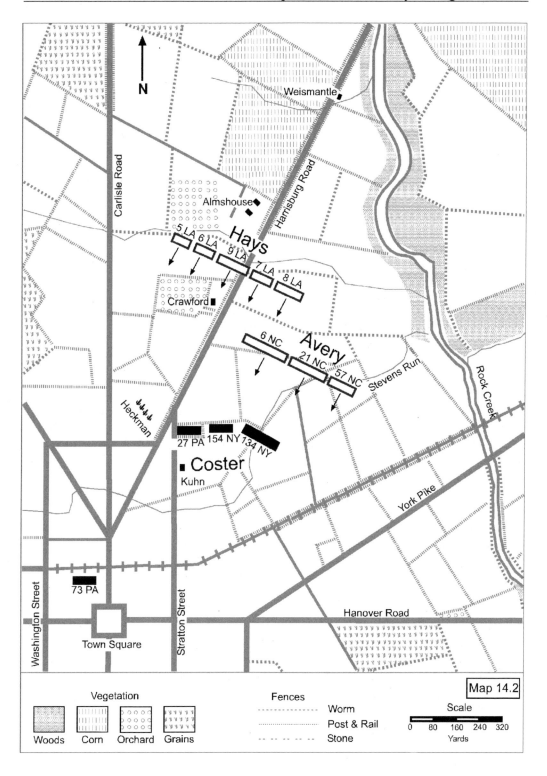

Map 14.2

Map 14.3

At about the same time that the 57th North Carolina enveloped the 134th New York on the east end of Col. Charles Coster's line, Brig. Gen. Harry Hays' Louisianans approached the 27th Pennsylvania from the north. The right end of Hays' long line (held by the 5th Louisiana) extended all the way to Carlisle Road—well beyond the left flank of the Pennsylvanians. Coster could now see the futility of remaining in his position and ordered an immediate withdrawal.

The men of the 27th Pennsylvania heard the order and began heading for the rear. As a result, the Louisianans on the right end of Hays' line did not experience much resistance. Because of the noise and smoke, however, the 154th New York in the center of Coster's line of battle did not get the message to retreat and remained in place. The men of the 134th New York on the right who had not yet fled also attempted to hold fast on Coster's defensive line.

Colonel Godwin of the 57th North Carolina recalled the men of the 134th New York "stubbornly holding their position until we had climbed over into their midst." Firing from the left front of Coster's line was Captain Heckman's Federal battery. When Heckman realized the game at the brickyard was played out, he ordered his pieces to safety. He was a few minutes too late, and some of Hays' soldiers captured two of his guns. During the thirty minutes of action, the battery fired 113 rounds at the Confederates.[9]

With the brigades of Col. Isaac Avery and Harry Hays overlapping the two ends of the Federal line, the defenders could see that they were in danger of being surrounded. It was now every man for himself. To the Confederates, who were within 30 yards of the defensive position, the Federal troops "raised up like a flock of blackbirds" and fled for safety. "We entered the road [Harrisburg Pike], and fierce hand to hand conflict ensued," remembered Lt. Alanson Crosby of the 154th New York.

Most of Coster's Federals did not yet realize that Hays had moved much of his brigade around their left flank and was now in their rear. According to Crosby, the "opposing forces were mingled in promiscuous confusion. Four color-bearers in the 154th New York were shot down in rapid succession. The only resource left was to cut through the enemy's ranks. The bayonet was used, but alas, what could a mere handful of men do against thousands that surrounded us on all sides." Another private agreed. "[When] we got to the road it was full of Rebels and they were coming up behind us, so there we had to stay, and but few got away." As one Louisiana veteran wrote with slight exaggeration, "we ran them thro town & caught more prisoners than we had men in the brigade."[10]

Coster's brigade sustained horrific losses in its short sojourn at the brickyard. Of the 922 men in the three regiments who took part in the fight, only 359 made it back to the safety of Cemetery Hill—a loss of 61 percent. Only four Federal brigades lost a higher percentage of men during the three-day battle. The entire detachment of the 27th Pennsylvania sent to the center of Coster's line fell killed, wounded, or captured; the 134th New York lost sixty-three percent of its men; and the 154th New York suffered losses of eighty-four percent. Only one other Federal regiment, the 25th Ohio (Ames' brigade, Barlow's division, XI Corps), lost a higher percentage of men than the 154th New York, although most of the losses (178 out of 200) were captured rather than killed or wounded. Miraculously, not one of Coster's flags was lost. The 27th Pennsylvania on the left of the line and the only regiment to hear Coster's orders to withdraw left thirty-nine percent of its men in and around the brickyard.

The crushing defeat suffered by Colonel Coster and his brigade ended the fighting that day between the Federal XI Corps and Jubal Early's Confederate division.[11]

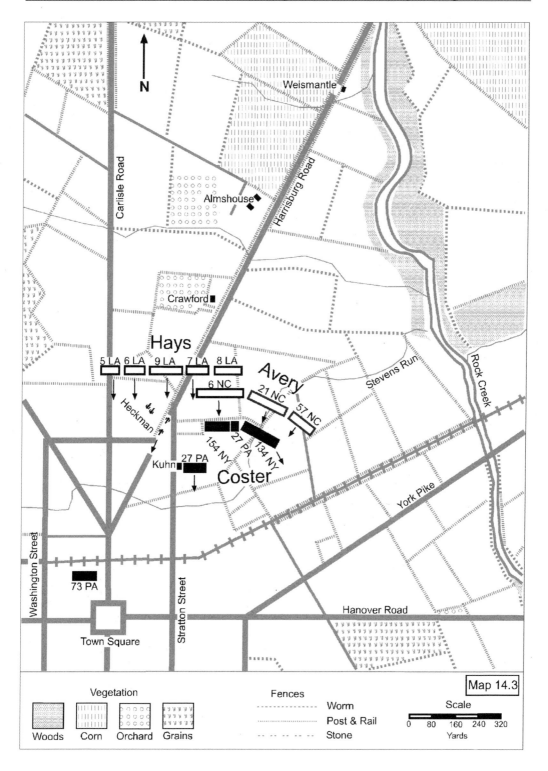

Map 14.3

Evening July 1 – Morning July 2

The first day's fighting ended when Lt. Gen. Richard Ewell, commander of the Confederate Second Corps, decided against attacking the hills southeast of Gettysburg. The sun set on a stunning Southern victory, though the cost was high. The 11,500 Federals of Reynolds' I Corps inflicted about 5,900 casualties in Heth's, Pender's, and Rodes' divisions—about the same number as their own losses, which included 1,600 captured or missing. The 8,500 men in Howard's XI Corps inflicted another 600 losses to Early's and Rodes' divisions, while suffering about 3,400 casualties, including 1,490 captured or missing. The head-on Southern attacks gained them the heights north and west of Gettysburg, but Federal troops now manned heights more commanding: Cemetery Hill and Culp's Hill.[1]

Not all of the combatants slept that night, for there was much work to be done. Many soldiers, primarily on the Confederate side, cared for the wounded and buried the dead. Field hospitals sprang up around the deadly fields as the surgeons plied their gruesome trade. On the Federal side, the men threw themselves into fortifying the heights southeast of town. "All night long the Federals were heard chopping away and working like beavers, and when day dawned, the ridge was found to be crowned with strongly built fortifications, and bristling with a most formidable array of cannon," a Southern staff officer recorded ominously in his journal. The passage of a quiet evening and night angered many Southerners, who were convinced that the heights could (and should) have been taken when they were driving the enemy the day before.[2]

Units in both armies, meanwhile, continued their trek to the battlefield while many of those already there assumed new positions. "All night it was tramp, tramp, tramp. The rumble of artillery moving to positions, wagons with supplies of all kinds needed by soldiers, coming up," complained a soldier in Pender's Division. On the Federal side, the XII Corps arrived late on the afternoon of July 1 and split itself: John Geary's division marched south to anchor the Federal line near the Round Tops, while Alpheus Williams' division occupied Culp's Hill. [3]

July 2 dawned bright, promising another hot day. The expected resumption of hostilities did not begin immediately. Both Lee and Meade spent hours positioning newly arriving troops and contemplating their options. Geary moved his division to Williams' left that morning, with units of the I Corps on his left. The XI Corps nervously guarded Cemetery Hill, which meant the III Corps anchored the Federal left. Unhappy with his low marshy position, Maj. Gen. Daniel Sickles advanced his men and guns toward Emmitsburg Road. When Maj. Gen. Winfield Hancock's II Corps arrived on the morning of July 2, it moved to Cemetery Ridge in the center of the Federal line. Major General George Sykes' V Corps reached the battlefield just after the II Corps during the early morning hours of July 2 and assumed a reserve position between Powers Hill and Rock Creek. By the middle of the afternoon, just before hostilities resumed, Meade had every corps on the field except Maj. Gen. John Sedgwick's VI Corps. The late afternoon battle was well underway by the time Sedgwick's infantry reached the southern end of the field.[4]

Like Meade, General Lee also carefully arranged his units as they arrived on the field. Richard Ewell's Second Corps continued to hold the northern portion of the battlefield, facing Cemetery Hill and Culp's Hill. A. P. Hill's Third Corps occupied the sector west of Gettysburg. Two divisions of Longstreet's First Corps would strike the initial blow against what Lee believed was the vulnerable Union right. The attack would roll northward en echelon, brigade by brigade, spilling across the front of Hill's Third Corps as the Southern infantry sought to break through Meade's line. Lee sent Longstreet's two divisions under Maj. Gens. Lafayette McLaws and John B. Hood on a march around the right when they arrived from the Chambersburg-Fayetteville area. Concerned that Union spotters on Little Round Top would see his men, Longstreet approached his jump-off position via a circuitous march that took hours to complete. "Old Pete's" third division under Maj. Gen. George Pickett was not yet on the field.

Late on the afternoon of July 2 the battle resumed in earnest, as Lee attempted to drive the Federal army off the heights before him.

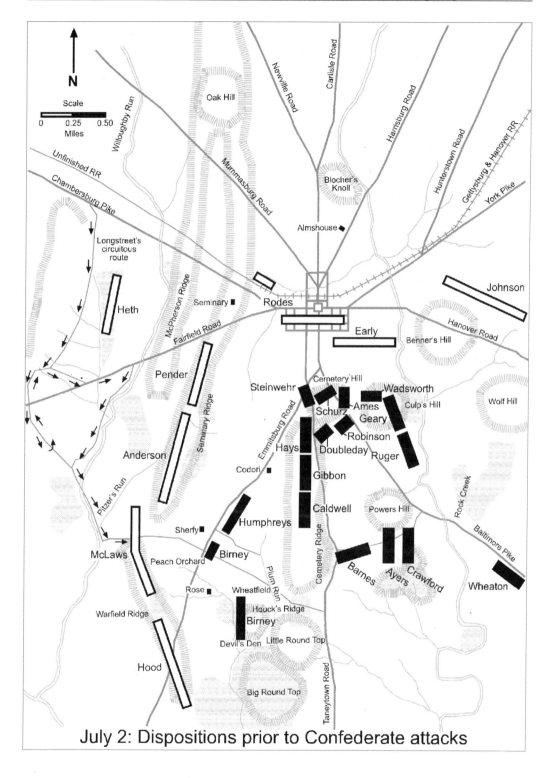

July 2: Dispositions prior to Confederate attacks

Map Set 15: Little Round Top

Map 15.1

The long march to the southern portion of the battlefield positioned the First Corps under Lt. Gen. James Longstreet on the right flank of the Army of Northern Virginia. Holding Longstreet's own right flank was Brig. Gen. Evander Law's Alabama brigade, deployed from left to right as follows: 4th Alabama – 47th Alabama – 15th Alabama – 44th Alabama – 48th Alabama. On Law's left flank was Brig. Gen. Jerome Robertson's Brigade, deployed from left to right as follows: 3rd Arkansas – 1st Texas – 4th Texas – 5th Texas. Their objective was the capture of Little Round Top.

According to General Robertson, his division commander, John Hood, ordered him to "keep my right well closed on Brigadier General Law's left, and to let my left rest on the Emmitsburg Pike." Robertson immediately ran into problems. Emmitsburg Road, reported Robertson, "bears sharply to the left . . . while Law on my right bore to the right." The 3rd Arkansas on Robertson's left stubbornly held its left on Emmitsburg Road, while the 5th Texas on the opposite end of the brigade maintained its connection with Law. Realizing that his brigade was too small to cover the widening gap that was developing, Robertson ordered the 4th Texas to remain with its sister 5th regiment, while the 1st Texas advanced with its left snugly against the 3rd Arkansas' right, both regiments heading for Houck's Ridge. The result was that the brigade broke into two wings during the advance, each fighting independently of the other. General Law eventually shifted the 44th and 48th Alabama regiments from the right side of his brigade all the way to his left to plug the growing gap.

The devastating effectiveness of Capt. James Smith's battery on Houck's Ridge also affected the alignment when Law's Alabama regiments shifted left to avoid the fire. On Law's extreme right, Col. William Oates' 15th Alabama was ordered to "hug the base of Great Round Top and go up the valley between the two mountains, until I found the left of the Union line, to turn it and do all the damage I could."

The 47th Alabama, a small unit, stayed with the 15th Alabama, advancing on its left flank.[1]

A tenacious skirmish line west of the Slyder farm manned by the 2nd U.S. Sharpshooters blocked the route to Little Round Top. The Federal rifles were so effective that when the Confederates stepped within 100 yards, they had little choice but to charge the sharpshooters. The Federals held their ground until the Alabamians came within fifty paces before retreating. Many halted at a stone wall at the foot of Big Round Top, where they opened again on the advancing 15th and 47th Alabama regiments, buying what proved to be valuable time for Federal reinforcements to reach Little Round Top.[2]

Little Round Top was devoid of Federal infantry when five Confederate regiments, about 2,000 men, approached it from the south and west. General Gouverneur Warren recognized the hill's importance and solicited help from the nearby V Corps. The Third Brigade commander, Col. Strong Vincent, intercepted a messenger bound for his division commander and, without orders, sent his 1,336 effectives from the vicinity of the Wheatfield toward the rocky heights. Approaching the summit of the hill via an old logging road, Vincent quickly deployed his brigade from left to right as follows: 20th Maine – 83rd Pennsylvania – 44th New York – 16th Michigan. The 44th New York was in the rear during this march, but its colonel asked permission to fight beside the 83rd Pennsylvania. As the brigade deployed, Vincent made it very clear to Col. Joshua Chamberlain that his 20th Maine, situated on the "spur" of Little Round Top, was the left-most regiment of the Army of the Potomac's entire defensive line.[3]

Vincent's men occupied a good defensive position protected in front by large rocks. These boulders also dotted the side of the hill, and would soon disrupt Confederate battle lines as they scaled the heights. Colonel Chamberlain did not care for his position. His men faced the "saddle" between Little Round Top and Big Round Top, which he called, "rough, rocky, and stragglingly wooded." Chamberlain sent Capt. Walter Morrill's Company B out on the skirmish line to his left to prevent a surprise attack against his flank and rear.[4]

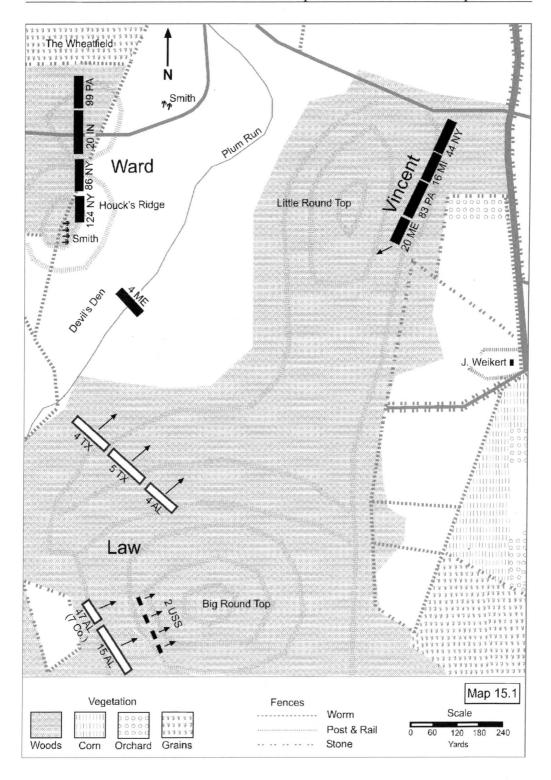

The Wheatfield

N

Smith

99 PA

20 IN

Ward

86 NY

124 NY

Plum Run

Houck's Ridge

Smith

Little Round Top

Vincent

44 NY

16 MI

83 PA

20 ME

Devil's Den

4 ME

J. Weikert

4 TX

5 TX

4 AL

Law

Big Round Top

47 AL
(7 Co.)

2 USS

15 AL

Vegetation				Fences		Scale

Vegetation

Woods   Corn   Orchard   Grains

Fences

.... Worm
.... Post & Rail
– ·· – ·· – ·· Stone

Map 15.1

Scale

0   60   120   180   240
Yards

Map 15.2

When he reached the base of Big Round Top, Col. William Oates ignored his brigade commander's orders and sent his 15th Alabama directly up the steep and rocky hill after the retreating 2nd U.S. Sharpshooters. The 47th Alabama followed suit.

The sharpshooters stopped periodically to fire at their pursuers, but in shooting downhill they aimed too high, and inflicted few casualties. About halfway up the hill, the sharpshooters broke into two groups, one circling around to the opposite (eastern) side, while the other moved south on Oates' right flank. Because the latter movement threatened his exposed flank, Oates ordered Company A to deal with this detachment while the rest of the 15th Alabama completed its ascent to the top of the hill. The men had already marched thirteen hours to get to the battlefield, and the trek up Big Round Top was itself arduous. To make matters worse, most of the men did not have any water. Many fell from the ranks before reaching the summit of the hill, some fainting from their exertions. For a variety of reasons, three companies of the 47th Alabama on the skirmish line never rejoined the regiment, reducing the numbers of the already small unit.[5]

Meanwhile, the 4th Texas, 5th Texas, and 4th Alabama regiments drove toward Little Round Top. After briefly halting to dress their lines, the men scaled the heights. The 16th Michigan, 44th New York, and 83rd Pennsylvania were waiting for them to step into killing range. "As we arrived on top," recalled Lt. Charles Salter of the 16th Michigan "[we] saw a long line of rebels coming over and down a range of hills opposite us. If we had been 5 minutes later, the enemy would have gained the ridge we were on."[6]

The steep hill, studded with numerous large rock formations, made it difficult for the Confederates to maintain anything resembling well-dressed ranks. Some of the granite boulders were so large that the troops had to halt and file through gaps between them. "The huge rocks forming defiles through which not more than 3 or 4 men could pass abreast, thus breaking up

our alignment and rendering its reformation impossible," observed Lt. Col. King Bryan of the 5th Texas. A Southern private recalled that the hill was so steep that "a mountain goat would have reveled" in it. The heavy terrain forced the Confederates to fight Indian-style, loosely organized into knots of soldiers while fighting from behind rocks and trees. Because the regiments had broken into small clumps of men, their firepower was dispersed and largely ineffective.

Strong Vincent's troops returned the fire, which Colonel Bryan likened to "being showered like hail upon us." A private in the 5th Texas grimly watched as the Federal troops held their position and continued "pouring volley after volley into the gray line." Another private noted that the "trees were barked and thousands of bullets blew to atoms against the hard rocks." Many of the Southern veterans sized up the situation before them and realized that taking these hills, on this line, was an all-but impossible task. According to one Texan, "we could hardly have gone over them if there had been no Yankees there."[7]

The first attack probably hit the 44th New York and 83rd Pennsylvania regiments. A soldier from the latter outfit recalled that as the Confederate foot soldiers advanced, "a sheet of smoke and flame burst from our whole line, which made the enemy reel and stagger, and fall back in confusion."

With the first attack stymied, Confederate officers pulled their men back to the woods at the base of the hill. Major Jefferson Rogers, who had taken command of the 5th Texas after its colonel and lieutenant colonel both fell wounded, pulled his men back only when the withdrawal of the other regiments left both of his flanks unsupported.

When the Confederate forces fell back, some quick-thinking Federal troops rushed down the rough slope and scooped up prisoners before they had a chance to retire to the base of the hill.[8]

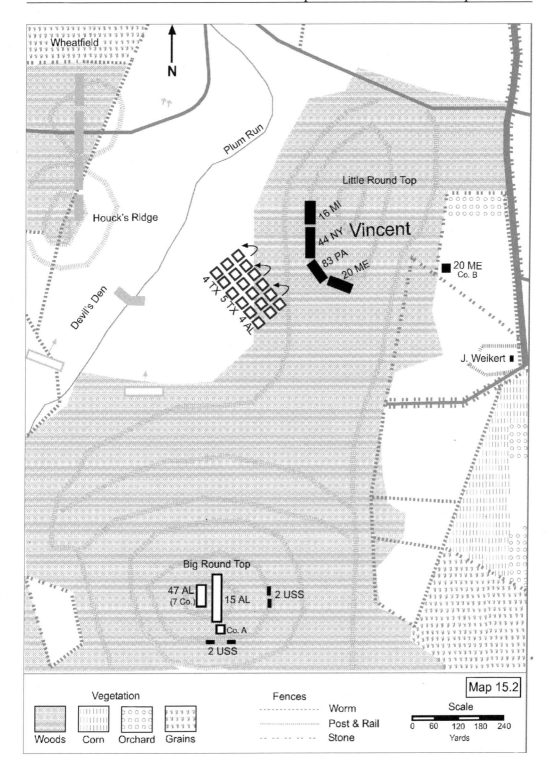

Wheatfield

N

Plum Run

Little Round Top

Houck's Ridge

16 MI

44 NY Vincent

83 PA

20 ME

4 TX 5 TX 4 AL

20 ME
Co. B

Devil's Den

J. Weikert

Big Round Top

47 AL
(7 Co.)

15 AL

2 USS

Co. A

2 USS

Map 15.2

Vegetation

Fences

Scale

Worm

Post & Rail

Stone

Woods   Corn   Orchard   Grains

0   60   120   180   240
Yards

Map 15.3

The 4th Alabama, 4th Texas, and 5th Texas regiments launched a second attack against Little Round Top across terrain strewn with the bodies of their dead comrades. The Federal defenders remained defiant and held their position, peppering the attackers with a deadly fire. This attack was also repulsed, but not before it spread well to the left and sucked the 16th Michigan into the fight. One Texan noted after the battle that it would have been impossible to take the heights "had the enemy only been armed with rocks." Many Confederates took refuge behind boulders on the slope, from which they could neither advance nor retreat. A few held up white handkerchiefs to surrender.[9]

As the firing continued, Lt. Charles Hazlett's 5th United States, Battery D, approached Little Round Top. He had originally protested the order to scale the hill, asking that a different battery be sent in his stead. At the top of the hill, he conversed with General Warren, who did not think it was possible to depress the gun barrels enough to fire into the Confederates below. According to Warren, it was "no place for efficient artillery fire." Perhaps that was true, but Hazlett knew "the sound of my guns will be encouraging to our troops and disheartening to others, and my battery's of no use if this hill is lost."[10]

While Hazlett was positioning his artillery, a Confederate staff officer rode up Big Round Top and ordered the 15th and 47th Alabama regiments to attack Little Round Top from the south. Colonel Oates initially protested, claiming that if artillery unlimbered on the hill they now occupied, it could rain deadly missiles down on the Federal position. He was overruled.

Lieutenant Colonel Michael Bulger moved the 47th Alabama down the northeast face of Big Round Top, using rocks and trees to conceal his men. He hoped to get as close as possible to the enemy line before launching his attack. The plan unraveled when the regiment came face to face with the left flank of the 83rd Pennsylvania and the right and center of the 20th Maine. Although the 15th Alabama on the right of the 47th Alabama had not yet come up, Colonel Bulger launched his attack alone. Colonel Joshua Chamberlain of the 20th Maine reported that Bulger's men "burst upon us in great fury." The subsequent fighting between the 20th Maine and 47th Alabama was bitter and often hand-to-hand.[11]

As the 47th Alabama attacked Little Round Top, Oates' 15th Alabama streamed down the north side of Big Round Top. Seeing this threat, the left side of the 20th Maine opened a strong fire upon the unsuspecting Southern infantry. Chamberlain extended his line to the left and refused two companies so that his defensive line was almost double its original length, although far more thinly spread. Not recognizing the enemy's new alignment, the 15th Alabama took the full brunt of another volley only 40 or 50 paces from the Federal line. The bullets staggered the Alabamians, striking many and causing some to flee to the rear.

Oates ordered his troops to close ranks and return fire, which hit many of Chamberlain's men. After a second volley crashed into the 20th Maine's two left companies, the Federal line began to waver; Oates ordered his men to charge. According to Chamberlain, the enemy "burst forth again with a shout, and rapidly advanced, firing as they came . . . pushed up to within a dozen yards of us before the terrible effectiveness of our fire compelled them to break and take shelter." Oates agreed with Colonel Chamberlain's assessment: the fire, reported the Alabama colonel, was "so destructive that my line wavered like a man trying to walk against a strong wind." The thinning Alabama line finally halted and started backward.[12]

Oates' battle line was shy a company, detached during the descent from Big Round Top to fall upon Federal ordnance wagons parked well off his right. As luck would have it, the timing could not have been worse. Company A not only failed to capture the wagons, but was unavailable for the critical assault against the far right flank of the Army of the Potomac.

Colonel Oates had unwittingly deprived himself of about ten percent of his men at what would prove to be one of the pivotal points in the battle.[13]

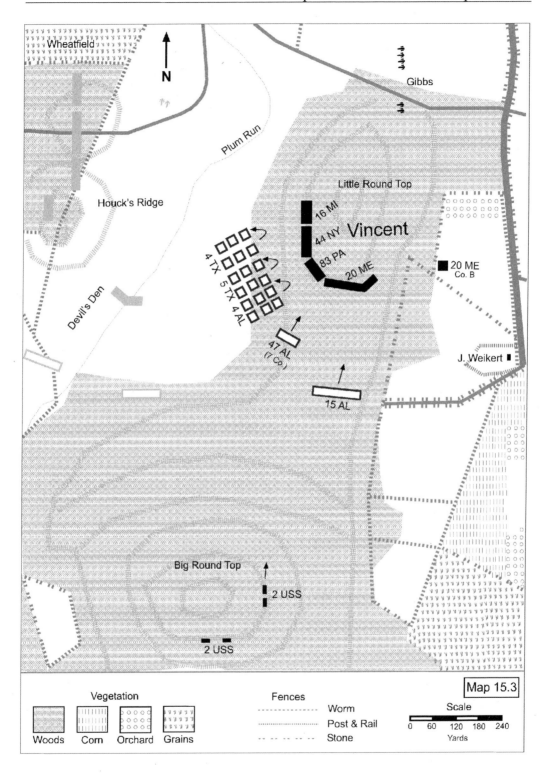

Wheatfield

N

Plum Run

Houck's Ridge

Little Round Top

16 MI

44 NY

83 PA

Vincent

20 ME

Gibbs

20 ME
Co. B

4 TX 5 TX 4 AL

Devil's Den

47 AL
(7 Co.)

J. Weikert

15 AL

Big Round Top

2 USS

2 USS

Map 15.3

Vegetation

Woods   Corn   Orchard   Grains

Fences

--------------- Worm
.... Post & Rail
-- -- -- -- Stone

Scale

0   60   120   180   240
Yards

Map 15.4

The 48th Alabama of Law's Brigade arrived after helping neutralize Capt. James Smith's battery on Houck's Ridge. The 48th formed on the left of the 4th Texas. According to the Alabama regiment's adjutant, Henry Figures, the "enemy were upon the top of the mountain, the steepest place I ever saw in my life." The attacks of the 4th and 5th Texas and 4th Alabama regiments had been repulsed twice, but the forthcoming assault looked more promising because the 48th Alabama's left flank overlapped the right end of the 16th Michigan's regimental line. With a yell, Law's men again stormed the craggy and thus far unyielding heights.[14]

Fire from the men of the 44th New York stopped the 5th Texas to their front. Turning their attention to the right, the New Yorkers fired into the advancing flank of the 4th Texas as it attacked the 16th Michigan. "Although we had been engaged in other battles," wrote Lt. Charles Salter of the 16th Michigan, "we never had such a terrible, close bayonet fight before. It seemed as if every man, on both sides, was activated by the intensest [sic] hate, and determined to kill as many of the enemy as possible." The right side of the 16th Michigan began giving way, either because of the Confederate pressure on the flank or a mistaken order to withdraw. The Southern infantry quickly made its way toward the summit despite the 44th New York's devastating oblique fire.[15]

Seeing the right of his line collapsing, Colonel Vincent dashed over with his wife's riding crop in his hand. The officer mounted a large rock and yelled out to his men, "Don't give an inch, boys, don't give an inch!" Vincent had hardly uttered these words when a mortal shot struck him in the groin. Colonel James "Old Crazy" Rice of the 44th New York took command of the brigade.[16]

The situation was much different in the center of the Confederate line, where the 4th Alabama pulled back, exposing the left flank of the 47th Alabama. The 83rd Pennsylvania took advantage of the withdrawal by pouring an oblique fire into the vulnerable regiment. Another gap opened on the 47th Alabama's right flank. With its commander wounded, and now exposed to small arms fire raking its center and right from the 20th Maine and its left from the 83rd Pennsylvania, the 47th Alabama was in a terrible position. It had charged the 20th Maine four times and had been driven back on three occasions. The outcome of the fourth assault was becoming painfully clear for the Alabama soldiers. According to one Confederate officer, the men "were completely exhausted before they began this [final] charge & they fainted on the field by the hundreds."[17]

Unable to break through on the fourth attempt, the 47th Alabama began its slow retreat. Colonel Oates ordered his four left companies to change position to fire into the 20th Maine's right flank to cover their withdrawing comrades. These companies soon received return oblique fire from the 83rd Pennsylvania. Recognizing the dangerously exposed position of his men, Oates passed through his line to the front and yelled with his sword drawn, "Forward, men, to the ledge!" According to Oates' postwar account, his men drove the Maine soldiers five times, and five times the enemy countercharged to regain their positions. On two occasions, the fighting was so close, claimed Oates, that bayonets were freely used.[18]

The 20th Maine fought desperately to hold its exposed position. According to Colonel Chamberlain, "squads of the enemy broke through our line in several places, and the engagement was literally hand to hand. The fight was like ocean waves—rolling back and forth." He admitted that several times his men were forced back, but they counterattacked to reclaim their original positions. One soldier recalled the scene as a "terrible medley of cries, shouts, groans, cheers, curses, bursting shells, whizzing rifle bullets and clanging steel."

Running low on ammunition, the Union and Confederate soldiers began scrounging through the cartridge boxes of their fallen comrades. A concerted push by Colonel Oates' right flank knocked Colonel Chamberlain's left flank back so far that the 20th Maine's line resembled a hairpin.[19]

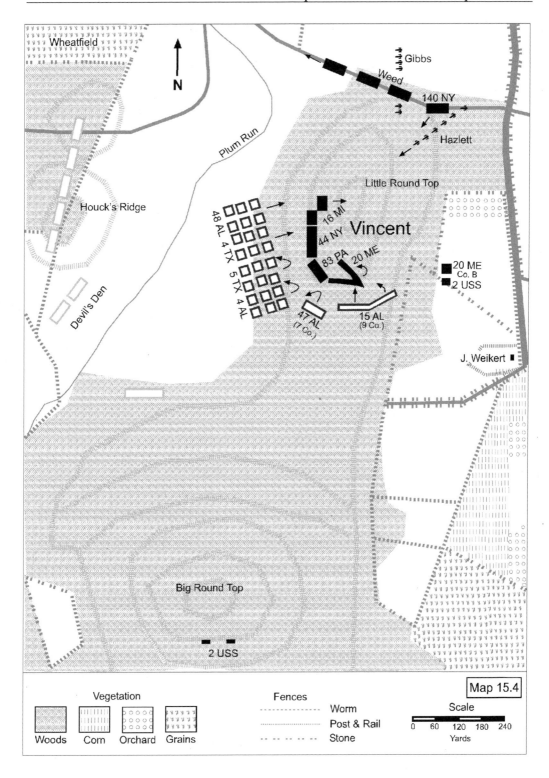

Map 15.4

Map 15.5

Although some of the Confederates were having difficulties reaching the enemy line, victory danced within sight as the 48th Alabama and 4th Texas surged toward the summit of Little Round Top. General Warren was not done with his heroics, however. Rushing down the northern slope of the hill, he encountered his old brigade, now under Brig. Gen. Stephen Weed (Ayres' division, V Corps). Weed was up ahead, so Warren sought out Col. Patrick O'Rorke, commander of the 140th New York. "Paddy, give me a regiment," Warren yelled. O'Rorke hesitated, telling Warren that Weed had ridden ahead for orders. "Never mind that, bring your regiment up here and I will take responsibility," Warren insisted. O'Rorke obeyed and led his 140th New York toward Little Round Top.[20]

Climbing the slope in a column of fours, the New Yorkers presented a colorful sight in their new Zouave uniforms. Two companies immediately followed O'Rorke up the steep hill. When they reached the summit, the men halted to level their rifled-muskets into the advancing 48th Alabama and 4th Texas, who were in the process of flanking Vincent's brigade. The enemy was only about 40 feet away when O'Rorke's men opened fire. It was a terrible sight. "The wild cries of charging lines, the rattle of musketry, the booming of artillery, and the shrieks of the wounded were orchestral accompaniments of a scene . . . like very Hell itself," noted a Federal officer. O'Rorke quickly drew his sword and yelled, "Down this way, boys!" as the men approached the right of the 16th Michigan. The fight was brief and at close range—and in some cases hand-to-hand. Absorbing fire from both flanks and in front, the Confederate charge withered away. Other companies of the 140th New York arrived on the hill, where the remainder of Weed's brigade joined them. O'Rorke, however, fell mortally wounded during the charge.[21]

While the infantry battled for the heights, Hazlett's gunners struggled to ascend the difficult slope. The cannoneers wrestled their guns up the hill by sheer hand power, assisted by some of General Weed's infantrymen. When the guns were finally in position and opened fire, Vincent's men let out a cheer. "No military music ever sounded sweeter," remembered a New Yorker.[22]

Over on the Union left, however, Chamberlain and his men were fighting for their very existence. Aware of his rapidly depleting ranks, dwindling supply of ammunition, and with 15th Alabama poised for yet another attack Chamberlain "ordered his men to fix bayonets." The soldiers of the 20th Maine began charging down the hill, first in small groups, and then by full companies. As Chamberlain later put it, "the effect was surprising; many of the enemy's first line threw down their arms and surrendered . . . . Holding fast by our right, and swinging forward our left, we made an extended 'right wheel,' before which the enemy's second line broke and fell back, fighting from tree to tree, many being captured, until we had swept the valley and cleared the front of nearly our entire brigade." Colonel Oates told a slightly different story. Seeing that his support had disappeared, and with the enemy swarming near his left flank, he ordered a withdrawal—even as the 20th Maine launched its final assault.[23]

The survivors of the 15th Alabama quickly made their way to the rear. Some came close to Company B of the 20th Maine, who along with some men from the 2nd U.S. Sharpshooters had taken position in the saddle between the Round Tops to the left of Chamberlain's main line. These sixty or so men opened fire and charged, creating even more havoc as they captured scores of Oates' men.[24]

This action effectively ended the direct attacks against Little Round Top. After the battle, the Federal troops who had fought on the hill were shocked to see the effects of their small arms fire. According to one, "the scene where our volley first struck the enemy's line was one of sickening horror. Their dead and wounded tumbled promiscuously together, so that it was difficult to cross the line where they fell without stepping on them. . . . I pray to God that I may never witness such a scene again."[25]

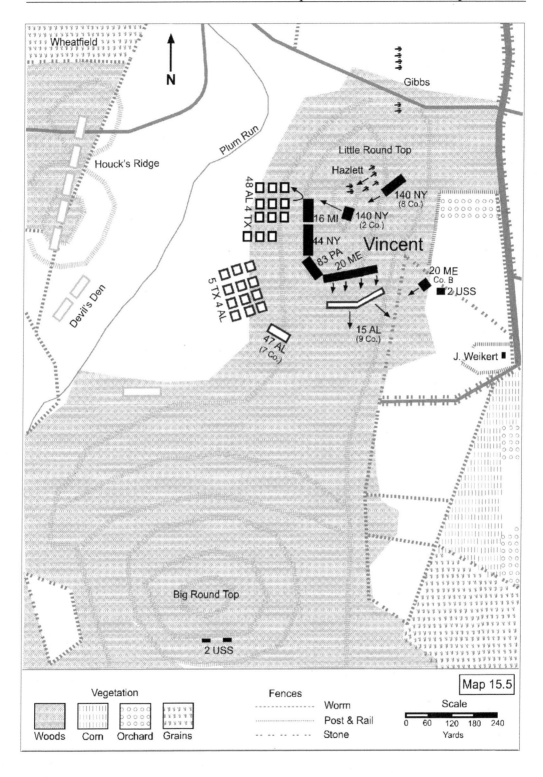

Map 15.5

Map Set 16: Devil's Den and the Slaughter Pen

Map 16.1

Brigadier General Hobart Ward's brigade (Birney's division, III Corps) had the dubious distinction of holding the Federal army's left flank on the afternoon of July 2. Instead of anchoring the left of the Federal line on Little Round Top as originally ordered, III Corps commander Maj. Gen. Dan Sickles advanced his entire corps to higher ground to his front.

When the move was finished, Ward's brigade was 300 yards west of Little Round Top. His left flank hung in the air in the boulder-strewn Devil's Den. The balance of his line ran north, stretched along Houck's Ridge. It ended in Rose's Woods, where his right flank rested in the air beside a large field of summer wheat. The 4th Maine (on the far left) and 124th New York occupied the high ground near Devil's Den, while the 86th New York, 20th Indiana, and 99th Pennsylvania (holding the far right) extended the line north. Captain James Smith's battery arrived and deployed in front of Ward's left. However, because of the ridge and rocky topography, Smith could only bring up four of his six guns. The remaining two unlimbered in the rear in Plum Run Valley to cover Ward's left flank. The 2nd U.S. Sharpshooters, also part of Ward's brigade, held the skirmish line.[1]

From his vantage point in front of the 4th Maine, Captain Smith realized that his four guns could not defend the open ground between his left flank and the wooded slopes of the Round Tops. He asked permission to have the 4th Maine occupy the woods at the base of Little Round Top. Col. Elijah Walker liked his current position and declined the request. Smith next sought out General Ward, who ordered Walker to move his regiment to the left and occupy Plum Run Valley, facing Devil's Den and the gorge. Walker made his way to Ward and "remonstrated with all the power of speech I could command," but there was no time to reconsider.

With the enemy quickly approaching, Walker reluctantly obeyed the order to leave the high ground. He placed his right wing on Devil's Den, anchored on a large rock formation, with the rest of the regiment stretched toward the base of Big Round Top. The change in position left a gaping hole in Ward's line, which Smith thought he could defend with his four guns.[2]

Parts of two Southern brigades belonging to Evander Law and Jerome Robertson approached the left flank of Ward's brigade. When Law's Alabamians began attacking Little Round Top, Smith's Union battery opened fire. The barrage was so intense that Law ordered the two regiments making up his right flank—the 44th and 48th Alabama—to pass behind the rest of the brigade and advance to remove the potentially dangerous artillery fire. The shifting regiments also filled a hole that had developed within Robertson's advancing brigade line.[3]

While the right wing of Robertson's brigade (the 4th and 5th Texas) approached Little Round Top, the left wing (the 1st Texas and 3rd Arkansas), advanced against Houck's Ridge and Rose's Woods to the northwest. The Arkansas regiment swept toward the positions of the 20th Indiana and 86th New York in Ward's center, while the 1st Texas approached a triangular field fronting the position held by the 124th New York.[4]

Before the Southern infantry attacked, Smith's battery dueled with their Confederate counterparts deployed along Seminary Ridge and Warfield Ridge. Counter-battery fire forced the 124th New York to move to the right to seek the cover of Rose's Woods, which widened the gap between it and the 4th Maine. When the Confederate infantry stepped into view, Smith's guns blasted away at their closed ranks. The guns first threw case shot at the enemy, then shells when they entered the woods, and finally canister when they tramped with easy killing range. The canister did little harm to the Confederates, however, because of the large number of rocks and boulders.

As Smith's ammunition dwindled, his excited voice could be heard above the din of battle, "Give them solid shot! Damn them, give them anything!"[5]

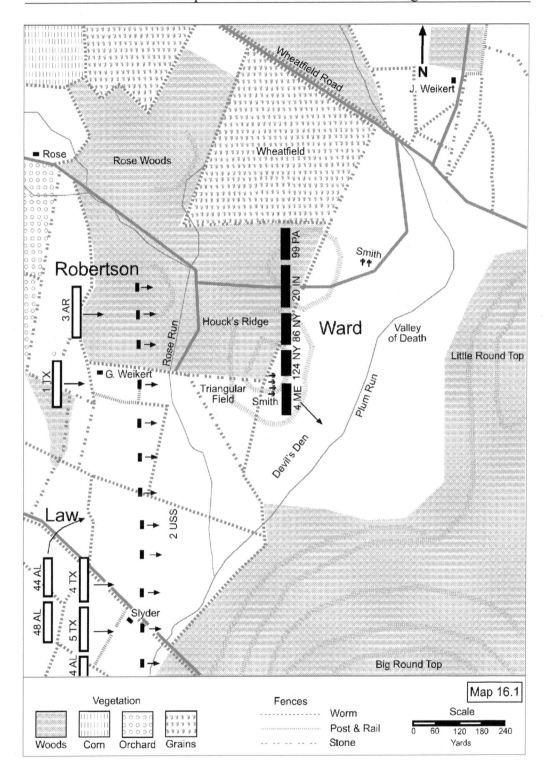

Map 16.1

Map 16.2

Colonel Van H. Manning's 3rd Arkansas of Brig. Gen. Jerome Robertson's Brigade engaged the enemy first, routing the Federal skirmishers near the Timbers house before pushing into the southern portion of Rose's Woods. The Arkansans traversed the soggy ground around Plum Run and approached Brig. Gen. Hobart Ward's main defensive line on Houck's Ridge.

Waiting for these Southern soldiers were three regiments: the 86th New York, 20th Indiana, and 99th Pennsylvania. These 1,130 Federal soldiers were more than a match for the roughly 500 men of the 3rd Arkansas and a handful of others from a company of the 1st Texas who somehow ended up fighting on Manning's left flank. General Ward ordered his men not to fire until they could plainly see the enemy; the 4th Maine and 124th New York on the left of the line were directed to wait until the enemy had closed to within 200 yards.[6]

The 3rd Arkansas walked into a withering frontal and oblique fire on its left flank. Colonel Manning ran to the left and ordered the last three companies to refuse their flank to face this new threat. The noise was so loud that Manning had to push the men into position because they could not hear his orders. None of it mattered however, for a sudden counterattack by the 86th New York, 20th Indiana, and 99th Pennsylvania drove the Arkansans back about 75 yards. While the exultant Federals returned to their former positions atop Houck's Ridge, Manning used the time to reorganize his infantry and resume the advance. None of them saw the 17th Maine (de Trobriand's brigade, Birney's division, III Corps) arriving in the Wheatfield on their left and taking position behind a stone wall.[7]

After suffering moderate losses from Smith's guns atop Houck's Ridge, the 1st Texas came up on the 3rd Arkansas' right flank and took refuge behind a stone wall at the base of the Triangular Field. Fortunately for the Texans, Smith's cannon could not depress their barrels enough to fire into them as they crouched behind the wall. The Texans opened fire on Smith's gunners and silenced the battery. According to Private A. C. Sims of the 1st Texas, "we loaded and fired, the front rank on their knees and the rear standing." The left of the 86th New York and the 124th New York, to the right of Smith's Union battery, faced the Texans and opened fire. The small arms and artillery shells forced them to stay put behind the wall on the west side of the Triangular Field.[8]

Two additional units, the 44th and 48th Alabama, approached Devil's Den from the southwest. These men belonged to the two regiments Law had shifted from his right flank to his left to close the gap with Robertson's Brigade. Although both came from Law's Brigade and had shifted at the same time, the two regiments were operating independently. Colonel William Perry of the 44th Alabama had orders to take Smith's battery, so he wheeled his line about 45 degrees left about 200 yards from the Federal position. Perry's left flank now approached the sector between the Triangular Field and Devil's Den. The 44th Alabama's right wing had some difficulty as it picked its way through the boulders leading to Plum Run gorge. Perry did not like the terrain on his right flank, calling it "a valley destitute of trees and filled with immense bowlders between them."[9]

Meanwhile, the 48th Alabama advanced to the south of its sister regiment. The 48th moved northeast, with the woods at the base of the Round Tops to its right and Plum Run to its left. Colonel James Sheffield called the route along which they marched a "very rough and rugged road—the worst cliffs of rocks there [that] could have been traveled over."

That same terrain was also a blessing in disguise for the Southern infantry. Because of the trees and the rugged terrain, the 4th Maine, which was defending the left end of General Ward's line, did not see the approaching Alabama troops.[10]

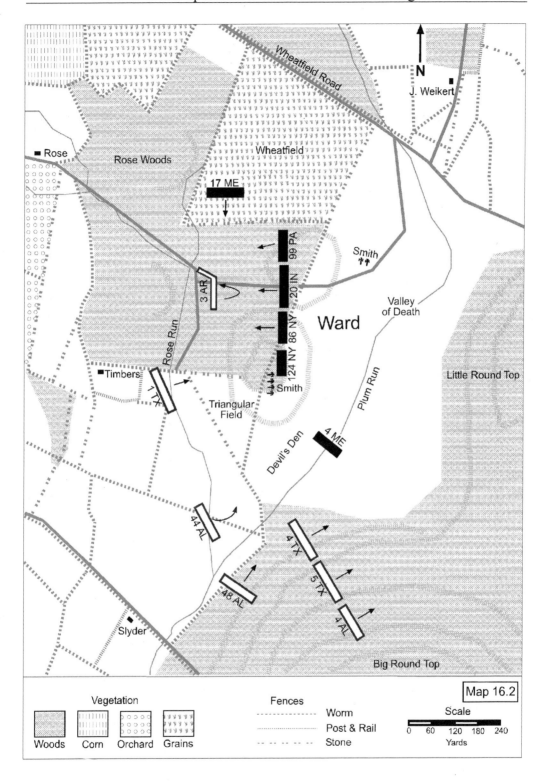

Map 16.2

Map 16.3

Colonel Van Manning decided to flank Brig. Gen. Hobart Ward's brigade line by extending his 3rd Arkansas to the left until it was almost double its original length. The Federal troops on Houck's Ridge immediately opened fire, as did the 17th Maine in the Wheatfield, forcing the Arkansans to retreat a second time. After regrouping, Manning pushed his men ahead for another attack, but this too was unsuccessful. He halted his bloodied regiment and ordered his men to fire at the Federal line until reinforcements arrived.[11]

After regaining their breath, the men of the 1st Texas continued their assault on Smith's four guns on Houck's Ridge. They climbed over the wall and advanced into the Triangular Field. When they were within 50 yards of the ridge, the 124th New York rose and fired shattering volley. "[I]t cost us dearly, for as we lay in close range of their now double lines," remembered one Texan, "the enemy poured a hail of bullets on us, and in a few minutes a number of our men were killed or wounded." One New Yorker wrote that the "crash of riflery [sic] perceptibly thinned their ranks and brought them to a stand . . . it seemed to paralyze their whole line." Undeterred, the Texans continued their advance.[12]

The 124th New York's commander, Col. A. Van Horne Ellis, tried to calm his men by standing nonchalantly with his arms folded as he watched the Texans advance. His second in command approached him twice to suggest a counterattack, but both times Ellis rebuffed him. Realizing, however, that an audacious counterattack was perhaps his only hope against the larger 1st Texas, Colonel Ellis called for his horse and ordered a charge. The other field officers also mounted up. When a captain protested about going into the fight on horseback, Ellis replied, "The men must see us to-day." The New Yorkers dashed forward with a cheer, smashing into the 1st Texas and sending it reeling 200 yards to the rear. There the Texans reformed and, as the New Yorkers continued to advance, cut them down with devastating volleys, killing or wounding about a quarter of the regiment. One New Yorker described the chaos as "roaring cannon, crashing rifles, screeching shots, bursting shells, hissing bullets, cheers, shouts, shrieks, and groans." The situation for the New Yorkers was precarious. They had already sustained a number of casualties and they occupied an advanced and very vulnerable position with both of the regiment's flanks hanging unsupported in the air.[13]

The 44th Alabama, meanwhile, approached Plum Run Gorge intent on capturing Smith's cannon blazing atop Houck's Ridge. When they finally spotted the approaching Alabamians, the men of the 4th Maine opened a fire that forced the attackers to quickly dive for whatever cover was at hand. Walker sent scouts to the left, who quickly returned with news that another Confederate column was not more than 50 yards distant and approaching rapidly from the direction of Big Round Top. Walker immediately refused his left flank in an effort to confront the enemy.[14]

The Confederates Walker was preparing to meet belonged to the 48th Alabama, which was moving against the Union regiment from the southwest. The two regiments opened fire when they were barely 60 feet apart. Rolling terrain had protected each from the other until the range was point-blank. The volleys were especially intense on the left of the 48th Alabama in the area known today as the Slaughter Pen. Hit hard, the men holding that sector of the regimental line either fell to the ground dead or wounded or stumbled rearward to avoid the killing fire. The remainder of the regiment eventually followed suit. The 48th Alabama made two more attacks, but neither was able to drive the 4th Maine from the gorge.[15]

Just as matters seemed beyond rescue on this part of the field, help for the blunted Confederate assault appeared in the form of Brig. Gen. Henry Benning's Georgia brigade. The Georgians were advancing northeast into the gap yawning between the right of the 1st Texas and the left of the 44th Alabama. Benning's thrust was also aimed directly at the even wider gap that existed in the Federal line beyond the right flank of the embattled 4th Maine.[16]

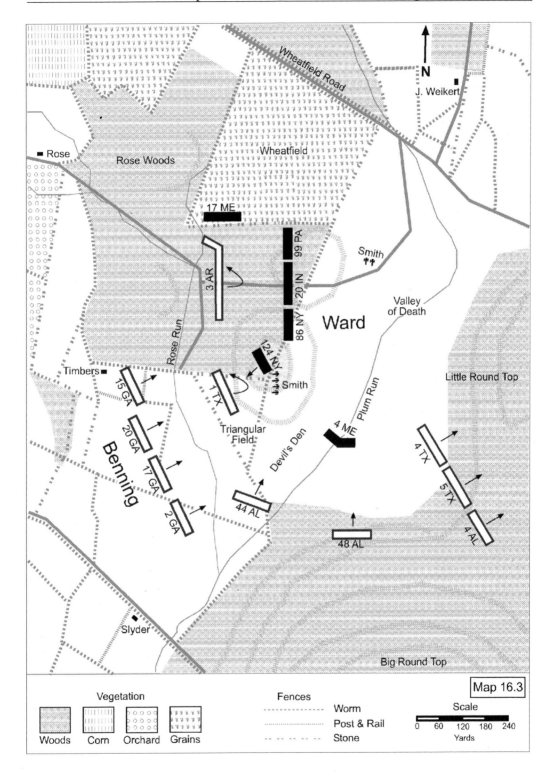

Map 16.3

Vegetation

| Woods | Corn | Orchard | Grains |

Fences

- - - - - - - - - - - Worm
····················· Post & Rail
- - - - - - - - Stone

Scale

0   60   120   180   240
Yards

Map 16.4

Joined by the 15th and 20th Georgia regiments from Brig. Gen. Henry Benning's Brigade, the 1st Texas renewed its advance. The Texans, however, quickly commingled with the 15th Georgia and despite the efforts of their officers, could not be separated. The regiments fought the rest of the day together. "We raised a deafening yell and went over the rock fence and up the hill shouting and yelling like demons," wrote a Georgia private.

The 124th New York collided with the Confederates in the Triangular Field. Because of their losses, the New Yorkers probably numbered no more than 150 by this point and were no match for the three Confederate regiments. They quickly retreated to Ward's main line on Houck's Ridge. Scores of men fell killed and wounded during the brief but sharply-fought action including Colonel Ellis, who was shot from his horse and killed outright.[17]

A screaming Confederate shell damaged one of Smith's guns, which several men manhandled out and dragged to the rear. The remaining cannoneers came under fire from Confederate sharpshooters. Fearing that his guns would be captured by the enemy onslaught, Smith rushed over to the New Yorkers and pleaded for their help. The infantry, however, were busy trying to maintain their own position. Smith knew retreating with his guns was impossible. Without any viable options, he decided to hold his position on the ridge as best he could.[18]

Meanwhile, the 48th Alabama renewed its attack on the 4th Maine as the 44th Alabama slid to its left, around the 4th's right flank. The move shoved Federal skirmishers out of Devil's Den, capturing about 40 of them in the process. Watching his left repulse yet another charge of the 48th Alabama, Colonel Walker shifted his regiment to the right. From his new vantage he could see the 44th Alabama approaching Houck's Ridge, moving into the gap between the 4th Maine and the 124th New York. Smith's guns were in imminent danger of being overrun. If this wasn't enough, some in the 44th Alabama were working their way around his right flank

and into his rear. Walker took immediate action, pulling his regiment back after it had fired about 25 rounds at the 48th Alabama. He quickly reformed the men and ordered them to fix bayonets. "I shall never forget the 'click' that was made by the fixing of bayonets, it was as one," he wrote after the war. When his men were ready, Walker ordered a right oblique charge up the slope of Houck's Ridge—the same area he did not want to vacate in the first place. "Our principal loss was in this place," wrote Lieutenant Charles Sawyer. His men went down by the score.[19]

The Devil's Den sector was an especially perilous place on the afternoon of July 2 because artillery on both sides focused their tubes there. Colonel Perry ordered his 44th Alabama to move down the slope where the men could find better shelter. Just as he was about to give this order, Georgians from Benning's Brigade arrived. The 20th Georgia moved directly against Smith's guns "with promptness and alacrity," while the 17th Georgia on its right passed the 44th Alabama "gallantly and with impetuosity." Benning's right-most regiment, the 2nd Georgia, entered Plum Run Gorge.[20]

Realizing that he needed additional support, General Ward had earlier sent a desperate plea for assistance to his division commander, Maj. Gen. David Birney. The result yielded the 40th New York from de Trobriand's brigade and the 6th New Jersey from Burling's, and both rushed to the area to bolster Ward's flagging prospects. Although there were no guides to lead them to Ward's left, the sound of Smith's cannons clearly marked the route.[21]

The Federal V Corps volunteered to send some troops toward the Wheatfield, which permitted Ward to move the 99th Pennsylvania from his right to his endangered left. When immediate help did not materialize, the commander of the 20th Indiana stretched his regiment to the right to cover the gap in the line. Losses sustained by the Federals battling the 3rd Arkansas were severe. The 20th Indiana lost 146 of 400 men in less than 30 minutes.[22]

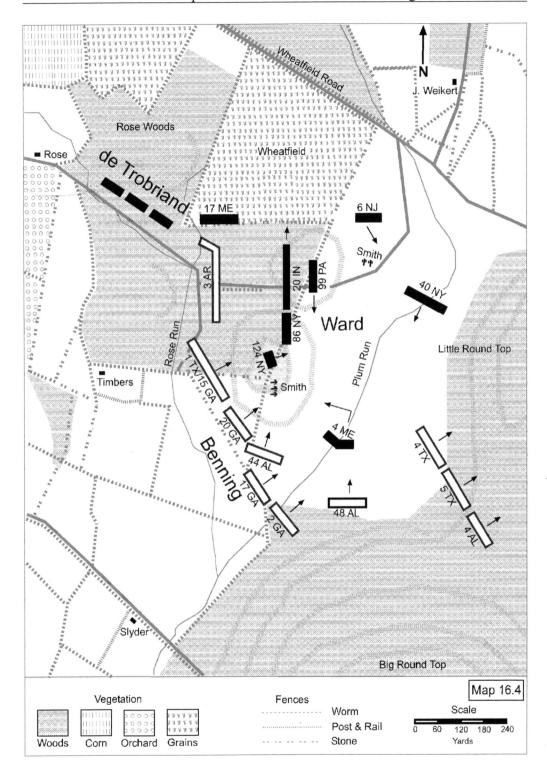

Map 16.4

Map 16.5

Major General John B. Hood's final brigade, commanded by Brig. Gen. George "Tige" Anderson, advanced toward the Wheatfield in line of battle on Benning's left. The movement attracted the attention of the 17th Maine, which in turn relieved the pressure on the 3rd Arkansas' left flank. Joined with the 1st Texas, 15th Georgia, and the left of the 20th Georgia, the 3rd Arkansas renewed its attack against General Ward's right and center. When it became obvious he could no longer hold his position, Ward ordered the 20th Indiana, 86th New York, and 124th New York to abandon Houck's Ridge. More than 140 men were captured before they could slip away to safety.[23]

Moving at a right oblique, the 4th Maine approached Smith's now-silent battery (the 1st Texas had driven away its gunners). The 99th Pennsylvania formed on its left and remnants of the 124th New York may have formed on its right. The three regiments attacked a portion of the 1st Texas, 15th Georgia, and 20th Georgia near Smith's guns and swept them from the ridge. The men of the 99th yelled, "Pennsylvania and our homes!" as they attacked. One Pennsylvanian recalled that his regiment fired "one volley, and with a dash . . . were into the thick of the fight. Above the crack of the rifle, the scream of shell and the cries of the wounded could be heard the shout for 'Pennsylvania and our homes.'" The Confederates took a few minutes to regroup before attacking again. The fighting quickly became hand-to-hand, and after a short time Southern numbers prevailed and the Federal troops finally abandoned the southern end of Houck's Ridge.[24]

Federal reinforcements finally began to arrive. The 600-man 40th New York deployed in the 4th Maine's former position in the Plum Run Valley. Captain Smith again begged for assistance in saving his guns, but Col. Thomas Egan had his own worries. The 48th Alabama was to his left and the 2nd and 17th Georgia regiments swamped Devil's Den in front of him. Colonel Egan couldn't withdraw, and standing pat was suicide. His alternative was to charge, and he took it. A sergeant in the 2nd Georgia recalled

the moment when his regiment encountered the 40th New York. "Above us then, quite twenty feet, on the edge of the rock stood a line of blue coated United States regulars firing straight down at our line which had become broken in passing over and around the huge boulders which barred our way." In this "Slaughter Pen," men on both sides fell in large numbers. The last two guns of Smith's battery that had been left in the rear opened a blistering fire on the advancing Confederates, shooting southwest into the valley. The two Georgia regiments fell back, taking position in the large rock formations of Devil's Den. Smith's other three guns on Houck's Ridge had already fallen into Confederate hands, and soon the other two fell silent, masked by the advance of the 40th New York.

The charge by Egan's men broke down as it approached strong Confederate defensive positions in the large rocks, although the New Yorkers tried several times to drive the enemy from Devil's Den. The 6th New Jersey (Burling's brigade) arrived and took position in the rear of the 40th New York. From that position it opened an oblique fire against the Alabamians near Devil's Den. With its attack halted and now threatened on its right flank by the Confederate troops who had captured Houck's Ridge, the 40th New York withdrew under the cover of fire from the 6th New Jersey.[25]

The 40th New York and the 6th New Jersey regiments retreated. The Devil's Den–Houck's Ridge sectors and three of Smith's cannon were now in Confederate hands. Worse still for the Federals was the fact that there was no sign of reinforcements to recapture this part of the battlefield.

The Confederates appeared to have driven away all organized opposition.[26]

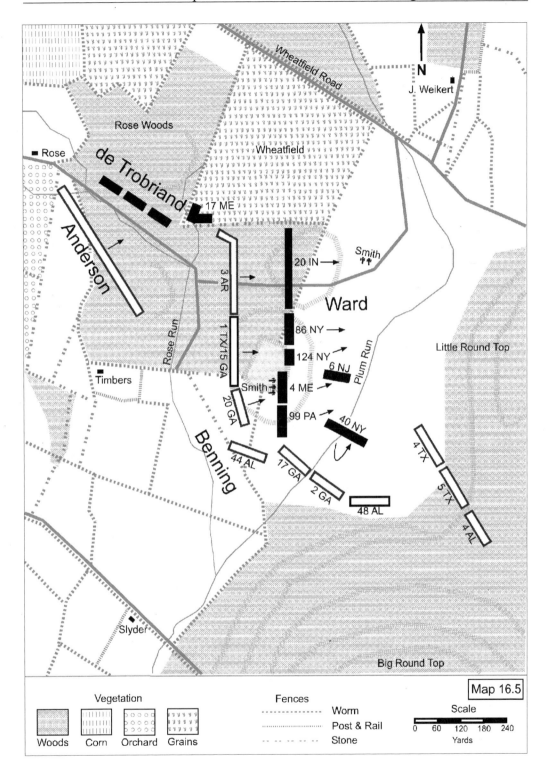

Map 16.5

Map Set 17: The Wheatfield and Stony Hill

Map 17.1

Colonel P. Regis de Trobriand's brigade (Birney's division, III Corps) held the sector between Ward's brigade on Houck's Ridge and Graham's brigade in the Peach Orchard. This area included Stony Hill and the Wheatfield.

Throwing the 3rd Michigan out on the skirmish line to the northwest, de Trobriand deployed the rest of the brigade along Rose Run facing southwest. The 110th Pennsylvania was on the right of the line, with the 5th Michigan on its left. The 40th New York and 17th Maine occupied the rear. The latter rushed to a stone wall in the Wheatfield as the Confederate attack began, helping repel the attack of the 3rd Arkansas (Robertson's Brigade) by firing into its left flank. The 40th New York was sent south to help defend Devil's Den, leaving a yawning gap between the 17th Maine and 5th Michigan.[1]

The Confederate brigade under Brig. Gen. George "Tige" Anderson moved forward to support Robertson's advance. Anderson, however, was unsure exactly where Robertson was fighting, so he did the next best thing and marched to the sound of the guns, which was most pronounced in the Wheatfield-Stony Hill sector. His men quickly stepped across the open fields toward the Federal positions with fire from Captain George Winslow's battery in the Wheatfield and from massed artillery in the Peach Orchard harassing every step. The brigade deployed from left to right as follows: 9th Georgia – 8th Georgia – 11th Georgia – 59th Georgia. The 8th and 9th Georgia regiments headed toward Stony Hill, while the 11th Georgia pointed toward the Wheatfield. The 59th Georgia on the right of the line fell in line with the 3rd Arkansas to take on the right side of Ward's brigade.[2]

Crossing Rose Run, Anderson's men encountered irregular ground with large rocks that wreaked havoc on the dressed ranks. It was in this area that Federal infantry now opened fire on Anderson's men. "Our line did not waver under the galling musketry, but came on almost at a run, firing vigorously," noted one Confederate soldier.[3]

After helping repel the initial attack of the 3rd Arkansas on their left, the men of the 17th Maine in the Wheatfield watched the 11th Georgia approaching on their right, "concealing themselves as much as possible, and using the shelter of the bank of the main branch of Plum Run," remembered an officer.[4]

As the 8th and 9th Georgia approached Stony Hill, the 115th Pennsylvania and 8th New Jersey of Col. George Burling's brigade arrived to fill the gap between the 17th Maine and 5th Michigan. The 8th Georgia attacked the 115th Pennsylvania and 8th New Jersey, while the 9th Georgia hit the 5th Michigan and 110th Pennsylvania.[5]

Colonel de Trobriand described this position on the right as a "strong one, in a wood commanding a narrow ravine, which the enemy attempted in vain to cross under our fire." Deadly Federal fire forced the Confederates to take cover behind the banks of Rose Run. The right of the 110th Pennsylvania extended beyond the left flank of the 9th Georgia, and according to one Confederate officer, "bullets were coming from our front; enfilading from our left; and also diagonally from our rear." Anderson refused his left three companies to face this threat.[6]

Finding a gap on the right of the 8th New Jersey, the right side of the 9th Georgia and part of the 8th Georgia quickly exploited it, forcing the New Jersey soldiers to abandon their position and pull back. The 115th Pennsylvania soon followed, retreating through the Wheatfield before halting to support Winslow's belching guns. The 17th Maine held firm, refusing its right flank and throwing enfilade fire into the Georgians. The 5th Michigan and 110th Pennsylvania at the other end of the line also sent volleys into the attacking enemy formations.

With little to show for his hour of fighting the stubborn enemy except scores of dead and wounded soldiers, "Tige" Anderson pulled his brigade rearward to reform it and await the arrival of reinforcements.[7]

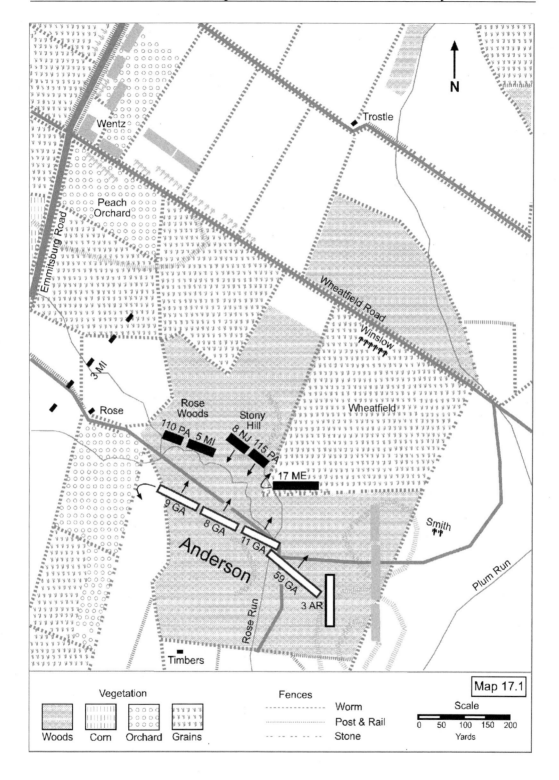

N

Trostle

Wentz

Peach
Orchard

Emmitsburg Road

Wheatfield Road

Winslow

3 MI

Rose

Rose
Woods

Stony
Hill

8 NJ 115 PA

Wheatfield

110 PA 5 MI

17 ME

Smith

9 GA

8 GA

Anderson

11 GA

59 GA

Plum Run

Rose Run

3 AR

Timbers

Vegetation				Fences			Map 17.1

Worm

Post & Rail

Stone

Scale

0   50   100   150   200
Yards

Woods   Corn   Orchard   Grains

Map 17.2

Federal reinforcements from Maj. Gen. George Sykes' V Corps moved south from their reserve positions to counter "Tige" Anderson's attacks on Stony Hill and the Wheatfield. The men of the 8th New Jersey could see Col. William Tilton's and Col. Jacob Sweitzer's brigades of Barnes' division approaching, but continued their flight away from Anderson's Georgians. Colonel Tilton's men took position on Stony Hill's southern slope with the 22nd Massachusetts forming the left, the 1st Michigan the center, and the 118th Pennsylvania the right. The latter regiment's right flank was refused to conform to the irregular edge of Stony Hill, facing west. The 18th Massachusetts remained in reserve behind the 1st Michigan, facing southwest. The 110th Pennsylvania and 5th Michigan were to the front and right of Tilton's men, extending the line toward the Rose farm house. Colonel Sweitzer's brigade faced west, deploying with the 32nd Massachusetts on the left, the 62nd Pennsylvania in the center, and the 4th Michigan on the right. Colonel Sweitzer did not like either the low open position held by the 32nd Massachusetts or its exposed left flank, so he refused the regiment at right angles to the rest of the brigade. His flank now faced southwest, in the approximate position previously occupied by Burling's pair of two now departed regiments.[8]

General Joseph Kershaw's South Carolina brigade, part of McLaws' Division, began advancing from Seminary Ridge about the time Anderson's men launched their second attack on the Federal positions in the Wheatfield and Stony Hill. Kershaw intended to throw his entire brigade against Stony Hill. Brigadier General William Barksdale's delayed advance, however, forced Kershaw to direct his left wing, composed of the 2nd and 8th South Carolina regiments and the 3rd South Carolina Battalion, to neutralize the massed Federal artillery in the Peach Orchard. The right wing, composed of the 3rd and 7th South Carolina, continued its advance to the left of the 9th Georgia of Anderson's Brigade.[9]

The men of the 118th Pennsylvania, holding the right of Tilton's Federal brigade line, heard the Rebel advance before they could see it. "The musketry rolled in continuous roar, volley after volley was poured in heavily as nearer and near the enemy approached the right. The ground trembled, the trees shook and limbs quivered," wrote an enlisted man. Joseph Kershaw's South Carolinians emerged through the smoke, "moving with a shout, shriek, curse and yell," recalled the unit's historian. The men also saw that the enemy "were moving obliquely, loading and firing with deliberation as they advanced, begrimed and dirty-looking fellows, in all sorts of garb, some without hats, others without coats, none apparently in the real dress or uniform of a soldier." Tilton's men opened fire, grinding the enemy advance to a stop. The Pennsylvanians stood erect when they fired, their accurate delivery causing the casualties to mount within Kershaw's ranks. Tilton's men were successfully thwarting Kershaw to their front, but movements beyond their left flank were increasing their concern.[10]

Colonel Jacob Sweitzer's men were barely in position when Anderson's Georgians attacked them. Sweitzer ordered his brigade realigned, with the 62nd Pennsylvania and 4th Michigan regiments assuming a supporting position along the slope toward Wheatfield Road behind the 32nd Massachusetts.[11] Anderson's left wing, composed of the 8th and 9th Georgia, moved past the 5th Michigan and 110th Pennsylvania of de Trobriand's brigade and engaged Sweitzer's 32nd Massachusetts. Two of de Trobriand's regiments, the 5th Michigan and 110th Pennsylvania, continued throwing enfilade fire into the flank of the 9th Georgia, disorganizing the line until it finally stopped advancing altogether.

By this time if not before, Anderson realized he needed help if he was going to break through the enemy position. He found it in the form of Kershaw's 15th South Carolina. On the Federal left, the 17th Maine continued holding out against the 11th Georgia and possibly the right flank of the 8th Georgia.[12]

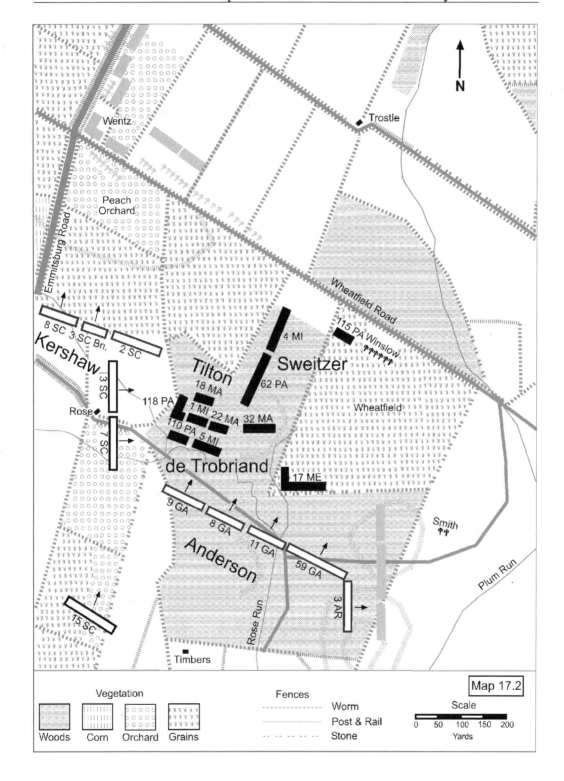

N

Wentz

Trostle

Peach
Orchard

Emmitsburg Road

Wheatfield Road

Kershaw

8 SC 3 SC Bn. 2 SC

3 SC

118 PA

Rose

7 SC

4 MI

115 PA Winslow

Tilton

Sweitzer

18 MA

62 PA

1 MI 22 MA 32 MA

110 PA 5 MI

Wheatfield

de Trobriand

17 ME

9 GA

8 GA

11 GA

59 GA

3 AR

Smith

Anderson

Rose Run

Plum Run

15 SC

Timbers

Vegetation				Fences			Map 17.2

Vegetation

Woods   Corn   Orchard   Grains

Fences

- - - - - - - - Worm
.... Post & Rail
- - - - - - Stone

Map 17.2

Scale

0   50   100   150   200

Yards

Map 17.3

Brigadier General Joseph Kershaw's South Carolina brigade was having a tough time of it. Split into two wings, three regiments veered north to attack the Peach Orchard, while the other wing of two regiments attacked due east toward Stony Hill and the poorly aligned Federal troops there. The latter pair of regiments somehow entangled themselves during the advance, forcing Kershaw to order the 7th South Carolina to "move to the right a little to open out the line." This accomplished, the attack on Stony Hill continued.[13]

A nervous Colonel Tilton, who had never commanded a brigade in combat before, sent an aide back to Brig. Gen. James Barnes with word that he did not think he could hold his position. Not a lion on this day, Barnes sent orders for Tilton to withdraw his brigade. This order relieved the men. "Shot, shell and bullets flying pretty thick here. Men are dropping pretty fast," an anonymous soldier in the 1st Michigan noted in his diary. "We are outflanked both right and left and fall back." Colonel de Trobriand could not believe his eyes when he saw Tilton's men withdrawing. He tried to no avail to get them back to their positions.[14]

Not all of Colonel Tilton's men were happy when told to vacate their position on Stony Hill. Members of the 118th Pennsylvania shouted, "No retreat! No retreat! We're on our own soil!" When most of the others pulled back, however, they had no choice but to obey. The unit joined the rest of Tilton's brigade in the Trostle Woods and all three regiments continued their retreat, heading northeast toward Cemetery Ridge. Tilton's withdrawal exposed the left flank of Sweitzer's brigade. Barnes ordered Sweitzer to pull back also, which he did by marching his men out by the right flank.[15]

The 110th Pennsylvania and 5th Michigan suddenly found themselves in a very hazardous position with enemy infantry approaching their front and both flanks. They too turned and headed for the rear. Riding over to the 17th Maine along the stone wall in the Wheatfield, de Trobriand ordered it to withdraw. Almost as soon as the unit reached Wheatfield Road, Maj.

Gen. David Birney ordered it back into the Wheatfield. The regiment was soon joined by the 5th Michigan and 115th Pennsylvania, and all three exchanged fire with Anderson's men, who had taken the stone wall that had previously sheltered the 17th Maine. Winslow's battery kept the Confederates at bay behind the safety of the wall. In the meantime, Kershaw's 3rd and 7th South Carolina continued their advance and took possession of Stony Hill. Just as it looked as though the Federal position was unraveling, help arrived for Birney's men in the form of Brig. Gen. John Caldwell's entire II Corps division, marching rapidly from its former position on Cemetery Ridge.[16]

General Caldwell halted his division along Wheatfield Road and deployed his men. Colonel Edward Cross, whose brigade led the column south, was on the left, aligned from left to right as follows: 5th New Hampshire – 148th Pennsylvania – 81st Pennsylvania – 61st New York.

Although Brig. Gen. Samuel Zook's brigade was the last in Caldwell's column, it had been diverted by a III Corps staff officer and reached its position just after Cross. Zook deployed his brigade in two lines. From left to right, the first line was composed of three regiments: 66th New York – 52nd New York – 140th Pennsylvania. Only a shadow of their former selves, the three New York outfits were so small they had been consolidated into one (although they retained their unit designations). The 57th New York formed the second line.

Colonel Patrick Kelly's Irish Brigade, which had marched behind Cross, took position between these two brigades. Kelly's brigade was deployed from left to right as follows: 63rd New York – 69th New York – 88th New York – 28th Massachusetts – 116th Pennsylvania.

General Caldwell's fourth brigade, under Col. John Brooke, formed the division's reserve.[17]

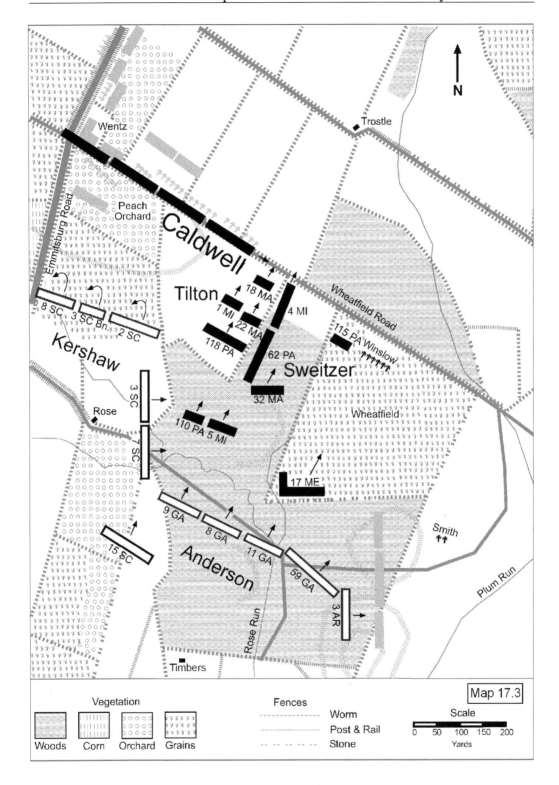

Trostle

Wentz

Peach
Orchard

Caldwell

Emmitsburg Road

Tilton

18 MA

1 MI

22 MA

4 MI

118 PA

62 PA

Wheatfield Road

115 PA Winslow

8 SC   3 SC Bn.   2 SC

Kershaw

Sweitzer

3 SC

32 MA

Rose

110 PA 5 MI

Wheatfield

7 SC

17 ME

9 GA

8 GA

Anderson

11 GA

Smith

15 SC

59 GA

Rose Run

3 AR

Plum Run

Timbers

Map 17.3

Vegetation

Fences

Worm

Post & Rail

Stone

Scale

0   50   100   150   200

Yards

Woods   Corn   Orchard   Grains

Map 17.4

Following Brig. Gen. John Caldwell's orders, Col. Edward Cross advanced his brigade across the Wheatfield, moving southwest in an oblique. As a result, the right side of the line was farther into the Wheatfield than the left side. The latter, composed of the 5th New Hampshire and part of the 148th Pennsylvania, entered the northeast corner of the Rose's Woods while the remainder of the brigade advanced through the open and unprotected field. Because the movement into the Wheatfield was so rapid, Cross did not have time to throw out a skirmish line. Seeing the Federals advancing, Anderson's Georgians dove behind the shelter of the stone wall at the opposite end of the Wheatfield, which had previously sheltered the 17th Maine, and opened fire.[18]

Brigadier General Samuel Zook's brigade advanced next toward Stony Hill, moving gingerly through Col. Jacob Sweitzer's prone men along Wheatfield Road. The 66th and part of the 52nd New York on the left of the line marched through the northeast corner of the Wheatfield, while the 140th Pennsylvania moved with considerable difficulty through the woods leading to Stony Hill. A soldier in the 140th Pennsylvania recalled the "scores of huge uprising boulders, so thickly set that we had great difficulty to preserve our alignment."[19]

As Zook's men advanced toward Stony Hill, they could see "through a dense pall of smoke and stifling heat . . . a blaze of light in front, revealing the dark forms of a double line of men who were actively engaging the enemy." The dark forms were men from the Irish Brigade on their left, which plugged the gap between Zook's and Cross' brigades.[20]

Because the Irish Brigade, commanded by Col. Patrick Kelly, was obliquing through the Wheatfield in the same alignment as Cross' brigade, only the New York regiments on the left had to march a considerable distance through the open ground. The right side of the brigade, comprised of most of the 28th Massachusetts and the 116th Pennsylvania, soon left the open Wheatfield and advanced through the woods leading to Stony Hill. Two Federal lines collided

there, the 116th Pennsylvania mingling with the 66th New York of Zook's brigade, forcing the Pennsylvanians to undertake a "right flank movement."[21]

As the two Federal brigades advanced against Stony Hill, the 3rd and 7th South Carolina of Kershaw's Brigade scrambled up the heights after scattering the last of de Trobriand's men from the sector. Because of the speed of the Federal advance, the South Carolinians were unable to take up proper defensive positions before being attacked on two sides. Kershaw requested help from Brig. Gen. Paul Semmes' Brigade (McLaws' Division) and attempted to get his 15th South Carolina into the fighting.[22]

According to an officer on the left of Zook's line, "we pressed steadily forward through wheat-fields, woods, over rail fences 10 feet high, stone walls, ditches, deep ravines, rocks, and all sorts of obstructions, every one of which had served as cover for the enemy, and from which a murderous fire was poured upon us as we advanced, but without avail, as nothing could stop the impetuosity of our men."[23]

Meanwhile, "Tige" Anderson's Georgians continued firing at Cross' men advancing across the open Wheatfield. One of Caldwell's staff officers recalled that "every rock, tree and bush concealed a sharpshooter and the moment the heads of Cross' line appear above the crest of the hill the edge of the wood along his entire front and right flank is fringed with a blaze of musketry."

After advancing a short distance into the field, Cross ordered his men to level their rifled muskets and return the enemy's fire. In a field of breast-high ripening wheat, a private from the 148th Pennsylvania recalled "how the ears of wheat flew in the air all over the field as they were cut off by the enemy's bullets." Federal casualties were heaviest on the right side of the line, where the 61st New York lost nearly two-thirds of its men.[24]

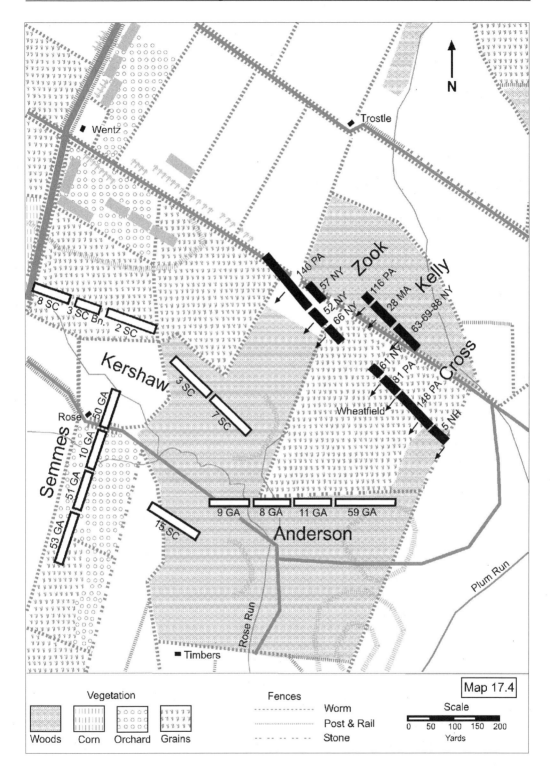

Map 17.4

Vegetation

Woods   Corn   Orchard   Grains

Fences
.... Worm
.... Post & Rail
.... Stone

Scale
0   50   100   150   200
Yards

Map 17.5

With his men falling by the score, Colonel Cross realized that to stand was suicide and retreat offered possibilities nearly as unpalatable. He realized his only viable option was to charge the enemy and drive them from the perimeter of the Wheatfield.

Cross walked to the left of his line to order his former regiment, the 5th New Hampshire, to advance. A bullet drilled into his body, mortally wounding the colonel. The charge went off without him. Because the stone wall protecting "Tige" Anderson's men stood at approximately a forty-five degree angle to Cross' advance, the 5th New Hampshire and part of the 148th Pennsylvania rolled up Anderson's right flank. Within a short time the entire Southern brigade began making for the rear. A private in the 148th Pennsylvania recalled how "the rebels continued to fire into the right of our line until we leaped on the wall and took them in flank." Colonel H. Boyd McKeen, who had assumed brigade command when Cross fell, halted the men when the brigade's right flank reached the crest of the knoll, about midway into the Wheatfield. McKeen's left flank at this time occupied the stone wall.[25]

Joe Kershaw's two Confederate regiments on Stony Hill opened fire on Zook's brigade, but their initial volleys were too high and ineffective. The men settled down and the fire became more deadly. "Men reeled and fell on every side, but with daunting courage those who survived stood their ground until the order came to fall back," recalled a Federal soldier. Zook's men returned the enemy fire. On the right of the line, the 140th Pennsylvania battled the 3rd South Carolina to its front while suffering under a deadly flanking fire from the 2nd South Carolina to the southwest.[26]

Because Zook's brigade occupied the South Carolinians' attention, Colonel Kelly's Irish Brigade advanced undetected and unharmed. The 7th South Carolina finally saw this movement and loosened a volley that flew harmlessly over the heads of the men on the right of the brigade. The Irish Brigade returned a more deadly fire, forcing the right of the 7th South Carolina to be refused to face this new threat. According to an officer in the 69th New York, "after our line delivered one or two volleys, the enemy were noticed to waver, and upon the advance of our line (firing) the enemy fell back, contesting the ground doggedly. One charge to the front brought us in a lot of prisoners."

Meanwhile, the 116th Pennsylvania on the right side of the line quietly approached the 7th South Carolina, opening fire from about forty feet away with its deadly short-range "buck and ball" ammunition. As Maj. St. Clair Mulholland aptly put it, "a blind man could not have missed the mark." The two sides blazed away at each other at point-blank range for about ten minutes. According to General Kershaw, the two sides exchanged fire from less than thirty paces. The fighting forced Kershaw to refuse the right flank of the 7th South Carolina even more, until "the two wings of the regiment were nearly doubled on each other."[27]

Kershaw knew a tight spot when he saw one. He sorely needed help if he was going to maintain his position. Luckily for the South Carolinians, help was on the way as Brig. Gen. Paul Semmes' Brigade stepped quickly to his assistance. The 50th Georgia on the left rushed toward Stony Hill at the double-quick and opened fire on the enemy. The 50th's left flank, however, did not connect with the refused right flank of the 7th South Carolina. The result was a gap about 100 yards wide yawning invitingly between the two regiments. Veterans of the Irish Brigade spotted the tactical opportunity and quickly worked to exploit it.[28]

After holding its position for about half an hour, the right side of Cross' brigade was almost out of men and ammunition. Caldwell threw in Col. Edward Brooke's brigade to relieve it. The 5th New Hampshire and part of the 148th Pennsylvania on the left of Cross' line retained their positions and continued blazing away at Anderson's Georgia troops, while the rest of the brigade drifted rearward through the smoke and confusion.[29]

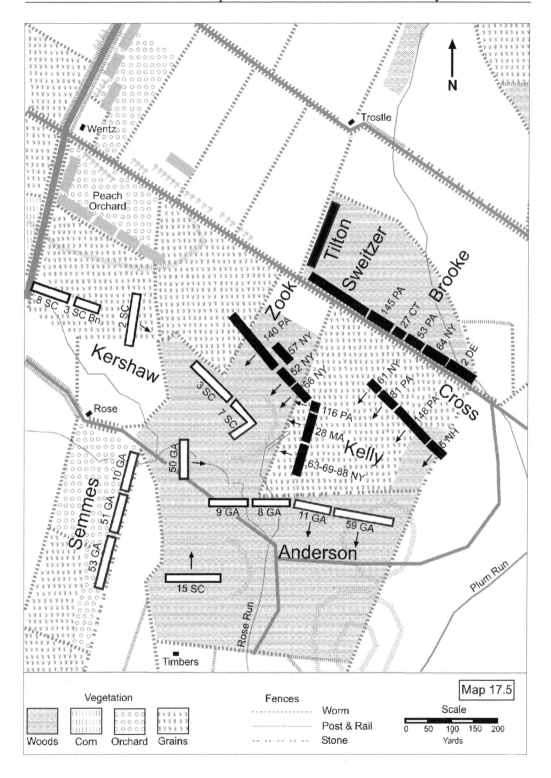

Map 17.5

Map 17.6

The 853 men of Col. John Brooke's small brigade (Caldwell's Second Division, II Corps), deployed from left to right as follows: 2nd Delaware – 64th New York – 53rd Pennsylvania – 27th Connecticut – 145th Pennsylvania, and advanced rapidly through the Wheatfield. Brooke recalled that his brigade spanned almost the entire width of the field. Reaching Cross' position about half way into the field, Brooke ordered his men to "Halt, fire at will!" for about five minutes. Brooke then moved the brigade forward after ordering his men to fix bayonets. "It was a deafening roar, and it was very difficult to hear the commands given, and took some effort to start the line forward into another charge," recalled a soldier in the 64th New York. In the ear-splitting noise and smoky chaos, Brooke grabbed the 53rd Pennsylvania's colors and carried them forward. The entire brigade rose and followed, driving Anderson's Georgians into and through Rose's Woods.[30]

As Brooke's men scrambled through the timber after Anderson's men, large rocks and ledges disordered their formations. The advance continued until the brigade reached the edge of the woods adjacent to the open pasture north of the sprawling patch of timber. There, the men observed Semmes' fresh Georgia brigade "drawn up in readiness just beyond [the woods], within pistol range" in the open field in front of them. Semmes' Brigade deployed from left to right as follows: 10th Georgia – 51st Georgia – 53rd Georgia. The 50th Georgia was farther to the left (north), supporting Kershaw's two regiments on Stony Hill. "[W]e then advanced about 60 yards and stopped behind some rocks, which however, did not afford much protection because they only projected from 12 to 18 inches above the surface," wrote one of the Georgians. The two lines immediately exchanged volleys, but the Southerners were standing in the open. The lead missiles tore into their ranks and dropped dozens of men. A soldier from the 10th Georgia observed that "many fell along this line." General Semmes had already suffered what would prove to be a mortal wound, and several other field officers were knocked out of action.

Semmes' line buckled, held for a few moments, and then fell back.[31]

On Stony Hill, the 2nd South Carolina arrived on Kershaw's left flank. After crossing Emmitsburg Road, the regiment suffered terribly from a pounding delivered by Federal artillery deployed near the Peach Orchard. When they reached the front, the South Carolinians took position on the left flank of the 3rd South Carolina in time to help take on Zook's large 140th Pennsylvania.

Meanwhile, just south of Stony Hill, Col. Patrick Kelly ordered his Irish Brigade to charge the South Carolinians, driving northwest in the direction of Emmitsburg Road. According to Major Mulholland of the 116th Pennsylvania, "in charging we had literally ran right in among them." Trapped in a nutcracker as Federal troops closed on them from two sides, the three South Carolina regiments began to break apart. Unable to withstand the simultaneous pressure in front and along its right flank, the 7th South Carolina broke for the rear. The 3rd South Carolina refused its right flank, but it too was overwhelmed and forced to join in the retreat. The last of the three regiments, the 2nd South Carolina, had no choice but to withdraw or stand firm and be surrounded and destroyed. It, too, fell back. Most of these men gathered to reorganize around the Rose farmstead.[32]

More Federal reinforcements were about to be fed into the Wheatfield cauldron, Regular Army soldiers to a man. Colonel Hannibal Day's brigade of 1,557 men and Col. Sidney Burbank's brigade, 954 strong (both of Barnes' division, V Corps) approached the Wheatfield from the south and took up positions well to the east of Brooke's brigade along the eastern fringe of Rose's Woods. They faced the Wheatfield.

Burbank's brigade was in the first line, deployed from left to right as follows: 17th U.S. – 11th U.S. – 10th U.S. – 7th U.S. – 2nd U.S. Day's brigade formed a supporting line, deployed from left to right as follows: 14th U.S. – 12th U.S. – 6th U.S. – 4th U.S. – 3rd U.S. The appearance of 2,500 veterans threatened to tip the balance in favor of the Federals.[33]

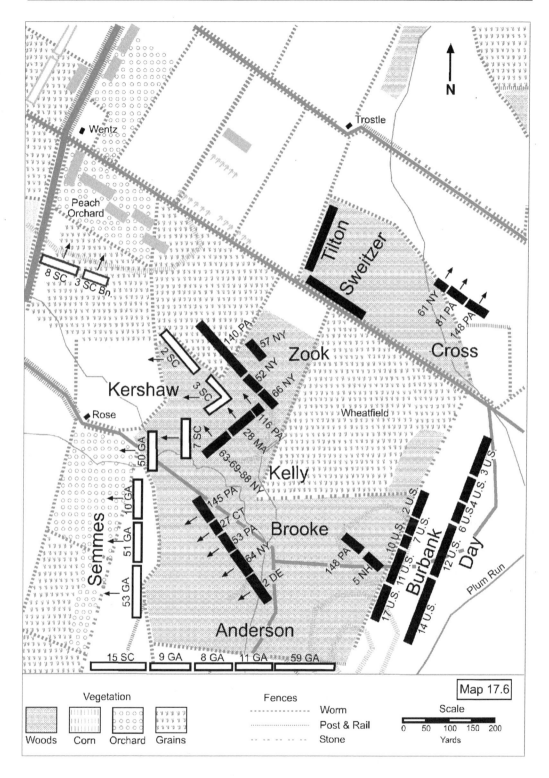

Wentz

Trostle

N

Peach
Orchard

Tilton

Sweitzer

8 SC 3 SC Bn.

61 NY 81 PA
148 PA

Cross

140 PA

57 NY

2 SC

52 NY

Zook

Kershaw

3 SC

66 NY

Rose

7 SC

116 PA

Wheatfield

28 MA

50 GA

63-69-88 NY

Kelly

145 PA

10 GA

27 CT

Brooke

4 U.S. 3 U.S.

Semmes

51 GA

53 PA

64 NY

2 U.S.

6 U.S.

10 U.S. 7 U.S.

12 U.S.

Burbank

Day

53 GA

2 DE

148 PA

5 NH

17 U.S. 11 U.S.

14 U.S.

Plum Run

Anderson

15 SC   9 GA   8 GA   11 GA   59 GA

Vegetation

Woods   Corn   Orchard   Grains

Fences

············ Worm
············ Post & Rail
― ― ― ― Stone

Map 17.6

Scale

0   50   100   150   200

Yards

Map 17.7

By this time in the fighting, Col. John Brooke's line resembled something of a crescent, with the 53rd Pennsylvania at the advanced center of the bulging line. While successfully clearing its front of Confederates, Brooke's rapid advance had outpaced Federal support on either side. The rapid advance left both of his flanks hanging in the air. Brooke had another problem: ammunition was down to an average of five rounds per man.

Brooke knew he needed reinforcements and quickly requested them from General Caldwell. Failing their arrival, he at least required additional ammunition to try and hold his position. Before he received a reply, word reached Brooke that a large body of enemy troops (probably a portion of Anderson's Georgia brigade) was descending on his left flank. Small arms fire began ripping into that part of the line. Before Brooke could rearrange his troops to deal with this threat, another aide brought news that Confederate troops (almost certainly regiments from Paul Semmes' brigade) were bearing down on his exposed right flank. The ridge, wrote a Federal soldier in his diary, was "the hottest place we came across that day." The firing was so intense the men "loaded their pieces under shelter of the brow of the hill, then rising up, delivered their fire." Brooke refused the 2nd Delaware's left, while he stood on a large boulder near the left-center of his line to better direct the action.[34]

More Confederate troops poured into the sector. Brigadier General William Wofford's Brigade (Lafayette McLaws' Division) swept east down Wheatfield Road, a 400-yard battle line that cleared everything in its front. Wofford's units were aligned from left to right as follows: Cobb Legion – Phillip's Legion – 24th Georgia – 18th Georgia – 16th Georgia. Wofford's left skirted the Peach Orchard while his right moved toward Stony Hill and the Wheatfield. "Our Men charged the Enemy with a terrific Yell, peculiar to the Southerners on all such occasions," a Southern surgeon recalled. The left wing of Kershaw's Brigade, comprised of the 2nd and 8th South Carolina regiments and the 3rd South Carolina Battalion, reentered the fighting on Wofford's right.[35]

The men of the 140th Pennsylvania, fighting on the right of Zook's line, were the first to see Wofford's grand approach. Because they came from the general direction of the Peach Orchard, where Graham's brigade was engaging the Confederates, the Pennsylvanians initially received orders to hold their fire. The men realized the error when "a volley of musketry which enfiladed our line and revealed the enemy, [which] envelop[ed] our flank in such a way as to make escape impossible," noted an enlisted man. Lieutenant Colonel John Fraser, now in command of the brigade because General Zook had received a mortal wound, saw that he was about to be flanked and ordered a retreat. As a soldier in the 140th Pennsylvania put it, "we were completely flanked and cut our way out." The regiment lost nearly half of its men during its short sojourn in the Wheatfield.[36]

As the right wing of Zook's brigade collapsed, the officers of the 116th Pennsylvania (part of the Irish Brigade) ordered each man to "look to his own safety, pointing out the direction they were to take towards Little Round Top." A staff officer arrived and yelled at the men, "You are surrounded; retreat and save as many men as possible!"[37]

As Wofford's Brigade closed on his right flank, and Anderson's, Semmes', and Kershaw's brigades assailed his front and left, Colonel Brooke realized that he could no longer hold his position. His brigade had spent fifteen brutal minutes on the ridge, each minute preciously purchased. The historian of the 2nd Delaware proudly wrote that Brooke's brigade "reached the farthest point gained by any of the Union troops during the day." Enveloping Confederate forces forced Brooke's soldiers to run a terrible gauntlet of fire that dropped scores of men killed and wounded. Many more were captured.

Colonels Sweitzer, Burbank, and Day, however, had their respective brigades aligned on the eastern periphery of the Wheatfield, ready to enter the fight.[38]

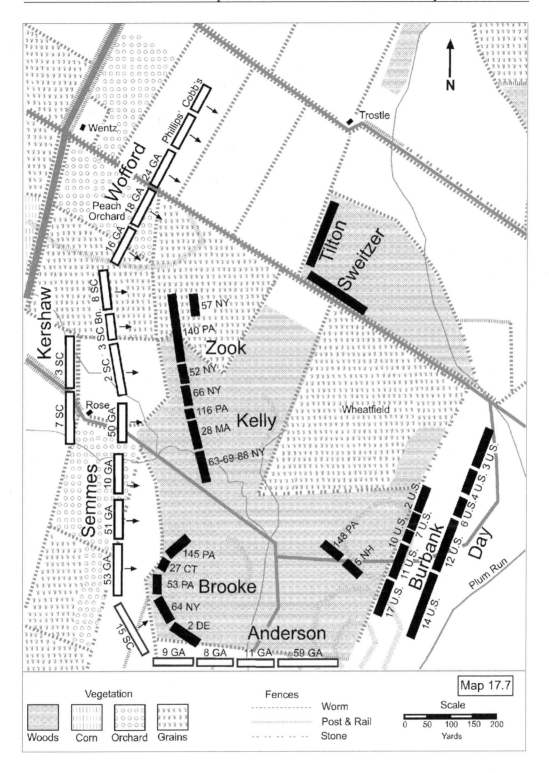

N

Wentz

Trostle

Wofford

Phillips' Cobb's

24 GA

18 GA

16 GA

Peach
Orchard

Tilton

Sweitzer

Kershaw

8 SC

3 SC Bn.

3 SC

2 SC

57 NY

140 PA

Zook

7 SC

Rose

50 GA

52 NY

66 NY

116 PA

28 MA

Kelly

Wheatfield

63-69-88 NY

Semmes

10 GA

51 GA

53 GA

148 PA

5 NH

10 U.S.

2 U.S.

7 U.S.

11 U.S.

12 U.S.

6 U.S.

4 U.S.

3 U.S.

Burbank

Day

145 PA

27 CT

53 PA

Brooke

64 NY

17 U.S.

14 U.S.

Plum Run

2 DE

Anderson

15 SC

9 GA   8 GA   11 GA   59 GA

Vegetation

Woods   Corn   Orchard   Grains

Fences

------------ Worm

.... Post & Rail

– – – – – – Stone

Scale

Map 17.7

0   50   100   150   200
Yards

Map 17.8

Desperately seeking assistance, General Caldwell recalled Colonel Sweitzer's brigade back into the bloody Wheatfield. With the 32nd Massachusetts on the left, the 4th Michigan on the right, and the 62nd Pennsylvania in the center, the front of the 1,000-man brigade probably stretched about 300 yards, which covered most of the Wheatfield. Sweitzer's infantry quickly reached the stone wall where the 17th Maine had earlier taken up its position.[39]

Sweitzer's arrival was too late to alter the course of events there. The last of Caldwell's division streamed past his reinforcements. Soon after Zook's fleeing men passed them, a deadly flank fire hit the 4th Michigan's right flank. Sweitzer believed this fire was from "our troops aimed over us at the enemy in the woods beyond and falling short." The unit's flag bearer shouted, "Colonel, I'll be _____ if I don't think we are faced the wrong way; the rebs are up there in the woods behind us, on the right." Through the din of battle, remembered one Federal soldier, the men heard the "rattling of canteens and a heavy tread of infantry . . . in our rear, observing a little closer, we saw that they wore the gray uniform and were not over 10 rods distant. They were on double quick passing through the woods out into the wheat field east of us." The heavily treading infantry was Wofford's Georgians, who had already flanked Caldwell's division and were in the process of doing the same to Sweitzer.[40]

When he spotted the danger, Sweitzer ordered the 4th Michigan and 62nd Pennsylvania to face right to confront the new threat. Most of four Confederate brigades (Anderson's, Kershaw's, Semmes', and Wofford's) were now advancing against Sweitzer's three regiments. Some of Anderson's men could see a Federal flag bearer six feet in front of the main line. Stepping back into line, the Georgians knew what was coming next. "With the precision of a dress parade, that magnificent line of Federals lowered their pieces and the volley came." Most of the Georgians had already taken cover behind the bank of Rose Run, so most of the bullets passed harmlessly overhead. Anderson's men returned the fire, and it appeared to them that every shot hit its mark. According to one officer's exaggerated boast, "there was not one of the enemy left standing in our front."

Sweitzer had earlier dispatched an aide to find his division commander, Brig. Gen. James Barnes, to seek immediate help. Instead of finding Barnes, the aide found enemy infantry and quickly returned to inform Sweitzer that Confederates were also in his rear. Realizing how desperate the situation had become, Sweitzer ordered his men to fall back. The movement, he later reported, "was done in order, the command halting and firing as it retired." The colonel was likely putting the best spin on a bad situation. A private in the 32nd Massachusetts recalled the order this way: "Left face, and every man get out of this the best way he can." Getting out proved a deadly affair, and many men were killed, wounded, or captured attempting to do so.

John Coxe of the 2nd South Carolina recalled that as the men rushed forward to engage the Federal troops, a "tremendous Rebel yell went up from our powder-choked throats." Hand-to-hand combat was common up and down the line during this desperate period. Colonel Harrison Jeffords of the 4th Michigan saw his regimental colors captured and turned back to retrieve them, but was bayoneted during the resulting melee and later died. A soldier in the 4th Michigan recalled that when his regiment had to run the gauntlet, "the crash came—a storm of lead swept through our ranks like hail. Many of our noble boys fell to the ground." As the Confederate line advanced, the infantrymen discovered "a long blue line on the ground so close together that anyone could have walked over them as far as their front extended, without touching the earth."[41]

Meanwhile, the 5th New Hampshire and 148th Pennsylvania of Cross' brigade began vacating their positions in Rose's Woods just to the south (left) of Sweitzer's men. Southeast of the Wheatfield, Day's and Burbank's Regular brigades anxiously awaited orders to engage the enemy.[42]

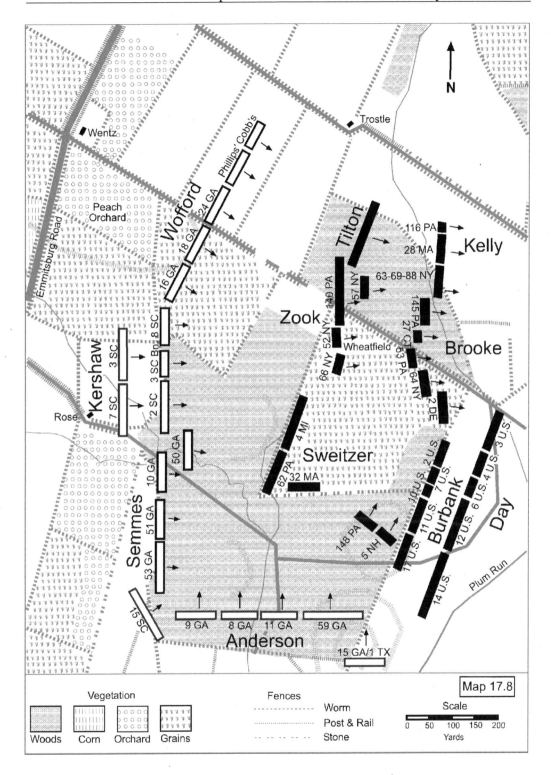

N

Wentz

Trostle

Phillips' Cobb's

Peach
Orchard

Wofford

24 GA

18 GA

16 GA

Tilton

116 PA

28 MA

Kelly

63-69-88 NY

145 PA

27 CT

Zook

140 PA

57 NY

52 NY

Wheatfield

Brooke

63 PA

Kershaw

3 SC Bn

8 SC

3 SC

99 NY

64 NY

2 DE

3 SC

7 SC

2 SC

Rose

50 GA

4 MI

Sweitzer

62 PA

32 MA

3 U.S.

2 U.S.

Semmes

10 GA

7 U.S.

10 U.S.

Burbank

6 U.S.

4 U.S.

51 GA

148 PA

11 U.S.

12 U.S.

Day

5 NH

53 GA

17 U.S.

14 U.S.

Plum Run

15 SC

9 GA

8 GA

11 GA

59 GA

Anderson

15 GA/1 TX

Map 17.8

Vegetation				Fences		Scale

Woods   Corn   Orchard   Grains

Worm

Post & Rail

Stone

0   50   100   150   200

Yards

Map 17.9

Swinging his line to the left, Col. Sidney Burbank moved his brigade into the Wheatfield, perpendicular to its original reserve position, to face down Anderson's and Semmes' advancing brigades. The 2nd and 7th U.S. formed the right of his brigade in the Wheatfield, while the other regiments occupied the northeastern portion of Rose's Woods. Burbank believed the section of woods in front of him had to be filled with the enemy, so he ordered his men to fire a volley into it. When no reply was forthcoming, he ordered his men to cease firing. Meanwhile, Col. Hannibal Day moved his brigade forward to occupy Burbank's former position on the periphery of Rose's Woods. The 5th New Hampshire and a portion of the 148th Pennsylvania continued moving to the rear to rejoin Colonel Cross' battered brigade. Colonel Sweitzer continued moving survivors of his beleaguered brigade out of the Wheatfield.[43]

By now, matters were utterly confused (much more so than battle reports indicate or convey). Elements from Semmes' and Anderson's brigades charged through the woods against Burbank's Regulars, but an effective volley stopped them in their tracks. According to the commander of the 2nd U.S., "a fresh column of the enemy at this time appearing upon our right, we were ordered to retire. The word was scarcely given when three lines of the enemy, elevated one above the other on the slope to our right, poured in a most destructive fire, almost decimating my regiment." The firing was from Wofford's men and perhaps some of Kershaw's South Carolinians. According to a soldier in the 11th U.S., the order to withdraw was to "face about and wheel to the right at the double quick and form on the general line of battle." In his report, Colonel Burbank wrote that this withdrawal was made "as rapidly and in as good order as the nature of the ground would permit."

Some of the men, particularly those in the center, did not see the threat on the right and complained about the order. The sheer noise and confusion was another problem. According to Captain William Clinton of the 10th U.S. in the center of the brigade, "the roar of musketry was so extensive that a great portion of our command did not hear the order to fall back until some minutes after it had been given. The enemy at this time was in front and on both our flanks."[44]

General Romeyn Ayres, commander of the division, could see that his two remaining brigades were in danger of annihilation and ordered their retreat. A young Federal lieutenant recalled that the Regulars "moved off the field in admirable style, with well-aligned ranks, facing about at times to deliver their fire and check pursuit . . . in this action the regulars sustained severe losses, but gave ample evidence of the fighting qualities, discipline, and steadiness under fire which made them the pattern and admiration of the entire army."[45]

The retreat heartened Anderson's and Semmes' exhausted men, who fired several volleys into the backs of the withdrawing Regulars and inflicted heavy casualties doing so. An officer in the 11th U.S. characterized it as an "almost semi-circle of fire . . . almost a sheet of fire . . . the slaughter was fearful." The survivors reformed near the signal station on Little Round Top. In an odd twist, Colonel Day's brigade never engaged the enemy because it was ordered to follow Burbank's brigade to the rear.[46]

Three of Burbank's regiments—the 7th, 10th, and 17th U.S.—lost more than fifty percent of their men in the short time they spent in the Wheatfield; the others lost in excess of thirty-four percent. Burbank's total losses amounted to forty-seven percent. Given the Confederate encirclement of the brigade, the losses could have been much higher. The same could be said for Sweitzer's brigade, which lost more than four of every ten men engaged. The 4th Michigan, hit on two sides, lost nearly half of its men. Day's brigade, which occupied a relatively safe supporting line and so was never directly engaged, still lost twenty-five percent of its men. Most of these losses occurred during the retreat from the Wheatfield sector.[47]

After some of the bloodiest and hardest-fought combat of the war, the Confederates had finally wrested control of the Wheatfield and Stony Hill from their adversaries.

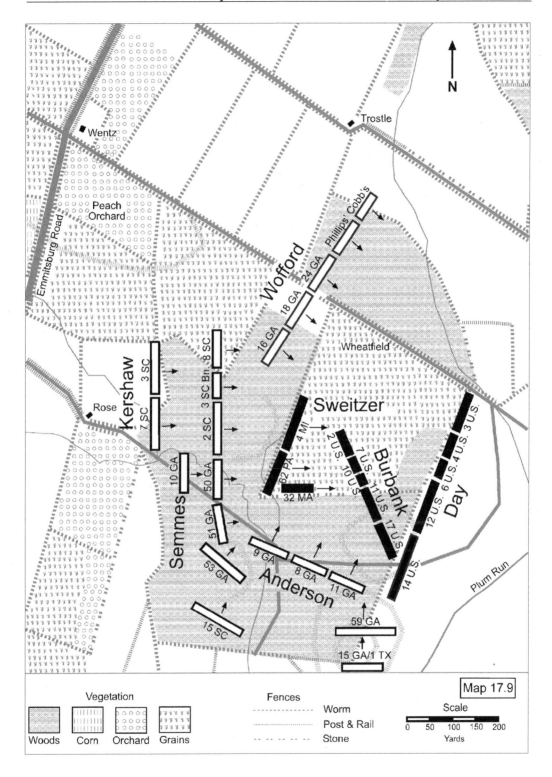

N

Wentz

Trostle

Peach
Orchard

Emmitsburg Road

Wofford

Phillips'   Cobb's

24 GA

18 GA

16 GA

Wheatfield

Kershaw

3 SC

8 SC

3 SC Bn.

2 SC

7 SC

Sweitzer

Rose

4 MI

2 U.S.

62 PA

10 U.S.

Burbank

7 U.S.

3 U.S.

4 U.S.

6 U.S.

Day

10 GA

50 GA

32 MA

11 U.S.

17 U.S.

12 U.S.

Semmes

51 GA

9 GA

8 GA

11 GA

14 U.S.

Anderson

53 GA

59 GA

15 SC

15 GA/1 TX

Plum Run

Map 17.9

Vegetation

Woods   Corn   Orchard   Grains

Fences

- - - - - - - - Worm

.... Post & Rail

- -- -- -- -- -- Stone

Scale

0   50   100   150   200

Yards

Map Set 18: The Peach Orchard

Map 18.1

Major General Dan Sickles did not like the position General Meade had assigned his III Corps. Well to his front was higher ground running along Emmitsburg Road. Perhaps Sickles recalled how his troops had taken a pounding from enemy guns firing from a higher elevation at Chancellorsville. Whatever the reason, Sickles resolved to move his corps forward. His decision to redeploy his corps created a vulnerable salient. Like Francis Barlow, Sickles and his men would pay a terrible price for leaving the Corps' assigned position.

The move westward deposited three of Brig. Gen. Charles Graham's six regiments along Emmitsburg Road facing west. The 114th Pennsylvania formed the left of the line behind four guns of Lt. John Bucklyn's battery. The 57th Pennsylvania came next, deployed across the road (east) from the Sherfy house in support of Bucklyn's other two cannon and two more from Capt. James Thompson's battery deployed on the north side of the house. The third regiment, the 105th Pennsylvania, occupied the right of the brigade, with its own right resting on the Trostle farm lane. The 141st Pennsylvania formed at right angles to the remainder of the brigade and faced south along Wheatfield Road. Graham's fifth regiment, the 68th Pennsylvania, formed behind the 141st. The brigade's final regiment, the 63rd Pennsylvania, was on the skirmish line west of the brigade's main line of battle.[1]

The 2nd New Hampshire of Col. George Burling's brigade filled the gap in the line at the salient to the left of the 114th Pennsylvania and the right of the 141st Pennsylvania. The regiment initially faced south. Because its right flank was in the air, Col. Edward Bailey refused it to connect with the 114th Pennsylvania along Emmitsburg Road. The south side of the Peach Orchard salient was weak, so Graham threw out the 3rd Maine of Brig. Gen. Hobart Ward's brigade and the 3rd Michigan of Colonel Trobriand's brigade in a heavy skirmish line in front of his left flank.[2]

Two other batteries had already unlimbered. After briefly unlimbering in the Peach Orchard and throwing some shots at Seminary Ridge, Capt. Judson Clark shifted his battery northeast of the orchard near the 141st Pennsylvania and 68th Pennsylvania. Captain Nelson Ames' six-gun New York battery replaced Clark's battery amongst the fruit trees.

Colonel William Brewster's New York "Excelsior Brigade" (Maj. Gen. Andrew Humphreys' Second Division) deployed on Graham's right. The 72nd and 71st New York formed on the right of the 105th Pennsylvania along Emmitsburg Road northwest of the Trostle Farm lane. The brigade's other three regiments remained nearby in a reserve position.

While Graham's men rested, Maj. Gen. Lafayette McLaws deployed his division on Seminary Ridge. Brigadier General Joseph Kershaw's Brigade occupied Biesecker's Woods, Brig. Gen. William Barksdale's Brigade was in Pitzer's Woods, and two supporting brigades led by Brig. Gens. Paul Semmes and William Wofford formed behind them. Artillery battalions under William Cabell and E. Porter Alexander deployed in front of the infantry.

While the infantry deployed, Confederate artillery opened fire on the Federal line. The guns did not inflict much damage, but they did trigger commands to bring up more Federal artillery support for the sector. The guns that arrived included Capt. John Bigelow's Massachusetts battery, which unlimbered on the left of the line, Capt. Charles Phillips' battery, which deployed on Bigelow's right, and Capt. Judson Clark, whose pieces unlimbered next in line. Captain Patrick Hart's battery deployed slightly in front and to the right of Clark's position. On Hart's right front were the remaining four guns of Thompson's battery. The 7th New Jersey (Burling's brigade) deployed behind Clark on the left of the 68th Pennsylvania (Graham's brigade). It was an impressive collection of firepower.

Between artillery salvos, the men could hear the growing sounds of the infantry battle developing well to the south. By 5:30 p.m., the 63rd Pennsylvania had expended most of its ammunition and pulled back from the skirmish line. Although a Confederate attack was imminent, orders arrived that sent the regiment to the rear—and out of the fight.[3]

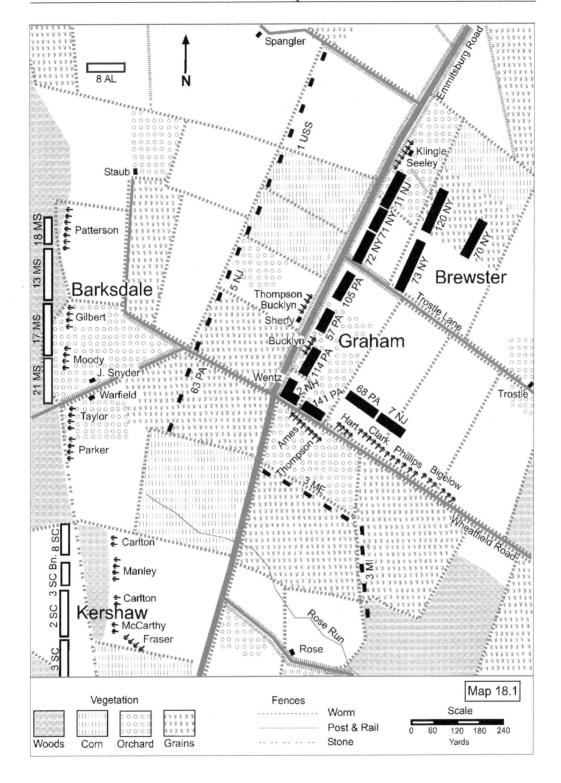

Map 18.1

Vegetation

Woods Corn Orchard Grains

Fences

---------- Worm
·········· Post & Rail
- - - - - Stone

Scale

0   60   120   180   240
Yards

Map 18.2

To the southwest, Brig. Gen. Charles Graham's men could see Brig. Gen. Joseph Kershaw's South Carolina brigade stepping off on its attack from Seminary Ridge. While Kershaw's right-most regiments approached the Wheatfield and Stony Hill, the 2nd and 8th South Carolina and the 3rd South Carolina Battalion drove straight for the Peach Orchard salient.

As the South Carolinians approached, the 3rd Maine and 3rd Michigan on the skirmish line pulled back beyond the Peach Orchard. Approximately thirty-two artillery pieces opened fire on the South Carolinians. Kershaw recalled that his men marched "majestically across the field . . . with the steadiness of troops on parade." As they advanced, however, the tremendous weight of Federal artillery fire "rendered it difficult to retain the line in good order." A soldier in the 2nd South Carolina called it "the most terrible fire to which they ever were exposed."[4]

Captain Nelson Ames' battery expended all its ammunition in short order and withdrew from the Peach Orchard, replaced by Lt. Malbone Watson's battery. Watson's stay in this vital area would be short.[5]

As the South Carolinians charged the enemy, a miscommunication caused the 2nd South Carolina to veer right, where its flank lay exposed to massed artillery fire. According to its commander, Col. John Doby Kennedy, the carnage was almost unspeakable. "We were in ten minutes or less, terribly butchered," he wrote. "I saw half a dozen at a time knocked up and flung to the ground like trifles . . . there were familiar forms and faces with parts of their heads shot away, legs shattered, arms torn off, etc." The battered unit's survivors took refuge in a depression, shaken by the intensity of the flying metal that had cut its ranks into ribbons.[6]

Meanwhile, the 8th South Carolina and the 2nd South Carolina Battalion on the left of Kershaw's line drove forward, pushing back the 3rd Maine and 3rd Michigan on the skirmish line. With the 2nd South Carolina turning off to the right, these two units had become isolated, which may have contributed to what happened next.

Seeing the enemy approach, Colonel Bailey of the 2nd New Hampshire sought out Graham and asked permission to charge. Graham purportedly replied, "Yes, for God's sake, go forward!" The last thing the South Carolinians expected to see was a line of screaming Federals running at them. The tactic halted the Palmetto soldiers in their tracks. According to a man in the 2nd New Hampshire, Kershaw's men "did what any other body of troops would have done under like circumstances—about-faced and went back as fast as they could run, for a new start."[7]

With the quick (albeit temporary) repulse of Kershaw's left wing, the Peach Orchard sector grew relatively quiet. During the brief lull, the 68th Pennsylvania crossed Wheatfield Road and took up position in the Peach Orchard facing Emmitsburg Road, its right touching Wheatfield Road. It now formed the left flank of Graham's line along Emmitsburg Road; the 114th Pennsylvania was on the 68th's right flank.[8]

The quiet did not last for long. In Pitzer's Woods, Barksdale's Brigade waited, aligned from left to right as follows: 18th Mississippi - 13th Mississippi - 17th Mississippi - 21st Mississippi. Their general was anxious to attack, and had been very vocal about doing so, pleading for permission to launch his brigade. His request was made first to division leader McLaws, and then to James Longstreet, the commander of the First Corps. Longstreet counseled patience. "Wait a little," he replied, "we are all going in presently." Barksdale brightened considerably when he finally received permission to assault the Federal positions opposite him along Emmitsburg Road. When he gave the signal, his men responded with alacrity. As one veteran put it, the Mississippians were "yelling at the top of their voices, without firing a shot, the brigade sped swiftly across the field and literally rushed the goal."[9]

A soldier in the 17th Mississippi recalled the men stepped off "in perfect line" only to meet a storm of fire crossing the open fields. "They would knock great gaps in our line. Then we would fill up the gaps and move on." Another soldier agreed. "When a solid shot tore a gap in your ranks it was instantly closed up, and the Brigade came on in almost perfect line."[10]

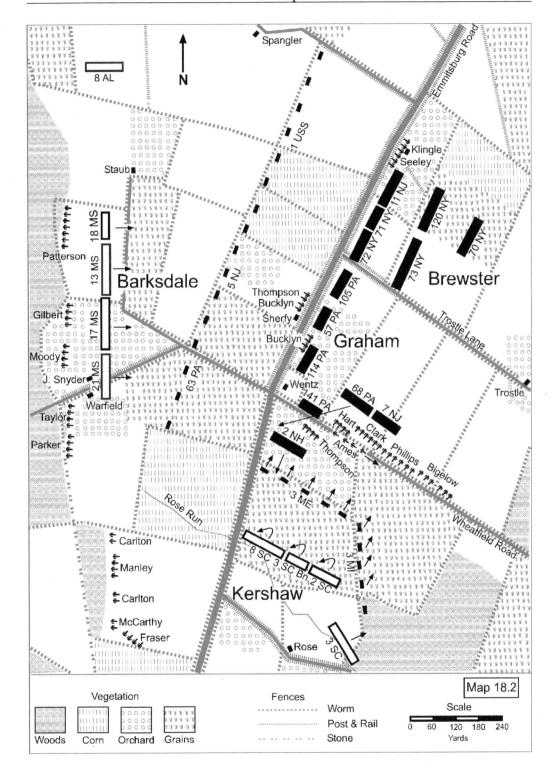

Map 18.2

Vegetation

Woods   Corn   Orchard   Grains

Fences

--------------- Worm
.... Post & Rail
-- -- -- -- -- Stone

Scale

0   60   120   180   240
Yards

Map 18.3

As he watched Brig. Gen. William Barksdale's heavy lines of infantry advance, III Corps artillery commander Capt. George Randolph feared for the safety of Bucklyn's battery. Randolph rode up to the commander of the 114th Pennsylvania and shouted, "If you want to save my battery, move forward. I cannot find the general [Graham]. I give the order on my own responsibility." Captain Edward Bowen immediately led his men across Emmitsburg Road to the Sherfy farm to buy time and lay a covering fire for the battery to withdraw. "The regiment sprang forward with alacrity and passed through and to the front of the battery, which hastily limbered up and [went] to the rear," an officer wrote after the war. The 57th Pennsylvania and the 105th Pennsylvania also crossed the road to take up positions on the right of their sister regiment. These Pennsylvanians engaged immediately with Barksdale's 13th, 17th, and 18th Mississippi regiments, which were approaching rapidly from the west.[11]

From its new position on the south end of the line, the 68th Pennsylvania watched the 21st Mississippi approach. The men were told to "reserve their fire until [the enemy] reach[ed] a certain point, when a destructive fire was opened, the enemy halting and dropping behind a fence." As the 21st Mississippi advanced against the 68th Pennsylvania's front, the 17th Mississippi hit its right flank. Punched from two sides simultaneously, the Pennsylvania regiment crumbled quickly and the men retreated to the east side of the Peach Orchard, reforming behind the batteries lining Wheatfield Road.[12]

The south side of the salient came under renewed attack as the left wing of Joe Kershaw's Brigade, which had reformed to the southeast, renewed its advance. In response, the 141st Pennsylvania crossed Wheatfield Road and formed in line of battle with the 3rd Michigan on its left and the 3rd Maine on its right. The line faced south and advanced in an attempt to connect with the left of the 2nd New Hampshire on the edge of the Peach Orchard. The 8th South Carolina and 2nd South Carolina Battalion moved to meet them and the two sides opened

fire. Veterans from the 141st Pennsylvania recalled how their volleys staggered the advancing South Carolinians. "So deadly and unexpected was our 'assault that the enemy halted, reeled, and staggered like drunken men, then scattered and ran in every direction like a flock of frightened sheep," wrote one of the soldiers. "We gave several rousing cheers and felt decidedly good."[13]

The Pennsylvanians were dismayed and then outraged to see the 3rd Michigan on one side and the 3rd Maine on the other halt their advance, turn, and head for the rear. The 141st's Col. Henry Madill noted matter-of-factly in his report, "I found myself alone, with a small regiment of about 180 men." Madill tried to hold his position but it proved impossible, so he led his redoubtable Pennsylvanians to a new position behind the 68th Pennsylvania, which had moved by the left oblique to take on the right flank of the 21st Mississippi. Seeing that it was unsupported, the 2nd New Hampshire also pulled back, turning periodically to fire before finally taking up a position on slightly higher ground in the Peach Orchard.[14]

The rest of Graham's embattled brigade had its hands full farther north near the Sherfy farm along Emmitsburg Road, where the 105th Pennsylvania and 57th Pennsylvania battled the advancing 13th and 18th Mississippi regiments. While the 114th Pennsylvania slugged it out with the 13th Mississippi along its front, the 17th Mississippi delivered a devastating oblique fire against the 114th's exposed left flank. The men naturally crowded to the right to try and escape this fire, which in turn compromised the 114th's integrity.

West of Emmitsburg Road, meanwhile, gunners from several batteries watched as the Federal battle line shielding them from the Confederate attack began to collapse. Several of the batteries in the sector began limbering up and pulling back to avoid being trapped when the sagging line broke.

The 73rd New York of Brewster's brigade moved from its reserve position just north of Trostle Lane to bolster Graham's weakening line along Emmitsburg Road.[15]

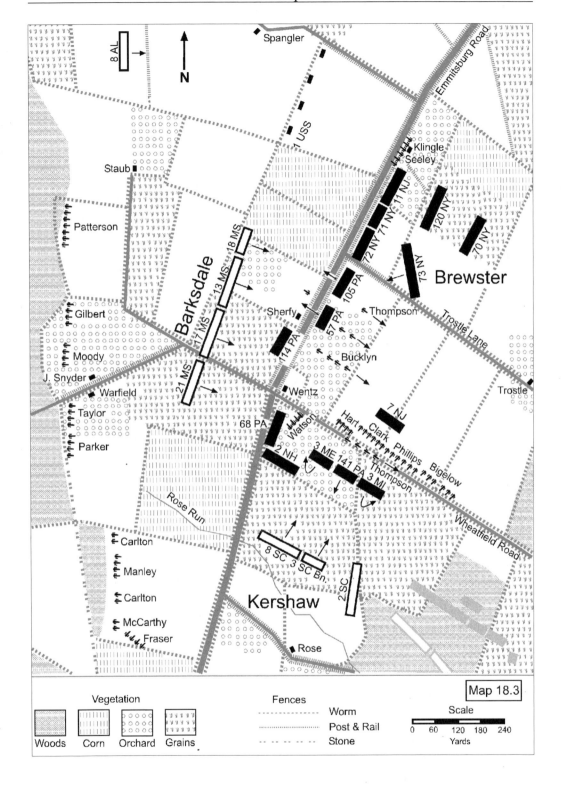

Map 18.3

Map 18.4

The 73rd New York of Col. William Brewster's brigade stormed toward Emmitsburg Road. Although it advanced on an oblique toward the 13th and 17th Mississippi regiments, they could not shoot because the 114th Pennsylvania was directly in their path. That was not a problem for Barksdale's men, however, and some of them opened fire, felling a number of the New Yorkers. One Federal officer recalled how the 13th Mississippi charged, "firing and shrieking like Indians."[16]

The men of the 114th Pennsylvania realized they could no longer hold their position and began retreating north up Emmitsburg Road. With its front cleared, the 73rd New York opened fire, its volleys temporarily checking the screaming Mississippians. Orders arrived for the New Yorkers to ready a charge, but there was no time for that. Pressure on their left and front from the 13th and 17th Mississippi regiments was more than they could handle. Just before they were overwhelmed, orders arrived for them to retreat. The New Yorkers halted periodically to throw volleys into Barksdale's men as they withdrew.[17]

Farther north and just west of Emmitsburg Road, two Confederate regiments closed on the 57th Pennsylvania. The 18th Mississippi struck its front and the 13th Mississippi its left flank. The 57th Pennsylvania received assistance from the 105th Pennsylvania on its right (Graham's right-most regiment along Emmitsburg Road), which threw an enfilade fire into the left flank of the 18th Mississippi, but it was insufficient to halt the Mississippians. The 57th Pennsylvania could not maintain its position under this intense pressure, and it too was forced to pull back. With the 18th Mississippi moving around the north side of the Sherfy barn, and the 13th and 17th Mississippi advancing south of it, Barksdale's three regiments finally reached Emmitsburg Road and wheeled to the north to take on the 105th Pennsylvania.[18]

After exchanging heavy volleys with the 21st Mississippi, the 2nd New Hampshire took a new position behind a rise near the Peach Orchard. The 68th Pennsylvania formed about fifteen yards to its right and rear, and the 3rd Maine formed on the 2nd New Hampshire's left and rear, forming something of a triangle and a defense in depth. The 141st Pennsylvania took up a position behind the 68th Pennsylvania. These soldiers took on the 21st Mississippi in their front and the 17th Mississippi along their front and right flank.

The commander of the 2nd New Hampshire recalled that his regiment and the 21st Mississippi fired volleys into each other at a distance of not more than 20 yards. Behind the Confederates, the men could see more enemy soldiers approaching: an entire brigade of fresh troops. The body of men was William T. Wofford's Georgia brigade approaching rapidly behind the Mississippians. The pressure was just too great, and orders issued to the Pennsylvanians directed them to abandon the makeshift line and make for the rear. With the rest of the Federal line falling back, Bailey ordered his New Hampshire troops to retire, "which was done quite rapidly, yet coolly, and without excitement." The 2nd New Hampshire's line in the Peach Orchard was visible after the battle, its dead neatly lining the ground.[19]

To the right and rear, the commander of the 68th Pennsylvania, Col. Andrew Tippin, encountered General Graham as his regiment vacated its position in the Peach Orchard. Graham ordered Tippin to "engage the enemy coming down on our right flank." The Pennsylvanians complied, charging toward the 17th Mississippi across Emmitsburg Road near the Sherfy farm. In fierce fighting, "the artillery having retired, and the ranks very much decimated by the fire of the enemy," the Pennsylvanians were repulsed. Colonel Bailey ordered his regiment to retire. When Graham fell wounded in the general retreat, Tippin assumed command of the First Brigade.[20]

The situation was becoming increasingly dire for Dan Sickles' III Corps sector, and only a portion of the First Brigade remained there to contest the Confederate advance.

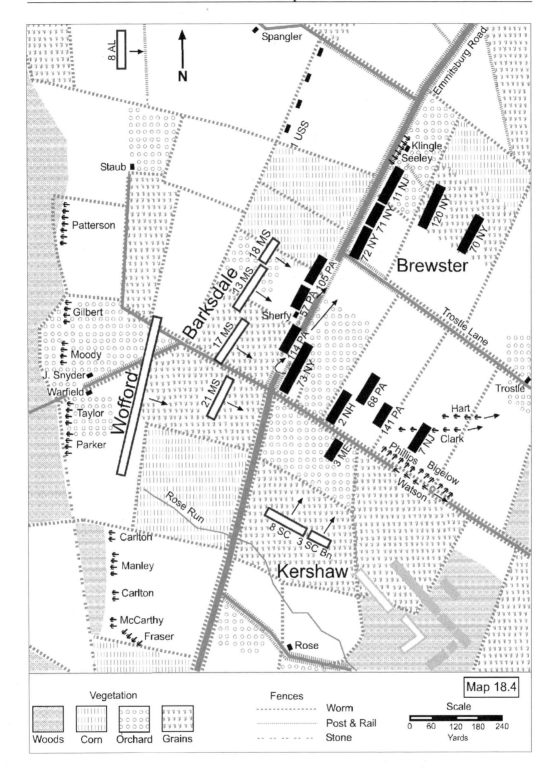

Map 18.4

Map 18.5

With the 2nd New Hampshire, 3rd Maine, and 68th Pennsylvania gone, the 141st Pennsylvania faced the advance of the 21st Mississippi alone. A captain rushed up to the regiment's commander, Col. Henry Madill, and begged him to pull the regiment back to safety. "I have no order to get out," Madill replied. "If I had my full regiment here we could whip the whole crew." Seeing troops on their right flank beyond the smoke, the men opened fire. An officer who thought the troops were Federals quickly ordered the firing to halt. The mistake was costly, as a subsequent volley from Barksdale's men brought down more than a score of Pennsylvanians.

After holding his position for what he believed to be twenty minutes, Colonel Madill finally accepted that to remain was suicide and ordered his men to pull back. "It was at this point that my regiment suffered so severely," Madill recalled. General Sickles watched the men retreat and asked, "Colonel! For God's sake can't you hold on?" With tears in his eyes, Madill replied, "Where are my men?"[21]

Meanwhile, the 105th Pennsylvania offered the last organized resistance from Graham's brigade along Emmitsburg Road. As Barksdale's victorious troops wheeled about and approached from the southwest, Col. Calvin Craig ordered his men to "retire slowly, a short distance, and changed front to the rear on the first company," which resulted in a new line of battle across Emmitsburg Road, approximately where it intersected with Trostle Lane. Members of the 57th Pennsylvania joined the men of the 105th there, and together they opened fire on the enemy. One Confederate recalled that the Pennsylvanians were "posted behind an embankment, and they killed lots of our boys." The Mississippians nearly engulfed the short makeshift defensive line. To stay meant annihilation, so Colonel Craig ordered his men to withdraw. "The regiment being so small and both flanks being entirely unprotected, I ordered the regiment to retire slowly," Craig recalled. The regiment managed to reform a short distance in the rear and again opened fire. One veteran

estimated that the regiment performed this maneuver eight to ten times. In the continuous firefight, the Mississippians gave as good as they got, and the 105th Pennsylvania lost almost half of its men.[22]

One Confederate veteran recalled that the Federal troops "fought back bravely, retiring slowly until the firing was at close quarters, when the retreat became a rout in which our men took [a] heavy toll for the losses inflicted on them." Barksdale's infantry captured sizeable numbers of Federal soldiers during this portion of the attack, including the wounded General Graham. Colonel Tippin was surprised that Graham did not get out for, "after dismounting, he walked with apparently little difficulty."[23]

With the Peach Orchard salient crushed, the 21st Mississippi continued its eastward advance, colliding with the 7th New Jersey of Burling's brigade, which had been supporting the Federal batteries. These troops had already had a share of excitement when Clark's battery, with its horses, cannons, and caissons, barreled through their line in its haste to reach safety. Men scrambled to avoid being crushed or trampled. Seeing the 21st Mississippi approach, Col. Louis Francine threw his right wing forward, and the entire regiment opened fire. After firing a few volleys, Francine ordered a charge. One Federal officer recalled that it was folly as "the enemy's fire was so severe that we were compelled to fall back a short distance." The regiment reformed, but the 21st Mississippi continued its attack, overlapping by a wide margin the 7th New Jersey's right flank. The unit finally retreated, but only after losing about 40 percent of its men.[24]

The 21st Mississippi continued advancing east along Wheatfield Road. The remainder of General Barksdale's Brigade swept north along Emmitsburg Road, attacking the exposed left wing of Humphreys' division, composed of the rest of Brewster's brigade.

Another threat appeared from the west: the brigades of Brig. Gen. Cadmus Wilcox and Col. David Lang were attacking off Seminary Ridge. Their infantry was about to join General Barksdale in catching the Federals in a vise.

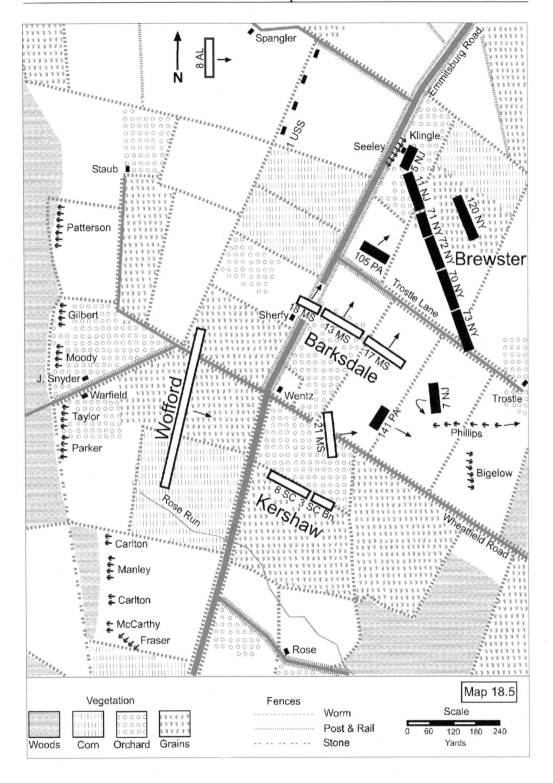

N

8 AL

Spangler

Emmitsburg Road

71 USS

Staub

Patterson

Klingle

Seeley

5 NJ

11 NJ

71 NY

72 NY

120 NY

105 PA

Brewster

70 NY

Trostle Lane

18 MS

Sherfy

13 MS

17 MS

Barksdale

73 NY

Wofford

Warfield

Moody

J. Snyder

Taylor

Parker

Wentz

7 NJ

Trostle

141 PA

Phillips

21 MS

Bigelow

Rose Run

8 SC 3 SC Bn.

Kershaw

Wheatfield Road

Carlton

Manley

Carlton

McCarthy

Fraser

Rose

Gilbert

Map 18.5

Vegetation

Woods   Corn   Orchard   Grains

Fences

Worm

Post & Rail

Stone

Scale

0   60   120   180   240

Yards

Map Set 19: Crushing Humphreys' Division

Map 19.1

Along Emmitsburg Road, Maj. Gen. Andrew Humphreys faced a dire situation. His division was already short-handed. Colonel George Burling's brigade had been detached, its regiments scattered to several sectors that needed reinforcements. That left Humphreys with but two brigades, about 3,500 men, to defend the area along Emmitsburg Road north of the Peach Orchard. In addition, his units faced northwest, and three Confederate brigades were closing on him from two directions.

Two regiments of Col. William Brewster's brigade, the 72nd and 71st New York, aligned to the right of Brig. Gen. Charles Graham's brigade along Emmitsburg Road. Next came Brig. Gen. Joseph Carr's brigade, deployed from left to right as follows: 11th New Jersey (on the right of the 71st New York) – 12th New Hampshire (on the right of the Klingle house) – 16th Massachusetts – 11th Massachusetts (behind the Rogers house) – 26th Pennsylvania. A detachment of 100 men from the 16th Massachusetts moved south to occupy the area around the Klingle house, flanking the 12th New Hampshire on two sides. Three regiments were on the skirmish line covering Carr's wide front. The 1st Massachusetts was on the right, and to its south (left) were the 1st U.S. Sharpshooters of Brig. Gen. J. H. Hobart Ward's brigade, and the 5th New Jersey of Burling's brigade. To protect Carr's right, which dangled in the air, the 74th New York of Brewster's brigade moved into position behind the 26th Pennsylvania. Three batteries sporting eighteen guns also defended the area. Lieutenant Francis Seeley's battery deployed just south of the Klingle house and John Turnbull's battery unlimbered about 250 yards to the north between the 16th Massachusetts and 11th Massachusetts north of the Spangler farm lane and south of the Rogers house. Farther north, Lt. Gulian Weir's six guns prepared to open fire on the enemy.[1]

Advancing on Humphreys' division from Spangler's Woods were Brig. Gen. Cadmus Wilcox's Alabama brigade and Brig. Gen. Edward Perry's small Florida brigade. Because General Perry had fallen ill, Col. David Lang of the 8th Florida was in command of the brigade. Wilcox's men had already fought with units of the III Corps when it approached Pitzer's Woods earlier that day. Prior to the arrival of James Longstreet's First Corps, Wilcox's infantry formed the right wing of the army. At that time the 8th and 10th Alabama faced south and its sister regiments—the 9th, 14th, and 11th Alabama—fronted east. Prior to the main attack against the Emmitsburg Road defenders, Wilcox moved his brigade north and reassembled near Perry's (Lang's) Floridians. Wilcox's pre-attack deployment was from left to right as follows: 9th Alabama – 14th Alabama – 11th Alabama – 10th Alabama – 8th Alabama. The 10th Alabama formed to the right of the 11th Alabama, but since the 8th did not follow this movement, a 200-yard gap formed between it and the rest of the brigade. As a result, when the 8th Alabama finally advanced against the Federal position, it moved out independently and with unfortunate consequences.[2]

Colonel Lang later reported that his orders were to "throw forward a strong line of skirmishers, and advance with General Wilcox, holding all the ground the enemy yielded." The 740 men in the three Florida regiments to the left of Wilcox's brigade deployed from left to right as follows: 2nd Florida – 8th Florida – 5th Florida. Unlike most of the brigadiers in Lee's army, Lang was inexperienced at brigade command.[3]

When Wilcox's and Lang's 2,500 men stepped to assault Humphreys' line, Barksdale's Mississippians were devastating Graham's brigade in the Peach Orchard. Brewster could see the disaster unfolding and sent the 73rd New York south in an attempt to shore up the line. The move proved too little too late, and the New Yorkers were forced to pull back. Flush with victory, Barksdale's men advanced up Emmitsburg Road, closing in on Humphreys' exposed left flank while Wilcox and Lang approached from Seminary Ridge to the west.[4]

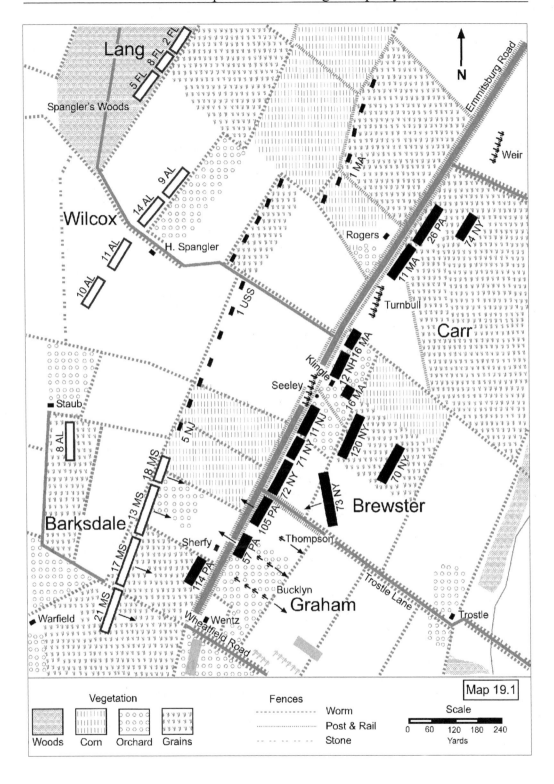

Map 19.1

Map 19.2

As he was desperately trying to shore his collapsing line, III Corps commander Maj. Gen. Daniel Sickles was struck by a cannonball that mangled his right leg. The stricken general was placed on a stretcher while someone applied a tourniquet to stem the heavy bleeding. He was carried to a field hospital chewing on a cigar; his leg was amputated later that day. David Birney, one of Sickles' division leaders, assumed command of the embattled corps as it was being squeezed from the west and from the south.

When he saw Brig. Gen. William Barksdale's Confederates moving north up Emmitsburg Road toward Trostle Lane, he ordered General Humphreys to refuse his left flank. According to Humphreys' report, his orders were to "throw back my left, and form a line oblique to and in rear of the one I then held, and I was informed that the First Division would complete the line to the Round Top ridge." He only had minutes to execute the move.

On the left of Carr's brigade, the 11th New Jersey line pulled back behind the Klingle house facing south and four other regiments aligned on it. Two regiments from Brewster's brigade, the 71st and 72nd New York, formed to its left (southeast). The 70th New York, which had been in the reserve, formed on their left, and the 73rd New York, which had rushed forward to support Graham against Barksdale's attack only to be quickly driven back, formed as the last regiment on the left of the line. The only regiments available to Brewster for a reserve were the 120th New York, already a reserve in this sector, and the 74th New York, which was pulled from the extreme right of Carr's brigade to form behind the left of Brewster's refused line. Humphreys now had Carr's brigade deployed along Emmitsburg Road to face Wilcox's and Lang's approaching onslaught, and Brewster's brigade at an almost right angle to it facing Barksdale's advance from the south.[5]

Colonel David Lang watched for the start of Wilcox's charge. As one of his men recalled, "there goes Wilcox's Brigade, and soon all to the right is hidden by dense smoke, and the rebel yell can be heard above the rattle of musketry."

Almost immediately, the Floridians heard the orders: "Attention, forward, charge!" and the men began their attack.[6]

As they stepped out of the tree line, Seeley's, Turnbull's, and probably Weir's batteries stationed along Emmitsburg Road, pounded both brigades. For a time the 5th New Jersey, 1st U.S. Sharpshooters, and 1st Massachusetts on the skirmish line held their positions, dropping Confederates with each step, but they were finally forced to fall back before the irresistible advance. The 1st Massachusetts reformed in front of the 26th Pennsylvania, but later shifted to the right, uncovering the Pennsylvanians. The 5th New Jersey retreated from the skirmish line and formed near Seeley's battery to protect the guns from the growing threat. The Federal fire was intense, as one Confederate foot soldier later remembered: "[The] enemy's guns are making great gaps in our lines, and the air seems filled with musket balls, our men are falling on all sides."[7]

Comparatively little has been written about Barksdale's demolishment of the Federal left above the Peach Orchard, but at least one source does not believe the New Yorkers held their positions very long. According to the 72nd New York's historian, "the division changed front and rallied three times, but was compelled to fall back to the second line."[8]

As the 70th, 71st, 72nd, and 73rd New York regiments melted away before the advancing Mississippians, and Brewster's line with them, the 120th New York was called up from its reserve position. It advanced about 50 yards to a position behind a low stone wall. According to one New Yorker, the "order came and the whole line rose as a man and poured into their ranks such a terrible fire of musketry, as to bring them to a standstill when within a few rods of us."

The 11th New Jersey to the right, and the 74th New York to the left, struggled to hold their positions. It was particularly difficult for the 11th New Jersey. The unfortunate regiment was caught in a crossfire at the tip of the salient, with Barksdale's men firing from the south and Wilcox's infantry firing from the west.[9]

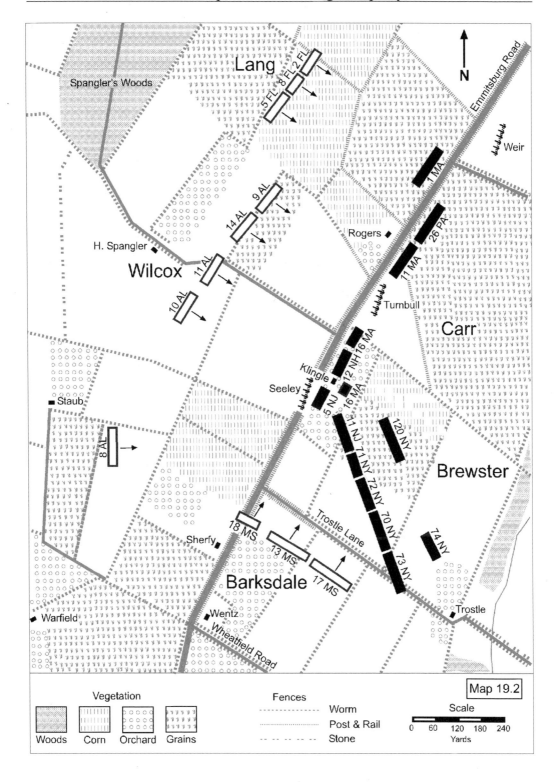

Map 19.2

Vegetation

Woods   Corn   Orchard   Grains

Fences
---------------- Worm
.... Post & Rail
-- -- -- -- -- Stone

Scale
0   60   120   180   240
Yards

Map 19.3

The 11th New Jersey opened fire on the enemy, its men firing volleys by rank, rear rank first. Soldiers from both sides fell in droves, but Barksdale's infantry continued advancing. As the Confederates closed in, Seeley's battery limbered up and galloped to safety. The 11th New Jersey, 120th New York, and 74th New York could no longer hold their positions and also drifted rearward.[10]

As the situation deteriorated, General Birney ordered Humphreys' men to fall back to Cemetery Ridge. The order irked Humphreys, who believed he could hold the Emmitsburg Road line. But there was no chance of that, for his left flank was no longer there. One soldier recalled the order was to "change fronts to the rear," and that it was immediately carried out. The regiments making up the right of Carr's line insisted that they never received orders to fall back, but did so when their positions became untenable. Turnbull's battery lost so many horses that some of the infantry had to help drag the guns and caissons to the rear.[11]

Confederate success created a problem when the brigades of Wilcox and Barksdale began overlapping. The former spotted the difficulty when his right flank began crowding Barksdale's advancing left. He remedied the situation with a quick adjustment, ordering his line "to incline slightly to the left."[12]

Lang's Floridians, facing the right of Carr's line, contributed mightily to the Federal retreat. Seeing that the Florida brigade extended far beyond their right, the 1st Massachusetts and 26th Pennsylvania attempted to wheel their line to meet this new threat. Lang reported that his men "opened a galling fire upon them, thickly strewing the ground with their killed and wounded. This threw them into confusion, when we charged them, with a yell, and they broke and fled in confusion into the woods and breastworks beyond, leaving four or five cannon in my front." These guns were from Turnbull's battery. The right side of Carr's line had no choice but to pull back to safety, which the men performed in a relatively orderly fashion.[13]

With Barksdale's Brigade pushing them from the south, and Wilcox's from the west, Carr's regiments on the left of his line also relinquished their positions along Emmitsburg Road. Most of the Federal units still had enough fight in them to turn periodically and face the enemy. Much of that was because of Humphreys. The general was everywhere during the retreat, inspiring his soldiers with orders to halt periodically and fire into the enemy that followed relentlessly in their wake. After firing several volleys in this manner, the men continued their retreat.[14]

The victorious Confederates continued pressing the Federals, but their ranks were by now in much disarray. In particular, the 10th and 11th Alabama regiments were thoroughly mixed. One officer noted that the regiments were in "marked confusion, mixed up indiscriminately, officers apart from their men, men apart from their officers, but all pushing forward notwithstanding." Separated from the rest of Wilcox's Brigade, the 8th Alabama had informally attached itself to Barksdale's Brigade. When the men spotted the flags of their comrades to the left, the regiment undertook a "half-wheel" maneuver and rapidly closed the distance.[15]

Humphreys' division lost more than forty percent of its men during this fairly brief action. Although circumstances beyond his control dropped the division in an untenable position, many of the enlisted men blamed Humphreys for their defeat. Confederate losses are difficult to ascertain because Wilcox's Brigade was engaged later that evening and, together with Lang's Floridians, attacked Cemetery Ridge again on the afternoon of July 3.[16]

The tactical situation facing the Federals was now critical. Major General Dan Sickles' entire III Corps and Brig. Gen. John Caldwell's division of the II Corps had been shattered and driven from their positions. Three Confederate brigades had pierced the left center of the Union line and were vigorously moving to press their advantage. Cemetery Ridge rose invitingly before them.

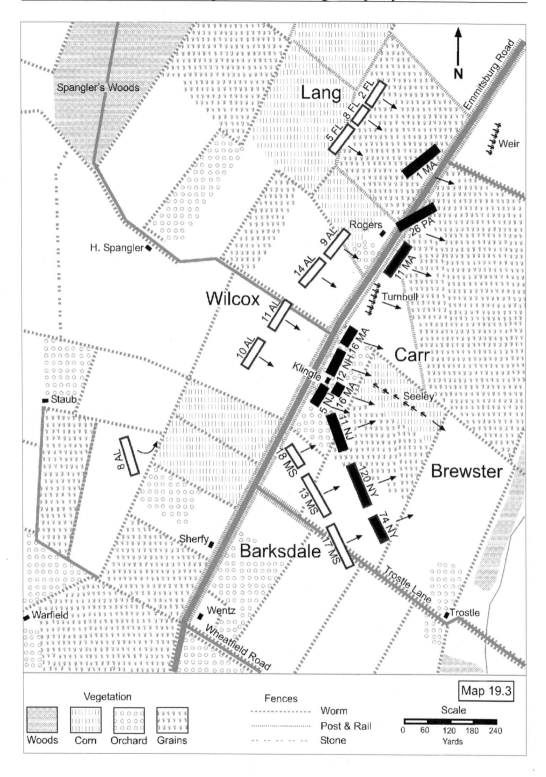

Map 19.3

Vegetation

Fences

Scale

Woods Corn Orchard Grains

Worm
Post & Rail
Stone

0 60 120 180 240
Yards

Map Set 20: The Fight Along Plum Run

Map 20.1

Four Confederate lines of battle breached the Federal line along Emmitsburg Road and continued eastward to press their attacks.

On the Confederate right, Brig. Gen. William Barksdale's Brigade broke into two parts. Pushing aside all resistance, the 21st Mississippi advanced southeast along the Trostle farm lane toward Capt. John Bigelow's battery. Bigelow was making a desperate stand to buy time for Col. Freeman McGilvery to establish a new artillery line in the Plum Run Valley. To the north, the remainder of Barksdale's Brigade pushed toward Cemetery Ridge deployed from left to right as follows: 18th Mississippi – 13th Mississippi – 17th Mississippi. On Barksdale's left (north) was Brig. Gen. Cadmus Wilcox's Brigade deployed from left to right as follows: 9th Alabama – 14th Alabama – 11th Alabama – 10th Alabama. Colonel David Lang's Brigade extended the line north, aligned from left to right as follows: 2nd Florida – 8th Florida – 5th Florida. The small band of Floridians had nearly destroyed Brig. Gen. Joseph Carr's brigade (Humphreys Division, III Corps) and now approached southern Cemetery Ridge.

II Corps commander Maj. Gen. Winfield Hancock cast about for units to assist the beleaguered III Corps and plug the hole yawning wide on his left. He had already sent Brig. Gen. John Caldwell's entire division to the Wheatfield, and now he rounded up several isolated regiments and set them to work. He positioned the 19th Maine 800 yards east of Emmitsburg Road in support of Captain Weir's battery. Although they had been in the army about one year, these soldiers had yet to engage the enemy.[1]

The Maine soldiers watched with some anxiety as Humphreys' men retreated. One member recalled that Carr's soldiers "swept over us, they stepped over us, they stepped on or between the men and even tumbled over us, having no regard to dignity or military order, or to pick out reasonable paths to walk in, as their only object seemed to be to get to the rear, out of reach of their relentless pursuers."[2]

In a search for more reinforcements, Hancock rode north along Cemetery Ridge until he found Col. George Willard's Third Brigade of Brig. Gen. Alexander Hays' Third Division in reserve north of the Copse of Trees. Hancock led the four New York regiments south. Captured at Harpers Ferry the year before and subsequently paroled, these troops had recently returned to the army with a stained reputation and a strong desire for redemption.

Colonel Norman Hall sent two small regiments, the 19th Massachusetts and 42nd New York, south to help Humphreys stem the advance. These veterans knew an impossible task when they saw it. Deploying behind a small knoll about 1,000 yards east of the Rogers house, the 360 men tried to halt Wilcox's 1,500. The Federals went prone, waited, rose, fired two volleys into the Alabamians—and promptly retreated. If this action slowed Wilcox's advance, it was only for a few moments.[3]

The men of the 19th Maine now stood alone. To their front were Lang's approaching Floridians. They waited until the Floridians were about thirty-five yards distant before opening fire. Although the lead storm staggered the enemy, Lang's men continued advancing. A mistake in communication caused the 19th Maine to withdraw about twenty yards, but it quickly turned back to face Lang's men.[4]

The 21st Mississippi, meanwhile, approached Bigelow's battery. The guns were deployed in a semi-circular line near the Trostle house. One gun was disabled and sent to the rear while the others continued firing at the advancing Mississippians. "[H]e smites and shatters, but cannot break the advancing line," a newspaper writer extolled about Bigelow. "[H]e falls back on spherical case, and . . . he holds his position. They are within six paces of the guns—he fires again . . . and he blows devoted soldiers from his very muzzles. . . . They spring upon his carriages and shoot down his forces." Bigelow recalled how his canister blew the enemy away where it ripped through their lines, but yelling like "demons," they threw themselves against the battery and ultimately captured it.[5]

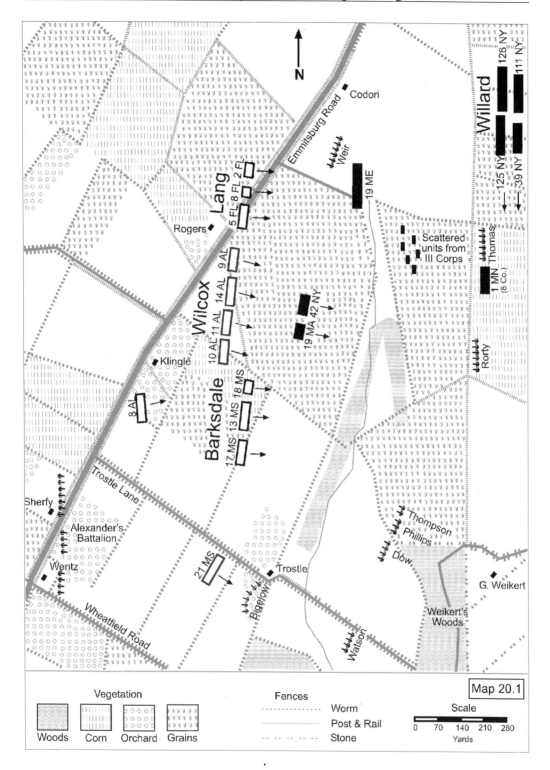

Map 20.1

Vegetation

| Woods | Corn | Orchard | Grains |

Fences

- - - - - - - - - - - Worm
.... Post & Rail
- - - -- -- Stone

Scale

0   70   140 210 280
Yards

Map 20.2

From Cemetery Ridge, Maj. Gen. Winfield Hancock watched as Brig. Gen. Cadmus Wilcox's Confederates broke through Brig. Gen. Joseph Carr's line. Hancock realized that he needed additional reinforcements to plug the hole and looked desperately for any available troops. Eight companies of the 1st Minnesota, a total of 262 men, stood in support of Lt. Evan Thomas' battery. They, too, had witnessed Humphreys' defeat. "[I] never felt so bad in my life," a Minnesota sergeant wrote. "I thought sure the day was gone for us." Many shared the sentiment that they would rather die than be disgraced by a defeat on Northern soil.[6]

Seeing these eight companies, Hancock rode over to the regiment's commander, Col. William Colvill. He pointed back at the Confederate battle flags coming toward Cemetery Ridge and shouted, "Advance and take those colors!" Colvill yelled, "Attention, First Minnesota; right shoulder shift; arms. Forward, double quick march!" The Minnesotans rushed toward Plum Run, where a volley from the Alabamians greeted them. The Southern infantry was shooting uphill and most of the rounds were aimed too high. But Wilcox's men were veterans and their aim quickly improved. According to one Minnesotan, "the bullets were coming like hailstones, and whittling our boys like grain before the sickle." Realizing the lopsided odds, Colvill ordered his men to charge. It was a desperate act, but the moment called for desperate measures. The sudden attack shocked Wilcox's first line, and caused it to fall back. As one officer noted, "men were never made who will stand against leveled bayonets coming with such momentum and evident desperation."[7]

To the northwest, the 19th Maine watched the advance of Lang's Brigade. One soldier described its movement as "snail-like." He did not realize that its commander, Col. David Lang, had halted his men "for the purpose of reforming, and allowing the men to catch breath before the final assault on upon the heights."[8]

Colville, meanwhile, expected a counterattack and ordered his 1st Minnesota to take cover along Plum Run. The two sides exchanged gunfire for several minutes. Casualties mounted, particularly in the 1st Minnesota, whose front and both flanks were exposed. The Alabamians did not charge, however. One Federal soldier hypothesized that the "ferocity of our onset seemed to paralyze them for a time, and though they poured in a terrible and continuous fire from the front and enveloping flanks, they kept at a respectful distance from our bayonets." According to Wilcox, the 1st Minnesota charged his men three times, and three times they were stopped.[9]

Dispatched by Hancock and tramping due south "by the left flank," Willard's brigade halted just north of Weikert Woods. The brigade had retained its original deployment: 125th New York on the left of the first line, with the 126th New York on its right. The 39th New York formed behind the 125th New York, and the 111th New York formed on its right. The brigade advanced toward the Plum Run thickets. Unbeknownst to any of them, three of Barksdale's regiments were approaching on the opposite side of Plum Run.[10] Barksdale's fourth regiment, the 21st Mississippi, continued east on Trostle lane after capturing Bigelow's battery. Lieutenant Malbone Watson's battery lay in its path, and the Mississippians quickly advanced and captured its guns before their owners could drag them to safety.[11]

Willard initially left his second line in reserve near Weikert Woods and advanced toward Plum Run with his 125th and 126th New York regiments. An aide to General Birney approached the 39th New York with orders to move to the left, attack the 21st Mississippi, and recapture Watson's lost guns. "By whose orders?" demanded the commanding officer.

"By order of General Birney," replied the aide.

"I am in General Hancock's Corps," replied the officer.

The aide quickly replied, "Then I order you to take those guns, by order of General Hancock."

Realizing the seriousness of the situation, the officer ended his dialog with the aide and ordered his men to the left.[12]

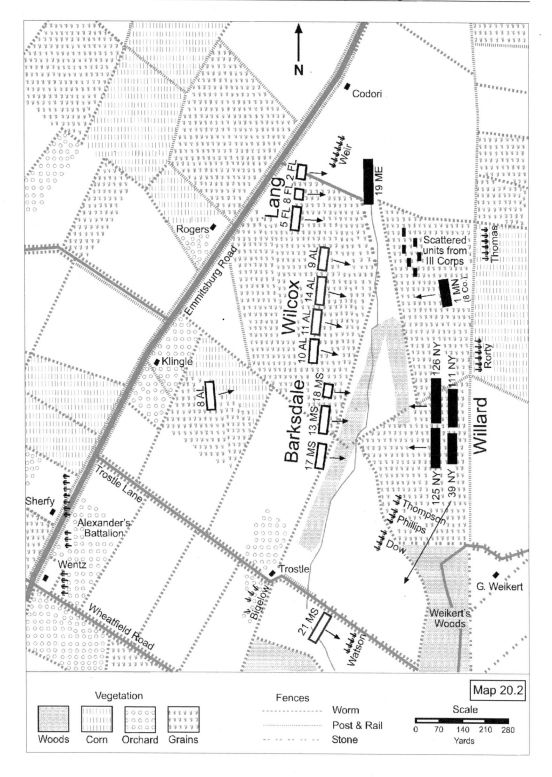

N

Codori

Weir

Lang

2 FL
8 FL
5 FL

19 ME

Rogers

Scattered
units from
III Corps

Thomas

Emmitsburg Road

9 AL

1 MN
(8 Co.)

1 MN

Wilcox

14 AL

10 AL 11 AL

Klingle

Rorty

126 NY

111 NY

8 AL

Barksdale

18 MS

Willard

13 MS

17 MS

Trostle Lane

125 NY

39 NY

Sherfy

Thompson

Phillips

Alexander's
Battalion

Dow

Wentz

G. Weikert

Trostle

Weikert's
Woods

Bigelow

21 MS

Wheatfield Road

Watson

Map 20.2

Vegetation

Woods   Corn   Orchard   Grains

Fences

- - - - - - -   Worm

· · · · · · ·   Post & Rail

- · - · - · -   Stone

Scale

0   70   140   210   280

Yards

Map 20.3

Help was on the way for the 1st Minnesota in its desperate battle against Cadmus Wilcox's Alabama infantry.

General Hancock ordered the 111th New York to leave its reserve position and drive toward the right, plugging the hole between the 126th New York and the 1st Minnesota. Wilcox could see the New Yorkers arrive and, looking to his right, the rest of Willard's brigade advancing on Barksdale's Brigade. His men could not turn the 1st Minnesota's right flank because of blasts of canister from Thomas' battery. Captain James Rorty's battery had also opened on them. Scattered units from Humphrey's division were also firing into Wilcox's left flank. With no fresh troops coming to his aid and despite several pleas to his division commander, Maj. Gen. Richard Anderson, Wilcox believed he had no viable choice but to break off the attack, return to Emmitsburg Road, and reorganize his regiments. "[W]ith a second supporting line, the heights could have been carried," lamented Wilcox after the war. The 1st Minnesota's daring tactics had successfully blunted Wilcox's penetrating charge, but the price was tremendous. More than two-thirds of the regiment's officers and men lay dead or wounded.[13]

Moments after Colonel Lang discovered Wilcox's withdrawal, an aide arrived with more ominous news: the enemy was attempting to get behind his right flank. This information, along with the presence of the 400-man 19th Maine in his front, convinced Lang to also break off the attack and withdraw.[14]

Of the three brigades, only Barksdale's continued its victorious advance. The Mississippian halted his men as they approached tree-and bush-lined Plum Run. By this time the summer sun was already setting. Unbeknownst to the Mississippians, the 125th and 126th New York approached on the opposite side of Plum Run. They opened fire on the Mississippians, but Willard mistakenly believed that the men to his front were Federal troops, so he ordered his infantry to cease firing. The reprieve gave the Mississippians time to reload and prepare for the new Federal force in front of them.[15]

When the Mississippians opened fire, New Yorkers fell by the score. "[C]ontrary, as is evident, to the expectations of the brigade commander [Willard]," wrote Lt. Col. James Bull after the war, "the rebels in considerable force were found in the underbrush." When he realized his mistake, Willard ordered the two regiments forward, firing as they went. The men cried out "Remember Harper's Ferry!" as they renewed their charge. Crashing through the underbrush, and with artillery fire supporting them, they advanced with fixed bayonets. The stand by Bigelow's battery had allowed Lt. Colonel McGilvery to cobble together a line of guns. When they opened, the concentrated cannon fire blew Barksdale's line apart. Barksdale fell from his horse with a mortal wound and many Mississippians threw down their weapons and surrendered in the face of the sudden and ferocious Federal attack. Others ran to the rear.[16]

The New Yorkers charged after the fleeing Mississippians, but soon encountered artillery fire from some of E. P. Alexander's First Corps cannon that had advanced from Seminary Ridge to the Peach Orchard. A large iron fragment smashed into Willard, carrying away most of his face and part of his head, killing him instantly. The two New York regiments halted and returned to Plum Run.[17]

Dense masses of blue-clad figures materialized in front of the 21st Mississippi. These men included the 39th New York of Willard's brigade and Brig. Gen. Henry Lockwood's brigade (Maj. Gen. Henry Slocum's XII Corps), which had been pulled from its position on Culp's Hill. The Confederates turned Watson's guns to fire into the new arrivals, only to find that the artillerists had removed the rammers and friction primers before abandoning the battery.

Realizing they were in an impossible situation, the men of the 21st Mississippi began retreating. In their wake were the two recently captured Union batteries.[18]

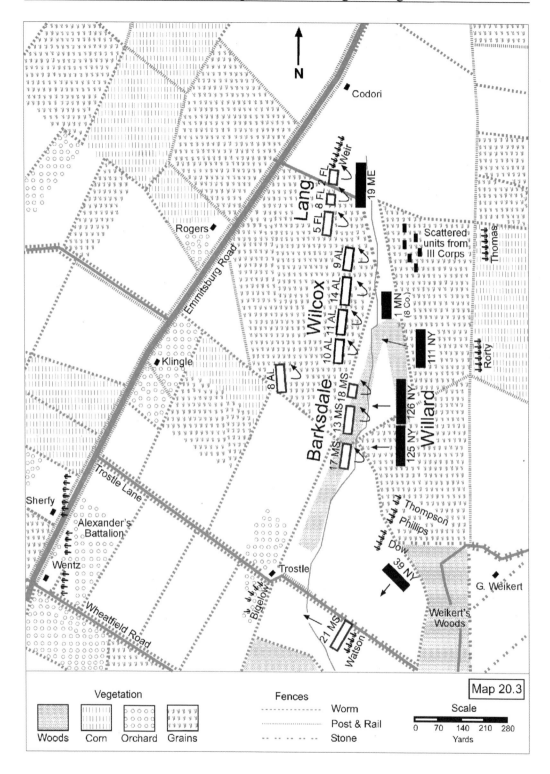

Codori

N

Weir

Lang

FL
5 FL 8 FL 2 FL

19 ME

Rogers

Scattered
units from
III Corps

Thomas

Wilcox

9 AL

14 AL

11 AL

1 MN
(8 Co.)

Emmitsburg Road

Klingle

10 AL

111 NY

Rorty

Barksdale

8 AL

18 MS

13 MS

125 NY 126 NY

Willard

17 MS

Sherfy

Trostle Lane

Alexander's
Battalion

Thompson

Phillips

Dow

Wentz

39 NY

G. Weikert

Trostle

Bigelow

Weikert's
Woods

Wheatfield Road

Watson

21 MS

Vegetation				Fences		Scale	Map 20.3

Vegetation

Woods Corn Orchard Grains

Fences

- - - - - - - Worm
· · · · · · · · · Post & Rail
-- - -- - -- Stone

Scale

0   70   140   210   280
Yards

Map 20.3

Map Set 21: Wright Tries the Union Center

Map 21.1

The sweeping Confederate attack of July 2 continued rolling northward en echelon, with brigades unleashed one by one similar to a falling row of dominos. The initial attack by Lt. Gen. James Longstreet's First Corps was designed to defeat the enemy, capture important terrain, and siphon southward Federal reinforcements from other areas of the line. This, it was hoped, would weaken Cemetery Ridge and other points along the right side of the Federal line so that when those sectors were struck by subsequent assaults, they could be more easily broken and carried.

Longstreet's attack captured Devil's Den, the Wheatfield, the Peach Orchard, and a large section of the enemy front along Emmitsburg Road. However, Little Round Top and the southern end of Cemetery Ridge remained in Federal hands. With Longstreet's First Corps fully committed, the en echelon attack rolled northward into A. P. Hill's Third Corps sector. Major General Richard H. Anderson kicked off Hill's attack by launching Cadmus Wilcox's and David Lang's brigades against Emmitsburg Road. They helped Barksdale drive A. A. Humphreys' division from its position along the road, but could not capture Cemetery Ridge.

Anderson's third brigade under Brig. Gen. Ambrose Wright stepped off Seminary Ridge between 6:15 and 6:30 p.m. to attack Cemetery Ridge. Wright's line was aligned from left to right as follows: 48th Georgia – 3rd Georgia – 22nd Georgia. The 2nd Georgia Battalion, on the skirmish line behind a fence between Seminary Ridge and Emmitsburg Road, had orders to form on the left of the 48th Georgia as it swept by. Instead, the battalion lost its cohesion and dissolved into the rest of the advancing brigade.[1]

The brigade halted briefly to redress its lines when it reached the fence line held by the 2nd Georgia Battalion. When the attack was renewed, the Georgians came under fire from Lt. Fred Brown's battery near the Codori House and Lt. Alonzo Cushing's and Capt. William Arnold's

batteries on Cemetery Ridge. Undulations in the ground screened the Georgians at times, but they lost many men. Wright's attack was so unexpected that Lieutenant Brown was only able to shift his left and center sections to meet the movement.[2]

Portions of three Federal brigades lay in front of Wright's Brigade. About 600 men of the 15th Massachusetts and 82nd New York (Brig. Gen. William Harrow's brigade, Brig. Gen. John Gibbon's division, II Corps) had formed in line along Emmitsburg Road just north of the Codori house. Gibbon sent them to this vulnerable position directly in front of the main Federal line on Cemetery Ridge to support the embattled III Corps fighting on his left. Realizing the precariousness of their situation, the veterans threw up breastworks. Flimsy at best, most did not survive the enemy artillery fire that rained down on them. From their position just east of Emmitsburg Road, however, the Federal infantrymen could not see Wright's Georgians approach because tall grass obstructed their view. The Federal artillery on Cemetery Ridge continued firing, but the gunners occasionally misjudged the range (particularly when the Confederates neared the road) and some of the rounds dropped among their own troops.[3]

Three Federal regiments crouched behind a low stone wall on the forward slope of Cemetery Ridge. The 69th Pennsylvania, part of Brig. Gen. Alexander Webb's Philadelphia Brigade, held the right of the line in front of the Copse of Trees, with the 7th Michigan and 59th New York of Col. Norman Hall's brigade on the 69th's left. Webb's other three regiments rested on the reverse slope of the ridge in column, aligned west to east as follows: 71st Pennsylvania – 72nd Pennsylvania – 106th Pennsylvania.[4]

Brigadier General Carnot Posey's Brigade of Mississippians (Anderson's Division) was next in line on Seminary Ridge to assault across the valley. The Mississippi regiments were arranged left to right as follows: 12th – 16th – 19th – 48th. The men captured the Bliss house and barn. The 19th Mississippi and a small part of the 48th Mississippi continued on "400 paces" beyond the farm buildings, where they opened fire on the gunners firing from Cemetery Ridge (probably Arnold's battery), killing and wounding a number of them and driving the rest from their pieces.[5]

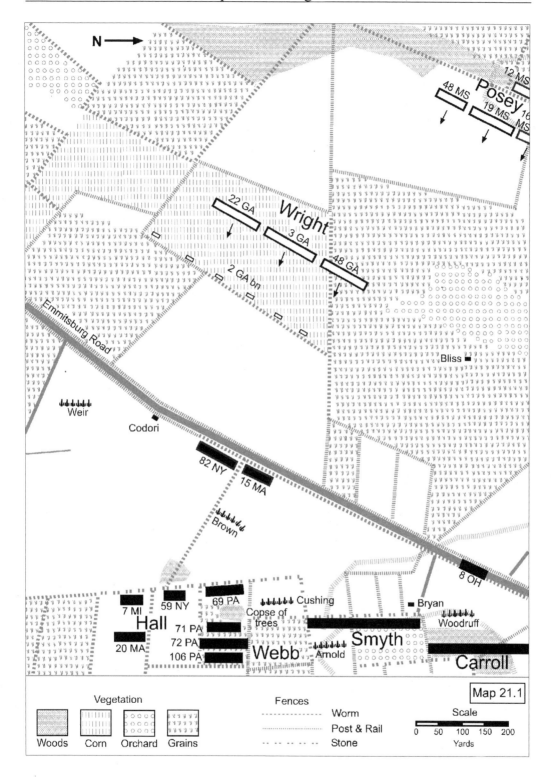

N→

12 MS

Posey

48 MS
19 MS
16 MS

22 GA
Wright
3 GA
48 GA
2 GA bn

Emmitsburg Road

Bliss

Weir

Codori

82 NY
15 MA

Brown

8 OH

7 MI
59 NY
69 PA
Cushing
Bryan
Hall
71 PA
Copse of trees
Woodruff
Smyth
72 PA
20 MA
106 PA
Webb
Arnold
Carroll

Map 21.1

Vegetation

Woods   Corn   Orchard   Grains

Fences

--------- Worm
.... Post & Rail
-- -- -- Stone

Scale

0   50   100   150   200
Yards

Map 21.2

Brigadier General Ambrose Wright's men let go a "demoniac yell" as they approached the two Federal regiments along Emmitsburg Road. The Massachusetts and New York veterans responded with a deadly volley, sending scores of Wright's men sprawling in the grass. One Federal soldier called it "one of the most destructive volleys I ever witnessed . . . they hesitated, then reeled, they staggered and wavered slightly, yet there was no panic." Undeterred, the Georgians pressed on.[6]

Because Wright was at the head of an entire brigade, his line of battle far overlapped the narrow front held by these two Federal regiments. Attacked in front and against the left flank, the 82nd New York's line crumbled first. This made the 15th Massachusetts' position on the 82nd's right untenable, and the men quickly made for the rear. The retreat turned into a foot race, as the Georgians chased down retreating Federal troops. One soldier recalled that we "retired in some disorder, being pressed so closely that we lost quite a number of prisoners, captured by the enemy."[7]

Many Georgians turned their attention to capturing Brown's battery, their interest so intent they ignored Federal soldiers trying to surrender. The artillerists worked feverishly, ramming spherical case shells into their guns. Each shell was filled with seventy leaden or iron balls set to explode in four seconds. One gunner recalled that as Wright's men advanced, "our fuses were cut at three, two, and one second, and then canister at point blank range, and finally, double charges were used."[8]

The cannon fire tore large gaps in Wright's line, but the Georgians' advance continued. "As artillery fire cut down their men," remembered one of the artillerists, "they would waver for a second, only to close up and continue their advance, with their battle flags flying in the breeze, and the barrels of their muskets reflecting the sun's dazzling rays." A foot soldier who participated in the charge recalled that "shells around us tore our bleeding ranks with ghastly gaps . . . we pressed on, knowing that the front was safer now than to turn our backs, and with a mighty yell, we threw ourselves upon the batteries and passed them, still reeking hot."[9]

As the Confederates closed in on his exposed position, Lieutenant Brown ordered his men to limber up the guns and gallop to the rear. One gun commander decided to fire one last shot, but in the few seconds it took to do so, several horses fell wounded or killed. "The boys had to look out for themselves, as the Johnnies were all around us, and the bullets flew very lively," he later wrote. Another gun was abandoned near the wall in front of the Federal position.[10]

When Wright's men overran Brown's two abandoned Napoleons, they tried to turn them around to fire at the Federal infantry on Cemetery Ridge. However, Alonza Cushing's and William Arnold's batteries pivoted and opened fire on Brown's position with single canister charges. One of Cushing's gunners wrote that "this movement was so rapidly executed that it staggered the Confederates (who, by the way, were in the act of training those pieces on us), and they fled to the rear in short order, totally broken up." The rest of the Georgians, however, continued moving east against Cemetery Ridge.[11]

Posey's Mississippi brigade, however, was not in position to support Wright's stunning advance because Posey had lost control of his brigade. "Get up and fight!" yelled some of the Georgians when they realized that Posey's Mississippians were not advancing with them on their left. "Come forward Mississippians!" screamed others. According to one veteran from the 48th Mississippi, at least part of his regiment formed on the left flank of the 48th Georgia as it rushed past them toward the ridge. The bulk of the Mississippi brigade, however, remained stationary around the Bliss buildings. In all likelihood, few if any Mississippians crossed Emmitsburg Road.

The withdrawal of Colonel Lang's Floridians on the right and General Posey's failure to advance on the left meant that both of General Wright's flanks were unprotected. He anxiously dispatched requests to his division commander, Richard Anderson, for reinforcements.[12]

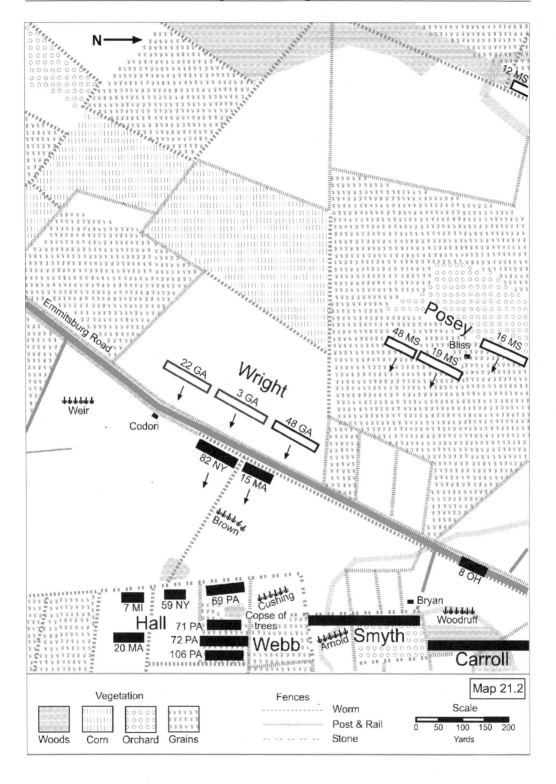

N→

12 MS

Posey

Emmitsburg Road

48 MS   16 MS

Bliss

19 MS

22 GA   Wright

3 GA

Weir   48 GA

Codori

82 NY

15 MA

Brown

8 OH

7 MI   59 NY   69 PA   Cushing   Bryan

Hall   71 PA   Copse of   Woodruff
                          trees

20 MA   72 PA   Webb   Arnold   Smyth

106 PA   Carroll

Map 21.2

| Vegetation | | | | Fences | | Scale |

Woods   Corn   Orchard   Grains

Worm

Post & Rail   0   50   100   150   200

Stone   Yards

Map 21.3

The Federal defenders behind the stone wall on Cemetery Ridge quietly watched the Georgians approach on their left front. The Irishmen of the 69th Pennsylvania could not open fire until Brown's guns thundered past them. Once their front was clear, the 69th's color-bearer calmly shook the folds out of the green flag as his comrades opened fire. The gunners who took refuge in front of the stone wall looked up to see, as one witness put it, a "vivid flame sending messengers of death to the foe."

Brigadier General Ambrose Wright's Georgians were also exhausted. Winded from their trek from Seminary Ridge and their earlier attacks against the 15th Massachusetts, 82nd New York, and Brown's battery, Wright's men now faced the main Federal line at the base of Cemetery Ridge. A sizeable percentage of the brigade was already down, killed and wounded during the earlier fighting.[13]

One Confederate explained what it was like to charge against Cemetery Ridge that day. "Wild with enthusiasm and ardor, on we pressed, while every instant the enemy thundered their shot and shell in our midst," he wrote. "Shells amongst us, shells over us and shells around us tore our bleeding ranks with ghastly gaps. . . . The ground roared and rumbled like a great storm, and the shower of minie balls was pitiless and merciless."[14]

The redoubtable Georgians pressed on "until they reach point-blank range of our rifles," remembered the historian of the 69th Pennsylvania. "We met their charge with such a destroying fire that they were forced back in confusion. They rally again and make a second effort and again are their lines broken and thinned as we pour volley upon volley into their disordered rank, until they finally retire a dispirited mob." The rhapsody of his memory notwithstanding, these steadfast Pennsylvania volleys did not stop the tramping Georgians, who continued moving toward the wall.[15]

Brigadier General Alexander Webb could see that his 69th Pennsylvania was about to be overwhelmed by the 48th Georgia and quickly

called forward his three reserve regiments from the reverse slope of Cemetery Ridge. The 71st Pennsylvania took position behind a low stone fence to the right of the Copse of Trees, with its right flank connecting with Arnold's battery. Alonzo Cushing's guns were in front, farther down the slope. The 72nd Pennsylvania rushed to the left of the trees and the 106th Pennsylvania advanced to the crest of Cemetery Ridge, just to the right of the knot of timber that would soon become the most famous stand of trees in American military history.[16]

On the far left of the Federal line, the 7th Michigan and 59th New York poured a rapid and destructive fire into Wright's 3rd and 22nd Georgia regiments. Behind these two regiments was the 20th Massachusetts, which also opened fire. Brown's surviving guns stood unlimbered and ready for action just south of the Copse of Trees.[17]

The men of the 22nd Georgia and some of the 3rd Georgia noticed a gap in the line to the right of the 59th New York, where John Caldwell's division was deployed before being sent south to bolster the III Corps. Driving toward it, the 22nd Georgia reached the base of Cemetery Ridge and shoved its way up the slope toward its summit.[18]

Five companies of the 13th Vermont, part of Brig. Gen. George Stannard's brigade (Maj. Gen. Abner Doubleday's Division, I Corps) was rushing toward Cemetery Ridge from Cemetery Hill. One of General Meade's aides spied them earlier in the day and orders finally reached them to move immediately to Cemetery Ridge. As the 340 men approached the ridge, they encountered II Corps commander Maj. Gen. Winfield Hancock, who directed Col. Francis Randall and his men to the desired area. Although inexperienced in battle, Randall and his Vermont infantry were anxious to throw back the enemy assault.[19]

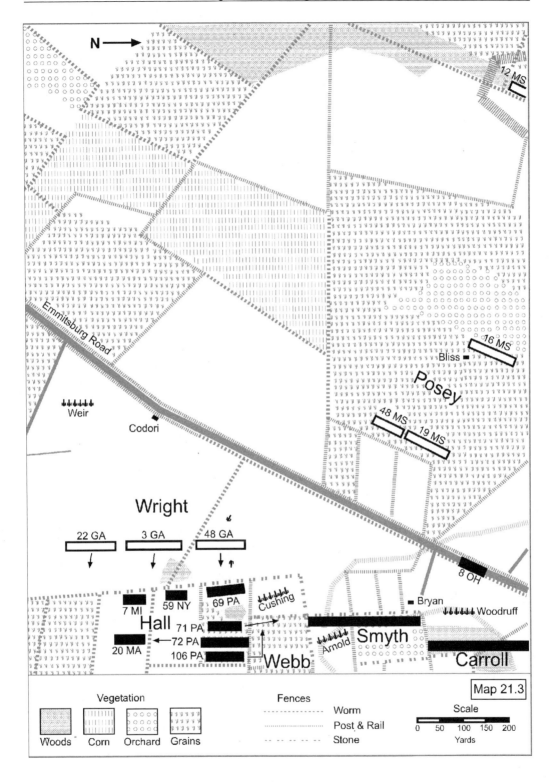

N→

12 MS

Emmitsburg Road

16 MS

Bliss ▪

Posey

Weir

Codori ▪

48 MS   19 MS

Wright

22 GA   3 GA   48 GA

8 OH

7 MI   59 NY   69 PA   Cushing   Bryan ▪   Woodruff

Hall   71 PA   Smyth

20 MA   72 PA   Arnold

106 PA   Webb   Carroll

Map 21.3

Vegetation   Fences   Scale

············   Worm   0   50 100 150 200
··················   Post & Rail
Woods   Corn   Orchard Grains   ·· ·· ·· ··   Stone   Yards

Map 21.4

When it reached the top of the ridge to the right (north) of the Copse of Trees, the 106th Pennsylvania opened fire on the 48th Georgia (Ambrose Wright's Brigade) as it approached the 69th Pennsylvania's position behind the stone wall. Colonel William Curry, the 106th's commander, observed a falter in the Georgians' advance after these volleys and decided to seize the moment. "Seeing his lines waver, I ordered bayonets fixed and a charge to be made, which movement resulted in a complete success, the enemy retiring in confusion to his original position in the woods," he later reported.

The sight of the Pennsylvanians attacking their left flank with bayonets fixed, while the 69th Pennsylvania continued firing into their faces, was too much for the exhausted infantrymen of the 48th Georgia. They had reached the high-water mark of their attack. The Georgians began the long and dangerous retreat back to Seminary Ridge. Fifty-seven percent of the Southern regiment, together with its battle flag, remained on the slope of Cemetery Ridge.[20]

On the right of the 48th, however, the 22nd and part of the 3rd Georgia regiments continued ascending Cemetery Ridge. Five companies of the just-arrived 13th Vermont suddenly materialized in front of them. When the surprised Georgians opened fire, Colonel Randall's horse went down, temporarily pinning him to the ground. When his men tried to extract him, Randall angrily yelled, "Go on boys, go on. I'll be at your head as soon as I get out of this damn saddle."[21]

Most of the bullets fired by the clearly rattled Georgians were poorly aimed and ineffectual. Rather than halt to return the fire, the Federal troops rushed forward with fixed bayonets. "When my men sprang forward with the bayonet with so much precipitancy . . . they [the Georgians] appeared to be taken wholly by surprise," wrote the regiment's commander. The attack was so sudden that many of Wright's men simply surrendered, while others turned and rushed west toward Seminary Ridge. Vermonter Edwin Palmer summarized the charge by writing, "they [the 13th Vermont] now charge down the sloping hill, over the dead and dying, shouting, firing into the foe . . .

it seemed but a moment till the rebel lines were breaking all along and flying back in dismay."[22]

Not content to watch Wright's men retreat, the victorious 106th and 71st Pennsylvania regiments followed after them. They swept past Brown's cannons in the process and continued after the Georgians, many of whom had halted at the Codori farm. On the southern end of the line, the 13th Vermont surged forward, recapturing the guns of Weir's battery overrun earlier in the evening.[23]

Wright's losses were staggering. All but one of his regimental/battalion commanders were killed, and about half of his 1,400-man brigade had been killed, wounded, or captured. On the Federal side, the 15th Massachusetts and 82nd New York, formed along Emmitsburg Road, sustained losses approaching fifty-five percent. Despite withstanding the worst of Wright's assault, the 69th Pennsylvania fought protected by a low stone wall and lost only about ten percent of its original complement of 284 men.[24]

Ambrose Wright complained bitterly about his lack of support on July 2, his barbs aimed squarely at Brig. Gen. Carnot Posey's tactical failures. "I have not the slightest doubt but that I should have been able to have maintained my position on the heights, and secured the captured artillery, if there had been a protecting force on my left, or if the brigade on my right had not been forced to retire." He had good cause to complain about Posey's failure on his left. Poor brigade-level leadership allowed a skirmish line manned by the 8th Ohio to interrupt and stop the advance of Posey's Mississippians. The brigade that had advanced on Wright's right flank under Colonel Lang had been repulsed at Plum Run after heavy fighting.

Although he did not know it on the evening of July 2, Wright would one day take some pride in accomplishing what many more troops under George Pickett and other commanders could not achieve the following day: reach the summit of Cemetery Ridge, however briefly.

Wright never forgot his lost opportunity at Gettysburg.[25]

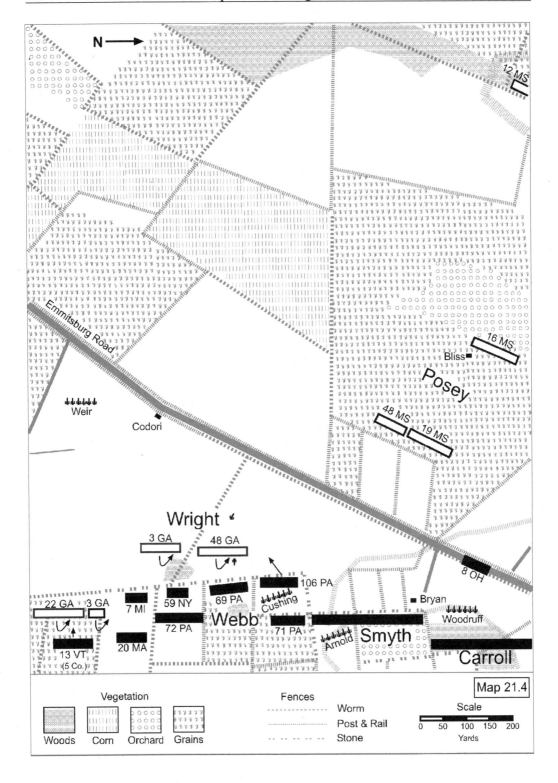

N →

12 MS

Emmitsburg Road

16 MS

Bliss■

Posey

Weir

Codori

48 MS   19 MS

Wright

3 GA   48 GA

106 PA

8 OH

22 GA 3 GA   7 MI   59 NY   69 PA   Cushing   Bryan■   Woodruff

72 PA   Webb   71 PA   Smyth

13 VT   20 MA   Arnold   Carroll
(5 Co.)

Map 21.4

Vegetation

Woods Corn Orchard Grains

Fences

------------- Worm

.... Post & Rail

-- -- -- -- Stone

Scale

0   50   100   150   200
Yards

Map Set 22: The Valley of Death

Map 22.1

After bitter fighting through most of the late afternoon and early evening, Confederate troops finally achieved uncontested control of the Wheatfield. Looming in front of them was what many considered the grand prize and anchor of the Federal left—Little Round Top.

The sun was setting when the Southern infantry advanced in two groups. To the south, remnants of Brig. Gens. Joseph Kershaw's, Paul Semmes', and George "Tige" Anderson's brigades pressed toward the rocky heights. Some historians describe this group as a little more than a mob. The units had lost their cohesion and many field officers had been killed or wounded. To the north was Brig Gen. William Wofford's Brigade, likely deployed from left to right as follows: Cobb's Legion – Phillips' Legion – 24th Georgia – 18th Georgia – 16th Georgia. Flushed with victory after driving the last Federals from the Wheatfield, they advanced east on Lt. Aaron Walcott's six-gun battery unlimbered on a rise on the north side of Wheatfield Road. Walcott's gunners threw rounds of canister into the Georgia ranks, but its position was too advanced and its infantry support non-existent. When he failed to slow Wofford, Walcott ordered his men to retreat—but not before spiking his guns.[1]

Federal troops arrived to bolster the sector's defense. Two brigades from Maj. Gen. Samuel Crawford's Third Division (Maj. Gen. George Sykes' V Corps) took up a position on Little Round Top's northwest slope. Colonel Joseph Fisher's Third Brigade of the Pennsylvania Reserve division faced the enemy north of the hill, while Col. William McCandless' First Brigade formed behind Fisher. Elements of Maj. Gen. John Sedgwick's VI Corps also streamed into the area. Brigadier General Frank Wheaton's brigade, under Col. David Nevin (Maj. Gen. John Newton's division), took position behind McCandless. Brigadier General Joseph Bartlett's Second Brigade (Brig. Gen. Horatio Wright's Division), deployed on Nevin's right.[2]

Captain Frank Gibbs' Battery L unlimbered on the northern slope of Little Round Top. As McCandless' men climbed the hill, an officer from the battery, worried that his unit would suffer the same fate as Walcott's, ran up to them and shouted, "Dunder and blixen, don't let dem repels took my batteries!" Colonel Samuel Jackson of the 40th Pennsylvania told him to "double-shot his guns, hold his position, and we would see to their safety." Hearing this, Jackson's men yelled out, "Stand by your guns, Dutchy, and we will stand by you."[3]

General Crawford received orders to send help to Strong Vincent's embattled brigade on the southern portion of Little Round Top. He dispatched Fisher, leaving McCandless to face the enemy pressing from the west. McCandless quickly deployed his men in two lines. The first line was, from left (south) to right (north) as follows: 1st Pennsylvania Reserves – 11th Pennsylvania Reserves (from Fisher's Brigade) – 6th Pennsylvania Reserves. The second line was composed of the 13th Pennsylvania Reserves on the left and the 2nd Pennsylvania Reserves on the right. Colonel Nevin deployed his brigade behind McCandless and to the left of Bartlett as it arrived, from left to right as follows: 139th Pennsylvania – 93rd Pennsylvania – 62nd New York. Once formed, Nevin moved northwest toward Weikert's Woods. The 98th Pennsylvania separated from the rest of the brigade and deployed south of McCandless' second line.[4]

Captain Frank Gibbs waited impatiently until Burbank's and Day's brigades, retreating from the Wheatfield, cleared his front. "[A]n irregular, yelling line of the enemy put in his appearance," recalled Gibbs, "and we received him with double charges of canister. . . . So rapidly were the guns worked that they became too hot to lay the hand on."[5]

General Wheaton was also watching as Wofford's Georgians advanced. Seeing that Bartlett's men were not yet in position, Wheaton ordered Nevin to move to the right and quickly form in front of his sister brigade. Nevin immediately complied. An angry Bartlett later wrote that Nevin's troops "moved rapidly to the front and right, completely masking my troops, and rendering an advance unnecessary."[6]

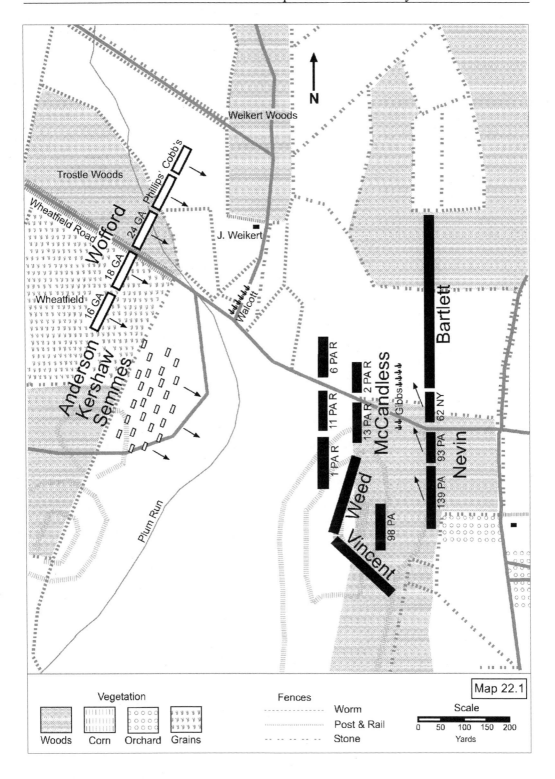

N

Weikert Woods

Trostle Woods

Wheatfield Road

Wofford

Phillips' Cobb's

24 GA

18 GA

16 GA

Wheatfield

J. Weikert

Walcott

Anderson
Kershaw
Semmes

Plum Run

6 PA R

11 PA R

2 PA R

13 PA R

1 PA R

McCandless

Gibbs

62 NY

Bartlett

93 PA

Nevin

139 PA

Weed

98 PA

Vincent

Vegetation

Woods   Corn   Orchard   Grains

Fences

------------   Worm
·················   Post & Rail
-- -- -- -- --   Stone

Map 22.1

Scale

0   50   100   150   200
Yards

Map 22.2

As Brig. Gen. William Wofford's infantry approached the rocky high ground, they could see that Little Round Top bristled with Federal troops from Maj. Gen. John Sedgwick's newly arrived VI Corps. Undeterred, Wofford pushed his men forward until a "terrible volley" from Col. David Nevin's brigade met them.[7]

Nevin's infantry had waited until Wofford's line tramped into range before, in the words of its commander, "deliver[ing] two volleys into the ranks of the advancing rebels, and immediately after charged their column, breaking the same and driving them in disorder down the hill." Confederate First Corps commander James Longstreet saw the futility of attacking Little Round Top and ordered Wofford to break off the advance and pull his men back to safety. The order bitterly disappointed Wofford and his soldiers. "[N]o troops went so far as my 16th," wrote Georgia Col. Goode Bryan after the war, "[T]here were no enemy either in front or on our right to cause us to fall back. . . . Seeing Longstreet some distance to my rear I went to him, and requested him not to order us back . . . his reply was I order you to fall back."

Because of the smoke, confusion, and wide brigade front (the 16th was on Wofford's far right), Bryan did not see the threat posed to the brigade's center and left flanks by Nevin's three Federal regiments. The Georgians' withdrawal was probably hastened when Nevin's men charged down the hill, crossed the Plum Run Valley, and continued about 100 yards before halting, recapturing Walcott's battery in the process.[8]

To the south, meanwhile, the remnants of three Confederate brigades continued their trek toward Little Round Top. A member of the 2nd South Carolina of Kershaw's Brigade, W. Johnson, saw "several lines of battle posted on the hillside [Little Round Top] so that they could shoot over the heads of the men in front. We got close up and kept the men who were attempting to fire some guns which were posted there thinned out so that they could not do much. But the lines of battle fired into us and many of our troops fell . . . we retreated in good order, loading and firing on the Yanks. We reached the edge of a woods and here we made a stand." Colonel Franklin Galliard of the same regiment recalled that the bullets "literally came down upon us as thick as hailstones."[9]

The Pennsylvania Reserves under Col. William McCandless also advanced. According to Evan Woodward, when the "enemy had advanced within fifty paces . . . the gallant Crawford, seizing the standard of the First, whose bearer had been shot down, waved it aloft and cried out, 'Forward, Reserves!' With a simultaneous shriek from every throat, that sounds as if coming from a thousand demons, who had burst their lungs in uttering it, on swept the Reserves."[10]

When McCandless' left flank of his first line came under a heavy fire, he moved the 13th Pennsylvania Reserves from the second line to the left of the first, where it joined its comrades in their attack. Captain Frank Bell called this advance "the most irregular line that ever made a charge. Many of the men stopping to drop behind a rock or some other cover and fire at the enemy on our left who were busy with their complements." The 98th Pennsylvania from Nevin's brigade, on the left of the 13th Pennsylvania Reserves, also joined this move but was too far south to encounter any resistance.[11]

The men from Brig. Gens. Kershaw's, Semmes', and Anderson's brigades had marched for much of the morning and half the afternoon before fighting until sunset in one of the most grueling offensive engagements of the war. Simply put, they had reached the end of their tether. The advance of McCandless' fresh brigade convinced the disorganized and exhausted Confederates that there was little choice left but to retreat.

The Federal advance finally halted at the stone wall midway through the Wheatfield, which had been so hotly contested for several hours earlier in the day. The bloody battle for the southern sector of the Gettysburg battlefield was over.

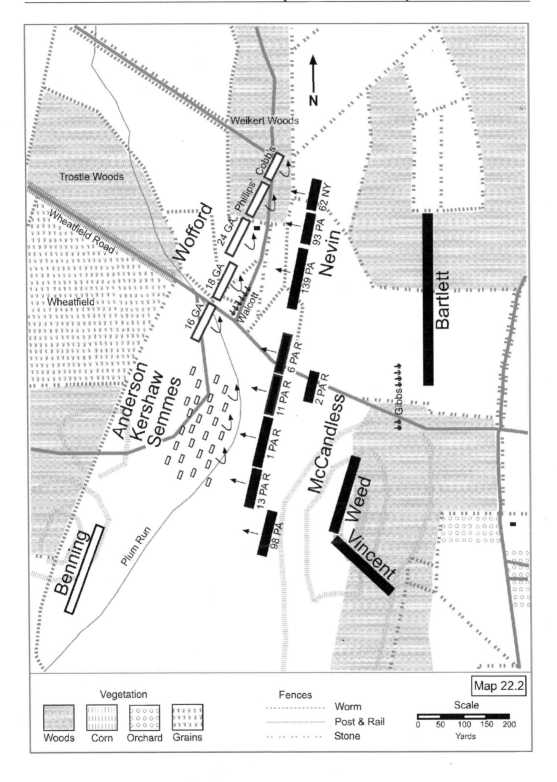

Weikert Woods

Trostle Woods

Wheatfield Road

Wofford

Phillips Cobb's

24 GA

18 GA

16 GA

Walcott

Wheatfield

Anderson
Kershaw
Semmes

Benning

Plum Run

62 NY

93 PA

139 PA

Nevin

Bartlett

Gibbs

6 PAR

2 PAR

11 PAR

McCandless

1 PAR

13 PAR

Weed

98 PA

Vincent

Map 22.2

Vegetation

Woods   Corn   Orchard   Grains

Fences

-------------- Worm

···················· Post & Rail

— — — — — Stone

Scale

0   50   100   150   200

Yards

Map Set 23: Cemetery Hill

Map 23.1

Cemetery Hill was the hinge of the entire Federal position, the joint upon which the defensive line turned from its north-south axis eastward before curving south onto Culp's Hill to form the well-known "fishhook" position. Although it bristled with guns and good fields of fire, it was defended by elements of Maj. Gen. Oliver O. Howard's XI Corps, which had been decimated at Chancellorsville two months earlier and again the previous day (July 1).

Brigadier General Adelbert Ames replaced the wounded Francis Barlow at the head of the First Division. Colonel Andrew Harris of the 75th Ohio took over command of Ames' First Brigade. Harris' new command had originally faced the town from the crest of the hill, but much of it was moved down closer to its base and deployed near Brickyard Lane. The 107th Ohio anchored the left of the line, facing generally north, with its left extending toward the top of the hill and its right running down the hill toward the lane. The 25th Ohio formed on its right behind a stone wall, its left flank facing northwest toward the town, and its right to the northeast. The 17th Connecticut was next in line, and the 75th Ohio formed the brigade's right flank. Behind them was the summit of the hill and battery after battery of Federal cannon. The most important artillery units for Ames' men were those facing northwest under Capts. Michael Wiedrich's, Robert Ricketts', and Gilbert Reynolds' batteries (the latter now under Lt. George Breck).[1]

Colonel Leopold von Gilsa's brigade occupied a low stone wall to the right (southeast) of Harris' brigade. Von Gilsa's Germans faced northeast. The 54th New York was on the left, and the 68th New York and the 153rd Pennsylvania extended the line to the right along Brickyard Lane. Von Gilsa's fourth regiment, the 41st New York, along with the 33rd Massachusetts of Col. Orland Smith's brigade, occupied Culp's Meadow to the northeast, probably to guard against an attack on Culp's Hill by Maj. Gen. Edward Johnson's Confederate division. Von Gilsa's position was especially poor. Isolated from the other units, von Gilsa's men could not be effectively covered by the Union guns on Cemetery Hill, and a knoll 120 yards in their front restricted their line of sight.[2]

For the defenders of Cemetery Hill, the day was quiet save for enemy sharpshooting from the town. About 4:00 p.m., Maj. Joseph Latimer's Confederate artillery battalion on Benner's Hill opened fire. According to a soldier in the 153rd Pennsylvania, the "enemy's shot and shells which, hitherto had injured us but little, were now doing terrible execution in our ranks. Everywhere men were seen writhing in the agony of death . . . wounded were shrieking for help which no one could render them." Some units moved frequently to reduce losses. The Federal artillery on the hill picked up the range of the enemy guns and drove them off, inflicting heavy losses and mortally wounding Major Latimer.[3]

Just before dark, General Ames noticed a gap between Harris' right and von Gilsa's left. He quickly ordered the 17th Connecticut to move to the right of the 75th Ohio. While this effectively sealed the gap between the two brigades, it created a new one between the 25th Ohio and the 75th Ohio, which was only partially filled by Colonel Harris, who ordered a "thinning of the line from the left, moving the regiments farther to the right except the left of the 107th Ohio." So thin was his line that "all of the men could get to the stone wall used by us as a breastwork, and have all the elbow room he wanted."[4]

While the Federals adjusted their lines, Maj. Gen. Jubal Early's Division (Lt. Gen. Richard Ewell's Second Corps) rested near the southeast corner of the town, readying its attack. Brigadier General Harry Hays' Louisiana Tiger brigade occupied the area behind Winebrenner's Run. Although no one left an account of its disposition, a reasonable guess is that it formed from left to right as follows: 6th Louisiana – 5th Louisiana – 9th Louisiana – 7th Louisiana – 8th Louisiana. Colonel Isaac Avery's Brigade was on Hays' left and retained the same alignment as the day before, from left to right as follows: 57th North Carolina – 21st North Carolina – 6th North Carolina. Brigadier General John Gordon's Brigade formed in reserve.[5]

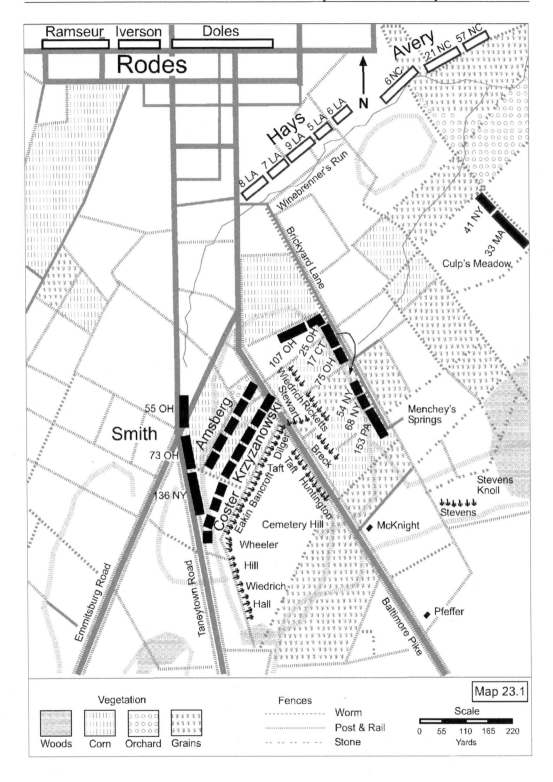

Ramseur Iverson Doles

Rodes

Avery

6 NC 21 NC 57 NC

Hays

8 LA 7 LA 9 LA 5 LA 6 LA

Winebrenner's Run

Brickyard Lane

41 NY
33 MA

Culp's Meadow

107 OH 25 OH 17 CT 75 OH

Wiedrich Stewart Ricketts

54 NY 68 NY 153 PA

Menchey's Springs

55 OH

Smith

Ansberg

Coster Krzyzanowski

73 OH

Eakin Bancroft Diltger Taft Breck Huntington

136 NY

Taft

Stevens Knoll

Stevens

Cemetery Hill

McKnight

Wheeler

Hill

Wiedrich

Hall

Emmitsburg Road

Taneytown Road

Baltimore Pike

Pfeffer

Vegetation

Woods Corn Orchard Grains

Fences

Worm
Post & Rail
Stone

Scale

0   55   110 165 220
Yards

Map 23.1

Map 23.2

The relative quiet was broken shortly before 8:00 p.m. when Maj. Gen. Jubal Early launched two brigades against Cemetery Hill. Col. Isaac Avery's regiments were ordered to strike from the northeast while Brig. Gen. Harry Hays' Louisiana troops assaulted from the north. Holding Gettysburg proper was Maj. Gen. Robert Rodes' Division. His task was to get his brigades out of town, deploy them, and assail Cemetery Hill from the northwest

A lieutenant in the 8th Louisiana received the orders to assault the high ground with dread. "I felt as if my doom was sealed, and it was with great reluctance that I started my skirmishers forward." Another officer put it this way: "the quiet, solimn mien of our men showed plainly . . . on every face was most legibly written the firm determination to do or die." Colonel Hamilton Jones of the 57th North Carolina recalled that when a bugle sounded the order to move out, "the line advanced in beautiful order, and as it pointed to the south-west there was a glint all along the line of bayonets that was very striking and marked how beautifully they were aligned."[6]

Hays' right flank probably followed the eastern side of Brickyard Lane for about 250 yards before wheeling to the right to approach the Federal line. The brigade's left flank was probably where the school sits today.[7]

Avery's Brigade probably marched astride the fence line that today is marked by East Confederate Avenue. After crossing an orchard, the North Carolinians traversed Culp's Meadow, where Colonel Avery halted the brigade to dress its ranks. He then wheeled his men to the right while Hays moved to the left to close the gap between the two brigades. The commander of the 57th North Carolina described the movement as one in "which none but the steadiest veterans could have executed under such circumstances." In a vulnerable position in Culp's Meadow, the 41st New York and 33rd Massachusetts pulled back and extended von Gilsa's line to the right.[8]

The Confederates sustained only light losses from the artillery and small arms fire and reached a low-lying area out of sight of the Federals remarkably unscathed. "But we are too quick for them, and are down in the valley in a trice, while the Yankee missiles are hissing, screaming & hurtling over our heads, doing but little damage," was how an officer in Hays' Brigade explained the thus-far successful attack.

Colonel Andrew Harris watched as Avery's line of battle appeared anew, stepping out of the low-lying area. "When they came into full view in Culp's meadow our artillery . . . opened on them with all the guns that could be brought to bear," Harris later wrote. "[S]till on they came, moving steadily to the assault, soon the infantry opened fire, but they never faltered. They moved forward as steadily, amid this hail of shot shell and minnie ball, as though they were on parade far removed from danger."[9]

Fully aware that his men were still recovering mentally and physically from the thrashing they had suffered on July 1, Colonel Harris rode along the line, reminding the soldiers about the "importance of our position, and that we must hold it all hazards." The colonel was not optimistic about his chances. Many of these same regiments had sustained heavy losses the day before, and some probably numbered fewer than 100 effectives.[10]

A wounded private watching the charge from the upper floor of a church left a graphic description of the effects of the Federal fire: "[H]eads, arms, and legs flying amid the dust and smoke . . . it reminded me much of a wagon load of pumpkins drawn up a hill and the end gate coming out, and the pumpkins rolling and bounding down the hill." At least four batteries poured a frontal and enfilade fire against the advancing Confederate lines. Avery's men were hardest hit, hammered by the batteries on Cemetery Hill and by Stevens' battery, firing from what is today known as Stevens Knoll.[11]

General Hays attributed the light losses suffered by his brigade to the growing darkness and rolling dense smoke. "Our exact locality could not be discovered by the enemy's gunners, and we thus escaped what in the full light of day could have been nothing else than horrible slaughter." The steep slope of East Cemetery Hill also protected Hays' men from the artillery on the top of the hill.[12]

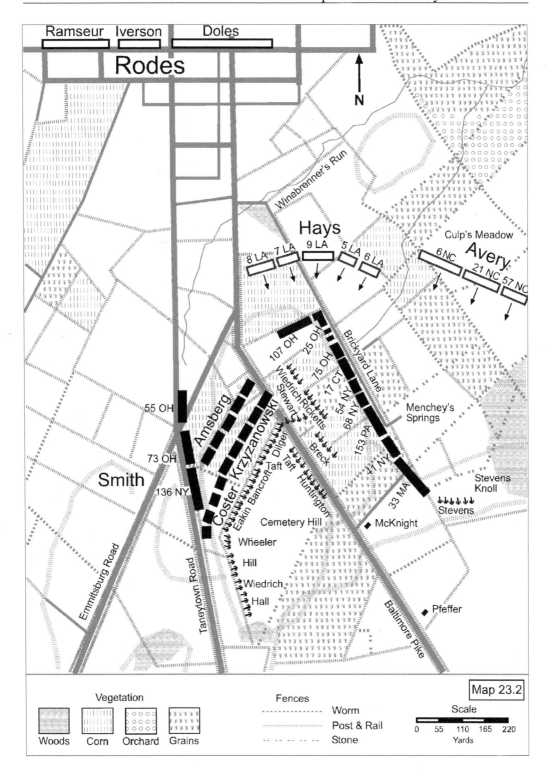

Ramseur Iverson   Doles

Rodes

N

Winebrenner's Run

Hays

Culp's Meadow

Avery

8 LA 7 LA 9 LA 5 LA 6 LA

6 NC 21 NC 57 NC

107 OH 25 OH 75 OH

17 CT

54 NY

68 NY

Brickyard Lane

Wiedrich

Ricketts

Stewart

153 PA

Menchey's
Springs

55 OH

Amsberg

Coster-Krzyzanowski

Dilger

Taft

Taft

Bancroft

Eakin

Breck

41 NY

33 MA

Stevens
Knoll

Stevens

73 OH

Smith

136 NY

Huntington

Cemetery Hill

McKnight

Wheeler

Hill

Wiedrich

Hall

Pfeffer

Emmitsburg Road

Taneytown Road

Baltimore Pike

Vegetation

Woods	Corn	Orchard	Grains

Fences

.... Worm
.... Post & Rail
-- -- -- -- Stone

Map 23.2

Scale

0   55   110   165   220
Yards

Map 23.3

Despite the concentrated Federal gunfire, the pair of Confederate brigades quickly traversed the 600 yards to Cemetery Hill. One of Brig. Gen. Harry Hays' soldiers wrote that upon approaching the stone wall, the enemy "did not want to leave . . . with bayonets & clubbed guns we drove them back." Some of the 7th and 9th Louisiana regiments found the thinly defended gap between Col. Andrew Harris' 25th Ohio and 75th Ohio regiments and exploited it. Sergeant George Clements of the former regiment recalled how the Confederates "put their big feet on the stone wall and went over like deer, over the heads of the whole . . . regiment, the grade being steep and the wall not more than 20 inches high."

Once over the wall, the Louisiana troops attacked the 25th and 107th Ohio from the rear. Captain John Lutz of the 107th Ohio insisted his men were ordered to pull back, "fighting step by step to the stone fence in front of Weidrich's Battery." The attack also forced back the 75th Ohio's two left-most companies.[13]

The rest of the 75th Ohio stood firm in its naturally strong position, as did the 17th Connecticut to its right. The men could not see their attackers, but they could certainly hear them. "They came on us about dark yelling like demons with fixed bayonets," noted Charles Ladley of the 75th Ohio. According to Major Allen Brady of the 17th Connecticut, "when within 150 paces of us, we poured a destructive fire upon them, which thinned their ranks and checked their advance." Hays' men regrouped and charged again. Although the fighting was hand-to-hand, the 17th Connecticut refused to give up the wall.[14]

Confederates who had breached the left of the brigade's line got into the rear of these two regiments. Meanwhile, the 6th North Carolina and the right of the 21st North Carolina struck the undersized and skittish 54th and 68th New York regiments. After a brief fight, the New Yorkers abandoned their positions and retreated up the hill. Battery commander Capt. R. Bruce Ricketts called their behavior "cowardly and disgraceful in the extreme . . . although they had a stone-wall in their front, [they] commenced running in the greatest confusion to the rear, hardly a shot was fired, certainly not a volley, and so panic stricken were they that several ran into the canister fire of my guns and were knocked over." A soldier from the 75th Ohio confirmed Ricketts' recollection, writing derisively, "those Germans could not face the bayonet. How they were slaughtered." The 153rd Pennsylvania on the New Yorkers' right attempted to hold its precarious position. One soldier recalled "muskets being handled as clubs; rocks torn from the wall in front and thrown, fists and bayonets used."[15]

Von Gilsa's defensive line sprang more leaks as the left portion of the 41st New York was also forced up the hill. However, the right side of the regiment and the 33rd Massachusetts on the flank held their positions. An "indentation" in the hill caused the 57th North Carolina's left flank to "swing round almost half a turn" before it struck these Federal units where they stood behind a sturdy stone wall. Colonel Adin Underwood of the 33rd Massachusetts recalled that the "enemy came on gallantly . . . my regiment opened a severe musketry fire on them, which caused gaps in their line and made it stagger back a bit. It soon rallied and bravely came within a few feet of our wall . . . and [my men] steadily poured in their fire. I ordered them to fix bayonets." Despite the concentrated small arms fire, the North Carolinians continued their advance. "Our colonel just gave the 33d, 'Fix bayonets and remember Massachusetts!' when Stevens' 5th Maine Battery to our right let go all six guns in one volley and swept our front clear of Rebels with canister," recalled John Ryder. That artillery volley all but ended the 57th North Carolina's attack against the stone wall.[16]

Meanwhile, three brigades from Maj. Gen. Robert Rodes' Division (led by Brig. Gens. Stephen Ramseur, Alfred Iverson, and George Doles) were moving out of Gettysburg to their jump-off point for the attack southeast of the town. The move was undertaken later than it should have been, and the logistics of untangling the masses of men from the narrow streets and deploying them for the attack took much longer than anticipated.

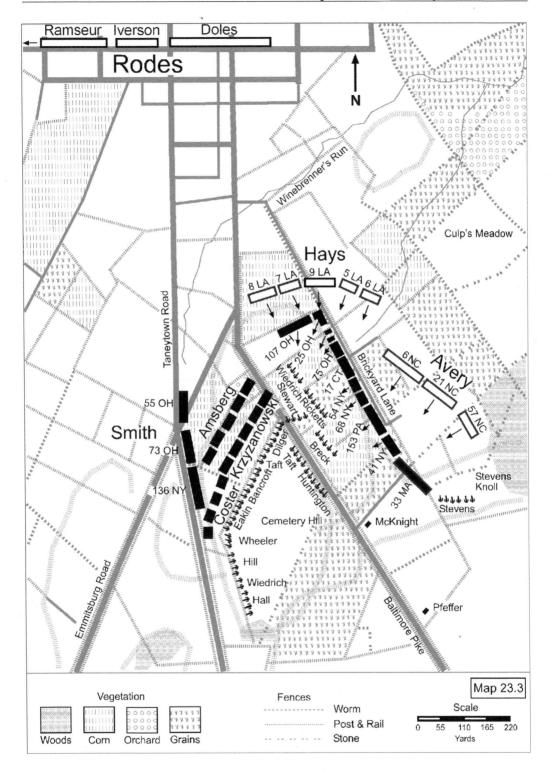

Map 23.3

Map 23.4

Fragments of Brig. Gen. Adelbert Ames' line continued to stand their ground at the stone wall—particularly the 75th Ohio and 17th Connecticut regiments on the left, and the 33rd Massachusetts coupled with elements of the 153rd Pennsylvania and the 41st New York on the right. The other regiments broke under the Confederate attacks and ran to the rear, up the slope to the top of the hill.

The 25th and 107th Ohio regiments took up positions behind a stone wall on the left flank of Captain Michael Weidrich's battery, facing north against Hays' Brigade. The flagbearer of the 107th Ohio, Sergeant Greibel, "stood flaunting them in the faces of the rebels" but was shot and the colors nearly captured. Realizing that his men were about to break, Capt. Peter Young sprang forward at the advancing Confederates and shot the 8th Louisiana's flagbearer, catching the colors before they hit the ground. Just seconds later, Young fell wounded in his left arm and lung. The fighting at the top of the hill was desperate and waged at close quarters. In the smoke and growing darkness, muzzle flashes illuminated the men. "It was almost impossible to distinguish who were Union, who were Confederate, to shoot and not kill our own men," wrote a Federal. "Artillerists fought with ramrods, wielding them like ball bats."[17]

The fight around Wiedrich's guns was especially frenzied. The Federal infantry and gunners fought with bayonets, clubbed muskets, pistols, rammers, and even rocks. One of Hays' men threw himself at a cannon muzzle, exclaiming, "I take command of this gun!" A German artilleryman yelled, "Du sollst sie haben!" and pulled the lanyard, blowing apart the soldier. The Louisianans ultimately claimed the guns. "Arriving at the summit, by a simultaneous rush from my whole line," the Louisiana general triumphantly wrote in his official account of the battle, "I captured several pieces of artillery, four stands of colors, and a number of prisoners. At that time every piece of artillery which had been firing upon us was silenced."[18]

It appears as though only portions of the 7th and 8th Louisiana regiments scaled the hill in the growing darkness, while about 75 men from the 6th North Carolina and a small contingent from the 21st North Carolina penetrated the line at the point formerly held by the 54th and 68th New York regiments before moving farther up the hill. The Tarheels could only see the artillerymen of Captain Ricketts' battery when the guns fired. With a final rush, these Confederates threw themselves on the battery's left section. The fighting there was hand-to-hand, with the gunners refusing to abandon their pieces. The Confederates captured at least one gun and spiked another during the bloody confrontation.[19]

By this time, after a stunning dusk attack and night fighting rarely witnessed during the war, two separate groups of Confederates held the summit of Cemetery Hill. To the north, men from the 7th and 8th Louisiana regiments held the area around Wiedrich's battery, where they continued fighting elements from the 25th and 107th Ohio regiments. Just to the south, about 75 men from the 6th North Carolina, a dozen or so from the 9th Louisiana, and possibly some from the 21st North Carolina, occupied the stone wall near Ricketts' guns. Both General Hays and Maj. Samuel Tate of the 6th North Carolina knew they had accomplished something substantial, but that without immediate and strong reinforcements, they would not be able to hold the summit. Their men were tired, too few in number, and it would be only a matter of minutes before the Federals counterattacked. Urgent requests for reinforcements were dispatched to General Early. Although they could not have seen it, help was on the way in the form of three brigades from Rodes' Division, slowly approaching from the northwest.[20]

As Hays feared, Federal reinforcements were also streaming into the sector. From the II Corps position just south of Cemetery Hill, Maj. Gen. Winfield Hancock quickly dispatched three regiments from Col. Samuel Carroll's brigade along with the 106th Pennsylvania from Brig. Gen. Alexander Webb's Philadelphia Brigade. General Howard was also at work, rounding up XI Corps troops from Cols. W. Krzyzanowski's and Charles Coster's brigades and rushing them to the hill.[21]

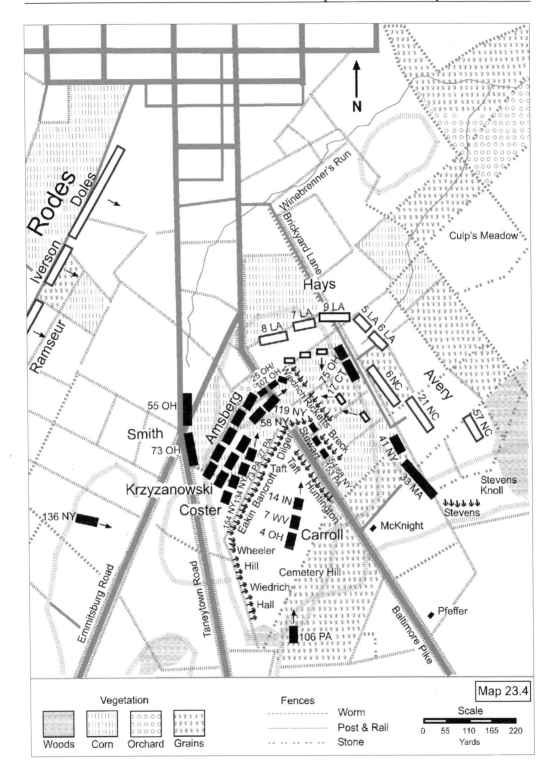

N

Rodes
Doles
Iverson
Ramseur

Winebrenner's Run
Brickyard Lane
Culp's Meadow

Hays
7 LA   9 LA   5 LA 6 LA
8 LA
25 OH/
107 OH   73 OH
Wiedrich   75 OH
17 CT   6 NC   Avery
55 OH   119 NY   Rickets Breck   21 NC
Smith   58 NY   Steward   57 NC
73 OH   27 PA   Diley   41 NY
Amsberg   Taft   Taft   153 PA
68 NY
Krzyzanowski   33 MA
Coster   14 IN   Stevens Knoll
154 NY 134 NY 73 PA   7 WV   Huntington   Stevens
136 NY   Eakin Bancroft   4 OH   Carroll   McKnight
Wheeler   Cemetery Hill   Pfeffer
Hill
Wiedrich
Hall
106 PA

Emmitsburg Road
Taneytown Road
Baltimore Pike

Vegetation

Woods   Corn   Orchard   Grains

Fences
---------- Worm
.... Post & Rail
— - — - — Stone

Scale
0   55   110   165   220
Yards

Map 23.4

Map 23.5

An eerie quiet descended around Brig. Gen. Harry Hays' position atop Cemetery Hill. The welcomed lull lasted only a short time.

As the Louisianans took stock of their new surroundings, they heard the sounds of troops massing in the darkness and moving in their direction. Were they reinforcements from Maj. Gen. Robert Rodes' Division or perhaps Brig. Gen. John Gordon's Brigade? Was the enemy already counterattacking? Unsure, General Hays ordered his men to hold their fire. A scattered volley was discharged toward the Louisianans. Hays stood firm. A second volley was discharged, and still Hays refused to allow his men to return it. When a third volley ripped through his line from less than 100 yards away, Hays finally determined to his satisfaction they were under attack by Federal troops. He ordered his men to open fire. "[The] Yankee line melted away in the darkness," recalled one officer.[22]

Another line soon appeared in their front and others approached on their flanks. These Federals were the 25th and 107th Ohio regiments and other XI Corps units. Major General Oliver O. Howard led the 119th New York and 58th New York regiments of Col. W. Krzyzanowski's brigade. The 27th and 73rd Pennsylvania regiments of Col. Charles Coster's brigade also arrived and threw themselves at the Louisianans. Hays knew his small command was about to be surrounded. With great reluctance, he ordered his men to fall back.[23]

The North Carolinians around Captain Ricketts' captured battery were also nervously awaiting reinforcements that would never arrive. Because of the darkness and dense smoke, noted an officer in the 6th North Carolina, "we could not see what the enemy was doing, but we could hear him attempting to rally his men . . . soon they came over the hill in pursuit, when we again opened fire on them, and cleared the hill a second time." These Federals were probably from Col. Leopold von Gilsa's brigade, which was driven back in the original attack. Behind them, Col. Samuel Carroll's brigade streamed through the archway of the cemetery.[24] The 14th Indiana led the brigade, followed by the 7th West Virginia and 4th Ohio. As the men neared the cemetery's gate house, Carroll yelled, "Halt! Front face! Charge bayonets! Forward, double-quick! March! Give them ———!" Carroll sent the West Virginians to the left to clear out the North Carolinians along the stone wall by Ricketts' guns. The 14th Indiana's Lt. Col. Elijah Cavins recalled the brief fight that followed: "it was a headlong dash in the dark—a yell—and a few rounds aimed at the flash of the enemy's guns, and all was over for the night." The 4th Ohio fought on the right of the Hoosiers. The 106th Pennsylvania of Webb's brigade and the 136th New York of Smith's brigade probably arrived too late to participate.[25] Overwhelmed by these reinforcements, Major Tate ordered his Tarheels to retreat. "Under cover of the darkness, I ordered the men to break and to risk the fire," he reported. "We did so, and lost not a man in getting out." Tate's infantry probably occupied the top of the hill for only 15 or 20 minutes.[26]

The stunning attack and short-lived victory on East Cemetery Hill generated heavy losses. One of those killed during the advance was Col. Isaac Avery, who was mounted on a conspicuous white horse. Wounded and pinned by his horse midway between the town and hill, Avery took out a scrap of paper and pencil and wrote his last words: "Major, tell my father I died with my face to the enemy." Although Avery did not make it to the summit, those who did and returned alive were upset that Gordon's Brigade did not advance to help them.

For reasons that are still perplexing, Rodes' division-size attack from the northwest did not materialize. Somehow, the experienced combat leader failed to prepare his men in time to march through the town and deploy properly to assault the heights while Jubal Early's infantry was doing the same thing from the north and northeast. By the time Rodes' brigades approached the hill, Early's men were being driven from its crest. Exactly why is not known, but Rodes turned over tactical command to Stephen Ramseur, one of his brigade commanders. The fiery officer marched more than halfway to the objective, but waved off the attack when he concluded they were too late to be of any help. Rodes' brigades pulled back to Long Lane.[27]

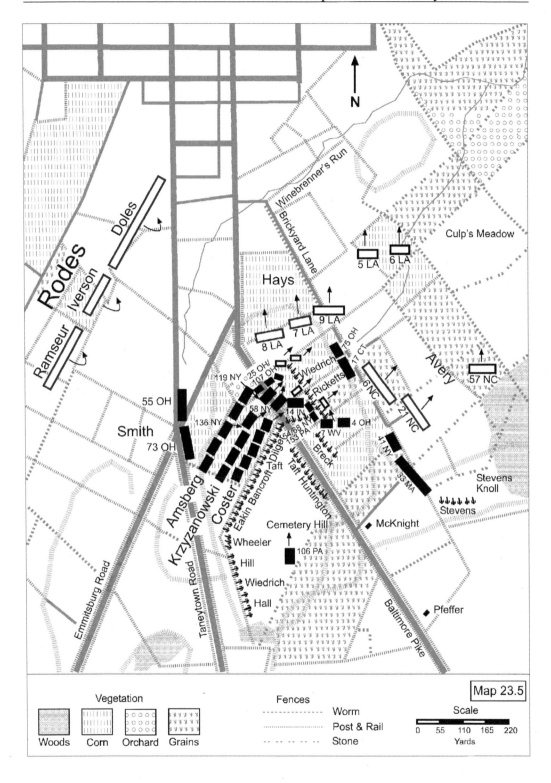

N

Rodes

Doles

Iverson

Ramseur

Smith

55 OH

73 OH

Hays

Winebrenner's Run

Brickyard Lane

Culp's Meadow

5 LA   6 LA

9 LA

7 LA

8 LA

119 NY   25 OH
107 OH
Wiedrich
Ricketts
136 NY   58 NY   14 N
54/68 N
153 PA   7 WV   4 OH
Taft   Breck

Amsberg

Krzyzanowski

Coster

Eakin   Bancroft   Dilger   Taft Huntington

Wheeler

Hill

Wiedrich

Hall

Cemetery Hill

106 PA

Emmitsburg Road

Taneytown Road

75 OH

17 CT

Avery

57 NC

6 NC

21 NC

41 NY

33 MA

Stevens Knoll

Stevens

McKnight

Pfeffer

Baltimore Pike

Vegetation

Woods   Corn   Orchard   Grains

Fences

------- Worm

·········· Post & Rail

— ·· — ·· — Stone

Map 23.5

Scale

0   55   110   165   220

Yards

Map Set 24: The Fight for Culp's Hill

Map 24.1

Major General Henry Slocum's Federal XII Corps arrived on the battlefield during the late afternoon of July 1. Despite its obvious importance, Slocum's corps did not occupy Culp's Hill until early the following morning. When he was elevated to command that sector, Brig. Gen. Alpheus Williams of the First Division took charge of the XII Corps. Brigadier General Thomas Ruger moved up to command the First Division, and Col. Silas Colgrove assumed control of the Third Brigade. Brigadier General John Geary commanded the XII Corps' Second Division.[1]

Culp's Hill is actually two hills, with a dip or wide "saddle" yawning between them. Geary's division occupied the higher of the two hills, with Brig. Gen. George Greene's brigade anchoring the left and Brig. Gen. Thomas Kane's brigade deployed on "Pap" Greene's right. Colonel Charles Candy's brigade dug in behind its sister units. Colonel Archibald McDougall's brigade of Ruger's First Division formed on Kane's right, with Col. Silas Colgrove's brigade occupying the Spangler Spring area farther to the right. An independent brigade under Brig. Gen. Henry Lockwood extended the line to the right, facing southeast.

From the top of the upper slope of Culp's Hill, Greene's men could look to their left and see Federals from the I Corps. Kane's brigade, now commanded by Col. George Cobham, deployed on Greene's right "at an angle of about 45 degrees forward, conforming its line to the crest of the ridge" in the "saddle" region between the higher and lower hills. Greene deployed his regiments along a 400-yard front from left to right as follows: 78th New York – 60th New York – 102nd New York – 149th New York – 137th New York. Kane's brigade deployed with the 109th Pennsylvania on the left and the 111th Pennsylvania on its right along the top of the lower hill. The latter regiment's right flank connected with the 123rd New York of McDougall's brigade. Kane's remaining regiment, the 29th Pennsylvania, deployed behind a stone wall about 100 yards to the rear. The 29th's right flank connected with the left flank of the 3rd Maryland Infantry of McDougall's brigade.[2]

The line of McDougall's brigade ran along the crest of the rocky, wooded lower hill with its right flank extending almost to Rock Creek. There, it connected at an angle with Colgrove's brigade. McDougall deployed his brigade in two lines of battle. The first line formed near the crest of the lower hill and contained, from left to right, the following regiments: 123rd New York – 20th Connecticut – 46th Pennsylvania. The second line settled behind a stone wall seventy-five yards in the rear, deployed, from left to right as follows: 3rd Maryland – 145th New York – 5th Connecticut.[3]

Colgrove's brigade extended the line to the right. A swale or marshy area divided the brigade into two parts. The 107th New York faced Rock Creek on the left at a 45-degree angle to McDougall's brigade, which it touched just north of Spangler's Spring. The 13th New Jersey was about 75 paces behind it, massed in double columns. To the southeast, on the other side of the swale in McAllister's Woods, were the remaining three regiments of Colgrove's brigade. According to Colgrove, the 2nd Massachusetts formed on the left, facing northeast, the 3rd Wisconsin formed in the center of the line facing east, and the 27th Indiana held the right flank, adjacent to Rock Creek and facing south. Because of this unusual alignment, Colgrove referred to the brigade's position as forming "three sides of an irregular square." Rock Creek's width and depth in this area convinced Colgrove the Confederates would not launch an attack in his sector.

Lockwood's unassigned brigade, composed of two large but green regiments, formed to the left of the 27th Indiana, extending the line almost to Baltimore Pike. The 1st Maryland Potomac Home Guard was on the right and the 150th New York formed on its left.[4]

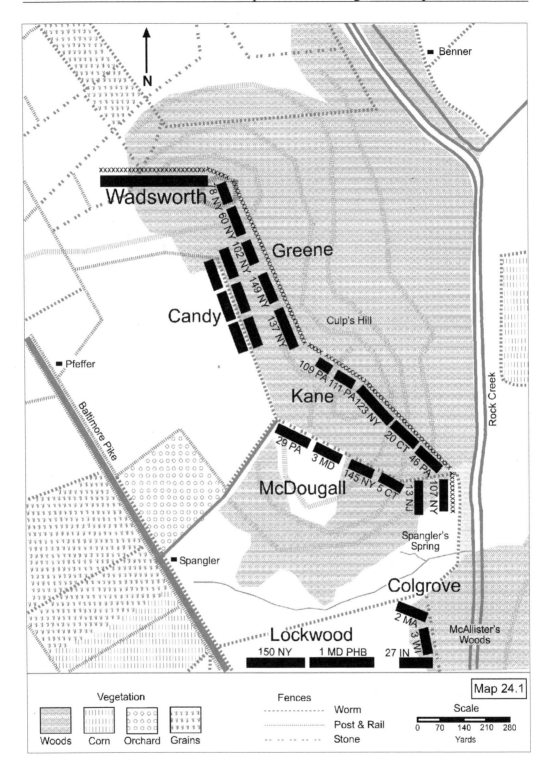

Benner

N

Wadsworth

78 NY

60 NY

102 NY

Greene

149 NY

Candy

137 NY

Culp's Hill

Pfeffer

109 PA

111 PA

123 NY

Kane

20 CT

Baltimore Pike

29 PA

3 MD

145 NY 5 CT

46 PA

107 NY

13 NJ

McDougall

Rock Creek

Spangler's
Spring

Spangler

Colgrove

2 MA

Lockwood

3 WI

McAllister's
Woods

150 NY   1 MD PHB   27 IN

Map 24.1

Vegetation

Woods   Corn   Orchard   Grains

Fences

- - - - - - - - - - -   Worm

....   Post & Rail

- - - - - - - -   Stone

Scale

0   70   140   210   280
              Yards

Map 24.2

While the Confederate troops on this end of the line spent July 2 resting, most of the Federal men with the XII Corps spent the morning building breastworks on Culp's Hill. The men worked methodically and diligently on their defenses. According to Capt. Jesse Jones of the 60th New York, "right and left the men felled the trees, and blocked them up into a close log fence. Piles of cordwood which lay near by were quickly appropriated. The sticks, set slanting on end against the outer face of the logs, made excellent battening." Areas with large rocks and stone ledges precluded the need for construction. The men completed most of the breastworks by noon on July 2 and were rewarded with a well-deserved rest.[5]

The veteran infantrymen of Maj. Gen. Edward Johnson's Division (Lt. Gen. Richard Ewell's Second Corps) knew they would likely be ordered to carry Culp's Hill, but could only shake their heads and complain about the delay in attacking the wooded heights. They could see and hear the Federals building their breastworks and knew that every passing minute would make their task more difficult. The four brigades in Johnson's Division deployed, from left to right as follows: Brig. Gens. James Walker, George Steuart, John M. Jones, and Francis Nicholls (under Col. Jesse Williams).[6]

Artillery from the two armies opened fire about 4:00 p.m. and quickly developed into a fierce counter-battery duel. Before long, the better placed and more numerous Federal guns on Cemetery Hill wreaked havoc on Joseph Latimer's artillery battalion on Benner's Hill. Although Johnson's soldiers sustained few casualties in their sheltered positions, the men watched the exchange with growing anxiety. "Perhaps nothing in battle is so trying to an infantryman's nerves and patience as the preliminary artillery fire that precedes it," explained Maj. William Goldborough of the 1st Maryland Battalion (CSA). Brigadier General Jones' Brigade moved from the division's main line to support Latimer's artillery on Benner's Hill.[7]

The XII Corps' rest ended about 6:00 p.m., when General Williams received urgent orders to pull most of his men from Culp's Hill and rush them south to help repel the savage Confederate attacks being launched along the Federal left and left-center. The thinning of troops from the northern end of the line was part of Lee's purpose behind the en echelon attacks, and it was working rather well. Ruger's division moved off the heights first. Two brigades of Geary's division were ordered to follow Ruger south, but confusion ensued and they ended up marching east across Rock Creek and off the battlefield. Geary compounded his error by sending his men into bivouac while fighting raged both north and west of his new position. Only George Greene's veteran New York regiments remained to defend Culp's Hill.[8]

With the departure of the rest of the XII Corps, General Greene had no choice but to throw the 78th New York out on the skirmish line in front of his brigade. He ordered the rest of his men to move "by the right flank." Steuben Coon of the 60th New York, which now held the left of the brigade, wrote that "now a singular thing took place . . . the commander of our brigade came riding up and ordered every regiment except the 60th to fall into line. He told our Colonel that the other regiments were needed in another place and that he must put the men in a single rank and far enough apart so [as] to cover the ground before occupied by the whole brigade. So away they all went, the last thing the General said, was that we must hold the position!" The 102nd New York and 149th New York regiments stretched to the right and the 137th New York shifted farther right into part of Kane's abandoned breastworks. Beyond the right flank of the 137th New York was an empty line all the way to McAllister's Woods.[9]

General Greene's line had been stretched far too thin to safely hold the high ground, but its weakness meant little for the Confederates because no orders had reached Edward Johnson to carry the hill. The afternoon stretched into evening while the Southern infantrymen sat unemployed.[10]

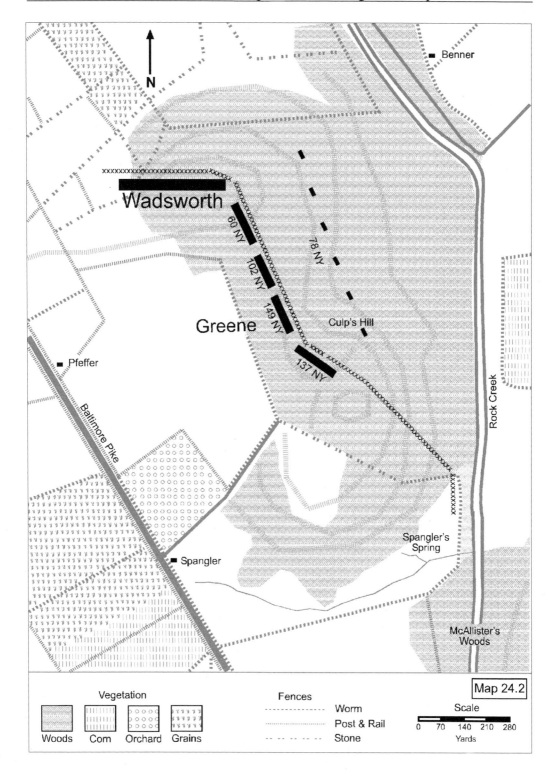

Benner

Wadsworth

60 NY

102 NY

149 NY

78 NY

Greene

Culp's Hill

Pfeffer

137 NY

Baltimore Pike

Rock Creek

Spangler's
Spring

Spangler

McAllister's
Woods

Map 24.2

Vegetation				Fences		Scale

Vegetation

Woods   Corn   Orchard   Grains

Fences

------------ Worm

············· Post & Rail

— ·· — ·· — Stone

Map 24.2

Scale

0   70   140   210   280

Yards

Map 24.3

Sometime after 6:00 p.m., Brig. Gen. John M. Jones marched his brigade back from Benner's Hill and took up a position on the right flank of Maj. Gen. Edward Johnson's division. The brigade deployed from left to right as follows: 21st Virginia – 48th Virginia – 42nd Virginia – 50th Virginia. (The position of the 44th Virginia is not known.) Francis Nicholls' Brigade, under Col. Jesse Williams, deployed on Jones' left, its disposition unknown except that the 1st Louisiana occupied the right flank. Brig. Gen. George Steuart's brigade was next in line, deployed left to right as follows: 10th Virginia – 37th Virginia – 23rd Virginia – 1st Maryland Battalion – 3rd North Carolina. Six companies of the 1st North Carolina formed as a reserve on the right side of the line, while its four remaining companies stayed on picket duty east of Rock Creek. James Walker's Stonewall Brigade held the left divisional front. The 2nd Virginia was engaged in a heavy skirmish with the 9th Massachusetts of Col. Jacob Sweitzer's brigade (James Barnes' division, Sykes' V Corps) and three cavalry regiments from Col. John McIntosh's brigade on Brinkerhoff Ridge. This action kept Walker's entire brigade out of the July 2 fight for Culp's Hill.[11]

When couriers arrived on lathered horses, Johnson's men knew what was in store for them. Commands rang out: "Forward—guide center!" The time was approaching 7:00 p.m. The initial part of the charge was most harrowing, as the men traversed open terrain under Union guns before crossing Rock Creek. Driving back the Federal skirmish line, the three Confederate brigades moved steadily forward. "Our whole line moved forward in handsome order," wrote Lt. Col. L. Salyer of the 50th Virginia, Jones' Brigade. More casualties fell from the ranks when the Confederate battle line encountered Federal infantry in position behind large rock formations. Driving them back, the line splashed across Rock Creek.[12]

The initial part of the attack was particularly difficult for "Maryland" Steuart's Brigade, driving generally west against the southeast sector of Culp's Hill. In order to bring his left

wing to bear, Steuart performed a "right half-wheel," rotating in a clockwise fashion while the 3rd North Carolina on the right maintained its connection with Nicholls' Brigade. The 1st Maryland Battalion maintained its connection with the North Carolinians, while the three Virginia regiments undertook this complex movement. This activity, performed while moving across rough terrain, disrupted Steuart's left regiments. The result was that the right wing portion of the brigade moved ahead faster than the left wing. Reaching the creek, the men splashed across in waist-high water and scrambled up the steep banks. Only Nicholl's (Williams') men indicated that they halted and reformed their ranks after crossing the stream.[13]

Because of the thick forest in front of them and the growing darkness, "Pap" Greene's men could not see what was going on at the bottom of the hill. They were experienced enough to know the significance of the gunfire along Rock Creek, followed a few minutes later by the sudden reappearance of the 78th New York, which had been on the skirmish line. The regiment formed in the "rear of our [102nd New York's] right wing." Word passed along the line that Greene's orders were to "hold the works under all circumstances." George Carr of the 149th New York could not see the Louisianans' initial approach, but recalled how the skirmish line "came running back followed by a Confederate line of battle, yelping and howling in its particular manner." Moments felt like years. "The pale faces, staring eye-balls, and nervous hands grasping loaded muskets, told how terrible were those moments of suspense."[14]

Help for the undermanned far right of the entire Union army was on the way. Realizing the terrible danger the army faced, General Howard quickly dispatched Col. George von Amsberg's brigade from Cemetery Hill to support Greene's men. A staff officer from the I Corps directed two regiments, the 61st Ohio and 157th New York, toward the right side of Greene's line. The remaining two regiments tapped to support Culp's Hill, the 82nd Illinois and 45th New York, were led astray by an XI Corps staff officer; they never entered the fight.[15]

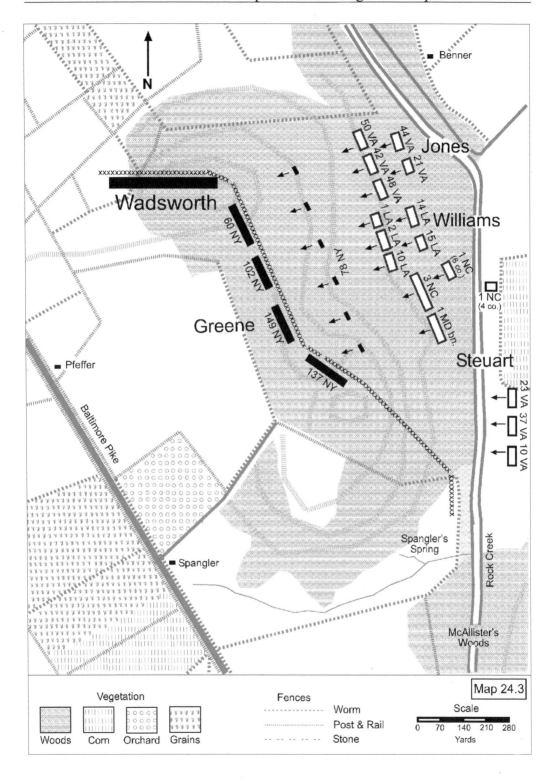

N

Benner

50 VA
44 VA
42 VA
21 VA
Jones
48 VA
14 LA
1 LA
2 LA
Williams
15 LA
10 LA
1 NC
(6 co.)
3 NC
1 NC
(4 co.)
1 MD bn.
Steuart
23 VA
37 VA
10 VA

Wadsworth

60 NY

102 NY

78 NY

Greene

149 NY

137 NY

Pfeffer

Baltimore Pike

Spangler

Spangler's
Spring

Rock Creek

McAllister's
Woods

Vegetation				Fences			Scale		

Woods   Corn   Orchard   Grains

Fences
---------------- Worm
.... Post & Rail
-- -- -- -- Stone

Map 24.3

Scale
0   70   140   210   280
Yards

Map 24.4

Captain Jesse Richardson of the 42nd Virginia of Brig. Gen. John M. Jones' Brigade recalled that his regiment "advanced up the mountain some 75 yards, when it opened fire upon the enemy. It continued loading and firing, pressing forward up the hill." The ill luck of position left Jones' Virginians to ascend the steepest part of Culp's Hill. Another officer recalled that the "works in front of our lines were of a formidable character, and in some places they could scarcely be surmounted without scaling-ladders. . . . All was confusion and disorder." The confusion was even greater on the left side of Jones' advancing brigade. As he rushed over to reassert control of the ragged advance, a Federal bullet fired from an unknown soldier tore into his thigh.[16]

Because of the less rugged terrain on its immediate front, Colonel Williams' Louisiana brigade probably outdistanced Jones' line, but Williams still had his share of problems. "With a yell," wrote one Louisiana officer, "our men rushed forward as best they could up the steep hill side over rocks and through the timber up to the enemy's line of works." The infantry ran from tree to tree and boulder to boulder in an attempt to avoid the minie balls raining down on them from the crest of the wooded heights. The men halted and dropped to the ground to return the fire about 100 yards from the Federal works. The 1st Louisiana regiment on the right side of the line apparently continued advancing, but within a short time Federal fire ground the effort to a halt.[17]

The 3rd North Carolina and 1st Maryland Battalion (the right regiments of George Steuart's Brigade) outdistanced the regiments on their left because of the latter's wheeling movement. As the men ascended the hill, "the heavens are lighted up by the flash of thousands of muskets and the deadly minnies tear and rend our ranks fearfully. Our column reeled and staggered like a drunken man," recalled an officer in the 1st Maryland when his men were hit by a deadly crossfire from the 137th and 149th New York regiments. "The fire thickens and the shrieking shells fill all the air with horrid sound, but still the line moves on over the huge projecting rocks, men falling at every step," remembered another officer. When the Southern infantry had advanced to within thirty yards of the enemy's breastworks, orders circulated through the ranks to lie down to avoid further casualties. Minie balls were "buzzing and hissing" all around them.[18]

According to Steuben Coon, a member of the 60th New York, "not a shot was fired at them until they got within about 15 rods. Then the order was given (Fire!) and we did fire, and kept firing. . . . The rebels yelled like wild Indians and charged upon us on a double quick. They acted bravely, they came as close as they could but very few got within 2 rods of us, those that did never went away again."[19]

George Greene's Federal infantry counted four separate attacks against their position that night. In between each, the men could hear the screams and pleadings of the Confederate wounded. As an officer from General Jones' Brigade recalled, "we tried again and again to drive the enemy from their position, but at length we were compelled to fall back, worn down and exhausted, but not till every round of cartridge had been discharged. At one time we were within a few feet of their works, but the fire was so heavy we could not stand it." The view from the top of the hill confirmed this observation. "[S]oon we heard the rebels coming again . . . this time they came with a rush—they had been reinforced, and thought to drive us out certain," wrote Steuben Coon of the 60th New York. "[T]hey charged again, and again retreated."

Concerned about the Confederate troops in his front that he could hear but not see, Col. Abel Godard of the 60th New York made a difficult decision. He ordered his infantry forward. "I ordered an advance of a portion of my regiment," explained the colonel, "who eagerly leaped the works and surrounded about 50 of the enemy . . . and took at the time two flags."[20]

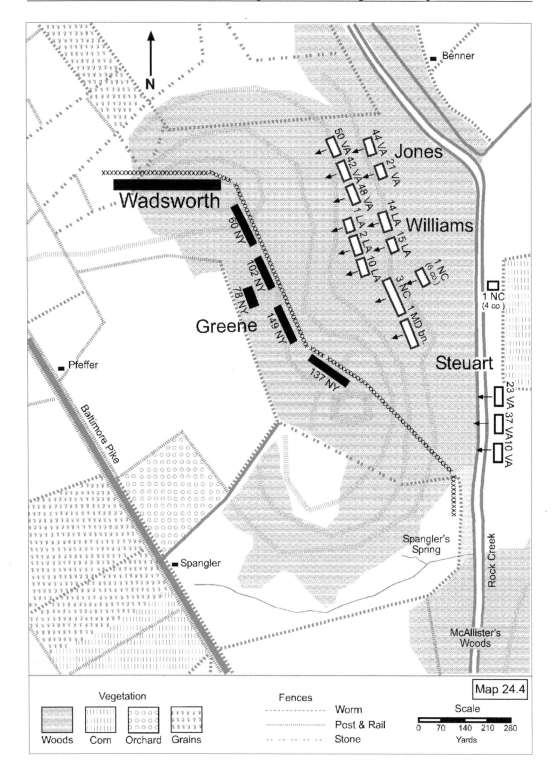

Vegetation

Woods Corn Orchard Grains

Fences

- - - - - - - - - - - - - - Worm
· · · · · · · · · · · · · · Post & Rail
— - — - — - — - Stone

Map 24.4

Scale

0   70   140   210   280
Yards

Map 24.5

By this time, the total darkness that enveloped the battlefield only added to the maddening confusion swirling about on the slopes of Culp's Hill.

East of Culp's Hill, Brig. Gen. George Steuart's right wing was pinned down, but his left wing crossed Rock Creek and ascended the slope on the lower hill. The 23rd Virginia arrived first, forming to the left of the 1st Maryland Battalion. The regiment was woefully understrength: in its ranks were only about fifty men—the rest had remained behind as skirmishers and as the brigade guard. After a time, the small band realized the breastworks in front of them were but weakly defended. Accompanied by three companies from the 1st Maryland Battalion, the Virginians swept up the hill, scattered the enemy soldiers in front of them, and scrambled into the works formerly held by Brig. Gen. Thomas Kane's brigade. The Federal troops driven from the works were probably from the 61st Ohio and 157th New York regiments of Col. George von Amsberg's brigade, which had taken position on the right of the 137th New York. (The 157th New York later lost its flag to the 37th Virginia during the fighting). The piercing of the line flanked the Federals on the right, forcing the two regiments there to retreat.[21]

The 71st Pennsylvania of Brig. Gen. Alexander Webb's Philadelphia Brigade (John Gibbon's division, Hancock's II Corps) arrived to bolster Brig. Gen. George Greene's right flank just as von Amsberg's men were withdrawing. The 37th Virginia could not see the Philadelphians advancing, but they could certainly hear them. Since they knew that no friendly troops would be coming from that direction, the Virginians fired at the noise. The Pennsylvanians quickly took shelter in Kane's abandoned earthworks. Blundering about in the darkness in close proximity to the enemy was apparently too much for the regiment's colonel, R. Penn Smith, who ordered his men to pull back to their position on Cemetery Ridge. When one of Greene's aides demanded to know what Smith was doing, he responded that he had orders to return to his brigade, which was certainly not the case.[22]

After capturing the works and seeing no enemy to his left or front, Lt. Col. Simeon Walton ordered his 23rd Virginia to file to the right to roll up the Federal flank. Forming a line perpendicular to the 137th New York, the Virginians continued advancing with the newly arrived 10th and 37th Virginia regiments. "We gained the enemy's breastworks and poured our fire up their line to our right, thus relieving our men of the other Regts. of the Brigade to our right from the murderous fire they were receiving—pinned down as they were," wrote Charles Raine of the 23rd Virginia after the war. Relieved of the crossfire it had been receiving for about forty-five minutes, and reinforced by the 1st North Carolina, the 1st Maryland Battalion was ordered to spring up and continue its attack in conjunction with the regiments stretching into the darkness beyond its left. The men struggled to their feet but were unable to breach the strong Federal position in front of them.[23]

As soon as the 10th Virginia came up on the extreme left of the line, orders arrived to move forward to a stone wall, where its men poured a destructive fire into the 137th New York's right flank and rear. Colonel David Ireland had already refused the right-most company (A) of the 137th New York to ward off an attack from that sector. The pressure on Company A was too great and it fell back from the earthworks. Each company on its left followed suit until only the left-most company remained in the breastworks (the rest of the line faced southeast).

Seeing the 137th New York's problems, Lt. Col. Charles Randall of the 149th New York attempted to change the orientation of his regiment's three right companies. Some of his company commanders misunderstood these orders and believed they had just been directed to retire. The movement to the rear was well underway before Randall realized the mistake and ordered the men back to their breastworks. It was a costly error. In the short time in the open away from their defensive works, the regiment sustained a number of casualties.[24]

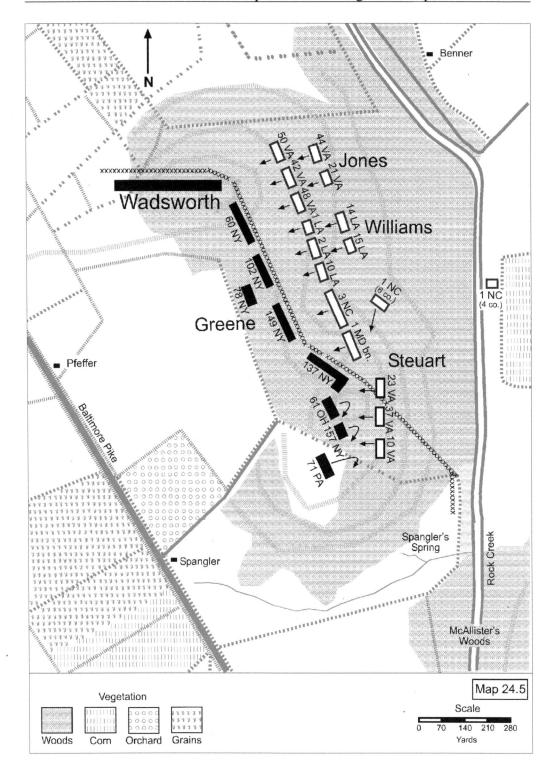

Map 24.5

Map 24.6

The pivotal moment in the battle for Culp's Hill was at hand. The Confederates had captured a portion of the Federal breastworks near the "saddle" area between the upper and lower slopes of Culp's Hill, and were pouring a destructive fire into General Greene's right flank. Reinforcements from the Federal I Corps were arriving about this time in the form of the 6th Wisconsin of the Iron Brigade, the 84th New York and 147th New York regiments of Brig. Gen. Lysander Cutler's brigade, and the 45th New York and 82nd Illinois regiments of Col. George von Amsberg's brigade.[25]

The 147th New York entered the works to the left of the 149th New York, and the 82nd Illinois and the 45th New York filled in the gap between the 60th and 102nd New York of Greene's brigade. Between them, they patched the line facing northeast. The other two I Corps regiments continued south toward the right of the 137th New York. As the 6th Wisconsin and 84th New York approached the breastworks, they quickly discovered the enemy occupied them. The encounter forced the commander of the 10th Virginia to change the orientation of his troops to beat back this new threat. The Confederates, "who were completely surprised at our sudden arrival, rose up and fired a volley at us, and immediately retreated down the hill," recalled Lt. Col. Rufus Dawes of the 6th Wisconsin.

Realizing that additional Federal troops were descending into the area, and with the growing confusion caused by the darkness, Brig. Gen. George Steuart ordered his men back to the captured breastworks. His decision ended the action between 10:00 and 11:00 p.m. From all available evidence of the confused fighting that night, it appears that Jones' Brigade had confronted the 60th New York and part of the 102nd New York; Nicholls' (Williams') Brigade had fought the 78th New York and 102nd New York, and Steuart's Brigade encountered the 149th and 137th New York—in addition to the reinforcements that arrived to block his thrust.[26]

Additional Federal help was streaming toward this end of the field. The remainder of Slocum's XII Corps was returning from its trek to the southern end of the field (where it was not needed because the fighting had ended). Slocum prepared his men to assail the lost breastworks in the morning. Kane's brigade arrived first and fired into Steuart's left wing, ending all thoughts the Confederates may have had of pressing their advantage that night.[27]

The arrival of Slocum and the repulse of Steuart's regiments ended the hostilities on July 2, although intermittent firing broke out along the line periodically throughout the night. "The firing ceased along the line about 9:30 p.m. During the night, about 1 a.m. and again at 2 a.m., volleys were delivered by both sides," wrote Capt. Lewis Stegman, commander of the 102nd New York.[28] Nowhere else on the battlefield did the Confederates hold as strategic or advanced a position as the captured Federal breastworks on Culp's Hill. The two sides rested and prepared for the fight everyone believed would erupt at daybreak.

While three of Johnson's brigades had assaulted Culp's Hill, his fourth brigade under Brig. Gen. James Walker sat on Brinkerhoff Ridge completely out of the main battle action. His presence was sorely missed and might have tipped the scales in the struggle for the wooded heights. "General Walker was directed to follow, but reported to me that the enemy were advancing upon him from their right, he was ordered to repulse them and follow on as soon as possible," was how General Johnson reported the absence of the Stonewall Brigade. Walker decided not to obey Johnson's orders. As he later explained it, "[O]ur flank and rear would have been entirely uncovered and unprotected in the event of my moving with the rest of the division, and as our movement must have been made in full view of the enemy, I deemed it prudent to hold my position after dark, which I did."

However prudent Walker's decision, his 1,400 men were on Brinkerhoff's Ridge and not on Culp's Hill on the evening of July 2. The 2nd Virginia returned about 8:00 p.m. and the entire Stonewall Brigade advanced toward Rock Creek to support Steuart's Brigade. Walker's infantry did not attack the Federal line that night.[29]

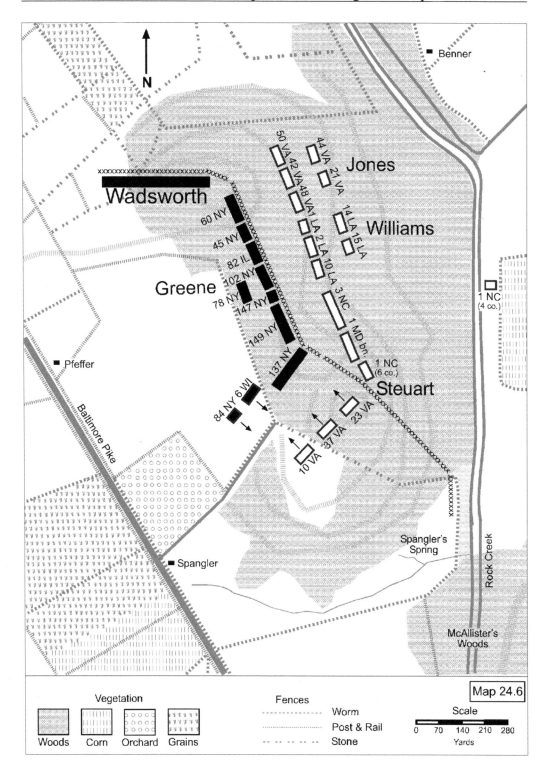

N

Benner

Wadsworth

50 VA 42 VA 48 VA 44 VA 21 VA   Jones

60 NY

45 NY

14 LA '5 LA   Williams

82 IL

102 NY

1 LA 2 LA

Greene

78 NY

10 LA 3 NC

147 NY

149 NY

1 MD bn.

1 NC
(4 co.)

Pfeffer

137 NY

1 NC
(6 co.)

Steuart

84 NY 6 WI

23 VA

37 VA

10 VA

Baltimore Pike

Spangler's
Spring

Spangler

Rock Creek

McAllister's
Woods

Vegetation

Woods   Corn   Orchard   Grains

Fences

.... Worm

.... Post & Rail

-- -- -- -- Stone

Map 24.6

Scale

0   70   140   210   280
Yards

Evening July 2 – Morning July 3

The intensity of the fighting on the southern and central portions of the battlefield belied its relatively short duration. During those few hours, eleven Confederate brigades had grappled with twenty-two Federal brigades during General Lee's effort to break up and drive away General Meade's left and center. Losses on both sides were heavy. Lee's army lost about 6,000 killed, wounded, and captured, while Meade's Federals suffered losses approaching 9,000 from all causes. General Ewell's attack against the Federal right on Cemetery Hill and Culp's Hill was much briefer and involved far fewer troops—five Confederate brigades against the better part of four Federal brigades. Because of advantageous defensive positions, the Federals lost fewer than 900 men, while Ewell's Corps left almost 1,600 casualties on the field attempting to charge head-long uphill. Southern soldiers had come close to capturing Little Round Top and had reached the summits of Cemetery Hill and Cemetery Ridge. Federal reinforcements had driven back every penetrating thrust. By the end of the day, the Confederates had gained significant terrain on the southern end of the field and controlled Houck's Ridge. On the northern end, they held a small section of the earthworks on Culp's Hill. Meade's army, however, was still intact.[1]

The men engaged in a variety of activities that night. Many roamed the fields searching for missing comrades, trying to locate their units, collecting weapons, or shuttling the wounded to makeshift hospitals. Some tried to fashion crude breastworks with whatever implements they could find. Most simply fell utterly exhausted to the ground. Sleep came to few. "All night long were heard the monotonous tramp of moving troops, the low rumble of the wheels of ambulances, the ammunition and supply trains, and the artillery over stony roads. The sharp command of the officers, the curses of teamsters heard above the murmur of many voices, the groans of the wounded and dying made a medley of weird and discordant sounds," recalled Henry Meyer of the 148th Pennsylvania (Col. Edward Cross' brigade, Hancock's II Corps). Everyone feared the dawn would bring more fighting.[2]

Meade assembled his corps leaders behind the center of his army at the Leister house. The Federals had narrowly escaped defeat and had lost heavily on each of the prior two days. Should the army remain at Gettysburg and continue fighting—or retreat? When a consensus was reached to stay and fight, Meade had orders for the army's deployment on July 3 drafted.

After two days of battle, Lee's options were very limited. He could not long remain in place because of logistical reasons, so assuming the defensive held little appeal—especially after two days of riding the razor's edge of victory. Withdrawing made little sense and was a risky proposition in front of a strong enemy. Resuming the offensive seemed his best option.

But attack where? Many details about how to strike Meade's center would not be ironed out until well after the sun was up, but Lee knew he would have fresh troops in Maj. Gen. George Pickett's Division (Longstreet's First Corps) and more artillery. Lee knew unmolested Federal guns and infantry would doom any attack across open terrain, so he decided to use a massive pre-attack barrage to soften the defenses. Lee's gunnery chiefs positioned their pieces during the night. Pickett moved south to a position near Spangler's Woods. General Longstreet protested Lee's decision, but Third Corps commander Lt. Gen. A. P. Hill endorsed it and offered infantry from his three battered divisions.

What Lee wanted was a simultaneous attack against Meade's center on Cemetery Hill and his right on Culp's Hill (the latter to either break through or prevent reinforcements from reaching the center). He ordered General Ewell to resume his attack against the wooded heights during the early morning hours of July 3. Portions of Gens. Rodes' and Early's divisions would march south from the town to add weight to the attack. Those who had charged up the hill the evening before were not eager to attempt the effort a second time.

On the Federal side, the rest of the XII Corps, which had marched south to reinforce other parts of the line on July 2, returned to Culp's Hill. These additional troops, coupled with the strong breastworks created during the night of July 2-3, made Culp's Hill all but impregnable.

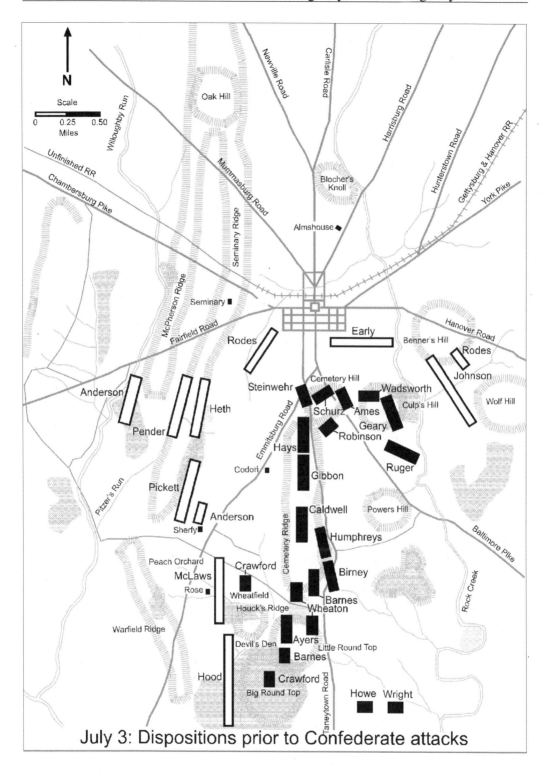

July 3: Dispositions prior to Confederate attacks

Map Set 25: Culp's Hill Remains in Union Hands

Map 25.1

Major General Henry Slocum's XII Corps could not reoccupy its former position on Culp's Hill when it returned during the night of July 2 because of the advanced position of Maj. Gen. Edward Johnson's Confederate division.

On the extreme right of the Federal line, Col. Silas Colgrove's brigade occupied McAllister's Woods just south of Spangler's Spring. The 3rd Wisconsin formed Colgrove's left wing, just behind and to the left of the 2nd Massachusetts. These two regiments faced northwest. The 13th New Jersey deployed on the right of the 2nd Massachusetts facing northeast toward Rock Creek. The 27th Indiana connected with the right of the 13th New Jersey, facing southeast toward McAllister's Woods. The brigade cobbled together into three sides of a square. Its fifth regiment, the 107th New York, was sent to support Col. Archibald McDougall's brigade forming along Baltimore Pike.[1]

McDougall deployed in a cornfield between Baltimore Pike and McAllister's Woods southwest of Colgrove's position. The brigade aligned from left to right as follows: 3rd Maryland – 145th New York – 20th Connecticut – 5th Connecticut – 46th Pennsylvania. The 123rd New York was in a slightly advanced position. During the early morning, the 20th Connecticut advanced to reconnoiter and possibly retake the lost breastworks.[2]

Just to the northwest, Brig. Gen. Henry Lockwood deployed his two regiments on either side of Lt. Sylvanus Rugg's Battery F and Lt. David Kinzie's Battery K, facing northeast on Baltimore Pike. The 1st Maryland Potomac Home Guard formed to the left of the guns near the Spangler House; the 150th New York formed to the right near the Lightner House.[3]

Colonel Charles Candy's brigade formed northeast of the 1st Maryland Potomac Home Guard. Two regiments, the 5th Ohio on the left and the 147th Pennsylvania on the right, deployed along Spangler's Lane behind a low stone wall. They faced southeast into an open field (later dubbed "Pardee Field" in honor of Col. Ario Pardee of the 147th Pennsylvania). The rest of the brigade marched northeast to form in a ravine behind Brig. Gen. George Greene's line. The disposition of these four regiments (the 7th, 29th, and 66th Ohio and 28th Pennsylvania) is not precisely known.[4]

The 109th Pennsylvania of Brig. Gen. Thomas Kane's brigade deployed on the left of the 5th Ohio, facing southeast at right angles to its original breastworks. The 29th Pennsylvania took up position to its left behind a stone fence. The 111th Pennsylvania formed as a reserve behind its sister regiments. Part of the brigade was in the "saddle" area between the upper and lower sections of Culp's Hill.[5]

The final XII Corps brigade under Greene did not vacate the hill the night before, so it occupied roughly its original position. The 60th New York was on the left. The rest stretching to the right included; 78th New York – 102nd New York – 149th New York – 137th New York.[6]

Southern reinforcements arrived during the early morning hours of July 3 when two brigades from Maj. Gen. Robert Rodes' Division and one from Maj. Gen. Jubal Early's Division took up position behind Johnson's men. Brigadier General Junius Daniel's Brigade formed behind Brig. Gen. John M. Jones' Brigade; Col. Edward O'Neal's Brigade formed behind Brig. Gen. Francis Nicholls' men. Brigadier General James Walker's Stonewall Brigade had already formed behind Brig. Gen. George Steuart's Brigade, and its 2nd Virginia occupied a stone wall across Spangler's Meadow from Colgrove's Federals. The exact deployment of these brigades is not known. Two Southern regiments from Brig. Gen. William "Extra Billy" Smith's Brigade were also making their way to this sector. [7]

Daniel's Tarheels moved up from the northeast. The 43rd North Carolina occupied the left of the first line with its left flank at an angle to the 3rd North Carolina of Steuart's line. The 45th North Carolina was on its right, followed by the small 2nd North Carolina Battalion. In the second line, the 32nd North Carolina formed behind the 43rd North Carolina, and the 53rd North Carolina behind the 45th North Carolina.[8]

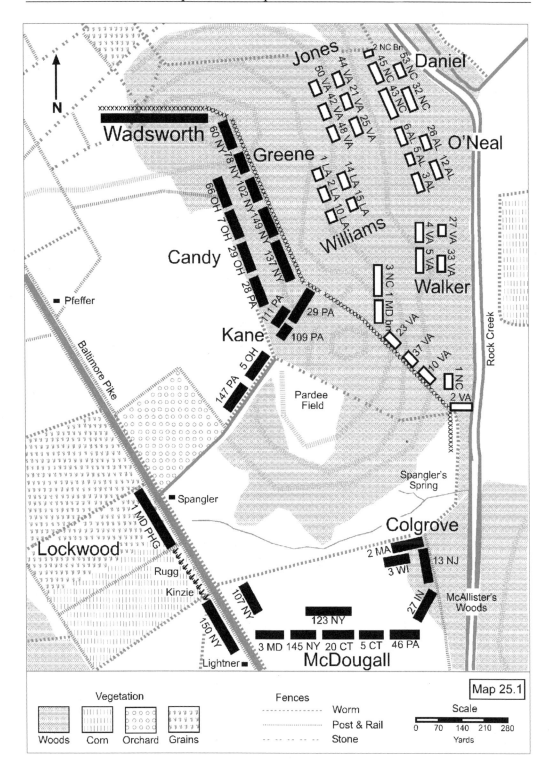

N

Wadsworth

Jones

2 NC Br

Daniel

44 VA
50 VA
21 VA
42 VA
25 VA
48 VA

45 NC
53 NC
43 NC
32 NC

60 NY

Greene

O'Neal

6 AL
26 AL
5 AL
12 AL
3 AL

78 NY
102 NY
149 NY

Williams

1 LA
2 LA
14 LA
15 LA
10 LA

66 OH

Candy

7 OH
29 OH
137 NY

27 VA
4 VA
5 VA
33 VA

Pfeffer

28 PA

3 NC
1 MD bn

Walker

111 PA
29 PA

23 VA
37 VA

Kane

109 PA

10 VA

Baltimore Pike

147 PA
5 OH

1 NC
2 VA

Pardee
Field

Spangler's
Spring

Rock Creek

Spangler

Colgrove

1 MD PHB

2 MA
3 WI

13 NJ

Lockwood

Rugg

Kinzie

27 IN

McAllister's
Woods

107 NY

150 NY

123 NY

Lightner

3 MD 145 NY 20 CT 5 CT 46 PA

McDougall

Vegetation				Fences		Scale

Woods Corn Orchard Grains

Worm
Post & Rail
Stone

0   70   140   210   280
Yards

Map 25.1

Map 25.2

The battle for Culp's Hill resumed about 4:30 a.m. when Federal artillery opened on the Confederate positions. According to Maj. Gen. Edward Johnson (Richard Ewell's Second Corps), this was the first of the three phases of the fight on Culp's Hill during July 3.

There is some doubt as to whether Brig. Gen. John M. Jones' Brigade (under the command of Lt. Col. Robert H. Dungan since Jones' wounding the day before), actually launched a full-scale assault on the Federal works. Most of the reports indicate that the men maintained a heavy fire, but only one indicated any forward movement.[9]

The same is true of Brig. Gen. Francis Nicholls' (Colonel Williams') Brigade. According to Lt. Col. David Zable of the 14th Louisiana, the brigade opened fire on Brig. Gen. George Greene's brigade about 4:00 a.m. on July 3 as part of a ruse. "Our best plan to mask our weakness would be to open fire on the enemy before daylight in the morning so as to cause them to believe that we were about to make another effort to capture the works," explained Zable. The net result was akin to prodding a hornet's nest with a stick, for the Federal returned fire, Zable recalled, was "the most terrific and deafening we ever experienced." The entire area was enveloped by smoke, and the noise was so intense that the officers could give orders only by yelling into the ears of their men. "Had the enemy fired with greater deliberation they would have annihilated the Brigade. . . . [O]ur foe were evidently demoralized, shooting wild into the tree tops so that the leaves and limbs were falling so thick and fast that it seemed it was raining," Zable concluded.[10]

The Federal troops were anything but demoralized. Freshly supplied with ammunition, Brig. Gen. George Greene's men put up quite a fight. Jones' Virginians may have been dissuaded from attacking when the 66th Ohio of Col. Charles Candy's brigade crossed the breastworks at their tallest peak and formed in line perpendicular to, and facing, Greene's line to the south. According to the 66th's commanding officer, Lt. Col. Eugene Powell, "we poured a murderous fire on the enemy's flank. After a short time, I found that the enemy had posted sharpshooters at the foot of the hill, behind a fence, who were annoying us very much. I ordered my regiment to take up a sheltered position behind trees and stones, and direct their fire on the sharpshooters, whom we soon dislodged."[11]

Unable to use their breastworks, most of Brig. Gen. Thomas Kane's men took position behind a protective ledge of rocks. Although the enemy remained largely unseen, Kane's defenders maintained a heavy fire into the wooded ravine in front of them for most of the morning.[12]

The 1st Maryland Potomac Home Guard moved east near Spangler's Spring to attack the 2nd Virginia (Brig. Gen. William Walker's Brigade), which was guarding Johnson's Confederate left flank. The large 700-man Federal regiment, its soldiers dressed in bright blue uniforms, immediately came under a heavy and sustained small arms fire from the Virginians, who were comfortably hunched behind a low stone wall. The attack was called off "to save it from the murderous fire to which it was exposed." As Brig. Gen. Henry Lockwood put it, "having already lost in killed and wounded some 80 men, and our ammunition being short, I withdrew the regiment, and returned to the turnpike." The brigade moved north and formed a supporting line behind General Greene's brigade.[13]

The 20th Connecticut of Col. Archibald McDougall's brigade approached Pardee Field from the southeast. Its orders were to "prevent the enemy from getting around the right of General Geary's forces in the entrenchments on our left, and holding the enemy back so that our artillery could have free play upon his columns without destroying our own troops." The regiment (which went in on the left of where the 1st Maryland Potomac Home Guard had fought) encountered the 10th Virginia of Brig. Gen. George Steuart's Brigade. The two sides locked fire for as long as five hours. Rocks and trees protected the combatants (especially the defenders) during this prolonged struggle.[14]

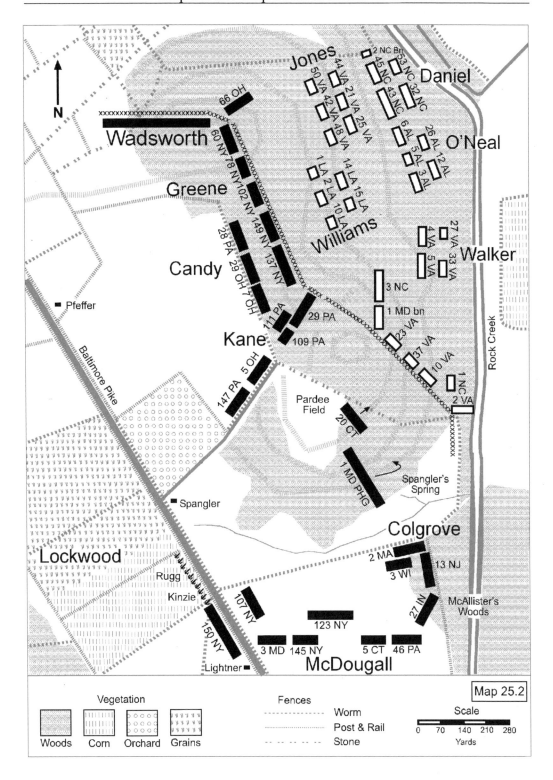

Jones
2 NC Bn
50 VA
44 VA
21 VA
45 NC
53 NC
32 NC
Daniel
42 VA
25 VA
43 NC
48 VA
6 AL
26 AL
O'Neal
66 OH
5 AL
12 AL
3 AL
Wadsworth
60 NY
1 LA
14 LA
2 LA
15 LA
Greene
78 NY
102 NY
10 LA
Williams
27 VA
4 VA
33 VA
Walker
149 NY
5 VA
28 PA
137 NY
Candy
29 OH
7 OH
3 NC
Pfeffer
1 MD bn
111 PA
29 PA
23 VA
Kane
109 PA
37 VA
10 VA
147 PA
5 OH
1 NC
2 VA
Pardee
Field
20 CT
Baltimore Pike
Rock Creek
1 MD PHG
Spangler's
Spring
Spangler
Colgrove
Lockwood
2 MA
Rugg
3 WI
13 NJ
Kinzie
107 NY
27 IN
McAllister's
Woods
150 NY
123 NY
3 MD
145 NY
5 CT
46 PA
Lightner
McDougall

Vegetation
Woods   Corn   Orchard   Grains

Fences
----------- Worm
··········· Post & Rail
- - - - - - Stone

Map 25.2

Scale
0   70   140   210   280
Yards

Map 25.3

By the time the sun was above the horizon, the entire Federal line had been ablaze for more than an hour. Brigadier General George Greene's men fired so rapidly their guns became fouled and their ammunition ran low. Brigadier General Alpheus Williams, temporary XII corps commander, compensated for these difficulties by rotating the troops from the front line to the "hollow" area to the rear, where the men rested, cleaned their muskets, and filled their cartridge boxes.

For example, soon after daylight, the 7th Ohio of Col. Charles Candy's brigade relieved the 60th New York of Greene's brigade. The Buckeyes remained on the firing line until about 8:00 a.m., when the 60th New York rotated back to relieve it. The 7th Ohio returned to the "hollow" and rested until 9:30 a.m. The 29th Ohio relieved the 137th New York of Greene's brigade in the breastworks at 5:45 a.m. The regiment remained there for about two hours and ten minutes before it was relieved by the 28th Pennsylvania. The 150th New York of Lockwood's brigade relieved the 78th New York. The result of this wise tactical decision was that regiments from four different brigades—Kane's, Greene's, Candy's, and Lockwood's—were able to shuttle back and forth while maintaining an intense rate of fire, all the while keeping the men and their weapons as fresh and clean as possible.

Few Federal casualties occurred during these swapping movements because of the method with which it was accomplished. According to Capt. Edward Hayes, the 29th Ohio "moved over the ridge at a run without firing a shot until fairly in the trenches, when it opened a heavy fire upon the enemy, under cover of which Colonel Ireland [of the 137th New York] was able to withdraw his regiment with but small loss."[15]

Looking behind them, the men of Brig. Gens. John M. Jones' and Francis Nicholls' brigades could see Col. Edward O'Neal's troops moving up the slopes to attack the summit of Culp's Hill. A Louisiana soldier noted, with some scorn, that O'Neal's Alabamans approached with a yell, which served "no other purpose but to intensify a galling fire in our front." Casualties mounted by the minute. O'Neal reported that the "brigade moved forward in fine style, under a terrific fire of grape and small-arms." The men may have made an admirable advance that morning, but Captain May of the 3rd Alabama called the action a "hopeless undertaking" that accomplished little except killing its participants. The officer could only look grimly "at our poor fellows and see them shot down one after another." An enlisted man wrote home soon after the battle, "I thought I had been in hot places before—I thought I had heard Minnie balls," he explained, "but that day [July 3] capped the climax. All day long it was one continuous roar."[16]

Brigadier General Junius Daniel (Rodes' Division), whose brigade had moved behind Nicholls', was alarmed when the sun rose and he realized the enormity of the task ahead of his men. His candid observation is telling: "The hill in front of this position was, in my opinion, so strong that it could not have been carried by any force." After waiting several hours, Daniel was ordered to file left and assist Brig. Gen. George Steuart's Brigade in taking the heavily reinforced heights. Both brigade leaders unsuccessfully protested the order to charge the hill.[17]

Steuart's men continued holding the left of the line. Only the three Virginia regiments, left-most in the brigade, crouched in protection within their captured earthworks. Ammunition was running low and the men had to scrounge from the dead and wounded scattered around them. The brigade maintained the same alignment as the night before, except that the six companies of the 1st North Carolina had moved from the right to the left side of the brigade.

Federal fire was incessant. One soldier from the 1st Maryland Battalion (CSA) recalled it this way: "The whole hillside seemed enveloped in a blaze. Minnie balls pattered upon the breastworks . . . like hail upon a housetop. Solid shot went crashing through the woods, adding the danger from falling limbs of trees to that from erratic fragments of exploding shells. The whole hill was covered with the smoke and smell of powder. No enemy could be seen."[18]

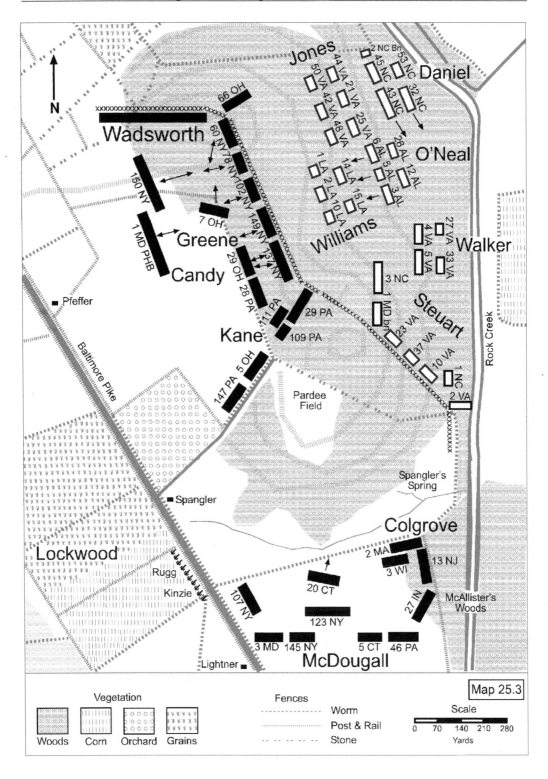

Map 25.3

Map 25.4

In preparation for his attack, Brig. Gen. George Steuart pivoted his 3rd North Carolina on the right and swung the remainder of the brigade in a clockwise manner to face Pardee Field. Steuart's 900 men could see a strong line of Federals on the opposite side of the field that included the 5th Ohio and 147th Pennsylvania regiments of Col. Charles Candy's brigade, and the three regiments from Brig. Gen. Thomas Kane's brigade.

When his line was ready to advance, it stood at right angles to the captured breastworks, aligned from left to right as follows: 1st North Carolina – 23rd Virginia – 37th Virginia – 1st Maryland Battalion – 3rd North Carolina. The 10th Virginia's orders were to protect the brigade's left flank by forming perpendicularly to the 1st North Carolina. The Virginians skirmished heavily with the 20th Connecticut.[19]

When Steuart's infantry emerged from the woods and advanced across Pardee Field, sheets of small arms and cannon fire swept the center and left side of the line. According to a member of the 147th Pennsylvania, "down the opposite slope they came in beautiful alignment, their officers gallantly leading. . . . There was no retreat for the poor fellows in the front ranks who, with blanched faces, came up to be mowed down by companies." The men halted and returned fire, but when they realized they could not remain exposed or move ahead with any hope of success, they began drifting to the rear. As Steuart wrote in his report, the left "did not maintain its position in line of battle." Some of his men decided to surrender rather than attempt to re-cross the deadly field of fire.[20]

The right side of Steuart's brigade, composed of the 1st Maryland Battalion and the 3rd North Carolina, continued its advance in the face of increasingly intense enemy fire. The devastation was almost indescribable, as the men were mowed down by fire from the front and both flanks. As one Pennsylvanian observed, the Marylanders fell in heaps. "[We] poured a deliberate and most deadly fire into their ranks," wrote a veteran from the 147th Pennsylvania. "This was done with cool and well-aimed

precision, such as old veterans alone could do, and the destruction of the rebel column was almost complete." The 29th Ohio arrived to provide support to its sister regiments along Spangler's Lane. What was left of Steuart's decimated brigade fell back and reformed behind a stone fence and some rocks.[21]

Because the attacks launched by Steuart and Daniel were not synchronized, the former was repulsed before the latter advanced. When Daniel's Tarheels moved forward, a heavy small arms fire from Kane's men on their left and front was unleashed upon them. The 43rd North Carolina on the left of the first line was overwhelmed and forced to pull back. The 2nd North Carolina Battalion on the right side of Daniel's line did not even attack, participating instead "chiefly as skirmishers."[22]

In the center of Daniel's front line, tucked between the 43rd North Carolina on the left and the 2nd North Carolina Battalion on the right, was the 45th North Carolina. When its members advanced, they spotted Federal troops to their front quickly sprinting from the first line of defenses to a second higher line. "At that time almost every man of the regiment [45th North Carolina] was firing into them as they passed the opening, certainly killing a number," wrote one of their officers. Daniel called it a "most destructive fire with the whole of the Forty-Fifth Regiment for five minutes upon a crowd of the enemy who were disorganized and fleeing in great confusion." Unable to exploit this situation and almost out of ammunition, the infantry of the 45th North Carolina was replaced by the men of the 32nd North Carolina, who slipped up and assumed a front line position.[23]

The 53rd North Carolina, meanwhile, moved up from the right side of Daniel's second line and charged the heights several times. According to one private, "our poor boys fall by our sides—almost as fast as the leaves that fell as cannon and musket balls hit them." Unable to make a dent in the Federal defenses, Daniel pulled his men back.[24]

Two regiments of Brig. Gen. William "Extra Billy" Smith's Brigade finally arrived and relieved the 2nd Virginia of the Stonewall Brigade, which then crossed Rock Creek.

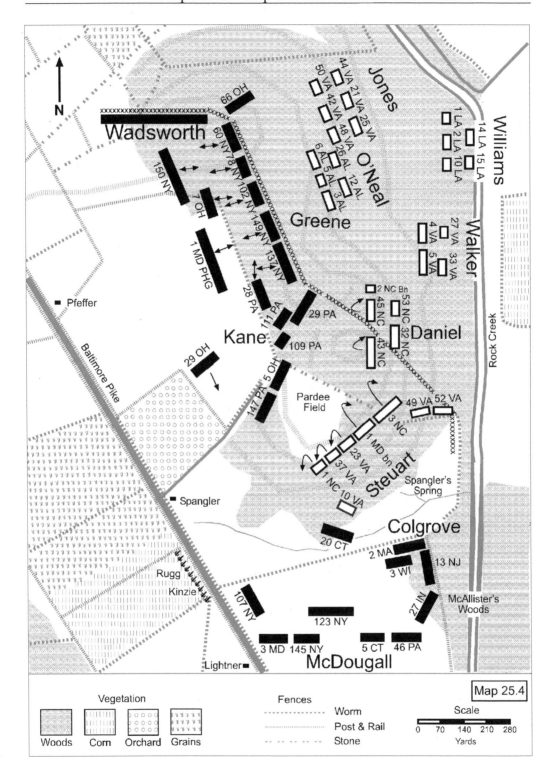

Map 25.4

Map 25.5

To the right of Brig. Gen. Junius Daniel's Brigade, James Walker's Stonewall Brigade shifted farther to the right and prepared to assail Culp's Hill. Although the brigade reached the field the night before, it did not attack Brig. Gen. George Greene's position. The disposition of Walker's regiments is not clear, except that the 5th Virginia probably occupied the extreme right. With the 2nd Virginia detached across Rock Creek, Walker took fewer than 1,000 men into battle.[25]

At least four Federal regiments, the 60th and 149th New York from Greene's brigade, and the 7th and 66th Ohio from Colonel Charles Candy's brigade, were waiting at the top for the Confederates. The 66th Ohio was deployed perpendicular to the others at the northern end of the line, and so could pour an enfilade fire into the right flank of the Stonewall Brigade. The Federal troops held their fire as Walker's men advanced unsteadily up the steep and rocky hill. When they stepped into killing range, gunfire exploded from the Federal regiments. So deadly was the barrage of small arms and artillery fire that many Federals recalled that the Confederate line simply melted away. Some of the Rebels dropped down to hide behind anything that could stop a bullet. Some of the men continued inching forward, protecting themselves by moving from rock to rock or tree to tree. A few brave souls made it to within fifteen yards of the breastworks. One sergeant actually reached the works and grabbed the flag of the 149th New York before a hail of bullets cut him down.[26]

Less than an hour passed before the men on the left side of Walker's line decided they could no longer withstand the murderous fire and began falling back. The 4th Virginia, which was probably deployed in the second line, moved forward to support the 33rd Virginia. It did not take Walker long to realize that the renewed attack "was done with equally bad success as our former efforts, and the fire became so destructive that I suffered the brigade to fall back to a more secure position, as it was a useless sacrifice of life to keep them longer under so galling a fire."

The order brought relief to some of the men, and many bounded down the hill. Others realized that they had advanced too far and decided to surrender rather than face probable death or maiming trying to retreat down the hill. Nearly seventy men from the 4th Virginia surrendered, and the regiment also lost its flag.[27]

Farther to the south, meanwhile, Col. Silas Colgrove received orders to attack the Confederate left flank, composed of the two regiments of Brig. Gen. William "Extra Billy" Smith's Brigade. The Southern infantry had taken up a position behind a stone wall across Spangler's Meadow. The order was apparently a mistake, but Colgrove didn't know that and directed the 2nd Massachusetts on the left and the 27th Indiana on the right to advance across the meadow.[28]

When he heard the orders, Lt. Col. Charles Mudge of the 2nd Massachusetts exclaimed, "Well, it is murder: but it's the order." Walking over to his men, Mudge yelled, "Up, men, over the works! Forward, double quick!" Because the 27th Indiana had to maneuver around the 13th New Jersey, its attack was not launched until after the 2nd Massachusetts was already well into the field.[29]

In addition to facing frontal fire from Smith's regiments, the two Federal regiments received an enfilade fire from George Steuart's Brigade. Men fell by the score, but still the two regiments continued their attack. They resisted the urge to halt and return fire until they reached the middle of the meadow. When they finally did stop, it proved a deadly mistake: the stationary targets only increased the bloodbath.

While the survivors of the 27th Indiana returned directly to the brigade, the remainder of the 2nd Massachusetts veered to the left, reached the woods on the opposite side of the meadow, and only later made their way back to their original positions. The smoke had hardly settled before General Smith ordered a counterattack. This, too, was ill-conceived and suffered the same fate as the Federal charge.

When the Southern attack ended, the firing fitfully dribbled to a close. The battle for Culp's Hill was over.[30]

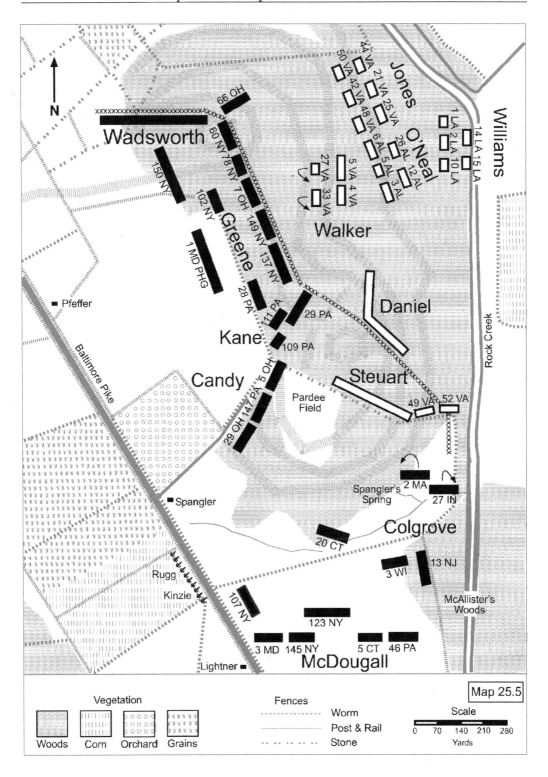

Map 25.5

Vegetation

Woods   Corn   Orchard   Grains

Fences
---------- Worm
.... Post & Rail
– – – – Stone

Scale
0   70   140   210   280
Yards

Map Set 26: The Pickett – Pettigrew – Trimble Charge

Map 26.1

Lieutenant General James Longstreet, the soldier Gen. Robert E. Lee called on the field of Sharpsburg (Antietam) his "Old War Horse," was in command of the July 3 offensive. The attack column included three fresh brigades from Maj. Gen. George Pickett's Division. Others from Lt. Gen. A. P. Hill's Third Corps were selected to go in with Pickett. Why these brigades were selected is unclear. Most had been roughly handled on July 1 and 2, and so were poor choices to participate in such an assault.

Pickett's Division deployed in front of Spangler's Woods, forming the right side of the attacking column. Brigadier General Richard Garnett's Brigade held Pickett's left front, aligned left to right: 56th Virginia – 28th Virginia – 19th Virginia – 18th Virginia – 8th Virginia. Brigadier General James Kemper's Brigade deployed on Garnett's right in the Spangler orchard, aligned left to right: 3rd Virginia – 7th Virginia – 1st Virginia – 11th Virginia – 24th Virginia. Brigadier General Lewis Armistead's Brigade formed behind Garnett aligned from left to right: 38th Virginia – 57th Virginia – 53rd Virginia – 9th Virginia – 14th Virginia.[1]

Four Third Corps brigades from Maj. Gen. Harry Heth's Division (under Brig. Gen. James Pettigrew) held the left front of the line deployed left to right as follows: Col. John Brockenbrough: 55th Virginia – 47th Virginia – 22nd Virginia Battalion – 40th Virginia; Brig. Gen. Joseph Davis: 11th Mississippi – 42nd Mississippi – 2nd Mississippi – 55th North Carolina; Pettigrew (under Col. James Marshall): 11th North Carolina – 52nd North Carolina – 26th North Carolina – 47th North Carolina; and Brig. Gen. James Archer (under Col. Birkett Fry): 5th Alabama Battalion – 7th Tennessee – 14th Tennessee – 13th Alabama – 1st Tennessee.[2]

Two brigades from Dorsey Pender's Division (under Maj. Gen. Isaac Trimble) formed behind Pettigrew's right, deployed left to right as follows: Brig. Gen. Alfred Scales (under Col. William Lowrance): 38th North Carolina – 13th North Carolina – 34th North Carolina – 22nd North Carolina – 16th North Carolina; Brig. Gen. James Lane's Brigade (Marshall): 33rd North Carolina – 18th North Carolina – 28th North Carolina – 37th North Carolina – 7th North Carolina.[3]

Facing this array of enemy infantry were parts of the Federal I and II Corps. On the south (left) front were two of Brig. Gen. George Stannard's Vermont regiments, deployed in the fields in front of the main line. The 14th Vermont advanced seventy-five yards to take advantage of the trees and bushes in the Plum Run Valley. The 16th Vermont split in two: half of its companies forming a picket reserve while the others rested behind the 14th Vermont. The 13th Vermont remained on the main line. On its right were the 80th New York and 151st Pennsylvania of Col. Chapman Biddle's brigade.[4]

Brigadier General John Gibbon's division extended the front northward. Brigadier General William Harrow's battered brigade occupied Gibbon's left, aligned from left to right: 15th Massachusetts – 1st Minnesota – 19th Maine – 82nd New York. Colonel Norman Hall's brigade was next, with the 7th Michigan and 59th New York in the front line and 19th and 20th Massachusetts and 42nd New York in support. The men of the 69th Pennsylvania, Brig. Gen. Alexander Webb's brigade, were on Hall's right. Webb's remaining regiments formed the reserve on the reverse slope of Cemetery Ridge.[5]

The division under Brig. Gen. Alexander Hays formed on Gibbon's right. The first line held Col. Thomas Smyth's brigade, deployed from left to right: 1st Delaware – 12th New Jersey – 108th New York (north of the Bryan house). The 14th Connecticut formed a second line behind the 1st Delaware. Except for the 126th New York, which formed to the right of the 108th New York, most of Col. George Willard's brigade (Col. Eliakim Sherrill), was in the second line, aligned left to right: 39th New York – 125th New York – 111th New York. George Woodruff's guns unlimbered in front of the 108th New York. The 8th Ohio of Col. Samuel Carroll's brigade and about 100 men of the 126th New York formed the skirmish line.[6]

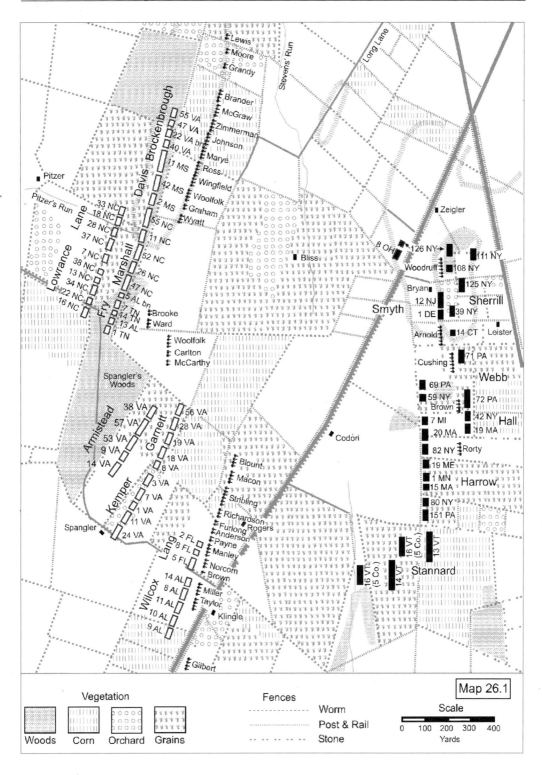

Lewis
Moore
Grandy

Brander
McGraw
Zimmerman
Johnson
55 VA
47 VA
22 VA btn
40 VA
1 MS   Marye
Ross
42 MS   Wingfield
2 MS   Woolfolk
55 NC   Graham
Wyatt

33 NC
18 NC
28 NC
37 NC   11 NC
7 NC   52 NC
38 NC   26 NC
13 NC   47 NC
34 NC   5 AL bn
22 NC   7 TN
16 NC   14 TN   Brooke
13 AL   Ward
1 TN

Woolfolk
Carlton
McCarthy

Pitzer

Pitzer's Run

Lowrance Lane

Marshall

F.TN

Davis

Brockenbrough

Stevens Run

Long Lane

Zeigler

8 OH   126 NY   111 NY
Woodruff   108 NY
Bliss   125 NY
Bryan
12 NJ   Sherrill
Smyth   1 DE   39 NY
Arnold   14 CT   Leister

Cushing   71 PA

Webb
69 PA
59 NY   72 PA
Brown   42 NY
7 MI   Hall
20 MA   19 MA

82 NY   Rorty

19 ME
1 MN   Harrow
15 MA
80 NY
151 PA

Codori

Spangler's
Woods

38 VA   56 VA
57 VA   28 VA
53 VA   19 VA
9 VA   18 VA
14 VA   8 VA
3 VA   Blount
7 VA   Macon
1 VA   Stribling
11 VA   Richardson
24 VA   Rogers
Furlong
2 FL   Anderson
8 FL   Payne
5 FL   Manley
Norcom
Brown
14 AL   Miller
8 AL   Taylor
11 AL
10 AL   Klingle
9 AL

Armistead

Garrett

Kemper

Lang

Wilcox

Spangler

16 VT
(5 Co.)   13 VT
16 VT
(5 Co.)   14 VT   Stannard

Gilbert

Vegetation

Woods	Corn	Orchard	Grains

Fences

- - - - - - - Worm
.... Post & Rail
- - - - - - Stone

Map 26.1

Scale
0   100   200   300   400
Yards

Map 26.2

An impressive array of Southern artillery rolled into position during the morning of July 3. General Lee believed a prolonged concentrated fire would drive away or destroy enemy infantry and artillery and make it easier to pierce the Union center. A 75-gun line attached to General Longstreet's First Corps extended from the Peach Orchard to the northeast corner of Spangler Woods. Some 35 of these were entrusted to First Corps artillerist Col. Edward P. Alexander, who had already placed the guns for the coordinated attack that failed to materialize earlier that day. For the grand bombardment, his guns (and others up and down the Southern line) redeployed to smother Union artillery on Cemetery Hill and along Cemetery Ridge.

Sixty guns from Lt. Gen. A. P. Hill's Third Corps continued the line north to Fairfield (Hagerstown) Road, and two Whitworth rifles deployed above it. Because Richard Ewell's Second Corps front offered fewer opportunities for effective artillery platforms, only twenty-four of his guns were in position to join the barrage. Perhaps 150 guns eventually participated. As many as fifty-six guns of the Second and Third Corps, however, would remain silent.[7]

Although the Federals were outnumbered in artillery along Cemetery Ridge, they had better terrain and better ammunition. Lieutenant Charles Hazlett's battery on Little Round Top and forty-three guns on Cemetery Hill had unobstructed fields of fire. II Corps batteries unlimbered between them. Colonel Freeman McGilvery established a strong 39-gun artillery line in Plum Run Valley. Fresh batteries from Maj. Gen. John Sedgwick's VI Corps and the army's artillery reserve awaited deployment.[8]

Skirmishing around the Bliss farm erupted while the infantry and guns prepared for the assault. Rebels had been harassing Federal troops from the Bliss barn between the ridges. Union infantry advanced to destroy it.

About 1:00 p.m., signal guns triggered the opening of the massive Southern barrage. The Army of the Potomac's chief of artillery, Brig. Gen. Henry Hunt, oversaw the methodical but effective 115-gun Federal response. Infantry on both sides hugged the ground to avoid shrapnel. Union fire struck prone Southern infantry on Seminary Ridge, killing and wounding many men before the attack even began.

The unprecedented cannonade "startled us, though we have been expecting it," recalled Randolph Shotwell of the 8th Virginia. Many Southern guns focused their fire against Union batteries around the Copse of Trees crowning Cemetery Ridge (the target, intentional or otherwise, of their infantry). The shelling forced several Union batteries to withdraw, but the heavy smoke blinded the Confederate gunners, who consistently overshot their targets. Hunt called it "a mere waste of ammunition." Armistead Long, a member of Lee's staff, was one of Hunt's artillery students before the war. In a talk after Appomattox, Hunt mentioned the shoddy Southern gunnery. "I remembered my lessons at the time," confessed Long, "and when the fire became so scattered, wondered what you would think about it." Despite the thunderous cacophony, many men were so tired they slept during the bombardment. Gunner Thomas Osborn barely recalled the noise. "I have often heard infantry officers speak of it, though I have but a faint recollection of it myself."[9]

General Hunt rode along the line and ordered his men to cease firing. It was better, he believed, to save his ammunition for the infantry attack sure to follow, and hope the enemy thinks his guns had been silenced. When Union artillery fire fell off, Colonel Alexander—whom General Longstreet tasked with judging the effect of the fire to determine when the Southern infantry should advance—was "elated" by the slackening fire. After exchanging messages with Alexander, General Pickett rode over to Longstreet. "General, shall I advance?" Longstreet was steadfastly against launching the attack, and could not bring himself to verbalize the command. Instead, he ordered Pickett forward with a nod of his head.

No one really knows how long the barrage lasted, or even what constituted an end to the cannonade because many guns continued firing even as the infantry advanced. A modern student of the attack estimates the bombardment effectively ended about 2:00 p.m.[10]

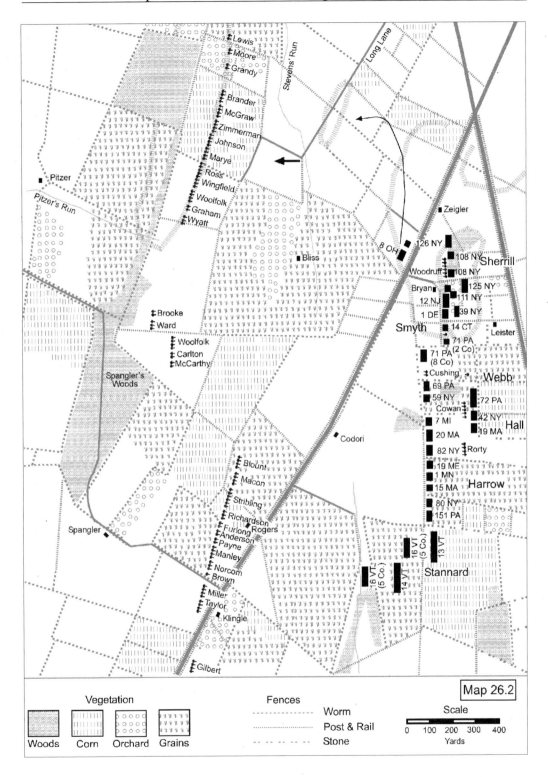

Map 26.2

Vegetation

Fences

Scale

Woods   Corn   Orchard   Grains

Worm
Post & Rail
Stone

0   100   200   300   400
Yards

Map 26.3

As the Southern fire fell off, the infantry stood to advance. Flagbearers moved four paces to the front. David E. Johnston of Kemper's Brigade remembers Pickett riding past and the "electrical" charge of his exhortation, "Up men, and to your posts! Don't forget today that you are from old Virginia!" The long lines of gray infantry started forward. Their orders were simple: "Go slow, do not cheer, and do not stop to fire." Soldiers knew their task would be difficult, but were generally confident of success.

Kemper had orders to dress on the left, which he did by shifting his line more than 100 yards north to meet Garnett's flank. Armistead moved forward directly behind Garnett. Like a giant comb, the Southern line of infantry parted its teeth to seep through the artillery line before closing the gaps and pressing on. Some of the artillerists doffed their headgear and cheered. The gesture, writes one historian, "was both an encouragement and a farewell."[11]

On the Confederate left, General Pettigrew's men moved out on a straight axis for the ridge nearly a mile distant. His front ranks advanced "in as magnificent style as I ever saw," recalled a member of the 26th North Carolina. Only two of the brigades (Marshall's and Fry's) advanced on time. Joe Davis was several minutes late getting started. His men rushed forward to catch up, but a realignment with Marshall's left seems never to have been firmly reestablished. Brockenbrough was also later and out of position. Pettigrew's left front sagged behind the rest of the line. Isaac Trimble's two brigades, however, crisply advanced on time behind Fry and Marshall.

Seeing the Confederates advance, Brig. Gen. Alexander Webb realized he had erred by not moving the 71st Pennsylvania to the front line. He did so now, sending it to the right of the 69th Pennsylvania. There was room there for eight companies, their right resting on the Angle. Remnants of Lt. Alonzo Cushing's battery stood ready for action between them. The remaining two companies settled in behind a stone wall behind and to the right of the rest of the regiment. Earlier during the cannonade, the 111th New York of Willard's brigade also changed its position so that its left wing moved behind the 12th New Jersey and its right was thrown forward to the right of the New Jersey troops on the front line. The 14th Connecticut had been in the second line, but now slid to the left to take the place of all but one gun of Arnold's battery. Brown's beaten-up battery to the south of the Copse of Trees finally vacated its position, replaced by Capt. Andrew Cowan's battery.[12]

Well into their advance, the Confederate infantry could plainly see the elevated Federal positions on Cemetery Ridge. Any illusions about the difficulty of their task were abruptly shattered when Federal artillery on both ends of the line opened. Kemper's advancing regiments, holding Pickett's right divisional front, and Brockenbrough's Virginians on Pettigrew's left received the brunt of this fire. "The havoc produced upon their ranks was truly surprising," wrote a Federal artillery officer.[13] "Shot, shell, spherical case, shrapnel and canister—thousands of deadly missiles racing through the air to thin our ranks!" recalled a Southerner. In places, eight, ten, or more men fell from the explosion of a single shell. Grass fires erupted. About half-way across the field, Federal skirmishers opened fire on the tramping Southern infantry.[14]

On the skirmish line with his 8th Ohio, Lt. Col. Franklin Sawyer ordered his men to advance and then pivot to take Brockenbrough's ragged line in the flank. The Buckeyes fired several volleys into the Virginians and charged. The 126th New York joined them. Demoralized by their high losses and poor leadership, many of Brockenbrough's men surrendered or fled. The careless decision to align a small and inherently suspect brigade on the column's left flank proved a costly mistake.[15]

Two houses along Emmitsburg Road disrupted Pickett's advancing lines. Kemper's 11th Virginia broke in two as it passed the Rogers house. Captain James R. Hutter found the maneuver exceptionally difficult to perform, particularly under heavy artillery fire. Kemper's entire brigade advanced south of the Codori house, while all but the right side of the 8th Virginia of Garnett's Brigade passed north of it.[16]

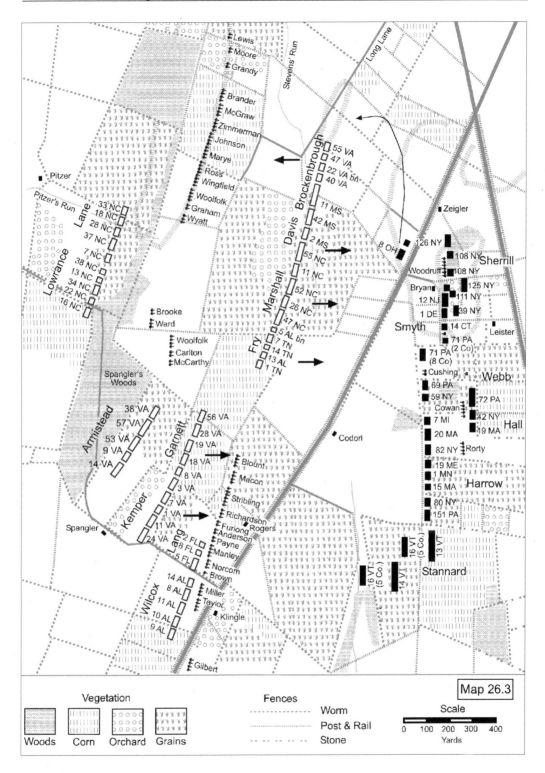

Lewis
Moore
Grandy
Brander
McGraw
Zimmerman
Johnson
Marye
Ross
Wingfield
Woolfolk
Graham
Wyatt

Pitzer

Pitzer's Run

Lowrance Lane

33 NC
18 NC
28 NC
37 NC
7 NC
38 NC
13 NC
34 NC
22 NC
16 NC

Stevens Run

Long Lane

Brockenbrough

Davis

Marshall

Fry

55 VA
47 VA
22 VA bn
40 VA

11 MS
42 MS
2 MS
55 NC
11 NC
52 NC
26 NC
47 NC
5 AL bn
7 TN
14 TN
13 AL
1 TN

8 OH

126 NY
108 NY
Woodruff 108 NY
Bryan 125 NY
12 NJ 111 NY
1 DE 39 NY
14 CT

Zeigler
Sherrill

Smyth

Leister

71 PA
(2 Co.)
71 PA
(8 Co.)

Cushing
69 PA
59 NY
Cowan
7 MI
20 MA

82 NY Rorty

19 ME
1 MN
15 MA
80 NY
151 PA

Webb

72 PA
42 NY
19 MA

Hall

Harrow

Brooke
Ward
Woolfolk
Carlton
McCarthy

Spangler's
Woods

Armistead

38 VA
57 VA
53 VA
9 VA
14 VA

Garnett

56 VA
28 VA
19 VA
18 VA
8 VA
3 VA
7 VA
1 VA
11 VA
24 VA

Blount
Macon
Stribling
Richardson
Rogers
Furlong
Anderson
Payne
Manley
Norcom
Brown

Kemper

Lang

2 FL
8 FL
5 FL

Spangler

Codori

Wilcox

14 AL
8 AL
11 AL
10 AL
9 AL

Miller
Taylor
Klingle

16 VT
(5 Co.)

16 VT
(5 Co.)

14 VT

13 VT

Stannard

Gilbert

Vegetation

Woods Corn Orchard Grains

Fences

---------- Worm
·········· Post & Rail
— — — — Stone

Scale

0 100 200 300 400
Yards

Map 26.3

Map 26.4

Because Emmitsburg Road angled northeast, Pettigrew's infantry reached it before Pickett's did. Two stout fences lined the road. When the Confederates began climbing the first fence, Federal infantry, who had been holding their fire, sent a storm of lead into the vulnerable attackers. One veteran described the ordeal at Emmitsburg Road as a matter of timing and luck. The men had to "climb up to the top of the fence, tumble over it, and fall flat into the bed of the road. All the while the bullets continued to bury themselves into the bodies of the victims and the sturdy chestnut rails."

After a few moments' respite, the men rose and repeated the process by climbing the fence on the opposite side of the road. One Federal soldier marveled at the bravery displayed when Marshall's men dressed ranks after traversing the second fence. The initial burst of fire was especially deadly because each Federal infantryman on the first line had two to five additional loaded guns. Some wondered how any of the Confederates survived these initial volleys. So tremendous was the gunfire that only some 1,000 of Pettigrew's men managed to cross the road and continue toward the Federal line. The remainder hunkered down along the road and opened fire on the Federal defenders, killing and wounding many. In Pickett's Division, a higher percentage of the attacking column advanced beyond Emmitsburg Road and up the final slope toward the crest of Cemetery Ridge.[17]

As his division approached Emmitsburg Road, Pickett ordered his 4,500 men to oblique to the left several hundred yards to link up with Pettigrew's Division. The maneuver was hard enough to perform on a parade ground; it was exceedingly difficult to execute while under fire from both artillery and small arms (some fired from as close as 200-300 hundred yards). The order seems to have been performed quite well, however, though some crowding and confusion occurred in the ranks—especially when the move exposed Kemper's right flank to artillery fire. The roughly 45-degree shift in direction also offered some of the men a better view of Pettigrew's column. With it came the disturbing image of hundreds of men (mostly from Colonel Brockenbrough's and Brigadier General Davis' brigades), scampering for the rear.

Still in reasonably good form, however, Pickett's three brigades slid past the left wing of the Federal II Corps.[18] According to modern scholarship, from this point forward the entire Confederate attacking column numbered perhaps 5,500 men. Arrayed against them were roughly equal numbers of Federals holding good defensive terrain well supported by artillery. Those odds did not bode well for General Lee's infantry.[19]

Seeing Kemper's right flank dangling in the air, Brig. Gen. George Stannard boldly ordered his 13th Vermont forward into the meadow, where the men "changed front forward on the first company." The order reformed the companies, one after the other, until they were perpendicular to the enemy flank. The maneuver was difficult to perform under the best of circumstances, yet the inexperienced Vermont soldiers pulled it off brilliantly. Some of the men in the 11th and 24th Virginia on the right of the line saw what was happening as they moved beyond the Codori house. The Virginians poured a deadly fire into the 13th Vermont as it rushed forward, but the Federals continued the realignment while the 16th Vermont formed on their left. The 14th Vermont did not participate in this movement; it held its place in line and fired into the oncoming enemy. [20]

The two Vermont regiments opened an enfilading fire that devastated Kemper's flank. "Those great masses of men seemed to disappear in a moment . . . the ground over which we passed after striking their flank was literally covered with dead and wounded men," recalled Col. Wheelock Veazey of the 16th Vermont. Many of Kemper's men threw down their arms and surrendered.

Kemper had immediately moved to the right of his brigade to organize a defense against the Vermont onslaught. A few minutes later and within 100 yards of the enemy, he would fall badly wounded (some feared mortally) with a ball in the groin. Southern infantry would later fight over his captured nearly paralyzed body to ensure his removal from the field.[21]

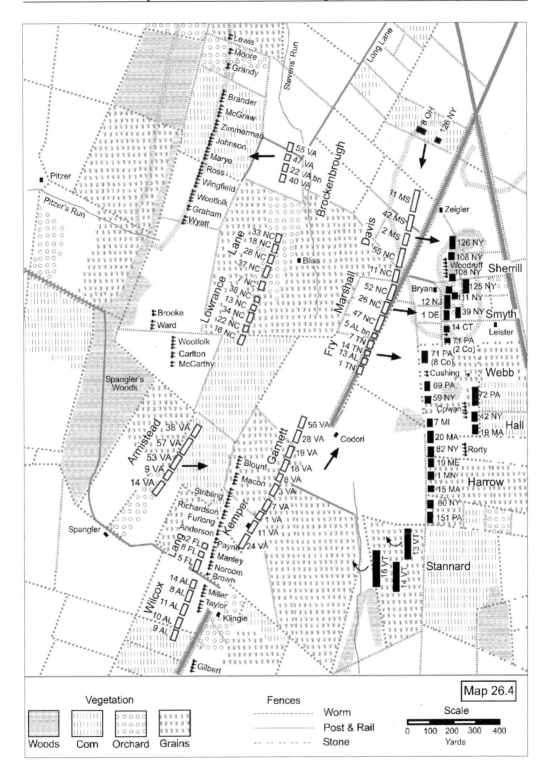

Map 26.4

Map 26.5

Pickett's Division, packed closely and rapidly losing the firm order it once possessed, continued advancing up the final slope toward the crest of Cemetery Ridge. The threat posed by the Vermont infantry against Kemper's right flank forced the Virginian to wheel the 24th Virginia and part of the 11th Virginia to it. When the 3rd Virginia's Col. Joseph Mayo learned of the threat, he moved some of his men to the right. Stannard's men refused to give ground. The "gray uniforms," wrote a Vermonter, "fall quick and fast and the front line hesitated, moved slowly and melted away."[22] Many of Kemper's men continued on, halting at a rough patch of ground in front of the Union position, where they opened a murderous fire on the defenders.

Some Federal commanders moved their units to meet the focal point of the attack. The 72nd Pennsylvania moved by the right flank, sliding northward to reach the northeast angle of the stone fence; the 19th Massachusetts and 42nd New York moved closer to the first line. Infantry manned at least one of Capt. James Rorty's remaining two guns, firing from near the stone wall south of the Copse of Trees. On Rorty's right, Cowan's fresh battery fired into the mass of Confederates surging toward the crest.[23]

After firing a few volleys from the broken ground, some of Kemper's men jumped up, issued a Rebel yell, and charged the wall. According to a soldier in the 7th Virginia the Federal troops "poured a murderous volley right into their faces. A moment the line halted and staggered as so many men went down, but . . . the whole line bent forward, gave the southern yell, charged and went over the stone wall."[24]

On Kemper's left, Richard Garnett's massed ranks also closed on the stone wall protecting the 69th and 71st Pennsylvania. A mortally wounded Lt. Cushing continued working his advanced guns, double-shotting them with canister. The giant shotgun-like discharge into the packed Virginians cleared a 50-foot wide swath in the human wave. Out of ammunition, Cushing's guns fell mute. The 28th, 56th, and part of the 19th Virginia, along with the right elements of Fry's Brigade (Pettigrew's

Division), struck the 71st Pennsylvania and the gap on its left. One of its companies broke for the rear as the two sides engaged in hand-to-hand combat on both sides of the wall. Seven other companies fell back to join the remaining pair behind them. The tip of Garnett's mass had reached the Federal line. When its members looked east up the ridge and saw the 72nd Pennsylvania in line of battle, they waited for Armistead to forge ahead with them. The fire of the newly-arrived Pennsylvania troops felled scores of Garnett's men. Somewhere in the chaos, smoke, and bloodshed, an enemy round found the mounted Garnett. (He was eventually buried in an unmarked grave.) General Webb sensed the vulnerability of the enemy and ordered the 72nd Pennsylvania to charge; the men refused.[25]

When he saw Garnett's men thronging along the wall, Armistead shepherded his brigade in that direction. The shift moved his Virginians parallel along the line held by the 69th Pennsylvania, which poured a killing fire into their packed ranks. At that range it was hard to miss, but many joined up with Garnett's soldiers. Fighting in front of the clump of trees, the 69th continued holding its position even though the pressure against it was nearly overwhelming.[26]

Farther to the north, some 1,000 men from Pettigrew's remaining brigades approached the ridge above the Angle. The defenders had waited until they reached the road (175 yards from the wall) before opening fire. According to Federal accounts, most of Pettigrew's men fell back before reaching the wall. Some in Marshall's command came within forty yards of it before being driven back. A few sprinted ahead but were shot down or captured. The enemy, said Colonel Smyth, "fought with a fierce determination that he had never seen equaled." On Pettigrew's left, Mississippians from Davis' Brigade advanced to the Bryan barn before being shot down, driven back, or captured.

The last of the infantry from the left wing of the attacking column, Isaac Trimble's demi-division consisting of Col. William Lowrance's and Brig. Gen. James Lanes' brigades, were now crossing Emmitsburg Road in support of a charge teetering on the brink of failure.[27]

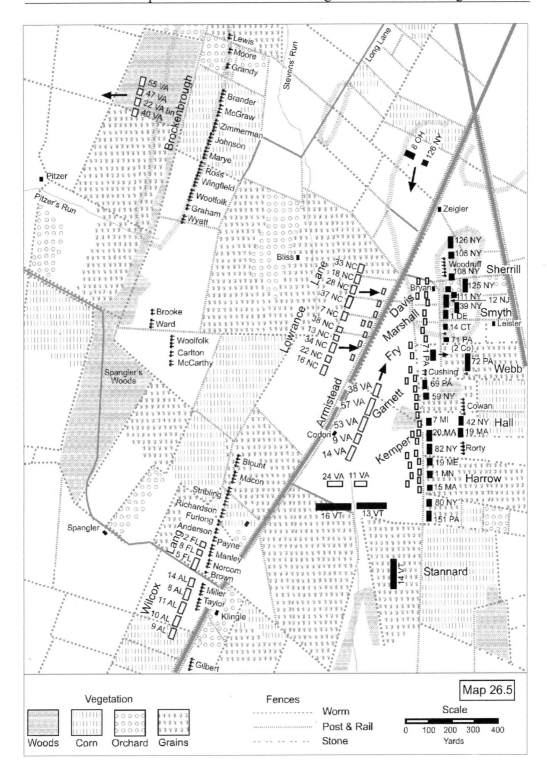

Map 26.5

Vegetation

Woods | Corn | Orchard | Grains

Fences

---------- Worm
·········· Post & Rail
- - - - - Stone

Scale

0 100 200 300 400
Yards

Map 26.6

Major General Isaac Trimble's brigades (led by Brig. Gen. James Lane and Col. William Lowrance) knocked down the first fence along Emmitsburg Road as they advanced into the killing cauldron ahead of them. Already exhausted and shocked by what was transpiring just to their front, only about half of the men climbed over the second fence. As they did so, Trimble's unfortunates received the same hail of gunfire Brig. Gen. James Pettigrew's men had encountered. Once across, those who dared continue stepped forward and merged into the extended masses of men making for the crest.

A serious miscommunication occurred when the 7th and part of the 37th North Carolina regiments of Lane's Brigade obliqued to their right to maintain a connection with Lowrance's left. Lane's remaining units, however, shifted to the left to fill a gap once held by Davis' Brigade. The gap thus created offered opportunities for Federal troops to pour enfilading fire into each group. Lane later claimed he led his brigade to within a few yards of the wall, but there is no evidence to support his postwar account. As a result, only some 400-500 of Trimble's men advanced beyond Emmitsburg Road. A short time later, Trimble was shot in the leg while riding west of the road surveying the course of his attack. His leg was later amputated.[28]

A couple hundred yards south around the Angle, survivors from Garnett's and Armistead's brigades massed along the stone wall and exchanged fire with the 72nd Pennsylvania near the crest of Cemetery Ridge, and with the 69th Pennsylvania, deployed along the wall to the right. Realizing the precariousness of his position, Armistead yelled, "Follow me boys! Give 'em the cold steel, boys!" and leaped over the wall. A number of men, perhaps as many as 100, followed him. The right companies of the 69th Pennsylvania turned to face Armistead's thrust on their right and rear, but the Virginians overwhelmed at least one company. Armistead fell mortally wounded while rushing through Cushing's abandoned battery.[29]

Although the pressure on the 69th Pennsylvania was heavy and its men fell back into the Copse of Trees, they refused to flee. One observer described the regiment as a "mob" at this point, but help was on the way. The 7th Michigan, 20th Massachusetts, and part of the 59th New York, which had been on the front line, formed at a right angle to their former positions and faced the knot of timber. Because of the chaos around them and with limited room to maneuver, these movements were confused and mixed elements of the units. The 19th Massachusetts and 42nd New York on the second line moved quickly to the right, connecting with the 72nd Pennsylvania.[30]

The balance of Brig. Gen. William Harrow's brigade together with the 80th New York and 151st Pennsylvania of Col. Chapman Biddle's brigade also rushed to the right to take on Pickett's men. The fighting along the wall in this sector was hand-to-hand. "Men fired into each other's faces; there were bayonet thrusts, cutting with sabres, hand-to-hand contests, oaths, curses, yells and hurrahs . . . grape and double canister . . . tore through the rebel ranks at only a few paces distant, the dead and wounded were piled in ghastly heaps," wrote a Southern soldier. "Still on they came up to the very muzzles of their guns; they were blown away from the cannon's mouth, but yet they did not waver."[31]

The bulk of the two sides stood less than fifteen paces apart. According to a private, "every time a man stoops to load, others crowd in ahead of him so that he will have to elbow his way through in order to get another chance to fire." Men were as likely to hit their comrades as the enemy. Regiments, per se, no longer existed because the units were intermingled. Large numbers of Confederates were streaming back to Seminary Ridge. Only devout handfuls fighting bravely along the wall singly, in pairs, and by the score remained.[32]

The 72nd Pennsylvania finally charged down the hill; other Federals also descended on the area. So close were the combatants that every musket discharge singed clothing and flesh. And then, quite suddenly according to survivors, the crisis passed. The remnants of Pickett's three brigades not yet negotiating the long return westward either surrendered or began the long dangerous scamper back to Seminary Ridge.[33]

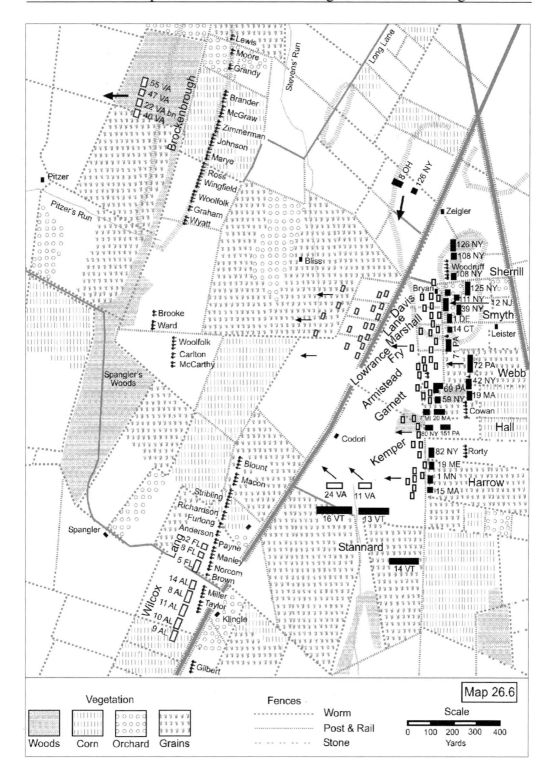

Map 26.6

Vegetation

Woods   Corn   Orchard   Grains

Fences

········· Worm
·········· Post & Rail
– – · – – · Stone

Scale

0   100   200   300   400
Yards

Map 26.7

As the survivors of the Pickett-Pettigrew-Trimble attack dribbled back toward Seminary Ridge, two Confederate brigades under Brig. Gen. Cadmus Wilcox and Col. David Lang moved out toward Cemetery Ridge. Both belonged to Maj. Gen. Richard Anderson's Third Corps division. Wilcox's Alabama soldiers, about 1,000 strong, held the right side of the column while Lang's Floridians, whittled down to only 400 men, held the left.

These brigades should have moved forward earlier to exploit any success and to protect Pickett's right flank against exactly what had befallen it: a flank attack of the variety delivered by Stannard's Vermont brigade. For some reason the two brigades did not step off until the Virginians were fighting for their lives near the stone wall. By then it was much too late. "Wilcox's brigade passed by us, moving to Pickett's support," recalled Colonel Alexander. By that time, noted the gunner, "There was no longer anything to support, and with the keenest pity at the useless waste of life, I saw them advance. The men, as they passed us, looked bewildered, as if they wondered what they were expected to do, or why they were there."[34]

Wilcox's Alabama regiments formed from left to right as follows: 14th Alabama – 8th Alabama – 11th Alabama – 10th Alabama – 9th Alabama. Lang's troops advanced from left to right as follows: 2nd Florida – 8th Florida – 5th Florida. The fifty-nine pieces of Federal artillery in front of this forlorn hope opened fire as the two brigades walked into view. "All of the enemy's terrible artillery that could bear on them was concentrated upon them from both flanks and directly in front, and more than on the evening previous," reported Wilcox. Casualties quickly mounted as case shot and shell, followed by rounds of canister (and then double canister) smashed through their ranks.[35]

When the Southern infantry reached the thickets surrounding Plum Run, Lang's men on the left side of the line dispersed to find shelter from the Federal guns. One of those keenly watching the new advance of the enemy was General Stannard. He ordered the 16th Vermont

to "double quick back to our original position and get in front of this new line," recalled its colonel, Wheelock Veazey. Four companies of the 14th Vermont moved forward to assist the 16th. The 13th Vermont held its position. The green troops rushed ahead without firing a shot and approached the 2nd Florida on the left of Lang's line. Colonel Veazey's order to charge the Floridians' flank inflicted heavy casualties and widespread confusion in the Confederate ranks. Colonel Lang had been trying desperately to move his brigade to safety, but the "noise of artillery and small-arms was so deafening that it was impossible to make the voice heard above the din, and the men were by this time so badly scattered in the bushes and among the rocks that it was impossible to make any movement to meet or check the enemy's advance." Lang also acknowledged that his orders were "not in time to save a large number of the Second Florida Infantry, together with their colors, from being cut off and captured by the flanking force on the left." His men did not go down easily, firing from behind rocks and trees until they were overwhelmed. Some of the Floridians were so stunned they willingly wandered east into the Union rear without guards.[36]

General Wilcox, meanwhile, rode back to the First Corps batteries along Emmitsburg Road to ask them to open fire on the Vermont troops. His request was impossible to fulfill because the guns were out of ammunition. "Not getting any artillery to fire upon the enemy's infantry that were on my left flank, and seeing none of the troops that I was ordered to support, and knowing that my small force could do nothing save to make a useless sacrifice of themselves, I ordered them back," he wrote. Although the Alabama troops had only faced artillery fire before retreating, Wilcox left more than 200 men on the field. Lang's losses were also heavy, particularly among the 2nd Florida. Two of his three regiments lost their battle flags.[37]

The repulse of Wilcox and Lang ended the last significant infantry fighting at the battle at Gettysburg.

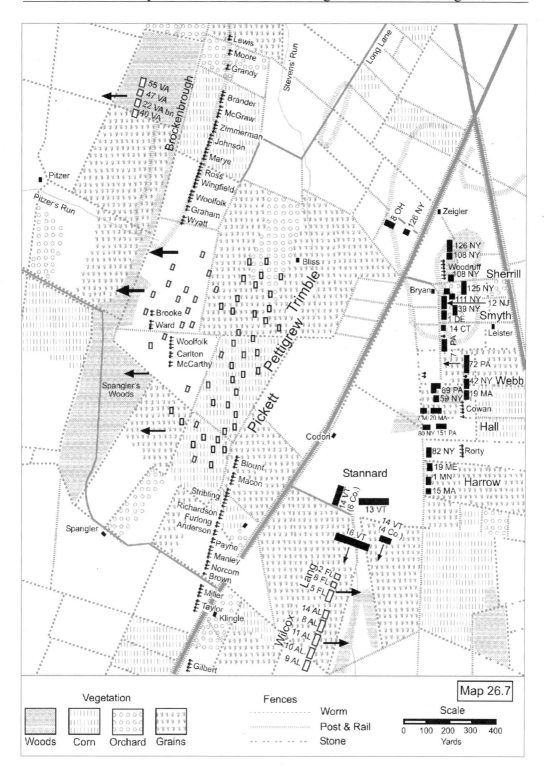

Map 26.7

Vegetation

Woods   Corn   Orchard   Grains

Fences
·········· Worm
·········· Post & Rail
— · — · — Stone

Scale
0   100   200   300   400
Yards

Map Set 27: East Cavalry Field

Map 27.1

The week leading up to Gettysburg was an arduous one for Maj. Gen. James Ewell Brown (Jeb) Stuart and his cavalry division. Stuart's task was gathering intelligence while screening the right flank of Richard Ewell's Second Corps as it moved north. Leaving two brigades behind under Brig. Gens. Beverley Robertson and William Jones to operate with Lee, Stuart mounted his remaining three brigades (about 5,600 men) early on June 24. The movement, based upon discretionary orders, would eventually become a long-distance ride around the entire Army of the Potomac.

Once the Union army moved north after General Lee's infantry, Stuart found it difficult to get around and ahead of its component pieces. Within a short time, he was effectively cut off from the Army of Northern Virginia. On June 28 near Rockville, Maryland, he captured 125 wagons loaded with supplies. The supplies were useful, but the wagons slowed him down. Unable to locate Lee, Stuart rode to York, Pennsylvania and then to Carlisle seeking information. Early on July 2, Stuart learned Lee was fighting a battle at Gettysburg. Between June 24 and July 2, his exhausted troopers and jaded horses rode 200 miles and fought a series of skirmishes (Thoroughfare Gap, Fairfax Court House, Rockville, and Carlisle), and three sharp actions: Westminster, Hanover, and Hunterstown.[1]

After riding all night from Carlisle, Stuart arrived at Gettysburg late on the afternoon of July 2 while preparations were underway to launch the en echelon attack against the Army of the Potomac. After a cold meeting between General Lee and his subordinate, a plan was crafted for Stuart to operate beyond the army's left flank, and to watch for any opportunity to assault the rear areas of the enemy. Back in their saddles early on July 3, Stuart's cavalry rode out on the York Pike. A portion of Albert Jenkins' cavalry brigade (which was under Lt. Col. Vincent Witcher, 34th Virginia Battalion), led the column. Behind Witcher rode Col. John Chambliss' Brigade, followed by Capt. William

Griffin's and Capt. Thomas Jackson's batteries. Next was Brig. Gen. Wade Hampton's Brigade, followed by a section of Capt. Charles Green's battery (which was not horse artillery). Brigadier General Fitz Lee's Brigade brought up the rear.[2]

Confronting Stuart's 6,000-6,500 men and thirteen guns were brigades under Cols. John McIntosh and Irvin Gregg, both of Brig. Gen. David Gregg's Second Cavalry Division. Gregg's brigade tangled with Ewell's Second Corps on July 2 at Brinkerhoff Ridge, and was now east of the ridge guarding the Army of the Potomac's right rear sector. McIntosh's brigade reached the field at 1:00 p.m. on July 3. General Gregg's orders were to move his division south to guard the right flank of the XII Corps, but he hesitated when he realized the strategic importance of this area. A brigade under Brig. Gen. George Custer and Lt. Alexander Pennington's battery (Brig. Gen. Kilpatrick's division), at Gregg's request, moved to occupy the pivotal position at the intersection of Hanover and Low Dutch roads. Dismounting two companies each from the 5th and 6th Michigan, Custer threw them forward down both roads.[3]

Stuart intended to leave York Pike and ride south to Hanover Road before riding toward Baltimore Pike. This move would place him close to Ewell's Corps and the Federal rear. When he reached Cress Ridge (between York Pike and Hanover Road) about noon, Stuart dismounted the 34th Virginia Battalion. The 170 men took possession of the Rummel barn, and shook out along a fence line left of the building. The remainder of the brigade deployed on both sides of the 34th Virginia Battalion. Chambliss' troopers took up a position behind Witcher. The former's right regiment, the 13th Virginia, extended to the George Trostle farm. Stuart deployed artillery and fired several shots in an unsuccessful effort to flush out the enemy.[4]

When Custer heard the firing he reoriented his brigade and the battery in its direction and sent the dismounted 5th Michigan across Hanover Road. Cavalry commander Maj. Gen. Alfred Pleasonton agreed to allow Gregg to return to his former position if Custer was released to return to Kilpatrick. Gregg agreed and his two brigades rode to the contested area.[5]

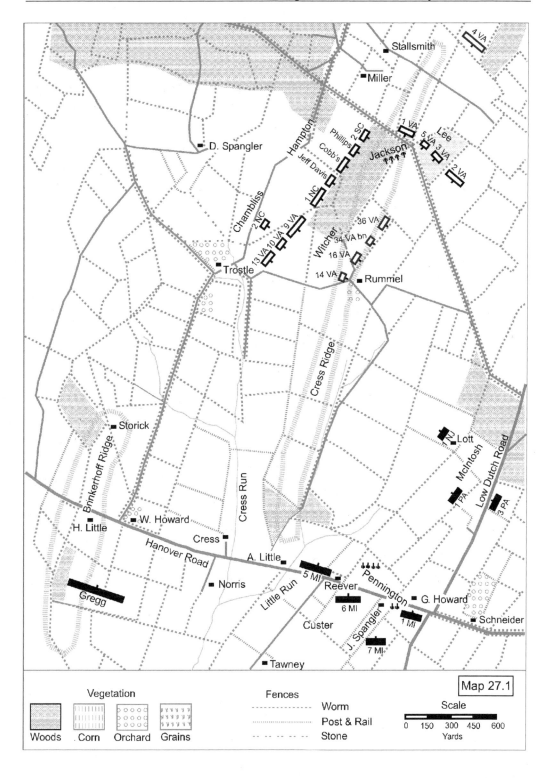

4 VA

Stallsmith

Miller

1 VA

Lee

5 VA 3 VA

2 SC Jackson

Phillips

Cobb's

2 VA

D. Spangler

Hampton

Jeff Davis

1 NC

Chambliss

2 NC 9 VA

36 VA

34 VA bn

Witcher

10 VA

13 VA

16 VA

Trostle

14 VA

Rummel

Cress Ridge

N.J. Lott

McIntosh

Low Dutch Road

Storick

Brinkerhoff Ridge

Cress Run

1 PA

3 PA

W. Howard

H. Little

Cress

Hanover Road

A. Little

5 MI

Reever

Pennington

G. Howard

Schneider

Norris

6 MI

Little Run

Gregg

Custer

J. Spangler

1 MI

7 MI

Tawney

Vegetation

Woods Corn Orchard Grains

Fences

Worm

Post & Rail

Stone

Map 27.1

Scale

0 150 300 450 600
Yards

Map 27.2

After some confusion, Col. John McIntosh's 1st New Jersey Cavalry replaced Brig. Gen. George Custer's 5th Michigan on either side of the Lott farmhouse. The rest of McIntosh's brigade deployed in column of squadrons in a clover field east of the farmhouse. Realizing he needed more troops, General Gregg convinced Custer to delay his departure. A section of Capt. William Rank's battery arrived and deployed south of Hanover Road, supported by the 1st Maine Cavalry and 10th New York Cavalry of Col. Irvin Gregg's brigade.[6]

Once in position, General Gregg decided to test the Confederates with Pennington's six guns. The four guns in Captain Jackson's Battery responded, but the Federal superiority in number of tubes and quality of ammunition became quickly obvious. Accurate Federal artillery fire disabled one of Jackson's guns on Cress Ridge, killing and wounding many of its men and horses. Outgunned and outranged, the Confederate battery fell back and was replaced by Green's Battery and a section of Capt. William McGregor's Battery. These guns quickly attracted the Federal artillery fire and half the horses were knocked quickly out of action. "The little artillery we used seemed of little service & I think most of it was soon silenced by the Federals," grumbled a Virginia cavalry officer. Federal horse artillery officers held a certain disdain for their Southern counterparts. "As a rule," wrote one, "their Horse Art'y was so badly handled in battle we Art'y officers paid but little attention to it." The uneven exchange forced five of the Confederate guns to withdraw and the others, for the most part, fell silent.[7]

The 34th Virginia Cavalry Battalion withdrew to replenish its ammunition, leaving behind the smaller 14th and 16th Virginia Cavalry regiments, which in the absence of Jenkins were also under Lt. Col. Vincent Witcher's command. As the Virginians withdrew, the Federal skirmish line quickly moved forward and attacked the dismounted Confederate cavalrymen behind the fence, forcing the men of the 34th Virginia Cavalry Battalion to sprint back to bolster the line. Their added firepower forced the Federal

skirmish line to drift back the way it had come. During this skirmish, Witcher was shocked to see the 14th and 16th Virginia regiments mount up and head for the rear. "The four-company detachment of the 16th Virginia did not exceed 50 men, as it was only a skeleton paper regiment," explained Witcher. As for the four companies of the 14th Virginia Cavalry, he continued, it was "never famous for its gallantry." The Federal artillery fire had become so annoying the 34th Virginia Battalion mounted a half-hearted charge to attempt to silence it. The effort was quickly repulsed and the men returned to their jump-off point. Witcher's men continued holding the area around the Rummel barn with support from Chambliss' men.[8]

With the artillery battle in full swing, General Gregg ordered the 1st New Jersey Cavalry forward toward Little Run, where it came under fire from the 34th Virginia Battalion and Witcher's other troops near the Rummel farm buildings. The 3rd Pennsylvania Cavalry, consolidated into five squadrons, deployed on both flanks of the 1st New Jersey. Stuart threw more troops from Chambliss' organization to the right of the 34th Virginia Battalion, overlapping the Federal line. When General Gregg learned the Confederate line extended beyond his left, he threw a portion of the 6th Michigan Cavalry forward and extended his own line accordingly. The 5th Michigan Cavalry advanced when the ammunition of the 1st New Jersey and 3rd Pennsylvania was nearly depleted. The two Michigan regiments were the only troops on the field with seven-shot repeating Spencer rifles. Their firepower convinced the Confederates they were facing more Federal troops than they really were. The Southern troopers had also been advancing, but the heavy fire quickly forced them to the safety of their main line. As one captured Confederate told a Federal cavalryman, "You'ns load in the morning and fire all day."

Seeing the Jerseymen and Pennsylvanians falling back, many of Witcher's Virginians mounted a charge. Some of Chambliss' troopers, including the 9th Virginia, joined them. However, the repeating rifles fired by the Michiganders quickly dampened their ardor, and they also broke off the assault.[9]

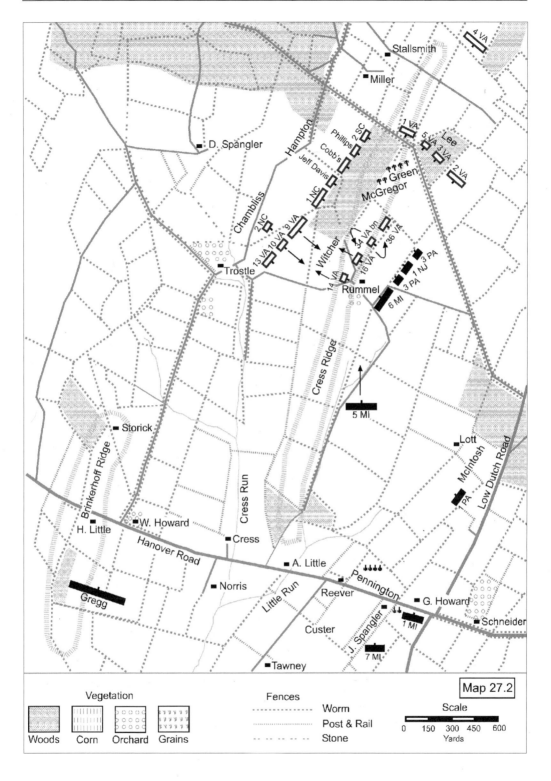

Map 27.2

Vegetation

Woods   Corn   Orchard   Grains

Fences

- - - - - - - -   Worm
· · · · · · · · · ·   Post & Rail
— - — - — -   Stone

Scale

0   150   300   450   600

Yards

Map 27.3

Captain Alanson Randol's four-gun Federal battery arrived and dropped trail just south of the Lott house, opening blistering fire on the Confederates on Cress Ridge. Pennington's battery joined in to good effect. "Never was there more accurate and effective fire delivered by the artillery than by the guns of Randol and Pennington," General Gregg wrote proudly.[10]

The retreat of the 1st New Jersey Cavalry, two squadrons from the 3rd Pennsylvania Cavalry, and 5th Michigan Cavalry was hastened by a charge from the 1st Virginia Cavalry of Lee's Brigade. Desperate for help, McIntosh called for his only reserve regiment—the 1st Maryland Cavalry. To his dismay, Gregg had moved the regiment and it was now too far away to be of service. Overcome with frustration, McIntosh "gave way to tears and oaths." All was not lost, however, for Custer's brigade remained on the field. Orders soon arrived for him to counterattack.

Appearing at the head of the 7th Michigan Cavalry, still a novice regiment, Custer yelled to his men, "Come on, you Wolverines!" The Virginians were also moving forward. The attack was "a more determined and vigorous charge . . . it was never my fortune to witness," recalled one Federal soldier. A stout fence stood between the combatants. The Michiganders reached it first, and when the first ranks halted, the rear ones plowed into them. "All were mixed in one confused and tangled mass," one of the Federals reminisced. The men knocked down sections of the fence and the two regiments engaged in hand-to-hand combat. "Bullets were flying mightily thick," noted a Federal trooper. The 5th Michigan, now on the Virginians' right flank, added a steady stream of small arms fire. Hit in front and flank, the Virginians finally retreated with the Michiganders hot on their tails.[11]

Looking ahead, the men of the 7th Michigan Cavalry spotted more Confederate troopers advancing toward them. These riders belonged to the 9th and 13th Virginia Cavalry regiments (Chambliss), the 1st North Carolina Cavalry and Jeff Davis Legion (Hampton), and the 2nd Virginia Cavalry (Lee). Reaching the farm lane that connected the Rummel Farm with Low Dutch Road, the Michiganders stopped because of both the barrier of the fence in front and the approaching Confederate reinforcements. Outnumbered and well in advance of their line, the 7th Michigan turned back. Riding forward past the Lott house, General Gregg tried to stop the withdrawal, yelling, "For God's sake, men, if you are ever going to stand, stand now, for you are on free soil!" His words had little or no effect.[12]

The advancing Southern troopers provided a tempting target for the Federal artillerymen, who opened fire with terrible effect. The iron tore into the charging squadrons, hurling horses and men into the air. On their right, the Confederates watched as a mass of Federal troops galloped toward their vulnerable flank. These men were four companies of the 5th Michigan Cavalry, followed by the rest of the regiment. The attack was hastily mounted, for just a short time earlier the Federals were facing what seemed an irresistible Confederate charge. The flank attack and the artillery barrage chewed up and slowed down the Southern attack until it finally ended altogether, the troopers turning away to return to safer territory on Cress Ridge.[13]

With the end of the Confederate cavalry charge, the Federal artillery turned its attention to the Southern batteries unlimbered on Cress Ridge, recently augmented by Capt. James Breathed's four-gun battery. Neither side gained a decided advantage in the exchange that ensued.[14]

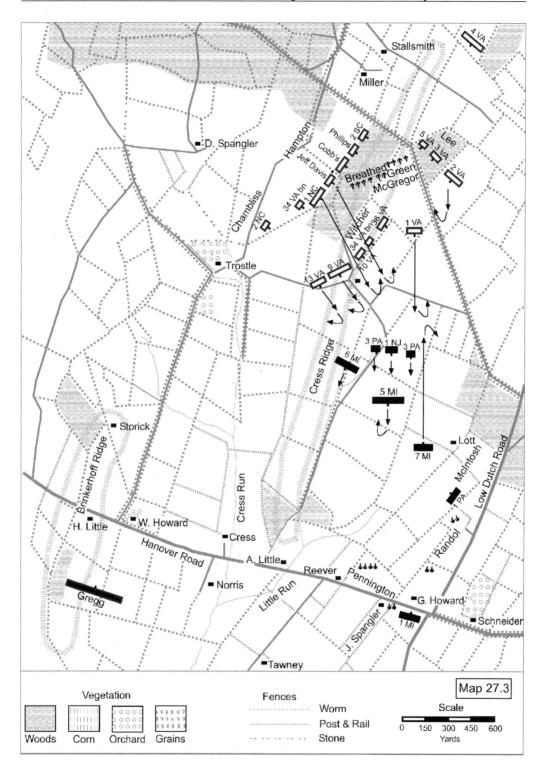

Map 27.3

Vegetation

Woods Corn Orchard Grains

Fences

--------- Worm
.... Post & Rail
-- -- -- -- Stone

Scale

0   150   300   450   600
Yards

Map 27.4

By this time it was approaching 3:00 p.m. General Lee's massive artillery barrage, in preparation for the Pickett-Pettigrew-Trimble infantry attack, was tapering off and the infantry was preparing to attack Cemetery Ridge. General Stuart, with three of his brigades, was poised just off the Federal army's right flank near the Rummel Farm.

Once formed, a long line of horsemen emerged from the woods on Cress Ridge at a walk, then a trot, and finally a gallop. The Federal cavalrymen watched in admiration. "A grander spectacle than their advance has rarely been beheld," admitted a Federal officer. "They marched with well-aligned fronts and steady reins. Their polished saber-blades dazzled in the sun." Another witness agreed, writing, "[T]he spectacle called forth a murmur of admiration."[15]

The Federal units quickly fell back to provide open fields of fire for Pennington's and Randol's gunners. General Gregg sent an aide to order the batteries to retreat. The message was greeted with derision. "Tell the General to go to Hell," answered the artillerymen as they shifted from shell to canister. The blasts knocked down troopers and horses alike, but others filled the gaps and the horsemen continued toward the Federals "as if nothing had happened."[16]

Posted behind the guns was the 1st Michigan Cavalry. Gregg ordered the regiment to meet the enemy charge. Asking a small veteran unit to take on more than eight Confederate regiments was a desperate, nearly suicidal, order. The 1st Michigan's commander, Col. Charles Town, tried to give a short speech but the men were in no mood to wait. The troopers launched into the attack even as pioneer details were busy pushing fences out of their way in front of them along Hanover Road. Crossing the road near George Howard's house, the Wolverines were joined by General Custer who wanted nothing more than to lead another charge.[17]

The two forces galloped toward each other at full speed. Their collision generated a tremendous crash of men, animals, and equipment. The impact reminded one soldier of "the falling of timber." Horses somersaulted into the air, throwing their riders to the ground; many were trampled. The wild melee that followed can only describe the chaos as the men hacked at one another with sabers and shot each other at close range with their pistols. Custer's horse went down, but he quickly mounted another as men cut and slashed on all sides of him.[18]

About this time, troopers from the 3rd Pennsylvania hit both Confederate flanks simultaneously. Some of McIntosh's own staff joined the small, 30-trooper band attacking the Confederate right. Slicing through the dense throng of enemy soldiers, they headed for a Confederate flag but lost about half their number in the process. An entire battalion of the 3rd Pennsylvania, which had been in the woods north of the Lott house, struck the Confederate left flank. The men had been ordered to hold these woods, but Capt. William Miller, the squadron's commander, saw an opportunity and seized it. The veteran enlisted men could also see what was occurring and began their attack before being ordered to do so. The 100 or so troopers slammed into the Confederate line about two-thirds of the distance from its center and rode through it, only to be engulfed on every side by screaming Confederate riders. Miller was later awarded the Medal of Honor for his actions.[19]

Other Federal units joined the swirling combat, including portions of the 5th and 7th Michigan regiments on the Confederate right flank and parts of the 1st New Jersey on the left. The vicious hand-to-hand combat continued for several minutes as both sides tried desperately to gain the upper hand. General Hampton, caught up in the middle of the action, took a severe saber slash to his head that knocked him out of the fight and nearly killed him. Attacked on three sides and unable to make any forward progress, the mass of Confederates began pulling back to Cress Ridge. The Federal troopers followed as far as the Rummel buildings.

Stuart decided it was time to abort his contest with Gregg. Each side suffered losses amounting to about ten percent of those engaged. "Mounted fights never lasted long," wrote Stuart, "but there were more men killed and wounded in this fight than I ever saw on any field where the fighting was done mounted."[20]

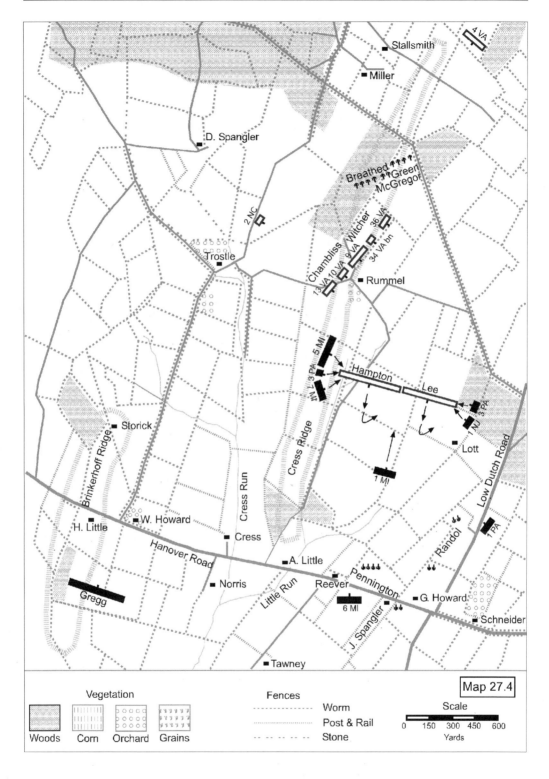

Map 27.4

Vegetation

Woods   Corn   Orchard   Grains

Fences

----------- Worm

················ Post & Rail

-- -- -- -- Stone

Scale

0   150   300   450   600

Yards

Map Set 28: South Cavalry Field
Map 28.1

About eight in the morning of July 3, Brig. Gen. Judson Kilpatrick, commander of the Federal cavalry's third division, received orders to operate on the Federal left flank at the southern end of the battlefield. Brigadier General Elon Farnsworth's brigade rode with him. Kilpatrick's other brigade under Brig. Gen. George Custer remained with Brig. Gen. David Gregg's division (at Gregg's request), and would later battle Jeb Stuart's troopers northeast of Gettysburg. Brigadier General Wesley Merritt's brigade of U.S. Regulars, part of John Buford's division, also arrived about this time. Buford and his other two brigades had already moved south into Maryland to guard the army's wagon trains.[1]

Farnsworth's men dismounted and took up positions in and around the Bushman Woods by 1:00 p.m. Lieutenant Samuel Elder's battery unlimbered on high ground, supported by the 5th New York Cavalry. The 1st Vermont Cavalry was on the right, followed by the 1st West Virginia and the 18th Pennsylvania. Farnsworth pushed out a skirmish line composed of four dismounted companies of the 1st Vermont Cavalry with two other mounted companies in support.[2]

The 1st Texas infantry (part of Brig. Gen. Jerome Robertson's Brigade, Maj. Gen. John B. Hood's Division, Longstreet's First Corps) watched from behind a low stone wall as the Federal horsemen gained in strength. The previous day's bloody fighting for Houck's Ridge had whittled down the regiment to fewer than 200 men. Their difficult orders were to hold a defensive line stretching about one-half mile. Skirmishers from the 47th Alabama were on their left. The Confederate troops in this sector were well supported by Capt. James Reilly's and Capt. William Bachman's batteries (Henry's artillery battalion). Sharp skirmishing erupted when the line of the 1st Vermont Cavalry advanced.[3]

General Merritt's brigade took its position to the west about the same time. Throwing eight companies of the 6th Pennsylvania Cavalry forward dismounted on the skirmish line, the rest of the brigade—the 1st U.S., 2nd U. S., and 5th U.S.—remained along the D. Currens farm lane just to the right of Emmitsburg Road. Graham's battery also added to the Federal buildup. The right side of the 1st Texas skirmish line and 9th Georgia Infantry of Brig. Gen. George "Tige" Anderson's Brigade (Hood's Division) on its right faced the Regular troopers. About 100 men from the 1st South Carolina Cavalry, detached from Brig. Gen. Wade Hampton's Brigade, supported by two guns from Capt. James Hart's horse artillery, were on the right of the Georgians. When he learned of the build-up of Federal troops, Brig. Gen. Evander Law, who was commanding in this sector, ordered other regiments of Anderson's regiments to reinforce the sector. Law also shifted a section of artillery from Reilly's battery behind the Georgians.[4]

The contingent of the 6th Pennsylvania Cavalry advanced about one-half mile up Emmitsburg Road before encountering the enemy infantry. Confederate artillery fire intensified, forcing the Pennsylvanians to grind to a halt. General Merritt ordered the rest of his brigade forward. The 2nd U.S. Cavalry formed on the right of Emmitsburg Road and the 1st U. S. Cavalry formed on the left, with the 5th U.S. Cavalry in support. The 6th Pennsylvania Cavalry moved forward again, and the weight of Merritt's brigade forced the 1st South Carolina Cavalry and Hart's guns to fall back. The 1st U.S. Cavalry proved especially irksome for the Confederates because it flanked the enemy's left.[5]

The men of the 9th Georgia regiment near the A. Currens farm watched Merritt's line of dismounted cavalrymen extending ominously beyond their right flank, threatening Hart's battery. The Georgians were relieved to see the 7th and 8th Georgia regiments marching at the double quick to take up positions on their right. The 1st South Carolina Cavalry on their right extended the line westward.[6]

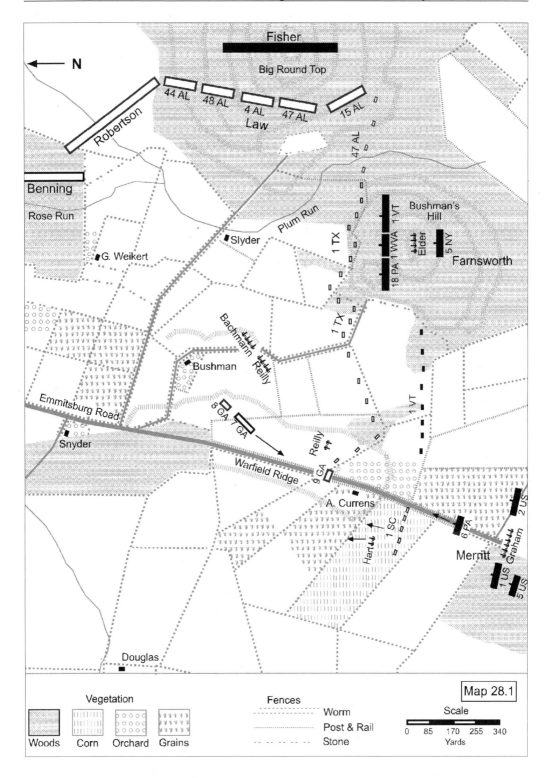

Map 28.1

Vegetation

Woods Corn Orchard Grains

Fences
- - - - - - - Worm
·············· Post & Rail
- · - · - · - Stone

Scale
0 85 170 255 340
Yards

Map 28.2

When Brig. Gen. Wesley Merritt saw the Confederate reinforcements arrive, he decided to flank the enemy by using the 5th U.S. on the left of the line. To fill the gap between the 5th U.S. and 1st U.S., Merritt deployed a skirmish line composed of companies from the 1st and 2nd U.S.

Meanwhile, Brig. Gen. George "Tige" Anderson's remaining regiments—the 11th Georgia and 59th Georgia—arrived and took position on the extreme right of the Confederate line. Brigadier General Evander Law was so concerned about this flank that he personally escorted the two regiments to their positions. It was now about 4:00 p.m., three hours since the low-intensity fighting began and about the time the Pickett-Pettigrew-Trimble attack was ending. The effects were beginning to show on the exhausted Georgians, who had marched and fought for hours in and near the Wheatfield the previous day. [7]

When his troops were in position, Law counterattacked by employing a left wheel movement by his right flank. His force was composed of the 11th and 59th Georgia regiments and the 100 troopers of the 1st South Carolina Cavalry. Caught off-guard by the strikes against its front and flank, the 5th U.S. Cavalry retreated. According to Law, his men "struck Merritt's skirmish line 'on its end and doubled it up' as far as the Emmitsburg Road." Not wanting to risk a general engagement, Law halted the advance. He was also concerned about suffering unnecessary losses to Graham's Federal artillery, which had "poured a steady stream of shot and shell into the ranks." [8]

"[T]hough everyone fought like a tiger . . . we had to fall back," Samuel Crockett of the 1st U.S. scribbled in his diary. General Merritt reorganized his line. The Pennsylvanians took position along a fence line south of the Currens house and remained there until after dark. Although the two sides skirmished for four hours, the casualties were fairly light—Merritt lost only 49 men, or three percent of those engaged. Confederate losses are unknown, but they were probably also light. [9]

Operating independently of Merritt, Brig. Gen. Judson Kilpatrick prepared a full-scale attack by General Farnsworth's brigade against the 1st Texas and, beyond it, the right flank of the Confederate army. Kilpatrick saw vulnerable Confederate artillery in front of him and an opportunity for glory. Law shifted the section of Reilly's battery near Emmitsburg Road to a position directly behind the Texans during this period. [10]

To the east, Farnsworth's 1st West Virginia launched its attack. According to one observer, the West Virginians attempted to "throw [down] the rails, tugging at the stakes, cutting with their sabers." Finally clear of the barrier, the West Virginians galloped toward the waiting Texans. Southern infantryman Thomas McCarthy recalled how "the ground trembled as they came, they rode down our skirmishers and charged us, and in a few seconds were on us." The Texans did not open fire until the horsemen were within sixty yards of their position. When the smoke cleared, large numbers of saddles were empty. [11]

The sheets of flame from the Texas barrels and the canister from Reilly's two pieces felled many West Virginians and their horses, but the momentum of the charge carried the horsemen onward and into the Texans. "They went right through us cutting right and left," noted McCarthy. Hand-to-hand combat swirled freely along the wall. While most of the West Virginians decided to retreat, Col. Nathaniel Richmond and a band of his men cleared the fence and found themselves trapped. Blocked by the wall to the east, they turned north. Confederate artillery and the 9th Georgia infantry near Emmitsburg Road blasted away at them as they rode. When he realized he was caught in a box, Colonel Richmond ordered his men to turn and cut their way through the line of Texans. Richmond's effort was ultimately successful, but his men sustained additional casualties making good their escape. [12]

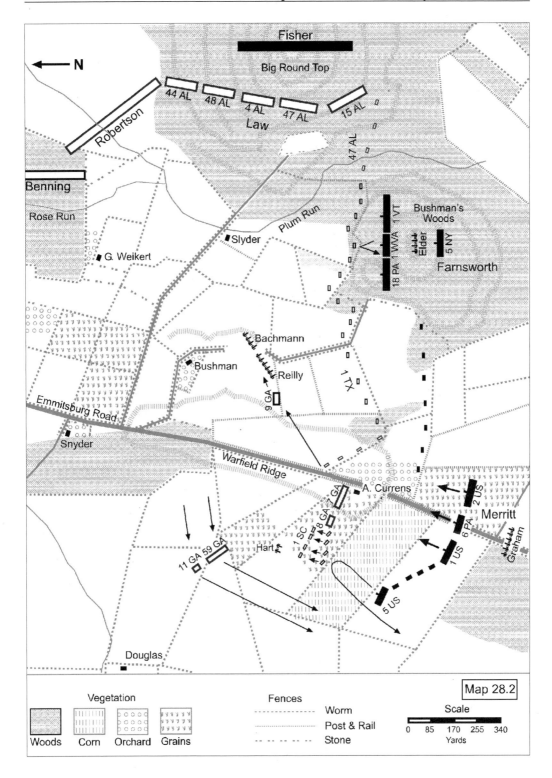

Fisher

Big Round Top

Robertson

44 AL   48 AL   4 AL   47 AL   15 AL

Law

47 AL

Benning

Rose Run

Slyder

Plum Run

1 VT
1 WVA
18 PA
Elder
5 NY

Bushman's
Woods

Farnsworth

G. Weikert

Bachmann

Bushman

Reilly

1 TX

9 GA

Emmitsburg Road

Snyder

Warfield Ridge

A. Currens

2 US

Merritt

7 GA

8 GA

6 PA

1 SC

Graham

11 GA 59 GA

Hart

1 US

5 US

Douglas

Map 28.2

Vegetation   Fences   Scale

----------- Worm   0   85   170   255   340

.... Post & Rail   Yards

Woods Corn Orchard Grains – – – – – Stone

Map 28.3

The 18th Pennsylvania Cavalry also charged the Texas line, advancing with a battalion of the 5th New York Cavalry on either side. Probably intended to coincide with the 1st Vermont's attack, the Pennsylvanians' assault went off prematurely.

According to Major John Hammond, the commander of the 5th New York, his orders were to "make a charge upon one of the enemy's guns, which was very troublesome. We moved forward some distance, when the enemy removed the piece, and we were ordered back, and took up a position in the rear of our battery [Elder's]." Given the few casualties suffered by the 5th New York, it seems likely the regiment pulled back before the 18th Pennsylvania troopers withdrew. The green Pennsylvanians came under the same intense fire that had earlier raked the 1st West Virginia Cavalry. Although the first volley fired by the Texans flew harmlessly above the Pennsylvanians' heads, the irregularity of the terrain and the inexperience of the men triggered a degeneration of the crisp battle line into an ineffective mob. After taking numerous casualties, the Pennsylvanians retired to their original positions.[13]

Because of the growing aggressiveness of Farnsworth's brigade, General Law began shifting his infantry to create a box. The 4th Alabama marched from the base of Big Round Top to the Slyder farm lane and faced the Plum Run Valley to the south. The rest of his old brigade did an "about face" and made some other minor movements to face east across the valley. Law ordered the guns of Bachmann's battery shifted to face east across the valley and brought over the 9th Georgia from Emmitsburg Road to support it. The 1st Texas closed the box to the south.[14]

While Law set his trap, Farnsworth divided the 1st Vermont Cavalry into three battalions, each with four companies. Captain Henry Parsons, Lt. Col. Addison Preston, and Major William Wells commanded the three battalions, respectively. Farnsworth rode with Wells (whose bravery this day would earn Wells a Medal of Honor). Only two battalions made the charge because Preston's second battalion remained dismounted and deployed behind a stone wall to provide support for the attacking troopers.[15]

As the Green Mountain men broke from the woods in columns of four, the Federal skirmishers begged them to halt. On the right, Captain Parsons' First Battalion slipped through the Alabama skirmish line east of the 1st Texas' position. Galloping north, they headed for Slyder's farm. They didn't know that the 4th Alabama had recently taken position there. The Alabamians opened fire. Their aim was high, however, so only a few of the cavalrymen fell. The second volley was much more deadly, forcing the Federal horsemen to ride south and then north again across the "D-shaped" field near Big Round Top.[16]

From this position, the troopers in the First Battalion could see Farnsworth and the Third Battalion to the east, closer to Big Round Top. Unable to join their commander, Parsons reluctantly ordered his men to retreat south to their original positions. Meanwhile, when the Third Battalion encountered several Alabama regiments at the base of the hill, the column turned north and headed toward the Slyder farm lane. Seeing the Confederate troops occupying Devil's Den, the battalion wheeled to the west and then southwest. This route took the battalion toward the 9th Georgia and Reilly's and Bachmann's batteries, which opened an accurate and deadly fire against it.

Thundering southward, the battalion smashed through the rear of the 1st Texas line and headed back to its original position. Farnsworth was not with the men when they returned. His horse was killed during the ride. When he was given another, he continued the charge into the D-shaped field. Farnsworth demanded the surrender of Lt. John B. Adrian, commanding the Confederate skirmish line, but Southern fire killed his replacement mount and wounded him in several places. Refusing to surrender, Farnsworth lay on the ground and died a short time later.

The foolhardy attempts to break the Confederate lines at the southern end of the battlefield were at an end.[17]

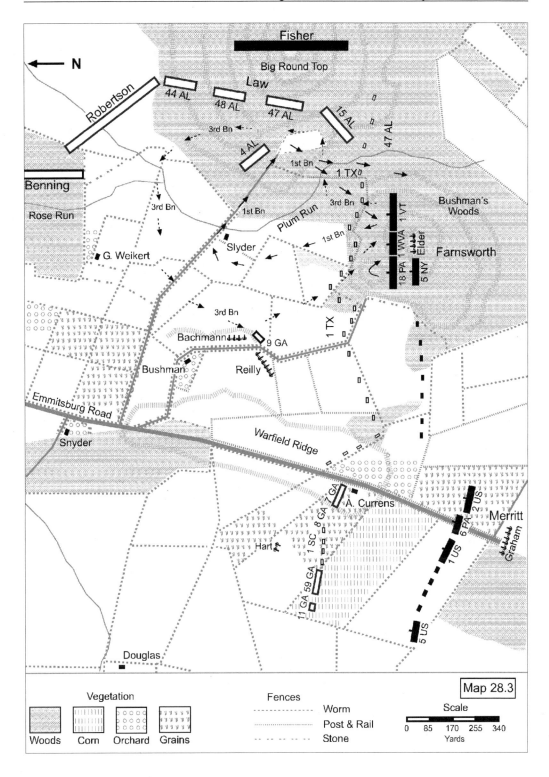

Map 28.3

Vegetation

Woods   Corn   Orchard   Grains

Fences
----------- Worm
·············· Post & Rail
– – – – – Stone

Scale

0   85   170   255   340
Yards

Map Set 29: The Retreat from Gettysburg

Map 29.1 (July 4)

General Robert E. Lee planned his army's retreat to Virginia after the Pickett-Pettigrew-Trimble Charge failed. Protecting his extensive wagon trains was foremost on his mind. He summoned Brig. Gen. John Imboden to his headquarters, where Lee arrived to greet him about 1:00 a.m. on July 4. Lee nearly sagged with fatigue. There was an "expression of sadness that I had never before seen upon his face," Imboden later wrote. He heard Lee utter, almost to himself, "Too bad! Too bad! Oh! Too Bad!"[1]

"We must now return to Virginia," the commanding general told Imboden. "As many of our poor wounded as possible must be taken home." With his 2,100 troopers and Capt. J. H. McClanahan's six-gun battery, Imboden was to escort the wagon train loaded with the wounded. Lee bolstered his command with seventeen guns from other artillery battalions. The cavalryman hoped to set out early on July 4, but it took a long time to assemble the wagons and he could not move out until 4:00 p.m. Imboden headed west along Chambersburg Pike. The slow-moving train of misery carried more than 12,000 wounded men. It stretched seventeen miles.[2]

Imboden placed the 18th Virginia Cavalry and a section of McClanahan's battery at the head of the column. Guns and a contingent of cavalry were inserted every one-third of a mile throughout the train. The wagons and troopers traveled through the night. Imboden avoided Chambersburg by taking a road to Greencastle, which the head of his column reached at daybreak on July 5. "During this one night I realized more of the horrors of war than I had in all the two preceding years," admitted Imboden.[3]

While Imboden gathered his wagon train, another long train filled with Lt. Gen. Richard Ewell's Second Corps supplies was rolling south along Fairfield Road. Ewell told Maj. John Harmon, his chief quartermaster, to get the train safely across the Potomac or "he wanted to see his face no more." The train began moving at 3:00 a.m. on July 4 with Brig. Gen. Iverson's Brigade rushing after it to provide support.[4]

Jeb Stuart left Gettysburg at nightfall on July 4 to screen the main army's retreat. Generals Fitz Lee and Wade Hampton led their brigades along Chambersburg Pike to guard the army's right and support Imboden. The brigades of Brig. Genls. Beverly Robertson and "Grumble" Jones rode toward the mountain passes near Fairfield, while Stuart rode with the brigades of Brig. Gens. Albert Jenkins and John Chambliss toward Emmitsburg, Maryland, to guard the army's left.[5]

The Federal army was also active. General George Meade was anxious to intercept Lee's slow and lightly defended trains. He sent Maj. Gen. Alfred Pleasonton's cavalry in pursuit. Brigadier General John Buford's division left Westminster for Williamsport to cut off the Confederate retreat on July 4. Judson Kilpatrick's division rode to Emmittsburg, which he reached about 3:00 p.m. He was joined there by Col. Pennock Huey's brigade of Brig. Gen. David Gregg's division. Kilpatrick rode to Monterey and attacked Ewell's wagons. He claimed (falsely) that "Ewell's large train was completely destroyed." Colonel Huey reported the capture of 150 wagons and 1,500 men.[6]

The bulk of the two armies remained on the battlefield, warily eyeing each other. Neither commanding general was sure the fighting was at an end. A truce permitted burial details to throw some of the dead into rough trenches and deliver the wounded to makeshift hospitals. Torrential rains soaked the field about noon.[7]

When darkness began to descend on Gettysburg it was clear to Lee that Meade was not going to attack. He began withdrawing his army to Fairfield Road, the shortest route to Hagerstown. Lieutenant General A. P. Hill's Third Corps led the retreat, which began after dark. When Maj. Gen. Richard Anderson's Division reached Fairfield at midnight, Lt. Gen. James Longstreet's First Corps, with the added responsibility of guarding some 4,000 Federal prisoners, began its retreat from Gettysburg. Its march was more difficult because Ewell's wagon train had cut deep grooves in the muddy road. Ewell's Second Corps impatiently waited for orders to begin its retreat.[8]

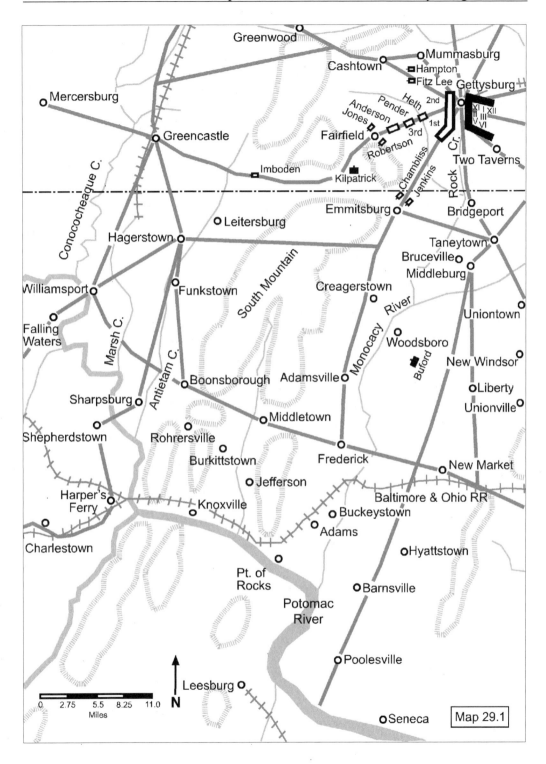

Map 29.1

Map 29.2 (July 5)

The attacks on General Lee's wagon trains continued on July 5. Early that day some 100 Union troopers and thirty to forty townspeople armed with axes attacked Imboden's wagons near Greencastle. The civilian-inspired attack destroyed the spokes of about a dozen wheels before Southern troopers drove the axe-wielding crowd away. Knots of Federal cavalry descended on the column in a series of hit and run attacks when the wagons reached Cearfoss. The audacious attack by an undersized Federal cavalry force at Cunningham's Crossroads, just below the Mason-Dixon Line, was finally repulsed, but not before it captured 100 wagons and their cargo of wounded men. The train finally reached Williamsport on the afternoon of July 5, but the Potomac River was swollen by heavy rains and Federal troops had destroyed the unguarded pontoon bridge. Imboden secured flatboats and began the tedious task of ferrying the wounded across the river.[9]

Federal cavalry attacked Ewell's wagons near Fairfield on July 5. Although driven off, the wagons experienced near-constant attack as they rolled their way south. Brigadier General Ambrose R. Wright's Brigade of Anderson's Division was dispatched to Monterey Gap to help Iverson's regiments defend the train.[10]

Two brigades of John Buford's division reached Frederick on July 5, where Merritt's brigade joined them. Riding south, General Kilpatrick deployed his division near Smithsburg on July 5. It fought a series of skirmishes there with Stuart's troopers. Sensing vulnerability, Kilpatrick withdrew toward Boonsborough, opening the road to the Potomac River. During the pursuit of Lee, the three brigades in David Gregg's cavalry division operated independently of each other. McIntosh's brigade rode to Emmitsburg, Maryland, missing Stuart's cavalry by several hours, before reconnoitering toward Fairfield. Huey's brigade rode with Kilpatrick's division, and J. Irvin Gregg's brigade traveled along Chambersburg Pike, skirmishing with Confederates near Greenwood.[11]

The entire Confederate army was now on the move. Hill's Third Corps led the column, marching all night. It reached the mountain gaps between Fairfield and Waynesboro, where it halted to protect these vital areas. The march continued later that day, reaching the base of South Mountain on the evening of July 5.[12]

Next in line was Longstreet's First Corps, which marched to the South Mountain passes and rested there on the night of July 4-5. The early minutes of July 5 found Ewell's Second Corps still in its positions west of Gettysburg. Ewell ordered his troops toward the Fairfield Road at 2:00 a.m., but they had to wait for the road to clear. The march finally began that morning, ending near Fairfield about 4:00 p.m. with its progress impeded by wagons. Brigadier General John Gordon's Georgia brigade (Maj. Gen. Jubal Early's Division) formed the rear-guard of the army.[13]

Early on July 5, General Meade ordered Maj. Gen. John Sedgwick's VI Corps to ascertain if the enemy still occupied the battlefield. When Sedgwick reported that only stragglers remained, Meade put four of his seven corps on the road after Lee's withdrawing army. The VI Corps departed first about 8:00 a.m. on the Fairfield Road, where about 5:00 p.m. it encountered Gordon's rear guard about two miles from Fairfield. The aggressive Federal advance caused Gordon to dispatch the 26th Georgia to hold the enemy in check near Fairfield while the wagon train and the rest of the army passed. A sharp fight ensued. Sedgwick claimed the capture of 250 Confederates during these rearguard actions, and both sides declared victory.[14]

Major General Winfield Hancock's II Corps began its march about noon on the Baltimore Pike, reaching Two Taverns that evening. The XII Corps under Maj. Gen. Henry Slocum also took this road about 1:00 p.m. and camped at Littlestown. Major General George Sykes' V Corps left about 5:00 p.m., marching about five hours to Marsh Creek.[15]

Major General Oliver Howard's XI Corps received orders to march the next day. Howard concentrated his men on Rock Creek about 5:30 p.m. on July 5. The shattered I and III Corps under Maj. Gens. Abner Doubleday and David Birney remained on the battlefield.[16]

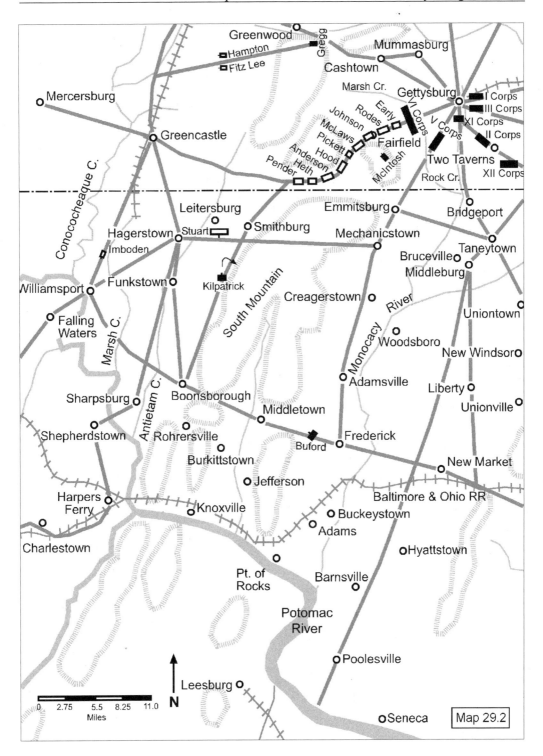

Map 29.2

Map 29.3 (July 6)

Dawn of July 6 found General Lee's army back on the road to Williamsport. Because of the rotation of his corps, Longstreet's First Corps led the infantry, but Ewell's Second Corps remained in the rear. Major General Robert Rodes' Division "act[ed] as rear guard, and repelled another attack of the enemy." The long column trudged through Waterloo and then to Hagerstown. It was slow going for the exhausted men and animals, and the roads were crowded and muddy. Longstreet's men reached Hagerstown at 5:00 p.m. and pressed on two additional miles south toward Funkstown along the Sharpsburg Turnpike, where they camped for the night along Antietam Creek. A. P. Hill's Corps camped between Leitersburg and Hagerstown. Ewell's Corps marched through Monterey Springs at the top of the mountain, then to Waynesboro, where it camped for the night.[17]

Stuart had already split his division once when he sent Fitz Lee and Hampton to guard the rear of Imboden's wagon train north of Williamsport. Now he split it again. Chambliss and Robertson occupied Hagerstown with their brigades while Jenkins' (under Ferguson) covered the road south of Hagerstown and Jones advanced south almost to Funkstown.[18]

July 6 was not a good day for Judson Kilpatrick. Earlier in the day while still at Boonsborough, he learned Buford was riding to Williamsport to attack Imboden's wagons. Kilpatrick moved his command to Hagerstown to engage the small cavalry brigades under Chambliss and Robertson. Passing through Funkstown and crossing Antietam Creek, Kilpatrick encountered pickets of the 9th Virginia Cavalry protecting the roads. About noon, Kilpatrick sent a squadron from the 18th Pennsylvania Cavalry into Hagerstown, where it engaged the Virginians. Kilpatrick fed in other units piecemeal, as heavy fighting broke out all around the town. He did not know that Iverson's North Carolina infantry brigade had rushed into the town to provide support. Although decimated on July 1, this veteran unit still counted more than 600 rifled-muskets and it

used them effectively. Realizing the folly of continuing the contest, Kilpatrick broke off the attack and rode west to assist Buford. The battle at Hagerstown is one of the few examples of severe urban street fighting during the Civil War.[19]

Lee was anxious to push his infantry because Imboden's wagon train at Williamsport was under attack. Buford's cavalry division, nearly 4,000 troopers in thirteen regiments and eighteen cannon, struck Imboden late that afternoon about 5:00 p.m., early enough for the Federal cavalry to inflict grave damage before nightfall. Buford began his ride from Frederick at 4:00 a.m. with orders to destroy the wagon train. A pitched battle now flared all along the line. Kilpatrick's division arrived and linked with Buford's right, but in the latter's words, "was of no consequence to either of us." To augment Imboden's small brigade, rifles were handed out to about 700 wagoneers and wounded men who joined the troopers. A daring counterattack drove back some of Kilpatrick's men and darkness ended the hostilities without the loss of a single wagon. The immediate crisis to the wagon train narrowly averted, Confederate reinforcements arrived to shore up Imboden's position. Some of Stuart's cavalry arrived as night fell. Imboden was also aided by Ewell's Second Corps infantry.[20]

Four of Meade's seven infantry corps remained in camp on July 6. The Federal III Corps remained at Gettysburg and the II and XII Corps were motionless along Baltimore Pike. The VI Corps began marching south toward Emmitsburg after dark, spinning off Brig. Gen. Thomas Neill's brigade of Brig. Gen. Albion Howe's division, which joined McIntosh's brigade in its pursuit of Lee's retreating column on the road from Fairfield. The XI Corps marched along Emmitsburg Road from the vicinity of Rock Creek, followed by the I Corps, which left Gettysburg at 7:00 a.m. Meade's V Corps marched from Marsh Creek to Moritz Cross Roads, just northeast of Emmitsburg, where it spent the night. The men marched at a fairly easy pace, and local citizens with food and water warmly welcomed the men.[21]

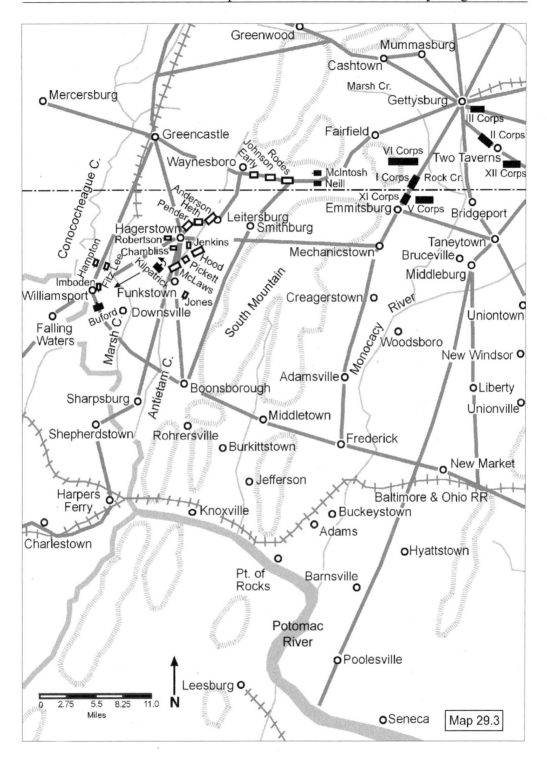

Map 29.3

Map 29.4 (July 7-8)

Richard Ewell's Second Corps continued its march early on July 7 with Robert Rodes' Division in the van, followed by the divisions of Jubal Early and Edward Johnson. The column reached Hagerstown about noon, camping north of the town. A. P. Hill's Third Corps also arrived, halting east of Hagerstown. James Longstreet's First Corps camped about two miles south of Hagerstown on the Hagerstown-Sharpsburg Road. George Pickett's Division of the latter corps marched the Federal prisoners to Williamsport, where they crossed the river. The remainder of Lee's army rested near Hagerstown for the next few days, strengthening its position while awaiting an attack.[22]

After resting near the Hagerstown-Boonsborough Road, four of Stuart's six cavalry brigades rode south to Downsville on July 7, where they deployed. From there, Stuart sent reconnoitering parties to locate Federal troops, which were purportedly moving toward the South Mountain gaps. Jones' and Robertson's brigades remained near Hagerstown.[23]

While Imboden continued to ferry the wounded across the swollen Potomac River on July 7, Buford could only watch in frustration while Confederate reinforcements poured into the sector. Buford's division later rode to Boonsborough, south of the accumulating Confederate infantry at Hagerstown. Here, Merritt's brigade skirmished with some of Stuart's cavalry on July 8. Skirmishing began at 5:00 a.m. and continued on and off for about twelve hours, becoming intense at times. Kilpatrick's division reunited with Buford's at Boonsborough later on July 8, forcing Stuart to break off his action and retire toward Funkstown as darkness fell on the region.[24]

With the departure of the Federal III Corps at 3:00 a.m. on July 7, the Gettysburg battlefield was left in the hands of the medical staffs and the undertakers. Thousands of dead and wounded from both armies remained behind. Meade left the battlefield on July 7 and rode to Frederick, Maryland. For the first time since the battle ended, the entire Federal army was on the move.[25]

The four Federal corps in the vicinity of Emmitsburg continued their trek south on July 7. The I and VI Corps reached the vicinity of Hamburg. The V Corps marched to Moritz Cross Roads, through Emmitsburg, and then on to Utica, northeast of Hamburg. The XI Corps made the longest march, from Emmitsburg to Middletown, between Boonsborough and Frederick. The two corps that had camped on the Baltimore Pike also marched south. The II Corps marched from Two Taverns to Taneytown. The XII Corps began its march at Littlestown and made its way south to Walkersville, east of the Monocacy River. The III Corps marched rapidly through Emmitsburg, camping for the night at Mechanicstown, Maryland. Buford's and Kilpatrick's cavalry divisions moved south to Boonsborough—the former deploying west of the town and the latter north of it. Reinforcements also moved into the sector. General William F. Smith's division of raw recruits from the Department of the Susquehanna marched south toward the Pennsylvania border, while 6,000 men from the Department of West Virginia under Brig. Gen. Benjamin F. Kelley approached Hancock, Maryland.[26]

Meade moved his headquarters from Frederick to Middletown on July 8 to keep pace with his hard-marching infantry. The five corps that had marched south through Emmitsburg continued marching south and west toward Lee's army. The I Corps moved from Hamburg to Turner's Gap in the South Mountain range. The VI Corps halted for the night at Middletown, just southeast of the Gap, where the V Corps, which had marched from Utica, joined it. The XI Corps made the shortest march—from Middletown to Turner's Gap—compensating for the prior day's long trek, although Carl Schurz's division was not so lucky, for it had to continue marching toward Boonsborough. The III Corps left Mechanicstown and marched to Frederick, camping about three miles south of it. It was joined here by the II Corps, which had marched from Taneytown. The XII Corps swung farther south and bivouacked at Jefferson, southwest of Turner's Gap.[27]

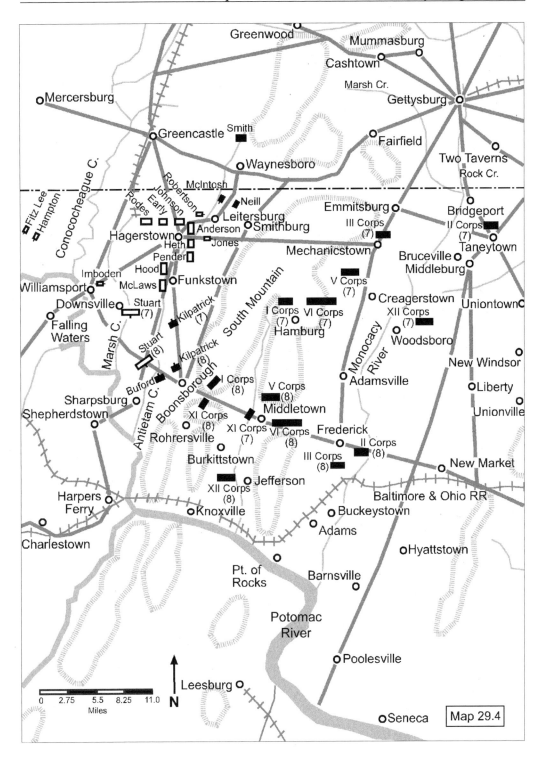

Map 29.4

Map 29.5 (July 9- 12)

The Federal army made shorter marches on July 9. Major General George Meade moved his headquarters to Turner's Gap, joining the I and XI Corps, which rested on July 9. The III Corps arrived from Frederick and the VI Corps leapfrogged over these troops, crossing the gap and marching to Boonsborough. The V Corps marched behind it. The II and XII Corps crossed South Mountain through Crampton's Gap to the south, and both rested for the night at Rohrersville.[28]

The swollen Potomac River was not going to recede any time soon, so General Lee ordered his engineers to complete a pontoon bridge. With his army exposed to attack and a flooded river at his back, General Lee selected a strong defensive line extending from west of Hagerstown south to Downsville. Richard Ewell's Second Corps took up position on the left of this line, with the divisions of Robert Rodes on the left and the divisions of Jubal Early and Edward Johnson extending the line to the right. Johnson's infantry line sprawled across the Williamsport-Hagerstown Pike. A. P. Hill's Third Corps made up the center, with Dorsey Pender's Division on the left, followed by Harry Heth's and Richard Anderson's divisions. Anderson's right flank was to the left (north) of Williamsport-Boonsborough Road. McLaws' Division of James Longstreet's First Corps was on the right of the road, and Hood's Division was beyond it on the south side. The defensive line was irregular because it followed the contours of Salisbury Ridge. It was, however, exceptionally strong. General Ewell reported that his men were in high spirits, "never better than at this time, and the wish was universal that the enemy would attack."[29]

Back in the saddle on July 10, Meade rode from Turner's Gap to Beaver Creek on the west side of Boonsborough. The I Corps and a brigade from Maj. Gen. French's division, which had been at Harpers Ferry through July 11, joined him here. The II Corps reached Tilghmanton on July 10, then marched to Jones' Cross Roads on July 11. The III Corps marched through Boonsborough on July 10 to Antietam Creek, near Jones' Cross Roads, where it remained behind the main Federal line on July 11. The V Corps left Boonsborough on July 10, marched to Delaware Mills on Antietam Creek, and remained there on July 11. The VI also left Boonsborough on July 10 and joined Meade and the I Corps at Beaver Creek. The XI Corps arrived later that day. The XII Corps, and last to arrive, marched from Rohrersville to Bakersville on July 10 and then on to the vicinity of Fair Play and Jones' Cross Roads.[30]

Buford attacked Stuart's troopers near Funkstown on July 10, forcing both sides to rush infantry to the sector. Buford's men fought until almost out of ammunition and were relieved by VI Corps infantry and Kilpatrick's troopers. Worried that Kilpatrick would loop around his right flank, Stuart broke off the action at nightfall and retreated.[31]

July 11 was fairly quiet for the cavalry, save that Buford's division moved to Bakersville, between Williamsport and Boonsborough. Kilpatrick deployed his division to the right of Sedgwick's VI Corps on the extreme right of the army. The Federal cavalry regained its aggressiveness on July 12, advancing on several roads. Stuart pulled his men out of the way, revealing the now entrenched Confederate infantry.[32]

Federal skirmishers and sharpshooters pressed the Confederate lines hard on July 12. The Federal front was complete now because the I, VI, and XI, which had been at Beaver Creek, moved west and north to Funkstown.

That evening, Meade called a council of war to discuss whether he should attack the strong Confederate position. To Meade's dismay, the majority of his lieutenants strongly advised against attacking the trapped Southern army. Meade concluded that he could not assume the responsibility for an attack so many of his commanders were unwilling to support.[33]

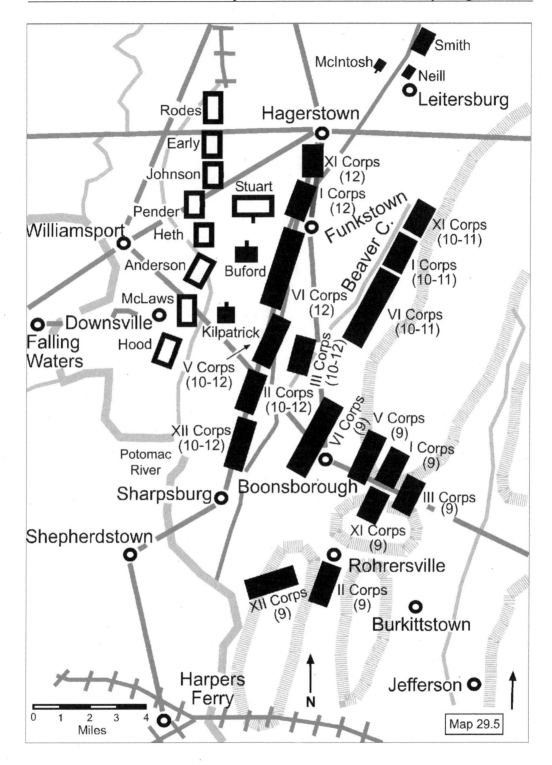

Smith

McIntosh

Neill

Leitersburg

Rodes

Early

Johnson

Pender

Heth

Anderson

McLaws

Hood

Williamsport

Downsville

Falling
Waters

Stuart

Buford

Kilpatrick

Hagerstown

XI Corps
(12)

I Corps
(12)

Funkstown

Beaver C.

XI Corps
(10-11)

I Corps
(10-11)

VI Corps
(12)

VI Corps
(10-11)

III Corps
(10-12)

V Corps
(10-12)

II Corps
(10-12)

XII Corps
(10-12)

Potomac
River

VI Corps
(9)

V Corps
(9)

I Corps
(9)

III Corps
(9)

XI Corps
(9)

Sharpsburg

Boonsborough

Shepherdstown

Rohrersville

XII Corps
(9)

II Corps
(9)

Burkittstown

Harpers
Ferry

N

Jefferson

0   1   2   3   4
Miles

Map 29.5

Map 29.6 (July 13-14)

July 13 found the Federal cavalry reconnoitering and the infantry entrenching. Only the VI Corps was in motion, marching from Funkstown toward Hagerstown.[34]

At 5:00 p.m., Lt. Gen. James Longstreet received orders to begin crossing his men on the pontoon bridge at Falling Waters after nightfall. Owing to the darkness and the single access road, movement was very slow. Longstreet personally supervised the crossing and ordered fires built at difficult parts of the road. Heavy rains returned to hinder the movement. A wagon loaded with wounded ran off the bridge in the darkness, throwing the unfortunates into the water and damaging the bridge. The men were rescued and the bridge was back in service within two hours. The last of Longstreet's soldiers crossed the river at 9:00 a.m. on July 14.

A. P. Hill's Third Corps tramped across the pontoon bridge next, completing the move by 11:00 a.m. even though sharp fighting broke out while the movement was underway. Richard Ewell's Second Corps made its way to the Williamsport ford after nightfall on July 13. Rodes was attacked during this movement, but beat off the Federal effort. When Ewell arrived, he found the crossing engulfed in confusion. Because the water was too deep for the wagons and artillery, they crossed on the pontoon bridge. The men carried ammunition across by hand and the armpit-high waters damaged much of it. Early's Division, the last of Ewell's infantry to cross, safely reached Virginia soil by 8:00 a.m. on July 14. Stuart's cavalry brought up the rear, crossing later that morning.[35]

John Buford's Federal cavalry division remained near Bakersville on July 13, periodically engaging Jeb Stuart's pickets near Downsville while Judson Kilpatrick's division, near Hagerstown, beat off several attacks. Buford received orders at 7:00 a.m. on July 14 to advance and test the enemy's strength. He learned the enemy had left its entrenchments by 7:30 a.m.[36]

When Kilpatrick learned that enemy pickets were withdrawing from his front about 3:00 a.m. on July 14, he mounted his men and drove them toward the Potomac, scooping up stragglers near Williamsport. When local citizens told Kilpatrick that large bodies of Confederate infantry had retreated toward Falling Waters, he rode in that direction. Major General Henry Heth's Division (Hill's Third Corps) was exhausted after a seven-mile march that had taken more than twelve hours to complete, followed by a tiring wait astride the road from Downsville for its turn to cross the river. Major General Dorsey Pender's Division under Brig. Gen. James H. Lane formed behind Heth, closest to the river. When Heth's men saw cavalry approaching, they assumed they were Stuart's men.

Kilpatrick could see two long lines of enemy infantry with their arms stacked. Realizing they were not ready for an attack, he ordered the 6th Michigan Cavalry of George Custer's brigade to charge. The troopers rode through the Rebel lines, engaging the enemy in hand-to-hand combat. Many of Custer's men were lost in the fight including their commander, Maj. Peter Weber, who was killed. Kilpatrick continued testing the enemy position, but each probe was repulsed. During the action, Brig. Gen. James Pettigrew was mortally wounded and hundreds of men from Col. John Brockenbrough's Virginia brigade were captured.[37]

Realizing that Kilpatrick's division was engaging Lee's rear guard, Buford sent word that he would attempt to attack the enemy's flank and rear. Buford's troopers captured a gun, caisson, and more than 500 prisoners, probably from Pender's Division, which had been sent back to help beat off the Federal cavalry. Brigadier General Alfred Scales' Brigade suffered the highest casualties, losing almost 200 captured.[38]

Although General Lee's army had escaped a potentially fatal trap, General Meade continued maneuvering his troops toward Williamsport—the destination of the I, V, VI, XI, and Williams' division of the XII Corps. The II Corps headed for Falling Waters, followed by the III Corps.[39] Seeing Lee's pontoon bridge in front of him, Buford ordered his men forward to capture it. "As our troops neared the bridge, the enemy cut the Maryland side loose, and the bridge swung to the Virginia side," Buford wrote.[40]

The Gettysburg Campaign was now the property of history.

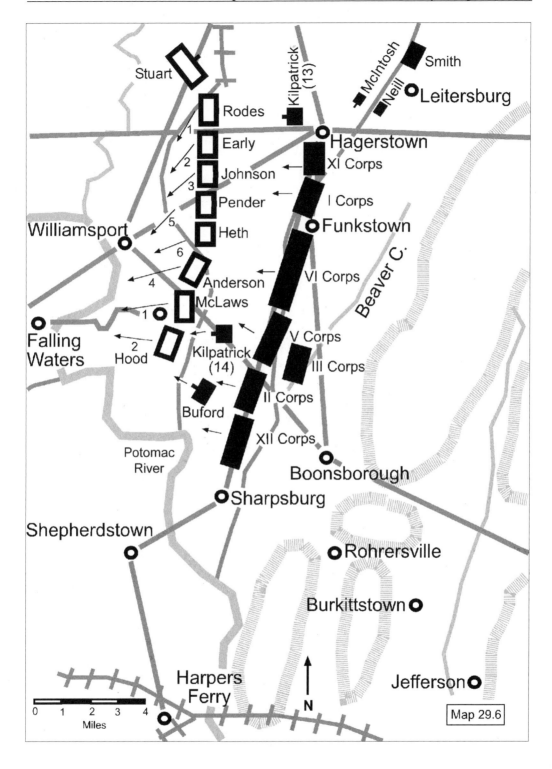

Map 29.6

Appendix

Order of Battle

ARMY OF THE POTOMAC
Maj. Gen. Joseph Hooker / Maj. Gen. George Meade

I Corps: Maj. Gen. John Reynolds / Maj. Gen. Abner Doubleday / Maj. Gen. John Newton

1st Division: Brig. Gen. James Wadsworth

1st Brigade: Brig. Gen. Solomon Meredith / Col. William Robinson
19th Indiana, 24th Michigan, 2nd, 6th, 7th Wisconsin

2nd Brigade: Brig. Gen. Lysander Cutler
7th Indiana, 76th, 84th, 95th, 147th New York, 56th Pennsylvania

2nd Division: Brig. Gen. John Robinson

1st Brigade: Brig. Gen. Gabriel Paul / Col. Samuel Leonard / Col. Adrian Root / Col. Richard Coulter / Col. Peter Lyle / Col. Richard Coulter
13th Massachusetts, 16th Maine, 94th, 104th New York, 107th Pennsylvania

2nd Brigade: Brig. Gen. Henry Baxter
12th Massachusetts, 83rd, 97th New York, 11th, 88th, 90th Pennsylvania

3rd Division: Brig. Gen. Thomas Rowley / Maj. Gen. Abner Doubleday

1st Brigade: Col. Chapman Biddle / Brig. Gen. Thomas Rowley / Col. Chapman Biddle
80th New York, 121st, 142nd, 151st Pennsylvania

2nd Brigade: Col. Roy Stone / Col. Langhorne Wister / Col. Edmund Dana
43rd, 149th, 150th Pennsylvania

3rd Brigade: Brig. Gen. George Stannard / Col. Francis Randall
12th, 13th, 14th, 15th, 16th Vermont

Artillery Brigade: Col. Charles Wainwright—guns: 28
2nd Maine Battery B, 5th Maine Battery E, 1st New York Batteries L and E, 1st Pennsylvania Battery B, 4th US Battery B

II Corps: Maj. Gen. Winfield Hancock / Brig. Gen. John Gibbon / Brig. Gen. John Caldwell / Brig. Gen. William Hays

1st Division: Brig. Gen. John Caldwell

1st Brigade: Col. Edward Cross / Col. H. Boyd McKeen
5th New Hampshire, 61st New York, 81st, 148th Pennsylvania

2nd Brigade: Col. Pennsylvania Patrick Kelly
28th Massachusetts, 63rd, 69th, 88th New York, 116th Pennsylvania

3rd Brigade: Brig. Gen. Samuel Zook / Lt. Col. John Fraser
52nd, 57th, 66th New York, 140th Pennsylvania

4th Brigade: Col. John Brooke
27th Connecticut, 2nd Delaware, 64th New York, 53rd, 145th Pennsylvania

2nd Division: Brig. Gen. John Gibbon / Brig. Gen. William Harrow

1st Brigade: Brig. Gen. William Harrow / Col. Francis Heath
15th Massachusetts, 19th Maine, 1st Minnesota, 82nd New York

2nd Brigade: Brig. Gen. Alexander Webb
69th, 71st, 72nd, 106th Pennsylvania

3rd Brigade: Col. Norman Hall
19th, 20th Massachusetts, 7th Michigan, 42nd, 59th New York

3rd Division: Brig. Gen. Alexander Hays

1st Brigade: Col. Samuel Carroll
14th Indiana, 4th, 8th Ohio, 7th West Virginia

2nd Brigade: Col. Thomas Smyth / Lt. Col. Francis Pierce
14th Connecticut, 1st Delaware, 12th New Jersey, 10th, 108th New York

3rd Brigade: Col. George Willard / Col. Eliakim Sherrill / Col. Clinton MacDougall / Lt. Col. J. Bull
39th, 111th, 125th, 126th New York

Light Artillery Brigade: Capt. John Hazard—guns: 28
1st New York Lieutenant Battery B, 14th New York Battery, 1st Rhode Island Battery A, Battery B,
1st US Battery I, 4th US Battery A

III Corps: Maj. Gen. Daniel Sickles / Maj. Gen. David Birney

1st Division: Maj. Gen. David Birney / Brig. Gen. Hobart Ward

1st Brigade: Brig. Gen. Charles Graham / Col. Andrew Tippin
57th, 63rd, 68th, 105th, 114th, 141st Pennsylvania

2nd Brigade: Brig. Gen. Hobart Ward / Col. Hiram Berdan
20th Indiana, 3rd, 4th Maine, 86th, 124th New York, 99th Pennsylvania,
1st, 2nd U.S. Sharpshooters

3rd Brigade: Col. Regis de Trobriand
17th Maine, 3rd, 5th Michigan, 40th New York, 110th Pennsylvania

2nd Division: Brig. Gen. Andrew Humphreys

1st Brigade: Brig. Gen. Joseph Carr
1st, 11th, 16th Massachusetts, 12th New Hampshire, 11th New Jersey, 26th Pennsylvania

2nd ("Excelsior") Brigade: Col. Wm. Brewster
70th, 71st, 72nd, 73rd, 74th, 120th New York

3rd Brigade: Col. George Burling
2nd New Hampshire, 5th, 6th, 7th, 8th New Jersey, 115th Pennsylvania

Artillery Brigade: Capt. George Randolph / Capt. Judson Clark—guns: 30
1st New Jersey, 2nd Battery B, 1st New York Battery D, 1st Rhode Island Battery E,
4th US Battery K, New York Light Artillery, 4th Battery

V Corps: Maj. Gen. George Sykes

1st Division: Brig. Gen. James Barnes

1st Brigade: Col. William Tilton
18th, 22nd Massachusetts, 1st Michigan, 118th Pennsylvania

2nd Brigade: Col. Jacob Sweitzer
9th, 32nd Massachusetts, 4th Michigan, 62nd Pennsylvania

3rd Brigade: Col. Strong Vincent / Col. James Rice
20th Maine, 16th Michigan, 44th New York, 83rd Pennsylvania

2nd Division: Romeyn Ayres

1st Brigade: Col. Hannibal Day
3rd, 4th, 6th, 12th, 14th U.S. Regulars

2nd Brigade: Col. Sidney Burbank
2nd, 7th, 10th, 11th, 17th U.S. Regulars

3rd Brigade: Brig. Gen. Stephen Weed / Col. Kenner Garrard
140th, 146th New York, 91st, 155th Pennsylvania

3rd Division: Brig. Gen. Samuel Crawford

1st Brigade: Col. William McCandless
1st, 2nd, 6th, 13th Pennsylvania Reserves

3rd Brigade: Col. Joseph Fisher
5th, 9th, 10th, 11th, 12th Pennsylvania Reserves

Artillery Brigade: Capt. Augustus Martin—guns: 26
5th U.S. Battery D, Battery I, 1st Ohio Battery L,
3rd Massachusetts Battery C, 1st New York Battery C

VI Corps: Maj. Gen John Sedgwick

1st Division: Brig. Gen. Horatio Wright

1st ("Jersey") Brigade: Brig. Gen. Alfred Torbert
1st, 2nd, 3rd, 15th New Jersey

2nd Brigade: Brig. Gen. Joseph Bartlett
5th Maine, 121st New York, 95th, 96th Pennsylvania

3rd Brigade: Brig. Gen. David Russell
6th Maine, 49th, 119th Pennsylvania, 5th Wisconsin

2nd Division: Brig. Gen. Albion Howe

2nd ("1st Vermont") Brigade: Col. Lewis Grant
2nd, 3rd, 4th, 5th, 6th Vermont

3rd Brigade: Brig. Gen. Thomas Neill
7th Maine, 33rd, 43rd, 49th, 77th New York, 61st Pennsylvania

3rd Division: Maj. Gen. John Newton / Brig. Gen. Frank Wheaton

1st Brigade: Brig. Gen. Alexander Shaler
65th, 67th, 122nd New York, 23rd, 82nd Pennsylvania

2nd Brigade: Col. Henry Eustis
7th, 10th, 37th Massachusetts, 2nd Rhode Island

3rd Brigade: Brig. Gen. Frank Wheaton / Col. David Niven
62nd New York, 93rd, 98th, 102nd, and 139th Pennsylvania

Artillery Brigade: Col. Charles Tompkins—guns: 48
1st Massachusetts Battery A, 1st, 3rd New York, 1st Rhode Island Batteries C & G,
2nd US Battery D, Battery G, 5th US Battery F

XI Corps: Maj. Gen. Oliver Howard / Maj. Gen. Carl Schurz / Maj. Gen. Oliver O. Howard

1st Division: Brig. Gen. Francis Barlow / Brig. Gen. Adelbert Ames

1st Brigade: Col. Leopold von Gilsa
41st, 54th, 68th New York, 153rd Pennsylvania

2nd Brigade: Brig. Gen. Adelbert Ames / Col. Andrew Harris
17th Connecticut, 25th, 75th, 107th Ohio

2nd Division: Brig. Gen. Adolph von Steinwehr

1st Brigade: Col. Charles Coster
134th, 154th New York, 27th, 73rd Pennsylvania

2nd Brigade: Col. Orlando Smith
33rd Massachusetts, 136th New York, 55th, 73rd Ohio

3rd Division: Maj. Gen. Carl Schurz / Brig. Gen. Alexander Schimmelfennig

1st Brigade: Brig. Gen. Alexander Schimmelfennig / Col. George von Amsberg
82nd Illinois, 45th, 157th New York, 61st Ohio, 74th Pennsylvania

2nd Brigade: Col. Wladimir Krzyzanowski
58th, 119th New York, 82nd Ohio, 75th Pennsylvania, 26th Wisconsin

Artillery Brigade: Maj. Thomas Osborn—guns: 26
13th New York, 1st New York Battery I, 1st Ohio Batteries I and K, 4th US Battery G

XII Corps: Maj. Gen. Henry Slocum / Brig. Gen. Alpheus Williams

1st Division: Brig. Gen. Alpheus Williams / Brig. Gen. Thomas Ruger

1st Brigade: Col. Archibald McDougall
5th, 20th Connecticut, 3rd Maryland, 123rd, 145th New York, 46th Pennsylvania

2nd Brigade: Brig. Gen. Henry Lockwood
1st Maryland Eastern Shore, 1st Maryland Potomac Home Brigade, 150th New York

3rd Brigade: Brig. Gen. Thomas H. Ruger / Col. Silas Colgrove
27th Indiana, 2nd Massachusetts, 13th New Jersey, 107th New York, 3rd Wisconsin

2nd Division: Brig. Gen. John Geary

1st Brigade: Col. Charles Candy
5th, 7th, 29th, 66th Ohio, 28th, 147th Pennsylvania

2nd Brigade: Col. George Cobham / Brig. Gen. Thomas Kane / Col. George Cobham
29th, 109th, 111th Pennsylvania

3rd Brigade: Brig. Gen. George Greene
60th, 78th, 102nd, 137th, 149th New York

Artillery Brigade: Lieutenant Edward Muhlenberg—guns: 20
1st New York Battery M, Pennsylvania Light Battery E, 4th US Battery F, 5th US Battery K

Artillery Reserve: Brig. Gen. Robert Tyler / **Capt. James Robertson**
1st Regular Brigade: Capt. Dunbar Ransom—guns: 24
1st US Battery H, 3rd US Battery F, K, 4th US Battery C, 5th US Battery C

1st Volunteer Brigade: Lt. Col. Freeman McGilvery—guns: 22
5th Massachusetts Battery E, 9th Massachusetts, 15th New York, Pennsylvania Light Battery C, F

2nd Volunteer Brigade: Capt. Elijah Taft—guns: 12
1st Connecticut Battery B, H, 2nd Connecticut, 5th New York

3rd Volunteer Brigade: Capt. James Huntington—guns: 20
1st New Hampshire, 1st Ohio Battery H, 1st Pennsylvania Battery F, G,
West Virginia Battery C

4th Volunteer Brigade: Capt. Robert Fitzhugh—guns: 24 guns
6th Maine Battery F, Maryland Battery A, 1st New Jersey Battery A, 1st New York Batteries G, K

Cavalry Corps: Maj. Gen. Alfred Pleasonton

1st Division: Brig. Gen. John Buford

1st Brigade: Col. William Gamble
8th, 12th Illinois, 3rd Indiana, 8th New York

2nd Brigade: Col. Thomas Devin
6th, 9th New York, 17th Pennsylvania, 3rd West Virginia

Reserve Brigade: Brig. Gen. Wesley Merritt
6th Pennsylvania, 1st, 2nd, 5th, 6th US

2nd Division: Brig. Gen. David Gregg

1st Brigade: Col. John McIntosh
1st Massachusetts, 1st Maryland, 1st New Jersey, 1st, 3rd Pennsylvania,
Purnell (Maryland) Legion, Co. A

2nd Brigade: Col. Pennock Huey
2nd, 4th New York, 6th Ohio, 8th Pennsylvania

3rd Brigade: Col. Irvin Gregg
1st Maine, 10th New York, 4th, 16th Pennsylvania

3rd Division: Brig. Gen. Judson Kilpatrick

1st Brigade: Brig. Gen. Elon Farnsworth / Col. Nathaniel Richmond
5th New York, 18th Pennsylvania, 1st Vermont, 1st West Virginia

2nd Brigade: Brig. Gen. George Custer
1st, 5th, 6th, 7th Michigan

Horse Artillery
1st Brigade: Capt. James Robertson—guns: 28
2nd US Batteries B, L, M, 4th US Battery E, 6th New York Battery, 9th Michigan Battery

2nd Brigade: Capt. John Tidball—guns: 20
1st US Battery E, G, K, 2nd US Battery A, 3rd US Battery C

THE ARMY OF NORTHERN VIRGINIA
Robert E. Lee

FIRST CORPS: Lt. Gen. James Longstreet

Hood's Division: Maj. Gen. John Bell Hood / Brig. Gen. Evander Law

Law's Brigade: Brig. Gen. Evander Law / Col. James Sheffield
4th, 15th, 44th, 47th, 48th Alabama

Robertson's Brigade: Brig. Gen. Jerome Robertson
1st, 4th, 5th Texas, 3rd Arkansas

Anderson's Brigade: Brig. Gen. George Anderson / Col. William Luffman
7th, 8th, 9th, 11th, 59th Georgia

Benning's Brigade: Brig. Gen. Henry Benning
2nd, 15th, 17th, 20th Georgia

Henry's Artillery Battalion: Maj. Mathis Henry—guns: 19
Latham's, Bachman's, Garden's, and Reilly's Batteries

McLaws' Division: Maj. Gen. Lafayette McLaws

Kershaw's Brigade: Brig. Gen. Joseph Kershaw
2nd, 3rd, 7th, 8th, 15th South Carolina, 3rd S.C. Battalion

Semmes' Brigade: Brig. Gen. Paul Semmes / Col. Goode Bryan
10th, 50th, 51st, 53rd Georgia

Barksdale's Brigade: Brig. Gen. William Barksdale / Col. Benjamin Humphreys
13th, 17th, 18th, 21st Mississippi

Wofford's Brigade: Brig. Gen. William Wofford
16th, 18th, 24th Georgia, Cobb's Legion, Phillips' Legion, 3rd Georgia Battalion Sharpshooters

Cabell's Artillery Battalion: Col. Henry Cabell—guns: 16
Manly's, Carlton's, Fraser's, McCarthy's Batteries

Pickett's Division: Maj. Gen. George Pickett

Kemper's Brigade: Brig. Gen. James Kemper / Col. Joseph Mayo
1st, 3rd, 7th, 11th, 24th Virginia

Garnett's Brigade: Brig. Gen. Richard Garnett / Maj. Charles Peyton
8th, 18th, 19th, 28th, 56th Virginia

Armistead's Brigade: Brig. Gen. Lewis Armistead / Col. William Aylett
9th, 14th, 38th, 53rd, 57th Virginia

Dearing's Artillery Battalion: Maj. James Dearing—guns: 18
Stribling's, Caskie's, Macon's, Blount's Batteries

First Corps Artillery Reserve: Col. James Walton / Col. E. Porter Alexander
Alexanders's Battalion: Col. E. Porter Alexander—guns: 24
Moody's, Gilbert's, Woolfolk's, Jordan's, Parker's, Taylor's Batteries

Eshleman's Battalion: Maj. Benjamin Eshleman—guns: 10
Washington Artillery of Louisiana: Squires', Richardson's, Miller's, Norcom's Batteries

SECOND CORPS: Lt. Gen. Richard Ewell

Rodes' Division: Maj. Gen. Robert Rodes

Doles' Brigade: Brig. Gen. George Doles
4th, 12th, 21st, 44th Georgia

Daniel's Brigade: Brig. Gen. Junius Daniel
32nd, 43rd, 45th, 53rd North Carolina, 2nd North Carolina Battalion

Iverson's Brigade: Brig. Gen. Alfred Iverson
5th, 12th, 20th, 23rd North Carolina

Ramseur's Brigade: Brig. Gen. Stephen Ramseur
2nd, 4th, 14th, 30th North Carolina

O'Neal's Brigade: Col. Edward O'Neal
3rd, 5th, 6th, 12th, 26th Alabama

Carter's Artillery Battalion: Lt. Col. Thomas Carter—guns: 16
Reese's, W. Carter's, Page's, Fry's Batteries

Early's Division: Maj. Gen. Jubal Early

Gordon's Brigade: Brig. Gen. John Gordon
13th, 26th, 31st, 38th, 60th, 61st Georgia

Hays' Brigade: Brig. Gen. Harry Hays
5th, 6th, 7th, 8th, 9th Louisiana

Hoke's Brigade: Col. Isaac Avery / Col. Archibald Godwin
6th, 21st, 57th North Carolina

Smith's Brigade: Brig. Gen. William Smith
31st, 49th, 52nd Virginia

Jones' Artillery Battalion: Lt. Col. Hilary Jones—guns: 16
Carrington's, Tanner's, Green's, Garber's Batteries

Johnson's Division: Maj. Gen. Edward Johnson

Steuart's Brigade: Brig. Gen. George Steuart
1st Maryland Battalion, 1st, 3rd North Carolina, 10th, 23rd, 37th Virginia

Nicholls' Brigade: Col. Jesse Williams
1st, 2nd, 10th, 14th, 15th Louisiana

Walker's (Stonewall) Brigade: Brig. Gen. James Walker
2nd, 4th, 5th, 17th, 33rd Virginia

Jones' Brigade: Brig. Gen. John Jones / Lt. Col. Robert Dungan
21st, 25th, 42nd, 44th, 48th, 50th Virginia

Snowden's Artillery Battalion: Maj. James Latimer / Capt. Charles Raine—guns: 16
Dement's, Carpenter's, Brown's, Raine's Batteries

Second Corps Artillery Reserve: Col. J. Thompson Brown
Dance's Battalion: Capt. Willis Dance—guns: 20
Watson's, Smith's, Cunningham's, A. Graham's, C. Griffin's Batteries

Nelson's Battalion: Lt. Col. William Nelson—guns: 10
Kirkpatrick's, Milledge's, Massie's Batteries

THIRD CORPS: Lt. Gen. Ambrose Powell Hill

Heth's Division: Maj. Gen. Henry Heth / Brig. Gen. James Pettigrew

Archer's Brigade: Brig. Gen. James Archer / Col. Birkett Fry / Lt. Col. Samuel Shepard
1st, 7th, 14th Tennessee, 13th Alabama, 5th Alabama Battalion

Davis' Brigade: Brig. Gen. Joseph Davis
2nd, 11th, 42nd Mississippi, 55th North Carolina

Pettigrew's Brigade: Brig. Gen. James Pettigrew / Col. James Marshall / Major John Jones
11th, 26th, 47th, 52nd North Carolina

Brockenbrough's Brigade: Col. John Brockenbrough
40th, 47th, 55th Virginia, 22nd Virginia Battalion

Garnett's Artillery Battalion: Lt. Col. John Garnett—guns: 15
Maurin's, Moore's, Lewis', Grandy's Batteries

Pender's Division: Maj. Gen. W. Dorsey Pender / Brig. Gen. James Lane / Maj. Gen. I. Trimble

McGowan's Brigade: Col. Abner Perrin
1st, 12th, 13th, 14th South Carolina, 1st South Carolina Rifles

Lane's Brigade: Brig. Gen. James Lane / Col. Clark Avery
7th, 18th, 28th, 33rd, 37th North Carolina

Scales' Brigade: Brig. Gen. Alfred Scales / Lt. Col. George Gordon / Col. William Lowrance
13th, 16th, 22nd, 34th, 38th North Carolina

Thomas' Brigade: Brig. Gen. Edward Thomas
14th, 35th, 45th, 49th Georgia

Pogue's Artillery Battalion: Maj. William Pogue—guns: 16
Wyatt's, J. Graham's, Ward's, Brooke's Batteries

Anderson's Division: Maj. Gen. Richard Anderson

Wilcox's Brigade: Brig. Gen. Cadmus Wilcox
8th, 9th, 10th, 11th, 14th Alabama

Perry's Brigade: Col. David Lang
2nd, 5th, 8th Florida

Wright's Brigade: Brig. Gen. Ambrose Wright
3rd, 22nd, 48th Georgia, 2nd Georgia Battalion

Posey's Brigade: Brig. Gen. Carnot Posey
12th, 16th, l9th, 48th Mississippi

Mahone's Brigade: Brig. Gen. William Mahone
6th, 12th, 16th, 41st, 61st Virginia

Lane's Artillery Battalion: Maj. John Lane—guns: 17
Sumter Artillery: Ross', Patterson's, Wingfield's Batteries

Artillery Reserve for Third Corps
McIntosh's Battalion: Maj. David McIntosh—guns: 16
Rice's, Hurt's, Wallace's, Johnson's Batteries

Pegram's Battalion: Maj. William Pegram / Capt. Edward Brunson—guns: 20
Crenshaw's, Marye's, Brander's, Zimmerman's, McGraw's Batteries

CAVALRY DIVISION: Maj. Gen. J.E.B. Stuart

Hampton's Brigade: Brig. Gen. Wade Hampton / Col. Lawrence Baker
1st, 2nd South Carolina, 1st North Carolina, Cobb's Georgia Legion, Phillips' Georgia Legion,
Jeff Davis' Mississippi Legion

Lee's Brigade: Brig. Gen. Fitzhugh Lee
1st, 2nd, 3rd, 4th, 5th Virginia, 1st Maryland Battalion

W. H. F. Lee's Brigade: Col. John Chambliss
9th, 10th, 13th Virginia, 2nd North Carolina

Jenkins' Brigade: Brig. Gen. Albert Jenkins / Col. M. J. Ferguson / Lt. Col. Vincent Witcher
14th, 16th, 17th Virginia, 34th, 36th Virginia Battalion, Jackson's Virginia Battery

Horse Artillery: Maj. Robert Beckham—guns: 15
Breathed's, W. Griffin's, Hart's, McGregor's, Moorman's Batteries

Notes

The Army of Northern Virginia Moves North

Map Set 1: The March to Gettysburg

1. Bradley M. Gottfried, *Roads to Gettysburg* (Shippensburg, Pa.: White Mane, 2001), 1.

2. Jedediah Hotchkiss, *Make Me a Map of the Valley* (Dallas: Southern Methodist University Press, 1988), 116; Clara E. LeGear, "The Hotchkiss Collection of Confederate Maps," *Library of Congress Quarterly Journal of Current Acquisitions* 6 (Nov., 1948): 19.

3. Douglas S. Freeman, *R. E. Lee* (New York: Scribners, 1935), vol. 3, 19, 23; U.S. War Department, *The War of the Rebellion: A Compilation of the Official Records of the Union and Confederate Armies.* 128 volumes (Washington: U.S. Government Printing Office, 1880-1901), vol. 27, part. 3, 858-859, hereafter *OR.*

4. Samuel Pickens Diary, copy in Brake Collection, United States Army Military History Institute (USAMHI).

5. *OR* 27 (2): 293; Gottfried, *Roads to Gettysburg*, 6, 8-9, 11, 13-14.

6. Gottfried, *Roads to Gettysburg*, 8-9; R. T. Coles, *From Huntsville to Appomattox* (Knoxville, Tenn.: University of Tennessee Press, 1996), 97

7. Jacob Hoke, *The Great Invasion* (New York: Thomas Yoseloff, 1959), 66; Wilbur Sturtevant Nye, *Here Come the Rebels!* (Baton Rouge, La.: Louisiana State University Press, 1965), 31.

8. Gottfried, *Roads to Gettysburg*, 11-14.

9. *OR* 27 (3): 12; Emil Rosenblatt and Ruth Rosenblatt, *Hard Marching Every Day* (Lawrence, Kans.: University Press of Kansas, 1992), 100.

10. *OR* 27 (3): 13.

11. *OR* 27 (2): 293, 546; Gottfried, *Roads to Gettysburg*, 16-17.

12. *OR* 27 (3): 17-18.

13. *OR* 27 (1): 33; *OR* 27 (3): 12, 18, 24, 27-28, 29.

14. Gottfried, *Roads to Gettysburg*, 21-22, 26-27.

15. Edward G. Longacre, *The Cavalry at Gettysburg* (Lincoln, Nebr.: Bison Books, 1993), 62-63, 65-86.

16. Gottfried, *Roads to Gettysburg*, 29-32.

17. Nye, *Here Come the Rebels!*, 73; Gottfried, *Roads to Gettysburg*, 33; *OR* 27 (3): 64.

18. *OR* 27 (2): 546; Gottfried, *Roads to Gettysburg*, 36-37.

19. *OR* 27 (1): 36; *OR* 27 (3): 58, 59, 60, 61, 67, 69; Hoke, *The Great Invasion*, 76; Nye, *Here Come the Rebels!*, 166; Longacre, *The Cavalry at Gettysburg*, 90.

20. *OR* 27 (2): 440, 546-547; Samuel Pickens Diary; Louis Leon, *Diary of a Tar Heel* (Charlotte, N.C.: Stone Publishing Company, 1913), 30.

21. *OR* 27 (3): 69, 70, 71, 72, 75, 77, 88.

22. William B. Jordan, *Red Diamond Regiment: The 17th Maine Infantry, 1862-1865* (Shippensburg, Pa.: White Mane Publishing. Co. 1996), 63

23. *OR* 27 (3): 78-79.

24. *OR* 27, pt. 2, 42-43, 69; Nye, *Here Come the Rebels!*, 74-77; Gottfried, *Roads to Gettysburg*, 42-43.

25. *OR* 27 (3): 88-89.

26. Gottfried, *Roads to Gettysburg*, 50, 52-54; Longacre, *The Cavalry at Gettysburg*, 100.

27. *OR* 27 (3): 88; Gottfried, *Roads to Gettysburg*, 52, 52-53, 54.

28. Gottfried, *Roads to Gettysburg*, 46-47; *OR* 27 (2): 546-548; Nye, *Here Come the Rebels!*, 128-129; Longacre, *The Cavalry at Gettysburg*, 94-96.

29. Gottfried, *Roads to Gettysburg*, 49-50; *OR* 27 (2): 460, 491, 499-500, 520, 524; Charles S, Grunder and Brandon H. Beck, *The Second Battle of Winchester* (Lynchburg, Va.: H. E. Howard, Inc. 1989), 29-30; Dennis Frye, *Second Virginia Infantry* (Lynchburg, Va.: H. E. Howard, Inc., 1984), 52-53.

30. *OR* 27 (1): 38, 39.

31. *OR* 27 (1): 797; *OR* 27 (3): 101; Gottfried, *Roads to Gettysburg*, 61-65; Ira S. Pettit, *Diary of a Dead Man* (New York: Eastern Acorn Press, 1976), 146; Diary of Sgt. Charles Bowen, copy in 12th U.S. folder, Gettysburg National Military Park (GNMP).

32. Ruth L. Silliken, *The Rebel Yell & Yankee Hurrah* (Camden, Maine: Down East Books, 1985), 90; William B. Jordan, *Red Diamond Regiment*, 63; Charles Mattocks, *Unspoiled Heart, The Journal of Charles Mattocks of the 17th Maine* (Knoxville, Tenn.: University of Tennessee Press, 1994), 38.

33. *OR* 27 (2): 548-49; Nye, *Here Come the Rebels!*, 130-135.

34. A. P. Smith, *The Seventy-Sixth Regiment, New York Volunteers* (Cortland, N.Y.: Truair, Smith and Miles, 1867), 226; Gottfried, *Roads to Gettysburg*, 73-74, 75; Longacre, *The Cavalry at Gettysburg*, 100.

35. Gottfried, *Roads to Gettysburg*, 74, 75, 77-78.

36. Gottfried, *Roads to Gettysburg*, 66-70; Longacre, *The Cavalry at Gettysburg*, 101.

37. Nye, *Here Come the Rebels!*, 137-142; Longacre, *The Cavalry at Gettysburg*, 97-98.

38. *OR* 27 (2): 549-550; Gottfried, *Roads to Gettysburg*, 67-69.

39. Bowen, "Diary of Captain George D. Bowen," 127; Britton and Reed, *To My Beloved Wife*, 102.

40. Gottfried, *Roads to Gettysburg*, 84-86; Longacre, *The Cavalry at Gettysburg*, 100.

41. Gottfried, *Roads to Gettysburg*, 79-82; J. G. de Roulhac Hamilton, ed. *Shotwell Papers* (Raleigh N.C.:

North Carolina Historical Commission, 1929-31), vol. 1, 479; Nye, *Here Come the Rebels!*, 169, 260.

42. Longacre, *The Cavalry at Gettysburg*, 98.

43. OR 27 (1): 48; OR 27 (3): 171, 181, 186, 191; Gottfried, *Roads to Gettysburg*, 90, 92-95.

44. Gottfried, *Roads to Gettysburg*, 88-89; OR 27 (2): 464.

45. OR 27 (3): 172; Nye, *Here Come the Rebels!*, 171-172.

46. Nye, *Here Come the Rebels!*, 169-170, 179-181, 188; Longacre, *The Cavalry at Gettysburg*, 104-109; OR 27 (2): 741.

47. Nye, *Here Come the Rebels!*, 181-185; Longacre, *The Cavalry at Gettysburg*, 111-113.

48. Longacre, *The Cavalry at Gettysburg*, 99.

49. Gottfried, *Roads to Gettysburg*, 100-101; Nye, *Here Come the Rebels!*, 237-238.

50. Gottfried, *Roads to Gettysburg*, 96-98; OR 27 (2): 464; Lippitt journal.

51. Nye, *Here Come the Rebels!*, 186-187, 188.

52. Longacre, *The Cavalry at Gettysburg*, 119-121.

53. Gottfried, *Roads to Gettysburg*, 107-108; Longacre, *The Cavalry at Gettysburg*, 121-125. Jones's brigade had been at Ashby's Gap.

54. Gottfried, *Roads to Gettysburg*, 102-105.

55. Gottfried, *Roads to Gettysburg*, 113-114; OR 27 (3): 229.

56. Gottfried, *Roads to Gettysburg*, 110-112; Nye, *Here Come the Rebels!*, 195-196.

57. Gottfried, *Roads to Gettysburg*, 118-120; Longacre, *The Cavalry at Gettysburg*, 125-132; Nye, *Here Come the Rebels!*, 197-211.

58. Gottfried, *Roads to Gettysburg*, 116-118; Thomas Lewis Ware, "Papers," Southern Historical Collection, University of North Carolina"; OR 27 (2): 366, 613.

59. OR 27 (3): 913; Longacre, *The Cavalry at Gettysburg*, 161.

60. Gottfried, *Roads to Gettysburg*, 122-123, 125-126; OR 27 (2): 464.

61. Gottfried, *Roads to Gettysburg*, 128-132; Longacre, *The Cavalry at Gettysburg*, 137-138; OR 27 (2): 464.

62. Longacre, *The Cavalry at Gettysburg*, 149-150, 162.

63. Gottfried, *Roads to Gettysburg*, 134-139; Longacre, *The Cavalry at Gettysburg*, 138.

64. Longacre, *The Cavalry at Gettysburg*, 150-151.

65. Gottfried, *Roads to Gettysburg*, 143-148, 164.

66. Charles E. Davis, *Three Years in the Army: The Story of the Thirteenth Massachusetts Volunteers from July 16, 1861 to August 1, 1864* (Boston: Estes & Lownat, 1864), 217; John M. Priest, *John T. McMahon's Diary of the 136th New York* (Shippensburg, Pa.: White Mane Pub. Co., 1993), 51 ; P. Regis de Trobriand, *Four Years*

With the Army of the Potomac (Boston: Ticknor and Company, 1889), 521.

67. Ware, "Papers"; Coles, *Fourth Alabama*, 101-102; Guy R. Everson and Edward W. Simpson, Jr. *Far, Far From Home* (New York: Oxford University Press, 1994), 249; Mark Nesbitt, *35 Days to Gettysburg* (Harrisburg, Pa.: Stackpole Books, 1992), 114; James W. Silver, ed. *A Life for the Confederacy* (Wilmington, N.C.: Broadfoot Publishing Company, 1991), 152; Gottfried, *Roads to Gettysburg*, 141-143. The men marched through parts of Virginia that Lincoln had annexed into the Union as West Virginia on June 20.

68. Longacre, *The Cavalry at Gettysburg*, 152-153; Nye, *Here Come the Rebels!*, 314-315.

69. OR 27 (1): 143, 156-161; OR 27 (3): 336.

70. Gottfried, *Roads to Gettysburg*, 149-155; OR 27 (2): 465; Earl Schenck Miers and Richard A. Brown, eds., *Gettysburg* (New Brunswick, N.J.: Rutgers University Press, 1948), 40-41.

71. Longacre, *The Cavalry at Gettysburg*, 153; Nye, *Here Come the Rebels!*, 316.

72. OR 27 (2): 143,170-175.

73. OR 27 (1): 59, 60.

74. Gottfried, *Roads to Gettysburg*, 165-170; Douglas Craig Haines, "The Advance of Ewell's Corps June 18 Through June 29," in *Gettysburg Magazine* (July 2005), Issue 33, 20-21.

75. OR 27 (3): 942-943.

76. Longacre, *The Cavalry at Gettysburg*, 153-154.

77. Priest, *John McMahon's Diary*, 51; Jacob Smith, *Camps and Campaigns of the 107th Regiment Ohio Volunteer Infantry* (n. p., n .d.), 84; OR 27 (1): 143-144.

78. Thomas B. Marbaker, *History of the Eleventh New Jersey Volunteers* (Hightstown, N.J.: Longstreet House, 1990), 89; Cornelius Van Santvood, *The One Hundred and Twentieth N.Y.S. Volunteers* (Rondout, N.Y.: Regimental Association & Kingston Freeman Press, 1894), 66; de Trobriand, *Fours Years in the Army of the Potomac*, 521.

79. Gottfried, *Roads to Gettysburg*, 185-189; Longacre, *The Cavalry at Gettysburg*, 166; OR 27 (3): 376-377.

80. OR 27 (2): 466-457, 492; Gottfried, *Roads to Gettysburg*, 176-183; Longacre, *The Cavalry at Gettysburg*, 145.

81. Longacre, *The Cavalry at Gettysburg*, 155-156; Nye, *Here Come the Rebels!*, 318-319.

82. Gottfried, *Roads to Gettysburg*, 194-200

83. Longacre, *The Cavalry at Gettysburg*, 168-170. 172.

84. Gottfried, *Roads to Gettysburg*, 191-194.

85. Longacre, *The Cavalry at Gettysburg*, 157-158; Nye, *Here Come the Rebels!*, 319-320.

86. Gottfried, *Roads to Gettysburg*, 204-209.

87. Longacre, *The Cavalry at Gettysburg*, 158-159, 170-171.

88. Gottfried, *Roads to Gettysburg*, 201-204.

89. Gottfried, *Roads to Gettysburg*, 212-214, 218.

90. Gottfried, *Roads to Gettysburg*, 211-213.

91. Gottfried, *Roads to Gettysburg*, 214-216, 219.

92. Gottfried, *Roads to Gettysburg*, 216-218.

93. Longacre, *The Cavalry at Gettysburg*, 193-197.

94. Longacre, *The Cavalry at Gettysburg*, 178, 204.

95. Longacre, *The Cavalry at Gettysburg*, 178, 200-201, 204.

96. *OR* 27 (2): 366; James Longstreet, *From Manassas to Appomattox* (Philadelphia, J. B. Lippincott, 1903), 365.

97. Timothy Reese, *Sykes's Regular Infantry Division, 1861-1864: A History of Regular United States Infantry Operations in the Civil War's Eastern Theater* (Jefferson, N.C.: McFarland, 1990), 239; Daniel G. Macnamara, *The History of the Ninth Regiment, Massachusetts Volunteer Infantry, Second Brigade, First Division, Fifth Army Corps, Army of the Potomac, June, 1861-June, 1864* (Boston: E. B. Stillings, 1899), 318; James L. Bowen, *History of the Thirty-Seventh Regiment, Mass., Volunteers, in the Civil War of 1861-1865.* (Holyoke, Mass.: C.W. Bryan & Co., 1884), 174; Gottfried, *Roads to Gettysburg*, 220-223.

The Confederates Clear the Valley

Map Set 2: The Battle of Second Winchester

1. *OR* 27 (2): 440, 460, 546-547; Grunder and Beck, *The Second Battle of Winchester*, 24-25.

2. *OR* 27 (2): 42.

3. *OR* 27 (2): 43; Grunder and Beck, *The Second Battle of Winchester*, 28.

4. Grunder and Beck, *The Second Battle of Winchester*, 28; *OR* 27 (2): 440.

5. *OR* 27 (2): 440, 499-500; Grunder and Beck, *The Second Battle of Winchester*, 28-29.

6. *OR* 27 (2): 57, 460, 477; Larry Maier, *Gateway to Gettysburg* (Shippensburg, Pa.: Burd Street Press, 2002), 151-152. Hays does not describe the deployment of his brigade, only mentioning that the 9th Louisiana was thrown out on the skirmish line (*OR* 27 (2): 477).

7. *OR* 27 (2): 80. Like Hays, Gordon did not reveal the disposition of his line of battle (*OR* 27 (2): 491).

8. Maier, *Gateway to Gettysburg*, 166-167.

9. *OR* 27 (2): 57-58, 105, 106; Maier, *Gateway to Gettysburg*, 166-167; 170-172.

10. *OR* 27 (2): 45, 477.

11. Maier, *Gateway to Gettysburg*, 177-178; *OR* 27 (2): 44, 45.

12. Maier, *Gateway to Gettysburg*, 178-179; Grunder and Beck, *The Second Battle of Winchester*, 35; *OR* 27 (2): 46, 440.

13. *OR* 27 (2): 477, 500; Maier, *Gateway to Gettysburg*, 183-185. In addition to the 18th Connecticut, Milroy sent the 5th Maryland and 87th Pennsylvania under the command of Colonel Ely to take on Johnson (*OR* 27 (2): 45-46).

14. Grunder and Beck, *The Second Battle of Winchester*, 39; Maier, *Gateway to Gettysburg*, 187-188.

15. Maier, *Gateway to Gettysburg*,192; *OR* 27 (2): 67, 68, 80.

16. *OR* 27 (2): 477. These were the same troops that Stonewall Jackson had used the year before to defeat the Federals at the first battle of Winchester. Hays' report does not indicate the deposition of his regiments in the line of battle.

17. Grunder and Beck, *The Second Battle of Winchester*, 41; *OR* 27 (2): 477; Maier, *Gateway to Gettysburg*, 194-195.

18. Maier, *Gateway to Gettysburg*, 196-200.

19. *OR* 27 (2): 61, 478.

20. Maier, *Gateway to Gettysburg*, 200-201.

21. *OR* 27 (2): 87.

Map Set 3: The Battle of Stephenson's Depot

1. *OR* 27 (2): 47; Grunder and Beck, *The Second Battle of Winchester*, 45.

2. Maier, *Gateway to Gettysburg*, 213-214; *OR* 27 (2): 47, 58, 61; Grunder and Beck, *The Second Battle of Winchester*, 45.

3. Maier, *Gateway to Gettysburg*, 215-216.

4. *OR* 27 (2): 441, 501, 517.

5. *OR* 27 (2): 501.

6. *OR* 27 (2): 58, 93.

7. *OR* 27 (2): 501, 507, 512-513; Maier, *Gateway to Gettysburg*, 221-222.

8. Maier, *Gateway to Gettysburg*, 222-224; *OR* 27 (2): 70.

9. Maier, *Gateway to Gettysburg*, 224-226; *OR* 27, 2, 62, 68, 99.

10. *OR* (2): 62, 501, 507; Maier, *Gateway to Gettysburg*, 229.There is some confusion about Keifer's initial attacks on Steuart's line. According to Nye (*Here Come the Rebels!*, 110) and Steuart's report (*OR* 27 (2): 507), the initial attack was repelled with few losses. Maier (*Gateway to Gettysburg*, 229) and Keifer's report (*OR* 27 (2): 62), the first attack successfully extracted the 10th Virginia. I am assuming that Nye and Steuart are correct and Maier and Keifer are referring to the second attack, which was greater in intensity.

11. *OR* 27 (2): 62, Nye, *Here Come the Rebels!*, 111.

12. Maier, *Gateway to Gettysburg*, 234, 236; *OR* 27 (2): 79, 512.

13. *OR* 27 (2): 62; Maier, *Gateway to Gettysburg*, 231. Upon receiving orders to retreat, the 116th Ohio, 12th West Virginia, and the 12th Pennsylvania Cavalry immediately left the area and few of their men were captured. *OR* 27 (2): 48.

14. *OR* 27 (2): 62, 507, 513.

15. Nye, *Here Come the Rebels!*, 115-116.

16. *OR* 27 (2): 517.

17. *OR* 27 (2): 517.

18. Maier, *Gateway to Gettysburg*, 241-243; OR 27 (2): 81, 152.

19. Nye, *Here Come the Rebels!*, 118-120; OR 27 (2): 502.

20. Edwin B. Coddington, *The Gettysburg Campaign: A Study in Command* (New York: Scribner's and Sons, 1968), 89; OR 27 (2): 49, 63, 68, 442; Grunder and Beck, *The Second Battle of Winchester*, 51-52.

The Battle of Gettysburg

July 1

Map Set 4: The Initial Fight West of Gettysburg and North of Chambersburg Pike

1. J. David Petruzzi, "John Buford: By the Book," *America's Civil War,* Vol. 18, No. 3 (July 2005), 24-27. Several Federal cavalrymen took credit for firing the opening shots. See Petruzzi, J. David, "Opening the Ball at Gettysburg: The Shot That Rang for 50 Years," *America's Civil War,* Vol. 19, No. 3 (July 2006), 24-30; Harry W. Pfanz, *Gettysburg—The First Day* (Chapel Hill, N.C.: University of North Carolina Press, 2002), 52-57; David G. Martin, *Gettysburg, July 1* (Conshohocken, Pa.: Combined Books, 1996), 63-67; John W. Busey and David G. Martin, *Regimental Strengths and Losses at Gettysburg* (Hightstown, N.J.: Longstreet House, 2005), 104; OR 27(1), 943.

2. Theodore W. Bean, "Who fired the opening Shots?" *Philadelphia Weekly Times,* February 2, 1878; Pfanz, *Gettysburg—The First Day*, 57-58.

3. Pfanz, *Gettysburg—The First Day*, 58; John H. Calef, "Gettysburg Notes: The Opening Gun," *Journal of the Military Services Institution of the United States,* January/February 1907, 42-44.

4. Petruzzi, "John Buford: By the Book," 28; Pfanz, *Gettysburg—The First Day*, 60; James McLean, *Cutler's Brigade at Gettysburg* (Baltimore, Md.: Butternut and Blue Press, 1994), 49.

5. Martin, *Gettysburg, July 1*, 74-83.

6. *New York Monuments Commission for the Battlefields of Gettysburg and Chattanooga—Final Report on the Battlefield of Gettysburg* (Albany, N.Y.: J. B. Lyon Company Printers, 1900), vol. 3, 991-992, 1002 (*NYG*); James McLean, *Cutler's Brigade at Gettysburg* (Baltimore, Md.: Butternut and Blue Press, 1994), 62, 64; Harry W. Pfanz, *Gettysburg—The First Day*, 76.

7. OR 27 (2): 649; Busey and Martin, *Regimental Strengths and Losses at Gettysburg*, 24, 299.

8. OR 27 (1): 282-282; John Kellogg to John Bachelder, November 1, 1866, Bachelder Papers, New Hampshire Historical Society; OR 27 (1): 285; *NYG*, 2, 615-616; *Pennsylvania at Gettysburg—Ceremonies at the Dedication of Monuments Erected by the Commonwealth of Pennsylvania* (Harrisburg, Pa: Wm. Stanley Ray State Printer, 1904), vol. 1, 220 (hereafter *PAG*); McLean, *Cutler's Brigade*, 70, 72; Walter Clark, ed. *Histories of the Several Regiments and Battalions from North Carolina in the Great War, 1861-1865* (Raleigh, N.C.: State of North Carolina, 1901), vol. 3, 297.

9. Clark, *N.C. Regiments*, 3, 297; OR 27 (1): 285; David L. Callihan, "Among the Bravest of the Brave: Maj. Andrew Jackson Grover of the 76th New York," *Gettysburg Magazine*, number 32 (January 2005), 51.

10. Coey, "Sketches and Echoes—Cutler's Brigade"; *National Tribune*, July 15, 1915; *NYG*, 3, 991, 1001, 1031; *McLean, Cutler's Brigade*, 79, 81.

11. OR 27 (1): 285; *NYG*, 2, 616; *PAG*, 1, 220; Busey and Martin, *Regimental Strengths and Losses*, 125.

12. *NYG*, 3, 991-993, 1001; J. Volnay Pierce to John Bachelder, November 1, 1882, Bachelder Papers, New Hampshire Hist. Soc.; McLean, *Cutler's Brigade,* 90-92, 95, 96; Pfanz, *Gettysburg—The First Day*, 87; Alfred Belo, "The Battle of Gettysburg," GNMP.

13. Maine Gettysburg Commission, *Maine at Gettysburg; Report of the Maine Commissioners Prepared by the Executive Committee* (Portland, Maine: The Lakeside Press, 1898), 18-19 (hereafter *Maine at Gettysburg*); David L. Ladd, and Audrey J. Ladd, *The Bachelder Papers* (Dayton, Oh.: Morningside Press, 1994), vol. 1: 891-892. Captain Hall and his brigade commander, Col. Charles Wainwright, blamed the infantry's ineptitude, particularly Maj. Gen. Wadsworth's, for the loss of his cannon.

14. OR 27 (1): 1031; John H. Calef, *Gettysburg Notes: The Opening Guns,* 49; David Schultz and Richard Rollins, "The Most Accurate Fire Ever Witnessed: Federal Horse Artillery in the Pennsylvania Campaign," *Gettysburg Magazine,* Issue 33 (July, 2005), 60.

15. OR 27 (1): 276, 286, 287, 296; C. V. Tervis, *The History of the Fighting Fourteenth: Published in Commemoration of the Fiftieth Anniversary of the Muster of the Regiment into the United States Service* (Brooklyn: Brooklyn Eagle Press, 1911), 83; McLean, *Cutler's Brigade*, 106-108; Rufus R. Dawes, *Service with the Sixth Wisconsin Volunteers* (Marietta, Oh.: E.R. Alderman and Sons, 1890), 166-167; James P. Sullivan, "The Sixth Wisconsin At Gettysburg," *Milwaukee Sunday Telegraph,* June, 21, 1885; Pfanz, *Gettysburg—The First Day*, 103.

16. Terrence J. Winschel, "Heavy Was Their Loss, Part 1," in *Gettysburg Magazine* (January 1990), Issue 2, 11, 17. Dawes, *Service with the Sixth Wisconsin Volunteers,* 166-167; Sullivan, "The Sixth Wisconsin At Gettysburg."

17. Winschel, "Heavy Was Their Loss," 11; Leander G. Woollard, "Journal of Events and Incidents as They Came to the Observation of the

'Senatobia Invincibles,'" Memphis State University Library; McLean, *Cutler's Brigade*, 109, 111; *OR* 27, 2, 649.

18. Loyd G. Harris, "With the Iron Brigade Guard at Gettysburg, *Gettysburg Magazine* (July 1989), Issue 1, 32; *OR* 27 (1): 276; Dawes, *Service with the Sixth Wisconsin Volunteers*, 167-168; Pfanz, *Gettysburg—The First Day*, 107.

19. W. B. Murphy Letter, copy in 2nd Mississippi folder, GNMP; B. T. Arrington, *The Medal of Honor at Gettysburg* (Gettysburg, Pa.: Thomas Publications, 1996), 8.

20. Beaudot William J. and Lance J. Herdegen. *An Irishman in the Iron Brigade, The Civil War Memoirs of James P. Sullivan* (New York: Fordham University Press, 1993), 95; Dawes, *Service with the Sixth Wisconsin Volunteers*, 169.

21. Clark, *N.C. Regiments*, vol. 3, 298; A. H. Belo, "The Battle of Gettysburg," *Confederate Veteran* (1900), vol. 8, 165; Ladd and Ladd, *Bachelder Papers*, vol. 1: 324; Busey and Martin, *Regimental Strengths and Losses*, 125.

Map Set 5: The Morning Fight Between Archer's Brigade and the Iron Brigade

1. *OR* 27 (2):637; Martin, *Gettysburg—July 1*, 60-61; Busey and Martin, 143, 144, 221, 224, 226, 228.

2. W. F. Fulton, *War Reminiscences of William Frierson Fulton II, 5th Alabama Battalion* (Gaithersville, Md., Butternut Press, 1986), 76; John T. McCall, "What the Tennesseans Did at Gettysburg"; *The Louisville Journal*, 1902; Martin, *Gettysburg—July 1*, 84; W. H. Bird, *Stories of the Civil War, Company C, 13th Regiment of Alabama Volunteers* (Columbiana, Ala., n.d.), 7; W. H. Moon, "Beginning the Battle at Gettysburg." In *Confederate Veteran* (1925), vol. 33, 449-450; J. B. Turney, "The First Tennessee at Gettysburg," in *Confederate Veteran* (1900), vol. 8, 535; Marc Storch and Beth Storch, "What a Deadly Trap We Were In," in *Gettysburg Magazine* (January 1992), Issue 6, 22; Clark Cooksey, "The Heroes of Chancellorsville: Archer's Brigade at Gettysburg," in *Gettysburg Magazine* (January 2007), Issue 36, 23.

3. James P. Sullivan, "The Old Iron Brigade at Gettysburg," *Milwaukee Sunday Telegraph*, December 20, 1864.

4. *OR* 27 (1): 267, 273, 279; O. B. Curtis, *History of the Twenty-Fourth Michigan of the Iron Brigade, Known as the Detroit and Wayne County Regiment* (Detroit, Mich: Winn and Hammond, 1891), 156; Cornelius Wheeler, "Reminiscences of the Battle of Gettysburg," Wisconsin MOLLUS, vol. 2, 210; Alan D. Gaff, "Here Was Made Out Our Last and Hopeless Stand," *Gettysburg Magazine*, (January, 1990), Issue 2, 25-32.

5. *OR* 27 (1): 273; Storch and Storch, "What a Deadly Trap," 21.

6. *OR* 27 (1): 286.

7. *OR* 27 (2) 646.

8. *OR* 27 (1): 273; Storch and Storch, "What a Deadly Trap," 21.

9. *OR* 27 27 (1): 279; Martin, *Gettysburg—July 1*, 146-149; McElfresh Gettysburg Map; *OR* 27 (2): 646.

10. W. H. Moon, "Beginning of the Battle of Gettysburg," 449; *OR* 27 (1): 274.

11. *OR*, 27, (1): 267, 273, 279; Pfanz, *Gettysburg—The First Day*, 96-98.

12. *OR* 27 (2): 279.

13. Moon, "Beginning of the Battle of Gettysburg," 449; Bird, *Stories of the Civil War*, 7; E. T. Boland, "Beginning of the Battle of Gettysburg," in *Confederate Veteran* (1906), vol. 14, 308.

14. *OR* 27 (2): 646; Turney, "The First Tennessee at Gettysburg," 535.

15. *OR* 27 (1): 279; William H. Harries, "The Iron Brigade in the First Day's Battle at Gettysburg," in *Minnesota MOLLUS*, vol. 4, 340; Cornelius Wheeler, "Reminiscences of the Battle of Gettysburg," vol. 2, 210; Ladd and Ladd, *Bachelder Papers*, vol. 3, 1806; Storch and Storch, "What a Deadly Trap We Were In," 25-26.

16. Storch and Storch, "What a Deadly Trap We Were In," 26-27; *OR*, 27 (2): 646.

Map Set 6: Oak Ridge: Initial Attacks

1. *OR* 27 (2): 552 566, 602-604; Pfanz, *Gettysburg—The First Day*, 155-160. There is some confusion about the deployment of General Daniel's Brigade on Oak Hill. Daniel did not describe it, so I followed the most commonly held convention (Doughtery, *Stone's Brigade and the Fight for the McPherson Farm*, 48; Martin, *Gettysburg, July 1*, 225; Robert Krick, "Three Confederate Disasters On Oak Hill," in Gary W. Gallagher, ed., *The First Day at Gettysburg* (Kent, Ohio: Kent State University Press, 1992) 96.

2. Krick, "Three Confederate Disasters On Oak Hill," 120, 125; *OR* 27 (2): 553, 592; Martin, *Gettysburg—July 1*, 221; Paul Clark Cooksey, "They Died As If On Dress Parade…" *Gettysburg Magzaine*, Issue 20, January, 1999), 91.

3. *NYG*, 1, 378; *OR* 27 (1): 734. The position of the six late-arriving companies of the 45th New York is unclear. According to the narrative in *New York at Gettysburg* (vol. 1, 379), these companies "moved obliquely to the left toward the gap between the First Corps right and our left." Pfanz (*Gettysburg—The First Day*, 167) puts these companies on the left of Mummasburg Road, but most other authors keep them on the right (Martin, *Gettysburg, July 1*, 266; Hall,

The Stand of the U. S. Army at Gettysburg, 55; Bachelder Maps). I have followed the latter convention.

4. Charles Wehrum, "The Adjutant of the 12th Massachusetts Replies to the Captain of the 97th N.Y.," *National Tribune*, December 10, 1885; Gary Lash, "Gen. Henry Baxter's Brigade at Gettysburg," *Gettysburg* Magazine (Issue 10, January, 1994), 15. Pfanz, in *Gettysburg—The First Day*, 167, places Baxter's regiments (88th and 90th Pennsylvania and 83rd New York) behind a stone wall about a hundred yards from facing Mummasburg Road. Other authors, such as Lash ("Gen. Henry Baxter's Brigade at Gettysburg," 15), Martin (*Gettysburg, July 1*, 216), Cooksey, ("They Died As If On Dress Parade…," 93), Hall, (*The Stand of the U. S. Army at Gettysburg*, 55); Krick, "Three Confederate Disasters On Oak Hill," 96) place these regiments near the road. I believe the latter interpretation is correct.

5. McLean, *Cutler's Brigade*, 128; Smith, *Seventh-Sixth Regiment*, 239; OR 27 (1): 282.

6. OR 27 (2): 553; John D. Vautier, "At Gettysburg." *Philadelphia Weekly Press*, November 10, 1886. Although John Vautier was not at Gettysburg with his unit, it appears that he relied heavily on the accounts of his comrades who were present. Therefore, I feel justified in using his extensive writing on the battle. ("Attack and Counterattack," *Gettysburg Magazine*, Issue 12 (January, 1995), 125.

7. OR 27 (2): 601; OR 27 (1): 734; Busey and Martin, *Regimental Strengths and Losses at Gettysburg*, 216, 291.

8. OR 27 (2): 553-554, 595, 602; Krick, "Three Confederate Disasters on Oak Hill," 128.

9. *NYG*, vol. 1, 378-379; John D. Vautier, *History of the Eighty-Eighth Pennsylvania Volunteers in the War for the Union, 1861-1865* (Philadelphia: J. B. Lippincott Company, 1894), 134; Vautier, "At Gettysburg."

10. Samuel Pickens, "Diary," 5th Alabama folder, GNMP.

11. *NYG*, vol. 1, 374, 379.

12. OR 27 (2): 566, 579; Martin, *Gettysburg—July 1*, 226.

13. John Vautier, "At Gettysburg"; Thomas L. Elmore, "Attack and Counterattack," in *Gettysburg Magazine* (July 1991), Issue 5, 128; Cooksey, "They Died As If On Dress Parade…" 96.

14. Charles Blacknall, "Memoir," Brake Collection, USAMHI; Clark, *N.C. Regiments*, vol. 2, 239; Krick, "Three Confederate Disasters on Oak Hill," 131-132.

15. Vautier, *History of the Eighty-Eighth Pennsylvania for the War for the Union*, 135; Vautier, "At Gettysburg"; Alfred Sellers letter, 90th Pennsylvania folder, GNMP; *PAG*, vol. 1, 487; Martin, *Gettysburg, July 1*, ";226, 227-228.

16. Clark, *N.C. Regiments*, vol. I, 635; George W. Grant, "The First Army Corps at Gettysburg," in *Minnesota MOLLUS*, vol. 5, 49.

17. Vautier, "At Gettysburg"; Grant, "The First Army Corps on the First Day at Gettysburg," 49; OR 27 (2): 566.

18. Vautier, "At Gettysburg"; Vautier, *History of the Eighty-Eighth Pennsylvania Volunteers,* 135; Blacknall, "Memoir"; George A. Hussey, *History of the Ninth Regiment N.Y.S.M.*(New York: J. S. Ogilvie, 1889), 270; *NYG*, vol. 2, 678.

19. Henry R. Berkeley, *Four Years in the Confederate Artillery* (Richmond, Va., 1991), 50; Clark, *N.C. Regiments*, vol. 1, 637-638; OR 27 (2): 579; Pfanz, *Gettysburg—The First Day*, 173.

20. OR 27 (2): 573, 576; Pfanz, *Gettysburg—The First Day*, 186.

21. Vautier, "At Gettysburg"; Grant, "The First Army Corps at Gettysburg," 50; Blacknall, "Memoir"; Clark; Grant, "The First Army Corps on the First Day at Gettysburg," 50.

22. Blacknall, "Memoir"; *N.C. Regiments*, vol. 2, 236.

23. Clark, *N.C. Regiments*, vol. 2, 236.

24. Blacknall, "Memoir"; Faison Hicks, "My War Reminiscences" USAMHI; Hicks, "Memoirs"; George Kimball, "Iverson's Brigade" *National Tribune*, October 1, 1885. McLean, *Cutler's Brigade*,138.

25. Hicks, "Memoirs."

26. Busey and Martin, *Regimental Strengths and Losses*, 289, 588.

27. OR 27 (2): 576; Martin, *Gettysburg, July 1*, 239-240; Pfanz, *Gettysburg—The First Day*, 186.

28. Richard A. Sauers, "The Sixteenth Maine Volunteer Infantry at Gettysburg." *Gettysburg Magazine*, Issue 13 (July, 1995), 35; Davis, *Three Years in the Army*, 227; *NYG*, 2, 753, 756.

29. OR 27 (2): 587. Based on a Union veteran's speech made long after the war, Cooksey (*Gettysburg Magazine*, Issue 20, 107) believed O'Neal made another attack on Baxter's right flank after Iverson was repulsed. However, none of the period reports or other letters or diaries support this claim.

Map Set 7: Along Chambersburg Pike

1. Scott D. Hartwig, "The Defense of McPherson's Ridge," *Gettysburg Magazine*, Issue 1 (July, 1989), 20; OR 27 (1): 247, 335; Bradley M. Gottfried, *Brigades of Gettysburg* (New York: DaCapo, 2002), 90; Pfanz, *Gettysburg—The First Day*, 195.

2. OR 27 (1): 356, 1031.

3. OR 27 (2): 566-567.

4. Busey and Martin, *Regimental Strengths and Losses*, 28, 210; OR 27 (1): 330, 342; Pfanz, *Gettysburg—The*

First Day, 197; Richard E. Matthews, *The 149th Pennsylvania Volunteer Infantry Unit in the Civil War* (Jefferson, N.C.: McFarland & Company, 1994), 87.

5. Hartwig, "The Defense of McPherson's Ridge," 20; "Chronicles of Francis Bacon Jones," USAMHI; Jones; Clark, *N.C. Regiments.*, vol. 4: 255; *OR* 27 (1): 330, 332; *OR* 27 (2): 566.

6. *OR* 27 (1): 342; *OR* 27 (2): 566.

7. *OR* 27 (1): 342; "Chronicles of Frances Bacon," Avery Harris Papers, USAMHI, 87-88.

8. John H. Bassler to John Bachelder, February, 1882 Bachelder Papers, New Hampshire Historical Society; Avery Harris Journal, USAMHI; *OR* 27 (1): 343; Pfanz, *Gettysburg—The First Day,* 201, 203.

9. *OR* 27 (1): 330.

10. *OR* 27 (1): 330, 335; Pfanz, *Gettysburg—The First Day,* 204.

11. James Stewart, "Battery B, Fourth United States Artillery at Gettysburg," Ohio MOLLUS, vol. 4, 185.

12. *OR* 27 (2): 572.

13. *OR* 27 (1): 332, 346; *PAG,* vol. 2, 748-749; John Kensill to John Bachelder, February 14, 1882, Bachelder Papers, New Hampshire Historical Society; Thomas Chamberlin, *History of the One Hundred and Fiftieth Regiment Pennsylvania Volunteers* (Philadelphia, 1895), 125-126; John F. Krumwiede, "A July Afternoon on McPherson's Ridge," in *Gettysburg Magazine* Issue 21 (July, 1999), 34-37; Busey and Martin, *Regimental Strengths and Losses,* 210.

14. Pfanz, *Gettysburg—The First Day,* 204-205.

15. Pfanz, *Gettysburg—The First Day,* 204-205.

16. *OR* 27 (2): 567, 572, 575; Clark, *N.C. Regiments,* vol. 2, 256.

17. PAG, vol. 2, 749-750; Krumwiede, "A July Afternoon on McPherson's Ridge," 37; "Memoranda of Lt. Col. Huidekoper Concerning the 150th Regt. PA," in Bachelder Papers, New Hampshire Historical Society; Pfanz, *Gettysburg—The First Day,* 206, 208.

18. *OR* 27 (1): 333; Allen Nevins, ed. *A Diary of Battle: The Personal Journal of Colonel Charles S. Wainwright* (New York: Harcourt, Brace, and World, 1962), 235.

19. Busey and Martin, *Regimental Strengths and Losses,* 126, 290; Pfanz, *Gettysburg—The First Day,* 194.

Map Set 8: The Fight for McPherson Ridge

1. *OR* 27 (1): 268, 274, 279; Curtis, *History of the Twenty-Fourth Michigan,* 157-159; Harries, "The Iron Brigade in the First Day's Battle of Gettysburg," *Minnesota MOLLUS,* volume 4, 210; William T. Venner, *Hoosiers Honor* (Shippensburg, Pa.: Burd Street Press, 1998), 170-171; Gaff, "Here Was Made Out Our Last and Hopeless Stand," 29.

2. *OR* 27 (1): 268, 274, 279, 317, 327; *Supplement to the Official Records of the Union and Confederate Armies* (Wilmington, N.C., 1994), vol. 5, 150, hereafter *OR Supp.*; Seward R. Osborne, *Holding the Left at Gettysburg: the 20th New York State Militia on July 1, 1863* (Hightstown, N.J.: Longstreet House, 1990), 7; Theodore B. Gates to John Bachelder, January 30, 1864, Bachelder Papers, New Hampshire Historical Society; *History of the 121st Pennsylvania Infantry Regiment, 1862-1865* (Philadelphia: Press of Burk & McFetridge Company, 1893), 45; Curtis, *History of the Twenty-Fourth Michigan,* 157-159; William H. Harries, "The Iron Brigade in the First Day's Battle of Gettysburg," vol. 4, 210; William T. Venner, *Hoosiers Honor,* 170-171; Gaff, "Here Was Made Out Our Last and Hopeless Stand," 29.

3. *OR* 27 (2): 607, 642-643; Clark, *N.C. Regiments,* vol. 2, 343-344, vol. 3, ";103-104; George Underwood, *History of the Twenty-Sixth Regiment of the North Carolina Troops in the Great War,1861-'65* (Goldsboro, NC: Nash Brothers, Book and Job Printers, 1901), 46; Homer D. Musselman, *Forty-seventh Virginia Infantry* (Lynchburg, Va.: H. E. Howard, Company, 1991), 50; Martin, *Gettysburg, July 1,* 368.

4. Underwood, *History of the Twenty-Sixth Regiment of the North Carolina Troops in the Great War, 1861-'65,* 49; Clark, *N.C. Regiments,* vol. 2, 351; vol. 3, 89, vol. 5, 119; John Lane, "Address at Gettysburg," John Lane Papers, Southern Historical Collection, University of North Carolina; *OR* (27) l: 268; R. Lee Hadden, "The Deadly Embrace," in *Gettysburg Magazine* Issue 5 (July 1991), 28; Curtis, *History of the Twenty-Fourth Michigan of the Iron Brigade,* 160.

5. Underwood, *History of the Twenty-Sixth Regiment of the North Carolina Troops in the Great War, 1861-'65,* 49.

6. Gaff, "*Here Was Made Out Our Last and Hopeless Stand,*" 29, 31; *OR* 27 (1): 244; Smith, *History of the Twenty-Fourth Michigan,* 129-130; *OR* 27 (1): 268, 279; Martin, *Gettysburg, July 1,* 354; John M. Vanderslice, *Gettysburg Then and Now* (New York: G.W. Dillingham Company, 1899), 120; Pfanz, *Gettysburg—The First Day,* 276, 277; *OR* 27 (2): 643; *OR Supp.*, vol. 5, 417; Venner, *Hoosiers' Honor,* 173-174; William Taylor letter, copy in 11th North Carolina folder, GNMP.

7. *OR* 27 (1): 274, 279; "The Iron Brigade-' 7th Wis. Infantry at Gettysburg, Pa.-Report of Lt. Col. John Callis," Bachelder Papers, New Hampshire Historical Society; Pfanz, *Gettysburg—The First Day,* 277-278.

8. Pfanz, *Gettysburg—The First Day,* 286.

9. Curtis, *History of the Twenty-Fourth Michigan,* 160, 182; Marc Storch and Beth Storch, "Unpublished Gettysburg Reports by the 2nd and 7th Wisconsin Infantry Regimental Officers," in *Gettysburg Magazine* Issue 17 (July, 1997), 22.

10. *OR Supp.*, vol. 5, 424-425; *OR* 27 (1): 268-269; Curtis, *History of the Twenty-First Michigan,* 160-162, 166; Smith, *History of the Twenty-Fourth Michigan,* 130-136; Venner, *Hoosier's Honor,* 179; Craig L. Dunn, *Iron Men, Iron Will* (Indianapolis, In.: Guild Press, 1995), 192-

193; Underwood, *History of the Twenty-Sixth Regiment of the North Carolina Troops in the Great War, 1861-'65*, 50-51; John Lane address; *OR Supp.*, vol. 5, 424; Archie K. Davis, *The Boy Colonel: The Life and Times of Henry King Burgwyn, Jr.* (Chapel Hill, N.C.: University of North Carolina Press, 1985), 332-333; Fred A. Olds, "A Brave Carolinian Who Fell at Gettysburg," *Southern Historical Society Papers* vol. 36 (1908), 245-247; Clark, *N.C. Regiments*, vol. 5, 119.

11. Musselman, *Forty-seventh Virginia Infantry*, 50; Martin, *Gettysburg, July 1*, 368; *OR* 27 (1): 274, 280; Storch and Storch, "Unpublished Gettysburg Reports," 22; Pfanz, *Gettysburg—The First Day*, 288.

12. Clark, *N.C. Regiments*, vol. 3, 106.

13. *OR* 27 (2): 646-647; Storch and Storch, "What a Deadly Trap We Were In," 25; Turney, "First Tennessee"; Pfanz, *Gettysburg—The First Day*, 289.

14. *OR* 27 (1): 327-328; "Movements of the 151st Penn. Vols. of Biddle's Brigade," Bachelder Papers, NH Hist. Soc.; "Report of Movements of 151st Pennsylvania," Bachelder Papers, NH Hist. Soc.

15. Musselman, *Forty-seventh Virginia Infantry*, 50; Martin, *Gettysburg, July 1*, 368; *OR* 27 (1): 274, 280; Storch and Storch, "Unpublished Gettysburg Reports," 22; Robert K. Beecham, *Gettysburg: The Pivotal Battle of the Civil War* (Chicago, A. C. McClung, 1911), 76-77.

16. *PAG*, 2, 661; Kevin E. O'Brien, "'Give Them Another Volley, Boys:' Biddle's Brigade Defends the Union Left on July 1, 1863, in *Gettysburg Magazine* Issue 19 (July, 1998), 43; *OR* 27 (1): 323; Frank Sterling, "Letter," State University of New Jersey, Rutgers Special Collections and Archives; *History of the 121st Pennsylvania*, 45-46; Clark, *N.C. Regiments*, vol. 3, 106; GNMP; Edwin R. Gearhart account, copy in 142nd Pennsylvania folder, GNMP; Hartwig, "The Defense of McPherson Ridge," 23; John Cook, "Personal Reminisces of Gettysburg," *Kansas MOLLUS*, 128.

17. *OR* 27 (1): 269.

18. O'Brien, "'Give Them Another Volley, Boys': Biddle's Brigade Defends the Union Left on July 1, 1863," 37-52; Sterling, "Letter"; *History of the 121st Pennsylvania*, 45-46.

19. *PAG*, 2, 661; *OR* 27 (1): 323; Sterling, "Letter"; *History of the 121st Pennsylvania*, 48; Clark, *N.C. Regiments*, 3: 89-90, 106; Biddle, "Supplemental Account," 151.

20. Edwin R. Gearheart, "Account," *Daily Times*, March 19, 1900 -August 6, 1990, Copy in the GNMP Library; Horatio N. Warren, *Two Reunions of the 142nd Regiment, Pennsylvania Volunteers* (Buffalo: The Courier Company, 1890), 22; Clark, *N.C. Regiments*, vol. 3, 89; Michael A. Dreese, *Like Ripe Apples in a Storm: The 151st Pennsylvania Volunteers at Gettysburg* (Jefferson, N.C.: McFarland & Co, 2000), 45-46.

21. *OR* 27 (1): 327-328; "Movements of the 151st Penn. Vols. Of Biddle's Brigade"; "Report of Movements of 151st Pennsylvania."

22. Jacob Hardenburgh "Letter," New York Historical Society; Gates, The "*Ulster Guard*," 442; Cook, "Personal Reminisces of Gettysburg," 326.

23. Gearheart, "Account"; Horatio N. Warren, *Two Reunions of the 142nd Regiment, Pennsylvania Volunteers*, 22.

24. Downey, Lethal Tour, 28, 31; Horatio N. Warren, *The Declaration of Independence and War History, Bull Run to Appomattox* (Buffalo: The Courier Company, 1894), 30; Gearhart, "Account"; Clark, *N.C. Regiments*, vol. 3, 90; Hartwig, "The Defense of McPherson Ridge," 25; Samuel P. Bates, *History of Pennsylvania Volunteers, 1861-5* (Wilmington, N.C.: Broadfoot Publishing. Co., 1993), vol. 7, 466.

25. *OR* 27 (1): 327-328; "Movements of the 151st Penn. Vols. Of Biddle's Brigade"; Pfanz, *Gettysburg—The First Day*, 292; Busey and Martin, *Regimental Strengths and Losses*, 126, 298.

Map Set 9: Seminary Ridge

1. Curtis, *History of the Twenty-Fourth Michigan*, 165; "'The Iron Brigade-' 7th Wis. Infantry at Gettysburg, Pa.-Report of Lt. Col. John Callis"; *OR* 27 (1): 327-328; "Movements of the 151st Penn. Vols. Of Biddle's Brigade."

2. *OR* 27 (1): 269, 280; Sterling, "Letter."

3. *OR Supp.*, 5, 151; *History of the* 121st *Pennsylvania*, 48; Sterling, "Letter"; *OR* 27 (1): 333, 336, 343.; Tervis, *History of the Fighting Fourteenth*, 85; McLean, *Cutler's Brigade at Gettysburg*, 140.

4. Pfanz, *Gettysburg—The First Day*, 297.

5. *OR* 27 (1): 934.

6. Busey and Martin, *Regimental Strengths and Losses*, 238.

7. Pfanz, *Gettysburg—The First Day*, 302-303. The brigade was closer the left of General Pender's line when it began its advance to support Heth's division. However, growing concern about his right flank caused Pender to shift the brigade in that direction. *OR* 27 (2): 656, 661; Martin, *Gettysburg—July 1*, 188).

8. *OR* 27 (2): 661.

9. *OR* 27 (2): 669; George H. Mills, *History of the 16th North Carolina Regiment (originally 6th N.C. Regiment) in the Civil War* (Hamilton, N.Y.: Edmonston Pub., 1992), 36; Alfred M. Scales to John Bachelder, February 22, 1890, Bachelder Papers, New Hampshire Historical Society.

10. *OR* 27 (2): 661.

11. *OR* 27 (2): 661; B. F. Brown, "Some Recollections of Gettysburg," *Confederate Veteran*, vol. 31 (1923), 53; Varina D. Brown, *A Colonel at Gettysburg*

and Spotsylvania (Columbia, S.C.: The State Company, 1931), 77; J. F. J. Caldwell, *The History of a Brigade of South Carolinians* (Marietta, Georgia: Continental Book Company, 1951), 97; Captain Shooter letter, *Drumbeat*, Newsletter of the Charleston Civil War Round Table, (June 1989), copy in 12th South Carolina file, GNMP; Brooks, *Stories of the Confederacy* (Columbia, S.C.: The State Company, 1912), 37; OR 27 (2): 661.

12. Brown, "Some Recollections of Gettysburg," 53; Shooter, "Letter."

13. Busey and Martin, *Regimental Strengths and Losses at Gettysburg*, 239, 240, 292.

14. Thomas M. Littlejohn, "Recollections of a Confederate Soldier," copy in 12th South Carolina file, GNMP.

15. Gaff, "Here Was Made Out Our Last and Hopeless Stand," 30; Storch and Storch, "Unpublished Gettysburg Reports," 22.

16. OR 27 (2): 661; Caldwell, *A Brigade of South Carolinians*, 96; Shooter, "Letter"; Nevins, *A Diary of Battle*, 236.

17. Augustus Buell, *The Cannoneer* (Washington, D.C.: The National Tribune, 1890), 67. (Buell wrote in the first person, but was not at Gettysburg—or even in the army—until he joined the battery in August 1863. See Coddington, *The Gettysburg Campaign*, 766, note 133. However, Buell interviewed his battery mates who were at Gettysburg, and so I have decided to include his observations, with this caveat.) C. V. Tervis, *History of the Fighting Fourteenth*, 85; Silas Felton, "The Iron Brigade Battery," in *Giants in Their Tall Black Hats: Essays on the Iron Brigade*, Alan T. Nolan and Sharon Eggleston, ed. (Bloomington: Ind.: Indiana University Press, 1998), 148-149.

18. OR 27 (2): 665; James S. Harris, *Historical Sketches: Seventh Regiment, North Carolina Troops* (Ann Arbor, Mich.: University Microfilms, 1972), 34; William K. McDaid, *Four Years of Arduous Service* (Ph.D. Dissertation, Michigan State U., 1987), 207-209; Martin, *Gettysburg—Day 1*, 426-427.

19. OR 27 (1): 280; Martin, *Gettysburg—July 1*, 398-399; OR 27 (1): 269, 280; Gaff, "Here Was Made Out Our Last and Hopeless Stand," 30; Storch and Storch, "Unpublished Gettysburg Reports," 22; Dawes, *Service with the Sixth Wisconsin Volunteers*, 175.

20. Buell, *The Cannoneer*, 68; Fairfax Downey, *The Guns at Gettysburg* (New York: David Mackay Co., 1958), 39-40.

21. Nathaniel Smith "Letter," Southern Historical Collection, University of North Carolina; Silas Felton, "The Iron Brigade Battery at Gettysburg," in *Gettysburg Magazine*, Issue 11 (July 1994), 60; OR 27 (2): 670. Historian David Martin does not believe Scales undertook a reconnaissance prior to the charge, because if he had, he would have called on the Confederate artillery to neutralize the guns.

22. OR 27 (2) 661-662; Daniel A. Thompkins, *Company K, Fourteenth South Carolina Volunteers* (Charlotte, N.C., 1897), 19-20.

23. Caldwell, *A Brigade of South Carolinians*, 97-98; Brown, *A Colonel at Gettysburg and Spotsyvania*, 80, 84.

24. Clark, *N.C. Regiments*, vol. 1, 698; *Maine at Gettysburg*, 85; Brown, *Colonel at Gettysburg and Spotsylvania*, 211.

25. Smith, "Letter"; Clark, *N.C. Regiments*, vol. 1, 698.

26. OR 27, 2, 662; Caldwell, *A Brigade of South Carolinians*, 98.

27. OR 27, 1, 280; Storch and Storch, "Unpublished Gettysburg Reports," 22; Gaff, "Here Was Made Out Our Last and Hopeless Stand," 30, 31.

28. Brown, *A Colonel at Gettysburg and Spotsylvania*, 212.

29. OR 27 (2): 662; Brown, *A Colonel at Gettysburg and Spotsylvania*, 79; Caldwell, *A Brigade of South Carolinians*, 98; Abner Perrin, "A Little More Light on Gettysburg," *Mississippi Valley Historical Review*, vol. 24 (1938), 522; J. Michael Miller, "Perrin's Brigade on July 1, 1863," in *Gettysburg Magazine*, 13 (July 1995), 31.

30. OR 27 (2): 662; Brooks, *Stories of the Confederacy*, 37; Shooter, "Letter."

Map Set 10: The Defeat of the Federal Troops on Oak Ridge

1. Gottfried, *Brigades of Gettysburg*, 533.

2. OR 27 (2): 587, 589, 595; Bennett, "Memoir"; John J. McClendon, "Memoir," copy in 14th North Carolina folder, GNMP; Frederick Phillips, "Letter," N.C. State Archive, copy in 30th North Carolina folder, GNMP.

3. OR 27 (2): 580; Pfanz, *Gettysburg—The First Day*, 190-191; Michael W. Taylor, "Ramseur's Brigade in the Gettysburg Campaign…," in *Gettysburg Magazine* Issue 17 (July 1997), 30, 33.

4. Pfanz, *Gettysburg—The First Day*, 185; Sauers, "The Sixteenth Maine Volunteer Infantry at Gettysburg," 38.

5. OR 27 (1): 292; Vautier, "At Gettysburg"; Grant, "The First Army Corps on the First Day at Gettysburg," 52; Pfanz, *Gettysburg—The First Day*, 185.

6. Austin Stearns, *Three Years with Company K* (Cranbury, N.J.: Fairleigh Dickinson University Press, 1976), 179-80; Pfanz, *Gettysburg—The First Day*, 187-188.

7. Octavus H. Tubbs, "Letter," 16th Maine folder, GNMP; Cyndi Dalton, *Sixteenth Maine Regiment, The Blanket Brigade: The Soldier's Story of the 16th Maine Infantry in the War Between the States* (Union, Me.: Union Pub Co., 1995), 134; Harold A. Small, *The Road to Richmond—The Civil War Memoirs of Major Abner R.*

Small of the 16th Maine (Berkley, Ca.: University of California Press, 1959), 101; OR 27 (1): 295.

8. Clark, *N.C. Regiments*, vol. 1, 719; J.D., Hufham, Jr. "Gettysburg," in *The Wake Forest Student* (1897), vol. 16, 454-455; Pfanz, Gettysburg—The First Day, 191; Small, *The Road to Richmond—The Civil War Memoirs of Major Abner R. Small of the 16th Maine*, 102; A.R. Small, *The Sixteenth Maine Regiment in the War of the Rebellion 1861-1865* (Portland, Me.: Thurston & Co., 1886), 118.

9. Small, *The Road to Richmond—The Civil War Memoirs of Major Abner R. Small of the 16th Maine*, 102; Small, *The Sixteenth Maine in the War of the Rebellion*, 118.

10. Lewis C. Bisbee, "War Reminiscences," 9, 16th Maine Folder, GNMP; Maine at Gettysburg, 43-44, 47, 51; Busey and Martin, *Regimental Strengths and Losses*, 240; Pfanz, *Gettysburg—The First Day*, 192-193.

Map Set 11: The Defeat of Barlow's Division on Blocher's Knoll

1. OR 27 (1): 701, 702, 707, 727; "Gen'l O. O. Howard's Personal Reminiscences in the War of the Rebellion," *National Tribune*, November 20, 1884; Schurz, *Reminiscences*, vol. 3, 6.

2. William R. Keifer, *History of the One Hundred and Fifty-Third Regiment Pennsylvania Volunteer Infantry* (Easton, Pa.: Press of the Chemical Publishing Company, 1909), 209-210.110

3. Martin, *Gettysburg—July 1*, 271; Keifer, *History of the One Hundred and Fifty-Third Regiment Pennsylvania Volunteer Infantry*, 209-210; William Warren, "Diary," 17th Connecticut folder, GNMP; M. Browne to John Bachelder, April 8, 1864, Bachelder Papers, New Hampshire Historical Society; Andrew Harris to John Bachelder, March 14, 1881; OR 27 (1): 727, 734, 738, 742, 745, 746; Alfred Lee to John Bachelder, February 16, 1888.

4. Busey and Martin, *Regimental Strengths and Losses at Gettysburg*, 85, 209; Hartwig, "The Defense of McPherson's Ridge," 37-38; OR 27 (2): 552-553, 581, 584, 597; C. D. Grace, "Rodes's Division at Gettysburg," *Confederate Veteran*, vol. 5 (1897), 614.

5. Barlow to mother, July 7, 1863, Barlow Papers, Massachusetts Historical Society, Boston; Busey and Martin, *Regimental Strengths and Losses*, 86; Schurz, *Reminiscences*, vol. 3, 9; Pfanz, *Gettysburg—The First Day*, 230.

6. Bates, *Pennsylvania Volunteers*, vol. VII, 775; J. Clyde Miller to John Bachelder, March 2, 1886, Bachelder Papers, New Hampshire Historical Society; Keifer, *History of the One Hundred and Fifty-Third Regiment Pennsylvania Volunteer Infantry*, 210-211; Martin, *Gettysburg—July 1*, 274; D. Scott Hartwig, "The 11th

Army Corps on July 1, 1863," *Gettysburg Magazine*, Issue 2 (January, 1990), 41.

7. OR 27 (2): 582; Henry W. Thomas, *History of the Doles-Cook Brigade, Army of Northern Virginia* (Atlanta, Ga.: Franklin Pub. Co., 1903), 7-8.

8. Martin, *Gettysburg—July 1*, 276-7, 288-289; OR 27 (1): 719; Andrew L. Harris to John Bachelder, September 18, 1882, Bachelder Papers, New Hampshire Historical Society.

9. OR 27 (2): 492; Alton J. Murray, *South Georgia Rebels: The True Wartime experiences of the 26th Regiment, Georgia Volunteer Infantry* . . . . (St. Marys, Ga.: Privately Printed, 1976), 134-135.

10. OR 27 (2): 492; Barlow to mother; Hudgins, Gettysburg Campaign," copy in 38th Georgia Folder, GNMP; G. W. Nichols, *A Soldier's Story of His Regiment* . . . (Jesup, Ga., n.p., 1898), 116; William R. Kiefer, *History of the One Hundred and Fifty-Third Pennsylvania Volunteer Infantry*, 213; Michael W. Hofe, *That There Be No Stain Upon My Stones* (Gettysburg, Pa.: Thomas Publications, 1995), 33-34.

11. Thomas, *History of the Doles-Cook Brigade, Army of Northern Virginia*, 7-8.

12. R. W. Tanner, "Reminiscences of the War Between the States," GNMP Library; Barlow to mother; OR 27 (2): 584, 586; Jeremiah William to John Bachelder, June 18, 1880, Bachelder Papers, New Hampshire Historical Society; Nichols, *A Soldier's Story of His Regiment*, 116.

13. Kiefer, *History of the One Hundred and Fifty-Third Regiment Pennsylvania Volunteers Infantry*, 211.

14. OR 27 (1): 748; OR 27 (2): 582; Pfanz, *Gettysburg—The First Day*, 232.

15. Nichols, *A Soldier's Story of His Regiment*, 116; Keifer, *History of the One Hundred and Fifty-Third Regiment Pennsylvania Volunteer Infantry*, 213.

16. Andrew Harris to John Bachelder, March 14, 1881; Anonymous, 75th Ohio folder, GNMP.

17. Warren, "Diary"; Charles P. Hamblen, *Connecticut Yankees at Gettysburg* (Kent, Ohio: Kent State University Press, 1993), 23-24; OR 27 (2): 492.

18. John B. Gordon, *Reminiscences of the Civil War* (New York: Scribner, 1903), 141; Andrew Harris to John Bachelder, March 14, 1881; OR 27 (2): 584.

Map Set 12: The Defeat of Krzyzanowki's Brigade

1. Theodore A. Dodge, "Left Wounded on the Field." *Putnam's Monthly Magazine*, vol. 4 (1869), 319; Alfred Lee, "Reminiscences of the Gettysburg Battle." *Lippincott's Magazine of Popular Literature and Science*, vol. 6 (1883), 56; Pfanz, *Gettysburg—The First Day*, 236-237.

2. OR 27 (1): 745; Dodge, "Left Wounded on the Field," 320-1; James S. Pula, *For Liberty and Justice—The*

Life and Times of Wladimir Krzyzanowski (Chicago: Polish American Congress Charitable Foundation, 1978), 100.

3. Dodge, "Left Wounded on the Field," 320-321; Pula, 100; Pfanz, *Gettysburg—The First Day*, 250; OR 27 (2): 585.

4. *OR* 27 (2): 585; *OR* 27 (1): 745; Busey and Martin, *Regimental Strengths and Losses*, 91, 214.

5. *OR* 27 (1): 747.

6. Lee, "Reminiscences of the Gettysburg Battle," 56; Pula, *For Liberty and Justice—The Life and Times of Wladimir Krzyzanowski*, 56; OR 27 (2): 585; OR 27 (1): 745.

7. *OR* 27 (2): 492.

8. Lee, "Reminiscences of the Gettysburg Battle," 56; Dodge, "Left Wounded on the Field," 321; OR 27 (2): 492; OR 27 (1): 746; Busey and Martin, *Regimental Strengths and Losses*, 141.

9. OR 27 (1): 745; OR 27 (2): 492; Arthur Lee to John Bachelder, February 16, 1888, Bachelder Papers, New Hampshire Historical Society; Pula, *For Liberty and Justice—The Life and Times of Wladimir Krzyzanowski*, 102-103; Dodge, "Left Wounded on the Field," 321.

10. Pula, *For Liberty and Justice—The Life and Times of Wladimir Krzyzanowski*, 102-103; Busey and Martin, *Regimental Strengths and Losses*, 141.

11. *OR* 27 (1): 753.

Map Set 13: The Defeat of the 157th New York

1. Martin, *Gettysburg—July 1*, 301-2; Jonathan Neu, "'But Few of This Force Escaped Us': An Account of Doles' Brigade and its Actions on July 1, 1863," in *Gettysburg Magazine* (January 2007), Issue 36, 48.

2. Pfanz, *Gettysburg—The First Day*, 254; Hartwig, "The 11th Army Corps on July 1, 1861," 47.

3. John Applegate, *Reminiscences and Letters of George Arrowsmith of New Jersey* (Red Bank, N.J.: John H. Cook, 1893), 211; D. Scott Hartwig, "The 11th Army Corps on July 1, 1861." *Gettysburg Magazine* (Issue 2, 1990), 47.

4. Martin, *Gettysburg—July 1*, 301.

5. Jonathon W. W. Boynton Memoir, Civil War Misc. Collection, USAMHI.

6. Martin, *Gettysburg—July 1*, 260, 301-2; John Applegate, *Reminiscences and Letters of George Arrowsmith of New Jersey*, 214-5; OR 27 (2): 584-5; Henry W. Thomas, *History of the Doles-Cook Brigade*, 475-476; James K. Swisher, "Brig. Gen. George Doles and His Georgia Brigade on July 1, 1863, Gettysburg, Pennsylvania," *Gettysburg Magazine*, Issue 27 (July 2002), 50.

7. Applegate, *Reminiscences and Letters of George Arrowsmith of New Jersey*, 217; Martin, *Gettysburg—July 1*, 302; Sidney J. Richardson, "Letter," Georgia Depart. of Archives and Records; *NYG*, vol. 1, 21.

8. Sidney J. Richardson, "Letter," Georgia Department of Archives and Records; *NYG*, vol. 1, 21; Busey and Martin, *Regimental Strengths and Losses at Gettysburg*, 140, 392; Boynton Memoir; OR 27 (2), 586.

Map Set 14: The Brickyard Fight

1. *OR* 27 (1): 721.

2. OR 27 (1): 729; Pfanz, *Gettysburg—The First Day*, 258-261.

3. *OR* 27 (2): 484.

4. R. Stark Jackson, "Letter," LSU Library.

5. OR 27 (2): 479, 484; Martin, *Gettysburg—July 1*, 310.

6. *NYG*, vol. 3, 1051; Charles W. McKay, "Three Years or During the War With the Crescent and Star." *National Tribune Scrap Book*, Washington, D.C., n.d., 131; Pfanz, *Gettysburg—The First Day*, 263.

7. Sheldon "Letter"; McKay, "Three Years or During the War With the Crescent and Star," 131; Wellman, "Letter."

8. McKay, "Three Years or During the War With the Crescent and Star," 131; *NYG*, vol. 3, 1051, 1055; George W. Conklin, "The Long March to Stevens Run: The 134th New York Volunteer Infantry at Gettysburg," *Gettysburg Magazine* Issue 21, (July, 1999), 52.

9. OR 27 (2): 484; *NYG*, vol. 3, 1055; *National Tribune Scrap Book: Stories of the Camp, March, Battle, Hospital and Prison Told by Comrades* (Washington, DC., 1909), 131; McKay, "Three Years or During the War With the Crescent and Star," 131; Conklin, "The Long March to Stevens Run: The 134th New York Volunteer Infantry at Gettysburg"; Pfanz, *Gettysburg—The First Day*, 264.

10. Wellman, "Letter," Crosby, "Letter"; Pfanz, *Gettysburg—The First Day*, 264; Mark H. Dunkelman and Michael J. Winey, *The Hardtack Regiment: An Illustrated History of the 124th Regiment, New York State Infantry Volunteers* (East Brunswick, N.J., 1981), 21; Jackson, "Letter"; Martin, *Gettysburg—July 1*, 311.

11. Busey and Martin, *Regimental Strengths and Losses*, 140, 392.

Evening July 1 – Early Morning July 2

1. Busey and Martin, *Regimental Strengths and Losses*, 20, 83; Pfanz, *Gettysburg—The First Day*, 350-351; Martin, *Gettysburg, July 1*, 566-567.

Pfanz's estimates of the size of the Federal forces (I Corps: 9,500; XI Corps: 7,000) are much lower than Busey's and Martin's. The latter's are used because of the exhaustive nature of their research.

2. *OR* 27 (2): 280; Jones, *Lee's Tigers: The Louisiana Infantry in the Army of Northern Virginia* (Baton Rouge, LA: Louisiana State University Press, 1987), 168-169; Seymour, "Journal."

3. Brooks, *Stories of the Confederacy*, 38.

4. Pfanz, *Gettysburg—The Second Day*, (Chapel Hill, NC: The University of North Carolina Press, 1987), 55-103; *OR* 27 (1): 592, 599-600; John L. Smith, *History of the 118th Pennsylvania Volunteers, Corn Exchange Regiment* (Philadelphia, 1909), 238.

July 2

Map Set 15: Little Round Top

1. William C. Oates, *The War Between the Union and Confederacy and its Lost Opportunites*, (New York: Neale Publishing Co., 1905), 210; William Oates "Letter," William Clements Library, University of Michigan; *OR* 27 (2): 392, 393; John D. Imhof, *Gettysburg, Day Two, A Study in Maps* (Baltimore: Butternut and Blue, 1999), 43; J. Gary Laine and Morris M. Penny, *Struggle for the Round Tops* (Shippensburg, Pa: White Mane Publishing Company, 1999), 49-50; *OR* 27 (2): 404, 405, 407; Jerome Robertson to John Bachelder, May 11, 1882, Bachelder Papers, New Hampshire Historical Society.

2. Oates, *The War Between the Union and Confederacy and its Lost Opportunities*, 210; J. W. Jackson letter, copy in 47th Alabama folder, GNMP; R. T. Coles, "History of the Fourth Regular Alabama Volunteer Infantry," Alabama Department of Archives and History, Chapter 12, 6-8; John J. Pullen, "Effects of Marksmanship—A Lesson From Gettysburg," in *Gettysburg Magazine* Issue 2 (January 1990), 56-58.

3. Busey and Martin, *Regimental Strengths and Losses*, 134, 260, 262; Theodore Gerrish, "The Twentieth Maine at Gettysburg," *Portland Advertiser*, March 13, 1882; Oliver W. Norton, *The Attack and Defense of Little Round Top* (New York: Neale Publishing Company, 1913), 264; Kevin E. O'Brien, "Valley of the Shadow of Death," in *Gettysburg Magazine*, Issue 7 (July, 1992), 46"; Amos M. Judson, *History of the Eighty-Third Regiment, Pennsylvania Volunteers* (Erie, Pa.: B. F. H. Lynn, 1865), 127; *OR* 27 (1): 623. The 44th New York should have fought next to the 16th Michigan. However, Col. James Rice requested that his New Yorkers be permitted to fight next to the 83rd Pennsylvania, which had usually been the custom. Colonel Vincent agreed, saying, "All right, let the Sixteenth pass you." Pfanz, *Gettysburg—The Second Day*, 213).

4. Gerrish, "The Twentieth Maine at Gettysburg"; *OR* 27 (1): 623; Thomas A. Desjardin, *Stand Firm Ye Boys From Maine* (Gettysburg, Pa.: Thomas Publications, 1995), 44.

5. Oates, *The War Between the Union and Confederacy and its Lost Opportunities*, 210-212; Jackson, "Letter"; Laine and Penny, *Struggle for the Round Tops*, 81-82; Desjardin, *Stand Firm Ye Boys From Maine*, 42.

6. *OR* 27 (2): 391, 411, 412; W. C. Ward, "Incidents and Personal Experiences on the Battlefield at Gettysburg," *Confederate Veteran*, vol. 8, (1900), 347-348; Charles H. Salter, "Letter," copy in 16th Michigan folder, GNMP. The 16th Michigan had originally deployed as a skirmish line on the left of the brigade, but was quickly sent north to form the right of Vincent's brigade (Desjardin, *Stand Firm Ye Boys From Maine*), 42, 43.

7. *OR* 27 (2): 411, 413; J. Mark Smither Letter, July 29, 1863, Confederate Research Center, Hill College, Hillsboro, Tex.; Imhof, *Gettysburg, Day Two*, 78, 80; John C. West, *A Texan in Search of a Fight* (Waco, Tex.: Press of J. S. Hill and Company, 1901), 94; Decimus et Ultimus Barziza, *The Adventures of a Prisoner of War 1863-1864* (Austin, Tex.: University of Texas Press, 1964), 45.

8. *OR* 27 (2): 413; Laine and Penny, *Struggle for the Round Tops*, 78.

9. Judson, *History of the Eighty-Third Regiment, Pennsylvania Volunteers*, 127.

OR 27 (2): 622, 630; Pfanz, *Gettysburg—The Second Day*, 222; *Michigan at Gettysburg, July 1st, 2d and 3rd, 1863* . . . (Detroit: Winn and Hammond, 1889), Rufus Felder to mother, July 9, 1863, Confederate Research Center, Hill College; Laine and Penny, *Struggle for the Round Tops*, 80.

10. *OR* 27 (1): 659; A. P. Martin, "Little Round Top," *Gettysburg Compiler*, October 24, 1899; Eugene G. Taylor, *Gouveneur Kemble Warren: The Life and Letters of an American Soldier* (Boston, Houghton-Mifflin, 1932), 129.

11. Oates, *The War Between the Union and Confederacy and its Lost Opportunities*, 212-213; Gary J. Laine and Morris M. Penny, *Law's Brigade in the War Between the Union and the Confederacy* (Shippensburg, Pa.: White Mane Publishing Company, 1996), 100-101; "General M. J. Bulger, A Hero" *New Orleans Picayune*, September 18, 1898; J. Jackson, "Letter," *Montgomery Daily Mail*, July 26, 1863; William C. Oates, "Gettysburg—The Battle on the Right." *Southern Historical Society Papers*, vol. 6 (1878), 176.

12. Ellis Spear, *The Civil War Recollections of General Ellis Spear* (Orona, Me.: University of Maine Press, 1997), 33; John J. Pullen, *The Twentieth Maine: A Volunteer Regiment in the Civil War* (Philadelphia: Lippincott, 1957), 117-118; Oates, *The War Between the Union and Confederacy and its Lost Opportunities*, 217-218; *OR* 27 (1): 623, 624; William C. Jordan, *Incidents During the Civil War* (Montgomery, Al.: The Paragon Press, 1909), 43; Oates, "Letter."

13. Oates, *The War Between the Union and Confederacy and its Lost Opportunities*, 222.

14. Henry L. Figures, "Letter," copy in Brake Collection, USAMHI.

15. *OR* 27 (1): 628, 630; Judson, *History of the Eighty-Third Regiment, Pennsylvania Volunteers*, 127; W. W. Colestock, "The 16th Mich. At Little Round Top," *National Tribune*, March 26, 1914; Pfanz, *Gettysburg—The Second Day*, 228; Charles H. Salter "Letter"; John Michael Gibney, "A Shadow Passing," *Gettysburg Magazine*, Issue 6 (January, 1992), 33.

16. Charles Sprague, "Letter," copy in the 44th New York folder, GNMP; *OR* 27 (1): 617; Bates, *Pennsylvania Volunteers*, volume IV, 1255; Eugene A. Nash, *A History of the 44th New York Volunteer Infantry* (R. R. Donnelley & Sons Company, 1911), 145.

17. "General M. J. Bulger, A Hero; J. Jackson, "Letter"; Oates, "Gettysburg—The Battle on the Right," 176.

18. *OR* 27 (1): 623; Oates, *The War Between the Union and Confederacy and its Lost Opportunities*, 218-219; Oates, "Letter."

19. *OR* 27 (1): 624; Joshua Chamberlain to John Bachelder, *Bachelder Papers*, vol. 3, 1885; Garrish, "Twentieth Maine"; Desjardin, *Stand Firm Ye Boys From Maine*, 67.

20. Joseph M. Leeper Statement, *Bachelder Papers*, New Hampshire Historical Society; Porter Farley, "Bloody Round Top," *National Tribune*, May 3, 1883.

21. Sprague, "Letter"; *OR* 27 (1): 617; Bates, *Pennsylvania Volunteers*, Volume IV, 1255; Nash, *A History of the 44th New York Volunteer Infantry*, 145; Norton, *Attack and Defense of Little Round Top, Gettysburg, July 2, 1863*, 260; Porter Farley, "Reminiscences of Porter Farley, 140th New York Infantry." *Rochester Historical Society*, vol. 22 (1944), 222; Laine and Penny, *Struggle for the Round Tops*, 92; Samuel R. Hazen, "Fighting the Good Fight," *National Tribune*, September 13, 1894; Brian A. Bennett, *Sons of Old Monroe: A Regimental History of Patrick O'Rorke's 140th New York Volunteers* (Dayton, Ohio: Morningside Books, 1992), 216.

22. Nash, *A History of the 44th New York Volunteer Infantry*, 145.

23. *OR* 27 (1): 624; Oates, *The War Between the Union and Confederacy and its Lost Opportunities*, 219-220; Oates, "Letter"; Jeff Denman, "Profile in Courage: The 15th Alabama Infantry at Gettysburg," in *Gettysburg Magazine* (January 2007), Issue 36, 60.

24. *OR* 27 (1): 624-425; Walter G. Morrill to John Bachelder, March 10, 1884, *Bachelder Papers*, New Hampshire Historical Society; Oates, *The War Between the Union and Confederacy and its Lost Opportunities*, 219-220; Oates, "Letter."

25. Bates, *Pennsylvania Volunteers*, Volume IV, 1255; Nash, *A History of the 44th New York Volunteer Infantry*, 153.

Map Set 16: Devil's Den and the Slaughter Pen

1. *OR* 27 (1): 506, 509, 511; Pfanz, *Gettysburg—The Second Day*, 127-128, 181.

2. Elijah Walker to John Bachelder, January 5, 1885, Bachelder Papers, New Hampshire Historical Society; *OR* 27 (1): 509; Pfanz, *Gettysburg—The Second Day*, 178.

3. *OR* 27 (2): 393-394; William F. Perry, "The Devil's Den." *Confederate Veteran*, vol. 9 (1901), 161; Pfanz, *Gettysburg—The Second Day*, 174.

4. Imhof, *Gettysburg, Day Two*, 42; A. W. Tucker, "Orange Blossoms—Services of the 124th New York at Gettysburg." *National Tribune*, January 21, 1886.

5. *OR* 27 (1): 588; A. W. Tucker, "Orange Blossoms."

6. Calvin C. Collier, *"They'll Do To Tie To!"—The Story of the Third Regiment Arkansas Infantry, C.S.A.* (Little Rock, Ark: Civil War Roundtable Associates, 1988), 140-141; *OR* 27 (1): 493; *OR* 27 (2): 407; Busey and Martin, *Regimental Strengths and Losses*, 50, 174.

7. *OR* 27 (1): 511, 522, 525; *OR* 27 (2): 407-408; Jerome Robertson to John Bachelder, April 30, 1876, Bachelder Papers, New Hampshire Historical Society.

8. A. C. Sims, "Recollections of A. C. Sims at the Battle of Gettysburg," copy in Brake Collection, USAMHI; Charles H. Weygant, *History of the One Hundred and Twenty-Fourth Regiment, N.Y.S.V.* (Newburgh, N.Y.: Journal Printing House, 1877), 175;. Tucker, "Orange Blossoms."

9. *OR* 27 (2): 394.

10. Laine and Penny, *Law's Brigade in the War Between the Union and Confederacy*, 90; *OR* 27 (2): 394, 395; Pfanz, *Gettysburg—The Second Day*, 183-184.

11. Collier, *They'll Do To Tie To!*, 140-141; *OR* 27 (2): 407.

12. James E. Smith, *A Famous Battery and It's Campaigns* (Washington, Lowdermilk and Company, 1892), 111-112; Garry E. Adelman and Timothy H. Smith, *Devil's Den—A History and Guide* (Gettysburg, Pa.: Thomas Publications, 1997), 34; *NYG*, vol. 2, 869; Joseph B. Polley, *Hood's Texas Brigade* (New York, Neale Publishing Company, 1910), 169; Tucker, "Orange Blossoms."

13. *OR* 27 (1): 493; Weygant, *History of the One Hundred and Twenty-Fourth Regiment*, 175, 176; *NYG*, vol. 2, 867, 869; Tucker, "One Hundred and Twenty-fourth New York"; Maj. Charles Bowery, Jr., "Encounter at the Triangular Field: The 124th New

York and the 1st Texas at Gettysburg, July 2, 1863." in *Gettysburg Magazine* (January 2004), Issue 30, 59.

14. OR 27 (1): 509-510; Elijah Walker to John Bachelder, January 5, 1885, Bachelder Papers, New Hampshire Historical Society; *Maine at Gettysburg*, 163; Perry, "The Devil's Den," 161-162.

15. OR 27 (2): 395-396.

16. OR 27 (2): 414-415, 421; Pfanz, *Gettysburg—The Second Day*, 190.

17. Sims, "Recollections of A. C. Sims at the Battle of Gettysburg"; OR 27 (1): 493, 506, 513; OR 27 (2): 394, 407, 408-409; Weygant, *History of the One Hundred and Twenty-Fourth Regiment*, 175, 176; William J. Fluker, "An Account of the Battle of Little Round Top Hill at Gettysburg," copy in 15th Georgia folder, GNMP; Kathleen G. Harrison, "Our Principal Loss Was in this Place," in *Gettysburg Magazine*, Issue 1 (July 1989), 62; Imhof, *Gettysburg, Day Two*, 102.

18. J. E. Smith, *A Famous Battery*, 104, 137-139; Thomas W. Bradley and Peter B. Ayars, "At Gettysburg," *National Tribune*, February 4, 1886; *NYG* vol. 3, 1291.

19. OR 27 (1): 509-510; Elijah Walker to John Bachelder; *Maine at Gettysburg*, 163.

20. OR 27 (2): 415, 424, 426.

21. OR 27 (1): 520, 526, 571, 577.

22. Pfanz, *Gettysburg—The Second Day*, 182.

23. OR 27 (2): 409, 421, 422; Pfanz, *Gettysburg—The Second Day*, 194; Weygant, *The One Hundred and Twenty-fourth New York*, 180.

24. Elijah Walker to John Bachelder; Peter B. Ayars, "The 99th Pennsylvania." *National Tribune*, February 4, 1886.

25. OR 27 (1): 494, 519, 526-527; William R. Houghton, *Two Boys in the Civil War and After* (Montgomery, Al.: The Paragon Press, 1912), 220; Pfanz, *Gettysburg—The Second Day*, 197-199.

26. Adelman and Smith, *Devil's Den—A History and Guide* (Gettysburg, PA: Thomas Publications, 1997), 50, 52; Erasmus Gibreath, "Recollections," copy in the Brake Collection, USAMHI.

Map Set 17: The Wheatfield / Stony Hill

1. *Michigan at Gettysburg*, 76; George W. Verrill, "The Seventeenth Maine at Gettysburg and in the Wilderness," *Maine MOLLLUS*, volume 1, 262. 263-264; John Pulford to John Bachelder, December 20, 1864, Bachelder Papers, New Hampshire Historical Society; Frederick C. Floyd, *History of the Fortieth (Mozart) Regiment, New York Volunteers* (Boston: Gilson Company, 1909), 201; OR Supp. 5, 185.

2. Travis Hudson, "Soldier Boys in Gray: A History of the 59th Georgia Infantry Regiment." *Atlanta Historical Society Journal*, Spring, 1979, 55-56;

George Anderson account, Ladd and Ladd, *Bachelder Papers*, vol. 1, 449; J. C. Reid diary, Alabama State Archives; Jay Jorgensen, *Gettysburg's Bloody Wheatfield* (Shippensburg, Pa.: White Mane Publishing Company, 2002), 54.

3. Reid diary.

4. Verrill, "The Seventeenth Maine at Gettysburg and in the Wilderness," 264-265; George W. Verrill to John Bachelder, February 11, 1884, Bachelder Papers, New Hampshire Historical Society; *Maine at Gettysburg*, 195, 212; Kevin E. O'Brien, "Hold Them with the Bayonet: de Trobriand's Brigade Defends the Wheatfield," in *Gettysburg Magazine*, Issue 21 (July, 1999), 84.

5. OR 27 (1): 526-527; Pfanz, *Gettysburg—The Second Day*, 242, 245; de Trobriand, *Four Years With the Army of the Potomac*, 498.

6. Imhof, *Gettysburg, Day Two*, 70; George Hillyer, "Battle of Gettysburg Address," *Walton Tribune*, 2, (copy in the 9th Georgia folder, GNMP), 6; "Letter From Captain Hillyer," *Southern Banner*, July 29, 1863; OR 27 (1): 520; OR Supp. 5, 185-186; Pfanz, *Gettysburg—The Second Day*, 246; John Dunne to John Bachelder, June 30, 1884, 1865, Bachelder Papers, New Hampshire Historical Society.

7. Reid diary; M. J. Bass letter, copy in the 59th Georgia folder, GNMP; Jay Jorgenson, "Anderson Attacks the Wheatfield," *Gettysburg Magazine*, Issue 14 (1996), 68-69.

8. Pfanz, *Gettysburg—The Second Day*, 244, 246; Samuel Toombs, *New Jersey Troops in the Gettysburg Campaign* (Orange, N.J.: Evening Mail Publishing House, 1888), 219-220; OR 27 (1): 610-611; Smith, *History of the 118th Pennsylvania Volunteers, Corn Exchange Regiment*, 242; Imhof, *Gettysburg, Day Two*, 91; Jay Jorgensen, *Gettysburg's Bloody Wheatfield*, 66. The veteran 9th Massachusetts of Sweitzer's brigade was not present as it was on picket duty near Power's Hill.

9. OR 27 (2): 368.

10. Smith, *History of the 118th Pennsylvania Volunteers, Corn Exchange Regiment*, 244; OR 27 (1): 520.

11. Francis J. Parker, *The Story of the Thirty-Second Massachusetts Infantry* (Boston: C. W. Calkins & Company, 1880), 168; OR 27 (1): 611.

12. OR Supp., 5, 191-192; *PAG*, vol. 1, 363; "The Sixty-Second Pennsylvania Volunteers Dedicatory Exercises at Gettysburg, September 11, 1889," 12-13; George Anderson account, Ladd and Ladd, *Bachelder Papers*, vol. 3, 1871; Pfanz, *Gettysburg—The Second Day*, 257, 263.

13. Joseph Kershaw to John Bachelder, *Bachelder Papers*, vol. 1, 452-458.

14. Smith, *History of the 118th Pennsylvania Volunteers, Corn Exchange Regiment*, 244; Anonymous diary, 1st Michigan folder, GNMP.

15. *PAG*, vol. 2, 634.

16. Silliken, ed, *The Rebel Yell & Yankee Hurrah: The Civil War Journal of a Maine Volunteer*, 101; *Maine at Gettysburg*, 197-198; Verrill, "Seventeenth Maine," 268.

17. Pfanz, *Gettysburg—The Second Day*, 269-274; OR 27 (1): 381.

18. OR 27 (1): 381; Charles Hale, "With Cross in the Gettysburg Campaign," copy at GNMP.

19. OR 27 (1): 394; Charles Freudenberg Account, *Bachelder Papers*, vol. 1, 667; Robert L. Stewart, *History of the One Hundred and Fortieth Regiment, Pennsylvania Volunteers (n.p.:* Regimental Association, 1912), 104

20. OR 27 (1): 394; Charles Freudenberg Account, *Bachelder Papers*, vol. 1, 667; Philippe de Trobriand to John Bachelder, May 2, 1882, in Bachelder Papers, New Hampshire Historical Society; Stewart, *History of the One Hundred and Fortieth Regiment, Pennsylvania Volunteers*, 104;

21. OR 27 (1): 386; Joseph G. Bilby, *Remember Fontenoy! The 69th New York, Irish Brigade in the Civil War* (Hightstown, N.J.: Longstreet House, 1995), 89; *PAG*, vol. 2, 625, 684.

22. OR 27, 2, 368; John Hard, Memoirs," copy in 7th South Carolina folder, GNMP; Augustus Dickert, *History of Kershaw's Brigade* (Newberry, S.C., Elbert H. Hull Company, 1899), 241.

23. OR 27 (1): 398.

24. OR 27 (1): 381, 384; Hale, "With Cross in the Gettysburg Campaign"; Charles A. Fuller, *Personal Recollections of the War of 1861 . . . In the 61st New York Volunteer Infantry* (Sherburne, N.Y.: News Job Printing House, 1906), 94; *PAG*, vol. 2, 729; William Wilson Account, *Bachelder Papers*, vol. 2, 1195; Joseph W. Muffly, ed., *The Story of Our Regiment: A History of the 148th Pennsylvania Volunteers* (Des Moines: Kenyon Printing and Manufacturing Company, 1904), 536, 537.

25. OR 27 (1): 381; Eric Campbell, "Caldwell Clears the Wheatfield." *Gettysburg Magazine*, number 3, 37; *PAG*, vol. 2, 729; Pfanz, *Gettysburg—The Second Day*, 273-274; William A. Child, *A History of the Fifth Regiment, New Hampshire Volunteers in the American Civil War* (Bristol, N.H.: R. W. Musgrove, Printer, 1893), 205, 206, 207.

26. Stewart, *History of the One Hundred and Fortieth Regiment, Pennsylvania Volunteers*, 105; Frederick, *Story of a Regiment*, 169; OR (1): 396, 398.

27. Bilby, *Remember Fontenoy!* 88-89; OR 27 (1): 389.

28. OR 27 (2): 368; J. B. Kershaw, J. B. "Kershaw's Brigade at Gettysburg." *Battles and Leaders of the Civil War*, vol. 3, 336, 337.

29. OR 27 (1): 383, 385; Muffly, *The Story of our Regiment*, 537, Child, *A History of the Fifth New Hampshire*, 206; John Brooke to John Bachelder, November 14, 1885, in Bachelder Papers, New Hampshire Historical Society; Pfanz, *Gettysburg—The Second Day*, 300.

30. OR *Supp.*, 5, 155; OR 27 (1): 400, 409; John Brooke to John Bachelder, November 14, 1885; S. A. Osborn, "The Battle of Gettysburg as I Remember It," *Shenango Valley News* (Greenville, Pa)., April 2, 1915; Diary of Martin Sigman, copy in 64th New York file, GNMP.

31. OR 27 (1): 400-401; Campbell, "Caldwell Clears the Wheatfield," 45; Imhof, *Gettysburg, Day Two*, 99; John D. Cochran, "The Tenth Georgia Regiment at Gettysburg," *Atlanta Journal* (February 23, 1901).

32. *PAG*, vol. 2, 625.

33. Richard Robbins, "The Regular Troops at Gettysburg"; *Philadelphia Weekly Times*, January 4, 1879; OR 27 (1): 640, 644-645, 646; Busey and Martin, *Regimental Strengths and Losses at Gettysburg*, 128, 134, 135.

34. OR 27 (1): 400-401; A. E. Clark, "The 27th Conn. At Gettysburg, "Connecticut Historical Society, copy in 27th Connecticut folder, GNMP; John Brooke to John Bachelder, November 14, 1885; Sigman, "Diary"; Winthrop D. Sheldon, *The "Twenty-Seventh," A Regimental History*, (New Haven Ct., Morris & Benham, 1866), 75; Pfanz, *Gettysburg—The Second Day*, 286-287.

35. Imhof, *Gettysburg, Day Two*, 163. The exact order of Wofford's alignment is unclear, and the deployment in the main text is based upon Imhof's assessment; William F. Shine diary, J. B. Clifton Collection, North Carolina Department of Archives and History.

36. Stewart, *History of the One Hundred and Fortieth Regiment, Pennsylvania Volunteers*, 107-108; Unknown writer's letter, Timothy Brooks Collection, USAMHI; J. Jackson Purman to John Bachelder, November 3,1871.

37. *PAG*, vol. 2, 626-627; Patrick O'Flaherty, *History of the 69th Regiment in the Irish Brigade, 1861-1865* (New York: n.p. 1986), 258-259; Paul Jones, *The Irish Brigade* (Washington, R. B. Luce, 1969), 196; OR 27 (1): 389.

38. OR 27 (1): 401, 410; Robert G. Smith, *A Brief Account of the Services Rendered by the Second Regiment Delaware Volunteers* (Wilmington, De., Historical Society of Delaware, 1909), 24-25.

39. *PAG*, vol. 1, 363; Pfanz, *Gettysburg—The Second Day*, 290.

40. *PAG*, vol. 1, 383; OR 27 (1): 611-612.

41. Pfanz, *Gettysburg—The Second Day*, ";292, 294-295; Hillyer Address, 8.OR 27 (1): 612; Pfanz, *Gettysburg—The Second Day*, 292; Oscar W. West, "On Little Round Top—The Fifth Corps Fight at Gettysburg—Particularly the 32nd Mass's Part." *National Tribune*, November 22, 1906; Bates, *Pennsylvania Volunteers*, Volume III 3, 458; John Coxe, "The Battle of Gettysburg," *Confederate Veteran*, vol. 21 (1913), 433-436.

42. Imhof, *Gettysburg, Day Two*, 177.

43. *OR* 27 (1): 645, 647, 649; Reese, *Sykes' Regular Infantry*, 256.

44. *OR* 27 (1): 645, 646, 647, 649; Pratt letter; Richard Robbins, "The Regular Troops at Gettysburg." *Philadelphia Weekly Times*, January 4, 1879.

45. *OR* 27 (1): 634; William H. Powell, *The Fifth Army Corps* . . . . (New York: G. P. Putnam's Sons, 1896), 535; *NYG*, vol. 1, 55.

46. *OR* 27 (1): 645; Pratt, "Letter"; W. H. Sanderson, "Sykes's Regulars," *National Tribune*, April 2, 1891.

47. Busey and Martin, *Regimental Strengths and Losses*, 134-135.

Map Set 18: The Peach Orchard

1. *OR* 27 (1) 497, 498, 499, 500, 502.

2. *PAG*, vol. 1, 356; Pfanz, *Gettysburg—The Second Day*, 314; Imhof, *Gettysburg, Day Two*, 13.

3. *OR* 27 (1): 497, 498; Bates, *Pennsylvania Volunteers*, vol. III, 495; Pfanz, *Gettysburg—The Second Day*, 322.

4. *OR* 27 (2) 368; Kershaw, "Kershaw's Brigade at Gettysburg," vol. 3, 335; Alex McNeill, "Letter," 2nd South Carolina folder, GNMP; Gregory Coco, *A Concise Guide to the Artillery at Gettysburg* (Gettysburg, Pa.: Thomas Publication, 1998).

5. Pfanz, *Gettysburg—The Second Day*, 317.

6. Joseph Kershaw to John Bachelder, April 3, 1876; Mac Wyckoff, *A History of the Third South Carolina Infantry, 1861-1865* (Fredericksburg, Va.: Sergeant Kirkland's Museum and Historical Society, 1995), 121-122; W. A. Johnson, "The Battle of Gettysburg," copy in the 2nd South Carolina folder, GNMP; W. T. Shumate, "With Kershaw at Gettysburg," *Philadelphia Weekly Times*." May 6, 1882; Gerald J. Smith, *One of the Most Daring of Men* (Murfreesboro, Tn., Southern Heritage Press, 1997), 83.

7. *OR* 27 (1): 574; Martin A. Haynes, *History of the Second New Hampshire Regiment: Its Camps, Marches, and Battles* (Manchester, N.H.: Charles F. Livingston Printer, 1865), 171, 176.

8. *OR* 27 (1): 498-499.

9. J. S. McNeily, J. S. "Barksdale's Mississippi Brigade at Gettysburg." *Publications of the Mississippi Historical Society*, vol. 14 (1914), 236; Lafayette McLaws, "Gettysburg." *SHSP*, vol. 7 (1879), 73.

10. McNeily, *Barksdale's Mississippi Brigade*, 236; George J. Leftwich, "The Carreer [sic] of a Veteran." *The Aberdeen Examiner*, August 22, 1913.

11. Bucklyn to Bachelder, December 31, 1863, Bachelder Papers, New Hampshire Historical Society; *OR* 27 (1): 502, 503.

12. *OR* 27 (1): 499, 502, 503, 505; Edward R. Bowen, "Collis' Zouaves—The 114th Pennsylvania Infantry at Gettysburg." *Philadelphia Weekly Times*, June 22, 1887; Bates, *Pennsylvania Volunteers*, vol. VI, 1183.

13. William E. Loring, "Gettysburg." *National Tribune*, July 9, 1885; *OR* 27 (1): 504-505; John D. Bloodgood, *Personal Reminiscences of the War* (New York: Hunt and Eaton, 1893), 138-139; Bates, *Pennsylvania Volunteers*, vol. VII, 442.

14. *OR* 27 (1): 505, 499; Gary G. Lash, "'A Pathetic Story'—The 141st Pennsylvania (Graham's Brigade) at Gettysburg." *Gettysburg Magazine*, Number 14 (1996), 91; Pfanz, *Gettysburg—The Second Day*, 328-329.

15. Imhof, *Gettysburg, Day Two*, 143, 145-146; *PAG*, vol. 1, 356; Bates, *Pennsylvania Volunteers*, vol. VI, 1183; Pfanz, *Gettysburg—The Second Day*, 329.

16. Frank E. Moran, "A Fire Zouave—Memoirs of a Member of the Excelsior Brigade." *National Tribune*, November 6, 1890; Given Diary, Philadelphia Civil War Library and Museum; Francis E. Moran, "About Gettysburg," *National Tribune*, November 6, 1890.

17. Moran, "About Gettysburg"; Pfanz, *Gettysburg—The Second Day*, 330.

18. *PAG*, vol. 1, 356; Bates, *Pennsylvania Volunteers*, vol. VI, 1183; Bowen, "Collis' Zouaves"; *OR* 27 (1): 497, 500-501.

19. *OR* 27 (1): 505, 574; Edward Bailey to John Bachelder, March 29, 1882, Bachelder Papers, New Hampshire Historical Society; Haynes, *History of the Second Regiment, New Hampshire Volunteers: Its Camps, Marches and Battles*, 142; Pfanz, *Gettysburg—The Second Day*, 332.

20. *OR* 27 (1): 499; Lash, "A Pathetic Story," 95.

21. *OR* 27 (1): 505; Bloodgood, *Personal Reminiscences of the War*, 140-141; Craft, *One Hundred and Forty-First Regiment*, 122, 123.

22. Bates, *Pennsylvania Volunteers*, vol. VI, 785; *OR* 27 (1): 501; Pfanz, *Gettysburg—The Second Day*, 331-332; McNeily, *Barksdale's Mississippi Brigade at Gettysburg*, 238; Busey and Martin, *Regimental Strengths and Losses*, 131.

23. McNeily, *Barksdale's Mississippi Brigade at Gettysburg*, 236-237; Pfanz, *Gettysburg—The Second Day*, 326; *OR* 27 (1): 499.

24. *OR* 27 (1): 578; Paul J. Lader, "The 7th New Jersey in the Gettysburg Campaign," *Gettysburg Magazine*, Issue 16 (1997), 61-70; Busey and Martin, *Regimental Strengths and Losses*, 133.

Map Set 19: Crushing Humphreys' Division

1. *OR* 27 (1): 543, 553, 555; Marbaker, *History of the Eleventh New Jersey Volunteers*, 121; Busey and Martin,

Regimental Strengths and Losses, 132; Pfanz, *Gettysburg—The Second Day*, 146, 366; OR Supp., vol. 5, 178; C. B. Baldwin to John Bachelder, *Bachelder Papers*, 1: 187-196.

2. Pfanz, *Gettysburg—The Second Day*, 355, 362-363.

3. OR 27 (2): 631; Busey and Martin, *Regimental Strengths and Losses at Gettysburg*, 740.

4. Pfanz, *Gettysburg—The Second Day*, 323; Busey and Martin, *Regimental Strengths and Losses*, 307, 308.

5. OR 27 (1): 533; Pfanz, *Gettysburg—The Second Day*, 347-348; A. A. Humphreys to John Bachelder, November 14, 1865, Bachelder Papers, New Hampshire Historical Society; Imhof, *Gettysburg, Day Two*, 143, 147.

6. OR 27 (2): 631; Johnson, "A Limited Review of What One Man Saw of the Battle of Gettysburg."

7. OR 27 (2): 631; Johnson, "A Limited Review of What One Man Saw of the Battle of Gettysburg"; Pfanz, *Gettysburg—The Second Day*, 358, 366; OR Supp., 5, 178.

8. Pfanz, *Gettysburg—The Second Day*, 347-349, 368; Henri L. Brown, *History of the 3d Regiment, Excelsior Brigade, 72d New York Volunteer Infantry, 1861-1865* (Jamestown, N.Y.: Journal Print. Co., 1902), 104.

9. C. D. Westbrook, "The 120th N.Y.'s Firm Stand on the Second Day at Gettysburg," *National Tribune*, September 20, 1900; Pfanz, *Gettysburg—The Second Day*, 367-369.

10. OR 27 (1): Henry N. Blake, *Three Years in the Army of the Potomac* (Boston: Lee and Shepard, 1865), 208; Pfanz, *Gettysburg—The Second Day*, 367-369; Cornelius VanSantvood, *The One Hundred and Twentieth N.Y.* (Rondout, N.Y.: Regimental Association & Kingston Freeman Press, 1894), 74; Imhof, *Gettysburg, Day Two*, 171.

11. OR 27 (1): 543, 553-554; Asa W. Bartlett, *History of the Twelfth Regiment, New Hampshire Volunteers in the War of the Rebellion* (Concord, N.H.: Ira C. Evans, Printer, 1897),124; OR 27 (1): 553-554; William H. Cudsworth, *History of the First Regiment Massachusetts Infantry* (Boston: Walker, Fuller and Company, 1866), 394; OR Supp., vol. 5, 179; Henry Blake, "Personal Reminiscences of Gettysburg," copy in the USAHMI. It is a testament to Humphreys that he was able to hold his position for as long as he did.

12. Cadmus M. Wilcox, "General C. M. Wilcox on the Battle of Gettysburg," *Southern Historical Society Papers*, vol. 6, 99.

13. OR 27 (2): 631; Pfanz, *Gettysburg—The Second Day*, 368.

14. OR 27 (1): 543; Blake, "Personal Reminiscences of Gettysburg"; John F. Langley Account, *Bachelder Papers*, vol. 1, 109; Charles W. Bardeen, *A Little Fifer's War Diary* (Syracuse: C. W. Bardeen, Publisher, 1910), 216; Pfanz, *Gettysburg—The Second Day*, 372.

15. George Clark, *A Glance Backward or Some Events in the Past History of My Life* (Houston: n.p., 1914),37; Bailey G. McClellan, *Civil War History of Company D, 10th Alabama Regiment* (Anniston Station, Al.: n.p., 1901), 2; Maurice S. Fortin, ed., "Colonel Hilary A. Herbert's History of the Eighth Alabama Volunteer Regiment, CSA" *The Alabama Historical Quarterly*, vol. 39 (1977), 116-117; OR 27 (2): 618.

16. Busey and Martin, *Regimental Strengths and Losses*, 132; Blake, *Three Years in the Army of the Potomac*, 209; Blake, "Personal Reminiscences of Gettysburg"; Gottfried, *Brigades of Gettysburg*, 580-581, 587.

Map Set 20: The Fight Along Plum Run

1. Francis Heath, "Letter," copy in 19th Maine file, GNMP; Francis Heath Account, *Bachelder Papers*, vol. 3, 1651.

2. Heath, "Letter"; John D. Smith, *History of the Nineteenth Regiment of Maine Volunteer Infantry*, (Minneapolis, Western Printing Company, 1909), 68-69; Silas Adams, "The Nineteenth Maine at Gettysburg," in *Maine MOLLUS*, vol. 4, 249-263.

3. OR 27 (1): 442, 443, 451; OR Supp., 5, 163; Busey and Martin, *Regimental Strengths and Losses*, 39, 235; Ernest L. Waitt, *History of the Nineteenth Regiment Massachusetts Volunteer Infantry* (Salem, Ma.: Salem Press Company, 1906), 230-231; Pfanz, *Gettysburg—The Second Day*, 376.

4. *Second Reunion of the Nineteenth Maine*, copy in the 19th Maine folder, GNMP, 10-11; Smith, *History of the Nineteenth Maine Volunteer Infantry*, 254-255; *Maine at Gettysburg*, 292, 293-294; Heath, "Letter"; OR 27 (2): 631-632.

5. Pfanz, *Gettysburg—The Second Day*, 338-339; McNeily, *Barksdale's Mississippi Brigade at Gettysburg*, 248; John Bigelow to John Bachelder, n.d., Bachelder Papers, New Hampshire Historical Society.

6. William Colvill, Jr. to John Bachelder, June 9, 1866, Bachelder Papers, New Hampshire Historical Society; William Lochren, "The First Minnesota at Gettysburg." Minnesota MOLLUS, vol. 3, 48-49; J. N. Searles, "The First Minnesota Volunteer Infantry," *Minnesota MOLLUS*, vol. 2, 106; Plumber, "Letter," August 26, 1863, 1st Minnesota File, GNMP.

7. William Colvill, Jr. to John Bachelder, June 9, 1866; Plumber, "Letter"; Lochren, "The First Minnesota at Gettysburg," 48-49; Searles, "The First Minnesota Volunteer Infantry," 106; Alfred Carpenter, "Letter," Minnesota Hist. Soc., Brake Collection, USAMHI.

8. OR 27 (2): 631-632; David Lang, "Letter To General Edward Perry," *Southern Historical Society Papers*, vol. 27 (1899), 195; William Pigman, "Diary," Pigman Papers, Georgia Historical Society.

9. Lochren, "The First Minnesota at Gettysburg," 50-51; William Colvill, "Statement," copy in Brake

Collection, USAMHI; Robert W. Meinhard, "The First Minnesota at Gettysburg," *Gettysburg Magazine*, Issue 5 (July, 1991), 82; *OR* 27 (2): 618; *OR* 27 (1), 475, 476

10. *NYG*, vol. 2, 905; R. L. Murray, *Redemption of the Harper's Ferry Cowards: The Story of the 111th and 126th New York State Volunteer Regiments at Gettysburg* (Wolcott, N.Y., 1994), 96-97; *OR* 27 (1): 474, 475.

11. McNeily, *Barksdale's Mississippi Brigade at Gettysburg*, 249.

12. *OR* 27 (1): 474, *NYG*, vol. 2, 906; W. F. Beyer, W. F. and O. F. Keydel, *Deeds of Valor* (Stamford, Ct.: Longmeadow Press, 1994), 240-241; Benjamin Humphreys to John Bachelder, May 1, 1876, Bachelder Papers, New Hampshire Historical Society; Pfanz, *Gettysburg—The Second Day*, 405-406; Imhof, *Gettysburg, Day Two*, 186.

13. R. I. Holcombe, *History of the First Regiment Minnesota Volunteer Infantry, 1861-1864* (Gaithersburg, Md.: VanSickle, 1987), 345, 364; William Colvill, Jr. to John Bachelder, June 9, 1866; *OR* 27 (2): 618; Pfanz, *Gettysburg—The Second Day*, 406; Imhof, *Gettysburg, Day Two*, 197-198.

14. Thomas L. Elmore, "The Florida Brigade at Gettysburg," in *Gettysburg Magazine*, Issue 15 (July 1996), 50; Pfanz, *Gettysburg—The Second Day*, 414; *OR* 27 (2): 631-632; Lang, "Letter To General Edward Perry," 195.

15. *NYG*, vol. 2, 886.

16. *NYG*, vol. 2, 906; *OR* 27, 1, 472; Arabella M. Willson, *Disaster, Struggle, Triumph: The Adventures of 1000 "Boys in Blue," from August, 1862, to June, 1865* (Albany: Argus Company Printers, 1870), 169; G. B. Judge, "The Battle of Gettysburg." *Waco Daily-Times Herald*, July 3, 1913; McNeily, *Barksdale's Mississippi Brigade at Gettysburg*, 243; William M. Abernathy, *Our Mess: Southern Gallantry and Privations* (McKinney, Tex.: McKintex Press, 1977), 33-34.

17. *NYG*, vol. 2, 906; Lewis Crandell, "Diary," copy in 125th folder, GNMP.

18. *OR* 27 (1): 474, *NYG*, vol. 2, 906; Beyer and Keydel, *Deeds of Honor*, 240-241; Benjamin Humphreys to John Bachelder, May 1, 1876, Bachelder Papers, New Hampshire Historical Society; Pfanz, *Gettysburg—The Second Day*, 405-406.

Map Set 21: Wright Tries the Union Center

1. *OR* 27, 2, 623, 630; Bradley M. Gottfried, "Wright's Charge at Gettysburg: Piercing the Union Line or Inflated Glory?" *Gettysburg Magazine*, Issue 17 (July 1997), 71.

2. John H. Rhodes, *The History of Battery B, First Regiment, Rhode Island Artillery* (Providence: Snow and Farnham Printers, 1914), 200-202.

3. *OR* 27 (1) 423, 436; *Augusta Daily Constitutionalist*, July 23, 1863; *OR* 27 (2) 627-9; Andrew E. Ford, *Story of*

the Fifteenth Regiment, Massachusetts Volunteer Infantry in the Civil War* (Clinton, Ma., Press of W. J. Coulter,1898), 267; Pfanz, *Gettysburg—The Second Day*, 385-6; Gregory Coco, *From Ball's Bluff to Gettysburg...* (Gettysburg, Pa. Thomas Publications, 1994), 196-201.

4. PAG, vol. 1, 415, 550-1; Joseph Ward, *History of the One Hundred and Sixth Pennsylvania Volunteers, 2d Brigade, 2d Division, 2d Corps, 1861-1865* (Philadelphia: Grant, Faires & Rodgers, 1883), 191; Anthony McDermott, Anthony. *A Brief History of the 69th Regiment Pennsylvania Veteran Volunteers....* (Ann Arbor, Mich.: University Microfilms, 1968), 28; *OR* 27 (1): 434; Gary Lash, "The Philadelphia Brigade at Gettysburg," *Gettysburg Magazine*, Issue 7 (July 1992), 100; Gottfried, "Wright's Charge at Gettysburg: Piercing the Union Line or Inflated Glory?" 71-72, 76.

5. *OR* 27 (2): 633-634.

6. Ford, *Story of the Fifteenth Regiment, Massachusetts Volunteer Infantry in the Civil War*, 267; Coco, *From Ball's Bluff to Gettysburg . . .*, 196-201.

7. *OR* 27 (1): 419-420, 425-426; *OR* 27, 2, 628, 629; Ford, *Story of the Fifteenth Regiment, Massachusetts Volunteer Infantry in the Civil War*, 268-269; Coco, *From Ball's Bluff to Gettysburg . . .*, 201-202; Wiley Sword, "Defending the Codori House and Cemetery Ridge: Two Swords with Harrow's Brigade in the Gettysburg Campaign," in *Gettysburg Magazine*, Issue 13 (July 1995), 46-47; *NYG*, vol. 2, 664.

8. Rhodes, *History of Battery B, First Regiment, Rhode Island Artillery*, 200-202.

9. Rhodes, *History of Battery B, First Regiment, Rhode Island Artillery*, 201; Frank Foote, "Marching in Clover." In *Philadelphia Weekly Times*, October 8, 1881.

10. Rhodes, *History of Battery B, First Regiment, Rhode Island Artillery*, 202-3.

11. Frederick Fuger, "Cushing's Battery at Gettysburg," *Journal of the Military Service Institution of the United States*, vol. 41 (1907): 406-7; Frederick Fuger, "Battle of Gettysburg, Recollections of the Battle," Webb Papers, Yale University Library, 20-21; *OR* 27 (2): 623.

12. *OR* 27 (2): 623-624, 634; Elwood W. Christ, *The Struggle for the Bliss Farm at Gettysburg, July 2nd and 3rd, 1863: "Over a Wide, Hot, Crimson Plain"* (Baltimore, Md:. Butternut & Blue, 1993), 38; Foote, "Marching In Clover"; Franklin L. Riley, *Grandfather's Journal...* (Dayton, Ohio: Morningside, 1988), 148.

13. *PAG*, vol. 1, 415, 550-551; Rhodes, *History of Battery B, First Regiment, Rhode Island Artillery*, 202-203.

14. Foote, "Marching in Clover."

15. McDermott, *A Short History of the 69th Regiment Pennsylvania Veteran Volunteers...*, 28.

16. Gottfried, "Wright's Charge at Gettysburg: Piercing the Union Line or Inflated Glory?" 77; *PAG*, vol. 1, 415, 550-551.

17. *OR* 27 (1): 436, 447-8; *OR* 27 (2): 628.

18. Gottfried, "Wright's Charge at Gettysburg: Piercing the Union Line or Inflated Glory?" 79.

19. Gottfried, *Brigades of Gettysburg*, 99.

20. Foote, "Marching in Clover"; 85; Ward, *History of the One Hundred and Sixth Regiment, Pennsylvania Volunteers*, 191-2; McDermott and Reilly, *History of the 69th Regiment, Pennsylvania Veteran Reserves*, 28; *PAG*, vol. 1, 550-551; OR 27 (1): 427, 434, 436, 447-448; OR 27, 2, 626; Anthony McDermott to John Bachelder, 2 July 1886, Bachelder Papers, New Hampshire Historical Society;; *PAG*, vol. 1, 550-551; Busey and Martin, *Regimental Strengths and Losses*, 311.

21. Gottfried, *Brigades of Gettysburg*, 99.

22. Pfanz, *Gettysburg—The Second Day*, 421; Ralph O. Sturtevant, *Pictorial History of the Thirteenth Vermont Volunteers, War of 1861-1865* (n.p., n.p., 1910), 267-269, 488, 499, 559-560; George H. Scott, "Vermont at Gettysburg," *Proceedings of the Vermont Historical Society*, vol. 1 (1930), 65; OR 27 (1): 349, 351-2; OR 27 (2): 623-625, 628; Edwin F. Palmer, *The Second Brigade or Camp Life* (Montpelier, Vt.: Printed by E.P. Walton, 1864), 196.

23. Gottfried, *Stopping Pickett* (Shippensburg, PA: White Mane, 1999), 162; OR 27 (1): 352.

24. Busey and Martin, *Regimental Strengths and Losses*, 311, 129; *Augusta Daily Constitutionalist*, July 23, 1863.

25. Gottfried, "Wright's Charge at Gettysburg: Piercing the Union Line or Inflated Glory?" 82; OR 27 (2): 623-624, 628; OR 27 (1): 423, 424, 426, 431.

Map Set 22: The Valley of Death

1. OR 27 (1): 660; John L. Parker, *Henry Wilson's Regiment: History of the Twenty-Second Massachusetts Infantry* (Boston: Press of Rand Avery Co., 1887), 313; Imhof, *Gettysburg, Day Two*, 180.

2. Pfanz, *Gettysburg—The Second Day*, 393.

3. H. N. Minnigh, *History of Company K, 1 st (Inft,) Penn'a Reserves* (Duncansville, Pa.: Home Print Publisher, 1891), 26; *PAG*, vol. 1, 278.

4. OR 27 (1): 653, 657, 685; Pfanz, *Gettysburg—The Second Day*, 394.

5. OR 27 (1): 662.

6. OR 27 (1): 671.

7. "Wofford's Georgia Brigade," *Richmond Daily Enquirer*, August 5, 1863; "Wofford's Georgia Brigade";

8. OR 27 (1): 685; Pfanz, *Gettysburg—The Second Day*, 398-399; Goode Bryan, "Letter," Southern Historical Collection, University of North Carolina.

9. OR 27 (2): 369; Johnson, "The Battle of Gettysburg"; Coxe, "The Battle of Gettysburg," 435.

10. OR 27 (1): 653, 657; Evan M. Woodward, *Our Campaigns—The Second Regiment, Pennsylvania Reserve Volunteers* (Philadelphia: J. E. Potter, 1865), 213.

11. Bell, "The Bucktails at Gettysburg"; Woodward, *Our Campaigns—The Second Regiment, Pennsylvania Reserve Volunteers*, 213; *PAG*, vol. 1, 279, 526; Captain Frank Bell, "The Bucktails at Gettysburg," (copy in the 42nd Pennsylvania folder, GNMP); Garry Adelman, "The Third Brigade, Third Division, Sixth Corps at Gettysburg." *Gettysburg Magazine*, Issue 11 (1994), 91-101.

Map Set 23: Cemetery Hill

1. Augustus Vignos to John Bachelder, April 17, 1864, Bachelder Papers, New Hampshire Historical Society; OR 27 (1): 716; Harry W. Pfanz, *Gettysburg: Culp's Hill and Cemetery Hill* (Chapel Hill: The University of North Carolina Press, 1993), 448-9, ft #27; Imhof, *Gettysburg, Day Two*, 222-223.

2. OR 27 (1): 714; David Martin, *Carl Bornemann's Regiment* (Hightstown, N.J.: Longstreet House, 1989), 150; Imhof, *Gettysburg, Day Two*, 228; Keifer, *History of the One Hundred and Fifty-Third Regiment Pennsylvania Volunteer Infantry*, 85, 86; Pfanz, *Gettysburg: Culp's Hill and Cemetery Hill*, 247-249, 260.

3. OR *Supp*, vol. 5, 217; Aldin Underwood, *Three Years' Service of the Thirty-Third Massachusetts Infantry Regiment* (Boston: A. Williams, 1881),123; Keifer, *History of the One Hundred and Fifty-Third Regiment Pennsylvania Volunteer Infantry*, 86.

4. OR 27 (1): 716, 718; Anonymous, *75th Ohio*; Andrew Harris to John Bachelder, March 14, 1881, Bachelder Papers, New Hampshire Historical Society; OR *Supp.*, vol. 5, 217-218; John J. Ryder, *Reminiscences Of Three Years' Service In The Civil War By A Cape Cod Boy* (New Bedford, Ma.: Reynolds Printing, 1928), 34-35; Pfanz, *Gettysburg: Culp's Hill and Cemetery Hill*, 249.

5. Pfanz, *Gettysburg: Culp's Hill and Cemetery Hill*, 237; Terry L. Jones, *Cemetery Hill* (New York, 2003), 69-70. Although the Bachelder maps show a substantially different deployment for Hays, subsequent events argue against Bachelder's placement (see also Imhof, *Gettysburg, Day Two*, 221).

6. Captain R. J. Hancock letter, John Daniel Papers, University of Virginia; R. Stark Jackson letter, LSU Library; William Seymour Journal, William L. Clements Library, U. of Michigan; copy in GNMP; Martin, *Carl Bornemann's Regiment*, 149-150; OR 27 (1): 713; William Simmers, *The Volunteers' Manual or Ten Months with the One Hundred and Fifty-Third Pennsylvania Volunteers* (Easton, Pa.: D. H. Neiman, 1863), 29; Pfanz, *Gettysburg: Culp's Hill and Cemetery Hill*, 250-251, 277-278; Clark, *N.C. Regiments*, vol. 3, 415.

7. Pfanz, *Gettysburg: Culp's Hill and Cemetery Hill*, 250-151.

8. OR 27 (2): 484; Pfanz, *Gettysburg: Culp's Hill and Cemetery*, 251-152, 255.

9. Seymour, "Journal"; Andrew L. Harris to John Bachelder.

10. Andrew Harris to John Bachelder.

11. Kiefer, *History of the One Hundred and Fifty-Third Pennsylvania*, 152; Pete Tomasak, "An Encounter with Battery Hell," in *Gettysburg Magazine*, Issue 12 (January 1995), 36-37.

12. OR 27 (2): 280; Hancock, "Letter"; Imhof, *Gettysburg, Day Two*, 234.

13. Andrew L. Harris to John Bachelder; OR 27 (2): 280; Jackson, "Letter"; Carol M. Becker and Ritchie Thomas, *Heath and Knapsack: The Ladley Letters, 1857-1880* (Athens, Ohio: Ohio University Press, 1988), 142; George S. Clements, "The 25th Ohio at Gettysburg." in *National Tribune*, August 6, 1891; Alfred Rider to John Bachelder, August 20, 1885, Bachelder Papers, New Hampshire Historical Society; Imhof, *Gettysburg, Day Two*, 240-241.

14. Pfanz, *Gettysburg: Culp's Hill and Cemetery Hill*, 257-258; OR 27 (1): 718; Becker and Thomas, *Hearth and Knapsack: The Ladley Letters*, 142.

15. R. Bruce Ricketts to John Bachelder, March 2, 1866, Bachelder Papers, New Hampshire Historical Society; OR 27 (1): 716; J. Clyde Miller to John Bachelder, March 2, 1886; Keifer, *History of the One Hundred and Fifty-Third Regiment Pennsylvania Volunteer Infantry*, 141-2; Clark, *N.C. Regiments*, vol. 2, 136-137; George Fox to John Bachelder, November 14, 1885, Bachelder Papers, New Hampshire Historical Society; Hamblen, *Connecticut Yankees at Gettysburg*, 60-61; *Anonymous account, 75th Ohio folder, GNMP*.

16. Clark, *N.C. Regiments*, vol. 3, 415; *OR Supp.*, vol. 5, 218; Martin, *Bornemann's Regiment*, 156; OR 27 (1): 714; OR 27 (2): 484; Ryder, *Reminiscences Of Three Years' Service In The Civil War By A Cape Cod Boy*, 35; *OR Supp.*, vol. 5, 218-219; Pfanz, *Gettysburg: Culp's Hill and Cemetery Hill*, 261.

17. Anonymous, 75th Ohio; Edward C. Culp, *The Twenty-Fifth Ohio Veteran Volunteer Infantry in the War for the Union* (Topeka, Ks.: G. W. Crane & Co., 1885), 78-79; Peter Young to John Bachelder, August 12, 1867; Smith, *Camps and Campaigns of the 107th Regiment Ohio Volunteer Infantry*, 101; OR 27 (1): 720.

18. OR 27 (2): 280; Jackson, "Letter"; Simmers, *The Volunteer's Manual...*, 30; Terry L. Jones, Terry L. *Lee's Tigers* (Baton Rouge, La.: Louisiana State University Press, 1987), 173; David L. Callihan, "Captain Michael Wiedrich's Company I, First New York Light Artillery at Gettysburg," in *Gettysburg Magazine* (July 2005), Issue 33, 87.

19. Pfanz, *Gettysburg—The Second Day*, 268-270; Clark, *N.C. Regiments*, vol. 1, 313-314.

20. Pfanz, *Gettysburg—The Second Day*, 262, 268-270; Clark, *N.C. Regiments*, vol. 1, 313-314, vol. 2, 136-137; J. Clyde Miller to John Bachelder, March 2, 1886; OR 27 (2): 486.

21. Anonymous, 75th Ohio; Edward C. Culp, *The Twenty-Fifth Ohio Veteran Volunteer Infantry in the War for the Union*, 78-79.

22. OR 27 (2): 280-281; Seymour, "Journal."

23. OR 27 (1): 743; OR 27 (2): 481; *NYG*, vol. 1, 431; James S. Pula, *The Sigel Regiment: A History of the Twenty-sixth Wisconsin Volunteer Infantry,1862-1865* (Campbell, Ca.: Savas, 1998), 176; Ralph Whitehead, "The 119th New York Volunteers and Their Participation in the Gettysburg Campaign, June 12-July 4, 1983," 119th New York folder, GNMP, 9-10; Pfanz, *Gettysburg: Culp's Hill and Cemetery Hill*, 268, 272; *PAG*, vol. 1, 420-421.

24. Clark, *N.C. Regiments*, vol. 1, 313-314; OR 27 (2): 486; J. Clyde Miller to John Bachelder, March 2, 1886.

25. OR 27 (1): 457, 459, 726; Elijah Cavins to John Bachelder, May 9, 1878 and "Statement of Lt. Col. Elijah H.C Cavins," in Bachelder Papers, New Hampshire Historical Society; J. L. Dickelman, "Gen. Carroll's Gibralter Brigade at Gettysburg"; *National Tribune*, December 10, 1908; David Beem letter, Indiana Historical Society); Keppler, *History of the Three Months and Three Years' Service . . . of the Fourth Regiment Ohio Volunteer Infantry in the War for the Union*, 128-129.

26. OR 27 (2): 486; Thomas E. Causby, "Storming the Stone Fence at Gettysburg," *Southern Historical Society Papers*, vol. 29 (1901), 340; "A Southern Keepsake," *Gettysburg Compiler*, December 13, 1909; Clark, *N.C. Regiments*, vol. 3, 416.

27. Jubal A. Early, *Autobiographical Sketch And Narrative Of The War Between The States* (Philadelphia: J. B. Lippincott Company, 1912), 75; John McPherson, "The Death of Colonel Isaac Avery," copy in the 6th North Carolina folder, GNMP; Robert W. Iobst, and Louis H. Manarin, *The Bloody Sixth: The Sixth North Carolina Regiment, Confederate States of America* (Durham, N.C.: Christian Printing Company, 1965), 138-139; Causby, "Storming the Stone Fence at Gettysburg," 340; Clark, *N.C. Regiments*, vol. 3, 416; OR 27 (2): 470, 486, 587-588.

Map Set 24: The Fight for Culp's Hill

1. OR 27 (1): 773; Alpheus Williams, *From the Cannon's Mouth: The Civil War Letters of General Alpheus S. Williams* (Detroit: Wayne State University Press, 1959), 228, 229. General Williams wrote: "General Lockwood being senior to General Ruger, then commanding First Division, and a stranger to the

division, I directed him to take his orders directly from me as an unassigned brigade during the pending operations." OR 27 (1): 766.

2. OR 27 (1): 825-826, 847, 854, 856, 860, 863, 864, 865; NYG, vol. 1, 450; Pfanz, *Gettysburg: Culp's Hill and Cemetery Hill*, 111-113, 211; David Mouart, "Three Years in the 29th Pennsylvania Volunteers," Historical Society of Pennsylvania; PAG, vol. 1, 569-570, 598.

3. OR 27 (1): 778, 783, 800; Hamblen, Connecticut at Gettysburg, 70-71; Pfanz, *Gettysburg: Culp's Hill and Cemetery Hill*, 428-429 (n. 44).

4. OR 27 (1): 812, 818, 819; Edmund R. Brown, *History of the Twenty-Seventh Indiana Volunteer Infantry* (Monticello: n.p., 1899), 370; Imhof, *Gettysburg, Day Two*, 22; Pfanz, *Gettysburg: Culp's Hill and Cemetery Hill*, 127.

5. *NYG*, vol. 3, 1013; Jesse H. Jones, "The Breastworks at Culp's Hill, in *Battles and Leaders of the Civil War*, vol. 3, 316; OR 27 (1): 856, 860.

6. OR 27 (3): 504.

7. OR 27 (1): 862, 863; OR 27 (2): 518, 526; William W. Goldsborough, *The Maryland Line* (Port Washington, N.Y.: Kennikat Press, 1972), 146.

8. OR 27 (1): 826-827.

9. OR 27 (1): 861, 862, 863, 865; NYG, vol. 3, 1013; Steuben Coon letter, copy in 60th New York folder, GNMP; Pfanz, *Gettysburg: Culp's Hill and Cemetery Hill*, 213.

10. OR 27 (3): 504.

11. OR 27 (2): 504, 518, 521, 532, 533, 537; OR Supp., vol. 5, 393, 394-395; Clark, N.C. Regiments, vol. 1, 148; Pfanz, *Gettysburg: Culp's Hill and Cemetery Hill*, 208-210. The deployment of Williams' brigade is problematic as the survivors left little information on this subject. I chose to follow Pfanz's map (207) showing the advance in two lines. The 23rd Virginia was considerably below strength because six companies had been detached (Pfanz, *Gettysburg: Culp's Hill and Cemetery Hill*, 210).

12. OR 27 (2) 536, 538, 539.

13. OR 27 (2): 509-10; *The Telegram*, n.d. (copy in 2nd Maryland Battalion folder, GNMP); Jones, *Lee's Tigers*, 170; David Zable Memoir, Tulane University; Pfanz, *Gettysburg: Culp's Hill and Cemetery Hill*, 216.

14. George K. Collins, *Memoirs of the 149th Regiment New York Volunteer Infantry* (Syracuse, N.Y.: Privated Printed, 1891), 138-139; OR 27 (1): 865.

15. OR 27 (1): 731; NYG, vol. 1, 63; Pfanz, *Gettysburg: Culp's Hill and Cemetery Hill*, 213.

16. OR 27 (2): 532, 537, 538.

17. Pfanz, *Gettysburg: Culp's Hill and Cemetery Hill*, 217; Zable, "Memoir"; Watha Rawlings, *War Stories, Being the Thrilling Experiences and Adventures of Captain Watha Rawlings During the War of 1861-1865* (McCauley, Tex.: Privately Printed, 1909), 3.; Jones, *Lee's Tigers*, 170.

18. *The Telegram*, OR 27 (2): 509-510; OR Supp., vol. 5, 394-395; Clark, *N.C. Regiments*, vol. 1, 195; Thomas L. Elmore, "Courage Against the Trenches," in *Gettysburg Magazine*, Issue 7 (July 1992), 86; George Thomas, "The Confederate Monument at Gettysburg." *Southern Historical Society Papers*, vol. 14 (1886), 445; William W. Goldsborough, "With Lee at Gettysburg," *Philadelphia Record*, July 8, 1900; William Zollinger, Lamar Hollyday, and D. R. Howard, "General George H. Steuart's Brigade at the Battle of Gettysburg," *Southern Historical Society Papers*, vol. 2 (1876), 106.

19. Collins, *Memoirs of the 149th N.Y. Infantry*, 138-139; Coon, "Letter"; Sergeant Sam Lusk letter, 137th folder, GNMP.

20. OR 27 (1): 861, 865, 867, 868; OR 27 (2): 539; Coon, "Letter."

21. Pfanz, *Gettysburg: Culp's Hill and Cemetery Hill*, 210, 213-4; Imhof, *Gettysburg, Day Two*, 245-246.

22. Pfanz, *Gettysburg: Culp's Hill and Cemetery Hill*, 220-21.

23. OR 27 (2): 510; OR Supp. vol. 5, 399; Lamar Holliday, "The Second Maryland Again," *The Telegram*, May 19, 1903; Charles Raine, "Memoir," Fredericksburg-Spotsylvania Military Park; Randolph McKim, "Steuart's Brigade at the Battle of Gettysburg." *SHSP*, vol. 5 (1878), 293; OR 27 (1): 866; Pfanz, *Gettysburg: Culp's Hill and Cemetery Hill*, 218-219.

24. OR 27 (2): 506; OR Supp., vol. 5, 401; George S. Greene, "The Breastworks at Culp's Hill," *Battles and Leaders of the Civil War*, vol. 3, 317; OR 27 (1): 827, 856, 857, 866; Jay Jorgensen, "Holding the Right as follows: The 137th New York Regiment at Gettysburg," in Gettysburg *Magazine*, Issue 15 (July 1996), 65; Collins, *Memoirs of the 149th N.Y. Infantry*, 139.

25. OR 27 (1): 857.

26. OR 27 (1): 861, 865; NYG, vol. 1, 451; Imhof, *Gettysburg, Day Two*, 269-270; Pfanz, *Gettysburg: Culp's Hill and Cemetery Hill*, 222-23; OR Supp, vol. 5, 397; Samuel Firebaugh, "Diary," Southern Historical Collection, UNC; Dawes, *Service with the Sixth Wisconsin Volunteers*, 172, 181-182; C. V. Tevis, *The History of the Fighting Fourteenth*, 91-92; Terrence V. Murphy, *Tenth Virginia Infantry* (Lynchburg, Va.: H. E. Howard, 1989), 78.

27. Pfanz, *Gettysburg: Culp's Hill and Cemetery Hill*, 223-224; Imhof, *Gettysburg, Day Two*, 271.

28. OR 27 (1): 865.

29. OR 27 (2): 504, 518-519, 521, 526.

Evening July 2 – Morning July 3

1. Pfanz, *Gettysburg—The Second Day*, 425, 429, 431; Busey and Martin, *Regimental Strengths and Losses*, 130, 139, 143, 278, 280, 282, 284, 286.

2. Hale, "With Cross in the Gettysburg Campaign"; Muffly, *The Story of our Regiment*, 539.

July 3

Map Set 25: Culp's Hill Remains in Union Hands

1. OR 27 (1): 815, 817, 820, 824; Brown, *History of the Twenty-Seventh Indiana Volunteer Infantry*, 377; Edwin C. Bryant, *History of the Third Regiment of Wisconsin Veteran Volunteer Infantry* (Madison, Wis.: Democrat Printing Company, 1891), 191; Toombs, *New Jersey Troops in the Gettysburg Campaign*, 79-80.

2. L. R. Coy letter, copy at GNMP; Henry C. Morhous, *Reminiscences of the 123rd Regiment, New York State Volunteers* (Greenwich, N.Y.: People's Journal Book and Job Office, 1879), 48; William Wooster to John Bachelder, December 19, 1886, Bachelder Papers, New Hampshire Historical Society.

3. Cook G. and Charles E. Benton, eds. *The "Dutchess County Regiment" in the Civil War* (Danbury, Ct.: Danbury Medical Printing Company, 1907), 32-33; Pfanz, *Gettysburg: Culp's Hill and Cemetery Hill*, 286; Alpheus Williams to John Bachelder, November 10, 1865.

4. J. R. Lynn, "What the 29th Ohio Did During the Three Days' Fighting," *National Tribune*, October 7, 1897; Kevin E. O'Brien, "A Perfect Roar of Musketry: Candy's Brigade in the Fight for Culp's Hill." *Gettysburg Magazine*, Number 9 (July, 1993), 87; Bates, *Pennsylvania Volunteers*, vol.VII, 552; OR 27 (1): 836-837, 839, 840; Pfanz, *Gettysburg: Culp's Hill and Cemetery Hill*, 228-229.

5. *PAG*, vol. 1, 220, 570-571; OR 27 (1): 849, 855.

6. OR 27 (1): 863, 864-5, 866, 868; Pfanz, *Gettysburg: Culp's Hill and Cemetery Hill*, 297.

7. Pfanz, *Gettysburg: Culp's Hill and Cemetery Hill*, 287-289. The precise alignment of Jones' and Williams' brigades is not known.

8. McKim, "Steuart's Brigade at the Battle of Gettysburg," 297; Pfanz, *Gettysburg: Culp's Hill and Cemetery Hill*, 311.

9. Pfanz, *Gettysburg: Culp's Hill and Cemetery Hill*, 291-292; OR 27 (2): 504, 533, 535, 536, 537.

10. Zable, "Memoir."

11. OR 27 (1): 837, 844; Eugene Powell to John Bachelder, May 15, 1878 and March 23, 1886, Bachelder Papers, New Hampshire Historical Society; John Mitchell to John Bachelder, August 15, 1887, Bachelder Papers, New Hampshire Historical Society.

12. OR 27 (1): 847, 849, 852, 855; Bates, *Pennsylvania Volunteers*, vol. I, 490.

13. OR 27 (1): 804-805, 806; *Report of the State of Maryland Gettysburg Monument Commission* (Baltimore: William K. Boyle and Son, 1891), 57-58.

14. William Wooster to John Bachelder, December 11, 1886; OR 27 (1): 784, 793; Hamblen, *Connecticut Yankees at Gettysburg*, 79-81; John Storrs, *The Twentieth Connecticut* (Ansonia, Ct.: Press of the Naugatuck Valley Sentinel, 1886), 92-93.

15. OR 27 (1): 841, 843, 863, 865, 867; Cook and Bartlett, *The "Dutchess County Regiment" in the Civil War*, 34-35.

16. Pfanz, *Gettysburg: Culp's Hill and Cemetery Hill*, 289; OR 27 (2): 518, 568, 593; 601.

17. OR 27 (2): 568; Thirty-Second Reg't Troops at the late Battles of Gettysburg, copy in 32nd North Carolina folder, GNMP; A. T. Marsh, "North Carolina Troops at Gettysburg," *Confederate Veteran*, vol. 16 (1908), 517.

18. OR 27 (2): 511; Clark, *N. C. Regiments*, vol. 1, 195; John Stone Memoir, Copy in 1st Maryland Battalion folder, GNMP; *The Telegram*

19. OR 27 (2): 511; Pfanz, *Gettysburg: Culp's Hill and Cemetery Hill*, 313, 315, 320; McKim, "Steuart's Brigade at the Battle of Gettysburg," 298; *The Telegram;* Thomas, "The Confederate Monument at Gettysburg, 445-446.

20. OR 27 (2): 511; *OR Supp.*, vol. 5, 397, 399; Thomas Rankin, *Twenty-Third Virginia* (Lynchburg, Va.: H. E. Howard, 1985), 68; Winfield Peters, "A Maryland Warrior and Hero," *Southern Historical Society Papers*, vol. 29 (1901), 248; *Reunion of the 28th & 147th Regiments, Pennsylvania Volunteers, Philadelphia, Nov. 24th, 1871* (Philadelphia: Pawson & Nicholson, 1872), 6; Goldsborough, *The Maryland Line*, 109.

21. Thomas Webb, "Letter," copy in 1st Maryland folder, GNMP; *PAG*, vol. 2, 718; OR 27 (1): 847, 849, 852; *PAG*, vol. 1, 220

22. OR 27 (2): 573-574, 578.

23. OR 27 (2): 568, 575.

24. James E. Green diary, copy at USAMHI; Leon, *Diary of a Tar Heel*, 36.

25. OR 27 (2): 519, C. A. Rollins, "A Private's Story," *Lexington Gazette and Citizen*, July 26, 1888.

26. Pfanz, *Gettysburg: Culp's Hill and Cemetery Hill*, 322-323; Collins, *Memoirs of the 149th Regiment New York Volunteer Infantry*, 141.

27. OR 27 (2): 519, 523; William G. Bean, *The Liberty Hall Volunteers* (Charlottesville, Va.: University of Virginia Press, 1964), 150; James I. Robertson, *The Fourth Virginia Infantry* (Lynchburg, Va.: H. E. Howard, 1982), 27-28; Pfanz, *Gettysburg: Culp's Hill and Cemetery Hill*, 323, 325-326; OR 27 (1): 841; Lawrence Wilson, "Charge Up Culp's Hill," *Washington Post*, July 9, 1899; S. R. Norris, "Ohio at Gettysburg." *National Tribune*, June 9, 1887; Norris, "Ohio at Gettysburg."

28. Thomas Ruger to John Bachelder, August 12, 1869, Bachelder Papers, New Hampshire Historical

Society; Thomas Ruger, "Letter," copy in 2nd Massachusetts folder, GNMP; *OR* 27 (1): 781; 813; W. M. Snow, "Letter," copy in 2nd Massachusetts folder, GNMP; Brown, *History of the Twenty-Seventh Indiana Volunteer Infantry*, 379.

29. Alonzo H. Quint, *The Record of the Second Massachusetts, 1861-1865* (Boston: James P. Walker, 1867), 180; Charles F. Morse, *History of the Second Massachusetts Regiment of Infantry* (Boston: George H. Ellis, 1882), 13; Everett W. Pattison, "Some Reminiscences of Army Life," in *Massachusetts MOLLUS*, 262-263; Brown, *History of the Twenty-Seventh Indiana Volunteer Infantry*, 380.

30. *OR* 27 (1): 813, 814; Brown, *History of the Twenty-Seventh Indiana Volunteer Infantry*, 383-384; Pfanz, *Gettysburg: Culp's Hill and Cemetery Hill*, 348; Quint, *Record of the Second Massachusetts*, 181; Morse, *History of the Second Massachusetts Regiment of Infantry*, 14-16; Bryant, *History of the Third Regiment Wisconsin Veteran Volunteer Infantry*, 195-196.

Map Set 26: The Pickett – Pettigrew – Trimble Charge

1. Kathy G. Harrison and John W. Busey, *Nothing But Glory* (Gettysburg, Pa.: Thomas Publications, 1993), 15-20.

2. *OR* 27 (2): 647 Clark, *N.C. Regiments*, vol. 3, 107; Billy Ellis, *Tithes of Blood*, (Nashville: Southern Heritage Press, 1997), 119; Baxter McFarland, "The Eleventh Mississippi at Gettysburg," *Mississippi Historical Society*, vol. 2 (1918), 550; Michael W. Taylor, "North Carolina in the Pickett-Pettigrew-Trimble Charge," *Gettysburg Magazine*, Issue 8 (January 1993); Gottfried, *Brigades of Gettysburg*, 611, 619, 630; Jennifer M. Murray, "'The General Plan Was Unchanged': General Lee's Plan For 'Pickett's Charge,' July 3, 1863." in *Gettysburg Magazine* (July 2005), Issue 33, 96-97.

3. *OR* 27 (2): 666, 671-672.

4. George G. Benedict, *Army Life In Virginia: Letters from the Twelfth Vermont Regiment and Personal Experiences of Volunteer Service in the War for the Union, 1862-63* (Burlington. Vt.: The Free Press Association, 1882); "An Account of the Reunion of the 14th Regiment Vermont Volunteers," copy in 14th Vermont file, GNMP; 11; *OR* 27 (1): 321-322, 349, 352; Hess, *Pickett's Charge*, 101.

5. Holcombe, *History of the First Regiment Minnesota Volunteer Infantry*, 364; *OR* 27, 1, 422; Stewart, *Pickett's Charge*, 50; *NYG*, vol. 2, 665

6. Earl Hess, *Pickett's Charge* (Chapel Hill, N.C.: University of North Carolina Press, 2002), 132; Wayne Mahood, *Written in Blood* (Shippensburg, Pa.: White Mane Publishing Company, 1997), 140; *NYG*, vol. 2, 907; Benjamin W. Thompson, "Personal Narrative of Experiences in the Civil War, 1861–65," copy in Brake Collection, USAMHI.

7. Edward P. Alexander, *Military Memoirs of a Confederate* (New York: C. Scribners & Sons, 1907), 418-19; *OR* 27 (2): 605, 619. The exact time of the beginning of the barrage is not knowable with certainty because no one synchronized their watches.

8. Thomas W. Osborn, *The Eleventh Corps Artillery at Gettysburg* (Herb S. Crumb, etc., Hamilton, N.Y.: Edmonston Publishing, 1991), 30; *OR* 27 (1): 883; David Shultz, *Double Canister at Ten Yards* (Redondo Beach, Ca.: Rank and File Publications, 1995), 6-7, 20; Hess, *Pickett's Charge*, 114.

9. Hess, *Pickett's Charge*, 128.

10. Hess, *Pickett's Charge*, 162.

11. Joseph T. Durkin, *John Dooley, Confederate Soldier, His War Journal* (Washington: Georgetown University Press, 1945), 104-105; J. R. Hutter, "Letter," Daniel Papers, University of Virginia; John Smith, "Account," *Southern Historical Society Papers*, vol. 32 (1904), 190; Catlett Conway, "The Battle of Gettysburg," in *Atlanta Journal*, December 7, 1901; James Walker, "The Charge of Pickett's Division by a Participant," Virginia State Library; Robert K. Krick, *Fortieth Virginia Infantry* (Lynchburg, Va.: H. E. Howard, Company, 1985), 27; Clark, *N.C. Regiments*, vol. 5,125; Johnston quote from Hess, *Pickett's Charge*, 166. About this time, instances were recorded of a handful of men losing their nerve and slipping to the rear.

12. Bradley M. Gottfried, *Stopping Pickett—The History of the Philadelphia Brigade* (Shippensburg, Pa.: White Mane Publishing Company, 1999), 169; *OR* 27 (1): 428, 432; George R. Stewart, *Pickett's Charge—A Micro-history of the Final Attack at Gettysburg, July 3, 1863* (Boston: Houghton Mifflin, 1959), 166; Andrew Cowan, "When Cowan's Battery Withstood Pickett's Splendid Charge," *New York Herald*, July 2, 1911; *OR* 27 (1): 439, 476; Hess, *Pickett's Charge*, 130-133. One of Cowan's guns was north of the Copse of Trees; the remaining five took Brown's place to the south of it.

13. Harold M. Walthall "Memoir," copy in 1st Virginia file, GNMP; Walker, "The Charge of Pickett's Division," 222; J. F. Crocker, "Gettysburg—Pickett's Charge and Other War Addresses," copy in 9th Virginia folder, GNMP, 42; John H. Lewis, "Memoirs," copy in Brake Collection, USAMHI; Harrison and Busey, *Nothing But Glory*, 54; *OR* 27 (1): 893.

14. William B. Robertson, "Account," Daniel's Papers, University of Virginia; John E. Divine, *Eighth Virginia* (Lynchburg, Va.: H. E. Howard, 1983), 22; Randolph A. Shotwell, "Virginia and North Carolina in the Battle of Gettysburg," *Our Living and Our Dead* vol. 4 (1876), 91-92; *OR*, 27 (2): 386.

15. Franklin Sawyer, *A Military History of the 8th Regiment, Ohio Volunteers Infantry: Its Battles, Marches, and Army Movements* (Cleveland: Leader Printing Company, 1881), 132; Thomas F. Galway, *The Valiant Hours: Narrative of "Captain Brevet," An Irish-American in the Army of the Potomac* (Harrisburg, Pa.: Stackpole, 1961), 116; Horace Judson to John Bachelder, October, 17, 1887, Bachelder Papers, New Hampshire Historical Society; Ezra D. Simons, *A Regimental History: The One Hundred and Twenty-fifth New York State Volunteers* (New York: E. D. Simons, 1888), 137-138.

16. Hutter, "Letter"; Hess, *Pickett's Charge*, 221.

17. *Report of Joint Committee to Mark the Positions Occupied by the 1st and 2nd Delaware at the Battle of Gettysburg* (Dover, De., 1887), 14, 15; Hess, *Pickett's Charge*, 209. Dr. Hess does not believe Marshall dressed ranks at this point, and "advanced only in a few clusters of men, probably as a group rather than in rank and file formation." E-mail to Theodore P. Savas, March 31, 2007; R. Penn Smith, "The Battle of Gettysburg—The Part Taken by the Philadelphia Brigade in the Battle," *Gettysburg Compiler*, June 7, 1887; Shotwell, "Virginia and North Carolina in the Battle of Gettysburg," 93; Gottfried, *Stopping Pickett—The History of the Philadelphia Brigade*, 170, 172; Lewis, "Memoirs"; Crocker, *Gettysburg—Pickett's Charge*, 43.

18. Hess, *Pickett's Charge*, 174, 219-220, 233, 236.

19. Hess, *Pickett's Charge*, 233.

20. *OR* 27 (1): 350; Stewart, *Pickett's Charge*, 232; Richard Rollin, *Pickett's Charge—Eyewitness Accounts* (Redondo Beach, Ca.: Rank and File Publications, 1994), 175.

21. Harrison and Busey, *Nothing But Glory*, 102, 116; Wheelock Veazey, "Letter," copy in the 16th Vermont file, GNMP; George G. Benedict, *A Short History of the Fourteenth Regiment, Vermont Volunteers* (Bennington, Vt., 1887), 11, 37; Wheelock Veazey to John Bachelder, December, 1863.

22. Charles T. Loehr, "The Famous Pickett Charge," *Richmond Times-Dispatch*, October 16, 1904; Ralh W. Gunn, *Twenty-fourth Virginia Infantry* (Lynchburg, Va.: H. E. Howard, Inc., 1987), 46; Joseph Mayo, "Report," Duke University; Joseph Mayo, "Pickett's Charge at Gettysburg," *Richmond Times-Dispatch*, May 6, 1906; Ralph O. Sturtevant, *Pictorial History of the Thirteenth Vermont Volunteers, War of 1861-1865* (n.p.: 1910), 301; Harrison and Busey, *Nothing But Glory*, 68; Veazey "Letter."

23. Edmund Rice, "Repelling Lee's Last Blow at Gettysburg," *Battles and Leaders of the Civil War*, 387; *OR* 27 (1): 439, 448; Hess, Pickett's Charge, 243.

24. Walthall, "Memoirs"; Durkin, *John Dooley, Confederate Soldier*, 106; Conway, "The Battle of Gettysburg"; Rawley W. Martin and John H. Smith, "Battle of Gettysburg and Charge of Pickett's Division," *Southern Historical Society Papers*, vol. 32 (1904), 191-192.

25. George W. Finley, "The Bloody Angle." Buffalo Evening News, May 29, 1894; William A. Young, *Fifty-sixth Virginia Infantry* (Lynchburg: H. E. Howard, Inc., 1990), 85; Frank A. Haskell, *The Battle of Gettysburg* (Boston: Houghton Mifflin Company, 1969), 112; Hess, *Pickett's Charge*, 245; Gottfried, *Stopping Pickett—The History of the Philadelphia Brigade*, 173.

26. Report of Lt. Col. Charles Morgan, Bachelder Papers, vol. 3, 1362; Anthony McDermott Account, Bachelder Papers, vol. 3, 1648, 1656-7; Stewart, *Pickett's Charge*, 222-223; *Survivors of the Seventy- second Regiment of Pennsylvania Volunteers, Plaintiffs vs. Gettysburg Battlefield Memorial Associa- tion* (1891), 135, 260, 266, 267.

27. Henry S. Stevens, "Letter," N.C. Department of Archives and History; *OR* 27 (1): 467; *OR Supp.*, vol. 5, 421; Hess, *Pickett's Charge*, 206-07, 251, 252.

28. James Lane, "Letter," Southern Historical Collection, University of North Carolina; William Morris, "Letter, "Southern Historical Collection, University of North Carolina; *OR* 27 (2): 666; John Turner, "Letter," Southern Historical Collection, University of North Carolina; James S. Harris, *Historical Sketches: Seventh Regiment, North Carolina Troops* (Ann Arbor, MI: University Microfilms, 1972), 37; *OR Supp.*, vol. 5, 451; Clark, *N.C. Regiments*, vol. 2, 74; Hess, *Pickett's Charge*, 248.

29. Martin and Smith, "The Battle of Gettysburg, 186-187; John B. Bachelder, "The Third Day's Battle," *Philadelphia Weekly Times*, December 15, 1877; *OR* 27 (1): 431; Gottfried, *Stopping Pickett—The History of the Philadelphia Brigade*, 175.

30. *OR* 27 (1): 443-444, 445-446, 450, 451; Hess, *Pickett's Charge*, 274-275; Hugh D. Purcell, "The Nineteenth Massachusetts Regiment at Gettysburg," (Essex Institute Historical Collections, October, 1963), 285; *OR supp.*, vol. 5, 165; Gottfried, *Stopping Pickett—The History of the Philadelphia Brigade*, 173-174.

31. David E. Johnston, *Four Years a Soldier* (Princeton, W.Va.: Privately Printed, 1887), 210.

32. *OR* 27 (1): 444; *OR suppl.*, vol. 5, 165; Waitt, *History of the Nineteenth Regiment Massachusetts Volunteer Infantry*, 240-243.

33. "Col. And Dr. R. W. Martin, of Virginia," *Confederate Veteran*, vol. 5 (1897), 70; J. Irving Sale, "Gettysburg"; in *Philadelphia Weekly Press*, July 4, 1887; James E. Poindexter, "General Armistead's Portrait Presented," *Southern Historical Society Papers*, vol. 37 (1909), 149; B. L. Farinholt, "Battle of Gettysburg–Johnson's Island," *Confederate Veteran*, vol. 5 (1897), 468; Shotwell, "Virginia and North Carolina in the Battle of Gettysburg," 94; Finley, "Bloody Angle

34. E. Porter Alexander, "The Great Charge and Artillery Fighting at Gettysburg," *Battles and Leaders of the Civil War*, vol. 3, 366.

35. *OR* 27 (2): 620; Hess, *Pickett's Charge*, 299-300.

36. *OR* 27 (1): 350; Veazey, "Letter"; *OR* 27 (2): 632-633; Clement A. Evans, *Confederate Military History—Texas and Florida* (n.p., n.d.), *vol. 11*, 152; Hess, *Pickett's Charge*, 300-303.

37. *OR* 27 (2): 620.

Map Set 27: East Cavalry Field

1. *OR* 27 (2): 692-697; Douglas Craig Haines, "Jeb Stuart's Advance to Gettysburg," *Gettysburg* Magazine, Issue 29 (July 2004), 55-58; Longacre, *The Cavalry at Gettysburg*, 156-159.

2. Longacre, *The Cavalry at Gettysburg*, 156-159, 220-221; *OR* 27 (2): 697.

3. *OR* 27 (1): 956; Marshall D. Krolick, "Forgotten Field: The Cavalry Battle East of Gettysburg on July 3, 1863." *Gettysburg Magazine*, Issue 4 (January 1991), 76, 78; David McMurtrie Gregg, *The Second Cavalry Division of the Army of the Potomac in the Gettysburg Campaign* (Philadelphia: 1907), 10; OR suppl., vol 5, 271; Ladd and Ladd, *Bachelder Papers*, vol. 2, 1206; vol. 3, 1532; Longacre, *The Cavalry at Gettysburg*, 223.

4. Longacre, *The Cavalry at Gettysburg*, 222; Ladd and Ladd, *Bachelder Papers*, vol. 2, 1237.

5. Longacre, *The Cavalry at Gettysburg*, 224-225. General Kilpatrick was not informed of Custer's detachment and spent most of July 3 waiting for his brigade to appear south of Gettysburg.

6. *OR* 27 (1): 1050.

7. Ladd and Ladd, *Bachelder Papers*, vol. 2, 1,079, 1,252; vol. 3, 1427; Robert J. Trout, *Galloping Thunder* (Mechanicsburg, Pa.: Stackpole Books, 202; 292-293; Jeffry D. Wert, *Gettysburg, Day Three* (New York: Simon and Shuster, 2001), 264; David Schultz and Richard Rollins, "The Most Accurate Fire Ever Witnessed: Federal Horse Artillery in the Pennsylvania Campaign," in *Gettysburg Magazine* (July 2005), Issue 33, 74-75.

8. Ladd and Ladd, *Bachelder Papers*, vol. 2, 1238, 1290.

9. Kevin E. O'Brien, "'Glory Enough for All': Lt. William Brooke-Rawle and the 3rd Pennsylvania Cavalry at Gettysburg," *Gettysburg* Magazine, Issue 13 (July 1995), 94-96; Krolick, "Forgotten Field: The Cavalry Battle East of Gettysburg on July 3, 1863," 84; Wert, *Gettysburg, Day Three*, 264-265.

10. O'Brien, "'Glory Enough for All': Lt. William Brooke-Rawle and the 3rd Pennsylvania Cavalry at Gettysburg," 96-97.

11. William E. Miller, "The Cavalry Battle Near Gettysburg," *Battles and Leaders of the Civil War*, vol. 3,

404; Wert, *Gettysburg, Day Three*, 267; O'Brien, "'Glory Enough for All': Lt. William Brooke-Rawle and the 3rd Pennsylvania Cavalry at Gettysburg," 97. The Virginians were not unscathed before meeting the 7th Michigan; three squadrons of the 3rd Pennsylvania Cavalry near the Lott house fired into their flank as they passed (Krolick, "Forgotten Field: The Cavalry Battle East of Gettysburg on July 3, 1863," 86).

12. O'Brien, "'Glory Enough for All': Lt. William Brooke-Rawle and the 3rd Pennsylvania Cavalry at Gettysburg," 97-98, 100; Wert, *Gettysburg, Day Three*, 267-268.

13. Ladd and Ladd, *Bachelder Papers*, vol. 1, 209; vol. 2, 1190, 1207, 1266; vol. 3, 1448, 1449; O'Brien, "'Glory Enough for All': Lt. William Brooke-Rawle and the 3rd Pennsylvania Cavalry at Gettysburg," 100.

14. Trout, *Galloping Thunder*, 294-295; Ladd and Ladd, *Bachelder Papers*, vol. 2, 1171.

15. Miller, "Cavalry Battle near Gettysburg," 404; Rawle, *Third Pennsylvania Cavalry*, 277. According to General Hampton's report, he was not aware of the attack order, and only learned of it when his troops were in motion (*OR* 27 (2): 725).

16. Ladd and Ladd, *Bachelder Papers*, vol. 1, 654-655; vol. 2, 1,079, 1,080, 1,087-1,090, 1,266, 1,667; Krolick, "Forgotten Field: The Cavalry Battle East of Gettysburg on July 3, 1863," 86.

17. Wert, *Gettysburg, Day Three*, 269; Ladd and Ladd, *Bachelder Papers*, vol. 3, 1434, 1,490.

18. Miller, "Cavalry Battle near Gettysburg," 404; Longacre, *The Cavalry at Gettysburg*, 238-239.

19. Longacre, *The Cavalry at Gettysburg*, 239; Wert, *Gettysburg, Day Three*, 270.

20. O'Brien, "'Glory Enough for All': Lt. William Brooke-Rawle and the 3rd Pennsylvania Cavalry at Gettysburg," 99; Wert, *Gettysburg, Day Three*, 271; Longacre, *The Cavalry at Gettysburg*, 239. Captain Miller had to wait thirty-four years for his Medal of Honor, awarded for his gallant actions in helping blunt the Confederate advance.

Map Set 28: South Cavalry Field

1. *OR* 27 (1): 992-993; Eric J. Wittenberg, *Gettysburg's Forgotten Cavalry Actions* (Gettysburg: Thomas Pub., 1998), 2; Eric J. Wittenberg, "Merritt's Regulars on South Cavalry Field: 'Oh, What Could Have Been.'" *Gettysburg Magazine*, Issue 16 (January 1997), 115.

2. *OR* 27 (1): 1009; Longacre, *The Cavalry at Gettysburg*, 241-242; Laine and Penny, *Struggle for the Round Tops*, 120-121.

3. W. T. White, "First Texas Regiment at Gettysburg," *Confederate Veteran*, vol. XXX (1922), 185; Paul M. Shevchuk, "The 1st Texas Infantry and

the Repulse of Farnsworth's Charge." *Gettysburg Magazine*, Issue 2 (January 1990), 85.

4. *OR* 27 (1): 943; *OR* 27 (2): 397; Laine and Penny, *Struggle for the Round Tops*, 129; Bradley M. Gottfried, "The Story of Henry's Artillery Battalion at Gettysburg, *Gettysburg Magazine*, Issue 34 (January 2006), 37, 39.

5. Ladd and Ladd, *Bachelder Papers*, vol. 2, 916; Laine and Penny, *Struggle for the Round Tops*, 130, 134; Wittenberg, "Merritt's Regulars on South Cavalry Field: Oh, What Could Have Been," 120.

6. *OR* 27 (2): 397; Laine and Penny, *Struggle for the Round Tops*, 132.

7. Laine and Penny, *Struggle for the Round Tops*, 130-131; Ladd and Ladd, *Bachelder Papers*, vol. 1, 119.

8. Law, "Round Top," *Battles and Leaders*, vol. 3, 328; Ladd and Ladd, *Bachelder Papers*, vol. 1, 496.

9. Samuel Crockett Diary, GNMP; Wittenberg, *Gettysburg's Forgotten Cavalry Actions*, 58; Busey and Martin, *Regimental Strengths and Losses*, 258.

10. Gottfried, "The Story of Henry's Artillery Battalion at Gettysburg," 39.

11. Henry C. Parsons, "Farnsworth's Charge and Death," *Battles and Leaders of the Civil War*, vol. 3, 394; Thomas McCarthy Memoir, copy in the 1st Texas folder, GNMP.

12. McCarthy Memoir; *OR* 27 (1): 1019; Shevchuk, "The 1st Texas Infantry and the Repulse of Farnsworth's Charge," 86.

13. *OR* 27 (1): 1009; Ladd and Ladd, *Bachelder Papers*, vol. 3, 1543; Laine and Penny, *Struggle for the Round Tops*, 144.

14. Longacre, *The Cavalry at* Gettysburg, 243; Gottfried, "The Story of Henry's Artillery Battalion at Gettysburg, 39.

15. Wittenberg, *Gettysburg's Forgotten Cavalry Actions*, 27.

16. Parsons, "Farnsworth's Charge and Death." 394.

17. Horace K. Ide, "The First Vermont Cavalry in the Gettysburg Campaign." *Gettysburg* Magazine, Issue 14 (January 1996), 17; Parsons, "Farnsworth's Charge and Death, 395-396; Longacre, *The Cavalry at* Gettysburg, 243.

July 4-13

Withdrawal to Virginia

Map Set 29: *The Retreat from Gettysburg*

1. John D. Imboden, "The Confederate Retreat From Gettysburg," *Battles and Leaders of the Civil War* (New York: Thomas Yoseloff, Inc., 1956), vol. 3, 420.

2. Imboden, "The Confederate Retreat From Gettysburg," vol. 3, 421-422.

3. Imboden, "The Confederate Retreat From Gettysburg," vol. 3, 423-4; John W. Schildt, *Roads from Gettysburg* (Shippensburg, Pa: Burd Street Press, 2000), 14.

4. Imboden, "The Confederate Retreat From Gettysburg," vol. 3, 425; Hotchkiss, *Make Me a Map of the Valley*, 158-159; *OR* 27 (2): 558.

5. *OR* 27 (2): 699.

6. *OR* 27 (1): 917, 928, 970, 993-994; *OR* 27 (2): 701; Schildt, *Roads from Gettysburg*, 16-18.

7. Schildt, *Roads from Gettysburg*, 2.

8. *OR* 27 (2): 309, 311, 625; Kent Masterson Brown, *Retreat from Gettysburg* (Chapel Hill: University of North Carolina Press, 2005), 69.

9. Imboden, "The Confederate Retreat From Gettysburg," 3:425-426; Schildt, *Roads from Gettysburg*, 16; Brown, *Retreat from Gettysburg*, 90-91.

10. *OR* 27 (2): 625.

11. *OR* 27 (1): 928, 943, 959, 967, 977.

12. *OR* 27 (2): 615.

13. *OR* 27 (2): 448, 471, 493; Brown, *Retreat from Gettysburg*, 174, 258.

14. *OR* 27 (1): 663, 666, 672; *OR* 27 (2): 493.

15. *OR* 27 (1): 145, 386, 429, 621, 834.

16. *OR* 27 (1): 145, 708.

17. *OR* 27 (2): 361, 448; Brown, *Retreat from Gettysburg*, 267.

18. *OR* 27 (2): 448, 473, 615; Brown, *Retreat from Gettysburg*, 213, 270.

19. *OR* 27 (1): 995; Schildt, *Roads from Gettysburg*, 55-56.

20. Imboden, "The Confederate Retreat From Gettysburg," 3: 422; *OR* 27 (1): 928.

21. *OR* 27 (1): 145, 296.

22. *OR* 27 (2): 448, 472, 615; Brown, *Retreat from Gettysburg*, 274.

23. *OR* 27 (2): 703.

24. *OR* 27 (1): 925, 928, 995; *OR* 27 (2): 703.

25. *OR* 27 (1): 146.

26. *OR* 27 (1): 146; Brown, *Retreat from Gettysburg*, 298-299.

27. *OR* 27 (1): 146.

28. *OR* 27 (1): 146.

29. *OR* 27 (2): 361, 448, 472, 505, 558, 615.

30. *OR* 27 (1): 147; Brown, *Retreat from Gettysburg*, 316-317.

31. *OR* 27 (2): 361, 704; *OR* 27 (1): 929, 996.

32. *OR* 27 (2): 704, 705; *OR* 27 (1): 929, 996.

33. *OR* 27 (1): 147; Brown, *Retreat from Gettysburg*, 326.

34. *OR* 27 (1): 147.

35. *OR* 27 (2): 361-362, 370, 449, 472, 558-559, 705. General Rodes estimated that his division lost 25,000-30,000 rounds of ammunition.

36. *OR* 27 (1): 929; 996.
37. *OR* 27 (1): 920; *OR* 27 (2): 640-641.
38. *OR* 27 (2): 609, 664, 672; *OR* 27 (1): 929.
39. *OR* 27 (1): 147.
40. *OR* 27 (1): 929.

Bibliography

Official Documents

United States War Department. *The War of the Rebellion: A Compilation of the Official Records of the Union and Confederate Armies.* 128 volumes. Washington: U. S. Government Printing Office, 1880-1901.

Supplement to the Official records of the Union and Confederate Armies. 100 vols. Wilmington, NC: Broadfoot Publishing Company, 1994.

Firsthand Accounts, Newspapers, and Secondary Sources

"A Letter From the Army." *The Savannah Republican*, July 22, 1863.

"A Southern Keepsake." *Gettysburg Compiler*, December 13, 1909.

Abernathy, Willliam M. *Our Mess: Southern Gallantry and Privations.* McKinney, TX: McKintex Press, 1977.

Adams, Silas. "The Nineteenth Maine at Gettysburg." Maine MOLLUS, vol. 4, 249-263.

Adelman, Garry. "The Third Brigade, Third Division, Sixth Corps at Gettysburg." *Gettysburg Magazine,* No. 11 (1994), pp. 91-101.

———, and Timothy H. Smith. *Devil's Den—A History and Guide.* Gettysburg: Thomas Publications, 1997.

Alexander, Edward P. *Military Memoirs of a Confederate.* New York: C. Scribners & Sons, 1907.

———. "The Great Charge and Artillery Fighting at Gettysburg," *Battles and Leaders of the Civil War,* vol. 3, 357-368.

Applegate, John. *Reminiscences and Letters of George Arrowsmith of New Jersey.* Red Bank, NJ: John H. Cook, 1893.

Arrington, B. T. *The Medal of Honor at Gettysburg.* Gettysburg: Thomas Publications, 1996.

Ayars, Peter B. "The 99th Pennsylvania." *National Tribune,* February 4, 1886.

Bachelder, John B. "The Third Day's Battle." *Philadelphia Weekly Times*, December 15, 1877.

Banes, Charles H. *History of the Philadelphia Brigade: Sixty-ninth, Seventy- first, Seventy-second, and One Hundred and sixth Pennsylvania Volunteers.* Philadelphia: J.B. Lippincott, 1876.

Bardeen, Charles W. *A Little Fifer's War Diary.* Syracuse: C. W. Bardeen, Publisher, 1910.

Bartlett, Asa W. *History of the Twelfth Regiment, New Hampshire Volunteers in the War of the Rebellion.* Concord, N.H.: Ira C. Evans, Printer, 1897.

Barziza, Decimus et Ultimus, *The Adventures of a Prisoner of War, 1863-1864.* Austin: University of Texas Press, 1964.

Bates, Samuel P. *History of Pennsylvania Volunteers, 1861-5.* Wilmington, NC: Broadfoot Publishing. Co., 1993.

Bean, Theodore W. "Who fired the opening Shots?" *Philadelphia Weekly Times*, February 2, 1878.

Bean, William G. *The Liberty Hall Volunteers.* Charlottesville: University of Virginia Press, 1964.

Beaudot William J. and Lance J. Herdegen. *An Irishman in the Iron Brigade, The Civil War Memoirs of James P. Sullivan…* New York: Fordham University Press, 1993.

Becker, Carol M. and Ritchie Thomas, ed. *Hearth and Knapsack: The Ladley Letters, 1857-1880.* Athens, Oh: Ohio University Press, 1988.

Beecham, Robert K. *Gettysburg: The Pivotal Battle of the Civil* War. Chicago, A. C. McClung, 1911.

Belo, A. H. "The Battle of Gettysburg." *Confederate Veteran* (1900), vol. 8.

Benedict, George G. *A Short History of the Fourteenth Regiment, Vermont Volunteers.* Bennington, VT: Co. F, 14th Vermont Regiment, 1887.

———. *Army Life in Virginia: Letters from the Twelfth Vermont Regiment and Personal Experiences of Volunteer Service in the War for the Union, 1862-63.* Burlington. VT: The Free Press Association, 1882.

Bennett, Brian A. *Sons of Old Monroe: A Regimental History of Patrick O'Rorke's 140th New York Volunteer.* Dayton, Oh: Morningside House, Inc., 1992.

Berkeley, Henry R. *Four Years in the Confederate Artillery.* Richmond: Virginia Historical Society, 1991.

Beyer, W. F. and O. F. Keydel, *Deeds of Valor,* Stamford, CT: Longmeadow Press, 1994.

Bilby, Joseph. G. *Remember Fontenoy! The 69th New York Irish Brigade in the Civil War.* Hightstown, NJ: Longstreet House, 1995.

Bird, W. H. *Stories of the Civil War, Company C, 13th Regiment of Alabama Volunteers.* Columbiana, Ala., n.d.

Blake, Henry N. *Three Years in the Army of the Potomac.* Boston: Lee and Shepard, 1865.

Bloodgood, John D. *Personal Reminiscences of the War.* New York: Hunt and Eaton, 1893.

Boland, E. T. "Beginning of the Battle of Gettysburg." *Confederate Veteran Magazine* (1906), vol. 14, 308-309.

Bowden, Scott and Bill Ward. *Last Chance for Victory: Robert E. Lee and the Gettysburg Campaign.* El Dorado Hills, CA, Savas, 2001.

Bowen, Edward R. "Collis' Zouaves—The 114th Pennsylvania Infantry at Gettysburg." *Philadelphia Weekly Times,* June 22, 1887.

Bowen, James L. *History of the Thirty-Seventh Regiment, Mass., Volunteers, in the Civil War of 1861-1865.* Holyoke, Mass.: C.W. Bryan & Co., 1884.

Bowery, Maj. Charles R. Jr. "Encounter at the Triangular Field: The 124th New York and the 1st Texas at Gettysburg, July 2, 1863." *Gettysburg Magazine,* Issue 30 (January 2004), 49-62.

Bradley, Thomas W. and Peter B. Ayars. "At Gettysburg." *National Tribune,* February 4, 1886.

Brooks, U. R. *Stories of the Confederacy*. Columbia, SC: The State Company, 1912.

Brown, B. F. "Some Recollections of Gettysburg." *Confederate Veteran*, vol. 31 (1923).

Brown, Edmund R. *History of the Twenty-Seventh Indiana Volunteer Infantry*. Monticello: n.p., 1899.

Brown, Henri L. *History of the 3d Regiment, Excelsior Brigade, 72d New York Volunteer Infantry, 1861-1865*. Jamestown, NY: Journal Print. Co., 1902.

Brown, Kent Masterson. *Retreat from Gettysburg*. Chapel Hill: University of North Carolina Press, 2005.

Brown, Varina D. *A Colonel at Gettysburg and Spotsylvania*. Columbia, SC: The State Company, 1931.

Bryant, Edwin C. *History of the Third Regiment of Wisconsin Veteran Volunteer Infantry*. Madison, WI: Democrat Printing Company, 1891.

Buell, Augustus. *The Cannoneer*. Washington, D.C.: The National Tribune, 1890.

Bulger, M. J. A Hero" *New Orleans Picayune,* September 18, 1898.

Busey, John W. and David G. Martin, *Regimental Strengths and Losses at Gettysburg*. Hightstown, NJ: Longstreet House, 2006.

Caldwell, J. F. J. *The History of a Brigade of South Carolinians*. Marietta, Georgia: Continental Book Company, 1951.

Calef, J. "Gettysburg Notes: The Opening Gun." *Journal of the Military Service Institute of the U.S.* (1907), vol. 40, 40-58.

Callihan, David L. "Among the Bravest of the Brave: Maj. Andrew Jackson Grover of the 76th New York," *Gettysburg Magazine*, Issue 32 (January 2005), 49-51.

——. "Captain Michael Wiedrich's Company I, First New York Light Artillery at Gettysburg." *Gettysburg Magazine,* Issue 33 (July 2005), 82-88.

Campbell, Eric, "Caldwell Clears the Wheatfield." *Gettysburg Magazine* (July, 1990), Issue 3, 27-50.

Causby, Thomas E. "Storming the Stone Fence at Gettysburg." *Southern Historical Society Papers* (1901), vol. 29, 339-341.

Chamberlin, Thomas. *History of the One Hundred and Fiftieth Regiment Pennsylvania Volunteers*. Philadelphia, 1895.

Child, William A. *A History of the Fifth Regiment, New Hampshire Volunteers in the American Civil War*. Bristol, NH: R. W. Musgrove, Printer, 1893.

Christ, Elwood W. *The Struggle for the Bliss Farm at Gettysburg, July 2nd and 3rd, 1863: "Over a Wide, Hot, Crimson Plain,* Baltimore, MD: Butternut & Blue, 1993.

Clark, George. *A Glance Backward or Some Events in the Past History of My Life*. Houston: n.p., 1914.

Clark, Walter, ed. *Histories of the Several Regiments and Battalions from North Carolina in the Great War, 1861-'65*. 5 vols. Raleigh, E. M. Uzzell, printer, 1901.

Clements, George S. "The 25th Ohio at Gettysburg." *National Tribune,* August 6, 1891.

Cochran, Hon. L. L. "The Tenth Georgia Regiment at Gettysburg." *Atlanta Journal,* February 23, 1901.

Coco, Gregory A. ed. *From Ball's Bluff to Gettysburg... And Beyond: The Civil War Letters of Private Roland E. Bowen, 15th Massachusetts Infantry 1861-1864.* Gettysburg: Thomas Publications, 1994.

———. *A Concise Guide to the Artillery at Gettysburg.* Gettysburg, Pa.: Thomas Publication, 1998.

Coddington, Edwin B. *The Gettysburg Campaign: A Study in Command.* New York: Charles Scribner's and Sons, 1968.

Coey, James. "Sketches and Echoes—Cutler's Brigade." *National Tribune,* July 15, 1915.

Coles, R. T. *From Huntsville to Appomattox.* Knoxville, Tenn.: University of Tennessee Press, 1996.

Colestock, W. W. "The 16th Mich. At Little Round Top." *National Tribune,* March 26, 1914.

"Col. and Dr. R. W. Martin, of Virginia." *Confederate Veteran*, vol. 5 (1897), 70.

Collier, Calvin C. *'They'll Do To Tie To!'—The Story of the Third Regiment Arkansas Infantry, C.S.A.* Little Rock, Ark: Civil War Roundtable Associates, 1988.

Collins, George K. *Memories of the 149th Regiment, New York Volunteer Infantry.* Syracuse, NY: Author Published, 1891.

Conklin, George W. "The Long March to Stevens Run: The 134th New York Volunteer Infantry at Gettysburg." *Gettysburg Magazine,* Issue 21 (July, 1999), 45-56.

Conway, Catlett. "The Battle of Gettysburg." *Atlanta Journal,* December 7, 1901.

Cook, John. "Personal Reminisces of Gettysburg." *Kansas MOLLUS.*

Cook, Stephen G. and Charles E. Benton, eds. *The "Dutchess County Regiment" in the Civil War.* Danbury, CT: Danbury Medical Printing Company, 1907.

Cooksey, Paul Clark. "They Died As If On Dress Parade..." *Gettysburg Magzaine*, Issue 20, January, 1999, 89-112.

———. "The Heroes of Chancellorsville: Archer's Brigade at Gettysburg." *Gettysburg Magazine,* Issue 36, January 2007, 22-31.

Coxe, John. "The Battle of Gettysburg." *Confederate Veteran* (1913), vol. 21, 433-436.

Cowan, Andrew. "When Cowan's Battery Withstood Pickett's Splendid Charge." *New York Herald,* July 2, 1911.

Craft, David. *One Hundred and Forty-First Regiment Pennsylvania Volunteers.* Towanda, PA: Reporter-Journal Printing Company, 1885.

Cudsworth, William H. *History of the First Regiment Massachusetts Infantry.* Boston: Walker, Fuller and Company, 1866.

Culp, Edward C. *The 25th Ohio Veteran. Volunteer Infantry in the War for the Union.* Topeka: G. W. Crane & Co., 1885.

Curtis, O. B. *History of the Twenty-Fourth Michigan of the Iron Brigade, Known as the Detroit and Wayne County Regiment.* Detroit: Winn and Hammond, 1891.

Dalton, Cyndi. *Sixteenth Maine Regiment; The Blanket Brigade: The Soldier's Story of the 16th Maine Infantry in the War Between the States.* Union, ME: Union Pub Co, 1995.

Davis, Archie K. *The Boy Colonel: The Life and Times of Henry King Burgwyn, Jr.* Chapel Hill, NC: University of North Carolina Press, 1985.

Davis, Charles E. *Three Years in the Army: The Story of the Thirteenth Massachusetts Volunteers from July 16, 1861 to August 1, 1864.* Boston: Estes & Lownat, 1864.

Dawes, Rufus R. *Service with the Sixth Wisconsin Volunteers.* Marietta, OH: E. R. Alderman and Sons, 1890.

Denman, Jeff. "Profile in Courage: The 15th Alabama Infantry at Gettysburg." *Gettysburg Magazine,* Issue 36 (January 2007), 50-60.

Desjardin, Thomas. *Stand Firm Ye Boys From Maine.* Gettysburg: Thomas Publications, 1995.

de Trobriand, P. Regis. *Four Years With the Army of the Potomac.* Boston: Ticknor and Company, 1889.

Dickelman, J. L. "Gen. Carroll's Gibraulter Brigade at Gettysburg." *National Tribune,* December 10, 1908.

Dickert, August. *History of Kershaw's Brigade.* Newberry, S.C.: Elbert H. Hull Company, 1899.

Divine, John E. *Eighth Virginia Infantry.* Lynchburg: H. E. Howard, Inc., 1983.

Dodge, Theodore, A. "Left Wounded on the Field." *Putnam's Monthly Magazine,* 4 (1869), 317-326.

Doughtery, James J. *Stone's Brigade and the Fight for the McPherson Farm.* New York: Da Capo Publishing Co., 2001.

Downey, Fairfax. *The Guns at Gettysburg.* New York: David Mackay Co., 1958.

Downey, James W. *A Lethal Tour of Duty: A History of the 142nd Pennsylvania Volunteer Infantry, 1862-1865.* M. A. Thesis —Indiana University of Pennsylvania, 1995.

Dreese, Michael A. *Like Ripe Apples in a Storm: The 151st Pennsylvania Volunteers at Gettysburg.* Jefferson, N.C.: McFarland & Co, 2000.

Dunkelman, Mark H. and Michael J. Winey. *The Hardtack Regiment: An Illustrated History of the 154th Regiment, New York State Infantry Volunteers.* East Brunswick, NJ: Fairleigh Dickinson University Press, 1981.

Dunn, Craig L. *Iron Men, Iron Will.* Indianapolis, In.: Guild Press, 1995.

Durkin, Joseph T. *John Dooley, Confederate Soldier, His War Journal.* Washington: Georgetown University Press, 1945.

Early, Jubal A. *Autobiographical Sketch and Narrative of the War Between the States.* Philadelphia: J.B. Lippincott Company, 1912.

Ellis, Billy. *Tithes of Blood.* Nashville: Southern Heritage Press, 1997.

Elmore, Thomas L. "Attack and Counterattack." *Gettysburg Magazine* (July 1991), Issue 5, 128.

——. "Courage Against the Trenches." *Gettysburg Magazine* (July 1992), Issue 7, 83-96.

——. "The Florida Brigade at Gettysburg." *Gettysburg Magazine,* Issue 15 (1996), 45-59.

Evans, Clement A., ed. *Confederate Military History...*12 vols. Atlanta: Confederate Publishing Company, 1889.

Everson Guy R. and Edward W. Simpson. Jr. *Far, Far From Home.* New York: Oxford University Press, 1994.

Farinholt, B. L. "Battle of Gettysburg- Johnson's Island." *Confederate Veteran* (1897), vol. 5, 467-470.

Farley, Porter. "Reminiscences of Porter Farley, 140th New York Infantry." *Rochester Historical Society* (1944), vol. 22, 199-252.

———. "Bloody Round Top," *National Tribune,* May 3, 1883.

Felton, Silas. "The Iron Brigade Battery at Gettysburg,*"* in *Gettysburg Magazine*, Issue 11 (July 1994), 56-70.

———. "The Iron Brigade Battery," in *Giants in Their Tall Black Hats: Essays on the Iron Brigade,* Alan T. Nolan and Sharon Eggleston, ed. Bloomington: Ind.: Indiana University Press, 1998.

Finley, George W. "The Bloody Angle." *Buffalo Evening News*, May 29, 1894.

Floyd, Frederick C. *History of the Fortieth (Mozart) Regiment, New York Volunteers…,* Boston: F. H. Gilson Company, 1909.

Foote, Frank. "Marching in Clover." *Philadelphia Weekly Times,* October 8, 1881.

Ford, Andrew, *Story of the Fifteenth Regiment Massachusetts Volunteers Infantry…* Clinton, MA: Press of W. J. Coulter, 1898.

Fortin, ed., Maurice S. "Colonel Hilary A. Herbert's History of the Eighth Alabama Volunteer Regiment, CSA" *The Alabama Historical Quarterly* (1977), vol. 39, 5-321.

Frederick, Gilbert. *The Story of a Regiment—The Fifty-Seventh New York Volunteer Infantry in the War of the Rebellion.* Chicago: C. H. Morgan Company, 1895.

Freeman, Douglas S. *Lee's Lieutenants.* 3 vols. Scribners, 1942-1944.

———. *R. E. Lee.* 4 vols. New York: Scribners, 1935.

Frye, Dennis. *Second Virginia Infantry.* Lynchburg, Va.: H. E. Howard, Inc., 1984.

Fuger, Frederick. "Cushing's Battery at Gettysburg," *Journal of the Military Service Institution of the United States,* vol. 41 (1907): 405-10.

Fuller, Charles A. *Personal Recollections of the War of 1861…in the 61st New York Volunteer Infantry.* Sherburne, NY: News Job Printing House, 1906.

Fulton, W. F. *The War Reminiscences of William Frierson Fulton II, 5th Alabama Battalion, Archer's Brigade…* Gaithersville, MD: Butternut Press, 1986.

Gaff, Alan D. "'Here Was Made Out Our Last and Hopeless Stand." *Gettysburg Magazine* (January, 1990), Issue 2, 25-32.

Galway, Thomas F. *The Valiant Hours: Narrative of "Captain Brevet," An Irish-American in the Army of the Potomac.* Harrisburg: Stackpole, 1961.

Gates, Theodore B. *The "Ulster Guard" (20th N. Y. State Militia) and the War of the Rebellion,…* New York: B. H. Tyrrel, printer, 1879.

Gerald, Judge B. "The Battle of Gettysburg." *Waco Daily-Times Herald,* July 3, 1913.

Gerrish, Theordore. "The Twentieth Maine at Gettysburg." *Portland Advertiser,* March 13, 1882.

Gibney, John Michael. "A Shadow Passing," *Gettysburg Magazine*, Issue 6 (January, 1992).

Goldsborough, William W. "With Lee at Gettysburg." *Philadelphia Record,* July 8, 1900.

———. *The Maryland Line.* Port Washington, NY: Kennikat Press, 1972.

Gordon, John B. *Reminiscences of the Civil War.* New York: Charles Scribner's Sons, 1903.

Gottfried, Bradley M. *Brigades of Gettysburg* (New York: DaCapo, 2002).

———. *Roads to Gettysburg.* Shippensburg, PA: White Mane Publishing Company, 2002.

———. *Stopping Pickett—The History of the Philadelphia Brigade.* Shippensburg, PA: White Mane Publishing, 1999.

———. "The Story of Henry's Artillery Battalion at Gettysburg," *Gettysburg Magazine*, Issue 34 (January 2006), 30-40.

———. "Wright's Charge on July 2, 1863: Piercing the Union Line or Inflated Glory?" *Gettysburg Magazine* (July, 1997), Issue 17, 70-82.

Grace, C. D. "Rodes's Division at Gettysburg." *Confederate Veteran* (1897), vol. 5, 614-615.

Grant, George W. "The First Army Corps on the First Day at Gettysburg." Minnesota MOLLUS, vol. 5, 43-58.

Greene, George S. "The Breastworks at Culp's Hill." *Battles and Leaders of the Civil War,* vol. 3, 317.

Gregg, David McMurtrie. *The Second Cavalry Division of the Army of the Potomac in the Gettysburg Campaign.* Philadelphia: 1907.

Grunder, Charles S, and Brandon H. Beck, *The Second Battle of Winchester.* Lynchburg, Va.: H. E. Howard, Inc. 1989.

Gunn, Ralph W. *Twenty-fourth Virginia Infantry.* Lynchburg, VA: H. E. Howard, Inc., 1987.

Hadden, R. Lee. "The Deadly Embrace." *Gettysburg Magazine* (July 1991), Issue 5, 43-58.

Haines, Douglas Craig. "Jeb Stuart's Advance to Gettysburg," *Gettysburg* Magazine, Issue 29 (July 2004), 26-61.

Haines, Douglas Craig. "The Advance of Ewell's Corps June 18 Through June 29." *Gettysburg Magazine,* Issue 33 (July 2005), 7-26.

Hall, Jeffrey C. *The Stand of the U. S. Army at Gettysburg,* Bloomington, Ind.: Indiana U. Press, 2003.

Hamblen, Charles P. *Connecticut Yankees at Gettysburg.* Kent, OH: Kent State University Press, 1993.

Hamilton, J. G. de Roulhac, ed. *Shotwell Papers.* Raleigh N.C.: North Carolina Historical Commission, 1929-31.

Harries, William H. "The Iron Brigade in the First Day's Battle of Gettysburg," in *Minnesota MOLLUS,* vol. 4, 335-350.

Harris, James S. *Historical Sketches: Seventh Regiment, North Carolina Troops.* Ann Arbor, MI: University Microfilms, 1972.

Harris, Loyd G. "With the Iron Brigade Guard at Gettysburg, *Gettysburg Magazine* Issue 1 (July 1989), 29-34.

Harrison, Kathleen R. "Our Principal Loss Was in this Place." *Gettysburg Magazine* Issue 1 (July 1989), 45-69.

Harrison, Kathy G. and John W. Busey. *Nothing But Glory.* Gettysburg, PA: Thomas Publications, 1993.

Hartwig, Scott. "The Defense of McPherson's Ridge." *Gettysburg Magazine* Issue 1 (July 1989), 15-24.

——. "The 11th Army Corps on July 1, 1863. *Gettysburg Magazine* Issue 1 (July 1989), 33-55.

Haskell, Frank A. *The Battle of Gettysburg.* Boston: Houghton Mifflin Company, 1969.

Haynes, Martin A. *History of the Second New Hampshire Regiment: Its Camps, Marches, and Battles.* Manchester, N.H.: Charles F. Livingston Printer, 1865.

Hazen, Samuel R. Fighting the Good Fight." *National Tribune,* September 13, 1894.

Herdegen Lance J. and William J.K. Beaudot. *In the Bloody Railroad Cut.* Dayton, OH: Morningside House, 1990.

Hess, Earl. *Pickett's Charge* (Chapel Hill, N.C.: University of North Carolina Press, 2002.

History of the 121st Pennsylvania Infantry Regiment, (1862-1865). Philadelphia: Press of Burk & McFetridge Company, 1893.

Hofe, Michael W. *That There Be No Stain Upon My Stones: Lieutenant Colonel William L. Mcleod, 38th Georgia Regiment, 1842-1863.* Gettysburg: Thomas Publications, 1995.

Hoke, Jacob. *The Great Invasion.* New York: Thomas Yoseloff, 1959.

Holcombe, R. I. *History of the First Regiment Minnesota Volunteer Infantry, 1861-1864.* Gaithersburg, MD: VanSickle, 1987.

Hotchkiss, Jedediah. *Make Me a Map of the Valley.* Dallas, Tex: Southern Methodist University Press, 1988.

Houghton, William R. *Two Boys in the Civil War and After.* Montgomery, AL: Paragon Press, 1912.

Hudson, Travis, "Soldier Boys in Gray: A History of the 59th Georgia Infantry Regiment." *Atlanta Historical Society Journal* (Spring 1979).

Hufham, J. D., Jr., "Gettysburg." *The Wake Forest Student* (1897), vol. 16, 452-454.

Hussey, George A. *History of the Ninth Regiment N.Y.S.M. Eighty-third N.Y. Volunteer).* New York: J.S. Ogilvie, 1889.

Ide, Horace K. "The First Vermont Cavalry in the Gettysburg Campaign." *Gettysburg Magazine,* Issue 14 (January 1996).

Imboden, John D. "The Confederate Retreat From Gettysburg," *Battles and Leaders of the Civil War* (New York: Thomas Yoseloff, Inc., 1956), vol. 3, 420-429.

Imhof, John D. *Gettysburg, Day Two—A Study in Maps.* Baltimore, MD: Butternut and Blue, 1999.

Iobst, Robert W. and Louis H. Manarin. *The Bloody Sixth: The Sixth North Carolina Regiment, Confederate States of America.* Durham, NC: Christian Printing Company, 1965.

Jackson J. "Letter." *Montgomery Daily Mail,* July 26, 1863.

Jones, Jesse H. "The Breastworks at Culp's Hill." *Battles and Leaders of the Civil War,* vol. 3, 316.

Jones, Paul. *The Irish Brigade.* Washington: R. B. Luce, 1969.

Jones, Terry L. *Lee's Tigers.* Baton Rouge, LA: Louisiana State University Press, 1987.

Johnston, David E. *Four Years a Soldier.* Princeton, WV:n.p., 1887.

Jordan, William B. *Red Diamond Regiment: The 17th Maine Infantry, 1862-1865.* Shippensburg, Pa.: White Mane Publishing. Co. 1996.

Jordan, William C. *Incidents During the Civil War.* Montgomery, AL: The Paragon Press, 1909.

Jorgenson, Jay. "Anderson Attacks the Wheatfield," *Gettysburg Magazine* Issue 14 (January 1996), 64-76.

——. "Holding the Right: The 137th New York Regiment at Gettysburg." *Gettysburg Magazine* Issue 15 (July, 1996), 60-67.

——. *Gettysburg's Bloody Wheatfield* (Shippensburg, Pa.: White Mane Publishing Company, 2002).

Judson, Amos M. *History of the Eighty-Third Regiment, Pennsylvania Volunteers.* Erie, PA: B. F. H. Lynn, 1865.

Keppler, Thomas. *History of the Three Months and Three Years' Service from April 16, 1861, to June, 1864, of the Fourth Regiment Ohio Volunteer Infantry in the War for the Union.* Cleveland, OH: Leader Printing Company, 1886.

Keifer, William R. *History of the One Hundred and Fifty-Third Regiment Pennsylvania Volunteer Infantry.* Easton, PA: Press of the Chemical Publishing Company, 1909.

Kershaw, J. B. "Kershaw's Brigade at Gettysburg." *Battles and Leaders of the Civil War,* vol. 3, 331-338.

Kimball, George. "Iverson's Brigade." *National Tribune,* October 1, 1885.

Krick, Robert. K. Fortieth Virginia *Infantry.* Lynchburg, VA: H. E. Howard, Company, 1985.

Krick, Robert K. "Failures of Brigade Leadership," Gary W. Gallagher, ed., *The First Day at Gettysburg.* Kent, OH: Kent State University Press, 1992.

——. "Three Confederate Disasters on Oak Ridge." *The First Day at Gettysburg.* Gary Gallagher, ed., Canton, OH: Kent State University Press, 1992.

Krolick, Marshall D. "Forgotten Field: The Cavalry Battle East of Gettysburg on July 3, 1863." *Gettysburg Magazine,* Issue 4 (January 1991), 75-88.

Krumwiede, John F. "A July Afternoon on McPherson's Ridge." *Gettysburg Magazine,* Issue 21 (July, 1999), 21-44.

Ladd, David L. and Audrey J. Ladd, *The Bachelder Papers.* 3 volumes. Dayton, OH: Morningside Press, 1994.

Lader, Paul J. "The 7th New Jersey in the Gettysburg Campaign." *Gettysburg Magazine* Issue 16 (January, 1997), 46-67.

Laine, J. Gary and Penny, Morris M. *Struggle for the Round Tops.* Shippensburg, Pa: White Mane Publishing Company, 1999.

Lang, David. "Letter To General Edward Perry, 19 July 1863." *Southern Historical Society Papers* (1899), vol. 27, 195-196.

Lash, Gary G. "The Philadelphia Brigade at Gettysburg." *The Gettysburg Magazine,* Issue 7 (July 1992), 97-113.

——. "Brig. Gen. Henry Baxter's Brigade at Gettysburg, July 1." *Gettysburg Magazine,* Issue 10 (January, 1994), 6-27.

——. "'A Pathetic Story'—The 141st Pennsylvania (Graham's Brigade) at Gettysburg." *Gettysburg Magazine* (January, 1996), Issue 14, 77-101.

Lee, Alfred. "Reminiscences of the Gettysburg Battle." *Lippincott's Magazine of Popular Literature and Science,* (1883), vol. 6, 54-55.

Leftwich, George J. "The Carreer [sic] of a Veteran." *The Aberdeen Examiner,* August 22, 1913.

LeGear, Clara E. "The Hotchkiss Collection of Confederate Maps," *Library of Congress Quarterly Journal of Current Acquisitions vol.* 6 (November 1948): 19.

Leon, Louis. *Diary of a Tar Heel.* Charlotte, NC: Stone Publishing Company, 1913.

Lochren, William. "The First Minnesota at Gettysburg." Minnesota MOLLUS, vol. 3, 41-56.

Loehr, Charles T. *War History of the Old First Virginia Infantry Regiment, Army of Northern Virginia.* Richmond, Va: William Ellis Jones, Printer, 1884.

——. "The Famous Pickett Charge." *Richmond Times-Dispatch,* October 16, 1904.

Longacre, Edward G. *The Cavalry at Gettysburg* Lincoln, Nebr.: Bison Books, 1993.

Longstreet, James. *From Manassas to Appomattox.* Philadelphia, J. B. Lippincott, 1903.

Loring, William E. "Gettysburg." *National Tribune,* July 9, 1885.

Lynn, J. R. " What the 29th Ohio Did During the Three Days' Fighting." *National Tribune,* October 7, 1897.

McCall, John T. "What the Tennesseans Did at Gettysburg." *The Louisville Journal,* 1902.

McClellan, Bailey G. *Civil War History of Company D, 10th Alabama Regiment.* Anniston Station, AL: n.p., 1901.

McDaid, William K. *Four Years of Arduous Service.* Ph.D. Dissertation, Michigan State U., 1987.

McDermott, Anthony. *A Brief History of the 69th Regiment Pennsylvania Veteran Volunteers…*Ann Arbor, MI: University Microfilms, 1968.

McFarland, Baxter. "The Eleventh Mississippi at Gettysburg." *Mississippi Historical Society* (1918), vol. 2, 549-568.

McKay, Charles W. "Three Years or During the War With the Crescent and Star." *National Tribune Scrap Book,* Washington, D.C., n.d.

McKim, Randolph. "Steuart's Brigade at the Battle of Gettysburg." *Southern Historical Society Papers* (1878), vol. 5, 291-300.

McLaws, Lafayette. "Gettysburg." *Southern Historical Society Papers* (1879), vol. 7, 64-90.

McLean, James L. *Cutler's Brigade at Gettysburg.* Baltimore, MD: Butternut and Blue, 1994.

McNeily, J. S. "Barksdale's Mississippi Brigade at Gettysburg." *Publications of the Mississippi Historical Society* (1914), vol. 14, 231-265.

Macnamara, Daniel G. *The History of the Ninth Regiment, Massachusetts Volunteer Infantry, Second Brigade, First Division, Fifth Army Corps, Army of the Potomac, June, 1861-June, 1864.* Boston: E. B. Stillings, 1899.

Mahood, Wayne. *Written in Blood.* Shippensburg, PA: White Mane Publishing Company, 1997.

Maier, Larry *Gateway to Gettysburg.* Shippensburg, Pa.: Burd Street Press, 2002.

Maine Gettysburg Commission, *Maine at Gettysburg: Report of the Maine Commissioners Prepared by the Executive Committee.* Portland, ME: The Lakeside Press, 1898.

Marbaker, Thomas B. *History of the Eleventh New Jersey Volunteers.* Hightstown, NJ: Longstreet House, 1990.

Marsh, A. T. "North Carolina Troops at Gettysburg." *Confederate Veteran* (1908), vol. 16, 516-517.

Martin, A. P. "Little Round Top," *Gettysburg Compiler,* October 24, 1899.

Martin, David G. *Gettysburg—July 1.* Conshohocken, PA: Combined Books, 1996.

———. *Carl Bornemann's Regiment: the Forty-first New York Infantry (DeKalb Regt.) in the Civil War.* Hightstown, NJ: Longstreet House, 1987.

Martin, Rawley W. and John H. Smith, "Battle of Gettysburg and Charge of Pickett's Division." *Southern Historical Society Papers* (1904), vol. 32, 183-195.

Matthews, *Richard E. The 149th Pennsylvania Volunteer Infantry Unit in the Civil War.* Jefferson, N.C.: McFarland & Company, 1994.

Mattocks, Charles. *Unspoiled Heart, The Journal of Charles Mattocks of the 17th Maine.* Knoxville, TN: U. of Tennessee Press, 1994.

Mayo, Joseph. "Pickett's Charge at Gettysburg." *Richmond Times-Dispatch,* May 6, 1906.

Meinhard, Robert W. "The First Minnesota at Gettysburg." *Gettysburg Magazine* Issue 5 (July, 1991), 79-88.

Michigan at Gettysburg, July 1st, 2d and 3rd, 1863… Detroit, MI: Winn and Hammond, 1889.

Miers, Earl Schenck, and Brown, Richard A., eds. *Gettysburg.* New Brunswick, N.J.: Rutgers University Press, 1948.

Miller, J. Michael. "Perrin's Brigade on July 1, 1863." *Gettysburg Magazine,* Issue 13 (July 1995), 22-32.

Miller, William E. "The Cavalry Battle Near Gettysburg," *Battles and Leaders of the Civil War,* vol. 3, 397-405.

Mills, George H. *History of the 16th North Carolina Regiment (originally 6th N.C. Regiment) in the Civil War.* Hamilton, NY: Edmonston Pub., 1992.

Minnigh, H. N. *History of Company K, 1st (Inft,) Penn'a Reserves.* Duncansville, PA: Home Print Publisher, 1891.

Moon, W. H. "Beginning the Battle at Gettysburg." *Confederate Veteran* (1925), vol. 33, 449-450.

Moran, Frank E. "A Fire Zouave—Memoirs of a Member of the Excelsior Brigade." *National Tribune,* November 6, 1890.

———. "About Gettysburg." *National Tribune,* November 6, 1890.

Morhous, Henry C. *Reminiscences of the 123rd Regiment, New York State Volunteers.* Greenwich, NY: People's Journal Book and Job Office, 1879.

Morse, F. W. *Personal Experiences in the War of the Rebellion, From December, 1862, to July, 1865*. Albany, NY: Munsell Printer, 1866.

Muffly, Joseph W. ed. *The Story of Our Regiment: A History of the 148th Pennsylvania Volunteers*. Des Moines, IA: Kenyon Printing and Manufacturing Company, 1904.

Murphy Terrence V. *Tenth Virginia Infantry*. Lynchburg, VA: H. E. Howard, 1989.

Murray, Alton J. *South Georgia Rebels: The True Wartime Experiences Of The 26th Regiment, Georgia Volunteer Infantry, Lawton-Gordon-Evans Brigade, Confederate States Army, 1861-1865*. St. Marys, GA: By Author, 1976.

Murray, Jennifer M. "'The General Plan Was Unchanged': General Lee's Plan For 'Pickett's Charge,' July 3, 1863." *Gettysburg Magazine,* Issue 33 (July 2005), 89-97.

Murray, R. L. *Redemption of the Harper's Ferry Cowards: The Story of the 111th and 126th New York State Volunteer Regiments at Gettysburg*. Wolcott, N.Y., 1994.

Musselman, Homer D. *Forty-seventh Virginia Infantry*. Lynchburg, VA: H.E. Howard, Company, 1991.

Nash, Eugene A. *A History of the 44th New York Volunteer Infantry*. Chicago: R. R. Donnelly & Sons Company, 1911.

Nesbitt, Mark. *35 Days to Gettysburg*. Harrisburg: Stackpole Books, 1992.

Neu, Jonathan. "'But Few of This Force Escaped Us': An Account of Doles' Brigade and its Actions on July 1, 1863." *Gettysburg Magazine,* Issue 36 (January 2007), 39-49.

Nevins, Allen, ed. *A Diary of Battle: The Personal Journal of Colonel Charles S. Wainwright*. New York: Harcourt, Brace, and World, 1962.

New York Monuments Commission for the Battlefields of Gettysburg and Chattanooga—Final Report on the Battlefield of Gettysburg. Albany, NY: J. B. Lyon Company Printers, 1900.

Nichols, G. W. *A Soldier's Story of His Regiment*. Jesup, Ga.: privately published, 1898.

Norris, S. R. "Ohio at Gettysburg." *National Tribune,* June 9, 1887.

Norton, Oliver W. *The Attack and Defense of Little Round Top*. New York: Neale Publishing Company, 1913.

Nye, Wilbur Sturtevant. *Here Come the Rebels!* Baton Rouge, La.: Louisiana State University Press, 1965.

Oates, William C. "Gettysburg—The Battle on the Right." *Southern Historical Society Papers* (1878), vol. 6, 72-182.

——. *The War Between the Union and Confederacy and its Lost Opportunites*. New York: Neale Publishing Co., 1905.

O'Brien, Kevin E. "A Perfect Roar of Musketry: Candy's Brigade in the Fight for Culp's Hill." *Gettysburg Magazine* Issue 9 (July, 1993), 81-97.

——. "'Give Them Another Volley, Boys:' Biddle's Brigade Defends the Union Left on July 1, 1863, in *Gettysburg Magazine* Issue 19.

——. "'Glory enough for All': Lt. William Brooke-Rawle and the 3rd Pennsylvania Cavalry at Gettysburg," *Gettysburg* Magazine, Issue 13 (July 1995), 89-107.

——. "'Hold Them with the Bayonet': de Trobriand's Brigade Defends the Wheatfield." *Gettysburg Magazine* , Issue 21 (July, 1999), 74-87.

——. "To Unflinchingly Face Danger and Death: Carr's Brigade Defends Emmitsburg Road." *Gettysburg Magazine* Issue 12 (January, 1995), 7-23.

——. "Valley of the Shadow of Death." *Gettysburg Magazine,* Issue 7 (July, 1992), 41-50.

Olds, Fred A. "A Brave Carolinian Who Fell at Gettysburg." *Southern Historical Society Papers* (1908), vol. 36, 245-247.

O'Flaherty, Patrick. *History of the 69th Regiment in the Irish Brigade, 1861-1865.* New York: n.p. 1986.

Osborn, S. A. "The Battle of Gettysburg as I Remember It. " *Shenango Valley News* (Greenville, PA), April 2, 1915.

Osborn, Thomas W. *The Eleventh Corps Artillery at Gettysburg.* Herb S. Crumb, etc., Hamilton, N.Y.: Edmonston Publishing, 1991.

Osborne, Seward R. *Holding the Left at Gettysburg : the 20th New York State Militia on July 1, 1863.* Hightstown, NJ: Longstreet House, 1990.

Palmer, Edwin F. *The Second Brigade or Camp Life.* Montpelier, VT: Printed by E.P. Walton, 1864.

Parker, Francis J. *The Story of the Thirty-Second Massachusetts Infantry.* Boston: C.W. Calkins & Company, 1880.

Parker, John L. *Henry Wilson's Regiment: History of the Twenty-second Regiment, Massachusetts Infantry.* Boston: Press of Rand Avery Company, 1887.

Parsons, Henry C. "Farnsworth's Charge and Death, *Battles and Leaders of the Civil War*, vol. 3, 393-396.

Pattison, Everett W. "Some Reminiscences of Army Life." *Massachusetts MOLLUS,* 262-263.

Pennsylvania at Gettysburg—Ceremonies at the Dedication of Monuments Erected by the Commonwealth of Pennsylvania. Harrisburg: Wm. Stanley Ray State Printer, 1904.

Perrin, Abner. "A Little More Light on Gettysburg." *Mississippi Valley Historical Review* (1938), vol. 24, 519-525.

Perry, William F. "The Devil's Den." *Confederate Veteran* (1901), vol. 9, 161- 163.

Peters, Winfield. "A Maryland Warrior and Hero." *Southern Historical Society Papers* (1901), vol. 29, 248.

Petruzzi, J. David. "Annihilation of a Regiment: The Battle of Fairfield, PA, July 3, 1863." *America's Civil War* (July 2007).

Pettit, Ira S. *Diary of a Dead Man.* New York: Eastern Acorn Press, 1976.

Pfanz, Harry W. *Gettysburg: The Second Day.* Chapel Hill, NC: The University of North Carolina Press, 1987.

——. *Gettysburg- Culp's Hill and Cemetery Hill.* Chapel Hill, NC: The University of North Carolina Press, 1993.

——. *Gettysburg—The First Day.* Chapel Hill, NC: University of North Carolina Press, 2001.

Poindexter, James E. "General Armistead's Portrait Presented." *Southern Historical Society Papers* (1909), vol. 37, 146.

Polley, Joseph B. *Hood's Texas Brigade.* New York: Neale Publishing Company, 1910.

Powell, William H. *The Fifth Army Corps…* New York: G.P. Putnam's Sons, 1896.

Priest, John M. *John T. McMahon's Diary of the 136th New* York. Shippensburg, Pa.: White Mane Pub. Co., 1993.

Pula, James S. *For Liberty and Justice—The Life and Times of Wladimir Krzyzanowski.* Chicago: Polish American Congress Charitable Foundation, 1978.

Pula, James S. *The Sigel Regiment: A History of the Twenty-sixth Wisconsin Volunteer Infantry, 1862-1865*. Campbell, CA: Savas, 1998.

Pullen, John J. "Effects of Marksmanship." *Gettysburg Magazine* (January, 1990), Issue 2, 55-60.

——. *The Twentieth Maine: A Volunteer Regiment in the Civil War*. Philadelphia: Lippincott, 1957.

Purcell, Hugh D. "The Nineteenth Massachusetts Regiment at Gettysburg." *Essex Institute Historical Collections*, (October, 1963), 277-288.

Quint, Alonzo, H. *The Record of the Second Massachusetts Infantry, 1861-1865*. Boston: James P. Walker, 1867.

Rankin, Thomas. *Twenty-Third Virginia*. Lynchburg, VA: H.E. Howard, Inc., 1985.

Rawlings, Watha. *War Stories, Being the Thrilling Experiences and Adventures of Captain Watha Rawlings During the War of 1861-1865*. McCauley, TX: n.p., 1909.

Report of the Joint Committee to Mark the Positions Occupied by the 1st and 2nd Delaware at the Battle of Gettysburg. Dover, DE: 1887.

Report of the State of Maryland Gettysburg Monument Commission. Baltimore, MD: William K. Boyle and Son, 1891.

Reese, Timothy J. *Sykes's Regular Infantry Division, 1861-1864: A History of Regular United States Infantry Operations in the Civil War's Eastern Theater*. Jefferson, N.C.: McFarland, 1990.

Re-union of the 28th & 147th Regiments, Pennsylvania Volunteers, Philadelphia, Nov. 24th, 1871. Philadelphia: Pawson & Nicholson, 1872.

Rhodes, John H. *The History of Battery B, First Regiment, Rhode Island Artillery*. Providence, RI: Snow and Farnham, Printers, 1914.

Rice, Edmund. "Repelling Lee's Last Blow at Gettysburg." *Battles and Leaders of the Civil War*, vol. 3, 387-390.

Riley, Franklin L. *Grandfather's Journal...* Dayton, OH: Morningside, 1988.

Robbins, Richard. "The Regular Troops at Gettysburg." *Philadelphia Weekly Times*, January 4, 1879.

Robertson, James, I. *The Fourth Virginia Infantry*. Lynchburg, VA: H. E. Howard, Inc., 1982.

Rollins, C. A. "A Private's Story." The *Lexington Gazette and Citizen*. July 26, 1888.

Rollins, Richard. ed. *Pickett's Charge—Eyewitness Accounts*. Redondo Beach, CA: Rank and File Publications, 1994.

Rosenblatt, Emil and Ruth. *Hard Marching Every Day*. Lawrence, KS: University Press of Kansas, 1992.

Ryder, John J. *Reminiscences of Three Years' Service in The Civil War By A Cape Cod Boy*. New Bedford, MA: Reynolds Printing, 1928.

Sale, J. Irving. "Gettysburg." *Philadelphia Press*, July 4, 1887.

Sanderson, W. H. "Sykes's Regulars." *National Tribune*, April 2, 1891.

Sauers, Richard A. "The Sixteenth Maine Volunteer Infantry at Gettysburg." *Gettysburg Magazine*, Issue 13 (July, 1995), 33-42.

——. *Fighting Them Over—How the Veterans Remembered Gettysburg in the Pages of the National Tribune*. Baltimore, MD: Butternut and Blue, 1998.

Sawyer, Franklin. *A Military History of the 8th Regiment, Ohio Volunteers Infantry: Its Battles, Marches, an Army Movements.* Cleveland, OH: Leader Printing Company, 1881.

Schildt, John W. *Roads from Gettysburg.* Shippensburg, Pa: Burd Street Press, 2000.

Schurz, Carl. *Reminiscences of Carl Schurz.* 3 vol. New York: McClure, 1906.

Schultz, David L. *Double Canister at Ten Yards.* Redondo Beach, Ca.: Rank and File Publications, 1995.

——, and Rollins, Richard. "The Most Accurate Fire Ever Witnessed: Federal Horse Artillery in the Pennsylvania Campaign. *Gettysburg Magazine*, Issue 33 (July, 2005), 44-81.

——, and Wieck, David F. *Battle Between the Farm Lanes: Hancock Saves the Union Center, Gettysburg, July 2, 1863.* Ironclad, 2006.

Searles, J. N. "The First Minnesota Volunteer Infantry." Minnesota *MOLLUS,* vol. 2, 80-113.

Sheldon, Winthrop D. *The "Twenty-Seventh," A Regimental History.* New Haven CT: Morris & Benham, 1866.

Shevchuk, Paul M. "The 1st Texas Infantry and the Repulse of Farnsworth's Charge." *Gettysburg Magazine*, Issue 2 (January 1990), 85.

Shotwell, Randolph A. "Virginia and North Carolina in the Battle of Gettysburg." *Our Living and Our Dead* (1876), vol. 4, 80-97.

Shumate, W. T. "With Kershaw at Gettysburg." *Philadelphia Weekly Times."* May 6, 1882.

Silliken. Ruth L. *The Rebel Yell & Yankee Hurrah.* Camden, Maine: Down East Books, 1985.

Silver, James W. ed. *A Life for the Confederacy.* Wilmington, N.C.: Broadfoot Publishing Company, 1991.

Simmers, William. *The Volunteers' Manual, or Ten Months With the One Hundred and Fifty-third Pennsylvania Volunteers.* Easton, PA: D. H. Neiman, 1863.

Simons, Ezra D. *A Regimental History: The One Hundred and Twenty-fifth New York State Volunteers.* New York: E.D. Simons, 1888.

Small, A. R. *The Sixteenth Maine Regiment in the War of the Rebellion 1861-1865.* Portland, ME: Thurston & Co., 1886.

Small, Harold A. *The Road to Richmond- The Civil War Memoirs of Major Abner R. Small of the 16th Maine.* Berkley, CA: University of California Press, 1959.

Smith, A.P. The Seventh-Sixth Regiment, New York Volunteers. Cortland, NY: Truair, Smith and Miles, Printers 1867.

Smith, Gerald J. *One of the Most Daring of Men.* Murfreesboro, TN: Southern Heritage Press, 1997.

Smith, Jacob. *Camps and Campaigns of the 107th Regiment Ohio Volunteer Infantry.* n.p., n.d.

Smith, James E. *A Famous Battery and Its Campaigns, 1861-1864.* Washington: W. H. Lowdermilk and Co., 1892.

Smith, John D. *The History of the Nineteenth Regiment of Maine Volunteer Infantry, 1862-1865.* Minneapolis, MN: Great Western Printing Company, 1909.

Smith, John L. *History of the 118th Pennsylvania Volunteers,Corn Exchange Regiment.* Philadelphia: J. L. Smith, Publisher, 1909.

Smith, John. "Account." *Southern Historical Society Papers* (1904), vol. 32, 193.

Smith, R. Penn. "The Battle of Gettysburg- The Part Taken by the Philadelphia Brigade in the Battle." *Gettysburg Compiler*, June 7, 1887.

Smith, Robert G. *A Brief Account of the Services Rendered by the Second Regiment Delaware Volunteers in the War of the Rebellion*. Wilmington, DE: Historical Society of Delaware, 1909.

Spear, Ellis. *The Civil War Recollections of General Ellis Spear*. Orona, Me.: University of Maine Press, 1997.

Stearns, Austin *Three Years with Company K*. Cranbury NJ: Fairleigh Dickinson University Press, 1976.

Stewart, George R. *Pickett's Charge*. Boston, MA: Houghton Mifflin Company, 1959.

Stewart, James. "Battery B, Fourth United States Artillery at Gettysburg," Ohio MOLLUS, vol. 4, 185.

Stewart, Robert L. *History of the One Hundred and Fortieth Regiment, Pennsylvania Volunteers*. Privately printed: Regimental Association, 1912.

Storch, Marc and Beth Storch. "What a Deadly Trap We Were In." *Gettysburg Magazine*, Issue 6 (January 1992), 13-28.

——. "Unpublished Gettysburg Reports by the 2nd and 7th Wisconsin Infantry Regimental Officers." *Gettysburg Magazine*, Issue 17 (July 1997), 20-25.

Storrs, John. *The Twentieth Connecticut*. Ansonia, CT: Press of the Naugatuck Valley Sentinel, 1886.

Sturtevant, Ralph O. *Pictorial History of the Thirteenth Vermont Volunteers, War of 1861-1865*. n.p., n.p., 1910.

Sullivan, James P. "The Iron Brigade at Gettysburg." *Milwaukee Sunday Telegraph*, December 20, 1884.

——. "The Sixth Wisconsin At Gettysburg," *Milwaukee Sunday Telegraph*, June, 21, 1885.

Survivors of the Seventy-second Regiment of Pennsylvania Volunteers, Plaintiffs. Vs. Gettysburg Battlefield Memorial Association...in Supreme Court of Pennsylvania, Middle District, May Term, 1891.

Swisher, James K. "Brig. Gen. George Doles and His Georgia Brigade on July 1, 1863, Gettysburg, Pennsylvania," *Gettysburg Magazine,* Issue 27 (July 2002), 50.

Sword, Wiley. "Defending the Codori House and Cemetary Ridge: Two Swords with Harrow's Brigade.

Taylor, Eugene G. *Gouveneur Kemble Warren: The Life and Letters of an American Soldier*. Boston, Houghton-Mifflin, 1932.

Taylor, Michael W. "North Carolina in the Pickett-Pettigrew- Trimble Charge at Gettysburg." *Gettysburg Magazine,* Issue 8 (January 1993), 67-94.

Taylor, Michael W. "Ramseur's Brigade in the Gettysburg Campaign: A Newly Discovered Account by Captain James I. Harris, Col. I, 30th Regt. N.C.T." *Gettysburg Magazine,* Issue 17 (July 1997), 26-40.

Teague, "Chaplain Chuck." "Brutal Clash at Blocher's Knoll." *Gettysburg Magazine,* Issue 32 (January 2005), 52-70.

Tervis, C. V. *The History of the Fighting Fourteenth: Published in Commemoration of the Fiftieth Anniversary of the Muster of the Regiment into the United States Service*. Brooklyn: Brooklyn Eagle Press, 1911.

Thomas, George. "The Confederate Monument at Gettysburg." *Southern Historical Society Papers* (1886), vol. 14, 439-446.

Thomas, Henry W. *History of the Doles-Cook Brigade, Army of Northern Virginia.* Atlanta, GA: Franklin Publishing Co., 1903.

Thompkins, Daniel A. *Company K, Fourteenth South Carolina Volunteers.* Charlotte, NC: Observer Printing and Publishing Company, 1897.

Tomasak, Pete. "An Encounter with Battery Hell." *Gettysburg Magazine*, Issue 12 (January 1995), 36-37.

Toombs, Samuel. *New Jersey Troops in the Gettysburg Campaign.* Orange, N.J.: Evening Mail Publishing House, 1888.

Trout, Robert J. *Galloping Thunder.* Mechanicsburg, Pa.: Stackpole Books, 2002.

Tucker, A. W. "Orange Blossoms—Services of the 124th New York at Gettysburg." *National Tribune,* January 21, 1886.

Turney, J. B. "The First Tennessee at Gettysburg." *Confederate Veteran* (1900), vol. 8, 535-537.

Underwood, Adin B.. *Three Years' Service of the Thirty-Third Massachusetts Infantry Regiment.* Boston: A. Williams, 1881.

Underwood,George. *History of the Twenty-Sixth Regiment of the North Carolina Troops in the Great War,1861-'65.* Goldsboro, NC: Nash Brothers, Book and Job Printers, 1901.

Vanderslice, John M. *Gettysburg Then and Now.* New York: G. W. Dillingham Company, 1899.

VanSantvood, Cornelius. *The One Hundred and Twentieth N.Y.S. Volunteers., A Narrative of its Services in the War for the Union.* Rondout, NY: Regimental Association & Kingston Freeman Press, 1894.

Vautier, John D. "At Gettysburg." *Philadelphia Weekly Press,* November 10, 1886.

Venner, William T. *Hoosier's Honor: The Iron Brigade's 19th Indiana Regiment.* Shippensburg: PA: Burd Street Press, 1998.

Waitt, Ernest L. *History of the Nineteenth Regiment Massachusetts Volunteer Infantry.* Salem, MA: Salem Press Company, 1906.

Ward, Joseph. *History of the One Hundred and Sixth Pennsylvania Volunteers, 2d Brigade, 2d Division, 2d Corps, 1861-1865.* Philadelphia: Grant, Faires & Rodgers, 1883.

Ward, W. C. "Incidents and Personal Experiences on the Battlefield at Gettysburg." *Confederate Veteran* (1900), vol. 8, 345-349.

Warren, Horatio N. *Two Reunions of the 142nd Regiment, Pennsylvania Volunteers.* Buffalo: The Courier Company, 1890.

Warren, Horatio N. *The Declaration of Independence and War History. Bull Run to Appomattox,.* Buffalo: The Courier Company, 1894.

Wehrum, Charles. "The Adjutant of the 12th Massachusetts Replies to the Captain of the 97th N.Y." *National Tribune,* December 10, 1885.

Wert, Jeffry D. *Gettysburg, Day Three.* New York: Simon and Shuster, 2001.

West, John C. *A Texan in Search of a Fight.* Waco, TX: Press of J. S. Hill and Company, 1901.

Westbrook, C.D. "The 120th N.Y.'s Firm Stand on the Second Day at Gettysburg," *National Tribune,* September 20, 1900.

Weygant, Charles H. *History of the One Hundred and Twenty-Fourth Regiment, N.Y.S.V.* Newburgh, N.Y.: Journal Printing House, 1877.

Wheeler, Cornelius. "Reminiscences of the Battle of Gettysburg." Wisconsin *MOLLUS*, vol. 2, 205-220.

White, W. T. "First Texas Regiment at Gettysburg," *Confederate Veteran,* vol. XXX (1922), 185;

Wilcox, C. M. "Letter." *Southern Historical Society Papers* (1877), vol. 4, 111-117.

Williams, Alpheus. *From the Cannon's Mouth.* Detroit, MI: Wayne State University Press, 1959.

Willson, Arabella M. *Disaster, Struggle, Triumph: The Adventures of 1000 "Boys in Blue," from August, 1862, to June,1865.* Albany: Argus Company Printers, 1870.

Winschel, Terrence J. "Heavy Was Their Loss: Joe Davis's Brigade at Gettysburg, Part 1." *Gettysburg Magazine*, Issue 2 (January 1990), 5-14.

———. "Heavy was Their Loss: Joe Davis' Brigade at Gettysburg, Part II." *Gettysburg Magazine,* Issue 3 (July 1990), 77-86.

———. Posey's Brigade at Gettysburg. Part II." *Gettysburg Magazine* , Issue 5 (July 1991), 89-102.

Wittenberg, Eric J. *Gettysburg's Forgotten Cavalry Actions.* Gettysburg: Thomas Publications, 1998.

———. "Merritt's Regulars on South Cavalry Field: Oh, What Could Have Been." *Gettysburg Magazine*, Issue 16 (January 1997), 111-123.

———, and Petruzzi, J. David. *Plenty of Blame to Go Around: Jeb Stuart's Controversial Ride to Gettysburg.* New York, Savas Beatie, 2006.

"Wofford's Georgia Brigade." *Richmond Daily Enquirer,* August 5, 1863.

Woodward, Evan M. *Our Campaigns—The Second Regiment, Pennsylvania Reserve Volunteers.* Philadelphia: J. E. Potter, 1865.

Wyckoff, Mac, *A History of the Third South Carolina Infantry, 1861-1865.* Fredericksburg, VA: Sergeant Kirkland's Museum and Historical Society, 1995.

Young, William A. *Fifty-sixth Virginia Infantry.* Lynchburg: H. E. Howard, Inc., 1990.

Zollinger, William, Lamar Hollyday, and D.R. Howard, "General George H. Steuart's Brigade at the Battle of Gettysburg, *Southern Historical Society Papers* (1876), vol. 2 (1876), 105-107.

Index